Pacuvii
3.74

THE
DONATIST CHURCH

THE
DONATIST CHURCH

A MOVEMENT OF
PROTEST IN
ROMAN NORTH AFRICA

BY

W. H. C. FREND

OXFORD
AT THE CLARENDON PRESS

Oxford University Press, Ely House, London W. 1

GLASGOW NEW YORK TORONTO MELBOURNE WELLINGTON
CAPE TOWN SALISBURY IBADAN NAIROBI DAR ES SALAAM LUSAKA ADDIS ABABA
BOMBAY CALCUTTA MADRAS KARACHI LAHORE DACCA
KUALA LUMPUR SINGAPORE HONG KONG TOKYO

FIRST PUBLISHED 1952
REPRINTED LITHOGRAPHICALLY IN GREAT BRITAIN
AT THE UNIVERSITY PRESS, OXFORD
BY VIVIAN RIDLER
PRINTER TO THE UNIVERSITY
1971

PREFACE TO THE SECOND IMPRESSION

IT is now nearly twenty years since the appearance of *The Donatist Church* and since then much valuable research has been undertaken on early Christianity in North Africa. The Iron Curtain has proved no barrier in this respect, for major works have been published on Donatism in East Germany as well as in Sweden, France, and Britain. The landmarks have been J. B. Brisson's *Autonomisme et Christianisme dans l'Afrique romaine*, Paris, 1958, followed by A. Mandouze's emphatic protest 'Encore le Donatisme!' published in *L'Antiquité classique* of 1960, H. J. Diesner's studies on the Circumcellions, published comprehensively in 1963, and Emin Tengström's detailed *Donatisten und Katholiken*, Göteborg, 1964. Finally, there have been the reassessments of Augustine's attitude towards religious coercion by P. R. L. Brown in his fine biography of St. Augustine and R. A. Markus in *Saeculum: History and Society in the Theology of St. Augustine*, Cambridge, 1970.

Apart from Diesner, the predominant tendency among scholars has been to concentrate once more on the ecclesiastical problem posed by the Donatists and to subject my emphasis on the importance of the North African background in influencing the success of the movement to detailed scrutiny. Brisson's work has demonstrated how far-reaching were the doctrinal links that bound Donatism to the main stream of African theological tradition represented by Tertullian and Cyprian. The African Catholics were the true schismatics, and the fanaticism of popular Donatism must always be understood in relation to previous North African ecclesiastical history. This view was supported from another angle in A. H. M. Jones' article 'Were ancient heresies national or social movements in disguise?' (*Journal of Theological Studies*, N.S. x. 2, 1959, 280–98), while five years later Emin Tengström undertook a searching examination of important aspects of my main thesis, particularly concerning the Numidian background of Donatism and the revolutionary character of the movement as exemplified by the Circumcellions. That the Donatists were not by nature political separatists who supported the rebel movements of Firmus and Gildo on principle may be agreed, though Tengström's failure to correlate texts from anti-Donatist sources with evidence from more impartial witnesses, such as Zosimus, regarding conditions in fourth-century North Africa, coupled with his inexperience in dealing with archaeological evidence, rendered his criticisms less valid than they might have been. Meantime the studies of H. J. Diesner of Halle University and his East German colleagues have continued to stress the importance of the whole range of non-theological factors that brought about the Donatist movement in North Africa.

The debate therefore continues. The main hindrance to further research is the difficulty of undertaking the necessary additional fieldwork in North Africa. The ever-varying political situation throughout the Arab world renders research projects in Algeria and Tripolitania hazardous, while there has been reluctance on the part of the British Academy to sponsor archaeological work in the more stable republic of Tunisia. The author's site of Kherbet Bahrarous north-west of Timgad remains, he understands, as he left it thirty years ago. Work on Romano-Berber village sites in Algeria which alone can settle some of the questions raised in *The Donatist Church*, particularly concerning the possible correlation of the rise of a Numidian village economy during the fourth century with the almost unanimous acceptance of Donatist Christianity in Numidia, has to await more settled political conditions. In retrospect, the historian must acknowledge his debt of gratitude to the work undertaken by the French archaeologists, largely inspired by MM. Louis Poinssot and André Berthier in the decade before the Second World War. Without their work the argument would still be confined mainly, as it had been since the Reformation, to the interpretation of the texts.

Despite two decades of research there are few changes I would want to make. A new book would follow Brisson's lead and pay more attention to the ecclesiastical and doctrinal aspects of the schism. From Tengström I would accept some changes of emphasis and amendments of detail. But the main lines of the book would stand. Hence, I have contented myself here with a few verbal corrections and the addition to the Bibliography of significant work published since *The Donatist Church* first appeared.

W. H. C. FREND

GLASGOW UNIVERSITY

August 1970

PREFACE

THIS work is in the main a development of a thesis written immediately before the Second World War, on 'The Social and Economic Background of Early Christianity in North Africa down to A.D. 430, with special reference to the Donatist Controversy'.[1] The writer had studied St. Augustine as his special subject in the Modern History School at Oxford, and had been impressed by the tenacity of the resistance of the Donatists to the Catholicism preached by Augustine. While the latter gained convincing victories over Manichees, Pelagians, Arians, and pagans, the Donatists defied him and survived to the end of Christianity in North Africa. Why was this so?

Thanks to the Craven Committee I was able to pursue my quest, first in Berlin under the direction of the late Professor Hans Lietzmann, and then in the Sorbonne, and finally under the tuition of MM. Poinssot, Berthier, and Martin in French North Africa. These gentlemen showed me every help and kindness, and it was due to them that I was able to study the Donatist culture in Numidia at first hand, and participate in the excavation of a Romano-Berber village and church at Kherbet Bahrarous. I wish to record my deepest gratitude to them and to the other French officials, notably M. Leschi and M. Logeart, who helped me.

The outbreak of war, however, practically put an end to these studies. Between 1940 and 1947 I was engaged on national service, though in 1943–4 I had a further chance of visiting some of the Numidian sites while engaged on intelligence duties in North Africa. My appointment, however, in March 1947 as a full-time member of an international Board of Editors engaged in selecting and publishing documents from the archives of the former German Foreign Ministry, seemed to close the door on further studies in early medieval history.

I was, however, constantly encouraged to revise my original thesis, in particular by my former supervisor, Professor N. H. Baynes, by the Principal of Brasenose, Professor Hugh Last, and by the Rev. T. M. Parker of Pusey House. Two accidents enabled me to turn to the Donatists once more. In the first place,

---

[1] The abstract is printed in vol. xiii of *Abstracts of Dissertations for the degree of Doctor of Philosophy*, O.U.P., 1947, pp. 42–48.

conditions in Berlin during the Blockade of 1948 imposed long periods of enforced leisure. I found that many people, both British and Germans, were interested in outside studies and were ready to help, and in these conditions I rewrote the narrative chapters (Chapters XI to XIX) of my work. I was, however, handicapped by lack of recognized authorities, particularly on the African Church Councils, and in some cases substitutes in the form of older and less complete reference works have had to be used.

Secondly, after the transfer of the German Documents Project to England in the autumn of 1948, the work of selecting documents, on which I was largely engaged, rapidly outpaced the process of final editing and publication. This fact, together with the congenial surroundings in the heart of Buckinghamshire in which the work was being done, enabled me to rewrite practically the whole thesis without trespassing on Government time.

In the last phase, my thanks are due to my wife for her patient work in compiling the index, to Frau Gertrud Opiela, to Mrs. Jean Duke, and to Mrs. Ethel Willshire for their help in typing a difficult manuscript; also to the officials of the Clarendon Press for their kindness and aid in preparing the work for publication; to my colleagues on the Documents Project, particularly to Dr. Paul Sweet, for their criticism of individual chapters; and to Professor Baynes for his help and advice on the footnotes. During the final revision I have had, too, the use of the Rev. G. G. Willis's *Saint Augustine and the Donatist Controversy*, a work whose value on the ecclesiastical aspects of the controversy I am happy to acknowledge.

W. H. C. F.

NOTTINGHAM UNIVERSITY

10 *November* 1951

CONTENTS

LIST OF MAPS
(at end)

ABBREVIATIONS OF ORIGINAL SOURCES

(For abbreviations of other works the reader is referred to the Bibliography at the end of this book)

CIL. *Corpus Inscriptionum Latinarum*, Africa, vol. viii, parts i and ii, ed. Wilmanns, 1881; Supplement 1 (Africa Pro-consularis), ed. Cagnat and Schmidt, 1894; Supplement ii (Numidia), Cagnat and Schmidt, 1894; Supplement iii (Mauretania), Cagnat and Dessau, 1904; Supplement iv (Proconsular Africa), Dessau, 1916.

CM. R. Cagnat and A. Merlin, *Inscriptions latines d'Afrique*, Paris, Leroux, 1923.

CSEL. *Corpus Scriptorum Ecclesiasticorum Latinorum*, Vienna, 1866– .

ILA. S. Gsell, *Inscriptions latines de l'Algérie*, tome i, Proconsular Numidia, Paris, on behalf of Government-General of Algeria.

ILCV. E. Diehl, *Inscriptiones Latinae Christianae Veteres*, Berlin, Weidmann, 1924–31.

MGH. *Monumenta Germaniae Historica*, Berlin, Weidmann, 1877– .

PG. J.-P. Migne, *Patrologia Graeca*, Paris, 1857–1934.

PL. J.-P. Migne, *Patrologia Latina*, Paris, 1843–90.

TU. *Texte und Untersuchungen zur Geschichte der altchristlichen Literatur*, Leipzig, 1882– .

INTRODUCTION

Ever since the Counter-Reformation the Donatist Church has attracted the interest of scholars. Donatists, if extinct in North Africa, have been resurrected to play their part in Protestant versus Catholic controversy. The Catholics from Baronius[1] onwards have claimed to recognize in Donatism the prototype of Protestant schism, a local community arrogating to itself superior virtue but cut off from the Church. The graphic descriptions of the discreditable origins of the dispute found in the writings of Optatus of Milevis and the arguments used by St. Augustine against his Donatist opponents have served the Catholics well. In the theological aspects of the debates the Protestants have not always been too happy. Perhaps had Newman's attention not been drawn to the article by Cardinal Wiseman on 'The Schism of the Donatists', published in the *Dublin Review*, the history of the Christian Church in England might have been different.[2]

But the controversy of the theologians has also served the general historian. For the last 250 years the texts on which any study of Donatism must be based have been published,[3] and increasing efforts have been made to establish an authentic record of events. It is with the texts themselves that modern critical study begins, and in this sphere the lay and Protestant historians have held their own. In 1883 Daniel Voelter published under the title of *Der Ursprung des Donatismus*[4] a detailed examination of the documents which formed the dossier used by the Catholics in their conference with the Donatists at Carthage in 411, and published by Du Pin as an Appendix to Optatus' works. These documents consisted of a record of the Synod of Cirta in 305, letters by the Emperor Constantine to officials in Africa after the outbreak of the dispute, and allegedly verbatim accounts of the proceedings in the African courts taken from the

---

[1] Baronius, *Annales Ecclesiastici*, Cologne, 1609, tome ii.

[2] On the influence of both the Monophysite and the Donatist controversies on Newman's conversion to Rome, see W. Ward, *The Life of John Henry Cardinal Newman*, Longmans, 1912, vol. i, p. 66. On the other hand, the Anglican view of the Donatists had been admirably set out by Hooker, *Ecclesiastical Polity*, v, chap. lxii, pp. 7–12 (ed. Bayne, 1902).

[3] Optatus' *De Schismate Donatistarum* was edited by E. Du Pin, Paris, 1700 and 1702.

[4] D. Voelter, *Der Ursprung des Donatismus*, Freiburg, 1883.

official archives. Voelter came to the conclusion that many of these documents had been falsified or interpolated at various stages of the controversy, and in consequence were of slight value as a record of events.[1] This view was examined in 1889 by Otto Seeck,[2] who, while upholding the authenticity of most of the dossier, agreed that the record of the Synod of Cirta and the instructions presumed to have been sent by Constantine to the authorities in Africa after the Council of Arles, which he placed in August 316, were open to suspicion. Next year, however, the Abbé L. Duchesne, using a ninth-century manuscript from the Abbey of Cormery near Tours, established that the documents included in the dossier formed a single whole and must have been compiled between the years 330 (the date of the last document) and 347, when the Catholics gained a period of ascendancy.[3] Duchesne's view is now generally accepted as correct, and the main facts regarding the outbreak of the schism may be taken as established.

Meantime, the problem was being approached from a different angle, as a native nationalist movement with a sociological background. Following a line of inquiry indicated by Döllinger,[4] a Westphalian Evangelical pastor named Wilhelm Thümmel[5] analysed Donatism as African nationalism representing inherent separatist trends prevalent during the Late Roman period. He drew attention to the origins of the dispute in Numidia, to the role played by the Numidians throughout its history, to the support given by the Donatists to the rebels Firmus and Gildo, and to the apparent coincidence of Donatism with areas in which a native language (Thümmel believed this to be Punic) was spoken. The present writer owes much to Thümmel's ideas, to which his attention was drawn by the late Professor Hans Lietzmann. The latter stressed in particular the importance of Thümmel's theory on the coincidence of a native language and a native form of Christianity.

---

[1] Voelter, op. cit., chaps. ii and iv.

[2] O. Seeck, 'Die Anfänge des Donatismus', *Zeitschrift für Kirchengeschichte*, x, 1889, pp. 526 ff.

[3] L. Duchesne, 'Le Dossier du Donatisme', *Mélanges d'Archéologie et d'Histoire de l'École française à Rome*, x, 1890, pp. 590 ff. (= *Mélanges*). This article supersedes both Voelter and Seeck, and with the exception of the letter 'Aeterna et religiosa' I have accepted Duchesne's findings in their entirety.

[4] J. J. von Döllinger, *Kirche und Kirchen*, München, 1861, p. 4.

[5] W. Thümmel, *Zur Beurtheilung des Donatismus*, Inaugural-Dissertation, Halle, 1893. Criticized by S. Gsell, *Mélanges*, xv, 1895, p. 325.

Unfortunately Thümmel lacked the archaeological evidence without which his conclusions could not be proved. He himself had too often to admit ignorance or support his ideas with improbable speculations. But at this very moment two French archaeologists, H. Graillot and S. Gsell,[1] were beginning a systematic study of the High Plains of central Algeria, the heart of ancient Numidia. Their reports showed that in the Later Roman period this area had been thickly populated by Christian village-dwellers who had developed a flourishing agriculture based on the cultivation of olives and barley. A number of inscriptions bearing the Donatist watchword 'Deo laudes' were found in churches whose ruins were planned and superficially explored. During the following years, thanks largely to the enthusiasm of local French archaeologists in Constantine, a great deal more was found out about the Algerian countryside in the Late Roman Empire.[2] An important inscription was discovered at Lamasba showing the type of landholding and irrigation practised by the Numidian farmers in the third century A.D. This information from southern Numidia was supplemented by the discovery of four inscriptions of great importance from the site of Imperial estates near the Tunisian-Algerian border. These inscriptions indicated the precise status and terms of tenure enjoyed by the African colonate as a whole.[3]

Thus material was accumulating which would enable Donatism to be studied not merely as a 'schism' but as a movement of opinion in relation to a given social and economic environment. In 1912 the Abbé Mesnage published a geographical description of Christian Africa in Roman and Byzantine times in which information on the distribution of Catholic and Donatist bishoprics was collated from all known archaeological and literary sources.[4] His colleague Canon Jaubert made a similar detailed study of Christian sites in the Department of Constantine.[5] I have used both of these works,

[1] H. Graillot et S. Gsell, 'Exploration archéologique dans le Département de Constantine', *Mélanges*, xiii, 1893, pp. 461–581, xiv, 1894, pp. 17–86.
[2] See the yearly reports of the Société archéologique du Département de Constantine, and in particular E. Mercier's article on the native population of Algeria in Roman, Vandal, and Byzantine times, in the *Recueil des Notices et Mémoires de la Société archéologique du Département de Constantine*, xxx, 1895–6, pp. 127–212 (= *Recueil de Constantine*).   [3] See below, pp. 41 ff.
[4] Le Père J. Mesnage, *L'Afrique chrétienne*, Paris, Leroux, 1912.
[5] Le Chanoine J. Jaubert, 'Anciens évêchés et ruines chrétiennes de la Numidie et de la Sitifienne', *Recueil de Constantine*, xlvi, 1912, pp. 1–218.

which, with Gsell's *Atlas archéologique de l'Algérie*, published in 1911, are still of basic importance.

It was in these years immediately preceding the First World War that Professor Paul Monceaux was beginning a systematic study of the literature and archaeology of the African Church. From the outset Monceaux had interested himself in the Donatists, and between 1908 and 1912 he published in the *Journal des Savants* and the *Revue de Philologie* a series of articles on the individual Donatist leaders, Donatus, Parmenian, Petilian, and Tyconius, together with material on Donatist epigraphy. The foundations were laid for his masterpiece, the seven volumes of the *Histoire littéraire de l'Afrique chrétienne*, which appeared at intervals between 1901 and 1923.[1]

Whatever else may be said of the period 1890–1914, it was one in which scholarship and the aim of establishing a true record of events took precedence over ideology and nationalism. French and Germans, Protestants and Catholics contributed towards furthering our knowledge of Roman Africa and the African Church. In the last four volumes of Monceaux's *Histoire littéraire* the reader will find not only a lucid and thorough account of Donatism but a permanent memorial to the great age of liberal scholarship that is passing away.

Between the Wars knowledge of the Donatists progressed in three directions. First, more was found out about the type of Christianity practised on the High Plains. A number of sites which were indisputably Donatist were identified and examined. Secondly, a few additional Donatist writings were identified, notably by the Italian scholar Pincherle,[2] and thirdly, the discovery of large numbers of Libyan and Romano-Libyan inscriptions in Numidia settled the controversy on the language spoken by the Numidian natives in St. Augustine's time in favour of Libyan or proto-Berber.

The present writer has gone to work with more materials a t his disposal than his predecessors a generation ago. But ther e are still significant gaps. Most serious is the complete loss of th e correspondence and written works of Donatus and his successor , Parmenian. We are still dependent on Catholic sources even

---

[1] P. Monceaux, *Histoire littéraire de l'Afrique chrétienne depuis les origines jusqu'à l'invasion arabe*. The author, however, did not bring the story down beyond the death of St. Augustine.

[2] See articles by A. Pincherle in *Bilychnis*, xxii, 1923, and *Ricerche Religiose*, i–iii, 1925–7.

for the barest outline of their personalities. We know practically nothing of the internal organization of the Donatist Church—the sort of detailed knowledge derived from Cyprian's letters on the African Church in the century before. We have no record from the Donatist side of the events that led up to the break with Caecilian. How did Donatus himself first come into the picture? What was happening in the years between the end of the Great Persecution and the death of Mensurius? At the other end of the story, the last years of Donatism are almost a complete blank. There is evidence to show that Donatism survived to the Moslem invasions, but of its leaders at this stage or the survival of Donatist traditions nothing is at present known.

Equally baffling is the period between the death of Cyprian and the outbreak of the Great Persecution when the great mass of the Numidian countryfolk were becoming Christian. I have decided not to follow some modern French scholars[1] in using Commodian to fill this gap. It is tempting to quote evidence supplied by the latter for the hatred felt by some Christians against the wealthy, and to point out how this led naturally to the attitude which inspired the writer of the *Passio Donati et Advocati*, and the Circumcellions a generation later. But the evidence about Commodian's origins is not watertight, and until it is, he must be left on one side.[2] Therefore one is thrown back on the traditional texts together with archaeological evidence, and the methods of dating sites in Algeria still leave a great deal to be desired. In telling the story of Donatism I have accepted as narrative the account of the origins and development of the movement found in the works of St. Augustine and Optatus of Milevis. That is to say, when Optatus describes a Donatist armed attack on the Catholics in Lemellefensis in 362, I accept this event as having taken place. Similarly, when Augustine asserts that Donatist clergy led the Circumcellions I see no reason to doubt this. The Donatists were sharp enough to take Augustine up on any inaccuracies of quotation,

---

[1] Notably J. P. Brisson, *Gloire et misère de l'Afrique chrétienne*, Paris, Laffont, 1949, pp. 132–41.

[2] My own inclination is to place him in late-third-century Africa, originating in an African town beginning 'Gad . . .' (such as *Gad*iaufala in Numidia). It is another matter, however, to support a thesis on this guess. See E. Buonaiuti, *Il Cristianesimo nell'Africa Romana*, Bari, 1928, pp. 268–78, and B. Altaner and A. Stuiber, *Patrologie*, (7th ed.), Freiburg im Breisgau, 1966, p. 182 (gives references).

B

but his facts are not challenged. Apart from questioning the value of the letter 'Aeterna et Religiosa', as representing Constantine's personal views on Christianity in 314,[1] I have also accepted the Catholic dossier published as an Appendix to Optatus as a record of events, and I have used non-African sources, notably Ammianus Marcellinus, Zosimus, and Salvian, where their statements can be corroborated by other evidence, e.g. from inscriptions or the Theodosian Code.

My divergence from the previous generation of scholars is in the field of interpretation. I have started from the facts that the Donatist movement did not end with the Conference of Carthage in 411, and that Christianity itself lasted only a relatively short time in North African history, between A.D. 200 and 700. I have therefore paid less attention to the theological and literary aspects of the controversy in favour of attempting to analyse the type of society in which Donatism flourished. Why did North Africa become Christian, and why was Numidia Donatist? Further, following Gautier,[2] I have attempted to relate the Donatist movement to the religious background of the Berbers in prehistoric times and in the early centuries of the Roman occupation, and also to examine whether there are links between Donatism and Islam in North Africa. Is Donatism part of a continuous native religious tradition, as fundamentally unchanging as the Berbers themselves in the routine of their daily life? Can one see in Donatus the forerunner of a Moslem Mahdi? Finally, I have asked myself how far Donatism and other movements of Christian dissent in the Late Roman Empire contributed towards bringing about the permanent cleavage in faiths between the peoples of the northern and southern shores of the Mediterranean. It is well to remember that 'Mediterranean civilization' means Islam as well as Roman Catholicism.

[1] See below, p. 152, n. 6.
[2] E. F. Gautier, *Le Passé de l'Afrique du Nord*, Paris, Payot, 1937.

I

THE PROBLEM OF DONATISM:
ORIGINS OF THE SCHISM

THE cleavage of faiths between Christianity and Islam has been one of the dominating factors in the history of the Mediterranean countries. As Pirenne has so cogently argued, the unity of the Mediterranean area was destroyed less by the Germanic invaders in the fifth century A.D. than by the victories of the Moslems over the Byzantines, of Khalid ibn el Walid in Syria and Sidi Okba in North Africa.[1] By the middle of the eighth century Christianity, which had reigned supreme throughout the Mediterranean, had been ousted from all but its northern shores. Though subsequently the balance altered in favour of the Christian Church, which reconquered Spain and Sicily, the rift between Christendom on the northern and western shores of the Mediterranean and Islam on its southern and eastern shores has lasted until today. The splendid ruins of the Roman cities, with their churches and temples, serve as a reminder of the eventual failure of both Christianity and classical culture to survive over large areas where they had once prevailed.

The object of this book is to discuss the opening phase of this development in a particular area, North Africa. For North Africa was one of the territories in which the Christian Church took deepest root. The works of Tertullian, Cyprian, and St. Augustine embody the teachings and traditions of Latin Christianity. In Pope Victor I (A.D. 189–99) Africa produced the first bishop of Rome who wrote in Latin, and in the age of Justinian the Latin viewpoint in the Three Chapters controversy found its most telling exponents among the African clergy. Yet from the eighth century onwards North Africa has been lost to Latinity and Christendom alike, and all efforts to win it back, either by St. Louis's crusaders or by the missionaries of more recent times, have been unsuccessful.

[1] H. Pirenne, *A History of Europe* (tr. Miall), London, Allen & Unwin, 1939, chap. iii. Also, *Mahomet and Charlemagne* (tr. Miall), London, Allen & Unwin, 1940, pp. 150 ff. For discussion and criticism of Pirenne's theories, with particular reference to this work, see A. Momigliano's review in *Journal of Roman Studies* (= *JRS.*), xxxiv, 1944, pp. 157–8.

Even before the Arab armies began to move against the Byzantine Empire the seeds of permanent religious division had been sown. Monophysites in Egypt, Monothelites, Manichees, and Nestorians in the other Eastern provinces, Donatists in North Africa, Priscillianists in Spain were already disputing the Byzantine dominions with the Catholic Church. In its early stages Islam was reckoned as another 'nationalist' heresy opposed to the creed declared orthodox by the Emperor. The real beginnings of religious divergence are to be found long before the Hegira, in the rise of various 'national' churches opposed to official Catholicism, which followed the adoption of Christianity as the religion of the Empire.[1] A study of the Donatist Church may help towards understanding the factors which led to this movement, and to the collapse of classical culture before the Mohammedan invaders in the seventh century A.D.

The Donatist Church had a known existence of nearly three centuries. The first texts record a disputed election to the see of Carthage in A.D. 312. The last indisputable written evidence is an appeal by Pope Gregory in 596 to the Emperor Maurice for sterner measures to stem the growing influence of Donatism in Numidia.[2] The tone of this letter, however, and other indirect evidence suggests that the Donatists held their ground until the arrival of Islam. The persistence of Donatism is remarkable. Other heresies and schisms flourished in North Africa, but only for limited periods. In the mid-fourth century, for instance, we are told by Optatus of Milevis (modern Mila in Dept. of Constantine) that the Marcionites and Valentinians, against whom Tertullian had fought, were almost forgotten in Africa.[3] Arians, despite the support of the Vandal rulers, Pelagians, and even Manichees[4] prospered for a short time and then vanished into obscurity. The Donatists remained. In A.D. 600 as in A.D. 400 their hold over Numidia was unshaken. And yet, except for the question of the validity of sacraments dispensed by non-orthodox

[1] On this subject, E. L. Woodward, *Christianity and Nationalism in the Later Roman Empire*, Longmans, 1916.

[2] Gregory, *Epistola* (ed. P. Ewald and L. M. Hartmann, Berlin, 1891–2), vi. 61.

[3] Catholic Bishop of Milevis, *fl.* A.D. 370, *De Schismate Donatistarum* (ed. C. Ziwsa, *Corpus Scriptorum Ecclesiasticorum Latinorum* (= *CSEL.*), xxvi, Vienna, 1893), i. 9, 'quorum per provincias africanas non solum vitia, sed etiam nomina videbantur ignota'. Translation, O. R. Vassall-Phillips, Longmans, London, 1917.

[4] The Manichees, however, linger on until the eighth century A.D., and are mentioned by Pope Gregory II among the refugees who sought asylum in Italy from the Moslem invaders (Gregory II, *Ep.* iv; *Patrologia Latina*, lxxxix, col. 502).

clerics, no serious theological difference separated them and the Catholics. There was no difference even of ecclesiastical organization, and it had been proved more than once that they had no legal case against their opponents. It was a matter of schism rather than heresy.[1] But despite centuries of repression by the authorities and the compelling logic of St. Augustine and other Catholic writers they remained defiant. When every allowance has been made—as Augustine himself made[2]—for the brilliance of the founder of the Donatist community, Donatus, and for the strength of inertia which could keep the movement in being after its causes had been forgotten, the survival of the Donatists requires an explanation. In Africa, moreover, the comparative abundance of literary and archaeological sources allows the historian to investigate both the ecclesiastical aspect of the schism and the social and economic environment in which the Donatist Church grew up.

The story of Donatism begins with the Great Persecution of A.D. 303–5.[3]

By this time Christianity had taken a firm hold in North Africa.[4] The Church had survived persecution under Severus, Decius, and Valerian, and was ceasing to be the religion of a poor minority. In contrast to the emptiness of pagan literature of this period there were the vigorous works of Cyprian, Arnobius, and Lactantius. The Church was making its impact felt on all classes and in the farthest corners of the Roman provinces in Africa. But with this missionary triumph a certain amount of the earlier zeal tended to disappear. There was little desire among the majority of new converts in the Roman cities to compromise themselves with the authorities.

Despite the premonition of approaching danger provided by the martyrdom of Maximilian of Theveste (modern Tebessa)

---

[1] The Donatists were only declared heretical in A.D. 405 in order to bring them within the scope of the general anti-heretical legislation in the Roman Empire.

[2] Augustine, *Enarratio in Psalmum 69*, 5 (Migne, *Patrologia Latina* (= *PL.*), xxxvi-xxxvii, col. 870), and *Epistola* 93. 43 (= *CSEL.* xxxiv, ed. Goldbacher, Vienna, 1898, p. 487).

[3] See Paul Monceaux, *Histoire littéraire de l'Afrique chrétienne*, Paris, Leroux, 1912, iv, chap. i, and Monsignor L. Duchesne, *Early History of the Christian Church* (English translation, ed. Murray, London, 1931), vol. ii, pp. 79–97. For the reasons behind the Great Persecution, N. H. Baynes, *Cambridge Ancient History* (= *CAH.*), xii, chap. xix.

[4] See Chapters VI and VII.

in A.D. 295,[1] and the publication of Diocletian's decree against Manichaeism in either A.D. 297 or 302,[2] the persecution caught the African Christians completely unawares. On 19 May 303[3] Diocletian's edict ordering the surrender of the Christian Scriptures, the registration of Church property, and probably the destruction of Church buildings arrived in Numidia. By 5 June[4] it was being enforced in the Proconsular Province as well. This was the *dies Traditionis*. In the autumn, or early in 304, a more severe edict arrived, ordering that everyone should perform some outward ritual act, such as throwing incense on a censer, as a mark of loyalty to the Emperors and to the gods under whose patronage they had placed the Empire[5] (the *dies Thurificationis*). Penalty for disobedience to this edict was death.

In the Roman cities the Emperor's orders appear to have been carried out firmly but not without tact. For the previous forty years Christians and pagans had lived side by side in relative peace. The Church had become almost an established institution. At Cirta (modern Constantine), the capital of the province of Numidia Cirtensis, the magistrate told Bishop Paulus to produce the lectors who were responsible for looking after the Scriptures. The reply was 'Everybody knows them'.[6] At Apthungi (modern Henchir Souar, in Tunisia),[7] the chief magistrate, the Duumvir Alfius Caecilianus, and the bishop Felix appear to have been on friendly terms, and indeed the official

---

[1] Ed. R. Knopf and G. Krüger, *Ausgewählte Martyrerakten*, 1929, pp. 86–87; P. Monceaux, *Histoire littéraire*, iii. 114–21.

[2] *Codex Gregorianus*, xv. 3 (ed. P. Krüger, *Collatio libr. juris antejustin.*, iii, 1890, pp. 187–8). Dating, see M. Besnier, *L'Empire romain de l'avènement des Sévères*, Paris, Les Presses Universitaires, 1937, p. 324. Besnier's conclusions are disputed by Wm. Seston in *Dioclétien et la Tétrarchie*, Paris, Boccard, 1946, p. 122.

[3] Dating, Pallu de Lessert, *Fastes des provinces africaines*, Paris, Leroux, 1901, ii. 1, p. 13.   [4] Ibid.

[5] This edict may have been due to Galerius' pressure on Maximian at the time of Diocletian's sickness. This would place it some time in the early part of 304. N. H. Baynes, *CAH*. xii. 668.

[6] *Gesta apud Zenophilum* (ed. Ziwsa, *CSEL*. xxvi. 186). 'Felix F. pp. Curator Paulo episcopo dixit, "Ostende lectores, aut mitte ad illos." Paulus episcopus dixit, "Omnes cognoscitis."'

[7] Identification, *Corpus Inscriptionum Latinarum*, viii (= *CIL*.), 23085. This places Apthungi in Byzacenia and not Proconsular Africa.

Other collections of Latin inscriptions used in this work are: (*a*) *Inscriptions latines de l'Algérie* (= *ILA*.), ed. S. Gsell, 1 volume only, published by the Government-General of Algeria, Paris, Champion, 1922; (*b*) *Inscriptiones latinae christianae veterae*, ed. Diehl, Berlin, 1924–31 (= *ILCV*.); (*c*) R. Cagnat et A. Merlin, *Inscriptions latines d'Afrique*, Leroux, 1923 (= *CM*.); (*d*) Dessau, *Inscriptiones latinae selectae*, Berlin, 1892–1916) (= *ILS*.).

did not know of the existence of the Emperor's edict until he was told about it by the Christians themselves.[1]

The records of this period are comparatively full. This was a critical period in the history of the rival Churches, and in future years both Catholics and Donatists maintained their dossiers complete. We therefore can gain a fair idea of what happened in different cities. At Cirta the immediate reaction of the Christian community to the edicts was flight.[2] Of those who stayed behind, the great majority sacrificed. Optatus of Milevis, who knew local Numidian conditions, said that the temples were not big enough to hold the crowds of apostates.[3] Then, on 19 May 303 Bishop Paulus was summoned before Munatius Felix, the Curator of the city.[4] He was ordered to hand over copies of the Scriptures. He prevaricated, gave up one copy and said the lectors had the rest. These were fetched and questioned. After a certain amount of argument, in which they tried to shield each other, they were persuaded to comply, and they brought out not only copies of the Scriptures but chalices, lamps, clothes kept by the congregation for the relief of the poor, and a sundry assortment of ecclesiastical objects. All these were duly inventoried. One of those who took part in the scene was Silvanus, a sub-deacon, who later became the Donatist bishop. He was not allowed to forget this incident.

Nothing further seems to have befallen Bishop Paulus, who, however, died soon afterwards. From the account of the conference of the twelve bishops who met on 5 March 305 to elect his successor, we gather that similar scenes were enacted elsewhere. Clergy and congregations hastened to comply with the edicts. Four of the twelve bishops admitted to having handed over the Bible to the authorities, one had actually thrown the Gospels into the fire, a fifth escaped only by pretending he was blind.[5] In the Proconsular Province it was the same. The

---

[1] *Gesta proconsularia quibus absolutus est Felix*, CSEL. xxvi, ed. Ziwsa, p. 199 (= *Gesta Proconsularia*).

[2] *Gesta apud Zenophilum*, p. 186, 'Cum incursum pateremur repentinae persecutionis fugivimus in montem Bellonae.'

[3] Optatus, *De Schismate*, iii. 8.

[4] A translation of the salient passages in these proceedings is given by A. H. M. Jones, *Constantine and the Conversion of Europe*, English Universities Press, 1948, pp. 51–54. On the office of Curator Reipublicae with reference to Munatius Felix, see Christian Lucas, 'Notes on the Curators in Roman Africa', *JRS*. xxx, 1940, pp. 56–74, at p. 67.

[5] The Acts of the Council of Cirta were cited by the Catholics at the Conference

Bishops of Furni,[1] Zama,[2] and Abitina[3] are stated to have yielded, and the Primate, Mensurius of Carthage, managed to salve his conscience by handing over some heretical tomes ('Novorum quaecumque reproba scripta haereticorum') to the waiting magistrates.[4] When in December 304 the Proconsul Anulinus[5] interrogated the confessor Crispina at Theveste, he could say with some justification that 'All Africa had sacrificed, so why should not she'.[6]

It would be unjust to decry the attitude of the African higher clergy as cowardly. Already, during the persecution under Decius and Valerian in A.D. 249 and 258, Cyprian had advised his colleagues against provoking the authorities, and he himself had retired to a landed estate until the worst was over.[7] The view was held that acts of fanatical zeal which might provoke reprisals were to be discouraged. If the magistrates could be satisfied by the production of medical or heretical treatises, so much the better. The congregation could remain quiet and undivided to resume activity as soon as the persecution ended.

But the prudence of the bishops did not by any means win the universal support of the Christian community. To many, the persecution was an opportunity for battle against the powers of evil, perhaps even of participating in the glories and horrors of the approaching end of the world.[8] Fanatics prominent in outlying districts attracted recruits looking for a chance of joining,

---

of Carthage with the Donatists in 411. Augustine gives a long fragment in *Contra Cresconium*, iii. 27, 30. (*PL.* xliii, cols. 510–11).

[1] *Gesta Proconsularia*, p. 199.

[2] Ibid. The site of both these towns is in western Tunisia between Mactar and Le Kef.

[3] *Acta Saturnini*, 3 (*PL.* viii, col. 691).

[4] Augustine, *Breviculus Collationis cum Donatistis*, iii. 13. 25 (*PL.* xliii, col. 638). Possibly Manichee writings, but the Carthaginian public were hardly to know that Mensurius had not in fact handed over the Scriptures.

[5] On Anulinus, see Pauly-Wissowa, *Real-enzyklopaedie der klassischen Altertumswissenschaft*, Stuttgart, 1894 (= *PW.*), col. 2651. Possibly Annius Anulinus, Consul in 295 and Praefectus Urbi under Severus and Maxentius.

[6] *Acta Sanctae Crispinae* (ed. P. Franchi di Cavalieri, *Studi e testi*, ix, Rome, 1902). Monceaux, *Histoire littéraire*, iii. 159.

[7] *Acta Proconsularia*, i (ed. Hartel, 1868–71, *CSEL.* iii. 3. cxi); *Ep.* 7 and 12.

[8] There appears to have been a good deal of veiled anti-Imperial eschatology in Africa at this time. The end of the world was approaching, it was said, and Asia would avenge herself on the West. See Lactantius, *Divinae Institutiones*, vii. 15. 11 and vii. 15. 19, ed. S. Brandt (*CSEL.* xix). Also Wm. Seston, *Dioclétien et la Tétrarchie*, pp. 123–4.

as they said, 'brethren who obeyed the precepts of God'.[1] In Carthage itself many rushed forward in enthusiasm and told the authorities that they had copies of the Scriptures which they refused to give up. In fact, they had not.[2] Others found prison and the consequent reputation of being a confessor a convenient way of evading debts to the treasury.[3] Economic stress as well as religious emotion seems to have driven many towards martyrdom. The popularity of the martyrs is attested by the great crowds which kept vigil outside the prisons. In A.D. 300 it seems that a large proportion of the lower classes at Carthage were Christian, and among them the fanatical element prevailed.

In one area of North Africa persecution seems to have been particularly severe. This was the southern part of Numidia, or Numidia Militana,[4] with its capital at Thamugadi (modern Timgad). Literary and archaeological evidence suggest that here the repression may have been on the scale of that witnessed by Eusebius in Palestine and Upper Egypt.[5] The governor, the *Praeses* Valerius Florus, seems to have been a convinced pagan and stern administrator of the Emperor's edicts. In the winter of 303–4 the *vicennalia* of Diocletian's accession was celebrated by the erection of triumphal arches in the main cities of the province.[6] At Timgad itself he restored a temple of Mercury[7] and dedicated altars to the Imperial Genii.[8] It seems clear that he had the support of the romanized citizen element, many of whom remained pagan throughout the fourth century. The *dies*

---

[1] *Acta Saturnini*, 5 and 14 (*PL*. viii, cols. 693, 698). This was the motive of the martyr Victoria, 'et illi sunt fratres mei qui Dei praecepta custodiant'.

[2] Mensurius' letter to the Numidian Primate, Secundus of Tigisis. Quoted by Augustine, *Breviculus Collationis cum Donatistis*, iii. 13. 25. (*PL*. xliii, col. 638).

[3] Ibid., col. 638: 'Quidam etiam in eadem epistola facinorosi arguebantur et fisci debitores, qui occasione persecutionis vel carere vellent onerosa multis debita vita . . ., vel certe acquirere pecuniam . . . .'

[4] On this temporary division of Numidia, Goyau's article in *Mélanges*, xiii, 1893, p. 251, is still useful. *Numidia Militana* probably disappeared *c*. 320 when Constantine put the military forces in Africa under the orders of a single officer, the *Comes Africae*.

[5] N. H. Baynes, *CAH*. xii, pp. 669–74.

[6] The *vicennalia* were celebrated in Rome on 20 Nov. 303. Inscriptions have been found at Macomades, Casae, and an unnamed site at Ksar el Ahmar. *CIL*. viii. 4764, 4324, and 18698. Florus' dates are not completely clear. If he had ceased to be *praeses* in Nov. 303 he could hardly be responsible for administering the later edict, for which he is famous. But see Pallu de Lessert, *Fastes*, ii. 1, pp. 312–14.

[7] Recorded in the *Bulletin archéologique du Comité historique des travaux historiques et scientifiques* (= *Bull. Arch. du Comité*), 1907, p. 274.

[8] *CIL*. viii. 2345–7.

Thurificationis was enforced, and the thoroughness with which the ceremonies were organized was not only noted by Optatus and Augustine, but recorded a century later on an inscription from the village of Castellum Elephantum (modern Rouffach).[1] Equally eloquent are the large number of inscriptions giving the names of native martyrs which have come to light in remote Numidian village churches. At Bir Aida there is 'Januaria et Comites', Migin at Bir Djedid, Florentius at Meharza, Primasius at Azrou Zaovia, Tertullus and Donatus at Mechta el Tein, and many others.[2] Few of these martyrs are on any regular canon, and some may be Donatists who perished at a later date. On the other hand, there is the contemporary statement of the Numidian Primate, Secundus of Tigisis, that many, including heads of families (*Patresfamilias*), had suffered martyrdom in Numidia,[3] and it is fair to assume that many of these *memoriae martyrum* refer to martyrs of this period. Just across the Proconsular border near Ammaedara (Haidra) an inscription names another group of thirty-four 'uncanonical' martyrs, recording explicitly that these 'suffered persecution under the divine laws of Diocletian and Maximian'.[4] It would appear that the thickly populated villages of the Numidian High Plains were severely handled, in much the same way as the Persecution in Egypt also seems to have fallen with a disproportionate weight on the native population outside the large centres.[5]

While this was happening in Numidia, events were taking place in Carthage which may be said to mark the beginning of the Donatist schism. At the end of 303 Bishop Fundanus of Abitina (probably Chaoud near Medjez el Bab in the Mejerda valley) had yielded to the authorities and become a *traditor* ('surrenderer')—that is, he had handed over the Scriptures.[6]

---

[1] *CIL.* viii, 6700 = 19353. Reference is made to 'martyrs of Milevis' who perished at this time: S. Gsell, *Bull. Arch. du Comité*, 1899, pp. 452–4.

[2] All these inscriptions were found during excavations conducted in central Algeria by MM. Berthier and Martin between 1933 and 1939. They have been published by the discoverers in *Les Vestiges du Christianisme antique dans la Numidie Centrale*, Algiers, 1943, Missions archéologiques, p. 210.
Monceaux, op. cit. iii. 170–5, shows that 60 out of 85 inscriptions recording martyrs found in North Africa (i.e. up to 1908) came from Numidia. The proportion has been maintained, and most appear to commemorate the Diocletianic period.

[3] Augustine, *Breviculus Collationis*, iii. 15. 27.

[4] 'Qui persecutionem Diocletiani et Maximiani divinis legibus passi sunt', *Bull. Arch. du Comité*, 1934, 69. Also, H. Delehaye, *Analecta Bollandiana*, liv, 1936, pp. 313–16.

[5] N. H. Baynes, *CAH.* xii. 675; A. H. M. Jones, op. cit., pp. 55–56.

[6] *Acta Saturnini*, 2 and 7.

The congregation, however, led by the presbyter Saturninus continued to meet at the house of a lector named Emeritus. One day they were surprised and forty-seven of them, including Saturninus and his four sons, were taken away to Carthage. The composition of the group is interesting. There was only one decurion (city councillor) among them, an individual named Dativus; the remainder appear to have been artisans or women,[1] the social groups least affected by romanization.

In February 304 the confessors were brought before the Proconsul Anulinus. The account of the trial, preserved in the *Acta Saturnini*, is one of the most moving testimonies of the Great Persecution.[2] The confessors show the same simplicity and constancy as the first martyrs of the African Church over a century before. Their attitude would appear to be in sharp contrast to the more Laodicean outlook of the episcopate. Popular imagination was fired and large numbers are said to have remained near their prison. The charge against them was disobedience to the Imperial laws. The confessors admit having met together for Divine worship. They are put to torture, but persist in their confession of faith. Anulinus asks the lector Emeritus: 'But why did you allow the others to enter your house?' 'Because they are my brethren and I could not prevent them from coming.' 'But you should have prevented them.' 'Certainly not,' Emeritus replied, 'we are not able to stand upright without celebrating the Lord. . . .' 'But', persisted Anulinus, 'the commands of the Emperors and Caesars come first.' 'God is greater than the Emperor,' was the reply. 'Have you any sacred text in your house?' 'I have them in my heart . . .', Emeritus said. Anulinus ordered them to be returned to prison, having achieved nothing.[3]

The eventual fate of the Abitinian martyrs is unknown, but the Donatists asserted that they were allowed to starve, and accused Mensurius' deacon Caecilian of using brutal methods in preventing the Christians from bringing them food.[4] The *Acta*

---

[1] Ibid. 2. P. Franchi di Cavalieri, *Studi e testi*, lxv, 1935, p. 3.

[2] For discussion of the *Acta*, A. H. M. Jones, op. cit., pp. 50–51, Monceaux, iii. pp. 140–7, and E. Buonaiuti, *Il cristianesimo nell' Africa Romana*, Bari, 1928, pp. 295–7. A large number of inscriptions have been found in Numidia in honour of these martyrs. Their *Acta* were produced by the Donatists during the conference at Carthage in 411 (*Gesta Coll. Carth.* iii. 434, 445–8 (*PL.* xi, col. 1253)).

[3] *Acta Saturnini*, 15 (*PL.* viii, col. 699).

[4] Ibid. 17 (*PL.* viii, cols. 700–1), 'Idemque [Caecilianus] lora et flagra cum armatis ante fores carceris ponit, ut ab ingressu atque aditu cunctos qui victum potumque in carcerem martyribus afferebant, gravi affectos injuria propulsaret.'

Saturnini, like the *Acta Perpetuae* a century before, were evidently written up by opponents of the Catholics later, but the subsequent events which they describe have an air of truth which it would be unwise to ignore.[1]

The Donatist writer of the *Acta* records that while in prison the confessors held a meeting among themselves, at which they condemned the *traditor* clergy in the strongest terms. Even to alter a single letter of the Scriptures was a crime, but contemptuously to destroy the whole at the command of pagan magistrates was to merit eternal punishment in Hell. Whoever, therefore, maintained communion with the *traditores*, they said, would not participate with them in the joys of Heaven.[2] In making these claims, the confessors were following in the footsteps of the confessors in the Decian persecution, but instead merely of assuming the right of pardoning the lapsed, they were now condemning bishops, among them their own Bishop Fundanus. The whole hierarchical principle was being attacked.

At the end of 304 the vigour of the Persecution began to flag. The last recorded trial of a Christian was that of Crispina of Thagora, held at Theveste on 5 December 304.[3] There are no recorded martyrdoms after that date, and in Proconsular Numidia, at all events, the Christian congregations seem to have been able to come into the open. By March 305 the Persecution had ended.[4] Its cessation did not bring peace to the Church in Africa. Too many people, including highly placed clergy, had sacrificed, and feeling against these *traditores* ('surrenderers') was intense. To understand it, one might quote the analogy of the feuds which sprang up in Western European countries after the Second World War between 'collaborators' and 'men of the Resistance'. These were irrational hatreds, and in both cases individuals used the opportunity to pay off old scores by de-

[1] Buonaiuti, op. cit., p. 297.

[2] *Acta Saturnini*, 18, 'Si ergo additus apex unus aut littera una dempta de libro sancto radicitus amputat, et sacrilegum facit et subvertit auctorem, necesse est omnes eos qui testamenta divina legesque venerandas omnipotentis Dei et Domini nostri Jesu Christi profanis ignibus tradiderunt exurendas aeternis gehennae ardoribus atque inextinguibili igne torqueri. . . . Si quis traditoribus communicaverit, nobiscum partem in regnis caelestibus non habebit.' The crime was apostasy, the surrender of the keys of salvation contained in the Lord's written word, cf. Augustine, *Contra Litteras Petiliani*, ii. 8. 17.

[3] Besnier, op. cit., p. 331.

[4] Optatus, i. 14. The exact date is uncertain, but Optatus' account of the synod of Cirta on 5 Mar. 305 suggests a sort of interregnum in which the churches remained confiscated but the clergy were none the less permitted to forgather.

nouncing their enemies as people who had worked for the wrong side. There were men, for instance, like the decurion Ingentius of Zigga Ziqua (Zaghouan, in Tunisia), who were prepared to have official *Acta* falsified in order to bring reckless charges of *traditio* against an unpopular cleric.[1] It was an unfailing weapon. But in Africa the situation was complicated by the growing and ambitious power of the Christian Church in Numidia, and also by the social cleavages which the Persecution had opened among the Christians themselves.

The first development took place in Cirta, where Bishop Paulus had died. The fanatics among the Christian community had now gained the upper hand and showed that they had no intention of waiting for the official cessation of Persecution before electing a successor.[2] Their choice fell on the sub-deacon Silvanus, who barely eighteen months before had been playing a willing part in handing over the property of his church to the pagan magistrates. The scene in which this man was acclaimed bishop was described by an eye-witness at his trial for simony, *traditio*, and abuse of office fifteen years later.[3] Silvanus was the nominee of the peasants and lower classes. He was known to have handed over silver chalices to the *curator* Munatius Felix and have boasted the fact.[4] He seems to have atoned for this in the eyes of the multitude by robbing pagan temples in the neighbourhood. He was only sub-deacon, and the citizens reasonably enough wanted a citizen like themselves and a man of better character, not a *traditor*, to be their bishop.[5] The mob would have none of it, and after two days of confusion the leading burghers were overawed and locked up in the cemetery of the martyrs.[6] Then, hoist on the shoulders of Mutus the quarryman, Silvanus was acclaimed bishop by a crowd of peasants, quarry workers, and women of the town.[7] He immediately accepted a bribe of

---

[1] *Gesta Proconsularia*, pp. 202–3.

[2] The date of this incident is not known, but it must have taken place before Secundus summoned his synod to consecrate Silvanus in Mar. 305.

[3] *Gesta apud Zenophilum*, (ed. Ziwsa, pp. 185–97). On the whole affair see Seeck, 'Die Anfänge des Donatismus', *Zeitschrift für Kirchengeschichte*, x, 1889, pp. 525–7, and P. Monceaux, *Histoire littéraire*, iv. 228–39.

[4] *Gesta apud Zenophilum*, p. 193: Victor dixit, 'Ibi [in the church] coepit alloqui populum, dicens, De quo dicunt me traditorem esse? de lucerna? de capitulata?'

[5] Ibid., p. 192: Victor dixit, 'Integrum petebamus, et civem nostrum.'

[6] Ibid., p. 194: Saturninus dixit, 'Ipse eum tulerunt et populus; nam cives in area martyrum fuerunt inclusi.'

[7] Ibid., p. 196: 'Campenses et harenarii fecerunt illum episcopum.... Prostibulae illic fuerunt.'

20 *folles* from a fuller named Victor and made him a presbyter.[1] This astonishing scene evidently went on without any reaction from the authorities, and Silvanus was accepted as bishop.

Here was a paradoxical situation. A self-confessed *traditor* had been chosen by fanatically Christian crowds as their bishop. Later, these same crowds would support Silvanus in making charges of *traditio* against Caecilian, the elected bishop of Carthage, thus forming the Donatist schism. There is no rational explanation for this, but a clue towards understanding Silvanus' popularity may be his association with a certain Bishop Purpurius of Limata. This man was an acknowledged brigand. He had murdered the two sons of his sister, and was later prepared to mete out the same treatment to the Catholic bishop of Carthage. He inspired terror among the Christians, but he also was prepared to carry the fight into the pagan camp. He and Silvanus had been concerned in robbing the Imperial treasury of vinegar which was stored in a temple of Serapis.[2] Among a population who had suffered cruelly at the hands of the authorities such a man might well come to the fore as leader, and his nominee would find ready acceptance by the crowd.

On 5 March 305, Cirta was also the scene of the next episode.[3] A synod was called together by the Numidian Primate,[4] Secundus of Tigisis, in order to consecrate Silvanus as bishop. By African tradition, twelve bishops were necessary for the ceremony.[5] But equally, for consecration to be valid the bishops performing the ceremony must themselves be in a 'state of grace'.[6] *Traditores*, or those who had in any way lapsed during

---

[1] *Gesta apud Zenophilum*, p. 195: 'Nam et Victor fullo, vestri praesentia et populi, dedit folles viginti ut factus esset presbyter.'

[2] Ibid., p. 196: Nundinarus dixit, 'In templo Serapis fuerunt, et tulit illas Purpurius episcopus, acetum quod habuerunt tulit eum Silvanus episcopus, Dontius presbyter et Lucianus.'

[3] Buonaiuti, op. cit., p. 301. The exact date is recorded by Augustine, *Breviculus Collationis*, iii. 17. 32, 'post consulatum Diocletiani IX et Maximiani VIII, tertio nonas Martii'. At the Conference of Carthage in 411 the Donatists urged that the *Acta* were forged, as no such synod could have been held during the Persecution. But as Optatus (i. 14) points out, the meeting took place in a private house in Cirta, and this was by no means improbable.

[4] His rank is given by Augustine, *Breviculus Collationis*, iii. 13. 25 (*PL*. xliii, col. 638): 'qui [Secundus] tunc habebat primatum episcoporum Numidarum.'

[5] Canon 39 of the Catholic Council of Carthage in 397 (ed. Bruns, p. 129): 'nonnisi a duodecim censeatis episcoporum celebrari ordinationes.' Cyprian, *Ep.* 67. 4 (ed. Hartel, *CSEL*. iii. 2. 738), gives the Scriptural basis for the usage, i.e. Acts vi. 2.

[6] Cyprian, *Ep.* 67 and 65. 2: 'If a priest is spotted with vice and sin (particularly, sacrifice to pagan gods) how can his prayers be heard by God?'

the Persecution, were held to have lost the Spirit and would not be eligible.

The synod is related by Optatus of Milevis to have met in a private dwelling, 'the home of Urbanus Carisius, as the churches were not yet restored'.[1] Secundus called upon his colleagues to prove themselves. Unfortunately his own record was open to challenge. During the Persecution he had been held a prisoner by the *stationarii* (custodians of Imperial granaries and posting stations), whose duty it seems to have been to take over the confiscated Church property. How had he been able to secure his release, if he had not given something up? As has already been recorded, four of the bishops present confessed to being *traditores*, but they claimed that as bishops they were answerable only to God. There was in fact no means, except by excommunication, of bringing a bishop to discipline. 'What are we to do about the martyrs? They gave nothing up. Therefore they were crowned', protested Secundus to Donatus of Mascula. 'Leave me to God. I will give my answer there,' was the reply.[2] The attitude of the offending bishops was comparatively humble, until Secundus reached Purpurius of Limata. 'It is said that you killed two of your sister's sons at Milevis', Secundus said. 'You think you can terrify me, as you did the rest. What did you do when the Curator and City Council demanded the Scriptures from you? . . . They did not release you for nothing. Yes, I did kill, and I will kill anyone who acts against me. Do not provoke me to say more. You know I'll have no truck with any man.' Secundus' nephew warned his uncle to let the matter drop, with the significant remarks: 'Do you hear what he is saying? He is ready to leave and start a schism, and not only he, but all those whom you have accused; I know they will dismiss you, and pass a sentence against you, and you will remain by yourself, a heretic.' Secundus took the hint, and the rest of the bishops were left without further ado to the judgement of God.[3] The idea of going into schism was one that came easily to the minds of those bishops present.

It would be probably at about the same time that an exchange of letters took place between Secundus and Mensurius of

[1] Optatus, i. 14: 'quia basilicae necdum fuerunt restitutae, in domum Urbani Carisi'.

[2] Augustine, *Contra Cresconium*, iii. 27. 30, 'Donatus Masculensis dixit, "Mitte me ad deum. Ibi reddam rationem." Secundus dixit, "Accede una parte."'

[3] Ibid.

Carthage. It seems that news of Mensurius' suspected *traditio* and lukewarm attitude towards confessors imprisoned in Carthage had begun to reach Numidia. Secundus asked for an explanation.[1] Mensurius informed him of his surrender of heretical works, and his reasons for discouraging the less reputable claimants to martyrdom. Secundus replied by giving his own version of his brush with the urban authorities. He had defied a centurion. (The man would probably be in no position to deny the fact.) His stand, he claimed, was comparable to that made by Eleazer, the martyr priest in the Maccabees (2 Macc. vi. 21), and he had declared to the emissary of the Curator, 'Christianus sum, et episcopus, non traditor.'[2] The tone of the correspondence was friendly, but it is not difficult to perceive evidence of suspicion and rivalry between the two primates which could become serious. Secundus had left no doubt that he was taking his stand with the more zealous Christians at Carthage.

The Great Persecution, however, ended without an open breach between Carthage and Numidia, but during the next five years the seeds of permanent schism began to germinate. It is the most obscure, yet one of the most important for the history of the Donatist Church, for it is the period in which opinions must have hardened in favour either of leniency towards the lapsed and the *traditores*, or of an imitation of the martyrs and a stern anti-hierarchical puritanism. One fragment of evidence should not be ignored. It is in this period that the name Donatus of Casae Nigrae is first heard.[3] The settlement of Casae was on the extreme southern edge of the High Plains of Numidia,

---

[1] Alternatively, Mensurius might have taken the initiative in writing, perhaps to consult on what was to be done now that the persecution was over. See Duchesne, op. cit., pp. 80–81.

[2] Augustine, *Breviculus Collationis*, iii. 13. 25.

[3] One must assume that Donatus led some sort of rigorist campaign in the Theveste area before moving to Carthage. In the capital he appears to have gone into opposition to Mensurius. 'Adhuc diacono Caeciliano schisma fecisse Carthagine' (ibid. 12. 24). At the Conference of Carthage there is an obscure allegation by the Donatists that Mensurius may have adopted an anti-puritan line: 'quid Mensurius Carthaginensis Ecclesiae episcopus, unitatis tempore persecutio effecerit, unde exstitit causa dissidii' (*Gesta Collationis Carthaginensis*, iii. 334 (*PL*. xi, col. 1249)). On the whole, however, it would be as well to accept Augustine's statement that there was no real trouble so long as Mensurius lived (*De Unico Baptismo*, 16. 29 (*PL*. xliii, col. 611)). In the fifth century, however, legend had made Mensurius into a *traditor* (Augustine, *Contra Litteras Petiliani*, ii. 92. 202 (*PL*. xliii, col. 323)).

about sixty miles due south of Theveste. It was in Florus' province, and the inhabitants had suffered under his rule. The cult of martyrs was as popular there as farther north on the Plains. An inscription from one village, Henchir Mertoum, refers to a 'long' and savage persecution in the reign of Constans or Constantius.[1] In October 313 Pope Miltiades pronounced Donatus guilty of rebaptizing clergy who had lapsed and of forming a schism,[2] and these activities may have taken place before Donatus arrived in Carthage, probably before 311.

In this year events began to move rapidly towards their climax. Though the usurper Maxentius had not continued the Persecution, and in Rome had ordered the return of movable Church property to the Bishop, his rule in Africa was not popular. His representative, the *Vicarius Africae*,[3] Domitius Alexander, revolted from him in the spring of 308 and declared for Galerius. The latter accepted his allegiance and promoted him to the rank of *praefectus praetorio*.[4] Shipments of corn to Rome were suspended, which reduced the city to low rations.[5] Maxentius was at first obliged to reconcile himself to this situation, but in 310 Spain, the main alternative source of supply for Rome, acknowledged Constantine as Emperor.[6] This may have been the reason for Maxentius' determination to restore his authority in Africa. His own *praefectus praetorio*, Rufius Volusianus, crossed to Africa in 311, defeated Alexander, and allowed the pillage of both Cirta and Carthage.[7] At Carthage, however, Alexander had firm adherents among the clergy, and Maxentius was attacked in pamphlets of Christian origin. One of Mensurius'

---

[1] Unfortunately the text is by no means certain. Professor L. Leschi, amending *CIL*. viii. 10706, considers it may refer to a Donatist persecution of Catholics. This, however, does not seem likely, and the choice would be between a reference to persecution under Constantius Chlorus, or under Constantius from 346 to 361. See L. Leschi, 'Inscriptions de la Plaine de Guert', *Soc. du préhistoire et d'archéologie de Tebessa, 1936–7* (1938), pp. 126–9. For a second inscription from the same area referring to religious persecution cf. ibid., pp. 124–5.

[2] Optatus, i. 24 (Ziwsa, p. 27).

[3] On the powers of these officials and their place in the Imperial hierarchy of the time see E. Stein, *Die Geschichte des spätrömischen Reiches*, i, Vienna, 1928, pp. 53 ff.

[4] Aurelius Victor, *De Caesaribus* (ed. Pichlmayr, 1911), 40. 17; Zosimus (ed. Mendelssohn, 1887), ii. 12; Besnier, op. cit., pp. 339–40.

[5] *Chronica Minora* (ed. Mommsen, Berlin, 1892, *Monumenta Germaniae Historica*), 1. 148: 'Maxentius imp. ann. vi . . . fames magna fuit.'

[6] Besnier, op. cit., p. 340.

[7] Aurelius Victor, *De Caesaribus*, 40; Zosimus, ii. 14; Pallu de Lessert, *Fastes*, ii. 1, p. 16.

C

priests, Felix, was discovered as the author of some of these scurrilous tracts and, threatened with arrest, threw himself on his bishop's mercy. Mensurius, with unwonted courage, refused to surrender him to the authorities. He was summoned by Maxentius to Rome. There, however, his mission was apparently a complete success. No further action was taken against Felix, and a promise of toleration for the Church was received from Maxentius. Before he could return home, however, Mensurius was taken ill and died.[1]

This event occurred probably at the end of 311 or early in 312. The next months were filled by an extraordinary series of intrigues, as rival parties and personalities jockeyed for the succession and the fruits of office. The facts would appear to be given by Optatus of Milevis. The first thing that happened was that the presbyters or *seniores*[2] of the church of Carthage, to whom had fallen the administration of the see in Mensurius' absence, tried to hurry through the election of one of their own number before the Numidians arrived on the scene.[3] This in itself suggests the strong rivalry between the churches of Numidia and Carthage at this moment.

Since Cyprian's time the Primate of Numidia had acquired the right of consecrating the new Primate of Africa at Carthage,[4] but this privilege was strenuously opposed by the Carthaginian clergy. These could claim that the custom of the African Church was for the consecration to be undertaken by bishops of the same province as the candidate,[5] and, as Augustine pointed out, they could also quote the custom of the Roman Church whereby each new bishop was consecrated by the neighbouring

---

[1] Optatus, i. 17.

[2] At this period it is not certain who the *seniores* were. In Tertullian's time they were a council of lay elders charged with administrative duties (*Apol.* 39. 4). There are some indications that this may have continued to be the case, but if that were so it is difficult to see what functions the presbyter could have had apart from parish work.

[3] Optatus, i. 18: 'Botrus et Celestius ut dicitur, apud Carthaginem ordinari cupientes, operam dederunt, ut absentibus Numidis soli vicini episcopi peterentur, qui ordinationem apud Carthaginem celebrarent.'

[4] When is uncertain, but the fact is stated by Augustine, *Psalmus contra Partem Donati*, ll. 44–46 (*PL.* xliii, col. 26). 'Cum Carthaginem venissent episcopum ordinare, | Invenerunt Caecilianum jam ordinatum in sua sede | Irati sunt quia ipsi non potuerunt ordinare.'

[5] Cyprian, *Ep.* 67. 5 (Hartel, p. 739): 'Quod apud nos quoque et fere per provincias universas tenetur, ut ad ordinationes rite celebrandas ad eam plebem cui praepositus ordinatur episcopi ejusdem provinciae proximi quique conveniant.'

Bishop of Ostia.[1] In fact, their own choice of a consecrator from outside the Proconsular Province was to make it impossible for them to base any case on these claims.

They had a more compelling reason to act quickly. Before he left, Mensurius had entrusted to them a number of gold and silver objects which could not safely be buried. These the *seniores* meant to realize for their own benefit.[2] Mensurius, however, had not felt complete confidence in them, and as a precaution had given a copy of the inventory to an old woman with instructions to hand it to his successor should he not return. Unfortunately for the *seniores*, they could not agree on a candidate. Two clerics, named Botrus and Celestius, put themselves forward, but neither won approval, and in the end the choice fell on Mensurius' archdeacon, Caecilian.[3] The old woman promptly handed over her inventory to him and the *seniores* were obliged to disgorge their plunder.

Caecilian was acclaimed by the citizen body[4] in Carthage, but he was not liked by the people. He seems to have been trusted by Mensurius, he was able and he held strong convictions, but his past career was against him. Even if some of the more sensational stories of his cruelty towards the confessors, and in particular the martyrs of Abitina, were untrue, he had for over a decade been known as an opponent of what he considered an exaggerated esteem of martyrs. Now, in addition, he was faced with the hostility of a party among the clergy. Unlike Cyprian in a similar situation after his own election as bishop, he could not count on popular support. He had made too many enemies.

[1] Augustine, *Breviculus Collationis*, iii. 16. 29: 'Cum aliud habeat Ecclesiae catholicae consuetudo, ut non Numidiae, sed propinquiores episcopos episcopum ecclesiae Carthaginis ordinent; sicut nec Romanae Ecclesiae ordinat aliquis episcopus metropolitanus sed de proximo Ostiensis episcopus.' The argument is interesting as showing the influence of the Roman See on local usages in the Catholic section of the African Church in Augustine's time. It is not, however, very convincing. Apthungi (Henchir es Souar) was not in Proconsular Africa at all, but fifty miles from Carthage in Byzacena, while Thuburbo Maius (Pont du Fahs) and Tyzica, the sees of Caecilian's other consecrators, were hardly 'neighbouring' Carthage.

[2] Optatus, i. 17.

[3] Ibid. This incident may perhaps indicate rivalry between presbyters and the deacons in the Church at Carthage such as existed in Cyprian's time, but there is no direct evidence for this. The election of the archdeacon (*archidiaconus*) was usual.

[4] Ibid., i. 19: 'cum Caeciliano tota civica frequentia fuerat'. Caecilian was thus in exactly the opposite situation to Silvanus of Cirta, whose even more questionable election had been acclaimed by the mob against the wishes of the citizens.

One of these, Lucilla, a rich Spaniard resident in Carthage, had never forgotten having been rebuked by him before the Persecution for kissing some alleged martyr's bone before receiving the Communion.[1] She decided her chance of revenge had come. One of her servants named Majorinus was a lector in Caecilian's office.[2] If popular clamour could be raised against Caecilian as an 'enemy of the martyrs', then a rival candidate might be found in Majorinus.

Meantime, Caecilian had been consecrated by three bishops, two from Proconsular Africa and one, Felix of Apthungi across the border in Byzacena.[3] None of these seems to have enjoyed a very high repute, and Felix was a suspected *traditor*. Nevertheless, no objection seems to have been raised at the ceremony, and Caecilian's embassies to other important sees announcing his consecration were well received.[4]

Secundus of Tigisis, however, was not prepared to accept a *fait accompli*. It is reasonable to assume with Duchesne that he had been kept informed of the situation by Donatus of Casae Nigrae, who was now an open opponent of Caecilian.[5] So when messengers from the opposition invited him to intervene he accepted with alacrity.[6]

Seventy Numidian bishops accompanied Secundus to Carthage.[7] They were a formidable and violent crew. They included Purpurius of Limata, and most of the others who had taken part in the Synod of Cirta. But nobody was to question them about their past. They found the city in a ferment and a prey to rumours damning the name of Caecilian.[8] The clergy who had formerly opposed Numidian participation so vigorously had changed their minds. The Numidian prelates were made to feel

[1] Optatus, i. 16, 'potens et factiosa femina'. See P. Monceaux, 'L'Église donatiste avant Saint-Augustin', *Revue de l'Histoire des Religions*, lx, 1909, p. 16.

[2] Optatus, i. 19: 'Majorinus, qui lector in diaconio Caeciliani fuerat, domesticus Lucillae, ipsa suffragante episcopus ordinatus erat.'

[3] Ibid.; Augustine, *Ad Donatistas post Collationem*, 22. 38 (*PL.* xliii, col. 676). The other bishops were Novellus of Tyzica and Faustinus of Thuburbo Maius, both of whom were also alleged *traditores*.

[4] Augustine, *Contra Epistolam Parmeniani*, 1. 3. 5 (*PL.* xliii, col. 37).

[5] L. Duchesne, op. cit., pp. 81–82. I accept the view that Donatus of Casae Nigrae and Donatus 'the Great' are one and the same person. See Dom J. Chapman, *Revue Bénédictine*, xxvi, 1909, pp. 13–23.

[6] Optatus, i. 19: 'Ad Secundum Tigisitanum missum est ut Carthaginem veniretur.'

[7] Augustine, *Ad Catholicos Epistola*, 18. 46 (*PL.* xliii, col. 426).

[8] Id., *Contra Epistolam Parmeniani*, 1. 2. 3 (*PL.* xliii, col. 36).

at home.[1] Soon Secundus heard not merely that the consecration had been undertaken by only three bishops instead of the usual twelve but that Felix of Apthungi was a *traditor*, and it was on this point that popular anger had fastened.

The first action Secundus took, therefore, was to consider Caecilian's election as unconfirmed, and to appoint an interim administrator (an *interventor*) to look after the see until the dispute was settled.[2] The *Interventor* was murdered in his church, allegedly by the Caecilianists.[3] Secundus replied by calling a Council of his bishops, which Caecilian was invited to attend.

The theory of episcopal equality to which Secundus' colleagues had successfully appealed in 305 was now applied against them by Caecilian himself. He refused to appear, and suggested that Secundus might come to his church and state his complaints there.[4] For Secundus to have accepted this would have been to acknowledge Caecilian as lawful bishop.

The deadlock was broken by what seems to have been a false move on Caecilian's part. He challenged his enemies to come out into the open and say what they had against him. He proposed that, 'if Felix of Apthungi had conferred nothing on him, let the Numidians ordain him as if he were still a deacon'.[5] Augustine saw the danger of this suggestion, and tried to prove that Caecilian was merely being sarcastic,[6] but it gave the Numidians the pretext they were looking for. In making this proposal, Caecilian seemed to admit that consecration by a *traditor* was not valid, and that though he suspected he might have been consecrated by one such he had continued to act as Primate of Africa. The reply of some of the Numidians was characteristic. Purpurius of Limata said he would break Caecilian's head in penance when he performed the consecration.[7] Secundus, fortified by what Augustine calls a 'seditious mob

---

[1] Optatus, i. 18, 'suscepti hospitio ab avaris'.

[2] Augustine, *Ep.* 44. 4. 8, 'dedisse quendam interventorem'. In *Sermo* 46. 15 Augustine calls him a *visitator*. On his role, *Codex Canonum Eccl. Africanae*, 74 (ed. Bruns, p. 174).

[3] Id., *Ep.* 44. 4. 8, 'Nunc ergo interventorem in suo conventiculo a nostris dicebat occisum.'   [4] Optatus, i. 19.

[5] Ibid. 'Si Felix in se nihil contulisset, ipsi tamquam adhuc diaconum ordinarent.'

[6] *Breviculus Collationis*, iii. 16. 29, 'Quod quidem sic dictum est, ideo dici potest ad illos irridendos.'

[7] Optatus, i. 19, Exeat huc, 'quasi imponatur illi manus in episcopatu et quassetur illi caput de poenitentia'.

drunk with its own wickedness',[1] proceeded to have Caecilian condemned by his Council. The alliance between the Carthaginian lower class and the Numidian clergy which persisted throughout the history of Donatism was coming into being. It is possible that Donatus himself served as the link between the Numidian and Carthaginian oppositions.[2]

Secundus' Council must have met in the autumn of 312. Reflecting African usages, each bishop recorded his view individually in a short speech.[3] One of these, that of a Bishop Marcian, has been preserved.

In His Gospel the Lord says, 'I am the true vine, and my Father is the husbandman. Every branch in me that beareth not fruit he cutteth off and casteth it away; and every branch that beareth fruit, he cleanseth it.' Thus, unfruitful branches are to be cut off and cast aside. So, *thurificati*, *traditores*, and those who being in schism are ordained by *traditores* cannot remain within the Church of God, unless they are reconciled through penance with wailing acknowledgement [of their fault]. Hence, no one ought to communicate with Caecilian who has been ordained by *traditores* in schism.[4]

The sentence illustrates the view of the Numidians and of the rigorist opposition to Caecilian. The *traditor* clergy were already considered schismatics. The Church was composed of those who had defied the Persecution, and to it the lapsed could only be admitted after severe penance. It followed in Marcian's mind that the action of Donatus in putting lapsed bishops and clergy to penance would be not only commendable in itself but the only means by which they could return to the Christian community.

Caecilian was unanimously condemned on the grounds that his consecration had been invalid and that, while deacon, he had denied food to the imprisoned martyrs of Abitina.[5] The Council,

---

[1] *Ep.* 43. 5. 14, 'furiosa et poculo erroris atque corruptionis ebria multitudo'.

[2] Dom J. Chapman, 'Donatus the Great and Donatus of Casae Nigrae', in *Revue Bénédictine*, 1909, pp. 13 ff.

[3] As had been the practice at Cyprian's Council at Carthage in 256.

[4] *Liber contra Fulgentium Donatistam*, 26 (*PL*. xliii, col. 774), 'In Evangelio suo Dominus ait, "Ego sum vitis vera, et Pater meus agricola; omnem palmitem in me non afferentem fructum, excidet et projiciet; et omnem manentem in me et fructum ferentem, purgat illum." Sicut ergo palmites infructuosi amputati projiciuntur, ita thurificati, traditores, et qui in schismate a traditoribus ordinantur manere in Ecclesia Dei non possunt, nisi cognito ululatu suo per poenitentiam reconcilientur. Unde Caeciliano in schismate a traditoribus ordinato non communicare oportet.'

[5] Augustine, *Breviculus Collationis*, iii. 14. 26, 'tanquam a traditoribus ordinatus,

allegedly influenced by a gift of 400 *folles*[1] from Lucilla, proceeded to elect Majorinus as bishop in Caecilian's stead. The money they received did not reach the poor for whom it may have been intended. Purpurius of Limata took 100 *folles* for himself and the rest was said to have been divided out among Silvanus of Cirta and his clergy.[2] The Council then sent embassies in Majorinus' favour to Rome, Spain, and Gaul, and letters announcing the decision of the Council were dispatched to the African provinces.[3] This done, the Numidians, satisfied that their rights had been vindicated, returned home.

The dispute over Caecilian's consecration had become a schism. In Optatus' picturesque phrase 'one altar was set up against another',[4] and when Majorinus died soon afterwards (probably as early as the summer of 313), Donatus of Casae Nigrae was immediately chosen in his place.[5] He was destined to preside over the fortunes of his Church for over 40 years, and it was from him that the Donatists took their name.

At this moment the African Church merely seemed to be following in the wake of other Churches where persecution had been severe. Apart from the personalities involved the immediate issue was factual. Was Felix of Apthungi a *traditor* or not? He himself was regarded by the opponents of Caecilian as 'the root of the whole evil',[6] and if he had lapsed during the Persecution, then it could be claimed from precedents in Cyprian's time that his consecration of Caecilian was invalid. If he were vindicated then Caecilian was bishop, and his opponents would have to give way with as good a grace as possible. There was no logical reason for schism.

There was much to be said for those, like Optatus of Milevis and the Roman authorities of the day, who took this optimistic view. In both the Severan and Decian persecutions there had

et quia cum esset diaconus, victum afferi martyribus in custodia constitutis prohibuisse dicebatur'.

[1] Clearly, 400 purses each containing a weight of coins. Four hundred individual Diocletianic *folles* would have been an insignificant sum. Augustine, *Ad Catholicos Epistola*, 25. 73 (*PL*. xliii, col. 443).

[2] *Gesta apud Zenophilum*, p. 194, 'Nundinarius dixit, "Purpurius episcopus tulit centum *folles*."'

[3] Augustine, *Contra Epistolam Parmeniani*, 1. 2. 2; Optatus, i. 20.

[4] Optatus, i. 15 and 19, 'et altare contra altare erectum est'.

[5] *Gesta apud Zenophilum* (Ziwsa, p. 185), 'Maiorinum, qui Donatus successit'.

[6] Augustine, *Breviculus Collationis*, iii. 14. 26 (*PL*. xliii, col. 639), 'fons malorum omnium diceretur'.

been temporary schisms in the African Church between the confessor or puritan party and the moderates. In Cyprian's time the question at issue had also been the treatment of the lapsed. But these storms had blown over and unity had been quickly restored. Moreover, in Palestine, Rome, and Alexandria there had been similar controversies, but these also were destined to leave little mark on the history of the Church in those places. Why was it to be so different in Africa? At Rome, at least, the confessors had had cause to complain of the conduct of the bishop and some of his clergy. Pope Marcellinus is reported in a number of sources actually to have sacrificed to the gods,[1] and for nearly three years between 308 and 311 the city was the scene of a struggle between Pope and anti-Pope. Only when both Eusebius and his rival Heraclius had died in exile did the moderates gain the upper hand and elect an African, Militiades, as bishop in July 311.[2] Then, as in Novatian's time, opposition faded away. Militiades himself was suspect as a *traditor*, and the parallel between his and Caecilian's positions should be borne in mind in assessing his attitude towards Caecilian's opponents.

In Egypt the early stages of the Melitian controversy recall vividly the story of Donatism.[3] There, Bishop Peter of Alexandria had been imprisoned in the early days of the Great Persecution, but had managed none the less to continue to administer his church. He was accused of lack of courage, and bolder spirits rallied to a certain Bishop Melitios of Lycopolis (Assiut) in Upper Egypt. In 305 this cleric defied his superior and began to tour the whole country, putting lapsed clergy to penance and conducting new ordinations. In this he was acting in exactly the same way as Donatus of Casae Nigrae. The

---

[1] The Donatists would appear to be on firm ground when they claimed this (Augustine, *Contra Litteras Petiliani*, ii. 92. 202, and *De Unico Baptismo*, 16. 27). The *Liber Genealogus* (ed. Mommsen, *Chronica Minora*, i, Berlin, 1892, p. 196), adds a further detail, that the deacons Strato and Cassian were with Pope Marcellinus when he sacrificed publicly to the pagan gods in the Capitol. The tradition of Marcellinus' conformity to paganism is also preserved in the *Liber Pontificalis* (ed. Duchesne, vol. i, part ii, p. 162) which records, 'De qua re et ipse Marcellinus ad sacrificium ductus est ut turificaret quod et fecit.' Later, it is asserted, he was martyred. There seems, however, to have been a real attempt to subject him to a *damnatio memoriae* after his death. See Jalland, *The Church and the Papacy* (S.P.C.K., 1944), pp. 185–6.

[2] L. Duchesne, *Early History of the Church*, ii, p. 76.

[3] On the Melitian schism, see H. Lietzmann, *Geschichte der alten Kirche*, iii. 103 ff. in the English translation. Sources quoted.

release of Bishop Peter, and the circular that he issued at Easter 306 criticizing (like Mensurius of Carthage) voluntary martyrdom and defining the terms under which the lapsed could be readmitted to Communion, added fuel to the flames. The persecution was renewed by Galerius. Melitios separated from the orthodox and threw his lot in with an incipient 'Church of the Martyrs' which was growing up among the confessors and their supporters. He was excommunicated by Peter, and the latter's death as a martyr in November 311 did not end the schism.

But the parallel breaks down at this point. The Melitians were not destined to play the same part in Egypt as the Donatists in North Africa. They embarrassed Peter's successor, Alexander, but never really threatened his authority. They were among the instigators of the proceedings against Arius whom they regarded as a renegade, and they later opposed Athanasius, but the twenty-eight bishops whom they mustered in 325 did not form the basis of a permanent 'national' church on the Donatist model. After the second Council of Nicaea in the autumn of 327[1] many of the Melitians accepted terms for readmission into the main body of the Church which were agreed there. Those remaining declined into a nuisance group, and gradually faded from history.

Not so the Donatists. Similar offers of reconciliation were made in 314 and 347 and they were rejected with scorn. No doubt Caecilian was infinitely more hated than Alexander, but the explanation of the Donatist obstinacy seems to lie outside the personalities of the main actors, and outside the legal and even the theological aspects of the controversy.[2] Felix of Apthungi was declared innocent of *traditio* in 315, Caecilian was formally vindicated after exhaustive inquiries by the Emperor Constantine in 316, and finally, in December 320, Silvanus of Cirta was proved in a trial before the governor of Numidia Militana to have been himself a *traditor*.[3] Within a generation, however, Donatism was the religion of 'nearly all Africa',[4] and neither

---

[1] H. Lietzmann, op. cit., p. 124. The Melitians were promised that their ordination would be recognized as valid when they returned to the Church; their bishops, however, must give way to Alexander's nominees, and Melitios was to withdraw to his own see of Lycopolis.

[2] For a critical appreciation of the personal factors that contributed to Donatism, see D. Voelter's *Der Ursprung des Donatismus*, p. 193.

[3] See below, Chap. XI.

[4] Jerome, *De Viris Illustribus*, 93 (*PL.* xxiii, col. 695).

force nor argument could root it out subsequently. The most likely method of approach to this problem seems to be the understanding of conditions in Numidia. Numidian bishops had condemned Caecilian, Numidian peasants had elected Silvanus as bishop, and Numidia had shown the most fanatical zeal for Christianity during the Persecution. Southern Numidia remained for three centuries the heart of Donatism. Proconsular Africa, on the other hand, remained generally loyal to Caecilian and to Catholicism. The geographical distinction is interesting, and perhaps the clue to Donatism may be found in a comparative study of economic and social conditions in these two provinces, and of the popular religion which flourished there.

II

CARTHAGE AND NUMIDIA

To the modern European Roman Africa means primarily Carthage. Memories remain of the Punic Wars, of Scipio and Hannibal, and perhaps even of the 'Numidian cavalry' that fought in Hannibal's armies at Lake Trasimene and Cannae. But the emphasis is on Carthage, and in later classical times on the Proconsular Province, the 'granary of Rome'. By the end of the Roman period, however, Carthage had become of little account. The battles between Byzantines and Arabs were fought on the plateaux, at Sbeitla (Lat. Suffetula) in 647 or near Biskra in 683. Carthage is mentioned once by Arab authors, in 698 when it was sacked.[1] The site was then ignored, for Tunis on the western extremity of the Lake of Tunis was less exposed and served equally well as a port. North Africa itself was known to the invaders merely as 'the isle of the West', the great land bridge between Mediterranean and desert that linked Kairouan with the main centres of Islam, Andalusia and Cairo. In the ninth and tenth centuries it was the corridor down which advanced the camel-mounted armies in campaigns fought over immense distances with Fez, Kairouan, or Cairo as the prize. The Donatists for their part had a third view of Africa, summed up in their interpretation of the verse in the Old Latin text[2] of Canticles i. 7, 'Tell me, O thou whom my soul loveth, where thou feedest, where thou makest thy flock to rest *in the south.*'[3] And 'the south' was Numidia, the land appointed by the Lord as His inheritance for His Bride, the Donatist Church.

These divergent views of North Africa are a reflection of its geography, which has allowed successively Roman cities, farming communities, and nomadic principalities to take root and flourish. Each in turn has become the predominant unit of society and its culture and religion have prevailed over the whole territory.[4]

[1] See E. F. Gautier, *Le Passé de l'Afrique du Nord*, Payot, Paris, 1937, pp. 247–54.

[2] The Donatists used the Old Latin Bible in use in Cyprian's time.

[3] Augustine, *Ep.* 93. 8. 24, and *Contra Donatistas, ad Catholicos Epistola*, 16. 40 (*PL.* xliii, cols. 421–2), 'ubi pascis, ubi cubas in meridie'.

[4] For the social geography of North Africa I have made use of the following: (a) S. Gsell, *L'Histoire ancienne de l'Afrique du Nord*, i, Paris, Leroux, 1913; (b) E. F.

Sandwiched between the Mediterranean and the Sahara, Barbary is in fact a long corridor, whose coastline extends 2,000 miles from the Gulf of Syrtes to Casablanca. Hardly one-fifth of that distance, however, separates the seaboard from the desert, and in parts the Sahara penetrates to within a bare hundred miles from the coast. The desert, stretching away 3,000 miles towards the Niger, has always been a more formidable barrier between the Libyans and the remainder of the African continent than was the Mediterranean against European influences. The climate and vegetation, too, are Mediterranean. North Africa may be reckoned as a part of the European, Mediterranean world, though an extremely backward part.

The two great mountain ranges running parallel from southwest to north-east the whole length of the country have kept North Africa sealed off alike from the desert and from Europe. How true this is of the northern range which runs along the coast can be tested by any traveller who crosses the Mediterranean from Marseilles to Algiers. There are few scenes more beautiful but less inviting than the distant view of the North African coast. Behind the forbidding grey of an unbroken line of cliffs, one sees rising tier on tier a tumbled waste of mountain, until crowning the horizon the snow-covered Djujuras sparkle and glisten in the early sunlight. The impression is not deceptive. From the Atlantic to the Tunisian headlands the coast is little more than cliffs indented here and there by small bays and narrow forelands. The mountain ranges of the Djebel Edough and Djebel Mjedja between Bone (Lat. Hippo Regius) and Collo (Lat. Chullu) or the Gouraya and Djebel Bissa in the Kabylie have always been forested, and shelving steeply to the sea leave no room for anchorages. Classical writers knew this shore as a 'sea without ports'.[1]

Access from Europe is also hindered by an almost complete lack of navigable rivers. Even the Mejerda (Lat. Bagradas) is

Gautier, *Le Passé de l'Afrique du Nord*, Paris, Payot, 1937; (c) A. Bernard, *Atlas de l'Algérie et de la Tunisie*, Algiers, 1924; (d) A. N. Sherwin-White, 'Geographical Factors in Roman Algeria', *JRS*. xxxiv, 1944, pp. 1–10. On Numidia (the Department of Constantine) A. Berthier, *Les Vestiges du Christianisme antique dans la Numidie centrale*, is useful, especially pp. 9–22; M. Cary, *Geographic Background of Greek and Roman History* (O.U.P., 1949), pp. 220–9, should also be consulted.

[1] Sallust, *De Bello Jugurthino*, 17 (ed. Ahlberg, Teubner, p. 53), 'mare inportuosum'. The small ports along the Algerian coast provided sailing-ships with little protection against the strong north winds encountered in the spring. Cf. Procopius, *De Bello Vandalico* (ed. Loeb, p. 132), iii. 15, 'ἀλίμενόν τε παντελῶς.'

reduced to a stream during the summer, and the Seybouse near whose mouth Hippo Regius grew up is blocked by rapids. The coastal settlements founded by the Carthaginians, like the Greek settlements on the Illyrian coast, were sited for defence and not for the purpose of trading with the interior. River estuaries were avoided.[1] Algeria in classical times turned its back on the Mediterranean and on Europe,[2] and the Berbers of the interior were never influenced by a spread of Punic or Latin influence inland from the long-established coastal towns.

In one quarter only does North Africa stand open to penetration from Europe. At Cap Blanc the African coast bends sharply southwards. The mountains lying between Bizerta and Hammam Lif are scarcely higher than foothills, and then beyond Sousse (Lat. Hadrumetum) the last outcrops of the mountains of Zeugitana give way to a vast level plain of quarternary limestone that extends as far south as the Gulf of Gabes. This coast, situated almost half-way between Egypt and Spain and only seventy-five miles from Sicily, was destined to become a centre of exchange between the peoples of Europe and the Near East.

By the ninth century B.C both Carthage and Utica were already in existence. In addition, the land behind both of these towns is comparatively low-lying, the soil is alluvial, and there is sufficient rain for abundant crops to be grown. But despite these advantages Carthage never achieved quite the same eminence in Roman Africa as, for instance, Alexandria achieved in Egypt or Antioch in Syria. It was impossible to rule all Africa from the north-east corner, and the Carthaginians themselves seem to have set greater store on the possession of Sicily than on the conquest of territory lying immediately to the west of the city. The problem of communications was insoluble. The Mejerda is not navigable and never developed into a commercial highway linking Numidia with Carthage. There were only two ways by which one could travel to Numidia by land from Carthage.[3] The first led round the coast via Hippo Diarrhytos

---

[1] Rusiccade, for instance, stands two and a half miles west of the mouth of the River Safsaf, and Hippo Regius about the same distance from the Seybouse. Thabraca was built on an island a few hundred yards from the Tunisian coast. Apart from necessities of defence, one of the main reasons for avoiding river-mouths was probably the presence of malaria near the estuaries.

[2] Sherwin-White, op. cit., pp. 5–6.

[3] Travel to Carthage from the interior was seldom by river. Goods were loaded

(Bizerta) and the other followed the Mejerda as far as Souk Ahras (Lat. Thagaste). But both ways were slow, and the southern or shorter route was made more hazardous by the thick forests which extend westwards from the border of the Proconsular Province into Numidia. As a result, Carthaginian, and later Roman, influence spread slowly into Numidia, and this province, whether in the time of Massinissa or in that of Firmus and Gildo, was able to hold its own politically against an administration centred at Carthage.

In addition, the areas open to intensive settlement in the Proconsular Province itself were divided off from each other by wide tracts of inhospitable country. The wilderness known as the Tractus Carthaginensis occupied a large part of the middle Mejerda valley, and this river, flowing sluggishly through the plain, furrows too deep a channel for use to be made of its waters for irrigation. In these sparsely cultivated lands the primitive Berber element survived in immediate proximity to the more civilized Carthaginian and Roman.

There was, however, an even more formidable barrier in the way of a common civilization growing up between Carthage and the interior. The country of forest and fertile valleys known as the Tell extends to a depth of about ninety miles from the Tunisian and Algerian coasts. Beyond that, lying between the mountain masses of the Kabylie to the north-west and the Aures mountains to the south, the country changes its character completely. The transformation from a well-watered and varied countryside between Constantine and Ain Mlila to the expanses of the High Plains that stretch away to the south is sudden and striking. On a journey from the Kabylie to Setif on the northern edge of the plains one has the impression of travelling *upwards* from amid mountains and forests to a vast barren plateau extending as far as the eye can see.

The general features of the High Plains do not vary. From a point west of the town of Bordj bou Arreridj to Sbeitla in Tunisia lie a series of plains, enclosed and broken by bare and eroded mountain spurs. Across the centre of this territory extends a belt of shallow salt lakes (*chotts*) formed by streams running north-

on to pack-animals or on clumsy two-wheeled vehicles. Trade between Carthage and Numidia must have been restricted. See the Oued Ramel mosaic (now in Bardo Museum), published in *Nouvelles Archives des Missions*, xv, 1907, p. 384 (transport in North Africa). Procopius, *De Bello Vandalico*, iv. 4. 26 (ed. Loeb, p. 240), indicates that Hippo Regius was ten days distant from Carthage by road.

wards from the Aures mountains and unable to find an outlet
to the sea. The presence of these chotts increases the salt
nature of the soil, and further subdivides the plains.

These plains average 2,700 feet above sea level, sloping
gradually from west to east from 3,100 feet near Setif to less
than 2,000 feet on the Tunisian-Algerian border. The inter-
vening mountains are not impressive, only one range, the
Djebel Guerioun, attaining a mean height of more than 4,500
feet. In primitive times they may have been wooded, but now
for the most part they consist of bare rocks reflecting an intense
heat which makes the summer intolerable for man and beast.

The division between the Tell and High Plains is not merely
physical but also one of climate and rainfall. All over the Tell,
and especially towards the east, rainfall is adequate. Very
heavy falls are experienced near the coasts, where the high
wooded mountain ranges extend down to the sea. In North
Africa the farmer needs a fall of about twenty to twenty-four
inches a year, spread between the autumn and late spring, to
assure a good wheat crop. Drought in the winter, and not heat
in the summer, is the danger.[1] The whole Tell attains this
amount on an average year, and so also does the strip of land
immediately north of the Aures mountains. This was signifi-
cantly enough the only part of southern Numidia which could
support towns as opposed to villages.

The boundary between the zone with an average rainfall of
more than twenty inches a year and that with less than twenty
inches coincides almost exactly with the boundary of Tell and
High Plains. It begins at the northern end of the Gulf of Hammamet in the east, passes through Djbebina and Kessera, thence
south-west to Thala before bending northwards to Mdaourouch
(Lat. Madauros), and then almost due west along the northern
edge of the plain by Ain Mlila, Saint-Arnaud, and Setif. South of
this line there are seldom more than 40 days' rain a year compared with 80 at Tunis and 100 at Algiers. Near Bone, in the
Edough mountains, even this figure is exceeded.

In addition, the cultivation of wheat on the High Plains was
made more difficult by wide variations in soil fertility. Around

---

[1] Cyprian, *Ad Demetrianum*, 3 (*CSEL*. iii. 1. 352), 'non hieme nutriendis seminibus
tanta imbrium copia est'. Augustine, *Enarratio in Ps.* 120. 15. See also F. G. de
Pachtère, 'Le Règlement d'Irrigation de Lamasba', *Mélanges*, xxviii, 1908, pp.
397–400.

Tebessa and on the plain of the Medjana near Setif there are considerable phosphate deposits, and good crops can be raised on very little rainfall. Classical writers[1] who commented on the fertility of the Numidian plains were not deceiving themselves. Natives scattering seed haphazardly on small plots of ground near their villages can raise sizeable crops, and the same is true even of the inhabitants of the oases on the edge of the Sahara. But the natural fertility of some areas is balanced by the brackishness of others. The salt of the chotts affects the country around them. A great part of the steppes in both Algeria and Tunisia is covered with a dry, salty crust, difficult to plough and unrewarding to normal cultivation.

There is no reason to think that the African climate has changed much since the Roman occupation, except possibly on the northern edge of the Sahara, where drought has increased.[2] In Roman times the wadis were no wider than they are today, and the chotts such as the Garaet el Tarf were no more extensive. One finds Roman ruins on their edges. What has failed has been the will to work, the ability to conserve available water and irrigate available land. The farmer has been replaced by the nomad.

Thus from the outset we are faced with two entirely different types of country in Roman North Africa.[3] The difference was well known to the ancients. Apuleius described his home, Madauros, as on the boundary of Libya and Gaetulia, that is, between the lands of sedentaries and the transhumants.[4] On the one hand there is Carthage, the coast and the river valleys. These are fertile, well watered, able to sustain a large urban population supported by mixed farming—wheat, vines, and stock-raising. There were the elements of a prosperous civilization accessible to influence from the other side of the Mediterranean. The Proconsular Province and parts of northern Numidia were first under Carthaginian influence and then the centres of Roman civilization in Africa.

---

[1] Columella, *De Re Rustica*, iii. 8. 4 (tr. Ash, ed. Loeb, 1941), 'Mysiam Libyamque largis aiunt abundare frumentis.' Cf. Arnobius, i. 16 (*CSEL*. iv. 12).

[2] S. Gsell, *Histoire ancienne*, i. 41–99. Also article by the same author, in the *Revue Africaine*, 1911, lv, no. 283, pp. 343–411, on the North African climate and rainfall in classical times.

[3] The parallel of the Highland and Lowland zones of Roman Britain is suggested as a similar situation to that of Numidia and Carthage.

[4] Apuleius, *Apologia* (ed. Helm, Leipzig, 1912), 24. Sallust, *Bell. Jug.* 18–19.

On the other hand the High Plains, which included southern Numidia, Mauretania Sitifensis, and part of Byzacena, could never support urban communities except immediately north of the Aures mountains. Lack of rainfall and sweet water imposed a lower standard of life on their inhabitants. Even today the Berber subsists on a low diet consisting largely of barley loaf (galetta) and figs. The plains themselves have been throughout history debatable land between nomads and farmers. The re-introduction of the camel[1] into North Africa, probably during the third century, gave the nomads the advantage right up to the French conquest. But in Roman times these territories were a land of villages and were densely peopled. Careful irrigation and the security of the Roman *limes* enabled settled farming communities to develop, with barley and olive cultivation as the basis of their livelihood. The olive-trees drive their roots several feet down and tap the moisture stored deep below the surface. The same crop was raised in the almost rainless areas of Byzacenia and Tripolitania. It is the key to the relative prosperity of all these districts during the Later Roman period.

But even so the inhabitants of the High Plains remained out of touch with Roman civilization. The influence of towns such as Timgad and Lambaesis hardly extended beyond their immediate borders. The Berber peasant used the same plough, dressed in the same type of hooded burnous, carried the same heavy club, and spoke the same Libyan language as he does today.[2] Above all, the inhabitant of the High Plains was conservative, rooted in customs and beliefs originating in a remote past, deeply attached to his independence, and inwardly despising the outlook of his conquerors. This antipathy could be expressed in religious disagreement, in Donatism in the fourth century A.D. and in Kharedjism four centuries later.

---

[1] Dating, Gautier, op. cit., pp. 200–27; S. Gsell, 'La Tripolitaine et le Sahara', *Mémoires de l'Institut national des Antiquaires de France*, xliii (1933), 149. In Strabo's time (Strabo, xvii. 3. 7) the desert tribesmen who came northwards to trade with Cirta used horses and donkeys to carry their packs. Cited from Cary, op. cit., p. 224.

[2] On these aspects of Berber conservatism throughout history, the following works may be useful: H. Basset, 'Les Influences puniques chez les Berbères', *Revue Africaine*, lxiv, 1921, pp. 340–75 (language); A. Berthier and F. Logeart, 'Gravures rupestres à Sila', *Troisième Congrès de la Fédération des Sociétés savantes de l'Afrique du Nord*, 1937 (= *Troisième Congrès*) (rock carvings showing the burnous as a garment approximately second century B.C.); J. Bérard, 'Mosaïques inédites de Cherchel', *Mélanges*, lii, 1935, pp. 113–42 (ploughs and native costume); A. Berthier, *L'Algérie et son passé*, Picard, 1951, chapter i (general).

III

TOWN AND COUNTRY IN ROMAN AFRICA

BEFORE discussing the geographical distribution of Donatist and Catholic communities, it is necessary to describe
the type of society which grew up on the Tell and High
Plains, and which formed the environment of the rival Churches.

As is well known, in Carthaginian times a civilization similar
to that of Roman Africa began to take shape along parts of the
Tunisian coast and down the river valleys leading inland from
Carthage itself.[1] The dominion of Carthage, as that of Rome
after her, tended to take the form of a confederation of cities.
These were organized administrative units, governed by a council
with executive officers known as Suffetes, reminiscent of the
Ordines and Duumvirates that succeeded them in the Roman
foundations. Sallust is careful to distinguish between the *urbes*
of the Carthaginians and the *castella* and *oppida* of the Libyan
natives.[2] Long before the Romans set foot in Africa, Utica,
Ruspe, Gigthis, and Leptis Magna on the coast were prosperous
towns and their inhabitants were proud of their status as citizens.[3] Their wealth may be assessed from the huge fine which
Caesar was able to levy against them.[4] Libyan society, on the
other hand, remained tribal, communities being governed by
councils of elders, *seniores*,[5] in much the same way as the *Djemaa*
presides over the affairs of a Kabyle village today.

Outside the boundaries of the Carthaginian towns were great
estates worked by slaves, the precursors of the Roman villas in
Africa. Agathocles' soldiers in 310 B.C., as they marched on

[1] On the Carthaginians in North Africa, S. Gsell, *Histoire ancienne de l'Afrique
du Nord*, iv (Paris, 1924), is recommended.

[2] Sallust, *De Bello Jugurthino* (ed. Ahlberg), 19. 3, 'post aliae Punicae urbes',
&c., as against 21. 2, 'Cirtam oppidum' and 'oppida castellaque munita adire',
ibid. 89. 2, when referring to Libyan settlements. Also Pliny, *Historiae Naturalis*
(ed. Mayhoff, 1906), 5. 1, 'populorum ejus [Libya] oppidorum nomina'.

[3] S. Gsell, *Histoire ancienne de l'Afrique du Nord*, ii, pp. 93 onwards. A Punic
inscription found in the countryside near Tigisis emphasizes that the dedicator was
a 'citizen of Tigisis', J. Chabot, *Recueil de Constantine*, lxiii, 1935–6, p. 197.

[4] [Caesar], *Bellum Africum*, 36. 2; 300,000 *modii* of wheat from Thysdrus.

[5] *CIL*. viii. 1616 (Nibber), and S. Gsell, *Histoire ancienne*, v. 70. *CIL*. viii. 4354 =
20216 shows the existence of *seniores* in Numidia in the late sixth century.

Utica and Carthage,[1] saw mansions surrounded by prairies, well stocked with cattle and horses. The same vision of wealth and abundance greeted Regulus' army fifty years later.[2]

The Roman occupation continued and intensified these beginnings. Rome discovered a second Sicily in North Africa, and the dispatch of some two-thirds of the annual wheat crop to Rome opened the way of prosperity to the growing towns of the Tell and the coast. It is noticeable that the early Roman roads were directed less to the needs of the interior than to the ports.[3] Connexions with Rome were strengthened, perhaps even at the expense of the settlement of the High Plains. As early as Strabo's time a great number of African ships were calling at Ostia.[4] A considerable African community came into existence in the capital, a fact which was not without importance in the development of Latin Christianity.

The export trade to Rome also meant that a large proportion of the best land must be kept in cultivation for corn-growing. The two centuries of peace which the Proconsular Province enjoyed from the reign of Augustus to the rebellion against Maximin in A.D. 238 enabled a wealthy urban civilization to grow up there. Around military posts, such as Sufes and Thala, along the roads leading away from Carthage up the Mejerda and Miliana valleys, from colonies of veterans, or from prosperous native settlements, Roman cities grew into being. It was no part of Rome's policy to urbanize the natives. The towns were useful as administrative and fiscal centres. Their rise was, however, in the nature of a gradual and spontaneous growth, due to the intelligent exploitation of the soil by the inhabitants.[5]

Two examples of this must suffice.[6] In the valley of the Oued Khalled which joins the Mejerda above Testour, about the area of Rutland, six important cities developed, Aunobaris (Henchir Douameus), Agbia (Ain Hedja), Thugga (Dougga), Thubursicum Bure (Teboursouk), Thignica (Ain Tounga), and Numululi (Hr. el Maatria). In a slightly larger area,

[1] Diodorus (ed. Dindorf, 1878), xx. 8. 3.

[2] Polybius (ed. Paton, Loeb Classical Library), 1. 29. 6–7. See also Caesar, *Bell. Af.*, 9. 2.

[3] Discussed by J. Toutain in *Les Cités romaines de la Tunisie* (Paris, 1895), p. 142. For roads converging on Hippo Regius, *Recueil de Constantine*, 1898, p. 154.

[4] Strabo (ed. Kramer, 1852), iii. 2. 6.

[5] J. Toutain, 'Le Progrès de la Vie Urbaine', *Mélanges Cagnat*, Paris, Leroux, 1912, pp. 319–47.

[6] Cited from J. Toutain, *Les Cités romaines*, pp. 33 f.

the basin of the Oued Jarabia, the towns of Bisica (Hr.
Bijga), Avitta Bibba (Hr. Bou Ftis), Telepte (Hr. bel Ait),
Abbir Cella (Hr. en Naam), Apisa Maius (Tarf ech Chua),
Thibica (Hr. Bir Magra), and Thuburbo Maius (Pont du Fahs)
were clustered together. In contrast to the sparsity of towns on
the High Plains, only three or four miles separated sizeable
centres such as Muzuc, Furni, and Zama Minor from each other.
All these towns were equipped with baths, fora, paved streets,
and triumphal arches on the Italian model. In the Mejerda
valley alone thirty-five towns acquired municipal status in the first
three centuries A.D.[1] During the second and early third centuries
it was the leading families of these towns, some of them little
more than romanized hill forts,[2] that produced many of the
rulers and literary men of the Roman Empire. The family, for
instance, of Pactumenus Fronto at Constantine, of Antistius
Burrus at Thibilis (Announa), of Severus at Leptis Magna, of
Albinus at Hadrumetum, and of Apuleius of Madauros all contributed to the maintenance of the splendour of the traditions
of Rome. It was with a justifiable pride that African traders
abroad could boast their nationality, *Civis Afer negotians*.[3]

But the inland cities were primarily agricultural centres. They
continued to be situated not from the point of view of commercial advantage, but from that of defence, or water-supply.
Apart from fulling and weaving which were carried on in Mactar,[4]
Carthage,[5] and Thuburbo Maius,[6] there is little trace of industry
in them. The citizens were landowners. Their ambition was to
be an 'agricola bonus',[7] or, on the coast, traders. The city, while
times were prosperous, provided an outlet for their social ambition, but their real interests lay on their estates.

Many of these big villas have been found on the Algerian and
Tunisian Tell. Some may have been just country mansions, but
the majority were centres of large estates run by slaves.[8] St.

---

[1] On Town and Country in general in North Africa, cf. M. Rostovtzev, *Social and Economic History of the Roman Empire*, O.U.P. 1926, pp. 274–93. A basic work.

[2] Tiddis, for example, was the birthplace of Lollius Urbicus, the builder of the Antonine Wall, *CIL*. viii. 6706; S. Gsell, *Atlas archéologique*, Paris, 1911, ff. 17, 86.

[3] *CIL*. iii. 5230; cf. *CIL*. iii. 13137 (Salona, civis Afer).

[4] *CIL*. viii. 23399.   [5] *Cod. Theod*. xi. 1. 24.

[6] *CM*. 243 (makers of common cloth). Simitthu is the only African city which can be regarded as a mining and industrial town.

[7] Inscription from Thubursicum Numidarum, A. Merlin, *Mélanges*, xxiii, 1903, p. 118.

[8] There was even a *collegium* of slaves on a senatorial estate near Sicca Veneria,

Augustine[1] and the writer of the Life of St. Melania the Younger[2] give interesting descriptions of the self-supporting villas that flourished in the fertile valleys near Constantine and Guelma (Lat. Calama). From mosaics also, such as that from the House of the 'Seigneur Julius' at Carthage, it is possible to gain an idea of the intensive form of mixed farming that was practised.[3] Different crops were grown in each season. In the summer sheep and goats were pastured, and the grain harvested. In the autumn the grapes would be gathered in, and in the winter the olives. The owner is shown spending his time hunting.

These cities and villas represent Roman civilization in Africa. The African city was laid out on the exact model of an Italian city, and some of the African villas, like Oued Athmenia, seem to have been planned according to the rules of Vitruvius.[4] The baths, the paved streets, the arches, and the fora are no different in Africa from what they are in Italy, and the same Italianate spirit is expressed in the mythological scenes portrayed on African mosaics, and by African literature and verse. It is interesting to note that the one portrait of Virgil comes from a mosaic in a house in Hadrumetum,[5] and that lines of the Aeneid are recorded on a funerary inscription from the out-of-the-way settlement of Narragarra.[6]

Wherever cities grew up, the original differences between Roman and Berber tended to die out. At Dougga,[7] at Numululi,[8] at Masculula,[9] at Uchi Maius,[10] and at Thuburbo Maius,[11] the

---

CIL. viii. 16292. On other large villas, P. Gauckler, *Monuments Piot*, iii, 1897, p. 177 (Uthina), and R. Cagnat, *Bull. Arch. du Comité*, 1928–9, pp. 51–55 (Gor, in Tunisia).

[1] Augustine, *In Ps.* 64. 8 (*PL.* xxxvi–xxxvii, col. 779). 'Fratres, constituamus nobis aliquam domum divitem; quantis bonis referta sit, quam copiosa sit, vasa quam multa ibi aurea, sed et argentea; quantum familiae, quantum jumentorum et animalium. Ipsa denique domus quam delectat picturis, marmore, laquearibus columnis, spatiis, cubiculis.'

[2] *Vita Sanctae Melaniae Junioris* (ed. Rampolla), 21, 'Possessio major erat civitati ipsius, habens balneum, artifices multos, aurifices, argentarios, et aerarios.' Rostovtzev, *Social and Economic History*, p. 290.

[3] A. Merlin, *Bull. Arch. du Comité*, 1921, pp. 95–114.

[4] J. Toutain, *Les Cités romaines*, p. 73; J. and P. Alquier, 'Les Thermes romains du Val d'Or', *Recueil de Constantine*, 1928–9, p. 291; P. Gauckler, *La Domaine des Laberii*, p. 217.

[5] P. Gauckler, *Inventaire des Mosaïques*, Paris, 1910, ii. 1, no. 133.

[6] *CIL.* viii. 4635.

[7] *CIL.* viii. 1495, 26591, 26622.   [8] *CIL.* viii. 26121.

[9] *CIL.* viii. 15775, 'conventus civium Romanor(um) et Numidarum qui Mascululae habitant'.   [10] *CIL.* viii. 15447.

[11] A. Merlin, 'Thuburbo Maius', *Cinquième Congrès International d'Archéologie*, 1930, p. 217.

native community and the colony of veterans which had settled beside it merged outwardly into a single whole. The process was a gradual one and probably at no time were the lower classes in the towns romanized to any extent.[1] The *pagus* of Roman veterans was at first content to choose the same patron as the native *civitas*;[2] only the *pagus* would acquire the right to receive legacies in its corporate capacity,[3] but finally the union of the two communities would be sealed in the *civitas'* attainment of municipal status. Then, the two *Ordines* would be amalgamated, and their union perhaps symbolized by a common dedication of the Capitol.[4] In the same way great native landowners such as the Arrii, north of M'Chira,[5] and the Pacati of Gigthis[6] entered the ranks of the senatorial nobility. Lesser men readily adopted Latin names and abandoned their native dress for the toga.[7]

The conversion, however, was less profound than outward appearances would suggest. The Carthaginian and Berber foundations on which Rome had built never disappeared completely. The transformation of the deities Baal and Tanit into Saturn and Caelestis or Juno was in name only, and in many other aspects of African life Roman civilization was little more than a façade. Even in flourishing towns such as Gigthis,[8] Punic remained an official language as late as the middle of the second century A.D., and the Latino-Punic, neo-Punic inscriptions[9] found in many parts of the Algerian Tell suggests that Punic continued to be spoken among the literate classes for a considerable time. We know in fact that two of Roman Africa's

[1] See, for instance, A. Belorgey's article on the native funerary caverns near Hippo in the Roman period, *Troisième Congrès des Soc. savantes*, 1937.

[2] As at Dougga, *CIL*. viii. 1494; *CM*. 556.

[3] The *ius capiendorum legatorum*, as at Dougga in A.D. 168, *CIL*. viii. 26528 b; L. Poinssot, 'Une Inscription de Dougga', *CRAI.*, 1911, pp. 496–503.

[4] Cf. A. Merlin, 'Thuburbo Maius', p. 218.

[5] On the Arrii, *CIL*. viii, 23831; *CM*. 279; *CIL*. vi. 1478 and iii. 6810–12; A. Merlin, *Bull. Arch. du Comité*, 1915, cxxxvii, and 1916, cxxxii.

[6] *CIL*. viii. 22729. Cf. L. A. Constans, 'Gigthis', *Nouvelles Archives des Missions*, xxii, 1916, p. 16, on senatorial families at Gigthis.

[7] This was a gradual process. Steles from the sanctuary of Saturn-Caelestis at Bir-Tlelsa (near el Djem) still show women worshippers wearing Carthaginian dress including the Punic conical hat (L. Poinssot, *Bull. Arch. du Comité*, 1927, pp. 32–36).

[8] P. Gauckler, *Nouvelles Archives des Missions*, xv, 1907, p. 325, no. 60. Also, *CIL*. viii. 15 (Leptis Magna).

[9] Such as *CIL*. viii. 793 (Hr. Brigita, third century A.D.); *CIL*. viii. 4636 (Narragarra); *CIL*. viii. 4936 (Thubursicum Bure).

greatest sons, Apuleius[1] and the Emperor Severus,[2] first learnt Latin at the schools, and that the women members of their families never mastered it. Carthaginian institutions seem also to have survived in Punic foundations, even in Volubilis in the far west.[3] Berber names and language forms appear often on Latin inscriptions. In speaking of Latin Africa it is perhaps as well to remember Monceaux's dictum: 'The Africans resembled Romans at a distance; they remained Moors and Carthaginians.'[4]

This Latino-Punic civilization of the Tell dominated North Africa for two centuries and a half, from the accession of Augustus to the revolt of the Gordians in A.D. 238.[5] It was a purely pagan civilization. Despite careful examination of Roman town sites there are practically no material traces of Christianity in the first two centuries A.D. The catacombs at Sousse (Hadrumetum) may be the only major exception to this rule, though there is little that can be assigned with certainty earlier than the third century A.D. The sub-Apostolic age remains the darkest in the history of the Christian Church in North Africa.

Pagan civilization in Africa reached its apogee at the turn of the third century A.D. The age of the Severi (A.D. 193–235) was a period of relative peace, abundance, and prosperity throughout Roman Africa. All over the Tell public buildings were being erected by wealthy citizens or by the patrons of the towns. The prosperity which allowed the building of the forum at Leptis Magna or the great baths at Bulla Regia spread down to the numerous agricultural towns that dotted the plains and river valleys.[6] These were the smaller settlements whose population ranged from between 3,000 to 10,000 inhabitants. They were agricultural units whose economic life probably resembled

---

[1] Apuleius, *Metamorphoses* (ed. Budé, Collection des Universités de France, 1940), Prologue.

[2] *Scriptores Historiae Augustae* (= *SHA*.), 'Vita Severi', 19 (ed. Hohl); Aurelius Victor, *Epitome*, 20; E. F. Gautier, *Le Passé de l'Afrique du Nord*, pp. 131–4.

[3] R. Chatelain, *CRAI.*, 1915, p. 396. Gales in Proconsular Africa is another example, *CIL.* viii. 23833, 23834.

[4] P. Monceaux, *Les Africains, Les Païens* (Paris, 1894), p. 98.

[5] For this period see in particular T. R. S. Broughton, *The Romanisation of Proconsular Africa*, Johns Hopkins, Baltimore, 1929; R. M. Haywood, *Economic Survey of Ancient Rome. North Africa*, Johns Hopkins, Baltimore, 1938.

[6] The forum of Leptis is Severan (P. Romanelli, *Leptis Magna*, Rome, 1925, pp. 21–22) and the baths of Bulla Regia were built by the daughter of the patron of the town in A.D. 186 (R. Cagnat, *CRAI.*, 1920, p. 326). The great era of building in North Africa is A.D. 175–215.

that of the smaller country towns in south Italy today. The population lived and worked on the adjacent lands, but used the town as their administrative and social centre. It was during this period that some of the tribal capitals such as that of the Nattabutes[1] and the Mizigi[2] became Roman *civitates*, while other centres which even today are extremely difficult of access, such as Henchir Okseiba (Civitas Popthensis),[3] found the means to set up public buildings which would have done credit to much larger cities. There was no need for defensive walls, even in the military station of Lambaesis guarding the passes from the Aures mountains. Town walls were put up as an embellishment just like any other public building. The general feeling of the age is expressed not merely by the exuberant utterances of Tertullian,[4] but by a graffito which somebody scratched on a dedication in the forum of Bulla Regia, *Quantam vim reipub(licae)*.[5] So, to all outside observers, it seemed. The strength of the Roman commonwealth and the *Pax Romana* might continue for ever.

The basis, however, of this civilization was fragile. The middle of the third century A.D. was to see the decline of the Roman cities in Africa as well as in other parts of the Roman Empire.[6] With the beginnings of this decline went also the decline of paganism and its progressive replacement by the Christian Church.

Meantime, the inland plains were beginning to support a relatively prosperous native society based on a dry-farming economy. The growth of the African villages in the first three centuries of Roman rule was not as spectacular as that of the towns, but it was more lasting. Being largely self-supporting and subsisting on barter, they were less affected by the financial crises of the third century A.D. Their history is exactly inverse to the history of settlement on the more favoured parts of the North African Tell.

There is evidence for a very considerable native population on the Plains even in prehistoric times. One gains a false im-

---

[1] *CIL*. viii. 4826.   [2] *CM*. 500, 'Civitas Miziga|tanorum'.

[3] J. Guey, 'Ksiba et à propos de Ksiba', *Mélanges*, liv, 1937, p. 75.

[4] As in *De Anima*, 30 (A.D. 213), 'Tantae urbes quantae non casae quondam. Iam nec insulae horrent, nec scopuli terrent, ubique domus, ubique populus, ubique respublica, ubique vita' (*CSEL*. xx. 350). Also *De Idololatria*, 8.

[5] *CIL*. viii. 25523.

[6] See F. Oertel's essay in *CAH*. xii, chap. vii and bibliography attached to that chapter.

pression when one reads the traditional descriptions of Gaetulia as being barren and inhospitable desert.[1] The vast cemeteries of megaliths—upwards of 10,000 tombs at Sigus and Sila, and as many round the Medracen in the Chott country—which have been found on the High Plains,[2] as well as the Libyo-Berber place-names of the Roman settlements[3] indicate a considerable degree of occupation.

At this stage, however, the inhabitants were transhumants, following their flocks into the mountains during the summer heat and transporting their reed-built huts with them.[4] It only needed the introduction of crops such as olives that could survive the summer heat, and at the same time provide shade, to persuade the inhabitants to remain on the plains for the whole of the year, and thus to develop from transhumance to agriculture. The opportunity arose in the early years of the second century A.D.

Two factors made this development possible. In the first place, the defeat of the native revolts and pacification of Numidia rendered the country sufficiently secure for settled life to be feasible. Secondly, the growth of a large class of native farmers was in the interests of both the cities and the Empire itself.[5] While sheep-owners whose flocks browsed on the cornfields belonging to a city were regarded as pests,[6] official encouragement was given to the creation of settled farming communities. The introduction of olive-cultivation gave the native a product completely adapted to the conditions of the High Plains.

This policy seems to have been carried out with coherence and continuity from the early second century A.D. onwards. In

[1] Sallust, *De Bello Jugurthino*, 89, 'ingentes solitudines' around Capsa.

[2] The prehistoric and Roman sites in southern Numidia were explored as long ago as 1890 by Gsell and Graillot. Their report was published in *Mélanges*, xiii, 1893, pp. 461–581, and xiv, 1894, pp. 18–86 and 501–95.

[3] The prefix 'Lam' appearing in names such as *Lam*baesis, *Lam*bafundi, and *Lam*asba probably means 'people of', in Libyan. '*Tha*' in *Tha*magaudi (Timgad) and *Tha*vagel is also a Berber prefix. S. Gsell and H. Graillot, *Mélanges*, xiii, 1893, p. 466.

[4] On the Libyan 'mappalia', Sallust, *De Bello Jugurthino*, 18; M. le Cœur, 'Les Mapalia des Numides', *Hespéris*, 1937.

[5] M. Rostovtzev, 'Studien zur Geschichte des römischen Kolonates', *Archiv für Papyrusforschung*, Erste Beiheft, Leipzig, 1910, pp. 381 f.

[6] Inscription from Henchir Snobbevr, *CIL*. viii. 23956. The citizens had complained of sheep-farmers who grazed their flocks on the municipal *territoria*, and offenders were informed that they rendered themselves liable to a heavy fine (line 14 of inscription).

the first thirty years of that century inscriptions indicate that steps were taken to settle the Berber tribes within certain defined boundaries and to see that they kept to them.[1] The Musulamii were pushed back into the area well south of Madauros,[2] the Zimicii were forbidden to cross the boundaries of the city *territorium* of Igilgilli,[3] and the *Gens Numidarum* were confined to a reservation near the town of Equizetum.[4] But these penal measures would not have succeeded had they not been accompanied by inducements to the natives to settle. These found their legal expression in two great agrarian enactments relating to Roman Africa, the *Lex Manciana* and the *Lex Hadriana*. The text of both of these laws can be reconstructed from the series of second-century inscriptions which were discovered on the Imperial estates in the valley of the Upper Mejerda, and they have been commented upon exhaustively.[5] The results may be summarized briefly.

The problem before the Roman authorities was to keep the land occupied and cultivated. The African native of the first century A.D. was already practising a system of mixed crops, planting his cereals interspersed among olive and fruit trees which were adapted to a dry climate.[6] All that was necessary was to extend this practice into hitherto uncultivated areas, and to give security to the farmer who settled on these less fertile lands. This was done. Peasants who took up land outside those parts which had been allotted to Roman colonists were granted a 'provisional title' (*usus proprius*) to it. This was defined as right of possession, enjoyment, mortgage, and bequest to heirs.[7] They were to pay a rent of one-third of their estimated crop. Their

---

[1] L. Poinssot, *Bull. de la Soc. nat. des Antiquaires de France*, 1923, p. 147.

[2] *CIL.* viii. 10667, 23246; *ILA.* 2988, 2989.

[3] *CIL.* viii. 8369.   [4] *CIL.* viii. 8813.

[5] Tenny Frank, 'The Inscriptions of the Imperial Domains of Africa', and 'A Commentary on the Inscription from Henchir Mettich', *American Journal of Philology* (=*AJP.*), xlvii, 1926, pp. 55–73 and 153–70; J. Carcopino, 'L'Inscription d'Ain el Djemala', *Mélanges*, xxvi, 1906, pp. 365–481, and *Klio*, 1908, pp. 154–85; A. Schulten, 'Lex Hadriana', *Hermes*, xxix, 1894, pp. 214–30; *Klio*, 1907, pp. 188–212; Ch. Saumagne, 'Sur la Législation relative aux Terres Incultes de l'Afrique romaine', *Revue Tunisienne*, 1922, p. 56.

[6] Pliny *N.H.* (ed. Mayhoff), xviii. 188. P. Monceaux, *Les Africains, Les Païens*, p. 167, cites lines from Manilius, *Astronomics*, Book V, to the same effect. The cereals benefit from the moisture transpired from the leaves of the trees above them.

[7] Henchir Mettich inscription, 'usum proprium', *CIL.* viii. 25902; Ain Ouassel (*CIL.* viii. 26416), ius 'pos|sidendi ac fru(en)di | (-) eredique s(uo) | relinquendi', ll. 8–10; Tenny Frank, *AJP.* xlvii, 1926, p. 166.

olives were to remain untaxed for ten years, and vines for five. Staple foods such as figs were free of all imposition. The scheme worked well. As population increased, more native farmers pressed for permission to take up lands on similar terms. Hadrian extended these privileges to all land, whether originally within the limits of centuriation or not, that had remained uncultivated for more than ten years.[1] Squatters (*inquilini*) were included among those on whom Mancian rights could be conferred, and the ten-year period of grace was granted in respect of wild olives and vines.

Under these conditions the position of the *colonus* on an Imperial estate in Africa was relatively enviable. The natives petitioned the Emperor to be allowed to become *coloni* under these terms. In 183 Roman citizens were numbered among the *coloni* on the Saltus Burunitanus. As Carcopino points out, even those who petitioned Hadrian must have been farmers of some means.[2] They possessed their own *villae*, and they were determined to see that the Emperor's bailiff, the *conductor*, shared with them the loss of crops destroyed by causes other than wilful damage. They speak also as men sure of their rights and confident that they will be respected.[3]

The *Lex Hadriana* was applied in its main principles to Imperial and private estates all over North Africa. Outside the Mejerda valley, on the Fundus Tapp...—at Jenan ez Zaytouna[4] above the Oued Chegaga—there were Mancian *coloni* in the early third century. In 319 the *Lex Manciana* was the legal basis on which peasant holdings rested, and it governed the relations between peasant and leaseholder on the Imperial estates.[5] At Ouled-Sidi-Thil, some sixty miles south-east of Theveste, the discovery of deeds of sale revealed that the Mancian colonate was a living institution in Numidia as late as the closing years of the fifth century.[6] It would seem probable that the Berbers

---

[1] Ain Ouassel inscription: Carcopino, *Klio*, 1908, p. 179. Hadrian was in Africa A.D. 129 and published a general law: 'De rudibus agris qui per decem annos continuos inculti sunt.'

[2] *CIL.* viii. 10570. 2. 14. Cf. inscriptions from the Saltus Massipianus mentioning *coloni* on that estate who possessed Latin rights at least, Th. Mommsen, *Hermes*, 1880, 393.　　　　[3] Carcopino, *Mélanges*, op. cit. 393.

[4] C. Saumagne, 'Les Inscriptions de Jenan ez Zaytouna', *CRAI.*, 1937, 292–301.

[5] *Cod. Just.* xi. 63 (62), 1.

[6] The deeds of sale referred to 'particelles agrorum ex culturis mancianis', E. Albertini, *Journal des savants*, Jan. 1930; C. Saumagne, 'La Paix vandale', *Revue Tunisienne* (nouvelle série, i), 1930, 183.

maintained their privileges despite the opposition of the Catholic Church and the landowners during the Byzantine period.[1] Small-holding by emphyteusis and the payment of rents in kind are the basis of Berber farming today.[2]

Throughout the Roman occupation the High Plains seem to have been occupied very largely by Imperial and senatorial estates. The western portion, Mauretania Sitifensis, still retained something of its character of being a part of the Imperial *res privata* until it became a separate province in 292.[3] In Numidia there were great estates around Theveste,[4] Mascula (modern Khenchela),[5] and Batna.[6] Timgad was the centre of a *regio*.[7] These areas fully deserved Frontinus' comment that in Africa the landed estates were sometimes more extensive than the urban *territoria*.[8]

These parts, however, benefited considerably from the Imperial decrees designed to encourage the native farmer. From the middle of the second century A.D. until after the end of the Byzantine period thousands of villages and small farms grew up in this part of North Africa. In southern Numidia, Gsell has listed over 1,200 occupied sites. Many more have been added to the map since he published his *Atlas archéologique* in 1911.[9] On the average one comes upon one Romano-Berber village every two and a half miles on the Numidian plains. In Mauretania Sitifensis sites are almost equally numerous, and south of the great Chotts, in country at present completely desert, the remains

---

[1] Cf. C. Saumagne, 'Du Rôle de l'Origo et du Census dans la Formation du Colonat', *Byzantion*, 1937, 534 and 'Observations sur deux Lois byzantines relatives au "Colonat" dans l'Afrique du Nord', *Actes du Deuxième Congrès des Sociétés savantes de l'Afrique du Nord*, 1936 (published 1937). Also *CIL*. viii. 4354 (Ain el Ksar, A.D. 578–82).

[2] M. Sumien, 'Un Souvenir de Droit romain en Tunisie', *Revue Algérien*, 1903, 201, on the *enzel* contract. Cf. Tenny Frank, *AJP*. xlvii, pp. 72–73, on the status of peasants round Dougga today. E. Masqueray, *La Formation des Cités de l'Algérie*, Paris, 1886, p. 21, points out that the Kabyle today is hardly ever a landowner in his own right, but nearly always a tenant having the usufruct of his land.

[3] A 'procurator rei privatae per Mauretaniam Sitifensem' is mentioned in the *Notitia Dignitatum* (ed. Seeck, Berlin, 1876), occ. xii. 25, in the late fourth century A.D.

[4] *ILA*. 3992.   [5] *CIL*. viii. 2232.   [6] Ibid. 4372, 4373.

[7] Ibid. 2757. Other estates are known to have existed near Ain Beida, R. Cagnat, *Bull. Arch. du Comité*, 1896, p. 228; Gibba = *CIL*. viii. 18548 and Lambafundi = *CIL*. viii. 2438, 17941.

[8] *In Controversia de Jure territorii*, ed. Lachmann, p. 53, 'In Africa, ubi saltus non minores habent privati quam reipublicae territoria.'

[9] S. Gsell, *Atlas archéologique*, feuilles 16, 26, 27, 37; A. Berthier, *L'Algérie et son passé*, p. 24.

of many farms and settlements have been found.[1] In Byzacena the wilderness which extends around the town of Sbeitla (Roman Suffetula) has yielded more than 120 Roman sites. As Berthier points out, if the native population of the High Plains in 1940 was about twenty-five to the square kilometre, it must have been at least equal to that in Roman times.[2] And in that period there were no sanitary and other services to maintain the numbers. The increase was entirely due to careful utilization of agricultural wealth. When Herodian commented in A.D. 240 on the dense population of the African countryside he could not have been exaggerating.[3]

In Mauretania Sitifensis the researches of Carcopino[4] and others have provided convincing evidence of the growth of native settlements in the first half of the third century A.D., and of the favourable treatment given to the native farmers by successive Emperors in this period. Inscriptions show that holdings on the Imperial estates were divided out among small proprietors.[5] Officials aided the irrigation of their lands,[6] and special protection seems to be implied in the terms *coloni imperatoris* by which many of these native farmers were known.[7] The latter responded to these evidences of goodwill. On the plain of the Medjana new sites came into occupation and existing settlements were enlarged. In A.D. 191 the *coloni* of the village of Castellum Thib(uzabetum?) dedicated an altar to the Emperor Commodus.[8] In A.D. 213 three tribes united in the solemn foundation of a new settlement named Castellum Aurelius Antoninianus.[9] Four further settlements appear to have come into existence in the next decade or so, the occupants of one of which (Castellum Cellense) were prosperous enough to build its walls.[10] Elsewhere, under the Gordians, houses began to extend beyond

[1] On the settlements in the neighbourhood of the Limes, the reader is referred to Part III of *Fossatum Africae*, by Jean Baradez, Government-Genera. of Algeria, 1949.   [2] A. Berthier, *Les Vestiges du Christianisme*, p. 25.

[3] Herodian, *Ab Excessu divi Marci* (ed. Stavenhagen), vii. 4. 14.

[4] J. Carcopino, 'Les Castella de la Plaine de Sétif', *Revue Africaine*, 1918, pp. 1 f.; A. Schulten, *Römische Grundherrschaften*, pp. 35 f.

[5] *CIL*. viii. 8812 (Bordj Bou Arreridj, Severus Alexander, A.D. 222–35), 'terminati(ones) (a)grorum defenicionis Matidinae adsignantur colonis Kasturre(nsibus)'; ibid. 9233 (Tiranadi). Also *SHA*. 'Vita Severi Alexandri', 58.

[6] *CIL*. viii. 8809.

[7] Ibid. 8425 (Saltus Horrerorum, Pertinax, A.D. 193); ibid. 8426 (same area, Caracalla, A.D. 208–17).

[8] Ibid. 8702.   [9] Ibid. 8425.

[10] Ibid. 8777 (reign of Gordian, 238–44), 'Murus constitutus a solo colonis eius'.

the original walled enclosure, and in the end at least one of these native settlements attained municipal status.[1] But this advance should not hide the fact that these communities were little affected even by the outward forms of Roman civilization. Their inhabitants still knew themselves by their tribal names, 'Leopard-hunters',[2] &c. This is true of Numidia also, where members of great tribal confederations such as the Suburbures and Musulamii retained their identity even when they were *coloni* on an Imperial estate.[3] At the end of the fourth century the area around Setif was one of those where a priest who did not speak the native language was useless.[4] But the relative material prosperity in the third century is undeniable. In contrast to the prevailing situation among the cities of the Tell, the period Gordian–Gallienus was the 'golden age of Mauretania', an age only temporarily interrupted by the Kabylie Revolt of A.D. 253–62.

In the Kabylie itself society remained in a primitive state. The native population was governed by its chiefs, whose authority seems to have been absolute. Archaeological evidence suggests the existence of communities similar to those that predominated on the Indian North-West frontier of our own day. The better-off lived inside a fortified farm-house[5] with their womenkind, cultivated by primitive methods a limited strip of ground, maintained constant blood feuds with their neighbours and relatives, and, when opportunity arose, swept down upon the villagers of the plains that lay within easy reach. It was from this 'frontier' within the bounds of the Roman province that the leaders of Berber particularism arose—the family of Firmus and Gildo.

We know something of the population which despite this family's tyranny and greed rallied to them against the Catholics and romanized landowners. Archaeologists have provided an insight into the conditions of life enjoyed by the farmers on the plains of Numidia and Mauretania. The villages themselves must have resembled the Kabylie or Aures village of today. The

[1] *CIL.* viii. 8809 (Lemellefense), in the reign of Philip, A.D. 244–9.

[2] 'Pardalarienses' (Ain Zada), ibid. 8426; J. Carcopino, op cit., p. 5, *CIL.* viii 8421.

[3] Dessau, *ILS.* 9380–1 for Suburbures; *CIL.* viii. 587. 23246; the Saltus Massipianus was 'in territorio Musulamiorum'.

[4] Augustine, *Ep.* 84. 2 (*CSEL.* xxxiv. 2, 393).

[5] For notes on these native castles in the Roman period, S. Gsell, *Atlas archéologique*, Fort National and adjacent sheets. For fortified farms in Tripolitania, R. G. Goodchild, 'The Limes Tripolitanus, ii', *JRS.* xl, 1950, pp. 34–38.

building techniques—walls of baked mud, a shallow-tiled pent-house roof, and earthen floor—have hardly altered. There is also the same lack of plan in both types of village. Buildings and narrow alleyways straggle in every direction. Some villages extended 500 yards or so in one direction across the plain but only one-tenth of the distance in another. Others, such as at Meharza on the Bled Faham, comprised separate groups of dwellings set round a fort. The population was as much as could be crowded into 100 acres or more in some large settle-ments, such as Kherbet Bahrarous or Bou Takrematem, or into twenty to thirty acres which is the average size of a village on the Plain of Bou Lhilet. The area was governed by the supply of fresh water. The trial holes dug by the natives at Oued R'zel and Bir Younken in their effort to reach the water level suggest that water was as scarce as it is in those parts today.[1]

The villages on the High Plains are of a single general type. The buildings are of a purely rustic character. Very occasionally the natives put up a triumphal arch or altar in honour of the Emperor,[2] but more usually their efforts seem to have been directed to building communal storehouses which bear a strong likeness to the tighremts found in Morocco, except that a church occupied the place of the mosque.[3] Dwellings probably belong-ing to individuals were rudely built. At Kherbet Baharous and Kherbet bou Addoufen buildings excavated in 1939 contained a single olive-press, a stone vat for storing oil, and another room used for keeping grain. The floors were of beaten earth, and the pottery of the plainest ware.[4] These dwellings resembled the agri-cultural unit cultivated by the native in the Kabylie or Aures today.

Signs of individual wealth such as villas, bath-buildings, and

---

[1] These particular observations were made by the writer in 1938–9 working under the guidance of M. André Berthier, Keeper of the Musée Gustave Mercier in Con-stantine. Published by M. Berthier in *Les Vestiges du Christianisme*, pp. 23–24.

[2] For instance, at Henchir Tikoubi (Gsell and Graillot, *Mélanges*, xiv, 1894, pp. 36–37), altar, to Carus, Carinus and Numerian (A.D. 283); Fundus Massi-pianus, *CIL.* viii. 587, a triumphal arch; Fundus Turris Rotunda, C. Saumagne, *Bull. Arch. du Comité*, 1927, p. 105, a triumphal arch.

[3] The writer excavated one such at Kherbet Bahrarous in 1939. The rooms round the three sides of the courtyard contained remains of large storage jars. The fourth side was occupied by a church. One wonders whether a similar building at Ain Tamda farther to the west was in fact a 'monastery', as suggested by M. William Seston, and not a Romano-Berber tighremt. ('Le Monastère d'Ain Tamda', *Mélanges*, li, 1934, pp. 79–113.)

[4] Briefly noted by Berthier, op. cit., p. 26.

even farms equipped with a cement floor are rare.[1] Everything, indeed, points to the existence of a primitive and equalitarian form of society. The well-known Lamasba inscription dated to the reign of Elagabalus (A.D. 218–22), with its division of plots of land between 89 owners and the rigorous administration of available water supply, confirms this view.[2]

Such wealth as existed was derived from the olive. The oil-press and the church are the typical ruins of a Romano-Berber village. Latin and Arab authors agree that the High Plains stretching the whole way from Tripolitania to Tangier resembled a continuous forest of olive trees.[3] The number of presses one finds in the Numidian villages is remarkable. At Oued R'zel, Henchir Djerouda, and Henchir Boulilet on the southern shores of Garaet ank Djemal there was an olive-press at every twenty yards.[4] At Kherbet Bahrarous the writer found eighty-five presses; eight miles to the south, at Bir Younken, an afternoon's search revealed another twenty in the same area; at Mrabta Hadda and Kherbet bou Addoufen there were as many, though the presence of growing crops prevented an accurate count. In other parts of the steppe in Byzacena more than 1,000 oil-presses are stated to have been found on sites round Suffetula.[5] Great numbers have also been discovered in the villages south of Theveste. The production of oil must have been on a considerable scale, and again the main advance seems to have taken place during the third century A.D.

Before that date Africa produced oil, but its harsh quality made it unsuitable for any purpose but lighting. Rome supplied herself from Spain, Istria, and Italy. The Monte Testaccio in Rome has provided an enormous quantity of amphora-sherds from southern Spain but few from Africa. But African oil improved in quality, and at the same time land seems to have gone out of cultivation in Italy. The Roman market became more accessible. In the early third century the presence of statues of Mercury in the walls of oil-presses at Madauros might suggest

[1] Two villas and two bath-buildings have so far been located among the scores of village sites investigated in central Numidia, cf. Berthier, op. cit., p. 27.

[2] F. G. de Pachtère, 'Le Règlement d'Irrigation de Lamasba', Mélanges, xxviii, 1908, pp. 373–455.

[3] Cited by Gautier, op. cit., pp. 16–17. The olive had much the same importance in Numidia as sugar-cultivation has in the West Indies today.

[4] Berthier, Les Vestiges du Christianisme, p. 25.

[5] M. Dubiez, Bull. Arch. du Comité, 1897, 385–6.

that Africa was beginning to trade more widely in that commodity.[2] At this time the richness of the Tripolitanian countryside was enabling the citizens of the coast towns of Leptis Magna and Tripolis to send large quantities of oil to Italy as a free gift.[2] This practice continued throughout the third century. At the end of that period Arnobius mentioned that Africa's chief sources of wealth were olive-culture and sheep-rearing.[3] Towards the year 350 the writer of the *Expositio Totius Mundi et Rerum*,[4] while praising Africa as being *dives in omnibus*—corn, fruit, trees, slaves, and cloth-working—shows that the country was above all famed for its oil. 'Paene ipsa omnibus gentium usum olei praestat.' This testimony is confirmed by all that is known of a Numidian village, and provides a further reason why the latter continued to evolve while the Roman towns declined. The great oil-fabrics of Henchir Brisgane, Bir Sgaoun, Hr. el Guiz, and Hr. bou Sboa suggest that one of the chief exporting centres may have been the country south of Theveste, where a special effort was made to improve communications at the end of the third century,[5] and the villages appear to have been particularly prosperous. It was from these parts that Donatus of Casae Nigrae came, and Donatism originated.

It is not intended here to do more than describe the conditions that developed in two important areas of Roman Africa. It is not difficult to see, however, that the villages had founded their future well-being on a firmer basis than had the towns. Even if one resists the temptation to regard the ruthless suppression of the revolt of the Gordians in 238 as an uncontrolled outbreak of ill feeling on the part of the Numidians, who formed a large portion of the Third Legion, against the romanized citizens,[6] it is clear that this event is of great significance in the history of North Africa. The cities never recovered from the pillage and sack which they suffered. From then on their decline was continuous, and the centre of relative prosperity began to pass from the corn-growing country of Proconsular Africa to the crowded villages of the inland plains. It is at this moment that the great changes in popular religion begin to take place.

[1] M. Christofle, *Essai de restitution d'un moulin à huile à Madaure*, Algiers, 1930, p. 9.
[2] *SHA*. 'Vita Severi', 18. 3; Aurelius Victor, *De Caesaribus*, 41.
[3] *Adversus Gentes*, i. 21.
[4] *Expositio*, ed. G. Lumbroso, Roma, 1903, 80–81.
[5] L. Leschi, 'Épigraphie du Pays de Nemencha', *Revue Africaine*, lxxii, pp. 262–294.   [6] J. Carcopino, *Syria*, vi, 1924, p. 53.

E

IV

THE GEOGRAPHICAL
DISTRIBUTION OF DONATISM

IT is against the background of different landscapes and cultures that one examines the geographical distribution of
Donatists and Catholics in North Africa. By far the most
valuable source is the verbatim record of the Conference of
Carthage, held between the two communities in June 411.[1] At
the start of proceedings the Donatists insisted on their rivals
identifying themselves individually and, thanks to their obstinacy, there exists almost a complete record of the African
bishoprics at the turn of the fifth century. Most of the sees can
be identified from inscriptions, or from literary evidence such
as the Antonine Itinerary, and from place-names. Even before
the introduction of modern archaeological methods, scholars
such as Mesnage[2] and Jaubert[3] were able to indicate satisfac-
torily the distribution of the rival bishoprics throughout North
Africa. Now, thanks to the work of Monceaux and, more
recently, to that of Berthier and members of the École française
de Rome,[4] more gaps in our knowledge have been filled. One
begins to know not merely where there was a Donatist or a
Catholic bishop, but also something about the type of worship
that took place in the remoter parts of the countryside. From
the geographical distribution of the two Churches one has a
clue to the social significance of each.

The literary evidence by itself shows conclusively the areas
in which the Donatists prevailed. Two incidents, the result of
heated exchanges at the Conference of Carthage, are significant.
In the first, the Donatist bishops had been acknowledging their
signatures on a document which had been drawn up for their
leaders immediately before the opening session. The President,

---

[1] Reproduced in *PL.* xi, cols. 1223–420. Cited as *Gesta Coll. Carth.*

[2] Le Père J. Mesnage, *L'Afrique chrétienne. Évêchés et ruines antiques*, Paris, Leroux,
1912.

[3] Le Chanoine Jaubert, 'Anciens évêchés et ruines chrétiennes de la Numidie',
Recueil de Constantine, xlvi, 1912, pp. 1–218.

[4] P. Cayrel, 'Une Basilique donatiste de Numidie', *Mélanges*, li, 1934, pp. 114–
42; M. Simon, 'Fouilles dans la Basilique de Henchir el Ateuch', *Mélanges*, li, 1934,
pp. 143–77; P. Courcelle, 'Une Seconde Campagne de fouilles à Ksar el Kelb',
Mélanges, liii, 1936, pp. 166–97.

Count Marcellinus, wanted to cut short proceedings. He asked that the remainder of the prelates should shout general assent.[1] At this Petilian, the Donatist bishop of Constantine, immediately protested: 'We mean to show we have no rivals in our sees.' It might be true that the *traditores* had many bishops in Proconsular Africa, but 'in Numidia nos ostendimus eos penitus non habere, aut habere certe sed in raris locis'.[2] The Donatists claimed to be an overwhelming majority in Numidia.

The second incident took place a few minutes later. The roll-call had gone on. More Donatist clergy had come forward. In turn, the Bishops of Tinisti, Castella, Mopti, and Jucundiana had acknowledged their signatures, when suddenly there was a protest from the Catholic side. Alypius, Bishop of Thagaste and friend of St. Augustine, broke in.

'All these men are bishops of estates (*fundi*) and manors (*villae*) not towns (*civitates*).'[3] Every bishop, in the Catholic view, was supposed to have his *civitas*.[4] These Donatist bishops came from villages, and therefore their right to be present was open to challenge. In a moment Petilian replied. 'Yes, you also have many bishops scattered over all the landed estates, but generally where you have them, they have no congregation at all.'

A little later Alypius repeated his challenge, and earlier in the proceedings the Catholic bishop of Musti had commented on the presence of a Donatist bishop of a *castellum* (fort or native settlement) within the territory of the Catholic see.[5] The information gained as a result of these exchanges is

---

[1] *Gesta Coll. Carth.* i. 164 (*PL.* xi, col. 1323), 'Marcellinus vir clarissimus, tribunus et notarius dixit, Quoniam longum est ire per singulos, hi decem qui se mandasse professi sunt, actis edicant utrum coram ipsis omnium sit facta subscriptio et praebeant in ea quae sunt gesta consensum.'

[2] *Gesta Coll. Carth.* i. 165 (*PL.* xi, col. 1323), 'Lucrum enim videtur his cedere qui multos se adversum nostros habere per hanc provinciam ostenderunt, si in provincia Numidia non [misprint for "nos"] ostendimus eos penitus non habere, aut habere certe sed raris locis.'

[3] *Gesta Coll. Carth.* i. 181 (*PL.* xi, col. 1326), 'Alypius episcopus Ecclesiae catholicae dixit, Scriptum sit istos omnes in villis vel in fundis esse opiscopos ordinatos, non in aliquibus civitatibus'; *Gesta Coll. Carth.* i. 182, Petilianus episcopus dixit, 'Sic etiam tu multos habes per omnes agros dispersos. Immo crebros ubi habes, sane et sine populis habes.'

[4] Pope Leo, *Ep.* 87. 2. For Augustine's pride in Hippo as a *civitas Romana* see *Contra litteras Petiliani*, ii. 83. 184.

[5] *Gesta Coll. Carth.* i. 121 (*PL.* xi, col. 1285). This was Turris Rotunda. On the site see C. Saumagne, *Bull. Arch. du Comité*, 1927, p. 106.

supported from other sources. In a letter written about A.D. 400 to the Roman senator Pammachius, Augustine refers to Numidia Consularis (i.e. Constantine and the High Plains) as the starting-point of the Donatist movement.[1] Elsewhere he admits that they 'preponderated in Numidia',[2] and this admission is supported by texts that show that the Donatist 'holy cities' were Timgad and Bagai in southern Numidia,[3] that important Donatist Councils were held in southern Numidian towns, and that it was in this area that Donatism revived to such effect in the late sixth century.[4] It is also well known that the most continuous organized resistance to the various efforts to enforce unity came from the Numidian and Mauretanian peasants. In 377 the Imperial authorities bewailed the fact that the Donatists, if expelled from the cities, 'went out into the countryside and there throve with unlawful fury, forgathering illegally in the villages (loca) attached to great estates or on the domains'.[5] The evidence from all these sources suggests that Donatism was principally a Numidian and agrarian movement.

Similarly, literary sources show that the Catholics were equally at an advantage in Proconsular Africa. Writing to Count Marcellinus on the eve of the Conference of Carthage, Augustine described the situation: 'Our clergy and our layfolk are certainly in the majority, above all in the Proconsular Province, although we are also more numerous in the other provinces of Africa with the exception of Consular Numidia.'[6] At the proceedings the claim regarding Proconsular Africa was amply justified.[7] In town after town, at Maxula,[8] Megalopolis,[8] Uchi Maius,[8] Canope,[8] and many others, the Donatists could

[1] Augustine, Ep. 58. 1.
[2] Id., Ad Catholicos contra Donatistas Epistola, 19. 51, 'Numidia ubi praepolletis' (addressing the Donatists). (PL. xliii, col. 431.)
[3] Id., Enarratio in Ps. 21, 26 (PL. xxxvi, col. 177).
[4] Optatus, ii. 18 (CSEL. xxvi. 52), Council held at Theveste in 363. Augustine, Ep. 34 (CSEL. xxxiv. 2. 26), Council at Milevis, 396. Augustine, Contra Cresconium, iv. 58. 69 (PL. xliii, col. 586), Council of Bagai, 394.
[5] Codex Theodosianus (ed. Mommsen and Meyer, Berlin, 1905), xvi. 6. 2.
[6] Augustine, Ep. 129. 6 (CSEL. xliv. 38), 'Hoc si aliquando a nostris dictum est, de his locis dici verissime potuit, ubi nostrorum coepiscoporum et clericorum atque laicorum longe major est numerus, et maxime in proconsulari provincia; quamquam excepta Numidia Consulari etiam in caeteris provinciis Africanis nostrorum numero facillime superentur.'
[7] In 411 the Catholics held 62 identifiable sees to the Donatist 34, with 61 divided between two claimants.
[8] Gesta Coll. Carth. i. 133.

claim to have only a priest or a deacon in the field against the Catholic bishop. It is to be noted, however, that the Donatists were strong in country areas near some of the towns, for instance near Bulla Regia.[1] On two occasions during his long tenure of office Aurelius of Carthage was able to muster more than 200 Catholic bishops for a Council, who were drawn from the Proconsular Province alone.[2] If the Donatists could boast their strength in Numidia, the Catholics had every right to point to the compact block which they formed in the Roman cities that clustered the river valleys and the immediate neighbourhood of Carthage.

The distribution map of bishoprics confirms the literary evidence. (Maps ii and iii.) In the two outlying provinces of Tripolitania and Mauretania Caesariensis the parties appear to have been of approximately equal strength. The Catholics held the cities of Tigava, Tipasa, and Sufasar in Mauretania Caesariensis while the Donatists controlled the native *castella* such as Numida, Lar Castellum on the coast, and Castellum Tingitanum—the last-named the site of some beautiful examples of fourth-century Christian architecture.[3] The Donatists also controlled some of the native agricultural settlements near the *limes*.[4] In Tripolitania the number of bishoprics held by both communities was equal, though recent discoveries indicate that here, too, the Donatists were in strength in the countryside.[5] Along the coasts in the Romano-Punic trading centres, neither Church can be shown to have gained a decisive advantage. Most of these towns, such as Leptis Minor, Hadrumetum, Curubis, Utica, Thabraca, and others along the Algerian coast, contained representatives of each community, though the Donatists tended to predominate in the isolated townships on the Kabyle coast such as Iomnium (Tigzirt) and Rusubiccari (Mers el Hadjedj).

---

[1] Augustine, *Ep.* 65. 1.

[2] In May 419 Aurelius mustered 217 bishops from Proconsular Africa. Nearly 200 attended the previous year: C. J. Hefele, *History of the Christian Councils* (tr. W. R. Clark, Edinburgh, 1872), ii, pp. 458, 467. On the strength of the Catholics in Proconsular Africa in general, P. Monceaux, *Histoire littéraire*, iv. 134-7.

[3] H. Leclercq, 'Orléansville', in *Dictionnaire d'archéologie chrétienne*, vol. 12, 2, col. 2728. In contrast the Catholics were strong at Beni-Rached near by, which was a centre of prosperous villas.

[4] Such as Ala Milaria: S. Gsell, *Les Fouilles à Benian*, Paris, 1901; *CIL.* viii. 21570-4.

[5] R. G. Goodchild found 'Laudes Deo Domino' on the lintel of a fortified farm which he excavated at Henchir Msuffin in 1949. To be published.

According to contemporaries, however, the Donatists in the coastal cities were inclined to follow the more moderate interpretation of their faith, and in A.D. 393 supported Maximian against the violence of Primian and the Numidians.[1]

The main division between the Churches is shown to be that between the Donatism of the inland plains and the Catholicism of the cities and towns on the Tell. To a less marked degree there is also a difference between the Berber-speaking areas of North Africa which were mainly Donatist, and the Latin- and Punic-speaking areas which were mainly Catholic. One can see at a glance that the Donatists were in a majority over the whole of the country of the High Plains, not merely in Numidia, but in their eastern and western extensions in the Roman provinces of Byzacena and Mauretania Sitifensis. They were strong also in the country of the Nemenchas extending south from Tebessa towards the Sahara desert. So far as existing knowledge goes, there were not more than some half-dozen sees in the whole of this vast area in which a Catholic bishop was in complete control. On the other hand, we know of thirty-seven unchallenged Donatist bishoprics. The Catholics were able to maintain themselves in the larger towns, such as Theveste (Tebessa), Mascula (Khenchela), Macomades (Ain Beida), and Thamugadi (Timgad), but their hold over the country populations was slight. They did not lack energetic leaders, such as Aurelius of Macomades, nor rare good fortune, such as the conversion of Maximian, Donatist bishop of Bagai, but opinion was against them. As the incident at Fundus Calviensis in A.D. 403[2] showed, they were unable to improve their position in face of popular feeling. From Augustine's letters we know too that the *coloni* on the great estates in northern Numidia were Donatist.[3] The Donatists also predominated even in fairly large settlements such as Cedias, Guzabeta, and Lambiridi. In Mauretania Sitifensis the majority of the native *castella*, whose growth was so favoured by the third-century Emperors, were unchallenged Donatist bishoprics, and Donatist inscriptions have been found on these sites.

The evidence derived from plotting bishoprics on a map finds additional support from the results of excavations in the

---

[1] Augustine, *Ep.* 93. 8. 24 and *Ad Catholicos Epistola*, iii. 6, records the predominance of Maximianism in Byzacena and Tripolitania. See below, p. 215.
[2] See below, p. 263.   [3] *Ep.* 88, 112 and 209.

villages on part of the plains lying between Batna and Châteaudun du Rummel. In eight years before the Second World War MM. Berthier and Martin[1] investigated seventy-two sites of Romano-Berber villages and established the plan of over 200 churches and chapels. The results show a remarkably uniform native Christian culture based on the veneration of martyrs and their relics. Between the fourth and seventh centuries the area must have been thoroughly Christianized. In the villages, churches and chapels, rudely constructed with mud and stone walls and floors of beaten earth, are crowded together. To date, no village that has been explored has failed to reveal traces of one or more churches. At Oued R'zel at the southern end of the Garaet Ank Djemal six have been located within the space of a quarter of a mile.[2] Some two miles away at Foum Seffane another three were found.[3] Four more were found at Henchir el Bahira,[4] and a further ten were planned in small villages clustered around freshwater wells on the plains of Ben Ziri and on the Djebel Azrouat. At Bir Younken the writer found the remains of two in the course of a short visit, and investigated two more at Kherbet Bahrarous. As Berthier quite reasonably suggests, these chapels must be the *basilicas non necessarias* to which Optatus of Milevis refers in his attacks on the Donatists.[5]

Many of these churches were undoubtedly Donatist. In about a dozen, as at Ain Ghorab,[6] Henchir Zoura,[7] Medfoun,[8] Henchir el Atrous,[9] Bir es Sedd,[10] Ain Mtirchou,[11] Foum el Amba,[12] and Oued R'zel vi,[13] the Donatist war-cry *Deo Laudes* has been found on inscriptions. At Henchir bou Said, the

---

[1] Results published in A. Berthier's *Les Vestiges du Christianisme*. The reader is referred in particular to the photographs published in this work.

[2] Berthier, op. cit., pp. 48–75, supported by the writer's own observations.

[3] Ibid., pp. 79–90.   [4] Ibid., pp. 107–11.

[5] Ibid., pp. 205–24.

[6] L. Leschi, 'Basilique et cimetière donatistes à Ain-Ghorab', *Revue Africaine*, xxviii, 1936, pp. 27–42.

[7] Le Commandant Guenin, *Nouvelles Archives des Missions*, xvii, 1909, 125.

[8] *CIL*. viii. 18660.

[9] P. Monceaux, 'Inscriptions chrétiennes de la Région de Tellidjen', *Bull. de la Soc. Nat. des Antiquaires de France*, lxix, 1909, 313.

[10] *CIL*. viii. 10694.   [11] Ibid. 17768.

[12] Berthier, op. cit., p. 77.

[13] Ibid., p. 206. Other *Deo Laudes* inscriptions include: *CIL*. viii. 2308 (Sef ed Dalaa), described by S. Gsell, *Mélanges*, 1893, pp. 498–502; Henchir Bekkouche (Comm. Guenin, *Nouvelles Archives des Missions*, xvii, 1909, 101), and Djemaa Titaya (J. Toutain, *Bull. Arch. du Comité*, 1894, 85, n. 4).

citizens and *peregrini* of an unnamed town seem to have combined to build a church in honour of a Circumcellion.[1] Elsewhere there are inscriptions quoting texts from the Old Testament, emphasizing that the dedicators were 'just' or 'saints', and that their sacrifices were 'pure'. Examples include the chapels at Henchir el Guis[2] and Henchir el Ogla.[3] Others breathe defiance at torture and persecution.[4] These are probably Donatist, and in addition there are inscriptions that employ a particular formula such as the curious 'B(onis) B(ene)',[5] which is sometimes associated with 'Deo Laudes', and thus suggests that the community was Donatist. Moreover, the village churches have one factor in common: the religion of their dedicators was centred on martyrdom. Most of the inscriptions found in these churches inform the finder that here was a *Memoria martyrum*. In all cases, the martyr's body lay beneath the altar, sometimes, as at Bou Takrematem, in a wooden coffin lined with olive-branches,[6] but more often in a plain stone sarcophagus, or a tiled grave. Next to the tomb were the relics; generally, as at Mechta Azrou, they consisted of grey powder or cloth enclosed in a cooking-pot. This had been hermetically sealed by plaster before being laid in a trough or some other receptacle. The site was marked by a flat stone called a *Mensa*, on which was often recorded the names of the martyrs venerated there. The *Mensa* was probably used also for sacrifices and feasts in their honour.

The inscriptions from these churches are inspired by martyrdom and martyrs. Even today one can feel the enthusiasm that lay behind 'Signu(m) Cristianu(m) et nomina martyru(m)'

---

[1] P. Monceaux, *Bull. de la Soc. Nat. des Ant. de France*, 1909, 210–16.

[2] *CIL*. viii. 10656, 'Adferte Dom(ino) mundum sacrificium, adferte D(o)m(ino) patriae gentium', *Ps*. 96. 7–8. Cf. P. Monceaux, *Revue de Philologie*, 1909, 128; *Histoire littéraire*, iv. 452.

[3] P. Monceaux, *Bull. de la Soc. Nat. des Ant. de France*, 1909, 277. Cf. *CIL*. viii. 10863 (Henchir Guessaria).

[4] For instance, from Ain Tellidjen (south-west of Tebessa), 'Si Deus pro nobis, nil mihi deerit', *CIL*. viii. 17610; also 'Exalta te, Do(mi)ne quia suscepisti me, et non jucundasti inimicos meos super me', *CIL*. viii. 8623–24 (Sitifis) and Ain Fakroun, *CIL*. viii. 18742. Cf. P. Monceaux, *Revue de Philologie*, 1909, 122.

[5] As at Henchir Guesses, *CIL*. viii. 17810; Ain Sfar, *CIL*. viii. 17801; Hr. Sidi el Hadjedj, *CIL*. viii. 2492; Bariha (E. Albertini, *Revue Africaine*, 1927, 99–101); Hr. bou Said, P. Monceaux, *Revue de Philologie*, tome xxxiii, 1909, p. 132; Ain Ghorab, L. Leschi, 'Basilique et cimetière donatistes', *Revue Africaine*, 1936; cf. P. Monceaux, *Histoire littéraire*, iv. 456.

[6] A. Berthier and M. Martin, *Recueil de Constantine*, lxiii, 1935–6, pp. 225 f.

from Henchir Guesses,[1] or the ecstatic dedication that begins, 'L(a)etamini Domino et exultate, justi', from the *castellum* of Thamallula in Mauretania Sitifensis (modern Tocqueville).[2] There is the tendency also to multiply the number of the dead, the *mensae* recording groups of victims such as 'Ianuaria et comites' at Bir Aida,[3] or Varagus and his companions at Henchir Sidi Naceur.[4] One notices the same tendency in Donatist *Acta Martyrum*. In addition, a large proportion of the saints honoured, like 'Misin and Sabinais', at Bir Djedid,[5] 'Lucitas' at Vazaivi,[6] or 'Stiddin, Miggin, and Cittin' at Henchir el Hamascha[7] and Ain el Ksar,[8] are clearly Berbers, and do not appear on official calendars of martyrs. From Augustine, however, we learn that the *natalitia* of these strange individuals were celebrated with immense enthusiasm by the Donatists.[9] The exact date of their *redditio* ('ransom') also is generally recorded on the inscriptions dedicated in their honour, suggesting a desire to keep an anniversary.

The impression one gains from these sites is that Donatism was the religion of the great majority of the inhabitants. There were Catholic minorities, even in towns such as Lamzelli where Gildo was buried,[10] and Catholicism was able to maintain itself as late as the records go. In northern Numidia we know that religion divided families, even Augustine's household.[11] Yet in the sixth century, when the population was living under the shadow of the Byzantine fortresses which guarded the passes north of the Aures mountains, Catholicism was not secure. The inhabitants lost no opportunity to demonstrate their veneration for Donatus. In the fourth and fifth centuries, when Imperial

---

[1] P. Monceaux, *Enquête sur l'épigraphie chrétienne*, no. 276; S. Gsell, *Bull. Arch. du Comité*, 1908, ccxxv.

[2] P. Monceaux, *Histoire littéraire*, iv. 455.

[3] As in the Donatist *Passio Cypriani*. Cf. R. Reitzenstein, 'Die Nachrichten über den Tod Cyprians', *Sitzungsberichte der Heidelberger-Akademie der Wissenschaften, Phil.-hist. Klasse*, 1913, p. 38.

[4] H. Jaubert, *Recueil de Constantine*, 1912, p. 159.

[5] *CIL*. viii. 8292; comment by M. Feraud, *Recueil de Constantine*, 1864, 83, no. 17. The inscription is in the bottom of the wadi, some 200 yards from the church.

[6] *CIL*. viii. 17653; Audollent and Letaille, *Mélanges*, x, 1890, 537. For the name 'Lucitas' in Numidia, cf. *CIL*. viii. 18617.

[7] *CIL*. viii. 10686-9 = 16742. Cf. A. Audollent, *Mélanges*, 1890, 445.

[8] *CIL*. viii. 20572, 10573; J. E. Baxter, *JTS*. 1924, p. 21, for the possibility that these martyrs were Circumcellions.

[9] Augustine, *Contra Epistolam Parmeniani*, iii. 6. 29 (*PL*. xliii, col. 106).

[10] *Gesta Coll. Carth*. i. 206.

[11] Augustine, *Ep*. 52 (*CSEL*. xxxiv, 149). Also, *Ep*. 33. 5.

control was less visible, Augustine indicates that the Donatist 'territories'[1] in southern Numidia were impervious to his arguments.

It may well have been so. In areas where tribal society prevailed, it would be hard to imagine much in the nature of religious division. The members of a clan would tend to accept the religion of their elders, and converts would be unpopular. At Mechta el Tein, Morsott, or Oued R'zel, where two or more churches have been found very close to each other, it is not necessary to conclude that one belonged to the Donatists and one to the Catholics. It may have been that the exclusive nature of the Donatist religion gave rise to the formation of small religious brotherhoods, such as exist in North Africa today. For instance, at the Red Village at el-Kantara seven mosques and koubbas exist for these brotherhoods in a population of some 5,000 inhabitants. Each of the chapels would then have been used by a separate brotherhood or sect.

If these conclusions are justified, then it seems that Donatism and Catholicism could to some extent be related to geographical and climatic conditions in North Africa. Divergence of religious belief thus coincided with divergence of environment and economic interest. There might seem to be an association between Donatism and the peasants who cultivated the unending forest of olive-trees that stretched across the country. Some of the olive-presses carry Christian inscriptions: one at Henchir Gosset bears the Donatist watchword, *Deo laudes*.[2]

Distribution maps of archæological remains in Numidia bring out another interesting fact, the coincidence of Donatism with the areas where pre-Roman Libyan remains are found in greatest profusion and where the Berber language was spoken.[3] In both southern and northern Numidia Donatist bishoprics existed in native settlements surrounded by vast cemeteries of dolmens and stone circles where Libyan inscriptions have also been found. The territory round the Libyan Royal Tomb known as the Medracen at the lower end of the Chott Djendeli (north of Timgad) contained five Donatist bishoprics, four of which were without Catholic challenge.[4] Farther north, near Sigus

[1] Augustine, *Contra Gaudentium*, 1. 24. 27 (*PL*. xliii, col. 722), 'in regionibus vestris'.
[2] *CIL*. viii. 2046.
[3] On this point see W. Thümmel, *Zur Beurtheilung des Donatismus*, pp. 63 ff.
[4] They were Ad Lacum Regium, Gibba, Lampsili, Casae, and Guzabeta. On the Medracen area, cf. S. Gsell, *Mélanges*, xiv, 1894, pp. 71–73. On Libyan inscrip-

and Sila, both Donatist sees, there are also enormous numbers of Berber prehistoric remains, and discoveries made immediately before the Second World War in the neighbourhood of Hippo Regius indicate the presence of a considerable native prehistoric population in a district which Augustine admitted was almost closed to Catholicism.[1] It may be a fact worth recording that, in contrast to the rough treatment accorded to many Roman statues, dolmens and Libyan inscriptions do not seem to have been disturbed even where they encroached on the immediate surroundings of the church.

There seems to be little doubt now that the language spoken by the natives of Numidia, and also in the mountainous districts of the Proconsular province around Mount Zaghouan where Donatism was also strong, was Libyan and not Punic. In Roman times, as at the present day, three languages were spoken in North Africa: Libyan, Punic, and Latin. Latin had been brought in by the conquerors from the northern shores of the Mediterranean as the official language, and it was probably spoken with the same fluency and enthusiasm by the native town-dwellers as French is by their Arab successors. But among themselves, whether in town or country, the normal speech of the natives seems to have been either a Semitic language, Punic, or the African language, Libyan, which is the direct ancestor of the modern Berber.[2]

Much confusion has been caused in the past by Augustine's identification of the native language spoken in the countryside as 'Punic'.[3] This was almost certainly the language of the people in Hippo itself, as it was in other Roman towns of Carthaginian origin. It was probably, too, the language spoken by members of a native aristocracy in pre-Roman times, as the Punic

tions in this area, F. Logeart, 'Nouvelles inscriptions libyques dans la Commune Mixte d'Ain Mlila', *Recueil de Constantine*, lxiii, 1935–6, pp. 187–96, and Gsell, *Atlas archéologique*, f. 28, Ain Beida, nos. 67–95.

[1] On the situation at Fussala in this area, before Augustine imposed Bishop Antonius, *Ep.* 209. 2–5 (*CSEL.* lvii. 348–50). The Libyan and Latino-Libyan inscriptions found in native cemeteries in these parts by M. Rodary are collated and published by the Abbé Chabot in his *Recueil des Inscriptions libyques*, Paris, Imprimerie nationale, 1940.

[2] See article by the writer, 'A Note on the Berber Background in the Life of Augustine', *JTS.* xviii, 1942, pp. 188–91.

[3] The evidence for the supersession, at least in part, of Libyan by Punic in Roman times is marshalled by Professor Gautier in his *Passé de l'Afrique du Nord*, pp. 134–57. Unfortunately he wrote before the full significance of M. Rodarys' discoveries in the Souk-Ahras area could be assessed.

inscriptions on the Royal Tombs at Dougga and the Medracen show. The Berbers also took to Punic personal names connected with the worship of Baal—just as their descendants call themselves 'Abdullah' or 'Mahomet'. But, by and large, the distribution of Libyan and Punic in Roman times could not have been very different from the modern distribution of Berber and Arabic-speaking areas, though Arabic is spoken more extensively than ever Punic was. Throughout historical times Libyan or Berber and not a Semitic or Latin language has been the mother tongue of the peoples of the Numidian plains.[1]

The clue is provided by the distribution of Libyan inscriptions. Knowledge of these has been considerably increased by discoveries made in the years immediately before the war, when over 250 were found.[2] Most of the new finds came from the forested and mountainous country between Souk-Ahras and Bone, that is, the area covered by Augustine's activities. More Libyan inscriptions have also been found on the Numidian High Plains, and even in Proconsular Africa. In the areas where these are found, Punic and neo-Punic inscriptions are lacking. The late date of some of these stones is suggested by the fact that bilingual Latino-Libyan inscriptions are by no means uncommon. If one also takes into account that modern Berber contains a few Latin loan-words, but practically none of Punic origin, it must be accepted that the villages with whom Augustine came into contact spoke Libyan.[3] The fact that to Romans the Libyan language was 'unpronounceable'[4] would make it easy to group all local languages under the heading of 'Punic'. Augustine's statement on the languages in use in the Donatist Church, 'Latinam et Punicam, id est Afram',[5] may have been a confession of ignorance rather than a statement of fact.

[1] Recent changes in favour of Arabic have been caused by the opening up of the Plains by road and railway.
[2] P. Rodary, 'Recherche des Inscriptions libyques dans la Région de Souk-Ahras', *Premier Congrès de la Fédération des Sociétés savantes de l'Afrique du Nord*, Alger, 1935 (= *Premier Congrès*), pp. 173–81, and pp. 415–23 in the transactions of the Third Congress held at Constantine, 1937, published at Algiers, 1938. These discoveries are also incorporated in the Abbé J. Chabot's *Recueil des Inscriptions libyques*. For Latino-Libyan inscriptions in Tripolitania, see R. G. Goodchild, *JRS*. xl, 1950, p. 32.
[3] See E. Mercier, *Recueil de Constantine*, xxx, 1895, p. 146; R. Basset, 'Les Influences puniques chez les Berbères', *Revue Africaine*, lxii, 1921, pp. 340–75.
[4] There is the statement in Pliny, *N.H.* 5. 1, 'Populorum eius [Libyae] oppidorumque nomina vel maxime sunt ineffabilia, praeterquam ipsorum linguis.'
[5] Augustine, *In Epistolam Ioannis ad Parthos*, ii. 3 (*PL*. xxxiv–xxxv, col. 1991).

It is interesting to note, in conclusion, that Donatism does not stand alone as an example of a dissenting form of Christianity which found acceptance in the villages and among a population little affected by classical culture. In Asia Minor, for instance, contrary to the general practice among the Catholics, the Novatian bishops often had their sees in villages, while their councils, at Pazos in 368[1] and Mylukomé in 515,[2] met in villages also. The epitaph of a Catharist priest Eugenius, at Bash Hüyük, speaks of the deceased as a 'tower of courage to the poor, and in the village pre-eminent over all'.[3] The tradition of dissent from the Catholic religion in some parts of the country seems to have been continuous. A prophetic Church was succeeded by a Montanist, and a Montanist by a Novatian. In Egypt, too, the centre of a similar tradition of dissent against the official religion of the Empire was in the Thebaid, in the villages of the Upper Nile, and its leaders, as Schnoudi, were Copts who knew of Greek civilization only in order to hate it.[4] In Egypt and Asia Minor, as well as in North Africa, the 'heretical' form of Christianity struck deepest root where native linguistic and cultural traditions were most vigorous.[5]

[1] Socrates, *Historia Ecclesiastica*, iv. 28 (*Patrologia Graeca* (=*PG*.), lxvii. 540). Cf. ibid. vii. 15; Sozomen, *Hist. Ecc.* vii. 9. 2.

[2] W. H. Buckler, *Journal of Hellenic Studies*, 1917, p. 95; W. Schepelern, *Der Montanismus und die phrygischen Kulte*, Tübingen, 1929, pp. 175–6.

[3] W. M. Calder, 'The Epigraphy of the Anatolian Heresies', *Anatolian Studies presented to Sir William Mitchell Ramsay* (Manchester University Press, 1923), 77.

[4] Cf. J. Leipoldt, 'Schenute von Atirpe', *Texte und Untersuchungen* (= *TU.*), xxv, 1904, pp. 26 ff.

[5] Cf. K. Holl, 'Das Fortleben der Volksprachen in Klein-Asien in der Nach-christlichen Zeit', *Hermes*, xliii, 1908, pp. 240–54, 'Aber es wird doch jedem auffallen, dass das Gebiet, aus dem die Sekten nicht zu vertreiben waren, ziemlich mit demjenigen sich deckt in dem wir die Volksprachen noch fortlebend fanden' (p. 253); and J. G. C. Anderson, *Studies in the History and Art of the East Roman Provinces*, Aberdeen, 1906, pp. 200 ff.

V

NORTH AFRICA IN THE
FOURTH CENTURY A.D.

THE existence of personal rivalries between the Numidian and Carthaginian clergy and the development of different types of society near Carthage and in Numidia would not in themselves account for the persistence of Donatism. These factors form part of the background to the misunderstandings that led to the outbreak of the schism, but they do not explain the tenacity with which the Numidian bishops maintained their cause, nor the violence with which the peasants defended it. We have noted in passing that contemporaries recognized economic motives, e.g. indebtedness to the fiscal authorities, among those who sought martyrdom during the Great Persecution. One may detect, too, an element of antipathy between the citizens of Cirta and the land-workers at the time of the election of Silvanus as bishop, and throughout the High Plains one is struck by the fanatical zeal shown by the village population in the cause of the martyrs. The prevailing economic conditions in Africa during the fourth and early fifth centuries are clearly relevant towards understanding the nature of Donatism.

The main trends in Africa during this period are the irrevocable decline of the Roman cities, and with them the pagan culture of the middle classes, the increase of taxation and the unrelieved oppression of the peasantry, and, finally, the growth of a small group of wealthy landowners who were able largely to avoid taxation and to live a life of comparative leisure. In the resulting social conflicts the Donatists and Catholics took different sides.

Sources for the study of the situation in North Africa in the fourth century are not lacking. The evidence of inscriptions and the results of excavations may be supplemented by the laws of the *Codex Theodosianus* and *Codex Justinianus*. Many of the Imperial decrees aimed at preventing corruption and administrative abuses were directed to officials in Africa. The correspondence of St. Augustine also adds lively details on conditions in northern Numidia. To these must be added the work of Optatus of Milevis, particularly valuable for the Circumcellion risings of 340–7, and non-African authors such as Zosimus,[1] Ammianus Marcellinus,[2] and Symmachus.[3] The last three may be considered impartial judges so far as concerns actual conditions in North Africa.

The failure of the revolt against the Emperor Maximin in the spring of A.D. 238 is one of the key events in the history of the Roman towns in Africa. Despite the effort made in the reign of Diocletian, these never appear to have recovered from the destruction and looting which befell them, nor was the citizen body ever again to unite in protest against the oppressive taxation which had been one of the main causes of the revolt.[4] Inscriptions of the late third and fourth centuries tell the same story of progressive decline. The appeals of the citizens for the aid of wealthy patrons fell on deaf ears.[5] Public buildings collapsed and were not repaired,[6] aqueducts fell into disuse,[7] dedications to the Emperors by prominent citizens became rarer,[8] a seat in the city council instead of being a coveted honour on which fortunes had been lavished became something to be shunned. Even in a large seaport such as Tipasa Latin usages seem to have become obsolescent. In the fourth century the Christian clergy were able to transform the epitaph of a well-to-do matron named Fabia Salsa aged sixty-three into that of the 'martyr', 'St.' Salsa aged thirteen, by a simple reinterpretation of conventional abbreviations on a tombstone.[9] Not a gap but a chasm separated the outlook of the African in the third century from that of his descendants a hundred years later.

---

[1] *Historia Nova*, ed. L. Mendelssohn, Leipzig, 1887.

[2] *Rerum Gestarum* Libri qui supersunt, tr. Rolfe, ed. Loeb, 1935. Ammianus is valuable for the misrule of Count Romanus and the revolt of Firmus.

[3] *Epistolae* (ed. Seeck in *MGH*. vi).

[4] Herodian, vii. 9; W. Ensslin, *CAH*. xii, p. 76. Revival under Diocletian, C. E. van Sickle, 'Public Works in Africa in the reign of Diocletian', *Classical Philology*, 1930, p. 173.

[5] For example, see the inscription from Henchir Belda near Musti in the Upper Mejerda, *CIL*. viii. 27432 (A.D. 242–4).

[6] e.g. the arch at Ad Maiores, collapsed in 267, not repaired until 297 (*CIL*. viii. 2480–1). Buildings in other towns such as Bulla Regia were begun but never finished, ibid. 25520.

[7] Ibid. 2572 (Lambaesis), 'multorum incuri|a dilapsum et per lo|ngam annorum seri|em neglectum'. Also ibid. 18328 (Macomades).

[8] At Thuburbo Maius, for instance, there is a gap in dedications between Gordian and Constantine. Other towns show similar gaps.

[9] H. Grégoire, 'Sainte Salsa', *Byzantion*, xii, 1937, pp. 213–24. The words 'Matri Sanct.' became 'Marturi Sanct.', and the dedicators 'F[ilii] et F[iliae] et n[epotes]' transformed into 'F[ilii] et F[ideles] et n[autae]'!

Individual governors such as Valerius Florus[1] and Ceionius Albinus[2] in Numidia attempted in vain to instil new life into the cities and repair their falling buildings. Archaeological evidence, however, shows that by the Vandal period towns as widely separated as Leptis Magna,[3] Gigthis,[4] Timgad,[5] Bagai,[6] and Zabi[7] were probably deserted. There is sometimes two feet of silt between the Roman and the Byzantine levels in North African towns, and the Byzantine often ignored the earlier Roman town-plan. When in 485 Victor, Bishop of Vita, wrote that 'most of the towns were peopled by few if any inhabitants',[8] he was writing the epitaph on what had once been a splendid and flourishing civilization.

The decline of the cities reflected the eclipse of the medium landowning class which had been their principal inhabitants. The middle classes were taxed out of existence. The practice of the Roman government was to devolve the collection and the apportionment of a tax on to the class that paid it.[9] The members of the local city council (curia) were responsible for assessing and collecting the amount due. Failure to meet the quota demanded involved confiscation of their personal property. Wherever possible the burden was passed on to someone else, and finally to the peasants, for in the last resort the peasant's

---

[1] See above, page 7.

[2] A considerable number of inscriptions dated between A.D. 364 and 367 testify to Ceionius' activity as a restorer of temples and public buildings—repairs, for instance, to a portico in front of the Capitol at Timgad, CIL. viii. 2388. Other inscriptions include: ibid. 2242, repairs at Khenchela; ibid. 6975, a Mithraeum at Constantine; ibid. 20156, a clothes-market at Djemila, and a basilica built near the temple of the Gens Severi, E. Albertini, CRAI., 1943, pp. 376–86; ibid. 7975, horrea at Philippeville (Rusiccade). For the failure of this initiative, however, see Cod. Theod. xv. 1. 15, addressed to Dracontius, Vicar of Africa, 16 Feb. 365.

[3] Procopius, De Aedificiis, 1. 1. When the Byzantines visited the site it was half covered with sand. Sabratha seems similarly to have been abandoned in the fifth century A.D.

[4] L. A. Constans, 'Gigthis', Nouv. Archives des Missions, 1916, p. 22.

[5] Procopius, De Bello Vandalico, iv. 13. 26 (tr. Dewing, ed. Loeb, ii. 320).

[6] Procopius, ibid. iv. 19. 7 (Loeb, p. 378).

[7] CIL. viii. 8805. The town was restored a fundamentis in Byzantine times.

[8] Victor Vitensis, Historia Persecutionis Africae provinciae (ed. CSEL. vii, 1881), 1. 3, 'Sed et urbes quam plurimae aut raris aut nullis habitatoribus incoluntur.'

[9] See Sir Samuel Dill's chapter on 'The Decay of the Middle Class', in his Roman Society in the Last Century of the Western Empire, Macmillan, 1919. Also, D. van Berchem, 'L'Annone Militaire dans l'Empire romain au iiie siècle', Mémoires de la Soc. Nat. des Antiquaires de France, lxxx, 1937, p. 117, and A. Déléage, La Capitation du Bas-Empire, Mâcon, 1945, chap. x.

crops provided the means by which the taxes were paid. The system is described in a sentence of Libanius addressing the Emperor Theodosius on behalf of the *coloni* of the administrative territory of Antioch (*c.* A.D. 390). 'Moreover, Sire, it is from the country that your tribute is drawn. It is to the cities that you address your orders for taxation, but the cities have to raise it from the countryside. Therefore, to protect the farmers is to protect your own interests; to maltreat them is to betray them.'[1] The *coloni* of the Saltus Burunitanus in the upper valley of the Mejerda had pointed out the same fact to the Emperor Commodus just over two centuries before.[2]

Circumstances in Africa, however, made the clash between those responsible for collecting the taxes and those who actually paid them particularly acute. The Africans were responsible for supplying both the city of Rome and the army in Africa. Since A.D. 308 there had been no mint in Africa,[3] and that increased the tendency for payments to the Imperial authorities for the troops and administration to be made in kind. Of these taxes the *annona* was the most important and the most burdensome. By A.D. 250 increases had become a matter for protest and lament.[4] An inscription from Rusguniae on the Algerian coast shows the citizens of that town thanking the governor because he had not permitted the amount of the *annona* to increase.[5] Another from Sitifis, the capital of Mauretania Sitifensis, dated A.D. 388–92 also indicates the onerous nature of the task of collection.[6] When the same individuals appeared in the guise of tax-assessors and custodians of the collecting-points (*stationes*) to which the produce must be sent, they would naturally appear to the countryfolk as oppressors. Salvian, writing about A.D. 440, may have expressed a general plaint when he asks, 'ubi non quot curiales fuerint tot tyranni sunt?'[7] In addition, many

[1] Libanius, *Oratio*, 50, *De Angariis* (ed. Foerster, iii, p. 487). Cited from W. E. Heitland, *Agricola*, Cambridge, 1921, p. 400.

[2] *CIL*. viii. 10570, 'ut beneficio maiestatis tuae rustici tui vernulae et alumni saltum tuorum non ultra a conductoribus agrorum fiscalium in quiete manere . . .'.

[3] H. Mattingly, *Roman Coins*, Methuen, London, 1928, p. 218.

[4] Cyprian, *Ad Demetrianum*, 10 (*CSEL*. iii. 1, p. 358), 'de captatis annonarum incrementis', &c. Cf. M. Besnier, *L'Empire romain*, pp. 196–7.

[5] *Année épigraphique*, 1928, no. 23, 'Rusg(unienses) et Rusgunis consistentes ob merita aere collato quod annonam frumenti passus non sit increscere'.

[6] *CIL*. viii. 8480.

[7] Salvian, *De Gubernatione Dei*, v. 18 (ed. and tr. Sanford, Columbia University Press, 1930); *MGH*. i. 58.

F

of these city magistrates were pagans, and the holders of priesthoods, in the midst of a strongly Christian countryside.[1]

The evidence shows that the African middle class made every
effort one way or another to rid themselves of their responsibilities. Carthage[2] and Constantine[3] are mentioned as two cities
whose Council (*Ordo*) was disastrously depleted by the middle
of the fourth century. Joining the army,[4] or the civil service,[5]
taking Holy Orders,[6] or placing oneself under the patronage
of a senator were among the expedients employed by the curials
in their efforts to escape their fate. It was in vain. Those discovered would be returned to their duties, but 192 decrees in
the *Codex Theodosianus* tell of their struggles to find another
occupation. He who sheltered the fugitive was committed to
the avenging flames.[7] It is interesting to note that both Donatists and Catholics attempted to have their enemies enrolled as
members of city councils.[8] Thus the class which in Africa had
been the backbone of the Roman cities in the Antonine and
Severan periods became stiffened into a caste whose function
was to squeeze revenue from the peasants or be squeezed
themselves.[9]

The two groups in the cities not immediately connected with
collecting taxes suffered less. Both the richest and the poorest
members of the urban community survived. The excavations,
for instance, at Djemila (Lat. Cuicul in Mauretania Sitifensis)
suggest that the inhabitants of the site in the late fourth and
fifth centuries were few, but were comparatively wealthy.[10] The
plateau on which the town was built was occupied by a few
sumptuous residences. The House of Amphitrates and the House

---

[1] As at Timgad and Calama, *CIL*. viii. 2403; Augustine, *Ep*. 90.

[2] *Cod. Theod*. xii. 1. 27 (A.D. 339).

[3] Ibid. 29 (A.D. 340).

[4] Ibid. 64 (to the Sitifensian Moors, 23 Apr. 368, 370, or 373).

[5] Ibid. 24, 26, 27, 31, 44, 45, 73, 95, and 149.

[6] Ibid. 59 and 60.

[7] Ibid. 179; Dill, *Roman Society*, p. 263.

[8] See below, p. 163.

[9] On oppression of the *curiales*, cf. *Cod. Theod*. xii. 6. 31; A. Déléage, *La Capitation du Bas-Empire*, pp. 245–8.

[10] Y. Allais, *Djemila*, Paris, 'Les Belles Lettres', 1938, p. 45. The larger houses
seem to have been occupied by Imperial notaries, and by individuals of senatorial
rank. A parallel to Djemila can be quoted in the town of Serdjilla in northern
Syria, where the later stage of Roman occupation is represented by a few large
houses and two churches. C. M. Cobern, *New Archaeological Discoveries*, New York
and London, 1921, p. 451.

of the Ass with their rich mosaics and carved pillars date to the fourth and fifth centuries. The only other permanent buildings in constant use were the churches, outstanding among which were the baptistery and basilica of the Catholic bishop, Cresconius (c. A.D. 420). From Augustine's works we learn that much the same situation prevailed in Hippo Regius and Thagaste. Augustine's next-door neighbour at Hippo was a senator named Julius,[1] and some of the owners of large estates round Thagaste, such as Augustine's benefactor Romanianus, could be qualified as 'very wealthy' (*praedives*).[2] The survival of these greater landowners is well known to any reader of Augustine's correspondence. We hear of ten large estates in the neighbourhood of Hippo, and there were others in the diocese of Calama.[3] The owners of these estates were relied on to convert by one means or another their tenants from Donatism to Catholicism.[4] That they lived well is shown by more than one text from Augustine.[5]

At the other end of the scale one has the impression that in some towns there was a considerable artisan element. One would expect cities such as Carthage to retain a large working population, but one is surprised to find evidence for its existence in the smaller towns. At Timgad, for instance, the final expansion of the city during the third to fourth century along the road leading southwards towards the Aures mountains was due primarily to the growth of an artisan quarter. In contrast to the carefully laid out plan of the second-century town, this suburb consisted almost entirely of small shops and dwellings. These were erected without any evidence of plan and leave the effect of a souk in a modern Arab-Berber village.[6] Yet this was the

---

[1] Augustine, *Ep.* 99, 'de domo clarissimi et egregii iuvenis Iuliani, quae nostris adhaeret parietibus' (*CSEL.* xxxiv. 2. 533).

[2] *Confessions*, vi. 14.

[3] They are the following: Hasna, *Ep.* 29. 2; Spanianum, 35. 2; Straboniana, 65. 1. 1; Thiava, 83. 1; Victoriana, 105. 3; Casphaliana, 105. 3; Urgi, 105. 3; Fussala, 209; Germaniciana, 251; Subsana 62. 4 (the figures refer to Letters). Near Calama there was Figuli and Olivetum next to it: *Ep.* 105. 4 (*CSEL.* xxxiv. 598). Cf. M. Rostovtzev, *Social and Economic History*, pp. 432–4.

[4] *Ep.* 89. 8 (*CSEL.* xxxiv. 424–5).

[5] *In Ps.* 32. 18 (*PL.* xxxvi–xxxvii, col. 295), 'Quando de fundis et de praediis aliquibus amplis atque amoenissimis quaerimus, "Est quidam senator, et illud aut illud vocatur, cuius est ista possessio": et dicimus, "Beatus ille homo."'

[6] Described by A. Ballu, *Sept années de découvertes à Timgad*, Paris, 1911, p. 21. Unfortunately the dating is not certain owing to failure to observe stratified deposits. It must have been in existence in the fourth century A.D., since one of the shops had a stock of Christian lamps.

quarter of the town which seems to have been most occupied in the later period, and the 15,000 poorly furnished Christian graves dug in the hillside immediately beyond suggest the existence of a relatively large population there. In other towns, too, such as Theveste,[1] and even in Mauretania Caesariensis at Castellum Tingitanum (modern Orléansville),[2] the magnificent scale on which the early-fourth-century churches were built is in itself a tribute to the strength and cohesion of the artisan guilds. These appear to have been responsible for the erection of a number of Christian buildings, in particular, small chapels in Numidia.[3] Their outlook was nearer to that of the Berber country-dweller than to the latinized middle and upper classes. They provided recruits for riots against unpopular clergy. During the Maximianist controversy[4] in 393–7 the Donatist extremists were apparently able to rely on the support of the crowd not only in Carthage but up country at towns such as Membressa and Assuras, to overawe their moderate opponents.

In the African towns during their decline there was thus the tendency for society to be divided into a small romanized group and a considerable native element. The Donatist sermon was addressed particularly to this latter group, while the Catholics found the majority of their supporters among the urban middle and upper classes.

Neither archaeological nor literary evidence suggests that the African villages were in the same exhausted condition as the towns. Indeed, the fourth and early fifth centuries were probably the periods of their greatest expansion. We find, for instance, that the churches and chapels in the villages generally stood on new ground and were solidly built by people who took an individual pride in their work. A vigorous native Christian art developed, an art which appears to have been inspired by the Donatist

---

[1] The cathedral of Theveste is one of the finest buildings of the Roman period in Africa. It was probably built in the first third of the fourth century. Every stone had been carefully hewn, and bears an individual mason's mark (published under *ILA*. 3100). The basilica has been described by A. Truillot, 'Autour de la Basilique de Tébessa', *Recueil de Constantine*, lxii, 1933–4.

[2] The church was dedicated on 21 Nov. 324, *CIL*. viii. 9708. Described by H. Leclerq, 'Orléansville', *Dictionnaire d'Archéologie chrétienne*, 12. 2, col. 2728.

[3] L. Leschi, 'Inscriptions de la Plaine de Guert' (south of Tebessa), *Recueil de Tébessa*, 1936–7, p. 120. Other inscriptions show that a chapel was built 'ex officina . . .'. For instance, at Henchir bou Said a church was built, 'ex officina Fortuni et Victori fili(i)' (H. Jaubert, *Recueil de Constantine*, 1912, p. 197), and at Er Rouis, 'ex officina Adriani' (ibid., p. 196).

[4] See below, p. 219.

Church, and whose tradition has survived down to the present day.[1] It was in this period that many of the olive presses were built, wells dug, and systems of canalization laid out. Some of the presses in Numidia and Byzacena were adorned with Christian symbols.[2] African oil was of paramount importance to Italy in the late fourth century.[3] Indeed, at this period Numidia was probably economically as productive as Proconsular Africa. In addition to the trade with Italy, southern Numidia was bene-fiting from an extensive caravan trade from the Sahara. Zarai was an important centre of this activity.[4] There is, too, a tendency in this province for communities which in the second and third centuries A.D. had apparently been Legionary settlements and had attained municipal status, to revert to the condition of vil-lages. The site of Bou-Takrematem on the High Plains south of Châteaudun is an example.[5] This settlement is over a mile long and covers an area of some 200 acres (i.e. as much as one of the larger Romano-British towns, such as Verulamium). Stamped Third Legion tiles have been found there, and so have some exceedingly fine marble columns, but the whole area is a mass of olive presses and buildings of a type found in Romano-Berber villages. Milestones and marble columns have been reused in the walls of one of the churches. In the later Roman period the site must have been a sort of Timbuctu—a vast, formless village with a teeming population.

There is not a great deal of evidence of African land falling out of cultivation.[6] Apart from the indications provided by the existence of extensive villages and carefully planned systems of irrigation to cultivate the hill slopes, the survey of the Imperial

[1] See article by the writer, 'The Revival of Berber Art', *Antiquity*, 1942, pp. 342–52.

[2] As at Henchir el Gouma and Henchir Khadem in western Tunisia, cf. P. Gauckler, *Bull. Arch. du Comité*, 1897, p. 385.

[3] Symmachus, *Ep.* ix. 58, 'ad egestatis levamen certum ex Africa olei modum decrevit antiquitas'. See E. Albertini, 'Un Témoignage de Saint Augustin sur la prospérité relative de l'Afrique au IVᵉ siècle', *Mélanges Thomas*, Bruges, 1930, pp. 1–5

[4] *CIL.* viii. 4508, and Haywood, *Economic Survey*, p. 79. Cf. *CIL.* viii. 10401 (Lamasba)—improvement of roads for the benefit of traders.

[5] The Christian churches on this site have been described by Berthier and Martin in *Premier Congrès de la Fédération des Soc. savantes de l'Afrique du Nord*, 1935, pp. 137–51. I visited Bou Takrematem on several occasions in 1938–9 and again in 1943. It would repay prolonged and scientific excavation.

[6] Lactantius, *De Mortibus Persecutorum*, 17, and the allusions by Augustine to peasants abandoning their holdings to join the Circumcellion bands (*Contra Gaudentium*, i. 28. 32 (*PL*. xliii, col. 725)) may be quoted.

estates in Proconsular Africa and Byzacenia in A.D. 422 leaves a favourable impression.[1] In the one province 9,002 *centuriae* were in cultivation and 5,700 waste, in the other 7,640 in cultivation and 7,615 waste.[1] In view of the exceptionally poor soil in the areas covered by these estates, this result may be considered as relatively satisfactory.

The cultivators themselves did not degenerate into serfs, but managed to retain their status as Mancian *coloni*.[2] Some, at any rate, felt themselves in no way bound to the soil but could work as hired labourers on special tasks such as harvesting and olive-picking.[3] These wandering bands of seasonal workers may have played a considerable role in the economy of the country, and they also acted as the bearers of rumours and agitators in favour of Donatism in the Numidian villages. For the rest, the peasants were often able to resist the encroachments of Imperial lease-holders,[4] and at the end of the Roman period Valentianian III could still speak of the 'privileges' of the Numidians and Sitifensian Moors.[5] The most able of their class could rise above their environment to high office in the Imperial service and to literary fame.[6]

The real causes of the anger and desperation of the village populations seem to be that, though their economy was relatively prosperous, they were continually subjected to acts of extortion and cruelty by tax-collectors, by soldiers, and by the unfortunate city councillors who were responsible for the quota of tax being levied. In addition, there were the constant attempts by the senatorial landowners to extend their own domains without regard to the claims of either the lesser landowners or the colonate.

Evidence for the oppressive character of the administration

---

[1] *Codex Theodosianus*, xi. 28. 13. See W. Barthel, 'Römische Limitation in der Provinz Afrika', *Bonner Jahrbücher*, 1911, p. 49.

[2] *Cod. Just.* xi. 63. 1; C. Saumagne, 'La Paix Vandale', *Revue Tunisienne*, 1930, pp. 167–84.

[3] An inscription from Mactar dated to mid-third century provides evidence for this class, *CIL*. viii. 11824. Also, Optatus, v. 7 (*CSEL*. xxvi. 135–6). On their association with the Circumcellions, cf. C. Saumagne, 'Ouvriers agricoles ou rôdeurs de celliers. Les Circoncellions d'Afrique', *Annales d'histoire économique et sociale*, vi, 1934, pp. 351–64.

[4] *Cod. Just.* xi. 63. 1 (A.D. 317–19).

[5] *Novel 13, De Tributis Fiscalibus*, 21 June 445.

[6] Aurelius Victor describes himself as, 'rure ortus tenui atque indocto patre in haec tempora vitam praestiti studiis tantis honestiorem' (*De Caesaribus*, ed. Pichlmayr, 20. 5). From Ammian (xxi. 10. 6) we learn that Aurelius Victor was Governor of Pannonia Secunda under Julian.

is consistent throughout the century and a quarter between the accession of Constantine and the end of Roman rule in Africa during the reign of Valentinian III. In one of the first constitutions of his reign Constantine drew attention to the rapacity of the tax-collectors in the cities. 'With the connivance of the wealthy the book-keepers (*tabularii*) of the cities are transferring the burden of taxation on to the shoulders of the lesser folk.'[1] This constitution, dated 18 January 313, is exactly contemporary with the outbreak of the Donatist controversy. Six years later the Emperor pointed out to the Proconsul Catullinus that 'the farms on the Imperial estates were being worn out by extraordinary exactions,' amounting to one-third or one-half of the farmer's total crop.[2] A good harvest was often feared as much as a drought.[3] In this period more successful farmers would find themselves forced to pay the taxes of a defaulter or 'promoted' to the local city council.[4] Their draught animals would be seized for the public transport.[5] In 322 some of the provincials are stated to have been forced to sell their children into slavery to save themselves from starvation.[6]

A generation later, the rescripts addressed by the Emperor Constantius to his officials in Africa show that no improvement had taken place. In 344 a decree addressed to Eubolida, *Vicarius Africae*, refers to officials extorting 'unheard-of sums' from the population. Particularly noxious were those in charge of security, the *Agentes in Rebus*.[7] Attempts to secure redress would only result in further exactions from members of other branches of the Imperial service who were charged with forwarding petitions (the *scholastici*).

[1] *Cod. Theod.* xiii. 10. 1. Ad Populum, 'Quoniam tabularii civitatum per conlusionem potentiorum sarcinam ad inferiores transferunt. . . .' The same abuse was rampant over a century later. See *Novel 10* of Valentinian III.

[2] *Cod. Theod.* xi. 16. 1, 'Patrimoniales fundos extraordinariis oneribus vel mediae vel tertiae portionis obsequiis fatigari non convenit, cum eosdem et auri speciem et frumenti plurimum modum constat persolvere.' Cf. ibid. 3. 1.

[3] Claudian, *In Rufinum*, 1. 190, 'metuenda colonis fertilitas' (tr. Platnauer, ed. Loeb, 1922).

[4] *Cod. Theod.* xi. 19. 1 and xii. 1. 133.

[5] Ibid. xi. 16. 4.   [6] Ibid. 27. 2.

[7] Ibid. viii. 10. 2, 'Praeter sollemnes et canonicas pensitationes multa a provincialibus Afris indignissime postulantur ab officialibus et scholasticis non modo in civitatibus singulis, sed et mansionibus dum ipsis et animalibus eorundem alimoniae sine pretio ministrantur.' Cf. *CIL.* viii. 17896 (regulation of fees to be paid to *scholastici*). A. Merlin, *Bull. Arch. du Comité*, 1918, p. ccxl, publishes an inscription from Thuburbo Maius showing arbitrary exactions by the *stationarii*, officials in charge of the storage of the *annona*.

From a contemporary African one learns something of the character of the men who were employed on the duties of collecting the *annona* from the peasants. They were 'evil, venal, cunning, deceitful, and avaricious, as if by nature endowed with the gift of perpetrating and concealing frauds'.[1] The laws of the *Codex Theodosianus* show them practising every type of malversation: dealing out fraudulent receipts,[2] exacting forced labour,[3] holding defaulters in private prisons,[4] and arbitrarily increasing the amounts due from the farmers. Between A.D. 412 and 415 three branches of the civil service were abolished in Africa, and tribunes were dispatched to round up deserters who had taken up their offices 'for the sake of loot'.[5]

The burden of heavy and unpredictable taxation placed the farmer at the mercy of his richer neighbours. He would either seek their patronage as a means of defence against the tax-collectors, or he would be obliged to raise a loan, often at an exorbitant rate of interest. These payments were enforced. From Augustine one learns how the poor were sometimes obliged to depend on the wealthy for their food,[6] and that failure to meet obligations entailed dispossession of the little previously owned. 'You are making your lives evil by stealing, in order that you may obtain a good villa', he told members of his congregation.[7] A century and a half previously Cyprian had described to his friend Donatus how the rich 'added estate to estate, excluding the poor from their boundaries and extending their domains in every direction'.[8] These men may have 'lived in perpetual dread', as Cyprian believed, but they also enjoyed considerable material comfort,[9] and it needed more than the bishops' rebukes to provide a remedy.

The true character of the social evils from which the African provinces were suffering are summed up at the very end of Roman rule in two different but complementary sources. First,

---

[1] Aurelius Victor, *De Caesaribus*, 33, 'nequam, venale, callidum, seditiosum, habendi cupidum atque ad patrandas fraudes velandasque quasi ab natura factum'. Their hostility to the peasants was proverbial. They were 'fortunis aratorum infestum.' [2] *Cod. Theod.* xi. 1. 2.

[3] Ibid. 16. 4. [4] Ibid. viii. 4. 2.

[5] Ibid. vi. 29. 11. [6] Augustine, *Ep.* 157. 38 (*CSEL.* xliv. 485).

[7] Augustine, *Sermo* 16. 2. 2 (*PL.* xxxviii, col. 122), 'Nam ut inhiando et male concupiscendo adipiscaris villam bonam, fraudando efficis vitam malam.'

[8] Cyprian, *Ad Donatum*, 12 (*CSEL.* iii. 1. 13), 'Sed et quos divites opinaris continuantes saltibus saltus et de confinio pauperibus exclusis infinite ac sine terminis rura latius porrigentes . . . '.

[9] Augustine, *In Ps.* 38, 2 (*PL.* xxxvi, col. 413).

there are *Novels 10* and *12* of Valentinian III, dated A.D. 441 and 443, and secondly the evidence of Salvian, who was writing of conditions in and around Carthage at this precise period. In the *Novels*, Africa is a territory characterized by the 'bankruptcy of all fortunes',[1] where 'those who united in themselves the riches of the world'[2] were oppressing those less prosperous. Rates of interest increased, and debtors were held at the mercy of their creditors. They were beaten, starved, tortured, and dispossessed. There was no possibility of legal redress. They were driven to surrender whatever was demanded from them by individuals whose cruelty, in the words of the rescript, exceeded that of the invading Vandals.[3] This same scene is described in terms equally severe by Salvian of Marseilles: 'Now we must consider also another charge of a serious kind, unlike this [vice and blasphemy] in its nature but not unlike it in gravity, unless its greatness sets it in a different class. I mean the proscriptions of orphans, the afflictions of widows, and the crucifixion of the poor. All these made their moan daily to God, and prayed for the end of their sufferings. Nay, what is worse, they were sometimes driven by their bitter woes even to pray for the arrival of the enemy.'[4] How blind many of the Catholic clergy were to this state of affairs is revealed by the description which Victor,[5]

---

[1] *Novel 12*, 'ubi omnium fortunarum diluvium'.

[2] Ibid., 'inlustribus titulis redunatis opulentia saeculi', &c.

[3] Ibid., 'De Pecunia Afris Credita et Fideijussoribus Eorum', 19 Oct. 443 to Albinus. Some relevant extracts: 'Si adflictis Afrorum fortunis, qui omnes facultates suas per acerbissima supplicia amittere sunt coacti, decet . . . consulere quanto dignius est infortunia eorum contra molestias improbas creditorum clementiae nostrae remediis sublevari? Quos enim constat pericula famis aliter non posse depellere, nisi ope aliena auxilioque recreentur, quam magnae acerbitatis putandum est hos ipsos inopes omnium rerum et precario victu egentes compelli ad [debita solvenda et adempta per] injuriam restituere ea quae improviso cladis impetu vis maior abstraxit sibique inter omnia spolia vindicavit?' The cruelty of the creditors, 'inmanitatem superet hostilem'. Therefore, Valentianian decrees, 'Ut nulli nomine chirograforum creditae pecuniae sive fideijussorum usque ad recuperationem rerum suarum quolibet pulsante teneatur,' &c. It is doubtful if these admonitions had much effect. Cf. *Novel 10* of Valentinian, 'usuris in majorem cumulum crescentibus'. It was against these precise abuses that the Donatist extremists revolted. See below, p. 172.

[4] Salvian, *De Gubernatione Dei* (tr. Sanford), vii. 16 (pp. 211–12). On the other hand, Salvian's value as an historical source is dubious. He was prepared to use any facts whether in context or not to prove the moral degeneracy of the Romans. In this instance, however, his testimony confirms what is already known from the Codex. On Salvian see P. Courcelle, *Hist. litt. des grandes invasions germaniques*, Hachette, 1948, pp. 127, 231.

[5] Victor Vitensis, *Historia Persecutionis*, i. 1. 3.

Bishop of Vita, gives of the province on the eve of the Vandal invasion. According to him, Africa was 'peaceful, quiet, and flourishing with the riches of the whole world'. The historical legend of the 'vandalism' of the Vandals has died hard.

This situation continued for over a century and a half and resulted in a spirit of desperation and revolt. It is not easy for the modern mind to grasp the idea of a static society ruled by custom, in which material conditions gradually grew worse from one generation to the next. The position of the African provincials in the time of Valentinian III seems to have been infinitely worse than it had been under Constantine. The form which revolt took was not merely flight and brigandage such as characterized the Bagaudic[1] movement in fourth–fifth-century Gaul and Spain, but was bound up with religious questions. The African always tended to see Imperial officials as 'servants of God' if they treated him justly or as 'powers of evil' or 'enemies of the Church' if they proved oppressive. Officials like Count Romanus were numbered among the latter by the Donatists.

The example of the revolt of Firmus in 372 may be quoted. Zosimus,[2] who was himself an *Advocatus fisci*, suggests that the main cause of the revolt of this Mauretanian chieftain was over-taxation, particularly through increases in the *annona*. This was aggravated by acts of oppression by officials, and by the garrisons which were stationed in the towns of the Chelif valley and which lived off the land. In addition, the armies in Africa were commanded by one of the most notorious administrators that even the Later Empire produced. Count Romanus governed for ten years. A comment on his rule comes from Ammianus Marcellinus. He outdid the barbarians in devastating the province.[3] Appeals against his blackmail and extortion resulted only in the execution of those who made them.[4] He had colleagues of the same brand. The Proconsul, Rusticus Julianus, was described

---

[1] On the Bagaudae in Gaul, C. Jullian, *Histoire de la Gaule*, vii, Paris, 1926, pp. 51–56. On Donatism as a movement of social revolution, F. Martroye, 'Une Tentative de révolution sociale en Afrique', *Revue des Questions Historiques*, lxxvi, 1904, pp. 353–416, and 1905, pp. 1–53.

[2] *Historia Nova*, iv. 16 (Mendelssohn, p. 171). It is interesting to note that in these years new Imperial granaries were erected at Rusiccade, presumably to store the product of the *annona* (*CIL*. viii. 7975).

[3] Ammianus Marcellinus, xxvii. 9. 1–2, 'saevitia morum multis erat exosus ... hac praecipue causa quod superare hostes in vastandis provinciis festinabat'.

[4] Ammianus Marcellinus, xxviii. 6. 7 and following, regarding Leptis Magna.

as an administrator, 'as greedy for human blood as a wild beast'.[1]

The revolt resembled a Bagaudic rising. Roman cities such as Caesarea were taken and burnt to the ground.[2] Roman administration ended, and those officials who were lucky enough to escape went into hiding. Firmus' Berber tribesmen were supported by the native villagers—the inhabitants, that is, of the *castella* such as Castellum Tingitanum[3]—and above all by the Donatist Church. While Ammianus merely says that the embassy dispatched by Firmus to the camp of the Roman general Theodosius included 'Christian bishops',[4] Augustine leaves no doubt that these bishops were Donatists. He narrates how the Donatist bishop handed over the town of Rusabiccari on the Algerian coast to Firmus,[5] and how the Donatists became nicknamed 'Firmiani' for their support of the rebel.[6] The Catholics and the landowners, on the other hand, rallied to the aid of Theodosius.[7] Firmus was checked at the town of Tipasa, a Catholic stronghold, allegedly by the intervention of Saint Salsa,[8] and Augustine was prepared to defend Count Romanus against Donatist attack.[9]

The extreme section of the Donatist Church did not merely support revolt but they fomented it themselves. The close link between these bands of fanatics known as Circumcellions and prevailing social grievances was obvious to contemporaries.[10] Augustine himself wrote in A.D. 408 to Macrobius, his Donatist rival in Hippo, who was at that time rated as a moderate. 'One flees unity', he says, 'so that the peasantry may rise boldly against their lords, and the slaves also, contrary to Apostolic precept. The fugitive slaves are not only alienated from their masters, but

---

[1] Id. xxvii. 6. 1.   [2] Id. xxix. 5. 42; Orosius, vii. 33 (*CSEL*. v. 516).
[3] Ammianus Marcellinus, xxix. 5. 12, 25 and 39. Castellum Tingitanum was a Donatist bishopric; *Gesta Coll. Carth*. 1. 180. Nearly all the fighting was centred on *fundi* or *castella* in Firmus' hands.
[4] Ammianus Marcellinus, xxix. 5. 15, 'Christiani ritus antistites oraturos pacem cum obsidibus misit'.
[5] Augustine, *Ep*. 87. 10 (*CSEL*. xxxiv. 406).
[6] Augustine, *Contra Epistolam Parmeniani*, i. 10. 16, 11. 17, *Ep*. 87. 10, and *Contra litteras Petiliani*, ii. 83. 184.
[7] Ammian, xxix. 5. 11 (landowners' support).
[8] *Passio Salsae* (*Catalogus Codicum Hagiographicorum*, Brussels, 1889, p. 351). S. Gsell gives the relevant extract in his article on 'Tipasa', *Mélanges*, xiv, 1894, pp. 311–12.
[9] Augustine, *Contra Litteras Petiliani*, iii. 25. 29.
[10] Optatus, iii. 4.

threaten their masters, and are not content with threats, but pass to the most violent attacks and robberies at their expense. They have for their leaders your confessors, the *agonistici* ("militants"), who honour you with shouts of *Deo Laudes*, and to *Deo Laudes* spill the blood of others.'[1]

Ten years later, in the brief period of triumph that followed the Conference of Carthage, Augustine wrote to Count Boniface a long letter in which he attempted to give him a complete account of Donatism.

Among the Donatists, he writes, herds of abandoned men were disturbing the peace of the innocent for one reason or another in the spirit of the most reckless madness. What master was there who was not compelled to live in dread of his own servant if he had put himself under the guardianship of the Donatists? Who dared even threaten one who sought his ruin with punishments? Who dared to exact payment of a debt from one who had consumed his stores, or from any debtor whatever, that sought their assistance or protection? Under the threat of beating, and burning, and immediate death, all documents compromising the worst of slaves were destroyed, that they might depart in freedom. Notes of hand [*chirographia*] that had been extracted from debtors were returned to them. Anyone who had shown a contempt for their hard words were compelled by harder blows to do what they desired. The houses of innocent persons were either razed to the ground or burned. Certain heads of families of honourable parentage, and brought up with a good education, were carried away half dead after their deeds of violence, or bound to the mill, and compelled by blows to turn it round after the fashion of the meanest beasts of burden. For what assistance from the laws rendered by the civil powers was ever of any avail against them? What agents ever exacted payment of a debt which they had been unwilling to discharge? What official ventured so much as to breathe in their presence? Whoever endeavoured to avenge those who were put to death in their massacres? Except, indeed, that their own madness took revenge on them, when some, by provoking against themselves the swords of men, whom they obliged to kill them under fear of instant death, others by throwing themselves over sundry precipices, others by water, others by fire gave themselves over on the several occasions to a voluntary death, and gave up their lives as offerings to the dead by punishments inflicted with their own hands upon themselves.[2]

[1] Augustine, *Ep.* 108. 6. 18 (*CSEL.* xxxiv. 632).
[2] Id., *Ep.* 185. 4. 15 (tr. Marcus Dods, Edinburgh, 1872, in vol. iii of *The Works of Aurelius Augustine*, pp. 491–2).

These are interesting passages. They give an insight into the mind of Augustine, conservative and a defender of established order, including slavery. In contrast, there is the connexion between Donatism, social discontent, and popular frenzy. It is the reaction one would expect from the situation described in the Codes, and is probably the key to the disappearance of Catholic Christianity in North Africa. We shall return to this subject. But sufficient is clear—the existence of a relationship between social and religious discontent in fourth-century Africa. Meantime, we pass on to the religious background of Donatism and examine the religious grounds for the fanaticism and even suicidal mania of some of its adherents.

VI

THE RELIGIOUS BACKGROUND
OF DONATISM

THE temples of the pagan gods in North Africa shared the fate of the other public buildings in the decaying Roman cities. The third and fourth centuries saw equally the collapse of official paganism and the ruin of the urban middle classes.[1] The picture of abandoned and derided temples, which Arnobius of Sicca paints at the end of the third century, could hardly have been exaggerated.[2] After A.D. 235 there is evidence for only a few dedications to the gods of the Empire, and for few temples built in their honour;[3] too often their shrines were stripped of their revenues and left to be pillaged and finally destroyed.[4] The place of the official religion was being taken by movements which expressed more fully the deep piety of the masses in town and countryside. All over the Roman Empire superstition, magic, and popular religious movements gathered strength as the decay of the Roman element became more pronounced. In Britain and Gaul this movement may have been Celtic and pagan in character, represented by the building of new shrines in abandoned hill forts like Maiden Castle,[5] and the repair and awakened interest in others such as those at Frilford,[6] Verulamium,[7] and Worth.[8] In the Mediterranean basin, how-

---

[1] On the subject, see J. Geffcken's *Ausgang des griechisch-römischen Heidentums*, Heidelberg, 1929, chap. ii.

[2] Arnobius, *Adversus Nationes*, i. 24 (*CSEL*. iv, p. 16), 'neleguntur dii, clamitant, atque in templis iam raritas summa est, iacent antiquae derisui caerimoniae et sacrorum quondam veterrimi ritus [caerimoniae] religionum novarum superstitionibus occiderunt'. Cf. *CIL*. viii. 12285 (Bisica).

[3] One might mention a temple at Dougga built in the reign of Gallienus, *CIL*. viii. 26559, another to Magna Mater at Mactar under Probus, ibid. 100, and possibly a temple at Thignica under Gallienus, ibid. 15246.

[4] Ibid. 15881, Sicca (robbery); *Gesta apud Zenophilum*, 193 (pillage); Herodian, vii. 9. 10 (confiscation of funds).

[5] R. E. M. Wheeler, 'Maiden Castle', *Reports of the Research Committee of the Society of Antiquaries*, xii, Oxford, 1943, pp. 72–76.

[6] J. S. P. Bradford and K. G. Goodchild, 'Excavations at Frilford, Berks.', *Oxoniensia*, iv, 1939, 35.

[7] R. E. M. Wheeler, 'Verulamium', *Reports of the Research Committee of the Society of Antiquaries*, xi, Oxford, 1936, 132.

[8] W. G. Klein, *Antiquaries Journal*, viii, 1928, 78.

ever, it was Christianity that triumphed, and in Africa victory was won at the expense not only of official paganism but also of the great national cult of Saturn and Caelestis.

This latter feature is of interest to the student of Donatism. Christianity was a phase in the religious history of the Berbers which lasted about 400 years. During this time its ascendancy was complete. At the turn of the fifth century there must have been more than 500 episcopal sees in North Africa, and the remains of churches can be numbered at well over a thousand. But in the early Roman Empire the prevalent religion was that of Saturn, and Christianity itself was to be displaced completely by Islam. Each in his turn, Saturn, Christ, and Mahomet, has obtained the undivided allegiance of multitudes of North Africans. In Numidia, where the rigorous and fanatical Kharedjite form of Islam succeeded Donatism, Saturn seems to have had particularly fervent worshippers.

Yet, underlying these seemingly complete changes in religious conviction, the Berbers have retained certain basic beliefs from prehistoric times down to the present day.[1] Their religion, so far as it can be traced back, has always tended towards monotheism, the cult of a single great and all-powerful deity. In Christian and Moslem times the deity was represented to the world through a single being, in whom were combined the concepts of prophet and teacher, Christ and Mahomet. Coupled with this has been veneration for a host of lesser saints and holy men, whether in the form of Christian martyrs or Moslem marabouts. Seers, prophets, and soothsayers have been assured popular following, and pilgrimages have always been made to their shrines. There has been, too, intense preoccupation with magic, and a fatalistic belief in the malevolent activities of djinns and spirits. Religious rites and practices designed to placate these spirits or to see into the future have remained unaltered from time immemorial. Offerings made to the dead, libations poured into their tombs, feasts partaken in the cemeteries have gone on in pagan, Christian, and Moslem periods alike. People slept at the tombs of ancestors or holy men in Herodotus' time, in the fourth century A.D., and do so at the present

[1] The reader is referred to A. Bel, *La Religion musulmane en Berbérie. Esquisse d'histoire et de sociologie religieuses*, i, Paris, Geuthner, 1938; E. Doutté, *Magie et religion dans l'Afrique du Nord*, Algiers, Jourdan, 1909; P. Westermarck, *Ritual and Belief in Morocco*, Longmans, 1926; also S. Gsell, *Hérodote*, Algiers, Jourdan, 1915, chap. iv.

day.[1] Magical symbols such as the 'Hand of Fatima' or the fish have retained their potency against the Evil Eye over centuries of political and religious change.[2] The transfer of outward religious allegiance has never meant in North Africa the complete abandonment of previously held convictions.

In the first half of the third century A.D. the cult of Saturn and Caelestis was almost universal in North Africa. Saturn, as has often been pointed out,[3] was not the Italian Saturnus. In Africa he was not merely a tribal deity, nor the god of crops and fields. These were among his attributes,[4] but he was infinitely greater. On dedications Saturn is termed Eternal (*Deus Aeternus*),[5] the Lord (*Dominus*),[6] Holy (*Sanctus*),[7] the Unconquered (*Invictus*),[8] or even Holy Spirit (*Numen sanctum*).[9] In the late fourth century the Grammarian Maximus of Madauros described him as 'summus, sine initio, sine prole naturae', the Supreme Being without beginning or descendant.[10] He was the god of the dead as well as the living.[11] On mosaics, as that from Moghrane near Zaghouan, he is shown presiding over the Sun and Moon.[12]

His origins cannot be sought in the classical pantheon. He belongs to religious concepts which were handed down from the remote past among the Berbers. In Carthaginian times he was worshipped under the name of Baal-Hammon. His female counterpart, 'the countenance of Baal' (*Tanit Pene Baal*), became romanized into *Caelestis*,[13] a goddess at once virgin and mother,

---

[1] For the custom in Herodotus' time, Herodotus (ed. Gsell), iv. 172. I have seen koubbas near Oran in 1943, where the practice still continues.

[2] E. F. Gautier, *Le Passé de l'Afrique du Nord*, pp. 148–9.

[3] J. Toutain, *Les Cultes païens dans l'Empire romain, Première partie, Les Provinces latines*, iii, Paris, Leroux, 1920. I have made use of this work throughout this chapter, and consider that Toutain's conclusions on the nature of Saturn as a god, and on the social level of his worshippers, have not been superseded.

[4] Saturn as 'Deus frugum', *CIL*. viii. 4581, or as a local deity, 'Genius Saltus Sorothensis', *Bull. Arch. du Comité*, 1896, p. 228, no. 19.

[5] *CIL*. viii. 2667 (Lambaesis); ibid. 21581 (Oued el Hamman).

[6] Ibid. 20969 (Caesarea); Toutain, op. cit., p. 17, points out that the title Lord, 'Dominus', is an exact translation of the Punic 'Ādhōn', used to address Baal on Punic and neo-Punic inscriptions. 'Dominus' is used on Christian inscriptions from Numidian chapels in the fourth century.

[7] *CIL*. viii. 8449, 9181 = 20820.   [8] Ibid.

[9] *Recueil de Constantine*, 1909, p. 293.   [10] Augustine, *Ep.* 21. 6.

[11] H-I. Marrou, 'La Collection Gaston de Vulpillières à el Kantara', *Mélanges*, l, 1933, pp. 81–86, at p. 83.

[12] J. Toutain, 'Le Sanctuaire de Saturnus Balcarensis', *Mélanges*, xii, 1892, pp. 95–96.

[13] J. Toutain, *Les Cultes païens*, iii, pp. 29–47.

the Queen of Heaven.[1] The same attributes, *aeterna*,[2] *sanctissima*,[3] and *domina*,[4] that were bestowed on Saturn were bestowed on her.

In the second and third centuries the hold which the cult of Saturn-Caelestis had on the Africans was immense. Dedications and offerings can be numbered in thousands. The intensity of popular religious fervour is indicated by the frequency with which the supplicant is shown on dedications in an attitude of prayer. Even in Christian times Saturn's name aroused feelings of superstitious terror. He was referred to only as *senex* (the Old Man).[5] The greater part of the Latino-African nomenclature both in the pagan and Christian periods was connected with his worship. Apart from Saturninus, names such as Donatus, Adeodatus, Honoratus, Rogatus, Concessus, Fortunatus, Habetdeus, which occur over and over again in Africa, are direct translations of Punic theophonic names. So Donatus or Adeodatus = Given of Baal or Iatanbaal, Fortunatus = favoured of Baal or Muthumbaal, Honoratus = Honoured by Baal, Hannibal (?), &c.[6] They suggest a certain fatalism in outlook, and an absolute subjection of the individual to the inscrutable decrees of the god.

All that is known of the worship of Saturn bears out this view. The god's bidding would be conveyed to the individual through a dream.[7] The worshipper might have committed some sin; he would be called upon to perform sacrifice, if necessary of his own children. As we know from Tertullian, human sacrifice continued in Africa in Roman times, possibly within Tertullian's own memory, i.e. to mid-second century.[8] But gradually, less terrible means were found to appease the divine wrath. In

[1] *CM*. 234 (Henchir Redir bir Fras), 'Cae[lesti] regi[nae au]g. sac.' E. F. Gauthier, op. cit., p. 146.

[2] 'Caelestis aeterna', *Année épigraphique*, 1913, no. 226.

[3] *CIL*. viii. 20745; Toutain, op. cit., pp. 29–30.

[4] *CIL*. viii. 20320.

[5] Augustine, *De Consensu Evangelistarum*, i. 23. 36 (*PL*. xxxiv, col. 1058), 'ut nec nominare illum velint [Mathematici] senem potius quam Saturnum appellantes tam timida superstitione, ut iam Carthaginenses pene vico suo nomen mutaverint, Vicum Senis crebrius quam Vicum Saturni appellantes'.

[6] On this subject, S. Gsell, *Histoire ancienne*, iv, p. 497.

[7] *CIL*. viii. 8201, 'somno monitus'; ibid. 8826, 'monitus sacra religione'; ibid. 8433 and 9650, 'ex praecepto numinis'—warning in a vision—'viso admonitus' from Bou Kournein.

[8] Tertullian, *Apologeticus*, 9. 2 (ed. Loeb, p. 46). I incline to the view that Tertullian was describing comparatively recent events. On the other hand, see Toutain, op. cit., pp. 78–80. Human sacrifice survived among the Moors in Byzantine times (Corippus, *Iohannidos libri*, viii. 308–9, ed. *MGH*. iii. 2).

the first half of the third century a series of inscriptions from N'gaous (Lat. Nicivibus) and el Kantara (Lat. Ad Calceum Herculis) in southern Numidia show how the full rigour of Saturn's demand was being modified.[1] In a ceremony known as Mochomor (meaning, in Punic, 'the promise of a ram'), performed at night, a lamb was sacrificed in substitution for a human being. But the text of the dedication indicates the redemptive character of the act. The lamb was offered *pro vicario*, that is, as 'representing' or 'in substitution for' the child. This is a technical religious term, probably a translation of a Semitic word, and it is interesting that Tertullian uses a similar term to define Christ's redemptive act upon the Cross.[2] The jingling formula employed, 'anima pro anima, sanguinis pro sanguine, vita pro vita' leaves no doubt as to the solemn and religious character of the deed. As Marrou has pointed out, this sacrifice was not merely in order to save life but to ensure salvation to the worshipper after death.[3] It was the Libyc-Phoenician version of the story of Abraham and Isaac.

The emphasis on correct ritual which this religion demanded is shown by other inscriptions. In one, the worshipper assures the god that he has performed his sacrifice with headgear duly arranged.[4] Abstinence and fasts are mentioned elsewhere.[5] No doubt the slightest deviation would have called down divine wrath, in the form of sickness or mishap. It can be no accident that Saturn is always depicted as aged and morose. He was in fact a jealous, implacable, and terrible being.

His worshippers would appear to have been drawn primarily from the lower classes in the towns and the countryfolk.[6] These were the two groups which in the later third century were to assure the victory of Christianity in Africa. As Toutain has calculated, not more than thirty of the 1,400 known dedications to Saturn were made by officials, veterans, or city magistrates.

---

[1] For discussion of this rite, H-I. Marrou, 'La Collection Gaston de Vulpillières à el Kantara', *Mélanges*, l, 1933, pp. 81–86; J. Guey, 'Ksiba et à propos de Ksiba', *Mélanges*, liv, 1937, pp. 83–103; J. Carcopino, *Revue de l'Histoire des Religions*, cvi, 1932, pp. 592–9; *Aspects mystiques de la Rome païenne* (Paris, Artisan du Livre, 1942), pp. 39–48; S. Gsell, *CRAI.*, 1931, pp. 21–26.

[2] *De Res. Carnis*, 8. On the significance of the term *pro vicario*, Carcopino, op. cit., p. 44. [3] Marrou, *Mélanges*, l, p. 83.

[4] P. Sempronius Quintus emphasized that he performed his sacrifice at Bou-Kournein 'capite ordinato'. Toutain, *Mélanges*, xii, 1892, insc. 17.

[5] A. Audollent, *Mélanges*, x, 1890, no. 100, p. 534.

[6] Toutain, *Les Cultes païens*, i. 3. 96–113.

This is a contrast to the frequency of dedications made in honour of the gods of the Roman pantheon by Roman citizens and officials in the towns.[1]

To date, there is evidence for one Municipium only, Thuburnica in the upper valley of the Mejerda, performing a collective sacrifice to Saturn.[2] Those bodies which rendered him homage were for the most part rural or non-citizen organizations. The majority of the worshippers were of humble status, people who could not write, and must content themselves with the offering of an inexpensive clay figure or a rough uninscribed dedication. Native African names are common among those which have been preserved. At shrines where the names of priests and faithful have survived these tell the same story. At Thignica (Ain Tounga) in Proconsular Africa, out of 287 dedications, including those of 157 priests, only two would appear to have been set up by individuals of citizen status.[3] At Henchir Rhobane near Tebessa, out of thirty-seven priests two have the Roman prae- and cog-nomen.[4] Here a number of purely native names, such as Cacaban and Cirippitad, were found. Even at Bou-Kournein outside Carthage dedications by Roman citizens were evidently rare. In contrast, at Sertei[5] in Mauretania Sitifensis and Siagu[6] in proconsular Africa, some of the dedicants appear to have been outwardly more romanized, but in these instances, too, few examples of the Latin *tribus* were found among the names which appeared on the inscriptions.

The non-classical background of the cult is also illustrated by the places of worship built for it. With few exceptions, the erection of a temple to Saturn would appear to have been a comparatively late development,[7] accompanying the drive for public

---

[1] Toutain, op. cit., pp. 100–2. No significant discoveries have been made since Toutain wrote, to necessitate revision of his conclusions.

[2] *Bull. Arch. du Comité*, 1906, p. ccxxi, no. 1; p. ccxxv, no. 16. Toutain, op cit., pp. 102–4.

[3] Toutain, op. cit., pp. 107–11.

[4] *ILA*. 3018. Gsell's comment, 'L'inscription même sent la plèbe', seems justified. For a similar verdict on the inscriptions from the shrine at Henchir Srira, C. Hautecœur, *Mélanges*, xxix, 1909. pp. 376–8.

[5] *CIL*. viii. 8826.

[6] *Bull. Arch. du Comité*, 1908, p. 410. But see also L. Poinssot, *Bull. Arch. du Comité*, 1927, pp. 32–35, on the social standing of most of the dedicants at this shrine.

[7] The only important exception is that at Uchi Maius, where a freedman Q. Urvinius Q. lib. Callistus had a temple erected in the reign of Nerva. A. Merlin and L. Poinssot, *Les Inscriptions d'Uchi Maius* (Paris, 1908), pp. 28–29, no. 7.

buildings in the last thirty years of the second century. It was in this period that the temples at Dougga,[1] Mactar,[2] Lambaesis,[3] Auzia,[4] Ammaedara,[5] and Thala[6] were built. Even so, the site selected was a high place outside the town, not in the centre of the community like most Roman temples. The plan of the building had little in common with the classical temple, even though Corinthian-type columns might be employed, and statues in Roman dress placed in the niches within. The basic element of the sanctuary seems to have been the sacred enclosure around which chapels would be built, and the whole was roofed over beneath a central dome. There was no central shrine, but a series of chapels in which the deity was believed to enter and take up his abode. A Punic inscription from a temple near Siagu in Tunisia refers to the 'gods entering the sanctuaries in the month of Mopha of the present year'.[7] The religious observance would resemble that of the Hebrew Tabernacle and, as Toutain points out, would be far removed from Greco-Roman ideas.[8] Generally, however, the sanctuary was not marked by any temple. It was simply an enclosure (*area*) on some high ground away from the town. That on the Bou Kournein, a crescent-shaped mountain twelve miles south of Carthage, or Mactar and el-Khenissia, south of Sousse, are typical of this type of religious centre. So different from Roman paganism, it is hardly accidental that Saturn was rarely associated with Jupiter and the other gods, nor, until the Severan age, with the Roman Emperors.

In Numidia the cult was popular, particularly in the early third century. Many hundreds of dedications have been found. Every major centre and also villages have provided evidence for Saturn-worship at this period, either in the form of a temple or a sanctuary.[9] In some places, such as Henchir Okseiba, both have been discovered;[10] large sanctuaries existed near Tebessa,[11]

[1] A.D. 194–5. Dr. L. Carton, 'Le Sanctuaire de Baal-Saturne à Dougga', *Nouvelles Archives des Missions*, vii. 360 f.

[2] Ph. Berger, 'Les Inscriptions de Maktar', *CRAI.*, 1890, p. 35; *Bull. Arch. du Comité*, 1891, p. 536, no. 9.

[3] *CIL.* viii. 2670 (A.D. 211–17).　　　　　[4] Ibid. 9015.

[5] Probably in A.D. 210, Piganiol and Vibert, *Mélanges*, xxxii, 1912, pp. 209–10.

[6] *Bull. Arch. du Comité*, 1915, p. clxxxvi. On all these sites, Toutain, op. cit., p. 115.

[7] Toutain, op. cit., p. 84.

[8] Ibid., pp. 55 and 85.

[9] For eastern Numidia and the Theveste area, the handiest reference is the Index of Gsell's *ILA.*, under 'Saturnus', p. 429.

[10] J. Guey, *Mélanges*, liv, 1937, p. 83.

[11] *ILA.* 3018; S. Gsell, *Bull. Arch. du Comité*, 1917, pp. 329–30.

Khenchela (Lat. Mascula),[1] Timgad,[2] Ain Zoui (Lat. Vazaivi),[3] Altavia,[4] and N'gaous[5] (Lat. Nicivibus) north of the Aures, and on the High Plains at Setif[6] and near Sillègue (Novar . . .), where several priestly families existed in the mid-third century.[7] In northern Numidia, Madauros,[8] Mons,[9] Khamissa (Lat. Thurbursicum Numidarum),[10] and Naragarra[11] were centres of the cult, and many lesser sanctuaries have been found in the forested country lying between Souk Ahras (Lat. Thagaste) and Bone (Hippo Regius).[12] These were also the main Donatist areas in the fourth century, but a hundred years previously Saturn was universally venerated. If it would be an exaggeration to consider his worship as 'the farthest removed from Roman ideas and entirely refractory to their influence',[13] it seems quite clear that the worship both in its religious ideas and in their outward expression belonged more to the native than to the Roman tradition.

Yet comparatively quickly, within a generation, between A.D. 240 and 275, worship of Saturn appears to have ceased almost entirely. The Severan age sees temples being built, priestly families founded, and evidence of popular religious fervour; then there is a sudden and complete break. The next datable inscriptions are Christian. The mass of the population seems to have changed its religious allegiance with startling suddenness. Both in Proconsular Africa and in Numidia the inscriptions and coins found in the sanctuaries tell the same story. At Bou Kournein the last dated inscription is A.D. 221,[14] at Auzia

[1] *CIL.* viii. 2232–8; S. Gsell and H. Graillot, *Mélanges*, xiii, 1893, p. 495, pl. vi.

[2] R. Cagnat et A. Ballu, *Le Musée de Timgad*, p. 20; S. Gsell and H. Graillot, *Mélanges*, xiii, 1893, p. 466.

[3] *CIL.* viii. 17619.   [4] *ILA.* 2926.

[5] J. Carcopino, op. cit., pp. 592–9.

[6] *CIL.* viii. 8434 (A.D. 234); Saturn is associated on this inscription with Jupiter. Also ibid. 8449, 8460.

[7] Ibid. 20432–48. The Latin name was very probably 'Nova Licinia' or 'Novaricia'. J. Mesnage, *L'Afrique chrétienne*, p. 370, argues in favour of this being the see of Cyprian's correspondent Jubaianus.

[8] *CIL.* viii. 16918.

[9] Ibid. 8658–63.

[10] Gsell and Joly, *Khamissa*, p. 20.

[11] *CIL.* viii. 16811; *Bull. Arch. du Comité*, 1901, p. cxcv.

[12] Romano-Libyan cemeteries with dedications to Saturn discovered and described by M. Rodary in papers submitted to the 1935 and 1937 Congrès des Sociétés savantes de l'Afrique du Nord.

[13] As Carcopino, in 'Le Limes de Numidie et sa garde syrienne', *Syria*, vi, 1925, p. 53.

[14] J. Toutain, *Mélanges*, xii, 1892, p. 110. Dated inscriptions range from A.D. 139 to 221.

A.D. 241,[1] Setif, A.D. 246,[2] Sertei, A.D. 247,[3] at Hadjeb el Aioun, A.D. 265,[4] and at Sillègue, A.D. 262 or 272.[5] At el-Khenissia[6] and Ain Tounga[7] the coin series from the sanctuary ceases in the mid-third century. The Numidian shrines such as N'gaous, el-Kantara, or Theveste have produced nothing that can be dated with any certainty later than this period.

It is interesting that one finds little evidence of a falling off of religious observance in the first third of the century. There is little overlap between the two religions. Tigzirt[8] on the coast, Cast. Tingitanum, and Sillègue[9] are three examples of places where Saturn-worship seems to have been succeeded almost without a break by Christianity. Unlike the other pagan cults, that of Saturn seems to have enjoyed no brief revival in the time of Diocletian.[10]

On the High Plains something like a real conversion *en masse* of the country population seems to have taken place. The great numbers of Christian churches in the villages, in some instances five or six in a single settlement, rule out all possibility of the two religions being practised together by the inhabitants in the fourth century. We find even that native tribes would combine to build a church where previously they might have made a sacrifice in common.[11] Moreover, we have already indicated how the brunt of the Great Persecution of A.D. 303–4 seems to have

---

[1] *CIL.* viii. 20744–6.   [2] Ibid. 8460.   [3] Ibid. 8826.

[4] L. Hautecœur, 'Les Ruines de Henchir es Srira près Hadjeb el Aioun (Tunisie)', *Mélanges*, xxix, 1909, p. 378.

[5] *CIL.* viii. 20435. The date of this inscription is A.D. 262 or 272 according to whether one accepts Toutain's or Poulle's reading.

[6] L. Carton, *Le Sanctuaire de Tanit à el Khenissia*, p. 115.

[7] R. Cagnat, *Mélanges*, ix, 1889, p. 251. The same dating may be accepted for the sanctuary of Mactar, Ph. Berger, *CRAI.*, 1890, p. 42, and of Siagu, *Bull. Arch. du Comité*, 1909, p. 69.

[8] P. Gavault, *Études sur les Ruines de Tigzirt*, pp. 85–86. Also at Lemellef, *CIL.* viii. 20606, 20607.

[9] Dated inscriptions in honour of Saturn end in 262–272. Christian inscriptions start in A.D. 324 (*CIL.* viii. 10930 = 20478). Bishop Jubaianus, Cyprian's correspondent, may have been bishop in 255.

[10] The brief pagan revival under the Tetrarchy is instanced by a restoration of a temple of Mercury at Timgad (*Bull. Arch. du Comité*, 1907, p. 274)—Dougga (*CIL.* viii. 26472), Calama (*CIL.* viii. 5290), and near Kairouan (*CIL.* viii. 11217). Zuccabar (*CIL.* viii. 2148). See J. Geffcken, op. cit., pp. 28–30, also V. Schultze, *Geschichte des Untergangs des griechisch-römischen Heidentums*, Jena, 1892, vol. ii, chap. vi.

[11] At Henchir Zerdan (position, Gsell, *Atlas archéologique*, f. 27, Batna, no. 279), three tribes, the Guzabetenses, Mucrionenses, and Venusianenses, combined to build a church (S. Gsell, *Monuments antiques*, ii. 341).

fallen on the villages of southern Numidia.[1] This was the territory over which the notorious *Praeses* Florus ruled, and the
area which has produced so many *memoriae* to the martyrs.
Faced with evidence for the popularity of the cult of Saturn up
to A.D. 250, and of fanatical Christianity fifty years later among
the same classes in the same area, one must conclude that the
great change took place in Numidia in the latter half of the
third century.[2]

A further interesting fact is that it was mainly the Donatist
religion which succeeded the cult of Saturn in these parts.
Though the evidence is not by any means complete, it is noticeable that many of those settlements which have produced traces
of a sanctuary of Saturn were later Donatist centres. Numidian
towns such as Theveste,[3] Mascula (Khenchela),[4] Sillègue,[5]
Zarai,[6] Vazaivi (Ain Zoui),[7] Nicivibus (N'gaous),[8] and Timgad[9]
were all Donatist bishoprics with negligible Catholic challenge.
Smaller settlements in southern Numidia such as Youks
(Aquae Caesaris),[10] Morsott (Vasampus),[11] and Henchir el Hamascha[12] have also provided evidence both for the cult of Saturn
and Donatism. In other centres such as Madauros, Thala, Setif,
Mactar, and Dougga the Donatist bishop follows hard on the
heels of the priest of Saturn.

[1] See above, p. 7.
[2] One is inclined to date the real movement towards Christianity to the post-
Cyprianic rather than the pre-Cyprianic period. The Numidians appear to play no
major part in the persecutions under Decius and Valerian, and as late as A.D. 283
coloni on an estate near Henchir Tikoubi between Timgad and Bagai set up an
altar to the three Emperors, Carus, Carinus, and Numerian (S. Gsell and H.
Graillot, *Mélanges*, xiv, 1894, pp. 36–37, no. 94). In the time of Constantine the
inhabitants of Ain Temoulha (Rotaria?) who set up a dedication to the Emperor
are Christian (*CIL.* viii. 22272).
[3] Theveste: Saturn-worship = *ILA.* 3018; Donatism: Optatus, ii. 18.
[4] Mascula: Saturn-worship = *CIL.* viii. 2232–8; Donatism: *Gesta Coll. Carth.*
1. 201, *CIL.* viii. 17718.
[5] Sillègue: Saturn-worship = *CIL.* viii. 20432–48; Donatism: ibid. 20482, 'Deo
Laudes Super Aquas'.
[6] Zarai: Saturn-worship = ibid. 4512; Donatism: *Gesta Coll. Carth.* 1. 201.
[7] Vazaivi: Saturn-worship = *CIL.* viii. 17619; Donatism: *Gesta Coll. Carth.* 1. 187.
[8] Nicivibus: Saturn-worship = J. Carcopino, op. cit., pp. 592–9. Donatism:
Gesta Coll. Carth. 1. 201.
[9] Timgad: Saturn-worship, Cagnat and Ballu, op. cit., p. 22; Donatism: Augustine, *In Ps.* 21. 26.
[10] Youks (Aquae Caesaris): Saturn-worship = *CIL.* viii. 2182, 17720; Donatism:
Gesta Coll. Carth. 1. 197.
[11] Morsott: Saturn-worship = *ILA.* 2872–3; Donatism: *ILA.* 2909.
[12] Henchir el Hamascha: Saturn-worship = *ILA.* 2963; Donatism: *CIL.* viii.
10689, *ILA.* 2965.

A detailed discussion of the causes of this transfer of allegiance needs a chapter of its own. Here one would point out that Africa does not stand alone in suggesting the mid- or late third century as the date for the mass conversion of the native peasantry from the worship of national deities to Christianity. In Egypt, for instance, there is no direct evidence for sacrifices at Philae after A.D. 253;[1] the last inscription relating to the worship of Sarapis at Aboukir is A.D. 247,[2] and the last inscription in hieroglyphics dates to A.D. 250.[3] The same area was the scene of the most bitter persecution a half-century later, and there is literary evidence of the conversion of 'thousands' of Egyptians to Christianity in the last years of the third century.[4] In Phrygia, the god Men occupied much the same place in the lives of the country people as Saturn in North Africa.[5] To such an extent did he appear to typify the province that local coins bearing his effigy were struck between A.D. 218 and 253 (Elagabalus–Trebonianus Gallus).[6] Like Saturn, he was an omnipotent being and a tyrant to his faithful. The slightest ritual offence was punished by sickness or death. Atonement could be performed only by a public acknowledgement of the offence, which was often inscribed on stone for future generations to heed. Yet in the third century his cult seems to have declined and disappeared. Its place was taken by Montanist and Novatianist Christianity —that is, by extreme and fanatical movements akin to African Donatism. As Schepelern[7] has indicated, the Montanists predominated in just that part of Phrygia, along the Mysian border, where previously the largest number of penitential inscriptions to Men had been found. It was also in this area that the native languages held their own against Greek. Thus in widely separated parts of the Empire the same period sees the downfall of hitherto all-powerful national cults before the same foe, an intense and fanatical form of the Christian religion. It can hardly be accidental that the Great Persecution raged with such violence in each of these three areas.

[1] J. Geffcken, *Der Ausgang des griechisch-römischen Heidentums*, p. 21.
[2] Ibid.
[3] J. Leipoldt, 'Schenute von Atripe', *TU.* xxv, 1903, p. 19.
[4] Quoted from *CAH.* xii. 675.
[5] W. Schepelern, *Der Montanismus und die phrygischen Kulte*, Mohr, Tübingen, 1929, p. 101 onwards; W. H. Ramsay, *Cities and Bishoprics*, Oxford, 1895–7, i. 148.
[6] Geffcken, op. cit., p. 25.
[7] Schepelern, op. cit., p. 104.

VII

THE EXPANSION OF CHRISTIANITY
IN NORTH AFRICA

BY the mid-third century A.D. the Christian Church was probably well on the way to gaining a predominant hold on the North African provinces. Its rise had been comparatively rapid. Despite the ease of communications which allowed the quick spread of ideas at least between the great seaport cities of the Empire, Christianity does not appear to have prospered in Africa before the second half of the second century A.D. So long as the creative power of Rome prevailed, the new religion found little response. Indeed, the origins of the Church at Carthage are as obscure as those of the great Patriarchates of Antioch and Alexandria.[1] It is uncertain, even, how Christianity first penetrated the province, whether direct from Rome, or step by step by way of the Jewish colonies in the coastal towns of Tripolitania and Tunisia. There is no mention of any Christian community whatsoever before A.D. 180, and no Bishop of Carthage is recorded prior to Agrippinus at the turn of the third century.[2] One can probably go no farther than saying that at this time Gnostic and Christian groups were present in many of the larger African towns, particularly in the Proconsular Province.[3]

The story of the African Church begins with martyrdom, and martyrdom was to be one of its major characteristics throughout. On 16 July A.D. 180, the Proconsul Vigellius Saturninus

---

[1] For discussion of the origin of the Church in Africa, see H. Lietzmann, *Die Geschichte der alten Kirche*, ii. 220, and P. Monceaux, *Histoire littéraire*, i. 3 f. I agree with Lietzmann's view that Africa probably received Christianity through Rome. See also J. Gagé, *Nouveaux aspects de l'Afrique chrétienne* (Gand, 1937), p. 185 (gives useful references).

[2] It would have been interesting had W. Bauer, in his *Ketzerei und Rechtgläubigkeit in den ältesten Kirchen* (Tübingen, Mohr, 1934), extended his researches on the Gnostic element in earliest Christianity to Africa. Were the reasons which prevented the see of Carthage from emerging from obscurity till the late second century similar to those which prevailed in the case of Alexandria and Antioch—that the 'orthodox' party had been previously a dissenting minority from the Gnostic Church?

[3] Optatus may have been Bishop of Carthage, *c.* 200. L. Duchesne, *The Early History of the Church*, i. 288.

found himself obliged to condemn to death a small group of Christians at Scilli (location unknown) for refusal to do sacrifice to the gods. From their names the victims, seven men and five women, seem to have been drawn from the purely native, non-citizen classes of the population.[1]

There followed an interval of twenty years of comparative peace, broken by sharp intermittent persecutions. But with each new batch of martyrs, numbers increased.[2] Men such as Tertullian, ardent characters and tired of the empty brilliance of the culture of their day, became converts to the new religion. On the administrative side the number of bishoprics increased rapidly. Seventy bishops met in Council under the presidency of Agrippinus of Carthage, some time after A.D. 200,[3] and at this time there would appear to have been Christian communities, not only in the cities of Latino-Punic Africa, such as Uthina,[4] Hadrumetum,[5] Thysdrus,[6] and Leptis Magna,[7] but also in parts of Mauretania, as at Setif[8] and Satafis.[9] Tertullian probably exaggerated the prosperity of the Church at the turn of the third century, when he asserted that the Christians were 'almost a majority' of the population in the towns;[10] there is, however, no doubt that the Church was now beginning seriously to gain ground.

The world, which in Tertullian's time was beginning 'to emerge from error, and to acknowledge God the Creator and Christ',[11] was taking the existence of the Church for granted

[1] *Acta Scillitanorum* (ed. Rendel Harris, *Texts and Studies*), Cambridge, 1891, i. ii. 106. The names of the martyrs were: Sparatus, Nartzalus, Cittinis, Veturius, Felix, Aquilinus, Laetantius, Ianuaria, Generosa, Vestia, Donata, Secunda. See P. Monceaux, *Histoire littéraire*, i. 63. Cf. A. Harnack, *Mission and Expansion of Christianity* (tr. Moffatt, London and New York, 1908), p. 278, n. 2. Another native martyr, Gudden, was executed in A.D. 203. M. Besnier, *L'Empire romain*, p. 52.

[2] It was to one such that Tertullian addressed the *Ad Martyres*, towards the year 197. On Tertullian's conversion, *Apologeticus*, 18.

[3] Cyprian, *Ep.* 71. 4, 73. 3 (*CSEL*. iii. 2. 774); P. Monceaux, *Histoire littéraire*, ii. 27–28. I have accepted the date suggested by Lebreton and Zeiller, *Histoire de l'Église*, ii (Paris, Bloud and Gay, 1948), p. 136.

[4] Tertullian, *De Monogamia*, 12 (*PL*. ii, col. 998).

[5] *Ad Scapulam*, 3 (*PL*. i, col. 780).   [6] Ibid. 4 (*PL*. i, col. 781).

[7] J. Mesnage, *Le Christianisme en Afrique*, p. 101.

[8] *ILCV*. 710 a and b.   [9] Ibid. 4038.

[10] *Ad Scapulam*, 2 (*PL*. i. col. 779), 'Tanta hominum multitudo, pars paene maior civitatis uniuscuiusque'. Also, *Apolog.* 2, de *Praescriptione*, 20. For full list of texts taken from Tertullian which show the expansion of Christianity in Africa during his lifetime, Harnack, op. cit. 276, n. 2.

[11] *Adversus Marcionem*, iii. 20, 'Aspice universas nationes de voragine erroris humani exinde emergentes ad deum creatorem, ad deum Christum.'

fifty years later. The long peace that lasted from the death of Septimius Severus to the accession of Decius may have witnessed in many African towns the conversion of the majority of religiously minded people to Christianity. The pagans saw their enemies gain ground continuously. Their opinion was perhaps best voiced by Caecilius, the pagan in the *Octavius* of Minucius Felix: 'Already—for ill weeds grow apace—decay of morals grows from day to day, and throughout the wide world the abominations of this impious conspiracy multiply.'[1] His friend Octavius admitted the accuracy of his statement: 'Nor need we plume ourselves upon our numbers; to ourselves we seem many; but to God we are very few.'[2] In the years which preceded the accession of Cyprian to the see of Carthage in 248, at least two Councils had been held, one of which was attended by ninety bishops.[3]

When persecution broke out in 249, it bore to a much greater degree the stamp of official action than formerly.[4] In 202-3 the crowd had been bitterly hostile to the martyrs Perpetua, Felicitas, and Saturus. They were infuriated by Saturus' threats against the Procurator Hilarianus, and demanded that the Christians should undergo additional rigours before being dispatched.[5] Under Decius and Valerian, however, there is a change of mood. Some indeed raised the cry, 'Cyprian to the lions',[6] but there was no general outcry against the Christian *areae*,[7] and officials and public alike were often prepared to do all in their power to save the Christians from the results of their folly. Cyprian himself was allowed to remain in retirement unharmed in 250-1, and could have saved himself by flight through the aid of influential friends in 258.[8] A part of the masses was

[1] Minucius Felix, *Octavius* (ed. Loeb, 1931, p. 337), 9. 1.

[2] Ibid. 33. 1, 'Nec nobis de nostra frequentia blandiamur; multi nobis videmur; sed deo admodum pauci sumus.'

[3] Cyprian, *Ep.* 1. 2 (*CSEL.* iii. 466); *Ep.* 59, 10.

[4] See N. H. Baynes, *CAH.* xii. 657-8.

[5] *Passio Perpetuae* (ed. J. A. Robinson, *Texts and Studies*, Cambridge, 1891), 18, 'ad hoc populus exasperatus, flagellis eos vexari pro ordine venatorum postulavit'. Cf. Tertullian, *Apolog.* 35 and 37. 3, 40. 2.

[6] *Vita Cypriani*, 7 (*CSEL.* iii. 3. xcvii), 'suffragiis saepe repetitis ad leonem postularetur'.

[7] As in Tertullian's time, 'areae non sint', *Ad Scapulam*, 3. Cf. *Apolog.* 37. 3.

[8] The fact that he had been given ample time in which to reconsider his opinion was emphasized by the Proconsul when condemning him: 'bonamque mentem habendam tanto tempore potuerunt revocare', *Acta Proconsularia*, 4 (*CSEL.* iii. 3. cxiii). Cf. *Passio Montani*, 12. 3.

clearly on the side of the Christians during this period. Cyprian had gone into retirement because he feared riots in Carthage if he stayed there;[1] while crowds assembled, and often hostile demonstrations against the judges took place as the martyrs were led away to execution.[2] As soon as the attention of the persecuting Emperor was diverted to other fields of activity, attacks against the Christians ceased.

The picture one gets of the social composition of the African Church in Cyprian's time is not by any means clear. There is evidence from Cyprian's writings that it had become a rich and powerful institution. It was well organized, and some of the parishes, like Felicissimus' on the Byrsa, were wealthy. It had funds enough at its disposal to pay its clergy a monthly stipend,[3] and it could organize relief in time of emergency, such as that sent to ransom prisoners taken by native insurgents during the Mauretanian revolt of A.D. 253.[4] In a period of increasing poverty in the towns, the Church was able to act as trustee for the fortunes of rich widows and as executor of their wills.[5] In his *De Lapsis*[6] Cyprian shows quite clearly not only that the Church was tolerated but that its leaders could live in prosperity. Some were obviously wealthy, and Cyprian denounces 'the very many bishops' who were 'increasing their fortunes by multiplying usuries', acting as procurators, or 'seizing estates by crafty deceits'.[7] His own clergy were able to travel freely at a time when contemporary society was becoming increasingly rigid and bound to the soil.[8] It seems that out of the ruin and disorder of this period the Church alone had the necessary organization, sense of purpose, and wealth to survive. In face of this, persecution degenerated into haphazard violence and was thus

---

[1] *Ep.* 7. 1, though the pagans rather than his own congregation were the more likely to provoke trouble.

[2] As in the case of Cyprian's, and also Montanus', execution, 'propter hoc tumultus fratrum exortus est', *Acta Proconsularia*, 5 (*CSEL*. iii. 3. cxiii). Cf. R. Reitzenstein, 'Die Nachrichten über den Tod Cyprians', *Sitzungsberichte der Heidelberger Akademie der Wissenschaften, Phil.-hist. Klasse*, 1913, 28.

[3] *Ep.* 34. 4 (*CSEL*. iii. 2. 571), 'divisione mensurna'.

[4] *Ep.* 62. See Harnack, op. cit. i. 185.

[5] *Ep.* 52. 1 (*CSEL*. iii. 2. 617).

[6] *De Lapsis*, 6 (*CSEL*. iii. 1. 241), 'habere argentum largiter velle'.

[7] *Ep.* 11. 1 (*CSEL*. iii. 2. 496), *De Lapsis*, 6.

[8] *Ep.* 75. 1. Cyprian was able to keep in touch with his allies in Asia Minor during the rebaptism controversy through the journeys of his deacon Rogatian. Also, Cyprian's enemies such as Novatus made frequent journeys between Rome and Carthage.

bound to fail. The Church was unaffected by the incessant civil wars, and the exhaustion of both citizens and soldiery alike was indirectly its gain.

But even so, at this period the main strength of the Christian Church continued to be from the lower classes and from women, that is, the most particularist and conservatively inclined portion of the population. There is the formal testimony to this effect from Minucius Felix,[1] there is the fact of Cyprian's rapid promotion to the rank of Bishop of Carthage,[2] and the illiteracy of some of his clergy and bishops.[3] This evidence is supported by that of the early Christian cemeteries. At Timgad and Sousse (Hadrumetum)[4] the great majority of the sepulchres are anonymous, unadorned even by a stone at the gravehead, like the poorest of the tombs in the contemporary pagan cemetery. The body was simply laid in liquid plaster and a small penthouse roof of tiles placed over it. At Timgad the uniformity of the cemetery, the 15,000 graves laid out row upon row, leaves the impression of a religious community whose members desired to remain brethren in death as they had been in life. It is clear from inscriptions and other sources that the magistracy of towns such as Timgad remained pagan.[5]

That numbers were increasing in this period there seems to be little doubt. Cyprian describes his own congregation in A.D. 249 as *copiosus*—abundant—and it must have been the case for so many to have lapsed.[6] Confessors were stated after the Persecution of 250–1 to have given out *libelli pacis* 'collectively' (*gregatim*).[7] Apostasies there were, but the Church was able to absorb them and move on again in a general advance.

---

[1] Caecilius in Minucius Felix, *Octavius*, 8. 4 (ed. Loeb, p. 335): 'Fellows who gather together illiterates from the dregs of the populace and credulous women....' Octavius agrees with his contention (ibid. 36. 3, Loeb, p. 425): 'That most of us are reputed poor is no disgrace.'

[2] He was 'adhuc neophytus', when called upon to be bishop. Pontius, *Vita Cypriani*, 5 (*CSEL*. iii. 3, p. xcv).

[3] *Ep.* 27. 1 (*CSEL*. iii. 2. 541), 'Aurelius litteras non nosset.' Yet Cyprian made him a lector: possibly he had ecstatic gifts of prophecy, and his duties as 'reader' did not entail any actual reading but of letting the Holy Spirit speak through him.

[4] At Sousse, the catacombs contain about 10,500 graves and date mainly to the third century A.D. H. Leclercq, article on 'Hadrumetum', *Dictionnaire d'archéologie chrétienne*, VI. ii, cols. 1981–2010.

[5] V. Schultze, *Geschichte des Untergangs*, ii. 148–9.

[6] Cyprian, *Ad Demetrianum*, 17 (*CSEL*. iii. 1. 363), 'copiosus noster populus ulciscitur'. See P. Monceaux, *Histoire littéraire*, ii. 7–10, for the advance of Christianity in Africa under Cyprian.

[7] Cyprian, *Ep.* 27. 1 (*CSEL*. iii. 2. 541).

They had little effect on the progress of the faith and were for the most part temporary.[1] As soon as the danger passed, the lapsed clamoured for readmission into the Church, and every respite brought new converts.[2] In the terrible plague which swept the African cities under Gallus and Valerian (A.D. 252–3) the valiant conduct of the Christian clergy, steadfast at their posts, tending believer and unbeliever alike, must have confirmed many in their resolve to adopt the new religion as their own.[3]

The list of eighty-seven bishops who took part in the great Council at Carthage, 1 September 256, shows that already the familiar features of the distribution of African bishoprics in the fourth century were emerging. The area round Carthage itself is not well represented, possibly because some of the sees, as Suturnuca and Didda, were in the hands of enemies of Cyprian.[4] Christianity, however, was making its way into those areas which later became its strongholds, the Latino-Punic cities of the coast and the Numidian and Mauretanian High Plains. On the coast, Tipasa,[5] Rusiccade, Hippo Regius, Hippo Diarrhytus, Hadrumetum, Girba, Sabratha, and Leptis Magna all had Christian communities. On the High Plains it may be too early to speak of any large conversion of the country populations, but the future Donatist centres north of the Aures, such as Theveste, Bagai, Mascula, Cedias, and Thamugadi, all sent representatives to the Council.[6] There were sees in the countryside also, as at Octava, a name associated with the Circumcellions a century later.[7]

There is little that would indicate any split between Numidian and Carthaginian Christianity in this period. Indeed, in 257, Cyprian was to find his warmest friends and supporters among

---

[1] It is interesting that these apparently sweeping but temporary apostasies occurred equally in the period of the conversion of North Africa from Christianity to Islam.

[2] Cyprian, *Ep.* 66. 5 (*CSEL*. iii. 2. 730), 'novus credentium populus'.

[3] *Vita Cypriani*, 9. Cf. Cyprian, *De Mortalitate*, 16.

[4] I have accepted Harnack's suggestion, op. cit. ii. 284. Suturnuca had been in the hands of the thoroughgoing apostate Repostus, *Ep.* 59. 10, and at Didda also there had been insubordination against Cyprian, *Ep.* 34. 1.

[5] The Bishop of Tipasa was not present at the Council, but a Christian community existed in A.D. 238 (*ILCV.* 3319) and was probably presided over by a bishop. Cf. L. Leschi, *L'Algérie catholique*, viii, Dec. 1936, on Bishop Renatus, and in *Bull. Arch. du Comité*, 1940, pp. 422 ff.

[6] See list of bishops at the Council given in Harnack, op. cit. ii. 287–93.

[7] Optatus, iii. 4. For Christian communities in the *castella* of Mauretania Sitifensis, such as Bamaccorra, see *Sententiae Episcoporum*, 33; at Thamalla, *ILCV.* 4156.

the persecuted Numidian bishops.[1] There is, however, evidence that suggests that the Numidians were beginning to act together. In A.D. 255, for instance, eighteen Numidian bishops sent a joint letter to Cyprian asking for his opinion on the question of the rebaptizing of reconciled heretics.[2] Cyprian called a Council before replying. In the next year the Numidians came to Carthage with their point of view well defined, and their leaders, Nemessianus of Thubunae (Tobna), Lucius of Castra Galbae, and Novatus of Thamugadi, all made comparatively long statements at the beginning of proceedings.[3]

The death of Cyprian was followed by no schism between Carthage and Numidia, and the cessation of persecution in Africa under Gallienus and his successors assured to the Church over forty years of unimpeded growth. The period, however, that saw the final triumph of the Church remains obscure. Pagans may have been becoming *iam rari*,[4] but, on the other hand, the lack of evidence of Councils, and hence of episcopal lists, prevents any attempt at the accurate tracing of the progress of Christianity. We have already indicated that this was probably the period which saw the change of allegiance from Saturn to Christ on the High Plains. It is clear also that Christianity was now becoming the religion of educated men,[5] of senators as Severian at Caesarea,[6] of men of letters, philosophers, and doctors like Victor the Grammarian at Cirta,[7] and of Arnobius and Lactantius. It may not be unwise to follow the judgement of Harnack, that the number of sees in North Africa doubled during the years which separated the death of Cyprian from the Great Persecution.[8] Certain it is that in the first half of the fourth century Donatus was able to gather 270 bishops for a Council at Carthage.[9] At the end of the third century there could hardly have been less than 250.

[1] *Ep.* 76–79. [2] *Ep.* 70.
[3] *Sententiae Episcoporum* 4, 5, and 7 (*CSEL.* iii. 1. 438–41).
[4] Arnobius, i. 24.
[5] Id. ii. 5, 'Tam magnis ingeniis praediti oratores, grammatici, rhetores, consulti iuris et medici, philosophiae etiam secreta rimantes magisteria haec expetunt spretis quibus paulo ante fidebant.'
[6] *CIL.* viii. 9585.
[7] *Gesta apud Zenophilum* (*CSEL.* xxvi. 185), Victor dixit: 'Professor sum Romanarum litterarum, grammaticus latinus.'
[8] Harnack, op. cit. ii. 286. [9] Augustine, *Ep.* 93. 43.

VIII

FACTORS RELATING TO THE CONVERSION OF NORTH AFRICA TO CHRISTIANITY

IN the previous two chapters we have seen how the victory of the Christian Church in North Africa was won probably in the latter half of the third century A.D. If that was the case, then it is also true that the change in religion coincided with economic and social changes, for it was in these years that the predominant unit in society ceased to be the city state and became instead the village and the villa. It is against this background that we must try to answer the question 'Why?' Why was it that the temples of the gods became deserted, the cult of Saturn abandoned, and the place of both taken by Christianity?

No clear-cut answer can be given. Among the minority of wealthy and educated men who became Christians during the third century A.D. two factors seem to have dominated. In an age of the deepest pessimism and uncertainty they accepted the Christian promise of immortality for the believer, and they admitted the moral superiority of the Christian teaching over the paganism of the day.

Terror of the unseen spiritual powers which were believed to regulate the lives of every individual was real. It is interesting that many North African funerary inscriptions of this period record not only the number of years an individual lived, but the months, days, and even hours.[1] This is probably due not to pedantry on the part of the relatives, but to a belief that the deceased had lived his predetermined span, a span minutely calculated by the conjunction of the stars under which he was born. Death came when the demons attached to these heavenly bodies decreed that it should. The power of the evil spirits could be neutralized only by access to secret knowledge granted to

---

[1] Such as the Urbanilla inscription from Lambiridi in southern Numidia, dated to the last third of the third century A.D. The psychology of Urbanilla and other adherents of Hermes in Africa is discussed by Carcopino in a brilliant chapter in *Aspects mystiques de la Rome païenne*, pp. 207–314.

mankind by a Saviour who himself was stronger than death. The key to immortality offered by Gnosticism, by the teaching of Hermes Trismegistos, and by Christianity was feverishly grasped at by individuals who felt that their lives were beset by demonic perils beyond their ken.[1]

But inscriptions like that from Lambiridi are rare in North Africa. It is clear that the message of Hermes could not have reached beyond a very limited circle. It lacked the mass appeal of Christianity, and to the majority the choice seems to have presented itself as—either paganism or the Church.

The mental process that led to conversion to Christianity is indicated clearly by Cyprian in his letter addressed to his friend Donatus, c. A.D. 245.[2] In his earlier years Cyprian, like Arnobius a generation later, had been an opponent of the new religion, and had spoken out against the Christians in public.[3] Gradually he began to heed the arguments on the other side and to compare the Christian outlook with the paganism which he was defending. He saw the society around him as barren, corrupt, and lacking in inspiration. He came into contact with the works of Tertullian and realized that his own life had been one of 'darkness, ignorance of self and estrangement'.[4] Then, to use his own words:

I seconded my own besetting vices, I despaired of improvement, I looked on my faults as natural and home-born. I even favoured them. But, as soon as the stain of my former life was wiped away by help of the birth-giving wave [of baptism], and a calm pure light from above flooded my purged breast, so soon as I drank of the spirit from Heaven and was restored to a new manhood by a second nativity, then marvellously doubts began to clear, secrets revealed themselves, the dark grew light, seeming difficulties gave way, supposed impossibilities vanished. I was able to recognize that what was born of flesh and lived under the rule of sin was of earth, earthy, while that which was animated by the Holy Spirit began to belong to God.[5]

---

[1] This fear of a spirit-beset unknown is well illustrated by the words 'σωθεῖσ[α] ἐκ μεγάλου κινδύνου'—Urbanilla's salvation from 'great danger'—that appear in the inscription quoted above.

[2] *Ad Donatum* (ed. Hartel, *CSEL.* iii. 1–16). On Cyprian during this earlier period, see Archbishop Benson's work, *Cyprian, His Life, His Times, His Work* (Macmillan, 1897), pp. 1–19.

[3] Jerome, *Commentarii in Jonam*, 3, 'adsertor idololatriae' (*PL.* xxv, col. 1145).

[4] *Ad Donatum*, 3 (Hartel, p. 5).

[5] Ibid. 4 (Hartel, p. 6). I have used the translation given in Archbishop Benson's *Cyprian, His Life, His Times, His Work*, p. 16.

Psychological experiences of this sort were not exceptional, nor confined to the wealthy. One finds the same strongly ethical outlook expressed on some of the south Numidian Christian inscriptions of the next century—peace on earth and goodwill towards men[1]—and also in the Acts of the Scillitan Martyrs. These latter had in their possession the Epistles of St. Paul, 'a righteous man', when they appeared before the magistrates.[2] Christianity was the one religion of the day that welcomed the sinner, and opened salvation to all men without distinction of birth, occupation, or race.[3]

The Christian catechumen, unlike the neophyte in a mystery sect, did not have to be in a state of ritual purity. That was reserved until preparation for baptism, which was often postponed until the believer was near to death. One of the commonest representations of Christ in the third century is as the Good Shepherd, the friend of sinners, and guide to Paradise.[4] Brotherly love,[5] a desire to live and worship as a community, a real regard for the sufferings of the poor, a pacifist outlook in an age characterized by perpetual wars,[6] these were some of the features of the nobler minds who accepted Christianity. The *Octavius* of Minucius Felix is the finest expression of their views.

Yet idealism, a spirit of self-criticism and self-examination, the feeling that the existing order was in irreparable decline, and the search for a creed which would give personal security, are the mental processes of thinking minds. The sensitive spirit might be moved by the horror of the martyrdom of Perpetua and Felicitas at Carthage in A.D. 203 or by some vile scene enacted on the stage,[7] but not the crowd that yelled encourage-

---

[1] *CIL.* viii. 4626, 10549, 10642, and 16720.

[2] *Acta Scillitanorum* (ed. J. Armitage Robinson, *Texts and Studies*, Cambridge, 1891, p. 114). Saturninus Proconsul dixit, 'Quae res in capsa vestra?' Speratus dixit, 'Libri et epistulae Pauli viri justi.'

[3] This point is made by K. Holl in 'Urchristentum und Religionsgeschichte', *Gesammelte Aufsätze zur Kirchengeschichte* (Der Osten, Halbband i, pp. 1–12).

[4] Christ as Good Shepherd is found on sarcophagi at Rusiccade (Gsell and Bertrand, *Le Musée de Philippeville*, no. 293), Tipasa, and Cap Matifou. See article, 'Pasteur', *Dict. d'Archéologie chrétienne*, vol. xiii. 2, cols. 2272–2390.

[5] Tertullian, *Apologeticus* (ed. Loeb, p. 176), 39. 'Vide, inquiunt, ut invicem se diligunt.' Also *Ad Scapulam*, 4 (aid to the poor).

[6] Cyprian, *Ad Donatum*, 13–14.

[7] Tertullian was probably influenced towards Christianity by the Martyrs. See *Apologeticus*, 50 (ed. Loeb, p. 226); T. R. Glover, *Conflict of Religions in the Early Roman Empire*, Methuen, 1909, p. 320.

ment to the beasts and demanded yet more gladiatorial shows. The thoughts of Cyprian and even Arnobius are those that lead to an 'elected silence', but they are not considerations that move great masses to abandon the national deities whom they have worshipped in dread for generations. Had Christianity in Africa been merely the religion of an earnest minority touching the same social groups as Lollardy in fourteenth-century England, then one would not have to look farther for the causes of its success. One would have placed it on the same level as its third-century rivals in Africa, Gnosticism and the cult of Hermes Trismegistos. But this was not the case. The important event in the third century was precisely the conversion of a large proportion of the mass of the inhabitants, and accompanying this the emergence of Numidia as a force in both the political and religious life of the territory.

Explanations are bound to be partial and unsatisfactory. The inarticulate strivings of the African peasants have left little mark on the literary or epigraphic sources. One can only state the facts as known and draw legitimate conclusions. Stéphane Gsell has suggested[1] that the monotheistic element in the worship of Saturn, bringing with it the submission of the individual to an all-pervading Divine Will, contributed to the readiness with which the North Africans accepted Christianity. This is suggested further, not merely by the persistence of symbols connected with the worship of Saturn in Christian churches, but by the emphasis which the African Christians laid on certain aspects of their new religion. The western European thinks of God as a loving Father who sent His only Son into the world as the Redeemer of mankind. The emphasis is on the love and mercy of God, the liberating power of Christianity, and the example of Christ's perfect life. But this was not the outlook of either Donatists or Catholics in Africa. Their religion seems to have been concentrated on the prospect of Judgement hereafter, and on the consequent necessity of propitiating the wrath of God. It was a religion of fear and dread, not of love.[2]

The problem may become simpler if one always bears in mind the temporary nature of Christianity in the history of

---

[1] S. Gsell, *Histoire ancienne*, iv. 498.

[2] So Tertullian in *De Cultu Feminarum*, ii. 2 (*CSEL*. lxx. 2. 74), 'Timor fundamentum salutis est.' While this attitude was common to Christians throughout the Mediterranean area, it seems to have taken on a more pronounced form in Africa.

North Africa—the Christian period had practically ended by A.D. 700. In every other aspect of their lives the Berbers have remained conservative and attached to ancient traditions. Furthermore, the late third century was a static and unprogressive age, and it would be surprising to find a sudden evolution in the religious beliefs of countryfolk dwelling in one of the remoter corners of the known world. It was an age, too, when magic, astrology, and animistic beliefs seem to have taken a greater hold on the minds of the literate and illiterate alike. In contrast to both official paganism and the cult of Saturn, the various forms of primitive African religion such as the worship of Draco at Tipasa,[1] or of Bacax in the grotto of the Djebel Thaya,[2] or the *Dei Mauri*[3] continued to be popular until the end of the century. How strong a hold belief in various forms of magic had even on the educated may be gleaned from Arnobius.[4] Perhaps Lucilla's bone would fall into the same category.[5] We are likely to be on firmer ground if we examine the acceptance of Christianity by large numbers of North Africans from the point of view of a transformed popular religion, rather than that of conversion to a new religion. The Christian message may have sounded to many as the restatement of age-old beliefs and hopes that were tending to become lost in the syncretist paganism of the third century, allied as this was to an administrative system that was becoming increasingly hateful and oppressive.[6]

The first task, then, is to investigate possible links between the cult of Saturn and African Christianity. One does not have to

---

[1] Despite the fact that there had been a Christian community in the town since about A.D. 230, the *Passio Salsae* states that at the time of the Great Persecution the mass of the inhabitants were worshippers of the native sea-god, Draco, and Christianity was still a *rara fides*. Gsell, *Mélanges*, xiv, 1894, p. 310. Draco appears also on an inscription from Caesarea: *CIL*. viii. 9326.

[2] The annual pilgrimage made by the magistrates of Thibilis to the grotto of Bacax went on down to A.D. 283 (*CIL*. viii. 5504-19, 18828-57; J. and P. Alquier, *Le Chettaba*, Constantine, 1928, pp. 141-88).

[3] *CIL*. viii. 21665 (Albulae, A.D. 292-305); Cyprian, *Quod Idola Dii non sint*, 20 (ed. Hartel, *CSEL*. iii. 1. 20, ll. 11-12).

[4] Arnobius, *Adversus Nationes*, i. 39 (*CSEL*. iv. 26), worship of elephant-bones, &c.

[5] Optatus, i. 16.

[6] The idea that Christianity was the original human religion, thus giving the believer the real name of God, seems to underlie much of Tertullian's Apology, with its attempts to prove that Moses was prior to Homer (*Apologeticus*, 19. 4). See W. R. Halliday, *The Pagan Background of Early Christianity*, Liverpool, 1925, p. 248. That they represented the *tradition* of African Christianity was, of course, one of the main arguments used by the Donatists.

look far in the works of the African Fathers for descriptions of the hereafter which would justify an attitude of mind hardly different from that produced by the worship of Saturn. The fate of the pagans, the philosophers, heretics, and persecutors was depicted in terrible terms—the more so if we remember that the Africans believed both as pagans and as Christians in literal bodily resurrection.[1] The passages in Tertullian's *Apologeticus* 18 and *De Spectaculis* 30 are echoed in Cyprian's *Ad Demetrianum*[2] and particularly in Lactantius' *De Mortibus Persecutorum*. Even Augustine's concept of the love of God is sometimes conditioned by the retributive element, that if the individual did not himself love God he would be dealt with ruthlessly in the next world.[3] He himself certainly feared that he would have to account for every sin of omission and commission at the Judgement.[4] The God of the African Church writers was conceived as a Being capable of the worst human passions, of implacable jealousy, rage, and desire for vengeance. Milder views were branded as heresy.[5]

These were not simply the personal ideas of controversialists anxious to press their opinions to a logical conclusion. They formed part of the basis of the doctrinal position of the African Church as a whole. The necessity for ritual fasts (the xerophagies), for harsh penances (the exomologeses), and for martyrdom itself would have been less pronounced but for the strong expiatory trend in African theology. As in many primitive religious systems, man's relations with the Creator were believed to be regulated by a sort of contract. The correct ritual would produce the desired benefit. Thus prayer became the employment of the proper formula to attract the attention of God. 'By our prayers we do God violence, as it were', claimed Tertullian.[6]

[1] In both pagan and Christian cemeteries the body was placed in a bed of wet plaster which preserved every detail of its outline. Tertullian, *Apologeticus*, 18, speaks of 'every man being raised, refashioned and reviewed' for Judgement at the Last Day (ed. Loeb, p. 91). Also *Apologeticus*, 23 (Loeb, p. 128).

[2] So Cyprian, *Ad Demetrianum*, 9 (ed. Hartel, *CSEL*. iii. 1, pp. 356–7). 'Manet postmodum carcer aeternus et jugis flamma et poena perpetua, nec audietur illic rogantium gemitus quia nec hic Dei indignantis terror auditus est.'

[3] Augustine, *Confessions*, i. 5, 'Amari se jubet Deus ab homine, et nisi faciat, minatur ingentes miserias.'

[4] Hence one of his reasons for persecuting the Donatists: *Ep.* 43. 2.

[5] Tertullian, *Adversus Marcionem*, i. 27, and *Adversus Praxean*, 7 and 10.

[6] *Apologeticus*, 39, 'Coimus in coetum et congregationem ut ad deum quasi manu facta precationibus ambiamus orantes. Haec vis Deo grata est.' This formula is not, of course, confined to Tertullian.

Similarly, a confessor who had borne witness to his faith before a pagan magistrate could claim a vision of Paradise as a right, without any intermediary action by the Church.[1] On the other hand, faults demanded the most stringent acts of propitiation. Post-baptismal sin could not be pardoned by the Church. The individual must settle his account with the Creator alone. As Tertullian expressed it, acts of penance were necessary, 'not because God is ignorant of the sins, but inasmuch as by confession satisfaction is settled, of confession repentance is born, by repentance God is appeased'.[2] The propitiatory sacrifice was, of course, one of the main features of the cult of Saturn.

The connexion between the old national cult and Christianity may perhaps also be sought in the attitude of the more rigorous Christians towards martyrdom. This was regarded both as the crowning achievement in the Christian's life and a personal sacrifice to God, which automatically released the sinner from all guilt.[3] The background may have been the reminiscence of human sacrifice, and in some passages of Tertullian this seems to have remained strong. 'Does God desire man's blood?' he asks, and his reply is in the affirmative. 'Yes, if man desires the Kingdom of God, if he desires a certain salvation, if he desires a second regeneration' (i.e. a second chance after baptism).[4] In another passage he exclaims, 'Happy is the man whom God has devoured,'[5] and so as to indicate that he meant this in a literal sense he appeals for justification to the pagan rites of human sacrifice practised in Gaul, Scythia, and also in Africa. A century later we hear of Donatist fanatics (Circumcellions) rushing in on pagan ceremonies not in order to break these up, but so as to be sacrificed to the gods.[6] One must bear in mind that the N'gaous inscriptions indicating the expiatory and redemptive

---

[1] *Passio Perpetuae*, 4, 'iam in magna dignatione es, ut postules visionem et ostendatur tibi an passio sit an commeatus'. See S. Gsell, *Histoire ancienne*, iv. 228, for the belief, in Punic religion, that man could coerce God through the exact performance of certain rites.

[2] *De Paenitentia*, 9 (tr. Roberts and Donaldson, Ante-Nicene Christian Library, Edinburgh, *Tertullian*, i, 1869, p. 273).

[3] Tertullian, *Scorpiace*, 6 (*CSEL*. xx. 158); *Apologeticus*, 50 (Loeb, p. 226).

[4] Tertullian, *Scorpiace*, 6 (*CSEL*. xx. 158), 'Sanguinem hominis Deus concupiscit? Et tamen ausim dicere, si et homo regnum Dei, si et homo certam salutem, si et homo secundam regenerationem.'

[5] Tertullian, *Scorpiace*, 7 (*CSEL*. xx. 160), 'et non beatum amplius reputasset quem Deus comedisset'.

[6] Augustine, *Ep*. 185. 3. 12. Augustine himself remarks that these acts were reminiscent of former (pagan) practices.

character of the ceremony of Mochomor are probably early third century, and therefore contemporary with Tertullian.[1] It is not perhaps surprising that in Augustine's time there were many alleged Christians who believed that the God that they were worshipping was in fact Saturn.[2]

If some of the characteristic features of African Christian doctrine may be traced back to the cult of Saturn, one would expect also to find evidence for religious continuity through liturgical practices and symbols. This seems to have been particularly the case in Numidia, where we have already indicated that fanatical devotion to Saturn was succeeded within a very short space of time by zeal for the Church of the martyrs. The archaeologist's interest is, for instance, aroused by the meticulous care with which the furnishings and reliquaries found in Numidian chapels have been covered with layers of white plaster.[3] Whitewashed altars seem to have been one of the characteristics of the Donatist Church,[4] and some reliquaries have been treated several times as though in accordance with a special ritual. An inscription from the sanctuary of Saturn at Hadjeb-el-Aioun (Byzacenia) indicates that the whitening of the cult objects formed part of the ceremonial.[5] There seems also to have been an element of continuity in Saturnian and Christian burial rites. The characteristic cupola-tomb is found in Numidia in both pagan and Christian cemeteries.[6] Similarly, the presence in Numidian reliquaries of earth and the bones of birds might also be due to a continuation of the same ritual in the worship of Saturn. Doves as well as lambs were sacrificed to him, and their bones buried in jars.[7] Religious formulas such as *Bonis bene* also appear in both Donatist and pagan contexts

[1] J. Carcopino, *Revue de l'histoire des religions*, lvi, 1932, p. 593. In a church at Lambaesis the bones of several young children were found sealed in a sarcophagus which had been buried in a place of honour under the altar. M. Christofle, *Rapport*, 1936, p. 366.

[2] Augustine, *De Consensu Evangelistarum*, i. 21. 29–30 (*PL*. xxxiv, cols. 1055–8). Salvian, *De Gubernatione Dei* (ed. Sanford), viii. 2, provides strong evidence for the worship of Caelestis by the Christian populace of Carthage just prior to the fall of the city to the Vandals in A.D. 439.

[3] See A. Berthier, *Les Vestiges du Christianisme*, pp. 194–5.

[4] Optatus, iii. 4 and 10 (*CSEL*. xxvi. 82 and 95), 'Dealbatae arae aut mensae.'

[5] 'Dealbavit petra(m) Saturni', *Bull. Arch. du Comité*, 1906, p. ccxxv, no. 16.

[6] H-I. Marrou, *Mélanges*, l, 1933, pp. 77–78.

[7] Ibid. Bird-bones were found in reliquaries at Meharza and Mechta Azrou. See Berthier, op. cit., pp. 198 and 223.

in Numidia,[1] and in some churches such as at Tigzirt, M'Chira, and Henchir Zora near Theveste, the curious crescent-shaped cake which was used in sacrifices to Saturn has been engraved on the chancel arch or altar.[2] Symbols such as the rosette, palm, dove, lion, and crown are common to both religions.[3] The title of 'Senex', reserved for the god himself, may perhaps have descended to the representative of God on earth, the Christian bishop.[4]

Apart from direct connexion with the cult of Saturn, one finds evidence of still more primitive beliefs having become embodied in African Christianity. If one may accept Tertullian, the life of the Christian in the third century was hedged about by a minute series of rules. Everyday acts had to be preceded by the sign of the cross;[5] evil spirits were believed to lodge in all sorts of harmless-looking places, whence they needed to be expelled. The rules for the Christian exorcist compare with the taboos of primitive tribes. Tertullian's emphasis on the exorcist's power suggests a considerable element of magic even in his own religious outlook.[6] He does not stand alone. If direct continuity with the worship of Saturn seems more in evidence in Donatism, subjection to magic and the occult was common to both Christian communities. It is interesting to see how magical formulas and symbols designed to ward off evil spirits, and in particular the Evil Eye, pass straight from pagan to Christian usage. For instance, the jingle, 'Invide, vive, vide ut possis plurima videre', is found associated with phallic symbols

---

[1] 'Bonis Bene', On dedications to Saturn, ILA. 2927 (Sidi Yahia near Theveste), 2977 (Ksar el Boum, Theveste), and 1669 (associated with fish symbol, at Thubursicum Numidarum). For Christian use, ILA. 3581 (Henchir Gosset, with 'Deo Laudes') and CIL. viii. 10932 (Sillègue). For Donatist associations, P. Monceaux, Revue de Philologie, 1909, pp. 116–32. Other references are given supra, p. 54, n. 5.

[2] Illustrated by Berthier, op. cit., pl. xxvii. For its place in the worship of Saturn, Ph. Berger and R. Cagnat, Bull. Arch. du Comité, 1889, p. 243 (Sanctuary at Ain Tounga). See also Comm. Guenin, Nouv. Archives des Missions, xvii, 1909, p. 194 (Henchir Zora).

[3] Berthier, op. cit., p. 34. The Berthaux inscription, on which numerous 'Christian' symbols are shown on a dedication to Caelestis, is now (1943) in the Constantine Museum.

[4] The title does not seem to have been reserved exclusively for provincial primates who were elected according to seniority as bishops. Innocentius, a bishop in Mauretania Caesariensis, is referred to as 'Senex' in a late-fourth-century Council, Codex Canonum, 97 (Bruns, Concilia, p. 185). So was Silvanus of Cirta.

[5] Tertullian, De Corona, 3. Cf. De Idololatria, 11 (Christians warding off evil spirits with their breath).

[6] Apologeticus, 23.

at Thala[1] and Henchir el Hammam,[2] in a sixth-century house at Carthage,[3] and in Christian mosaics in churches at Thubursicum Numidiarum[4] and Ain Regada in Numidia.[5] It was evidently believed to be a potent talisman against the Evil Eye, and the Evil Eye remained whether the African was pagan or Christian.[6] The same is also true of the fish, peacock, and hare, all of which appear among the stock-in-trade of both magician and Christian artist.[7] Perhaps it was no accident that Carthage and Sousse (Lat. Hadrumetum), two of the towns where Christianity made its earliest appearance, should also have produced more evidence for magical practices than any other centres.[8] In the popular view Christianity was often regarded as powerful magic, and Christ Himself as a pre-eminent wonder-worker.[9] As one member of Augustine's congregation admitted, 'To be sure, I visit the idols. I consult magicians and sooth-

---

[1] *CIL*. viii. 11683. [2] *ILA*. 864. See also ibid. 113.

[3] Guenin, *Nouvelles Archives des Missions*, xv, 1907, pp. 442–3. Also, A. Merlin, *CRAI.*, 1907, p. 801.

[4] *ILA*. 1971 (Byzantine date). [5] *ILA*. 3709.

[6] The reader is referred to two interesting articles on the subject of prophylactic magic in Christian and pagan environments: (1) L. Poinssot, 'Mosaïques d'el Haouria', *Premier Congrès*, 1935, pp. 183–206; (2) A. Merlin and L. Poinssot, 'Deux mosaïques de Tunisie', *Monuments Piot*, xxxiv, 1934, pp. 129–76.

[7] Apuleius, *Apologia*, 30. For this subject see A. Abt, *Die Apologie des Apuleius*, Giessen, 1908, pp. 135 ff., and J. Guey, 'Le Poisson sur une table chrétienne', *Revue Africaine*, lxxix, 1937.

[8] A. Audollent, *Defixionum Tabellae* (Paris, 1904), pp. 287 and 360, dealing with the curses and imprecations addressed to demons, found in the amphitheatres of Sousse and Carthage. *CIL*. viii. 12504–9. Also articles on 'Adjuration', by H. Leclercq, in *Dictionnaire d'Archéologie chrétienne*, i. i, col. 527, and 'Magie', ibid. x. i, cols. 1067–114.

[9] Arnobius, i. 44 (*CSEL*. iv. 29). The view of Christ which seems to have been held by the masses was that He was mortal ('hominum aliquem'), Tertullian, *Apologeticus*, 21. 3, or 'unus e nobis', Arnobius, 1. 45, and God's Representative from the beginning of time ('ab initio vicarius Patris', Tertullian, *Adv. Marcionem*, iii. 6). Inscriptions, using the phrase 'Dei atque Christi' (Henchir bou Sboa, *CIL*. viii. 2079), suggest a secondary position in regard to God the Father. This, however, did not entail Christ being of a different Nature from God; Christ was 'steeped in the Holy Spirit' (Tertullian, *Apologeticus*, 18. 13) and the Holy Spirit could not be other than God. On the other hand, a Prophet (such as Mahomet) could equally be steeped in the Spirit.

Inferior status combined with sameness of nature is further suggested by representations of Christ which occur in the *Acta Martyrum*, as a young man with radiant countenance carrying a baton. Sol, who always figures with Saturn on inscriptions, is also shown on mosaics, as that from Moghrane, as a youth holding a whip. It is interesting that the sun symbol occurs frequently in third-century Christian environments in Africa, for instance in the Sousse catacombs. In the popular imagination the relation Saturn–Sol may have been converted into God–Christ, and the same symbolism retained.

sayers, but I do not forsake the Church of God. I am a
Catholic.'[1]

The acceptance of Christianity, therefore, did not mean for
the majority any real break with the basic concepts of African
paganism. It was not conversion from heathendom to a higher
form of religion. Christianity was something of a transformed
popular religion, and one must look for other reasons why the
cult of Saturn-Caelestis should have forfeited popular favour.
We have pointed out that one of the main features of the old
religion was its independence of classical influences, and in this
it represented an underlying Berber antipathy towards Rome.
At the turn of the third century, however, this independence
was breaking down. The cult was becoming outwardly more
romanized. Instead of an open-air sanctuary, temples were
being built to Saturn. The god was being represented with the
round, moulded features of a classical deity, an imitation of the
Italian Saturnus.[2] One can, in fact, trace from large groups of
dedications, such as those found at Hippo and Henchir Okseiba,
the gradual transformation of the deity represented from a symbol to a fully romanized figure.[3]

His worship, too, was being associated not merely with that
of the other deities in the pantheon, but with the Emperors.
This was perhaps not surprising when the Emperor was an
African, like Septimius Severus, but the association continued
after Severus' death with his non-African successors.[4] The dedicants began to be shown as citizens in Roman dress, and the
inscriptions to Saturn in the third century are remarkable for
the high standard of execution, as though they had been set up
through some official authority. Those from N'gaous, for instance, are carved in a script which would have done credit to
an honorific dedication in a large city. At N'gaous, too, though
the ceremony to be performed is purely African, the opening
formula 'Quod bonum et faustum feliciter sit factum' is Roman
and, as Carcopino points out, a reminiscence of Cicero, *De Divi-*

---

[1] Augustine, *Enarratio in Ps.* 88, *Sermo* ii. 4 (*PL*: xxxvii, col. 1140), 'Ad idola
quidem vado, arreptitios et sortilegos consulo, sed tamen Dei ecclesiam non
relinquo; Catholicus sum.'

[2] As at el-Kantara. See H-I. Marrou, *Mélanges*, l, 1933, p. 76.

[3] J. Guey, *Mélanges*, liv, 1937, pp. 85 ff. (Henchir Okseiba). See le Capitaine
Maitrot, 'Le Musée d'Hippone', *Bulletin de l'Académie d'Hippone*, xxxiii, 1913–14,
pp. 158 ff. (Hippo), for further examples.

[4] *CIL*. viii. 2670 (Lambaesis, Caracalla, A.D. 211–17).

natione, i. 45. 102.[1] At the same time the god himself began to be assimilated into the Roman pantheon, and merged among a crowd of lesser deities. His priests no longer served at his altar alone, but, as one inscription shows, at those of the *Dei Mauri*, Silvanus, Mercury, Fortuna, and Victoria.[2] By the end of the century this syncretist tendency had gone so far that Arnobius could claim that Saturn could be equated with almost every deity in Heaven[3] —yet Arnobius received his command to become Christian in the usual manner of the god's commands, in a dream.[4]

One notes that these tendencies towards romanization take place in the last period of the cult of Saturn, and seem to increase as its extinction approaches. Datable and well-carved inscriptions in honour of the god are rare before the third century, but fairly numerous during that century. To judge from the defacement of busts of Saturn, the Berbers had no respect for an 'idol' carved in the form of a human figure.[5] Anepigraphic steles, however, or representations of Saturn as a symbol, or even as a figure in flat relief, are seldom found deliberately broken. The wearing of the toga by many of the dedicants in the latest period of the cult may afford another clue to its unpopularity. It is just at this moment that Christianity became identified by converts like Tertullian with a Punic cultural revival, manifested by the revival of the pallium or burnous as opposed to the toga.[6] As Apuleius shows,[7] there were many people who appear to have disliked the Latin language and institutions profoundly, and preferred their Carthaginian heritage. When the cult of Saturn itself became romanized, Christianity would make an additional appeal to

[1] Carcopino, op. cit., p. 593.

[2] *CIL*. viii. 8246 (Idicra = Aziz ben Tellis, near Constantine); ibid. 17619 (Vazaivi = Ain Zoui, near Khenchela); ibid. 9195 (Ksar Djuab).

[3] Arnobius, iii. 6 (*CSEL*. iv. 115), 'Saturnus inquit et Janus est, Minerva, Juno, Apollo, Venus, Triptolemus, Hercules, et alii ceteri.'

[4] Jerome, *Chron*. ad an. Abraham 2343(=327), 'ad credulitatem somniis compelleretur', *CAH*. xii. 607. Cf. *CIL*. viii. 9714 (Castellum Tingitanum), 8429 (Ain Turk), and 9703 (Quiza), for acts performed as the result of dreams.

[5] For defacement of statues of Saturn, el-Kantara, see H-I. Marrou, *Mélanges*, I, 1933, pp. 74–75. The N'gaous steles were also defaced, and the writer saw a number which had been treated similarly in the Tebessa area. For the revival of Berber artistic motifs in the third to fourth century, see article by the writer, *Antiquity*, 1942, pp. 342–52.

[6] Tertullian, *De Pallio*, 2, 'Sit nunc aliunde res ne Poenicum inter Romanos aut erubescat aut doleat'. Cf. M. Besnier, *L'Empire Romain*, p. 52.

[7] Apuleius, *Apologia* (ed. Helm), 98, 'Loquitur numquam nisi Punice et si quid adhuc a matre graecissat; enim latine loqui nec vult neque potest.'

these individuals. Perhaps official favour was as ruinous to the African national religion in the third century as was official favour shown by Constantine to the Catholics in A.D. 312. The Berber, like his Coptic contemporary, was always a dissenter.[1]

One of the most striking features of African Christianity in the third century was its uncompromising hostility to the institutions of the Roman Empire.[2] That is not to say that the Christians were disloyal in a political sense to the Empire itself. Tertullian, for instance, believed that it would last as long as human history, and that its existence afforded Christians an essential respite before the end of the world.[3] But it was otherwise with the Romans themselves and with various aspects of classical culture. The sharpest of contrasts was drawn between the Church and the pagan world. The concept of the Two Cities was alive in Africa long before it was systematized by Tyconius and Augustine. One detects a note of defiant hostility in Tertullian's claim, 'We turn our backs on the institutions of our ancestors' (Ad Nationes, ii. 1).[4] The idea of a Christian Caesar would have aroused his scorn. Even so urbane and courteous a debater as Octavius had hard words to say about pagan Rome. 'All that the Romans hold, occupy, and possess is the spoil of outrage; their temples are all of loot, drawn from the ruin of cities, the plunder of gods, and the slaughter of priests.'[5] In this instance, the attack may perhaps be discounted as formal polemic designed to discredit the argument that Rome had grown strong through her loyalty to the worship of the pagan gods. It is, however, hard not to believe that deeper feelings inspired the denunciations of Cyprian and Tertullian. To the latter, 'nothing could be more foreign to the Christian than the

---

[1] It is interesting to note that the Berber villages do not contain bath-buildings and theatres even of a primitive type such as those found in Romano-British country towns. As early as Severus' reign troops had to repair the baths of Seleucus at Youks (*CIL.* viii. 17727), while those at Mechta Azrou fell into decay in the third century. It seems that the Berbers, like another primitive people who adopted a dissenting form of Christianity, the Phrygians, never took kindly to Roman ways of life. (On the Phrygians, Socrates, *Hist. Ecc.* iv. 27.)

[2] On this theme, C. N. Cochrane, *Christianity and Classical Culture*, O.U.P., 1940, chap. vi.

[3] Tertullian, *Apologeticus*, 32 (Loeb, p. 154).

[4] Tertullian, *Ad Nationes*, ii. 1 (*CSEL.* xx. 94), 'Adversus haec igitur nobis negotium est, adversus institutiones maiorum, auctoritates receptorum, leges dominantium, adversus vetustatem, consuetudinem, necessitatem.'

[5] Minucius Felix, *Octavius*, 25. 5 (Loeb, p. 389).

[City] State'.[1] Acceptance of the Christian faith, in his view, entailed abstaining not merely from sacrifices and from watching gladiatorial combats, but from everything in any way connected with 'idolatry'.[2] In practice, this meant that the Christian should not accept municipal office, should not engage in a large number of trades more or less remotely associated with paganism, should renounce reading pagan literature, and should abjure all interest in the pagan philosophers. He should in fact cut himself off from the society of his fellows lest he share in their future damnation.

Forty years later, in Cyprian's time, these strong views had not undergone substantial change. To Cyprian's biographer Pontius, the penalty of exile, so dreaded by the pagan, was to be regarded by the Christian as a reward.[3] To Cyprian himself, as to Bishop Marculus and his fellow Donatists, acceptance of Christ meant the complete rejection of pagan civilization.[4] The Bible, like the Koran to the Berber today, was the source of all knowledge. All else was 'false learning'. Scriptural quotations play a tyrannical role in Cyprian's writings, but never once is a pagan author cited. The same hostile attitude was maintained by the Donatists.

The attitude of defiance and rebellion was developed to an extreme degree in Africa.[5] The powers of evil seemed to be personified in the Roman officials and magistrates.[6] Yet the Christians did not take up arms against their enemies. Martyrdom was their means to victory, in itself an act of vengeance, for martyrdom gave them hope of revenge hereafter, as the

[1] Tertullian, *Apologeticus*, 38 (Loeb, p. 172), 'At enim nobis ab omni gloriae et dignitatis ardore frigentibus nulla est necessitas coetus, nec ulla magis res aliena quam publica.'

[2] *De Idololatria*, 6–9. See T. R. Glover, *The Conflict of Religions in the Early Roman Empire*, pp. 329–30.

[3] Pontius, *Vita Cypriani*, 2, 'illis [the pagans] extra civitatem vivere gravis poena est; Christiano totus hic mundus una domus est'.

[4] Cf. *Passio Marculi*, i (*PL*. viii. 760), 'mox ubi primum beatae fidei rudimenta suscepit, statim mundanas litteras respuens, forense exercitium et falsam saecularis scientiae dignitatem suspensa ad caelum mente calcavit'.

[5] H. Leclercq, *L'Afrique chrétienne* (Paris, 1904), i. 301.

[6] *Acta Saturnini*, 6, 'Quid agis hoc in loco, diabole?'—Dativus to prosecuting counsel Pompeianus. Cf. *Passio Maximae, Secundae et Donatillae*, and Cyprian, *Ep*. 22, for Celerinus' attitude towards the Emperor Decius, 'ipsum anguem majorem, metatorem antichristi'. One must always remember that the African Christians believed that the 'idols' worshipped by the pagans were real malevolent demons (Tertullian, *Ad Scapulam*).

judges of the pagans.[1] It is difficult to see how Christianity could, in these circumstances, have made much appeal to the upper classes in the towns. The city magistrates as a whole, in the reign of Diocletian as in that of Severus, remained pagan, and carried out their duty of persecution firmly and without hesitation. Well into the fourth century this situation remained unaltered. In A.D. 365 no less than 47 out of 72 *curiales* recorded on the Album of Timgad were pagan priests.[2] The underlying bitterness between this once dominant class and the Christians is well illustrated by Augustine's letters to the City Councils of Sufes[3] and Calama.[4] On the other hand, despite the assertion by Secundus of Tigisis that *Patresfamiliae* were among the martyrs of A.D. 303-4,[5] there does not seem to be any very clear evidence for more than one decurion,[6] one member of the equestrian order,[7] and one grammarian being killed for their faith.[8]

One would ask what factors in the political and economic situation in third-century North Africa justified this attitude. In the next century there was a close connexion between Donatism and social unrest. Can the same be said of Christianity during the preceding period? In Egypt, some case has been made out long ago by Amélineau[9] and others that the mass of Egyptian peasants accepted Christianity out of protest against an alien rule and that, later, Monophysitism rested on the same foundation. The Egyptians were, in fact, renowned for their religious anarchism.[10] It may be noted that the revolt of Achilleus in A.D. 295-6 and the violent anti-Christian persecu-

---

[1] *Passio Perpetuae*, 17, Saturus, 'Notate tamen nobis facies diligenter ut recognoscatis nos in die illo', i.e. the Last Day. Cf. Tertullian, *Ad Scapulam*, 5, and *Scorpiace*, 12.

[2] *CIL.* viii. 2403.   [3] Augustine, *Ep.* 50.   [4] Id., *Ep.* 90 and 91.

[5] *Breviculus Collationis*, iii. 15. 27 (*PL.* xliii. 640), 'praesertim quia idem Secundus non quoslibet infimos, sed etiam patresfamilias . . . crudelissimis mortibus dixit ooccisos'.

[6] Dativus in *Acta Saturnini*, 2 and 6, 'Dativus qui et senator' (*PL.* viii. 691).

[7] Aemilian in *Passio Mariani et Jacobi*, 8. 1 (ed. Knopf, *Ausgewählte Märtyrenakten*, Tübingen, 1929), 'quamvis equestris ordinis gentilis haberetur'.

[8] Flavian in *Passio Montani*, 12, 16, 17, and 19.

[9] E. Amélineau, 'Le Christianisme chez les anciens Coptes', *Revue de l'histoire des religions*, xiv, 1886, pp. 308-45.

[10] *SHA.*, Flavius Vopiscus, *Quadrigae Tyrannorum* (ed. Hohl, Leipzig, 1927, p. 227), 7. 4, 'Aegyptii ut satis nosti (in)venti ventosi, furibundi, iactantes, injuriosi atque ideo vani, liberi, novarum rerum usque ad cantilenas publicas cupientes, versificatores, epigrammatarii, mathematici, haruspices, medici.'

tion seven years later took place in much the same parts of
Upper Egypt.[1] Though the African *colonus* was probably a good
deal better off than the Egyptian peasant, and might even be
termed relatively prosperous, there were certain parallels in
the condition of both. In each country any considerable rise
from subsistence level was threatened from two directions, first
by the extortions of the Emperor's tax-collectors and secondly
by the continuous incursions of neighbouring barbarian tribes.
The Quinquegentani and the Blemmyes play much the same
roles in the history of the North African High Plains and in
Upper Egypt respectively during this period. In North Africa
the final quarter of the third century seems to have been particularly distressing for the native cultivators.

The war against the Quinquegentani, which lasted nine
years, A.D. 289–97, caused much destruction in Mauretania
and western Numidia.[2] The rebels are recorded on an inscription as having penetrated into the town of Sitifis (modern
Setif) and destroyed temples there.[3] The country districts were
devastated. The *Passio Tipasii* speaks of the 'prostration' of
landowners and peasants alike owing to the war.[4] Yet it was
just at this time, about A.D. 292, that Diocletian reorganized
the provincial boundaries of Numidia and Mauretania and
tightened up the existing system of taxation.[5] The burdens
which fell on the inhabitants were considerably increased. The
peasants began to flee the land rather than pay.[6] Lactantius
records the exactions of the army of tax-gatherers that descended
on the African provinces and the hatred felt for them.[6] Fiscal
oppression was no new phenomenon in southern Numidia. At
Ain Zoui (Lat. Vazaivi), a *statio* north of the Aures mountains,
an inscription dated to the reign of Maximin (A.D. 235–8)
records the complaints of the peasants that 'extraordinary

---

[1] Cf. W. Seston, *Mélanges*, lv, 1938, pp. 184–200.

[2] On the effects, see Wm. Seston, *Dioclétien et la Tétrarchie*, pp. 115–28. I think
he may be exaggerating the speed at which the provinces recovered from the war.
Lactantius in *De Mortibus Persecutorum* paints a different picture of conditions in
these years.   [3] *CIL.* viii. 8457.

[4] *Passio Tipasii*, I (*Analecta Bollandiana*, ix, 1890, pp. 116–23), 'Praeterea in Siti-
fense provincia gentiles, qui semper pacati fuerant, et Quinquegentani vocantur,
direptis provincialibus facultatibus atque universis possessoribus incolisque pro-
stratis, latrocinia perpetrabant.'   [5] W. Seston, op. cit., pp. 261 ff.

[6] Lactantius, *De Mortibus Persecutorum*, 7 (*CSEL.* xxvii. 180), 'ut enormitate
indictionum consumptis viribus colonorum desererentur agri et culturae verte-
rentur in silvam'.

[7] Ibid. 23, 'censitoribus ubique diffusis, et omnia exagitantibus, hostilis tumultus'.

exactions' were being levied by the collectors (*exceptores*) as a matter of course, and that the kinsfolk and children of the debtors were being held in pledge until full payment was made.[1] It was this type of abuse that called the Circumcellions into being in the next century and made the Imperial officials hated in Numidia by the Donatist inhabitants. If one adds that the curial class there remained resolutely pagan up to and after the Great Persecution, one may be justified in including a measure of social and economic discontent as instrumental in bringing the Berbers to accept Christianity. In the incidents which took place at the election of Bishop Silvanus to the see of Cirta in A.D. 305 we have seen an indication of their fanaticism against paganism and also their antipathy towards the better-to-do townsfolk.

One final influence in the conversion of the provincials to Christianity in the late third century should not be omitted. Time and again in the *Acta Martyrum* and in Tertullian (e.g. *Apol.* 20) one reads of the immense veneration in which the Bible was held.[2] The Abitinian martyrs expressed their horror at the temerity of those who would change a single syllable of Holy Writ.[3] At the back of many people's minds was the belief that the Word of God had been recorded in a single work intelligible to ordinary humans and His Name thereby made known to them.[4] The Saviour was revealed as one who had been brought up in surroundings which had a familiar ring to most people. The social message of the Bible corresponded with prevailing conditions and must have found ready response among both the despairing and the oppressed. The North African countryside was an ideal field for this creed.[5] Not for

---

[1] *CIL.* viii. 17639, 'exactionibus inlicitis', &c.

[2] The Scillitan martyrs carried a copy of St. Paul's Epistles with them at their trial in A.D. 180. See above, p. 96.

[3] *Acta Saturnini*, 18.

[4] Knowledge of the 'name' of God was particularly important to the primitive mind. Arnobius 1. 46 indicates the use of Christ's name as a talisman against demons. The theory advanced by R. A. Knox, *Enthusiasm* (O.U.P., 1950), p. 53, that 'the very work that had gone into the fashioning of books enhanced their sacredness', strikes one as mistaken in this connexion. Copies of Scripture were widespread enough in the third and fourth centuries. Important was the secret conveyed in the text, and this is the case whether we are considering the Gospels of Christian Africa or the Koran in Moslem Africa.

[5] In our own more materialistic generation, we have seen how great populations of primitive-minded human beings have been converted to Marxism, that is to a rule of life based on a single 'Bible', which claims to explain all earthly difficulties,

nothing do inscriptions from village churches in Numidia repeat texts hailing Christ as a refuge from the toil and misery of the world. But from the outset of the history of African Christianity one can trace differences between those who accepted the words of the Bible literally to the exclusion of all other writing and experience, and those who regarded the authority of the Church as itself pre-eminent in their religion and were prepared to make compromises with the surrounding culture so long as it did not conflict with its doctrine. One can follow the development of this difference of outlook among African Christians from the time of Tertullian down to the moment when the dispute broadened into the Donatist controversy.

and at the same time appeals to their desire for social justice. The Bible and the Christian gospel may have had the same electric effect in Mediterranean countries in the late third century A.D. as Marxian Communism has in Central Europe today.

IX

AFRICAN CHURCH DIVISIONS
IN THE TIME OF TERTULLIAN

A.D. 197-225

So long as the threat of persecution remained, no permanent schism broke out in the African Church. But victory over paganism, and the exclusive favour shown by Constantine to the Caecilianist party in 312-13, set free forces of division within the Church which had long been active. At each successive crisis, under Septimius Severus, under Decius and Valerian, and under Diocletian, the Church in Africa split apart. The division produced two rival parties, the Catholics and the austerer party of the Confessors. Though on the two earlier occasions almost complete unity was quickly restored, an undercurrent of stress and disharmony remained. In the long periods of quiet which separated the persecutions, the peace of the Church was continually interrupted by fierce feuds among the clergy. The quarrel between Bishop Optatus and the presbyter Aspasius (c. A.D. 200)[1] and that which resulted in the deposition of Privatus of Lambaesis (c. A.D. 245)[2] were probably only two of the more notorious examples. Any one of these disputes, as Tertullian pointed out, might lead to schism.[3] The final breach over the question of Caecilian's election to the see of Carthage must be judged not as an isolated event but as the outcome of divisions in the African Church inherent since its foundation.

From an early stage there emerge two completely different interpretations of Christianity. On the one hand, there is the orthodox Catholic Church, prepared to compromise with the evils of this world for the sake of unity and peaceful progress. Its organization was based on an urban episcopate and an ordered hierarchy. On the other hand, there is the Church of the Holy

---

[1] *Passio Perpetuae*, 13 (ed. J. Armitage Robinson, p. 82).

[2] Cyprian, *Ep.* 59. 10.

[3] Tertullian, *De Baptismo*, 17, 'Episcopatus aemulatio schismatum mater est'; Lupton, 'Tertullian, *De Baptismo*', Cambridge, 1908, 47. Cf. Purpurius of Limata's threat to Secundus of Tigisis 'schisma facere' (*Contra Cresconium*, iii. 27. 30—*PL.* xliii. 511).

Spirit, of enthusiasm, of open hostility to the world, individualistic and intolerant.[1] Social cleavage tended to reinforce doctrinal cleavage, until the decision of the Caecilianist party at Carthage to accept Imperial favour rent the parties asunder in final schism. In the ensuing struggle both could with some justification be considered the true bearer of the original Christian message in North Africa.

We have seen that in the background of much of African early Christian thought stood the fear of active evil spirits and the dire need of propitiating God. The emphasis which the early Christians in Africa placed on the Third Person of the Trinity can only be understood if this dread of real malevolent spiritual powers is appreciated. It forms, indeed, the common ground between Christianity and Manichaeism in Africa. The doctrine of both religions included rules which the believer must observe in order to escape from their clutches. Union of the individual with the Divine attained through the medium of the Holy Spirit, in the first place through baptism, could only be secured by one who was himself in a ritually pure state. In the prevalent ideas of the day the Holy Spirit could not take up His abode with demons, and means more or less connected with current magical practices were employed to ensure the necessary ritual purity. Fasting, especially the xerophagy, the dry fast, was the means, Tertullian explains, at once of the Holy Spirit's incoming and of the evil spirit's exit.[2] This preoccupation with magic, and the belief in the presence of the Holy Spirit Himself in the waters of baptism, may explain much of the bitterness which surrounded the baptismal controversies.[3]

These ideas entailed a belief in the communication of God's will to the believers direct without intermediary, through him whom the Holy Spirit had entered.[4] Connected with the resulting tendency towards asceticism on the part of the early Christians went an emphasis on the importance of the prophet's

---

[1] For the connexion between Montanism and Donatism, with the movements towards enthusiasm in general in Christianity, see R. A. Knox, *Enthusiasm*, chaps. iii and iv. On the Donatists, Knox is inaccurate in detail, but the parallels he draws between the Donatists and Anabaptists and Camisards are valuable.

[2] *De Jejunio*, 8 (*PL.* ii, col. 1014), 'Quid enim mirum, si eadem operatione spiritus iniquus educitur, qua sanctus inducitur?'

[3] The Donatists believed in the special efficacy of their watchword 'Deo Laudes' in baptism (*CIL.* viii. 20482 (Sillègue)).

[4] Cf. *Adversus Praxean*, 30, the Spirit as 'oeconomiae [Trinitatis] interpretatorem, si quis sermones novae prophetiae ejus admiserit'.

gifts. Fasting, Tertullian pointed out, enabled Daniel to pro-
phesy and receive revelations.[1] He who was granted these
glimpses of the Beyond while possessed by the Spirit could
testify to the truth of Christ's Gospel and to the reality of
man's hope of immortality. It was, however, believed that the
supreme revelation of God's glory was granted only in the last
moments of one who had borne witness to his faith unto death,
and therefore become a μάρτυρ τοῦ θεοῦ:[2] St. Stephen, for
instance, declared that he saw the 'heavens opened, and the
Son of Man standing at the right hand of God'.[3] It was the
same vision of glory and power that Christ Himself had beheld
as He stood before the judgement seat of Pilate.[4] A Church of
the Holy Spirit, therefore, whose culminating honour was
martyrdom, must of necessity also have reserved an honoured
place for the prophet, and enjoined the practice of a stringent
moral code.

Associated with this view of Christianity was the belief in
the approaching end of the world, and the thousand-years' reign
of Christ among His elect.[5] This last factor sustained the Christians in their attitude of hostility to pagan Roman society. Ills
suffered in this world would be repaid in the Day of Judgement.
On the other hand, it enabled the more ascetic and puritanical
Christians to conceive of a Church encumbered with less
organization than that demanded by their laxer and more
philosophic opponents. There was no predilection in favour of
urban episcopacy among the rigorists. New Jerusalem might
descend in the wilds of Phrygia or in the up-country of Judaea.[6]
The bishops were indeed the successors of the Apostles, but their
powers were restricted to powers of administration of the visible
Church on earth.

On the other hand, if Christianity was to survive, separate
from the numberless mystery religions and Gnostic sects, there
was need for a far firmer organization. The increase of the

---

[1] *De Jejunio*, 9 (*CSEL*. xx. 283–4). So also the Donatist bishop Marculus (*Passio Marculi*—*PL*. viii, col. 763).

[2] Cf. K. Holl, 'Die Vorstellung vom Märtyrer und die Märtyrerakte in ihrer geschichtlichen Entwicklung', *Gesammelte Aufsätze*, Tübingen, 1927, Osten, Halb-band, ii. 70. The phrase was applied to the Apostles first, 1 Corinthians xv. 5–8, and then to those who died for the Faith. The end of martyrdom was the glory of God.   [3] Acts vii. 56.   [4] Mar. xiv. 62.

[5] Cf. Tertullian, *Adversus Marcionem*, iii. 24; *De Spectaculis*, 30; *Apologeticus*, 32 and 39; J. Berton, *Tertullien le Schismatique*, Paris, 1913, 60 ff.

[6] As suggested in *Adversus Marcionem*, iii. 24 (*PL*. ii. 384).

authority of the bishop, and the conception of the Church as a confederation of communities throughout the Roman Empire, meant in the long run that the Church must be focused in the large towns where communications were good. In Africa, Christianity first made its way to Carthage and to the Tunisian coast towns, and hence from the first was centred in them. The organization of the Church could hardly avoid becoming parallel with that of the city state, a Christian *respublica* over against the pagan city. It tended from the start to become an institution, whose interests were bound up with those of the city where it was, and its religious life was threatened by daily contact with the luxury and waste of the cities themselves. Moreover, as an institution, it could not be run permanently at a loss. Funds were necessary for good works, and property had therefore to be acquired. The city, and the law and order which it guaranteed, alone could give security for that property. One can see therefore that there must have been an inclination from the outset among some of the Christian leaders in the African towns to live at peace with the world, and refrain from provoking it unnecessarily.

In quiet times, however, there was no necessity for trouble to arise between the rigorists and the more liberal members of a Christian community. Little except enthusiasm separated the two parties.[1] Yet gradually, from the middle of the second century A.D. onwards, in Asia Minor and in North Africa, and also to a lesser degree in Gaul and Rome, the two conceptions of Christianity crystallized and came into opposition. Actual schism broke out first in Asia Minor, where the succession of prophets had kept pace with the succession of bishops,[2] but there is evidence to show that by the end of the century a like situation was threatening in Africa.

There, popular Christianity was developing into what may be termed a Church of the Spirit. Such scenes as Tertullian quotes as occurring in Asia Minor, where crowds of Christians demanded martyrdom at the hands of the magistrates, could not have been unknown at this period in North Africa.[3] The Christians were already earning the name of 'faggot fellows'

---

[1] The rigorists naturally formed the kernel of every Christian community. But this even in the second century was composed of widely differing elements. There was no doctrinal division between the rigorists and their more liberal fellow Christians. See C. Bigg, *Origins of Christianity*, Oxford, 1909, 80.

[2] W. M. Calder, *Philadelphia and Montanism*, pp. 329 ff.   [3] *Ad Scapulam*, 5.

and 'half-axle men',[1] through their spirit of desperation and contempt of death. Praise to martyrs was already in A.D. 200 tending to come second only to praise to God,[2] services were held in the *areae* wherein the martyrs were buried, and confessors in prison were believed to have a power to forgive sins even greater than that possessed by the Church.[3] If Reitzenstein's conclusions as to the origin and date of the tract 'On the Three Kinds of Fruit in a Christian Life' are accepted,[4] then by the end of the second century A.D. a militant body of martyrs and ascetics, the *agonisti*, may already have been developing into a caste apart within the Christian community.

One of the most important documents on this period of the African Church is the *Passio Perpetuae*.[5] Had this been written in A.D. 306 instead of A.D. 206 it would immediately have invited comparison with the *Acta Saturnini*, and have become known as one of the most interesting documents on the origins of Donatism. Nearly all the features of Donatism are represented. The *Acta* show clearly the connexion in the mental outlook between the rigorists of Tertullian's day and the 'Church of the Martyrs' in the time of Caecilian.

In the first place there is the voluntary surrender of Saturus, Perpetua's catechist, to the authorities.[6] Catholics had for half a century or more criticized such action,[7] and it will be remembered that this was one of the matters about which Mensurius of Carthage complained to the Primate of Numidia after the Great Persecution. Then the martyrs, like the Abitinian martyrs or the Donatist bishop Marculus in 347, are 'under the guidance of the Holy Spirit' from the moment they entered prison.[8] It is also clear that for them baptism was simply a

---

[1] Tertullian, *Apol.* 50. 3 (Loeb, 222), 'Licet nunc sarmenticios et semaxios appelletis.'   [2] *Scorpiace*, 7 (*CSEL*. xx. 159).

[3] *Ad Martyres*, i (*PL*. i. 695), 'Quam pacem quidam in Ecclesia non habentes, a martyribus in carcere exorare consueverunt.' Cf. *Ad Uxorem*, ii. 4, kissing martyrs' chains.

[4] R. Reitzenstein, 'Eine frühchristliche Schrift von den dreierlei Früchten des christlichen Lebens', *Zeitschrift für die neutestamentliche Wissenschaft*, xv, 1914, 73.

[5] I have used the editions of J. A. Robinson, *Texts and Studies*, Cambridge, 1891, and E. Knopf, *Ausgewählte Märtyrerakten*, Tübingen, 1929. For discussion of the *Acta*, cf. P. Monceaux, *Histoire littéraire*, i. 70 ff., and P. de Labriolle, *La Crise Montaniste*, Paris, 1913, 338 ff.

[6] *Passio*, 4, '(Saturus) qui postea se propter nos ultro tradiderat.'

[7] For instance, in *Acta Polycarpi*, quoted by Eusebius, *Historia Ecclesiastica*, iv. 15.

[8] *Passio Perpetuae*, 3 and 5. Cf. Tertullian *Ad Martyres*, 1, 'Nolite contristare spiritum sanctum qui vobiscum introiit carcerem.'

preparation for the tragedy and glory of martyrdom. They were to request nothing, it is stated, from the baptismal waters other than the suffering of the flesh.[1] Perpetua herself is represented throughout as being 'in great honour'[2] and filled with the Spirit. As a confessor she could *demand* a vision from the Lord and converse with Him.[3] The Donatist leaders, such as Donatus and Pontius, claimed likewise.

Perpetua's attitude towards the bishops and clergy is also clearly defined. They are indeed her superiors. The deacon Pomponius is called 'Pater',[4] and due respect is paid to Bishop Optatus, but their office is regarded mainly as one of administration. They have disciplinary functions directed to keeping the congregation free from compromise with the surrounding pagan world. 'Correct thy people', was the Angels' command to the priest Aspasius in Saturus' vision; 'they assemble before thee as if returning from a Circus, rioting over the factions.'[5] But theirs was an auxiliary role to that played by the martyr, unless, like the priest Saturus, they accompanied their flock to their appointed end.[6] Neither Aspasius nor Optatus goes to Paradise even when they have settled their dispute. Perpetua saw only martyrs there, as Tertullian emphasized.[7] The way, indeed, from earth to Paradise led not through the priesthood but only by combat with the powers of evil in the amphitheatre.

We know from comparison with other contemporary evidence that the religious ideas of Perpetua were not uncommon in North Africa at the time, and were not even confined to the Christian Church. Her assumption of male sex in the course of her visions, and her use of Greek as the language of Paradise find parallel in the beliefs of the followers of Hermes Trismegistos, such as the Urbanilla of the Lambiridi inscription in southern Numidia.[8] One is confronted by a general complex of

---

[1] 'Non aliud petendum ab aqua nisi sufferentiam carnis', *Passio Perpetuae*, 3.

[2] 'magna dignatione', ibid. 4.

[3] Ibid. 4. In a dream she sees her brother Dinocrates, who had died of a cancer, and he asks her to demand a vision, 'postules visionem'. Perpetua herself considered this justified. 'Agnovi me dignam esse et pro eo petere debere.'

[4] Ibid. 6.

[5] Ibid. 13. 3, Et dixerunt Optato, 'Corrige plebem tuam, quia sic ad te conveniunt quasi de circo redeuntes, et de factionibus certantes.'

[6] There is an interesting example of this attitude in the *Acta Saturnini*, 4. The writer praises the presbyter Saturninus for having associated himself with his fellow confessors as a martyr rather than claiming the privileges of his office.

[7] *Passio*, 11; Tertullian, *De Anima*, 55, 'solos commartyres'.

[8] J. Carcopino, *Aspects mystiques de la Rome païenne*, pp. 281–4. While Perpetua

religious ideas which, however, had their most lucid expression in the African version of Montanism in the early third century and in Donatism a century later. There seems little doubt that in their outlook as well as in their doctrinal beliefs Perpetua and her companions belonged to the Montanist party in the African Church.[1]

Perpetua and Felicitas were executed in A.D. 203, either on 2 February or 7 March.[2] Three years later Tertullian, who edited the account of their martyrdom, went over to the Montanists.[3] In a sense this period, 206–7, is almost as important in the history of the African Church as the outbreak of the Donatist controversy itself. For, with the adhesion of Tertullian, the dissenters found a leader who was prepared if necessary to defy the bishops, even the Bishop of Rome himself, and who has also left a record of their particular beliefs. The separation between the puritans and the moderates was thenceforth liable to be open.

It is not intended to give a detailed account of Tertullian's Montanism.[4] Of interest to the student of Donatism, however, is the fact that in this period one finds the beginnings of the arguments and counter-arguments on the nature of the Church that characterize the Donatist controversy.

Both as a member of the Great Church and as a Montanist

had been instructed to pronounce 'Hagios, Hagios, Hagios', on reaching Paradise, Urbanilla would say also in Greek 'Eu ter pius'.

[1] Cf. J. Armitage Robinson, op. cit., pp. 50–52. The episodes of Perpetua accepting Communion in the Montanist manner in sheep's milk and cheese and receiving baptism outside the times fixed by the Church, seem to fit quite naturally into the rest of the story of her martyrdom. One can hardly minimize this particular incident, since it is accompanied by a solemn 'Amen'. 'Amen' was always said after receiving Communion (cf. Tertullian, De Spectaculis, 25). A fourth-century mosaic from Matifou (Rusguniae) shows the Lord in Paradise milking sheep (Lieut. Chardon, Bull. Arch. du Comité, 1900, p. 142). For Roman Catholic views on Perpetua, see de Labriolle, La Crise Montaniste, p. 344, and W. H. Shewring, The Passion of SS. Perpetua and Felicitas, Sheed and Ward, 1931.

[2] The February date is given in the Greek Acta. Cf. S. K. Gifford and R. Harris, Acts of Perpetua and Felicitas, London, 1890, 39. 'Die nonarum Martiarum' in the short Latin Acta; cf. Aubé, Les Chrétiens dans l'Empire romain, Paris, 1881, p. 525. It should, however, be borne in mind that the Catholic tradition maintaining this date cannot itself be earlier than the fourth century, the date of the Depositio Martyrum of the Roman Calendar.

[3] H. Lietzmann, Geschichte der alten Kirche, ii. 222.

[4] The following general works are useful: J. Berton, Tertullien le Schismatique, Paris, 1928; K. Adam, Der Kirchenbegriff Tertulliens, Paderborn, 1907; P. Monceaux, Histoire littéraire; E. Buonaiuti, Il Cristianesimo nell'Africa Romana, chap. 5; A. Ehrhard, Die Kirche der Märtyrer, München, 1932, pp. 247–53.

Tertullian seems to have regarded the Church not merely as a school for salvation but as a community of saints awaiting the rapidly approaching end of the world. 'In prayer we await the trumpet of the angel', he writes in *De Oratione*.[1] The Christian organization which he describes in A.D. 197 in his *Apologeticus* was adapted to this outlook.[2] It was a brotherhood. Its rulers were 'elders' (*seniores*).[3] All property was held in common. The Christian had left 'the world' for good.

Tertullian's Apology contains no mention of bishops or of episcopal power, and a little later on, in *De Baptismo*, he appears to suggest that any Christian could dispense a valid sacrament when necessary.[4] The Holy Spirit was on the whole congregation, and the Church existed where 'two or three were gathered together in the unity of the Spirit'.[5] It followed, then, that a Christian who sinned ceased automatically to be a Christian.[6] He could expect no forgiveness except through martyrdom, the second baptism, this time of blood.[7]

From this subjective view of the Church one can see how Tertullian came to put forward arguments which were later developed by the Donatists. In his *De Baptismo* he defined what was to be the Cyprianic and Donatist view of baptism. The Holy Spirit was actually present in the waters,[8] and since no heretic by definition could be in possession of the Spirit, a baptism administered by a heretic or a person in mortal sin could not be valid.[9] Therefore anyone who had received baptism at the hands of a heretic must be rebaptized before he could be admitted to the Christian community. This view came to be adopted alike by friends and opponents of Tertullian,

---

[1] *De Oratione*, 29 (*PL*. i, col. 1304), 'Sub armis orationis tubam angeli expetemus.' Also *De Jejunio*, 17.

[2] *Apologeticus* (ed. Loeb, p. 174), 39.

[3] *Apol.* 39. 4. Cf. *De Corona*, 3, and *Passio Perpetuae*, 12, Saturus' vision of the Lord surrounded by *seniores*.

[4] *De Baptismo*, 17, 'Alioquin etiam laicis jus est.'

[5] Ibid. 6 and *De Exhortatione Castitatis*, 7. Cf. A. Harnack, *History of Dogma* (tr. Buchanan, 1896), ii. 7.

[6] *Apol.* 39. 4.

[7] Ibid. 50 (Loeb, p. 226), 'Omnia enim huic operi delicta donantur', and *Scorpiace*, 6 (*CSEL*. xx. 158). For similar views held by the Donatists see Petilian in *Contra Litteras Petiliani*, ii. 23. 51—(*PL*. xliii, col. 276), 'Cum enim nostra corpora occiditis, bis baptismum, sed baptismo nostro et sanguine baptizamur ut Christus.' This was the 'true baptism'.

[8] *De Baptismo*, 8 and 15.

[9] Tertullian, *De Baptismo*, 5 and 15. Cf. G. G. Willis, *Saint Augustine and the Donatist Controversy*, S.P.C.K., 1950, pp. 145–7.

and was confirmed by a decision of a Council held by Bishop
Agrippinus of Carthage, *c.* 220, at which bishops from Proconsular Africa and Numidia were present.[1] It was also the view
defended by the Donatists against Augustine.

Tertullian, however, did not see the question of baptism in
isolation. It was impossible for an individual in a state of sin
to remain in the Church at all. In words which were later to be
echoed by both Cyprian and the Donatists, the Church was the
'Bride of Christ, without spot or wrinkle'.[2] In a sentence, it was,
'ecclesia spiritus per spiritalem hominem, non ecclesiae numerus
episcoporum'.[3] The purity of the sacraments rather than numbers or geographical extent was the test whether an organization was the Church or not. At the Conference of Carthage,
Gaudentius, the Donatist Bishop of Thamugadi, was to maintain the same thesis.[4]

The reason for the expulsion of evil members from the
Church was that their evil was contagious. A priest was worthy
of his office if, said Tertullian, 'he knew how to administer in
sanctity'.[5] He quoted as his authority a prophecy of the Montanist prophetess, Prisca. Two centuries later Petilian, the Donatist Bishop of Constantine, was also to insist that 'what we look
for is the conscience of the giver of a sacrament administering
it in sanctity'.[6] Incestuous bishops in Tertullian's time[7] were as
intolerable as *traditor* bishops in the Donatist period. It was a
duty to withdraw from such brethren.[8]

That the Church was composed of a small company of the
elect was a matter of fact and not of necessity. The division
between the true Christians and the 'crowds' of 'Psychics' (Tertullian's name for the Catholic opposition)[9] and unbelievers
was moral and not geographical. The Spirit had made itself
manifest in Phrygia as well as in North Africa, and the maturity

[1] Cyprian, *Ep.* 71. 4 (Hartel, p. 774); Augustine, *De Baptismo contra Donatistas*,
ii. 9. 14 (*PL.* xliii, col. 135). Augustine argues that since Agrippinus had to summon a Council rebaptism had not previously been the custom of the Church.

[2] *De Pudicitia*, 18 (*PL.* ii. 1069), 'non habentem maculam aut rugam'. Cf.
Cyprian, *Ep.* 69. 2 (Hartel, pp. 750–1), and the Donatists in *Gesta Coll. Carth.* iii.
258 (*PL.* xi, col. 1409).

[3] *De Pudicitia*, 21.   [4] *Gesta Col. Carth.* iii. 102 (*PL.* xi, col. 1381).

[5] *De Exhortatione Castitatis*, 10, 'quod sanctus minister sanctimoniam noverit
ministrare'.

[6] Cf. Augustine, *Contra Litteras Petiliani*, iii. 8. 9, 'Conscientia sancte dantis
attenditur, quae abluat accipientis' (*PL.* xliii, col. 353).

[7] E.g. the Bishop of Uthina, *De Monogamia*, 12.   [8] *De Pudicitia*, 18.

[9] *De Fuga*, 14 (*PL.* ii, col. 142). Cf. *Adversus Praxean*, i (*PL.* ii, col. 179).

of the Church obtained through this New Prophecy was there for all to comprehend.[1] For the Donatists, Parmenian and the grammarian Cresconius[2] were to make similar claims. Circumstances, such as the support given to Caecilian by the see of Rome and other bishoprics overseas, had in fact placed heavy responsibilities on the Church in Africa, but it is doubtful whether any but the most fanatical of the Numidians believed that the Church would be confined for ever to a single province. The Donatist participation in the semi-Arian Council at Serdica in 342 and their election of a non-African, Parmenian, as Donatus' successor, c. 355, are indications to the contrary.[3]

As has already been stated, Christians in Tertullian's view must always be prepared for martyrdom.[4] Persecution and hatred by all men were their due. Martyrdom was the sole death worthy of a Christian and was that counselled by the Spirit.[5] Rather than die naturally a Christian should offer himself voluntarily to the judges.[6] He should join assemblies openly in time of persecution,[7] and if necessary he should be ready to take his own life.[8] These views found their logical development in Donatism, and in the extreme wing of the community, the Circumcellion movement.[9] The necessity of separation from the world and even hatred by it is further suggested by the title of Vitellius Afer's last work, written c. A.D. 350, 'De eo quod odio sunt mundi Dei servi.'[10]

Glorification of martyrdom did not, however, reduce the clergy to the level of ciphers. Tertullian was as hostile as Cyprian to the popular claim that a confessor could forgive deadly sins while still on earth.[11] Martyrs were only perfect when dead. A martyr could only purge his own sins, not

---

[1] De Virginibus Velandis, i (PL. ii, col. 938).

[2] Cresconius argued, for instance, that truth often originates with an insignificant minority (Augustine, Contra Cresconium, iv. 53. 63). Cf. Parmenian in Optatus, i. 5 and 6.

[3] See below, Chap. XII, p. 185; also Augustine, Ep. 44. 3. 6. Tertullian also quotes the decision of a Greek Council in De Jejunio, 13.

[4] De Spectaculis, 1, 'Christianos, expeditum morti genus.'

[5] De Fuga, 9. Cf. Scorpiace, 9 (CSEL. xx. 164). Much the same spirit animated the Berbers under Islam.

[6] Ad Scapulam, 5 (PL. i, col. 782), 'Nos haec [i.e. persecution] non timere sed ultro vocare.'   [7] De Fuga, 3 and 9.

[8] Ad Martyres, 4, and De Exhortatione Castitatis, 16 (example of Dido).

[9] See below, p. 175.   [10] Gennadius, De Scriptoribus ecclesiasticis, 4.

[11] De Pudicitia, 22 (CSEL. xx. 271). Cf. Lietzmann, Geschichte der alten Kirche, ii. 226.

forgive those of others.[1] In his earlier years, Tertullian would probably have left to the decision of a bishop the moment when the sinner should prepare himself for final reconciliation with the Lord through a martyr's death.[2]

The link between martyrdom and the bishop's office may perhaps be found in Tertullian's attitude towards the Apostles, and in particular Sts. Peter and Paul. The Apostles, he points out, were those who 'have the Spirit wholly in the works of prophecy and the efficacy of [healing] virtues and the evidences of tongues, not partially as all others have'.[3] The Apostles, moreover, were examples of martyrdom, the pillars of Christian discipline, and guides to reformation through the Spirit.[4] On the other hand, they were also bishops and the founders of the Churches whose authority was paramount. No doubt, in Tertullian's mind, whether as a member of the Great Church or as a Montanist, Rome was the symbol of the Church's authority.[5] But the powers granted to individual bishops were disciplinary rather than spiritual.[6] The Bishop of Rome had personally no special position. The keys of St. Peter were in the hands of all faithful Christians, not in his alone.[7] He could only claim St. Peter's personal authority when he showed that St. Peter's gifts had descended upon him.[8] The same combination of reverence for the see of Rome as the original see of the Christian Church coupled with denial of the special jurisdictional rights claimed by the Popes was characteristic of both Cyprian

[1] De Pudicitia, 22 (CSEL. xx. 271).

[2] De Labriolle's view, La Crise Montaniste, p. 410.

[3] De Exhortatione Castitatis, 4 (PL. ii. 969), 'Proprie enim Apostoli Spiritum sanctum habent, in operibus prophetiae et efficacia virtutum, documentisque linguarum, non ex parte, quod ceteri.'

[4] Scorpiace, 13 and 15; De Pudicitia, 16 (CSEL. xx. 253), 'Paulum, columnam immobilem disciplinarum.'

[5] De Praescriptionibus, 36 (PL. ii. 59), 'Romam, unde nobis quoque auctoritas praesto est.' Cf. with Scorpiace, 10 (PL. ii. 165), 'Nam et si adhuc clausum putas caelum, memento claves ejus hic Dominum Petro et per eum, Ecclesiae reliquisse.'

[6] De Pudicitia, 21 (CSEL. xx. 269), 'Quod si disciplinae solius officia sortitus es, nec imperio praesidere, sed ministerio, quis aut quantus es indulgere.' Cf. De Praescriptione, 32.

[7] Scorpiace, 10, 'claves . . . quas hic uniusquisque interrogatus atque confessus feret secum'.

[8] De Pudicitia, 21 (CSEL. xx. 269), 'Exhibe nunc apostolice, prophetica exempla, ut agnosco divinitatem et vindica tibi delictorum eiuscemodi remittendorum potestatem.'

G. Altaner, Patrologie (Freiburg i/B. 1938) p. 92, argues, but not to my mind convincingly, against the bishop attacked by Tertullian in the De Pudicitia being the Bishop of Rome.

and probably the Donatist bishop Parmenian.[1] It is interesting that one finds the Apostles Sts. Peter and Paul associated with Donatist martyrs on a series of inscriptions from southern Numidia. On the other hand, they are not found in Catholic areas.[2]

If one recognizes an outlook characteristic of the Donatists in the works of Tertullian, one may also see in his opponents the forerunners of what later became the orthodox party in the African Church. Clearly, the way of life preached by Tertullian was beyond the powers of many convinced believers.[3] The end of the world was an unwelcome thought, and if sacrifices to the gods were to be renounced, at least there was no harm in witnessing the scenes in the stadium or circus. These were 'a great refreshment to eye and ear' which God Himself looked down upon.[4] This attitude may have had the support of the African clergy,[5] especially when it was known that people were being dissuaded from becoming Christians by puritan teachings.[6] Already, by the time the *De Idololatria* was written, there were those who argued that the Church contained 'clean' and 'unclean'.[7] This was to be one of Augustine's major arguments against the Donatists.

There is, too, some evidence to show that those who bribed the magistrates and bought off arrest in time of persecution,[8] or who murmured at the obstinacy of the soldier in the *De Corona Militari*, on the grounds that he was endangering the peace of the Church,[9] were to be found among the richer members of the community. The poorer classes would hardly have been affected by Tertullian's arraignment of the laxer brethren in the *De jejunio*, because the foods which he describes would be beyond their means. Compromise with the Roman authority was natural for those who had much in this world to lose.[10]

---

[1] Optatus, *De Schismate*, I. 10.

[2] See article by the writer in *JRS*. xxx, 1940, pp. 32–49, at p. 41.

[3] See P. Monceaux, *Histoire littéraire*, i. 37–39.

[4] *De Spectaculis*, 1 and 2 (Loeb, pp. 230–2), 'sed et ipsi actus sub caelo Dei transiguntur'. Also, *De Spect.* 20.

[5] *De Idololatria*, 7 (*PL.* i, col. 745), 'Alleguntur in ordinem ecclesiasticum artifices idolorum.'

[6] *De Spect.* 2.

[7] *De Idololatria*, 24 (*PL.* i, col. 774). Tertullian's opponents quoted the example of the Ark containing snakes and dogs.

[8] *De Fuga*, 12.

[9] *De Corona Militari*, 1, 'Mussitant denique tam bonam et longam sibi pacem periclitari.'   [10] Cf. *De Laude Martyrii*, 17 (*CSEL.* iii. 3, p. 39).

Montanism, however, was but a phase in Tertullian's life. Before he died he had left the Montanist Church as he had left the Catholic, and gathered round himself a community of his own liking.[1] By a strange irony, he who had so persistently advocated the martyr's death seems to have died peacefully in extreme old age.[2] In the years of peace which divided the reign of Severus from that of Decius, the divisions in the African Church to which he had given expression had healed over. Yet in his writings are to be found the main elements of the doctrine of the purity of the Church, of the necessity for 're-baptism of heretics', of martyrdom, and the moral austerity which the rigorists of later generations were to develop. Though we know not whether Tertullian had any direct influence on the Donatists, their thought was in many ways but a continua-tion of his own. It is perhaps hardly an exaggeration to account him less a Catholic apologist than the forerunner and father of Donatism.

[1] Augustine, *De Haeresibus ad Quodvultdeum*, 86 (*PL.* xlii. 46).

[2] Jerome, *De Viris Illustribus*, 53 (*PL.* xxiii. 698), 'Ferturque vixisse usque ad decrepitam aetatem.'

X

THE AFRICAN CHURCH
IN THE TIME OF CYPRIAN[1]

THE period between 212 and 250, which Sulpicius Severus calls the '38 years' peace',[2] favoured the progress of the moderate party in the African Church. It was a period of appreciable advance for Christianity in the African cities, while in general the countryside still remained attached to the old national deities, Saturn and Caelestis. But the majority of new believers were not fitted to practise the faith as interpreted by the puritans of Tertullian's day. They accepted the instruction given to them, but otherwise continued to lead their ordinary lives. All over the Roman Empire one finds that the beliefs characteristic of the rigorists in the previous generation were falling into abeyance.[3] Sovereignty passed from the 'spiritual men' to the bishops and their clergy in the capital cities of the larger provinces. It can hardly be an accident that this age saw the future patriarchates of Antioch and Alexandria emerge from obscurity, and the episcopal list begin at Carthage. When the renewal of persecution under Decius ends the period of obscurity, we find Bishops Fabius of Antioch, Dionysios of Alexandria, and Cyprian of Carthage in the position of autocrats, secure in their hold over their subjects, while the fleeting Emperors were following fast upon each other's heels. At the same time, with the Decian persecution begins the development of the first of the puritan schisms on a provincial basis—Novatianism in Phrygia and North Africa.

The age of Cyprian foreshadows the Donatist controversy in two directions. First, during the Decian persecution the

---

[1] The following general works should be consulted: (a) E. W. Benson, *Cyprian, His Life, His Times, His Work*, Macmillan, 1897; (b) P. de Labriolle, *Histoire de la littérature latine chrétienne*, Paris, 1924, pp. 176–225; (c) P. Monceaux, *Histoire littéraire*, ii, 1902; (d) J. Lebreton and J. Zeiller, *Histoire de l'Église*, ii. 186–210.

[2] Sulpicius Severus, *Chronicorum* (ed. Halm, *CSEL*. i, p. 86), ii. 32.

[3] A. Harnack, *History of Dogma*, ii. 107, gives examples. For instance, it was asserted that 'the law and the prophets were until John'. Therefore, after that time prophecy had no place. The rigorist moral code was all very well, but it was suitable only to the priesthood.

confessors insisted on their claim in matters of Church discipline and they showed the way to the martyrs of Abitina fifty years later. Secondly, the dispute between Cyprian and Pope Stephen over the validity of sacraments administered by lapsed or sinful clergy and by heretics alined the African Church with the puritans in their interpretation of this doctrine. In that respect, Donatism was a continuation of the position maintained by the Council of Carthage in September 256. The Donatist claim to be the successors of the Cyprianic Church was to this extent justified.

The outbreak of the Decian persecution in January 250[1] found the African Church in a state comparable to that prevailing under Diocletian. There was the will towards martyrdom alongside of the much more general desire to comply with the requirements of the authorities. There was a section of the Christian community, drawn largely from the artisans,[2] whose ideas were akin to those that inspired the Carthaginian Montanists a generation before. Martyrdom and the powers of the martyr remained the centre of their religion. The *Passio Perpetuae* with its emphasis on the small chosen body of the elect and the communion of the confessor with the Holy Spirit seems to have been among the most popular Christian works of the day.[3] During the persecution almost ecstatic crowds kept vigil round the prisons,[4] and afterwards during the plague which ravaged Carthage in A.D. 252 many were tortured by the fear of losing their chance of martyrdom rather than by the prospect of death.[5] It was from among such as these that the Confessor party which caused Cyprian such embarrassment came into

---

[1] I have accepted Benson's dating (*Cyprian*, p. 65).

[2] For instance, Paula the mat-maker and Soliassus the mule-keeper, who were named by Cyprian as prominent supporters of the schismatic Felicissimus, Novatus' puritanical deacon (*Ep.* 42). The confessor Aurelius, among others, appears to have been illiterate and of humble parentage (*Ep.* 27. 1).

[3] Pontius, *Vita Cypriani*, i (*CSEL.* iii. 3, p. xc). I consider that 'certe durum erat, ut cum maiores nostri plebeiis et catechumenis martyrium consecutis tantum honoris pro martyrii ipsius veneratione tribuerint', is a reference to the *Passio Perpetuae*. Cf. R. Reitzenstein, *Die Nachrichten über den Tod Cyprians, Sitzungsber. der Heidelberger Akademie, phil.-hist. Klasse*, 1913, no. 14, p. 48. That the *Acta Perpetuae* were looked on as an almost canonical work in the fourth century is shown by Augustine (*De Anima*, i. 12; H. Delehaye, *Les Origines du Culte des Martyrs*, 430). Both the Greek version and the Shorter Latin version of the *Acta* must date not later than the mid-third century.

[4] *Ep.* 5. 2 and 20. 2; Benson, op. cit., p. 90.

[5] *De Mortalitate*, 17 (*CSEL.* iii. 1. 307).

being. On the other hand, scenes took place which find an exact parallel during the Great Persecution. In the *De Lapsis* we read of crowds besieging the Capitols in order to do sacrifice.[1] In one town, Suturnuca,[2] the bishop Repostus is reported to have led his flock in an act of mass apostasy. At Assuras (Zanfour) the bishop Fortunatianus also lapsed.[3] Many of those who accepted certificates that they had sacrificed (the *libellatici*) appear to have had little idea of sin or belief that divine punishment would follow from such acts.[4] They were prepared to sacrifice one day and receive Communion the next. Flight in persecution had ceased to be scandalous and was recognized as a reasonable course to be followed except by the clergy.[5]

The stories of the grim end of those wealthy *libellatici* who presented themselves for the sacrament without having done due penance are indicative of the hostility which these aroused in the popular mind.[6] But no permanent schism broke out on this issue. This may have been partly due to the attitude of the confessors themselves. From Cyprian's correspondence one gathers that these were more interested in doing their best for relations in need and in gaining popularity by remitting sins wholesale than in issuing anathemas against the clergy.[7]

Of interest to us is the claim made by the confessors to be empowered by the fact of their imprisonment to forgive sins, and the popular acceptance of this claim. The beginnings of this development we have already noted in Tertullian's reminder that a confessor was not perfect until he had become a martyr.[8] But no such inhibitions deterred the confessors from giving out 'letters of peace' (*libelli pacis*) collectively to the lapsed.[9] In A.D. 250 the name of the martyr Paulus was of greater weight than that of the official representatives of the Church—especially when these were absent. Indeed, we find

---

[1] *De Lapsis*, 8–10 (*CSEL*. iii. 1. 242–4). Cf. *Ep*. 18. 2 and 20.

[2] Site unknown, possibly Tuburnuc, about twelve miles from Carthage (*Ep*. 59. 10).   [3] *Ep*. 65.

[4] *De Lapsis*, 15, 'paenitentia de pectoribus exclusa est' (*CSEL*. iii. 1, p. 248). Cf. *De Lapsis*, 22.

[5] For criticism of Cyprian's retirement, *Ep*. 8. 2; Lebreton and Zeiller, op. cit., p. 190. See also *Ep*. 34. 4.

[6] *De Lapsis*, 24–26. For wealth as a motive for apostasizing, see *De Lapsis*, 6–12, 'decepit multos patrimonii sui amor caecus' (*CSEL*. iii. 1. 240–6). Quotation from *De Lapsis*, 11 (*CSEL*. iii. 244).

[7] *Ep*. 20, 21, and 27.

[8] Tertullian, *De Pudicitia*, 22. See *CAH*. xii, chap. xv, p. 538.

[9] Cyprian, *Ep*. 27. 1. Pardons were given out *gregatim*. See above, page 91.

K

the confessors recommending Cyprian to 'have peace with the holy martyrs'.[1] The challenge to episcopal authority was inherently as great as that delivered by Donatus and the martyrs of Abitina fifty years later.

There is one other incidental factor which is suggestive of the years immediately preceding the outbreak of Donatism. Cyprian's election had been opposed by five presbyters, headed by a certain Novatus. The latter is said, probably with truth, to have been an unscrupulous, energetic, and ambitious man.[2] His role turned out to be strangely similar to that played by his successors among the Carthaginian presbyterate at the time of Caecilian's election. At first he supported the confessors and advocated lenient treatment for the lapsed. Then, when Cyprian outmanœuvred him and regained the confessors' allegiance, he went to Rome and allied himself with Novatian, possibly returning to Africa later as the champion of the strictest puritanism.[3]

The success of the Novatianists in Africa was instantaneous and significant for later developments.[4] During 251 Novatian's missionaries travelled from town to town gaining support. They appear to have had no difficulty in setting up rival sees, and were even able to challenge Cyprian's authority in Carthage.[5] Their emphasis on stringent moral practices, on the inviolable purity of the Church, on the need for refusing readmittance of the lapsed and unhallowed to Communion, and for rebaptizing their converts,[6] found ready hearing. Not all the confessors had advocated leniency. Some, like Florentius,[7] had been as unbending as Novatian. Now, the latter's followers began to style themselves 'the Pure',[8] and this attitude was linked with a particular reverence for the Scriptures. They claimed to be the

---

[1] *Ep.* 23, 'Optamus te cum sanctis martyribus pacem habere.'

[2] *Ep.* 52. 2, 'Rerum novarum semper cupidus'; Benson, op. cit., pp. 110–17.

[3] I have assumed, though without direct evidence, that Novatus did return to Africa to lead the spread of Novatianism there. On Novatus in Rome, see Benson, op. cit., pp. 137–8.

[4] Cyprian, *Ep.* 44–48; H. Leclercq, *L'Afrique chrétienne*, i. 205–6; P. Monceaux, *Histoire littéraire*, ii. 34–35.

[5] Maximus was consecrated Novatianist bishop of Carthage (*Ep.* 59. 9). In the same letter, Cyprian records forwarding to Cornelius at Rome a list of bishops who were still loyal. He dared not publish Novatian's charges against Cornelius for fear of causing a riot (*Ep.* 45. 2).

[6] *Ep.* 73. 2.   [7] *Ep.* 66. 9.

[8] Eusebius, *H.E.* vi. 43, 'καθαροὺς ἑαυτοὺς ἀποφηνάντων' = Latin, 'Mundi'. The word is found on Donatist inscriptions, *CIL.* viii. 10656 (Henchir el Guiz); P. Monceaux, *Revue de Philologie*, 1909, p. 128.

'evangelical' Church, and Novatian himself an *assertor Evangelii*.[1] Here the African Novatianists showed themselves to be in the same line of Christian tradition as the Donatists.

A number of circumstances, however, prevented Novatus and Novatian from anticipating the work of Donatus. In the first place, the Numidian Church was much less powerful, and when late in 251 or in 252 the Five Presbyters finally came out in schism against Cyprian, the support of '25 Numidian bishops' for Fortunatus their candidate as anti-bishop was largely theoretical. Three apostates and two heretics were all that answered their call.[2] Cyprian's hold over Numidia and Mauretania never seems to have been threatened seriously. Furthermore, Novatus' allies, the confessors, were hardly prepared to press their more fantastic claims once the persecutions were over. They were for the most part ignorant, good-hearted fellows who enjoyed their fill of power and abundance while in prison, but otherwise were content to be reabsorbed into the main body of the Christian community.[3]

There was, too, a strong tendency within the African Church, especially among its wealthier members, to discount the value of enthusiasm and martyrdom in comparison with more practical virtues, such as almsgiving.[4] The worth of visions was becoming doubted.[5] Holl has long since drawn attention to the difference in tone between the *Passio Perpetuae* and some of the *Acta* of the Cyprianic generation of martyrs.[6] There is a certain formalism and even insincerity about these latter. The emphasis is less upon the visions of Paradise and struggles with the Devil, which are mentioned rather as a matter of course, than upon

---

[1] *Ep.* 44. 3 (*CSEL.* iii. 599), 'si se adsertores evangelii et Christi esse confitentur'. A good summary of Novatian's ideas is to be found in Harnack's article on 'Novatian', in Hauck's *Protestantische Real-Encyclopädie*, xiv, 1904, 223–42.

[2] *Ep.* 59. 11, 'dicentes viginti quinque episcopos de Numidia esse venturos qui sibi episcopum facerent' (*CSEL.* iii. 678). The relations between the two anti-bishops, Maximus the 'official' Novatianist and Fortunatus the 'Novatist', are not at all clear.

[3] For instance, Cyprian promoted two of the confessors, Celerinus and Numidicus, to Orders (*Ep.* 39. 1 and 40).

[4] *CIL.* viii. 20906 (Tipasa, mosaic from funeral chapel of Alexander, a third-century bishop); L. Leschi, *Bull. Arch. du Comité*, 1940, séance du 27 mai, pp. xii–xxi. Cf. Pontius, *Vita Cypriani*, i.

[5] *Ep.* 66. 10, 'quamquam sciam somnia ridicula et visiones ineptas quibusdam videri'.

[6] K. Holl, *Die Vorstellung vom Märtyrer und die Märtyrerakte* (Gesammelte Aufsätze), p. 85.

the humility and self-effacement of the martyrs.[1] The fact that they did *not* surrender to the authorities voluntarily is noted.[2] The priest takes precedence over the martyr, and the virtue of modesty and the inclination towards 'peace and unity' are emphasized.[3]

Even so, in 251/2 there were three rival bishops of Carthage, the Novatianist Maximus, the schismatic Fortunatus, and Cyprian himself. The Christian community was divided in its outlook between enthusiasts and laxists. The elements which went to make the Donatist schism were already active. Of decisive importance in preserving the unity of the African Church at this stage was probably the personality of Cyprian himself. A century later Cyprian was regarded with veneration by both Donatists and Catholics. The anniversary of his martyrdom was kept by both with equal enthusiasm.[4] The Catholics esteemed him as an example of ecclesiastical discipline and charity, to whom the unity of the Church had in practice meant more than the illusion of purity in its visible membership.[5] Augustine cites Cyprian's letter to the Confessors (*Ep.* 54) in three separate anti-Donatist works. In this, Cyprian denies the right of any man to separate himself from what he thinks to be 'tares' or 'earthen vessels' in the Church. Freedom to make good belonged to every soul.[6] One may also see an affinity between the views expressed by Cyprian in his letter to the confessor Florentius, and Augustine's sermon to the Donatist congregation at Caesarea in 418. Both stressed the impossibility of salvation outside the discipline of the Catholic Church. All else was possible—suffering, martyrdom, good works, divine service—and all else was equally valueless.[7]

---

[1] For instance, in *Passio Montani*, 13, Lucius 'de sua gloria nec sub ipsa passione praesumere', and *Passio Mariani*, 1, 'in notitiam fraternitatis per nos iusserunt, non quod in terris vellent coronae suae gloriam per iactantiam praedicari'.

[2] *Acta Proconsularia*, i, shows that Cyprian explicitly forbade this practice.

[3] *Vita Cypriani*, i, 'Cypriani tanti sacerdotis et tanti martyris passio praeteriretur, qui et sine martyrio habuit quae doceret.' Cf. A. Harnack, 'Das Leben Cyprians von Pontius' (*TU.* xxxix, 1913, p. 33).   [4] Augustine, *Ep.* 108. 3. 9.

[5] Id. *De Baptismo Contra Donatistas*, v. 23; *Ep.* 93. 41.

[6] Ibid. 108. 10; *Contra Cresconium*, ii. 43; and *Contra Gaudentium*, ii. 3. Cited from Benson, op. cit., p. 174.

[7] Cyprian, *Ep.* 66; Augustine, *Sermo ad Plebem Ecclesiae Caesareensis*, 8. See a valuable chapter on 'Saint Augustine's Doctrine of the Church', by G. G. Willis, in *Saint Augustine and the Donatist Controversy*, S.P.C.K., 1950, in which the author compares Cyprian's and Augustine's views on the nature of the unity of the Church.

On the other hand, the Donatists saw in Cyprian not merely the bishop and martyr but the supreme authority whose teaching provided a complete justification for their breach with Caecilian.[1] The decision of Cyprian's Council at Carthage in 256 was always quoted in defence of the practice of rebaptism. Very early in the controversy the Donatists seem to have put together a collection of Cyprian's letters to justify their attitude on the virtues of martyrdom and asceticism and the necessity of removing an unworthy bishop.[2] The Donatists regarded Cyprian himself as the perfect example of a bishop, whose martyrdom showed that his views had divine sanction. 'His merit is acknowledged by all and his doctrine is orthodox',[3] they told Augustine.

Where does the truth lie? It seems that the real measure of Cyprian's greatness is to be found in his own reconciliation of potentially rival conceptions of the Church. His power was derived from an ability to combine the qualities of episcopacy with those of spiritual enthusiasm. Originally a wealthy pagan advocate, with the repute of being a magician, he was nevertheless called to his high office by the acclamation of the people.[4] An upholder of a rigid and almost pagan sacerdotalism, he allowed his decisions to be guided by dreams and visions.[5] He surrounded himself with visionaries and ecstatics, and, like Donatus after him, he believed that he received his instructions direct from 'his Lord'.[6] Tertullian, and the puritan moral creed which he had represented, remained his spiritual guide throughout his life.[7] As Harnack points out, he held command of the two greatest powers existing in the Church, that of the Spirit

---

[1] Augustine, *De Baptismo contra Donatistas*, ii. 1. 2 (*PL.* xliii, col. 126); *Liber Genealogus*, i (Codex Florentinus, ed. Mommsen, *MGH.*, p. 160). Donatist dances round Cyprian's tomb on the anniversary of his martyrdom (Augustine, *Sermo* 311. 5).

[2] R. Reitzenstein, 'Ein donatistisches Corpus cyprianischer Schriften', *Nachrichten von der königlichen Gesellschaft zu Göttingen, phil.-hist. Klasse*, 1914, Heft 4, pp. 85–92. Also, K. Mengis, *Ein donatistisches Corpus cyprianischer Briefe*, Freiburg, 1916. That the Donatists in Hippo possessed such, Augustine, *De Baptismo*, I. i. 1.

[3] Augustine, *De Baptismo*, II. i. 2, 'Cyprianus, inquiunt, cujus tantum meritum novimus tantamque doctrinam.'

[4] *Vita Cypriani*, 5. On Cyprian as a magician, Prudentius, *Peristephanon*, xiii, ll. 21–4 (*CSEL.* lxi. 424). He was 'doctissimus artibus sinistris'.

[5] *Ep.* 57. 5, 'placuit nobis sancto spiritu suggerente et Domino per visiones multas et manifestas admonente . . .' (pardoning the lapsed). Also *Ep.* 16. 4 and 66. 10. For Donatus' visions, Augustine, *Ad Catholicos Epistola*, 19. 49.

[6] *Ep.* 66. 9.

[7] Jerome, *De Viris Illustribus*, 53 (ed. Richardson, *TU.* xviii. 31).

and that of episcopal office.[1] We may perhaps borrow the term used by the African confessors and the Proconsul at Cyprian's final trial, and call him the first 'Pope'.[2]

His central idea was the unity of the Church, expressing itself through a federation of bishops, all of whom were equally possessed and guided by the Spirit.[3] The Apostles had been bishops, and therefore their successors were the rulers of the Church.[4] As God's representatives they could judge His people *vice Christi*, and conversely they themselves could appeal, as the Numidian bishops did in 305, to the 'Judgement of God'.[5] Probably the clearest expression of Cyprian's views is to be found in his opening statement to his assembled colleagues at Carthage in September 256. 'It remains that upon this same matter [the validity of baptism given outside the Church] each of us should bring forward what we think, judging no man, nor rejecting any from the right of communion if he should think differently from us. For neither does any of us set himself up as a bishop of bishops, nor by tyrannical terror does any compel his colleague to the necessity of obedience; since every bishop, according to the allowance of his liberty and power, has his own proper right of judgement, and can no more be judged by another than he himself can judge another. But let us all wait for the judgement of our Lord Jesus Christ, who is the only one that has the power both of preferring us in the government of His Church, and of judging us in our conduct there.'[6] In the last resort, it was the Holy Spirit directing the ways of the Church

---

[1] A. Harnack, 'Cyprian als Enthusiast', *Zeitschrift für die neutestamentliche Wissenschaft*, iii, 1902, p. 182.

[2] *Ep.* 23; *Acta Proconsularia*, 3, Galerius Maximus Proconsul dixit, 'Tu papam te sacrilegae mentis hominibus praebuisti.'

[3] *De Unitate Ecclesiae*, 5 (*CSEL.* 213), 'Quam unitatem tenere firmiter et vindicare debemus, maxime episcopi qui in ecclesia praesidemus, ut episcopatum quoque ipsum unum atque indivisum probemus.' On Cyprian's view of the Roman primacy, I have followed H. Koch ('Cyprian und der Römische Primat', *TU.* xxxv. 1, 1910, 137 ff.), though the fact that Cyprian at one time held a decidedly 'papal' view is suggested by M. Bévenot, 'St. Cyprian's "De Unitate", chap. 4', *Analecta Gregoriana*, xi, 1938, 54 ff. For a summary of Cyprian's attitude, Lebreton–Zeiller, op. cit., pp. 206–9.

[4] *Ep.* 45. 3 (*CSEL.* 602), 'et laborare debemus ut unitatem a Domino et per Apostolos nobis successoribus traditam . . . .' Cf. *Ep.* 3. 3.

[5] *Ep.* 59. 5 and 55. 21.

[6] Cyprian's opening address to the Council of Carthage, 1 Sept. 256. Cited from *The Writings of Cyprian* (ed. Roberts and Donaldson, Ante-Nicene Christian Library, ii, p. 200). The text has been preserved in Augustine, *De Baptismo Contra Donatistas*, bks. vi and vii. It has been reconstructed by Hartel, *CSEL*. iii. i, pp. 433 ff.,

through bishops assembled in Council, and not the *fiat* of any individual bishop, even Peter's successor, the Bishop of Rome, that must prevail. Eighty years later Donatus allowed himself to be overruled in a Council on the same issue, and saw no reason to excommunicate those who dissented from his own views.[1]

This equality, however, was an equality among the bishops. It did not extend to the rest of the clergy, still less to the laity. The worst offence a Christian could commit was to be an 'enemy of the priests'.[2] This automatically branded him as a rebel against the Catholic Church. Cyprian made this clear to the confessors. He had already during his retirement written to his clergy that the 'glory of a confession of faith belonged to the Church as a whole', and that the 'principal share belonged to the bishop who was the Church's chief representative'. 'For although,' he stated, 'all the brethren ought to rejoice at this [the confession of Rogatian and his companions], yet in the common gladness the share of the bishop is greatest, for the glory of the Church is the glory of the bishop.'[3] On his return to Carthage at Easter 251 the Council which he summoned rejected all claims by the confessors to remit penances to the lapsed and laid down terms by which the latter could regain membership of the Church.[4]

The decision of this Council and that which followed the recurrence of the persecution in 252 had two important and contradictory results. On the one hand, it implied that the visible Church was to some extent a 'mixed body'. If *libellatici* could be readmitted, then the Church must also contain sinners as well as the righteous. That Cyprian was aware of this difficulty is suggested by a passage in the *De Lapsis*, where he maintained that for the sake of unity and peace some unworthy prelates had to be tolerated and left for divine censure. Confessors,

and H. von Soden, 'Sententiae LXXXVII Episcoporum', *Nachrichten von der kgl. Gesellschaft zu Göttingen*, 1909, pp. 247–307.

[1] See below, p. 168.

[2] Cyprian, *Ep.* 59. 4, 'qui sacerdotum hostes et contra ecclesiam catholicam rebelles'; *De Unitate*, xvii. 15. Cf. Willis, op. cit., pp. 97 ff.

[3] *Ep.* 13. 1 (*CSEL*. iii. 2. 504–5), 'nam cum gaudere in hoc omnes fratres oportet, tunc in gaudio communi maior est episcopi portio. Ecclesiae enim gloria praepositi gloria est.'

[4] Benson, *Cyprian*, pp. 158–9. The *libellatici* were to be subjected to individual inquiry as to their motives as well as to the facts. The *sacrificati* would be restored *in articulo mortis*.

as we have noted, had no right to separate themselves even from 'vessels of earth' in the Church. The Lord would divide the just and the unjust in due time.[1]

In the long run these ideas would mean the end of the concept of the Christian Church as an exclusive and austere body of the elect. As Augustine was quick to point out, the Church on earth was a mixed community extending throughout the world, united through common participation in the Sacraments. There would be no separation of the wheat from the tares until the Last Day.[2] Meantime, both must grow together. But Cyprian would have shrunk from this conclusion. Perhaps he drew a distinction in his mind between secular crimes such as oppressing one's neighbour and extorting high rates of interest, and ritual sins which were against the Holy Spirit. On individual cases he would consult his colleagues. There *might seem* to be tares in the Church.[3] That was all. The mercy shown to a penitent layman was not a free pass for fallen or heretical clergy.

Equally important, however, was the second conclusion which could be drawn from these early Councils. The readmission of the lapsed automatically involved a claim by the bishops in Council to be empowered to remit deadly sins, the *tria capitula* referred to by Tertullian.[4] These included adultery and apostasy. Some of the African bishops, notably a certain Antonian, who were otherwise loyal to Cyprian, dissented.[5] Once again, agreement to leave such differences to God was invoked. But the necessary consequence of this theory as it appeared at that time was that the bishops themselves must be personally in a state of grace. If not, the Holy Spirit could not speak through them, and their decisions would accordingly be null and void. No cleric could give what he himself did not possess. The Church, therefore, must be 'pure' as well as all-embracing.

---

[1] *De Lapsis*, 6, and *Ep.* 54. 3. Quoted by Augustine against the Donatists in *Contra Cresconium*, ii. 18 and iii. 40, and *De Baptismo*, iv. 9. 12.

[2] Augustine, *Breviculus Collationis*, iii. 8. 14; 9. 15; *Ep.* 93. 15; and *Gesta Coll. Carth.* iii. 269.

[3] *Ep.* 54. 3 (*CSEL.* iii. 2. 622), 'Nam etsi videntur in ecclesia esse zizania, non tamen inpediri debet aut fides aut caritas nostra ut quoniam zizania esse in ecclesia cernimus, ipsi de ecclesia recedamus. . . . Ceterum fictilia vasa confringere Domino solo concessum est.' Cf. Augustine, *Contra Cresconium*, ii. 38. 48; iii. 31. 35; iv. 56. 67.

[4] *Ep.* 75. 16 (Firmilian's opinion) (*CSEL.* 821), 'potestas ergo peccatorum remittendorum apostolis data est et ecclesiis quas illi a Christo missi constituerunt et episcopis qui eis ordinatione vicaria successerunt'.

[5] *Ep.* 55. 21.

The difficulties inherent in these two concepts could hardly be avoided once the Church ceased to be a persecuted minority.

Events conspired to throw Cyprian's attitude into sharper relief. In the first place, once the initial enthusiasm of Novatianism had subsided many Christians regretted being in schism from the Church governed by Cyprian. Some had been converted by the Novatianists, and the question arose whether baptism administered by persons outside the Catholic Church could be recognized as valid. Secondly, there was the problem of sacraments dispensed by a cleric in deadly sin and from whom the Holy Spirit must have departed. In 254 the congregations of the Spanish churches of Emerita (Merida) and Legio (León) appealed to Cyprian for advice as to whether sacraments given by their lapsed bishops were valid.[1] The new Bishop of Rome, Stephen, had been persuaded to restore these men to their offices and had enjoined the Christian communities to obey them.[2]

The dispute between Cyprian supported by the African bishops and Stephen supported equally firmly by the Roman tradition foreshadows the Donatist and Catholic standpoints of the following century. Stephen maintained that the Novatianists employed the same forms as those of the Catholic Church, and, moreover, were not separated by any difference of doctrine.[3] Their baptism was therefore valid. In addition, there was no reason for objecting to sacraments dispensed by the bishops of Legio and Emerita. The minister was simply the channel used for the administration of Divine Grace. The Sacrament itself was holy even if administered by a Marcionite.[4] It is interesting that Stephen and those who agreed with him quoted the same texts, such as Philippians i. 18 ('Whether in pretence or truth, Christ is preached'), in justification of their views as Augustine used in his anti-Donatist works.[5]

---

[1] *Ep.* 67. The appeal reached Cyprian in the autumn of 254.
[2] Ibid. 5. Stephen had succeeded Lucius as Bishop of Rome in May 254.
[3] His view can be reconstructed from Cyprian's *Ep.* 71, 73, and 74. See T. G. Jalland, *The Church and the Papacy*, pp. 168–78. I find it difficult, however, to follow Jalland's view that Cyprian's opening speech in the Council of 256 was directed at his opponents in Africa and not against Pope Stephen. Cyprian seems to have been on friendly terms in his correspondence with the African bishops who disagreed with him. With Stephen he was not; and it was against him that he called for support.
[4] *Ep.* 73. 4.
[5] *Ep.* 73. 14. Cf. Augustine, *De Baptismo*, iv. 7. 10 and vii. 50. 98.

These views were rejected by Cyprian and his colleagues, though a section of the Numidian and Mauretanian clergy felt some difficulty in repudiating Novatianist baptisms.[1] In a series of letters written in 255 and 256 Cyprian defined his attitude, and this received its formal endorsement in the unanimous opinion of the eighty-seven bishops who attended his Council at Carthage on 1 September 256. The best documents from which to study Cyprian's ideas are Letter 67 to the congregations of Legio and Emerita, and Letter 73 to Bishop Jubaianus. Both these were included, with good reason, by the Donatists in their various collections of Cyprianic works.[2]

The letter to the Spanish communities teaches the necessity of separating from an evil pastor who was by definition incapable of administering true sacraments.[3] If a cleric had not been duly elected by clergy and people, was not of moral integrity, and not in unity with his fellow bishops, he automatically ceased to be bishop, and another must be elected in his stead. The Church was 'a closed garden' whence profane elements were excluded. The clergy were the spiritual fathers of every member of their flock and responsible for their fate in the Day of Judgement. Thus the conscience of the priest who administered the sacraments was of prime importance for the welfare of his people. No priest could approach God's altar in an impure state. 'If a priest is spotted with vice and sin, how can his prayers be heard by God?'[4] He could in fact actually baptize his people into hell, for his evil was contagious.[5] The duty of a congregation faced with the presence of an apostate or schismatic bishop was to break with him and elect a worthier successor. There was no distinction between schism and apostasy or other forms of spiritual evil. All were equally outside the Church. Thus Donatus and Secundus of Tigisis were to break with Caecilian fifty years later, and thus the Maximianists were to claim against Primian and his adherents in 393.

The Donatists employed the same arguments. As Petilian of

---

[1] For instance, in 255 eighteen Numidian bishops ask whether the practice of rebaptizing heretics did not need reconsideration. The same point was made by Quintus, a Mauretanian bishop (Cyprian, *Ep.* 71).

[2] Reitzenstein, *Ein donatistisches Corpus cyprianischer Schriften*, p. 86; Willis, op. cit., p. 103.

[3] *Ep.* 67.

[4] Ibid. 1. Cf. *Ep.* 65. 2 and 69.2. For Cresconius the Donatist's use of the same metaphor, Augustine, *Contra Cresconium*, iv. 63. 77, 'Si conclusus est hortus . . .'.

[5] *Ep.* 67. 3. Cf. *Ep.* 65. 4.

Constantine stated, the bishop was the 'head and root' of every Christian.[1] *Traditor* bishops and their successors were spiritually dead, and therefore 'he that is washed [in baptism] by one who is dead, his washing profiteth him nothing'.[2] It was not that individuals were baptized twice but that the sacrament given by a *traditor* or persecutor was not baptism at all.[3] It was mere perversity to believe that one who was 'guilty through his own sins could make another free from guilt'.[4]

The letter to Jubaianus[5] deals more specifically with the question of rebaptism. It seems that this bishop in Mauretania enclosed a letter which may have survived under the title *Auctor de Rebaptismate*. In this, the writer suggested that the operation of God through baptism could not be confined within the bounds of the true Church. His grace might flow outside it.[6] A century later, Tyconius and Augustine were to argue along the same lines. Cyprian, however, pointed out that rebaptism was no new custom in the Church. Heretics being enemies of the Church could not possibly possess the Holy Spirit and the Church's baptism. Possessing nothing themselves they must receive baptism anew when they entered the true Church.

In the summer of 256 Cyprian summoned the bishops of North Africa to meet at Carthage for a Council which was to open on 1 September. Eighty-seven came, from the Proconsular Province, from Numidia, and from Mauretania, accompanied by priests and laity. It was probably the last time that the African Church was to meet in a single undivided assembly. The record has survived, thanks in part to the use made by the Donatists of the results. It is a tribute to the practical genius and piety of Cyprian. The proceedings were opened by the president reading his correspondence with Bishop Jubaianus and a letter to Stephen. Then every prelate, probably in order of seniority, gave his view. Their opinions were expressed in much the same

---

[1] Augustine, *Contra Litteras Petiliani*, i. 5. 6 (*PL.* xliii, col. 248), 'Qui fidem a perfido sumpserit, non fidem percipit, sed reatum. Omnis enim res origine et radice consistit, et si caput non habet aliquid, nihil est.'

[2] Ibid. ii. 7. 14, 'Qui baptizatus a mortuo; non ei prodest lavatio eius.' Donatus himself used this same quotation from the African Bible's version of Ecclesiasticus xxxiv. 30, Augustine, *Retractationes*, i. 21.

[3] *Contra Litteras Petiliani*, ii. 22. 49, 'vos quoque traditores similiter pacem et baptismum non habetis.'

[4] Ibid., ii. 35. 58.   [5] Cyprian, *Ep.* 73.

[6] *Auctor de Rebaptismate*, x; Willis, op. cit., p. 105.

form as that of Bishop Marcian at Secundus' council in 312, that is, Scriptural text, backed by argument.[1] In some, one finds the syllogisms which the Donatists were to use. For instance, Quietus of Baruch quotes Ecclesiasticus xxxiv. 30, in the same context as Petilian and Parmenian.[2] In others, there is an undertone of fear and fanaticism which foreshadows the conflicts of the next century. Two examples may be quoted as typical of the Council.

First, Caecilius of Bilta, who spoke as senior bishop directly after Cyprian's address.

> I know only one baptism in the church, and none out of the church. This one will be here, where there is the true hope and the certain faith. For thus, it is written: 'One faith, one hope, one baptism' (*Eph.* iv. 5), not among heretics, where there is no hope, and the faith is false, where all things are carried on by lying; where a demoniac exorcises, where one whose mouth and words send forth a cancer puts the sacramental interrogation; the faithless gives faith; the wicked bestows pardon for sins; and Antichrist baptises in the name of Christ; he who is cursed of God blesses; the blasphemer calls upon God; the profane person administers the office of the priesthood; the sacrilegious person establishes an altar. In addition to all these things, there is also this evil, that the priests of the devil dare to celebrate the Eucharist; or else let those that stand by them say that all these things concerning heretics are false. Behold to what kind of things the church is compelled to consent, and is constrained without baptism, without pardon of sins, to hold communion. And this thing, brethren, we ought to flee from and avoid, and to separate ourselves from so great a wickedness, and to hold one baptism, which is granted by the Lord to the Church alone.[3]

Secondly, one of the lesser delegates, Successus of Abbir Germanicana.

> Heretics can either do nothing, or they can do all. If they can baptise, they can also bestow the Holy Spirit. But if they cannot give the Holy Spirit, because they have not it themselves, neither

---

[1] See above, p. 20.

[2] Augustine, *De Baptismo*, vi. 34. 65; *Contra Litteras Petiliani*, ii. 7. 14.

[3] Cited from *The Writings of Cyprian* (Ante-Nicene Library), ii. 200–1. Latin in Hartel, *CSEL.* iii. 1. 436–7. Cf. Petilian's choice of words on the same issue, Augustine, *Contra Litteras Petiliani*, ii. 3. 6, 4. 8, and 7. 14, and Parmenian's, *Contra Epistolam Parmeniani*, ii. 14. 32, 'Numquam divinae legis censura patietur ut vivificare quemquam mortuus possit, curare vulneratus, illuminare caecus, vestire nudus, et mundare pollutus?'

can they spiritually baptise. Therefore we judge that heretics must be baptised.[1]

The opinion of the Council was unanimous. Against Stephen's threats the Africans found support in the Churches of Asia Minor. It is interesting how these two areas, geographically not dissimilar, should be developing their Christianity on parallel lines. In both, Councils had been held in favour of rebaptism of heretics,[2] in both a strong puritan element had accepted Novatianism. Both those areas, traditionally recalcitrant to classical influence, were to be strongholds of dissent.

But the issue of Carthage versus Rome was not to be pushed to extremes. In the summer of 257 Valerian renewed the persecution. On 2 August Stephen was martyred.[3] On 30 August Cyprian was summoned before the Proconsul, Aspasius Paternus, and after a short interrogation assigned an enforced residence at Curubis (Kurba, on the Gulf of Hammamet). He remained there for over a year. On 13 September 258 he was visited by two officials sent by the new proconsul, and the next day was brought to trial. A great crowd surrounded the judgement hall. The usual questions were put, and answered without hesitation. The sentence of death was met with a calm 'Deo Gratias'.[4] In the evening of 14 September Cyprian became the first bishop-martyr of Africa.

After his death, Cyprian was regarded by his friends as an example for all time of Christian 'temperies',[5] a bishop who throughout his administration had succeeded in steering a middle course between the Novatians and the confessors on the one hand, and the impenitent lapsed and intriguing presbyters on the other.[6] It is probable that he was opposed more by the puritanical elements in the Church than by the laxer. Yet he left, too, the reputation of being a proud and meddlesome man, continually experimenting in changes in ecclesiastical order.[7]

---

[1] *The Writings of Cyprian*, p. 205 (= *CSEL*. iii. 1. 443).

[2] Synnada, the site of the Council that decided in favour of rebaptism, was in the interior of Phrygia.

[3] *Liber Pontificalis* (ed. Duchesne), i. 69.

[4] *Acta Proconsularia*, 1 and 4; Lebreton–Zeiller, op. cit., pp. 209–10.

[5] *Vita*, 6, 'utrimque temperies'.

[6] Ibid. 8, 'Servatus est vir ingenii praeter cetera etiam spiritaliter temperati, qui inter resultantes conlidentium schismatum fluctus ecclesiae iter medium librato limite gubernaret.'

[7] Cf. auct. *de Rebaptismate*, 3 and 10.

Even his martyrdom did not silence the attacks.[1] Yet a closer examination of Cyprian's works has revealed something more than the orthodox ecclesiastic. It seems that he conceived the Church as a spiritual body, in which bishops and martyrs each had their appointed places. It was at once a brotherhood of the righteous and an institution presided over by bishops. In this he was both maintaining the former tradition of the Church as represented by Tertullian, and preparing the ground for the Donatists. His place in the history of Donatism may perhaps be compared to that of St. Cyril in the history of Monophysitism. Both men remained 'orthodox', and yet both could be claimed with some justice by the dissenters as the founders of their respective movements. Donatus himself was far more Cyprian's spiritual successor at Carthage than Caecilian, and it was in the Donatist Church that puritanism and emphasis on the martyr's crown combined with an awe of episcopal power were maintained. Cyprian took the leadership of the rigorist tradition in North Africa out of the hands of the ignorant confessors, where it would have perished, and made it the official policy of the Church. By his teaching, the superiority of the confessors and martyrs was maintained, and he himself by his own martyrdom preserved the glorious tradition of witness to the Lord.

[1] Cf. *Vita*, 1 and 7. The whole tendency of the *Vita* is to exalt Cyprian's 'opera' and 'merita' against attacks.

XI

CONSTANTINE AND THE DONATIST CHURCH

A.D. 312–37[1]

THE great Council of September 256 had done more than settle the question whether heretics should be rebaptized on their reconciliation, or not. It had shown that the African episcopacy was bent on maintaining the same puritan tradition and outlook that had characterized the Church a generation before. If the Church, it had then been emphasized, was indeed spread out over all the world[2] in extent and as regards its numbers, it could also be represented as a severe and exclusive body. Cyprian likened it to Noah's Ark, with the elect few saved within compared with the drowning multitudes without.[3] In the eyes of the Council it was not so much an institution as a spiritual brotherhood, with the Spirit manifesting Himself in the righteousness of the individual members of the priesthood, encouraging all to martyrdom and self-denial, abiding in them as they administered the Sacraments.

Nearly fifty years separated this Council from the outbreak of the Great Persecution. In that time great changes had taken place in the composition of the Christian Churches, changes calculated to sharpen the underlying differences between the puritan and moderate elements. Christianity was no longer confined to unprivileged and non-romanized groups. Its leaders were being drawn from all classes. The number of bishoprics had increased greatly. In the towns it was not possible for the Christians to break with the world, for the world itself was becoming Christian. By the turn of the fourth century, while

[1] Sources on this period in the history of Donatism: (a) L. Duchesne, 'Le Dossier du Donatisme', *Mélanges*, x, 1890, pp. 589–650; (b) Hans v. Soden, *Urkunden der Entstehungsgeschichte des Donatismus* (Kleine Texte 122, Bonn, 1913); (c) P. Monceaux, *Histoire littéraire*, iv, chap. 1; (d) N. H. Baynes, 'Constantine the Great and the Christian Church' (*Proc. of the British Academy*, 1929).

[2] Cf. Cyprian, *De Unitate Ecclesiae*, 5 (*CSEL*. iii. 1. 214), 'Sic et ecclesia Domini, luce perfusa per orbem totum radios suos porrigit.' Cited by Augustine, *Contra Cresconium*, iii. 65. 75.

[3] *Ep.* 74. 15 (*CSEL*. iii. 2. 809). For this as the Donatist view, cf. Augustine, *Ep.* 93. 27 and *Ad Catholicos Epistola*, v. 9 (*PL*. xliii. 397).

the theory of Church discipline remained as severe as it had been in the time of Cyprian, its practice tended to sink to the standard of the laxer members. When the Persecution broke out in the spring of 303 a large proportion of clergy and congregations hastened to sacrifice and surrender the Scriptures without evident fear of the consequences hereafter.

More serious from the point of view of the puritans was that the leaders of the Church at Carthage not merely were pliant towards the authorities, but actually decried the spiritual virtues which had been rooted in popular Christian sentiment for more than a century. Had Mensurius and Caecilian been content to restrain fanatics from rushing to their doom, or had they counselled prudent flight during the worst of the persecution, it is doubtful whether public opinion would have been so incensed. Cyprian had done no less himself. But these prelates seem to have cast doubts on the value of martyrdom as a means of securing forgiveness of sins.[1] Claimants to martyrdom were being carefully investigated before their virtues were acknowledged. The clerics pressed their views to their logical conclusion by driving off the crowds who were keeping vigil outside the prisons. No merit could be attached to watching round those whose deaths were in any case of little value—until they had been 'vindicated' by some competent ecclesiastical authority.[2]

In abandoning this aspect of North African Christian tradition the Carthaginian leaders could hardly help denying other cherished notions held by the Confessor party, such as the necessity of rebaptizing the lapsed, or those baptized by heretics. The Sacrament could only be lost to the individual in a Church which regarded itself as a body of the elect on earth. It was not the case in an organization which admitted that it was a 'mixed body' containing both good and evil. Lapse during persecution was no doubt a regrettable moral failure, but not a crime that automatically put the delinquent outside the Church until solemnly readmitted. The fifty years that separate Cyprian from the Great Persecution had brought the Carthaginian clergy firmly on the side of Rome on the question of rebaptism.

The election of Caecilian as Bishop of Carthage in succession

---

[1] Contrast the view suggested by Cyprian, *Testimonia*, iii. 16 (*CSEL*. iii. 1. 128–32), 'Liberat de malis animam martyr fidens', with Augustine's sceptical comment, 'et quasi abluere facinora sua' on the beliefs of imprisoned confessors at Carthage (*Breviculus Collationis*, iii. 13. 25 (*PL*. xliii. 638)). See above, p. 7.

[2] For instance, Lucilla's martyr was 'necdum vindicatus' (Optatus, i. 16).

to Mensurius in 312 was a victory not only for those who considered that compromise with the world was justified, but also for those who were prepared seriously to modify the teaching of Cyprian. If unchallenged, this would have entailed a complete break with the predominant doctrinal trends in the previous history of the African Church. The whole edifice of dogma and discipline laboriously established under Cyprian was in danger of collapse.

This threat to past traditions might well have succeeded, had it been opposed by the Carthaginian populace alone. The protests of the Abitinian martyrs could have proved as ineffectual as the activities of the illiterate confessors of Cyprian's day. But at this moment more powerful forces were arrayed in their defence. During the previous forty years Numidia had not merely become Christian, but had begun to exercise sufficient influence to attain ecclesiastical autonomy from Carthage. In 252, in a letter to Pope Cornelius, Cyprian had described his ecclesiastical province as including both Numidia and Mauretania.[1] There is in fact no mention of a Numidian primate in Cyprian's letters, and Cyprian seems to correspond with and give instruction to the Numidian clergy with the same assurance as he does to his own bishops in Proconsular Africa. But by A.D. 305 all this had changed. Secundus of Tigisis held an acknowledged position as Primate of Numidia,[2] and that he had some claim to consecrate the new Bishop of Carthage was never refuted by the Catholics. The Numidians threw their full weight on to the side of the opponents of Caecilian. It was the combination of Numidian leadership with the fanaticism of the Carthaginian lower classes that made Donatism possible.

The Church in Numidia, so far as one can tell, had always been rigorist.[3] In the 250's the Numidian bishops had been among those who held Cyprian's powers as a seer and a visionary in the highest esteem.[4] After their pro-Novatianist

---

[1] *Ep.* 48. 3 (*CSEL.* iii. 2. 607), 'Sed quoniam latius fusa est nostra provincia, habet etiam Numidiam et Mauretaniam sibi cohaerentes.'

[2] Augustine, *Breviculus Collationis*, iii. 13. 25.

[3] There is some evidence for a similar rigorist outlook in Mauretania at that time. At Caesarea clergy were buried round a martyr's tomb, and the inscription recording this has a severely exclusive ring: *CIL.* viii. 9585, 9586, 'Salvete fratres puro corde et simplici | Euelpius vos sa(lu)to *sancto spiritu* | *Eclesia fratruum* hunc restituit titulum.'

[4] As, for instance, in *Ep.* 78. 2. Cyprian's letters were 'filled with the Holy Spirit'.

L

scruples had been quieted they had been among his staunchest supporters in the Rebaptism Controversy, and, when called upon, they had gone unhesitatingly to martyrdom.[1] Their views of the Roman magistrates were those of the previous generation of martyrs and confessors,[2] and in their correspondence with Cyprian during the persecution under Valerian, one first comes across the use of the watchword 'Deo laudes' connected with the martyr's faith.[3] Now, in contrast to that of the Church of Carthage, the outlook of the Numidian clergy had not altered. The correspondence of Secundus of Tigisis with Mensurius in 303–4 and the Protocol of the Council of Cirta both illustrate this point. The Numidian bishops, moreover, were supported by a population who had accepted Christianity in its most intense forms. It seems they were prepared to forgive their bishops any personal weakness, so long as they showed themselves in public to be apostles of violence and leaders towards martyrdom. In 312, when Caecilian was declared Bishop of Carthage, the balance of forces between the puritanical and laxer parties in the African Church was just about even.

Meantime, news of the unsettled conditions in Africa had reached the Emperor Constantine in Milan. Material considerations, principally the need of provisioning Rome and Italy with oil and cereals from Africa, made the restoration of quiet extremely urgent. The new Emperor started with the advantage of being personally popular in Africa. The excesses of Maxentius' commanders had not been forgotten, and Carthage and Cirta had hastened to establish priesthoods in honour of the *gens Flavii*. Constantine set in hand the restoration of Cirta and renamed the city Constantina (modern Constantine).[4] Nevertheless, the goodwill of the Africans was liable to be fickle, and the Emperor evidently judged that the ecclesiastical dispute needed to be dealt with immediately.

---

[1] *Ep.* 76–79.

[2] They saw the Roman authorities as the Devil himself. Cyprian, *Ep.* 77. 2. It is interesting how often the three youths Ananias, Azarias, and Misael, who defied Nebuchadnezzar, are represented on Christian lamps in Numidia. For the connexion of this story with persecution at this period, Cyprian, *Ep.* 58. 5.

[3] *Ep.* 78. 2.

[4] Aurelius Victor, *De Caesaribus*, 41. An inscription from Lambaesis hails Constantine as 'the author of perpetual liberty and security' (*CIL.* viii. 7005 to 7010). Constantine's letter to Miltiades in the summer of 313 (Eusebius, *Hist. Ecc.* x. 5), after referring to the 'spontanea deditione' of the provinces, shows that he feared riots among the 'very numerous African populace' if the dispute were not settled quietly.

Without waiting to hear what the opposition had to say, Constantine decided that Caecilian was the rightful Bishop of Carthage. Probably while in Rome during the winter of 312-13, he instructed Ursus, the *rationalis* (financial officer) in charge of the Imperial Estates in Africa, to put 3,000 *folles* at Caecilian's disposal. In addition, Caecilian was authorized to apply to Heraclides the *procurator* of the Imperial Estates if he needed more. At the same time, lands of the Church which had found their way into the possession of the city councils and others during the Persecution were to be restored.[1] In letters addressed to Anulinus, Proconsul of Africa,[2] and Patritius the *Vicarius praefectorum* (deputy prefect) Constantine pointed out that he 'had heard of the attempts of some irresponsible individuals to corrupt the congregation of the most holy and Catholic Church with vile and base falsifications', and he ordered that any found 'suffering under this vain and bastard delusion' should be haled before the justices.[3] Caecilian himself was informed by the Emperor of what he had done, and assured that he was regarded as the 'representative of the most holy Catholic religion'.[4]

One may well ask why it was that Constantine so prejudged the issues. A possible clue is the fact that even at this time he was under the influence of Hosius, bishop of Corduba (modern Cordova). Throughout the controversy, the Donatists maintained that the Emperor had been prejudiced against them by this adviser. They pointed to the fact that Hosius had himself been forced to quit his see, and had been condemned by a Council of Spanish bishops, though later he had been rehabilitated by a Gallic Council.[5] The impression they wished to leave was that Hosius was for some reason hostile to their cause and was himself suspect. Certain it is that Hosius could not have sustained the role he assumed in the Arian controversy if he had

---

[1] Eusebius, *Historica Ecclesiastica* (ed. Schwartz, Leipzig 1908), x. 5. 15-17. Constantine was in Rome from 28 Oct. 312 to 17 Jan. 313.

[2] This Anulinus was Proconsul in 313 (Pauly–Wissowa, i. 2, col. 2561; Pallu de Lessert, *Fastes des Provinces africaines*, ii, pt. ii, pp. 18-19).

[3] Eusebius, *Hist. Ecc.* x. 6, 'καὶ ἐπειδὴ ἐπυθόμην τινὰς μὴ καθεστώσης διανοίας τυγχάνοντας ἀνθρώπους τὸν λαὸν τῆς ἁγιωτάτης καὶ καθολικῆς ἐκκλησίας φαύλῃ τινὶ ὑπονοθεύσει βούλεσθαι διαστρέφειν'.

[4] Eusebius, *Hist. Ecc.* x. 6, 'τῆς ἁγιωτάτης καθολικῆς θρησκείας'.

[5] *Contra Epistolam Parmeniani*, i. 4. 7, and i. 5. 10. The date of this Council is not known. After leaving Spain, Hosius evidently gained access to Constantine's court at Trier, and accompanied him on his campaign against Maxentius. By the end of 312 he was one of the Emperor's most trusted advisers.

ever been suspected of heresy, and one is left with the possibility of there being some incident during the Persecution which had alienated him from the Spanish Christians. Perhaps he himself had once felt the severity of the confessors' creed, though in later years he claimed to have been a confessor himself.[1]

In any case, Hosius was considered to have influenced the Emperor against the opposition to Caecilian. In March/April 313 Constantine took a further step which was to render it difficult for him to assume the role of arbiter later on. In a second letter to Anulinus he showed that he not only recognized Caecilian as bishop of Carthage, but was prepared to exempt all clergy in communion with him from municipal *munera*.[2] This, as we know, was an extremely important concession. It meant that from then on the Caecilianist clergy would be free from municipal levies, and would not be called upon to pledge their property against the city's quota of taxation. One sees in this step an instance of how the Emperor's policy of supporting the traditional social structure of the Empire was coming into conflict with his new-found zeal for the Christian Church. The priesthood soon became a refuge eagerly sought by the curial class.[3]

For the opponents of Caecilian the situation at once became more serious. Orthodoxy now brought with it financial privileges, and it was therefore desirable to avoid a direct sentence of unorthodoxy. Opinion rose against Caecilian and his supporters. In the words of a Donatist pamphleteer,[4] 'the Devil rewarded the lapsed clergy not only with the restoration of ecclesiastical honours, but also with royal friendship and earthly riches'. The Donatist appeal was hardly 'unprovoked', as Augustine would have his readers believe.[5]

The opposition decided to approach Constantine himself.[6]

[1] Letter written by Hosius to Constantius II in 357. Quoted by Athanasius, *Historia Arianorum*, 44. 1 (*PG.* xxv, col. 744).

[2] Eusebius, *Hist. Ecc.* x. 7; N. H. Baynes, *Constantine the Great*, pp. 68–69.

[3] *Cod. Theod.* xvi. 2. 3 (8 July 320 to Bassus).

[4] *Passio Donati* (*PL.* viii. 752–8, at col. 754), '(diabolus) non solum oblectans inani gloria miseros, sed et regali amicitia muneribusque terrenis circumscribens avaros'.

[5] Augustine, *Contra Epistolam Parmeniani*, 1. 5. 10, 'ultro fassus suos ipsos adivisse etiam Constantinum'. Similarly, *Ep.* 105. 2. 10.

[6] There was the precedent for Christians to appeal to the Emperor in an ecclesiastical dispute provided by the case of Paul of Samosata in 272. But there is nothing to show that this played any part in either Donatus' or Constantine's calculations.

On 15 April 313, 'a few days after' he had received the Emperor's order to exempt the Caecilianist clergy from the *munera*, the Proconsul was met by a crowd of Caecilian's opponents. The leaders handed him two packages. The first was sealed, and the second open. The one bore the title 'A document of the Catholic Church containing charges brought against Caecilian by the party of Majorinus'. The other was a brief petition:

> We appeal to you, good Emperor Constantine, for you come of a just lineage. Your father, unlike the other Emperors, had never persecuted, and Gaul remained free from that crime. In Africa quarrels have arisen between us and the other bishops. We appeal to your Piety to send us judges from Gaul. Given by Lucian, Dignus, Fidentius, Nasutius and Capito.

Anulinus duly forwarded both documents to Constantine.[1]

This is one of the decisive moments in the history of the early Church. Appeal had been made to the State in the person of a Christian Emperor. For the first time schism or unorthodoxy could become an offence punishable by law. The 'secular arm' stood at the disposal of whoever could prove himself orthodox. Constantine's Instruction to Anulinus was thus one of the major steps which brought about the alliance between Catholic Church and Roman Empire.

Constantine was at first very angry at this unforeseen consequence of his concession to the Caecilianists, but he decided to grant the petitioners at least part of their request. Anulinus was required to send Caecilian with ten bishops together with an equal number of his opponents to Rome.[2] There, the case could be judged by Bishop Miltiades, himself an African, and a certain Marcus,[3] having as assessors three Gallic bishops,

---

[1] The whole incident is related by Anulinus in his report to Constantine, dated 15 Apr. 313, and reproduced by Augustine, *Ep.* 88. 2 (*CSEL.* xxxiv. 408). The text of the petition is given in Optatus, i. 22, though this includes an additional final phrase 'et ceteris episcopis partis Donati'. Majorinus, however, was still alive. It is possible that Donatus himself was coming increasingly to the fore and had let his name be associated with the petition, though the addition looks like a gloss by the compiler of the dossier.

[2] Eusebius, *Hist. Ecc.* x. 5. Constantine's anger with the Donatists may have been due to a belief that they were splintering the mighty organism of the Faithful at the very moment when he was declaring his own allegiance thereto. See A. Alföldi, *The Conversion of Constantine and Pagan Rome* (trans. H. Mattingly), O.U.P., 1948, p. 50.

[3] Marcus is otherwise unknown. See Baynes, op. cit., p. 74.

Reticius of Autun, Maternus of Cologne, and Marinus of Arles.[1] Neither party appears to have raised any objection to appearing before a tribunal convoked by the Emperor. As Schwartz points out, the Lateran Council may be considered to have provided the pattern for Nicaea.[2]

Constantine informed Miltiades of his intention, and sent him copies of Anulinus' correspondence to help him in forming his judgement. As one recent writer points out, the letter reads like a minute to a civil servant. There is little sign of reverence in it.[3] Miltiades, however, appears to have used the opportunity to transform the small ecclesiastical tribunal which the Emperor convoked into a council under his presidency, dominated by Italian bishops. He summoned seven local (suburbicarian) bishops, together with eight from North Italy and three others whose sees are not known.[4] Constantine had already put the house of his wife Fausta on the Lateran at Miltiades' disposal, and it was there that the sessions opened on Wednesday, 30 September 313.[5]

Between April and October Majorinus appears to have died. Donatus of Casae Nigrae was chosen as his successor, but there was probably no time to consecrate him formally before the party set out on its way to Rome.[6] There, matters went against them. The fact that Caecilian was unpopular, and had been condemned by a Numidian Council sitting in Carthage, left the bishops unmoved. On the other hand, Donatus' own behaviour had been contrary to their views of ecclesiastical discipline. In the eyes of these Italians to sanction the rebaptism of even lapsed clergy would have been a dangerous innovation, though in fact Donatus was acting according to normal African and also Egyptian usage. At the end of the first session Donatus promised to produce witnesses to prove his charges against

[1] Baynes, loc. cit., also Optatus, i. 23.
[2] E. Schwartz, *Kaiser Constantin und die christliche Kirche*, Leipzig and Berlin, 1936, p. 78.
[3] A. H. M. Jones, *Constantine*, p. 108.
[4] Baynes's suggestion that the 'septem urbis Romae episcopi' (Optatus, i. 23) were those who probably received consecration at Rome, in contrast to the North Italian bishops, has been accepted (N. H. Baynes, *Constantine the Great*, p. 76). The sees which cannot be located are Quintiana, Ursinum, and Forum Claudii.
[5] Dating, Seeck, *Regesten*, p. 161; H. Lietzmann, *Geschichte der alten Kirche*, iii, p. 72.
[6] I have accepted Dom Chapman's reconstruction of the events (*Revue Bénédictine*, 1909, p. 23).

Caecilian, but next day he either thought better of it or, as his supporters later alleged, he was excluded from the meeting. Miltiades accordingly at the third session on 2 October passed sentence against him, Caecilian was vindicated, Donatus was condemned for disturbing discipline, rebaptizing clergy, and causing a schism. As a concession, however, ordinations which had been performed by Caecilian's opponents were allowed to stand, with the proviso that where there were rival appointments, the junior should give way and accept another congregation.[1] Miltiades could afford to be generous, for he had been able to enforce the Roman view of the validity of Orders on the Africans. The reverse suffered by Pope Stephen at the hands of Cyprian and his Council in 256 had been made good, and in Caecilian the Bishop of Rome had a dependent ally at Carthage.

Miltiades' judgement, however, was received with little satisfaction in Africa. The opposition clergy refused to accept Caecilian; rumours were spread defaming the judges.[2] Where they were strong enough the Donatists attempted to penalize their opponents by having them nominated to the city councils. Constantine's concession was quietly turned against the Catholics.[3] In Italy, though Donatus himself had been refused permission to return home,[4] his supporters felt themselves strong enough to appeal to the Emperor again. It is noticeable that neither they nor their Catholic opponents ever seem to have considered that a Papal judgement was binding. In fact, the Donatists accused Miltiades of being a *traditor* himself, and asserted that he had not heard the evidence against one of Caecilian's consecrators, Bishop Felix of Aptungi.[5] They also claimed that they had not been given Gallic judges as they had asked, and that more weight should have been given to the Council of seventy which had condemned Caecilian.

Constantine was angry and disillusioned at the appeal. He

---

[1] Optatus, i. 23; Augustine, *Ep.* 43. 5. 14–15. For the Donatist claim that they had been shut out of the proceedings, see Constantine's letter to the *Vicarius Africae* Aelafius (Ziwsa, p. 205).

[2] Augustine, *Ad Catholicos Epistola*, xviii. 46; *Contra Cresconium*, iii. 61. 67.

[3] *Codex Theodosianus*, xvi. 1. 2.

[4] C. H. Turner in *JTS.*, 1925, p. 283. I accept the rendering of Optatus, App. iii (Ziwsa, p. 205), 'ut istud post iudicium habitum Africam ipsos remeasse prohiber*em*.'

[5] Augustine, *Contra Epistolam Parmeniani*, 1. 5. 10, 'eundem Melchiadem crimine traditionis accusant'; *Ad Catholicos Epistola*, xviii. 46.

considered that the judgement of his commissioners had been fair. He was apparently scandalized at the idea of 'ministers of God wrangling among themselves like ordinary litigants'.[1] But the internal concord of the Church must be re-established for the benefit of the Empire, and Constantine gave way to the petitioners. By January 314, probably before Miltiades' death on 11 January had been reported to him, he had decided that a new Council should meet at Arles on 1 August at which all the provinces within his dominions should be represented.[2] Marinus the Bishop of Arles was to be president. Officials in the provinces were instructed to put the public posting service at the disposal of the bishops and their retinue. The decision which they were expected to give was to be regarded as final.

The directions which Aelafius, the Christian Vicar of Africa,[3] received would suggest that party feeling was running high, and that precautions were necessary to prevent the representatives of the two factions meeting on the way, or starting trouble in Carthage or Rome. Aelafius was ordered to send Caecilian and his opponents through Mauretania, and thence 'by a short sea journey' over Spain to Arles. It is certainly difficult to understand why they were not shipped from a North African port direct to Massilia. A 'short sea crossing' would hardly appear necessary on the Mediterranean in July.[4]

Meantime, the Emperor ordered an inquiry into the case of Felix of Aptungi. Was he a *traditor*, or was he not? There were many people still living, including the ex-*Duumvir* (magistrate) Alfius Caecilianus, who had held official appointments during the Persecution and who could be expected to remember what had happened in their town. These were to be called as witnesses. The record of the proceedings is preserved in a somewhat corrupt manuscript, but sufficient remains to see what took

[1] Optatus, i. 25, 'O rabida furoris audacia! Sicut in causis Gentilium fieri assolet, appellationem interposuerunt.' This phrase, however, occurs in Constantine's letter to the bishops after the Council of Arles in 314, and may have been taken out of its context by Optatus. One feels a good deal of hesitation in accepting the letter as genuine (see note 6 on p. 152).

[2] Constantine to Chrestus, Bishop of Syracuse, Eusebius, *Hist. Ecc.* x. 5. 21–22. The Emperor writes as though Miltiades were still alive.

[3] Optatus, Appendix iii (Ziwsa, p. 204).

[4] Ibid., 'data evectione publica per Africam et Mauretaniam inde ad Hispanias brevi tractu facias navigare'. See Baynes, *Constantine the Great*, p. 78. This is not a particularly satisfying explanation, for the Donatist bishops and their agents would be given a great opportunity of rallying support for their cause in Africa while on their way.

place.[1] The bitter partisan spirit which characterized the rank and file of the African Church is vividly displayed. The Donatists were determined to have Felix condemned. Before the inquiry opened, one of their agents, Ingentius, a town councillor from Zigga Ziqua (Zaghouan), had approached Alfius Caecilianus with the object of getting from him a document to the effect that Felix had burnt the Scriptures. The former *Duumvir* was not impressed by Ingentius and at first refused to see him. However, one of his friends intervened and said that Felix wanted to appropriate these valuable works for himself, and therefore needed a certificate to show that they had been burnt during the persecution. The old official was scandalized at this revelation of bad faith among Christians, but wrote a short note recording that the Scriptures and correspondence had been taken away and destroyed during the bishop's absence.[2]

This statement would not make Felix a *traditor*, and was thus of no use to Ingentius. The latter accordingly sat down and wrote a postscript. It was a childish fabrication which would not have deceived an impartial witness for a moment. In this Felix (though already stated in the letter to be absent) was supposed to have handed the keys of the church to the *Duumvir* and told him to take away the Scriptures, but for some reason added the request that the oil and wheat be left behind. Nevertheless, the Donatists used the letter, and in the preliminary inquiry before a pagan magistrate at the City Council at Carthage on 19 August 314 were able to have it certified and included in the official records.[3] Thus, even though matters were going badly for them at Arles, they were still able to hold their ground in Africa, and point to the suspicions that surrounded the person of Felix of Aptungi.

At Arles, however, their case was lost. The Gallic and other western bishops proved themselves no more sympathetic than the Italians had been in the previous year. The Donatists created a bad impression. Their representatives had included Bishops Fidentius and Capito, who were among the original petitioners to Anulinus against Caecilian, but the oratory and arguments

---

[1] Text in Ziwsa, Appendix ii, *CSEL*. xxvi. 197 ff. See also A. H. M. Jones, *Constantine*, pp. 113–15, and L. Duchesne, op. cit., pp. 90–92.

[2] *Gesta Proconsularia*, Ziwsa, p. 202.

[3] Ziwsa, p. 198, '[Volusiano] et Anniano consulibus XIIII kal. Sept.'

which roused the Numidian and Carthaginian crowds to enthusiasm merely annoyed the assembled bishops. In their report of the proceedings which they sent to Pope Silvester, they said that they found themselves dealing with dangerous men who had no respect for authority or tradition, and who could not prove any of the assertions they made. They were fit only for condemnation.[1]

Indeed, the arguments in favour of rebaptism, drawn from Cyprian's Councils, on which the Donatists may have relied, were out of date.[2] To Caecilian's supporters from Africa they had lost their force now that the Church was becoming the official religion of the Empire. The decisions of the Council were laid down in twenty-two canons. Caecilian was once more vindicated. The African custom of rebaptizing reconciled heretics was formally renounced (Canon 9).[3] Ordination by a *traditor* bishop was declared to be valid and a standard of proof was laid down as necessary before any cleric could be convicted as a *traditor* and deprived (Canon 13). Another blow at rigorist views was the clause which forbade Christians serving in the army from refusing their duty on religious grounds. The Council then turned to other topics, for example whether charioteers could be admitted to Communion, and the date of Easter.[4] The Emperor wearied of the whole affair (*taedians*) and sent them home. A few of the more moderate Donatists accepted the decision and made their peace with Caecilian; the majority, however, held firm to Donatus.[5]

Constantine may have written thanking the bishops for their work, though the letter 'Aeterna et religiosa' is not easy to accept as genuine throughout.[6] Much as he would have liked

---

[1] Optatus, Appendix iv (Ziwsa, p. 207), 'effrenatae mentis homines' and 'nulla in illis dicendi ratio subsisteret aut accusandi modus aut probatio conveniret'. Pope Silvester was represented by two legates. Bishop Marinus of Arles heads the list of signatories to the synodal letter. Caecilian had eight supporting African bishops present.

[2] I have accepted Reitzenstein's dating of the Corpus of pseudo-Cyprianic tracts which the Donatists published to justify their breach with Caecilian. The hearing before the Council of Arles would provide a motive for such a work (R. Reitzenstein, 'Ein donatistisches Corpus cyprianischer Schriften', *Nachrichten von der königlichen Gesellschaft der Wissenschaft zu Göttingen, phil.-hist. Klasse*, 1914, Heft 1, pp. 85–92).

[3] See C. H. Turner, *Ecclesiae Occidentalis Monumenta iuris antiqua*, Oxford, 1939, vol. i, fasc. ii, part ii, suppl. Niceno-Gallicum, pp. 387–8.

[4] Canons 3 and 1.   [5] Augustine, *Ep.* 88. 3.

[6] Ziwsa, pp. 208–10. The letter must have been compiled before 347, the prob-

to do so, the Emperor took no further action for the time being against the Donatists, for throughout the remainder of 314 he was engaged in war against Licinius. Opinion in Africa, however, continued to harden against the Catholic bishop. No more than in more modern communal disputes did the legal condemnation of the leaders of one of the creeds cause the defection of the mass of their following. The Berber reacted to Arles as the Copt did to Chalcedon in A.D. 451. Whatever the Emperor or foreign bishops might decree, the ordinary African was unable to grasp the fact that the Proconsuls and Imperial officials who oppressed him, and whom he had learnt to regard as emissaries of Satan, were now in 'Christian times' to be reverenced as servants of God. Nor was it right that clergy who had apostatized should be heaped with honours and restored to their rank and power. In Donatus himself the opposition found a real leader.

Very little is known about this remarkable man, who in Africa came to hold a position not unlike that achieved by his contemporary, Athanasius, in Egypt. In Donatus' case the Catholic *damnatio memoriae* has been particularly effective. His literary works have not survived, we know little of his background, his personal appearance, his friendships, and his way of life.[1] We do know that he was a great orator and leader of men; wherever he went the enthusiasm was such as to be remembered fifty years after his death.[2] In an age when religious controversy took something of the place occupied by ideological conflict in

---

able limiting date for the compilation of the Catholic *Acta* used by Optatus of Milevis. I remain unconvinced that Constantine wrote it. The tendency in the Emperor's other letters of this period on the Donatist controversy is to emphasize the need of conciliating the *summus Deus*, or the *divinitas caelestis*. References to Christ are conspicuously absent. The Emperor, moreover, is far from considering bishops as the exclusive judges in ecclesiastical disputes. His standpoint on this subject is made clear in his letter to Domitius Celsus the next year (Ziwsa, Appendix vii). One notices, too, that even Miltiades was greeted simply as 'τιμιώτατε', and not as 'frater carissime', the formula employed in this letter.

On the other hand, the allusions to Donatist 'arrogance', the activities of the Devil, and Divine Judgement could come more easily from an ecclesiastic than the Emperor. The whole letter reads like a sermon. Yet it is difficult to dismiss it as a later forgery. More likely it was drawn up by a cleric in Constantine's immediate entourage (possibly Hosius) to strike the right note at the Council.

[1] P. Monceaux, *Histoire littéraire*, v. 105 ff., has pieced together the available literary evidence which survives on Donatus.

[2] Augustine, *Enarratio in Ps. 69*, 5 (*PL*. xxxvi–xxxvii, col. 870), 'Apertissimis vocibus Donato dicuntur ista cantata, "Euge, Euge, dux bone, dux praeclare".' Cf. *Contra Cresconium*, i. 2. 3, 'eloquentiam Donati'.

providing an outlet for popular discontent, Donatus was a dominating figure. Just as the modern North African swears by 'the beard of the Prophet', so Donatus' followers swore by his 'white hairs'.[1] His writings against Caecilian were quoted in Augustine's time.[2] He seems to have personified popular loathing for the worldly ecclesiastics who thought that they would do well both in this life and the next. His own integrity and disinterestedness were acknowledged by friends and opponents alike. He was known as a religious reformer, the man who 'purged the Church of Carthage from error',[3] and at the same time was regarded by his followers as a 'seer wiser than Daniel' and a worker of miracles.[4] Donatus 'the Great' combined many of the attributes of a Moslem religious leader with a social and political cause. In his work and that of St. Augustine one sees the contrasting tendencies of North Africa in the late Roman Empire.

For the moment, however, things were against Donatus. Early in 315 the Caecilianists were able for the first time to challenge the credibility of the Donatists in Africa itself. Proceedings on the case of Felix of Aptungi had hung fire since August 314. The *Vicarius*, Aelius Paulinus, who had been originally charged with the inquiry had been replaced, and his successor Verus had fallen ill. The responsibility now lay with the Proconsul Aelian, who heard the case on 15 February 315.[5] The activities of the miserable Ingentius were unfolded and his accusations against Felix were shown to be a tissue of lies. His original aim had evidently been to shield the reputation of the Bishop of Utica whom Felix had accused of being a *traditor*. He became an impassioned opponent of the latter, and when Felix sided with Caecilian, Ingentius became one of Donatus' agents. The Caecilianist advocate Apronianus had some right to complain that his party had been the victim of terrorization and fraud. Ingentius confessed his misdeeds under threat of torture.

---

[1] Augustine, *Enarratio in Ps. 10*, 5 (*PL.* xxxvi–xxxvii, col. 134), 'per cujus canos jurant'. Cf. Optatus, iii. 3.

[2] Augustine, *Retractationes*, 1. 21 (*PL.* xxxii, cols. 617–18).

[3] Augustine, *Contra Cresconium*, iii. 56. 62, 'Cum Ecclesiae catholicae sanctitatem vir memoriae venerabilis ab errore perfidiae Donatus assereret', extract from the statement of the Donatist lawyer Nummasius in Carthage in 395. Cf. *Contra Litteras Petiliani*, ii. 39. 94, 'sobrietas Donati'.

[4] Augustine, *Ad Catholicos Epistola*, 19. 49, 'illa mirabilia fecit Donatus'. Also Petilian in *Gesta Coll. Carth.* iii. 32.

[5] *Gesta Proconsularia*, 197–204; Augustine, *Ep.* 88. 4; *Contra Cresconium*, iii. 70. 81, and *Ad Donatistas post Collationem*, 33. 56.

The Proconsul ordered his detention, and declared Felix innocent.[1] But from the point of view of vindicating Caecilian this
decision had come two years too late. Opinion was firmly on
the side of Donatus against the 'Pseudo-bishop'.[2] A rescript,
dated 25 February 315, instructing Aelian that the victims of
malicious tracts and pamphlets should not be prejudged, remained a dead letter.[3]

Meantime, no progress had been made in carrying out the
decisions arrived at in Arles. The autumn of 314 was spent in
war with Licinius and the Emperor was detained in the Danu-
bian provinces until midsummer 315. The Donatist delegates
were impatient to return to Africa. At last, on 21 July 315,
Constantine re-entered Rome to celebrate his *decennalia*.[4] The
Donatists beset him with daily appeals and requests,[5] and he
hesitated. At first he appears to have given permission for
their return to Africa and to have thought of sending officials
thither to try and find a settlement on the spot. A few days
later he changed his mind. Perhaps Donatist violence would
prevent a fair hearing from taking place. In the case of riots his
own prestige might become involved, a fact displeasing to God,[6]
Constantine claimed. In exasperation he ordered Probianus to
send the wretched Ingentius to him, so that Donatus and his
friends should hear from his own lips that their charges against
Caecilian were false.[7] But just as the whole issue, at least in its
legal aspect, seemed on the verge of being settled in his favour,
Caecilian failed to appear. There is no explanation for this, and
the Catholic writers prefer to gloss the incident over.[8] The
opportunity passed, and the Emperor began to get suspicious.
The Donatists were told that if they could prove one single

---

[1] *Gesta Proconsularia*, 204.

[2] In the *Passio Donati* (*PL*. xiii, col. 753), Caecilian is termed *Eudinepiso*. While
this might be some obscure term of abuse, the writer prefers in this case to follow
Seeck (*Untergang*, iii, p. 514) and accept a suggested emendation to 'pseudepiscopo'.

[3] *Cod. Theod.* ix. 34. 2 (dating, Seeck, *Regesten*, p. 163). In the early fifth century
the Donatists claimed that Felix had eventually been found guilty and sentenced
by a 'Proconsul Vincentius', and in any case Aelian's sentence was of no account in
an ecclesiastical dispute (Augustine, *Contra Cresconium*, iii. 69. 80, and *Ep*. 43. 4. 13).
The Donatists must have compiled their own version of the events of 313–16, but
this has been lost.   [4] Seeck, *Regesten*, p. 163.

[5] Augustine, *Contra Cresconium*, iii. 56. 67 (*PL*. xliii, col. 533), 'assiduis interpella-
tionibus accusarunt', and iii. 71. 83, 'diuturnis diebus interpellare non desistentes'.

[6] Baynes, op. cit., p. 15. I have used Baynes's chronology for this phase of the
conflict.

[7] Text of the Instruction is given by Augustine, *Contra Cresconium*, iii. 70. 81.

[8] Id. *Ep*. 43. 7. 20.

point against Caecilian, he would consider that they had gained their cause.[1] For the time being they were in favour, and some of the bishops took their chance to escape from Rome and return to Africa.

The Emperor's reaction to this move, however, was sharp. The reports which he had been receiving from Africa showed that the situation there continued to be unpromising in the extreme, and the arrival of additional Donatist firebrands would not improve it. In particular, religious strife had boiled up in Numidia. Domitius Celsus the new *Vicarius Africae* had sent a report to Constantine stating that Menalius, one of the bishops who had been present at Silvanus of Cirta's consecration in 305, was instigating anti-Caecilianist riots.[2] It was natural that precautions should be taken. The remainder of the Donatist party were put under guard and sent on to Milan, probably in the first days of October 315.[3] Constantine had left Rome on 27 September and was in Milan by 19 October.[4]

Once more the final decision was delayed. The Emperor did not stay long in the city and pressed on to Trier, where the Frankish incursions were claiming his attention.[5] The Donatists made good use of the respite, and succeeded in enlisting the support of some of the Court officials. One of them, Philumenus, who ten years later at Nicaea was one of Constantine's trusted advisers, suggested a compromise plan. For this he incurred the dislike of the Catholic apologists, and Optatus has branded him as a 'suffragator' of the Donatists.[6] Philumenus suggested that a commission of bishops should be sent to Africa to appoint a new candidate as Bishop of Carthage, Caecilian and Donatus meantime being both kept in Italy.

The proposal was accepted, and two prelates, Olympius and Eunomius, were chosen for the task and dispatched to Africa (winter 315/16).[7] They met with a hostile reception. The

[1] Optatus, Appendix vi, 'Constantinus Augustus, Episcopis: Polliceor autem vobis, quod si praesente ipso [Caeciliano] de uno tantum crimine vel facinore eius per vosmetipsos aliquid probaveritis, id apud me sit, ac si universa quae ei intenditis, probata esse videantur.'

[2] Constantine to Celsus, *Vicarius Africae* (Optatus, Appendix vii), 'Gravitatis scripta testata sunt', &c.

[3] Augustine, *Ep.* 43. 7. 20.

[4] Dating, Seeck, *Regesten*, p. 164; Baynes, op. cit., p. 15.

[5] Constantine reached Trier by the beginning of Jan. 316.

[6] Optatus, i. 26. Regarding Philumenus, see P. Batiffol, *Bulletin de la société nationale des Antiquaires de France*, 1914, pp. 209–11 and 226–7.

[7] Optatus, i. 26.

Donatists boycotted them, riots broke out in Carthage, and after a futile stay of forty days the mission returned, having accomplished nothing. Before they left, however, they communicated with the Caecilianist clergy. While they were there Donatus had requested to be allowed to return to Africa, but this had been refused.[1] His rival was meantime being held at Brescia at Philumenus' suggestion. Soon afterwards, however, Donatus escaped from detention and Caecilian quickly followed him back to Carthage.[2] From the point of view of the Emperor the situation in Africa was serious.

This disquieting news probably reached Constantine at Trier early in the year 316.[3] He may by this time have regarded neither side as trustworthy, and he was determined to come to Africa himself and settle the controversy on the spot. As a preliminary, on 27 February he had the Donatist bishops who were still at court provided with passports and sent home. The authorities in Africa were told to leave them in peace.[4] The instructions which were then sent to Domitius Celsus are of the greatest interest.[5] First, of course, the trouble started by Menalius must be suppressed. Then Constantine goes on to indicate that he had begun to understand something of the issues at stake. In one way or another, Caecilian's opponents had become associated in his mind with the martyrs—whether they had any claim to the blessing of the martyrs was the point they must prove.[6] But for the first and last time in the Emperor's correspondence they are put on the same level with Caecilian. Constantine declares his intention of coming to Africa, 'to demonstrate with unequivocal verdict as much to Caecilian as to those who seem to be against him, just how the supreme deity should be worshipped'.[7] There is no mention of Miltiades'

---

[1] Ibid. Lietzmann, *Geschichte der alten Kirche*, iii, p. 73, however, places this incident between Miltiades' Council and that of Arles.

[2] Optatus, i. 26. Later, the Donatists were to claim that Caecilian had been 'condemned' by Constantine and interned at Brescia (Augustine, *Breviculus Collationis*, iii. 20. 38).

[3] Baynes, *Constantine*, p. 15.

[4] Dating, Seeck, *Regesten*, p. 142; Baynes, op. cit., pp. 79–80.

[5] Optatus, Appendix vii (Ziwsa, p. 210).

[6] This seems to be indicated by the sentence: 'Cumque satis clareat neminem posse beatudines martyris eo genere conquirere, quod alienum a veritate religionis et incongruum esse videatur.' The Donatists had evidently been claiming the 'blessings of the martyrs' for themselves against Caecilian.

[7] Letter to Celsus, 'quod cum favente pietate divina Africam venero, plenissime universis, tam Caeciliano quam his, qui contra eum agere videntur, lecto dilucido

Council, or of Arles, or of Felix of Aptungi. Constantine would judge the case on its merits, and he considered it lay within his competence to pass such a judgement. 'What more can be done by me,' he concludes, 'more in accord with my constant practice, and with the very office of a prince, than after expelling error and destroying rash opinions, to cause all men to agree together to follow true religion and simplicity of life, and to render to Almighty God the worship which is His due?'[1] On this last duty rested the peace and security of the Empire, a conception which probably provides the clue to the Emperor's intervention into the details of this dispute. Constantine's instructions were to be applicable to all, priests and laymen alike.

The letter is of great interest in showing how the Emperor regarded the Christian Church. Constantine is in fact acting as though he were on a higher plane than the religious powers on earth, rather as God's own Vicar than an ordinary mortal.[2] The fourth century was to see the reversal of the roles. A few years after Theodosius had humbled himself to Ambrose at Thessalonica in 390, Augustine glossed over this letter from Constantine, claiming that 'the Emperor intended to apologize to the most reverend prelates for rejudging the case', after the Councils had passed their verdict.[3]

But the Emperor never put his resolve into effect. Perhaps he feared the repercussions which a decision given in Africa might have on the minds of a dangerously excited populace. Olympius' and Eunomius' experiences had been hardly encouraging to direct Imperial intervention. He may have felt, too, that the risk of becoming a partisan and appearing in Carthage as such was too great. At all events, in the autumn of 316 at Milan he

judicio demonstraturus sum, quae et qualis summae divinitati sit adhibenda veneratio, et cujusmodi cultu delectare videatur', Ziwsa, p. 211, ll. 22–24.

[1] 'Cum nihil potius a me agi pro instituto meo ipsiusque principis munere oporteat, quam ut discussis erroribus omnibusque temeritatibus amputatis, veram religionem universos, concordemque simplicitatem atque meritam omnipotenti Deo culturam praesentare perficiam.' Ibid. The same thought appears in Constantine's letter to Anulinus, and in that sent to the Synod of Tyre in 334 (Eusebius, *Vita Constantini*, iv. 42). Constantine's intentions are all the more interesting in view of the fact that the bishops at Arles claimed to be recording their own verdict in the presence of 'the Holy Ghost and His Angels'.

[2] On the conception of Constantine as representative of God on earth during this period of his reign, see A. Kaniuth, *Die Beisetzung Konstantins des Grossen*, Dissertation, Breslau, 1941, pp. 59 and 82.

[3] Augustine, *Ep.* 43. 7. 20, written A.D. 397.

once more reviewed the case of Ingentius and the charges brought by the Donatists against Caecilian. On 10 November he informed Eumalius, the new *Vicarius Africae*, of his decision. Caecilian was to be regarded as wholly innocent, and his opponents were 'calumniators'.[1]

THE FIRST PERIOD OF REPRESSION, 317-21

Having made up his mind who was the rightful bishop of Carthage, the Emperor quickly took steps to show Donatus 'the advantage of worshipping the Supreme Deity in the proper manner'. Probably in the spring of 317, a 'most severe' law was dispatched to North Africa. The churches held by the Donatists were to be confiscated and the Donatist leaders were to be sent into exile.[2]

At first, however, bribery was preferred to military force as a means of winning the opposition over.[3] But Caecilian was hated. Two events remained vivid in popular memory, the Persecution and the rule of Maxentius. Caecilian could not live down his attitude towards the Abitinian martyrs. Pamphlets, and that ever-effective weapon in the Near East, bazaar gossip, branded him as 'a man more cruel than the butcher (Anulinus), more brutal than the tyrant (Maxentius)'.[4] His next act was hardly likely to dispel these opinions.

Donatus, back in Africa, was determined on defiance. He refused to surrender the churches he held in Carthage. Caecilian appealed to the secular authorities. On 12 March between 317 and 321 he induced the *Dux* Leontius and the *Comes* Ursatius to place armed forces at his disposal.[5] These were seconded by

[1] Augustine, *Contra Cresconium*, iii. 71. 82. Dating, Augustine, *Ad Donatistas post Collationem*, xxxiii. 56. The word *calumniosissime* employed in the judgement may have had a technical character, denoting that the Donatists were guilty of the civil charge of *calumnia*. This point of view has been argued with learning, but without carrying conviction, by F. Martroye in an article on 'La Répression du Donatisme', in *Mémoires de la soc. nationale des Antiquaires de France*, viiie série, 3me tome, 1913, pp. 23–140.

[2] Augustine, *Ep.* 105. 9, 'Legem contra partem Donati dedit severissimam'; *Contra Litteras Petiliani*, ii. 92. 205; and *Ep.* 88. 3. The text has not survived.

[3] *Passio Donati*, 2 (*PL.* viii. 753 ff.), 'Mittit igitur pecunias quibus vel fidem caperet vel professione legis faceret occasionem avaritiae.'

[4] Ibid., 'carnifice crudelior, tyranno saevior [Caecilianus]'. Even in Optatus' time, Maxentius was regarded as 'tyrannus' (Optatus, i. 17).

[5] *Passio Donati*, 2, 'Caeciliano eudinepiso tunc instante, assentiente Leontio comite, duce Ursatio, Marcellino tunc tribuno'. Monceaux, *Histoire littéraire*, v. 60 ff., suggests 12 Mar. 317 as the most likely date for the incident described in the *Passio Donati*.

M

his own bodyguard, and by what the Donatist writers describe
as 'the Carthaginian magistrates, a heathen mob, and soldiery'.[1]
Churches were attacked, and in one which may have been
the *Basilica Maiorum*, situated on a mound outside the city, a
massacre took place.[2] In another, the Bishop of Advocata was
murdered, while in a third, Bishop Honoratus of Sicilibba was
struck down by an arrow alleged to have been shot by the commander of the guard, the tribune Marcellinus.[3]

The incident contributed to divide the African Christians
permanently into two rival Churches. Pleas that 'Christ was
a lover of unity'[4] carried no weight with those who saw the
Catholics working in alliance with pagan magistrates and
soldiers. This merely confirmed the Donatist claim that the
Catholics were 'schismatics'. Their Church became identified
with a hated idolatry, and with the persecution of the 'Church
of the Martyrs'. Donatist propagandists took care that the
events of the day were carefully preserved, and when, a few
years later, Ursatius fell in battle against barbarians, possibly
in Numidia, the Donatists saw in his death the hand of God
striking down the persecutor.[5]

Outside Carthage the persecution does not seem to have
been very severe. In Numidia, Silvanus of Cirta and all the
'old gang' of Donatist bishops who had consecrated him a dozen
years before were left in enjoyment of their sees. The pamphleteers were indeed censured by a law of 29 March 319, but
Donatus' position was secure enough, and not even a major
scandal could shake it.[6]

---

[1] Ibid., 'erat tunc videre militum manus traditorum furiis ministrantes'.

[2] Excavations in this church brought to light a well down which bodies had
been flung, together with fragments of an inscription dedicated to the martyrs
Perpetua and Felicitas (P. Monceaux, 'Épigraphie donatiste', in *Revue de Philologie*, année et tome xxxiii, avril–juillet 1909, p. 146).

[3] *Passio Donati*, 6. On Advocata, see S. Gsell, *Mélanges*, xix, 1899, p. 60.

[4] *Passio Donati*, 3, 'Christus, inquit [Diabolus], amator unitatis est'.

[5] On Ursatius cf. Augustine, *Contra Litteras Petiliani*, ii. 92. 202. Leontius, the
Dux, was probably a pagan (*CIL*. viii. 18219). On both these officials see also
Pallu de Lessert, *Fastes*, ii, pp. 174, 223, and Seeck, *Untergang*, iii, p. 514. One is
inclined to follow Seeck, that the Donatist writer has mixed up two or three
separate incidents; Leontius is more likely to have been concerned with the suppression of Menalius' riots in Numidia in 316. I do not accept Seeck's view, however,
that the tribune Marcellinus is the same as the Count Marcellinus who presided
over the conference of Carthage in 411. The writer of the *Passio* has in mind incidents that took place in Carthage in the lifetime of Caecilian and Leontius. There
seems little need to introduce characters who lived in the succeeding century.

[6] *Codex Theodosianus*, ix. 34. 1. The writer of the *Passio Donati* proclaimed his

This latter event took place in December 320.[1] Silvanus of Cirta had had the misfortune to quarrel with one of his deacons called Nundinarius. A man of violence, he had him stoned and finally excommunicated him. Nundinarius did not accept this treatment, and unfortunately for Silvanus he had a detailed knowledge of his bishop's career and his weak points. This was known to Silvanus' colleagues, who in vain implored him not to let the affair go too far. Purpurius of Limata, with murders and other crimes on his conscience, said bluntly, 'You will kill us all.'[2] Silvanus, however, was adamant, and failing to secure redress from the Numidian bishops, Nundinarius appealed to the law in the person of Zenophilus, *Consularis* of Numidia.

The case was heard at Thamugadi (Timgad) on 13 December 320. Silvanus was charged with *traditio*, simony, corruption, and theft, and from the *Acta* which have survived, the evidence was conclusive. The witnesses give a lively account of Cirta during the Persecution, detail how Silvanus became bishop, how he accepted bribes from candidates to the priesthood, how he embezzled for his own use money given by Lucilla for the poor, how he had allowed his episcopal throne to be used as a bargaining counter, and generally had led a discreditable life. He was found guilty and sent into exile.[3] But the Catholics were apparently completely unable to use this scandal to their advantage. The Donatists could even claim that Silvanus was a 'martyr', and that he had been forced into exile because he refused to communicate with Ursatius and Zenophilus. Within six months, on 5 May 321, Constantine recognized the hopelessness of trying to restore religious unity to Africa and granted the Donatists toleration.[4] By this time, the security of Africa in the event of war with Licinius had become more important than 'bringing madmen to reason'.[5] Constantine was prepared

intention of having the 'Caecilianist persecution' recorded until the end of time (*Passio*, 10).

[1] *Gesta apud Zenophilum* (Ziwsa, pp. 185-97).

[2] *Gesta apud Zenophilum* (Ziwsa, p. 189), 'omnes nos occiditis'.

[3] The account of the trial breaks off before the verdict is reached, but Augustine, *Contra Cresconium*, iii. 30, 34, makes it clear that Silvanus was sentenced to exile. 'Sed postea, inquis [Cresconius], Ursacio et Zenophilo persequentibus, cum communicare noluisset actus est in exilium'—another interesting example of Donatist propaganda among literate members of their community in the early fifth century.

[4] The sense of the decree is preserved in Augustine, *Post Collationem*, 32. 56. See also *Gesta Coll. Carth.* iii. 546-52 (*PL.* xi. 1257).

[5] Eusebius, *Vita Constantini*, i. 45 (ed. Heikel, Leipzig, 1902).

to admit his failure. In a circular letter addressed to the Catholics he counselled them to moderation and patience.[1] Donatus, if he had not secured the legal elimination of his rival, could afford to ignore him.

THE TRIUMPH OF DONATUS

The almost continuous narrative of events now breaks off for twenty years. Optatus has proved what he set out to prove, that the Donatists were themselves *traditores*, and that they were the authors of the schism.[2] He had no interest in following the progress of Donatus in establishing and ordering his Church. The result is that in this period of growth and expansion of Donatism the evidence is fragmentary.

Constantine continued to make occasional efforts to restore unity. In 324, shortly before the Council of Nicaea, he seemed to have intended to send Eastern bishops to Africa, but the Arian controversy now claimed his full attention.[3] He contented himself with expressing his confidence once more in Caecilian by inviting him to take his place among the bishops at Nicea.[4] Five years later, on 5 February 330, the Emperor wrote from Serdica his final letter of encouragement to the Catholic bishops. The Donatists had seized a basilica in Constantine which the Emperor had ordered to be built for the Catholics. Demands for restitution were made in vain, and the Emperor found that all he could do was to authorize the Catholics to apply to the *Rationalis* for funds with which to build a new church.[5]

The incident sheds some light on the position achieved by the Donatists in this period. They were gaining full benefit from the spread of Christianity. In the Numidian towns, churches of vast dimensions and magnificent construction were erected. At Theveste the basilica which seems to have been started in this period is one of the finest monuments in Roman Africa.[6] The massive stone blocks of which it was built stand today as sharp and unweathered as when they left the quarry. At

---

[1] Optatus, Appendix ix (Ziwsa, pp. 212–13).

[2] Optatus, i. 13, 'Primo loco audi, qui fuerunt traditores, et plenius auctores scismatis disce.'

[3] Eusebius, *Vita Constantini*, ii. 64–72. Batiffol, however, has long challenged the authenticity of this letter, *Bulletin d'ancienne littérature chrétienne*, iv, 1914, p. 83.

[4] Mansi, *Collectio Conciliorum*, ii. 696.

[5] Optatus, Appendix x (Ziwsa, pp. 213–16). Dating, Seeck, *Regesten*, p. 180.

[6] A. Truillot, 'Autour de la Basilique de Tébessa', *Recueil de Constantine*, lxii, 1934–5, p. 41.

Timgad, the great Cemetery-Basilica south-east of the town may also have been founded at this time, and the same would apply to many of the village churches and chapels in southern Numidia. In Mauretania, the church at Castellum Tingitanum (Orléansville) is precisely dated to A.D. 324,[1] and in other districts dated Christian inscriptions begin to make their appearance.[2]

In many of these areas, the triumph of Christianity meant the triumph of Donatus' Church. Congregations seem in general to have followed the lead of their bishop. In Constantine, as the grammarian Victor explained during the trial of Silvanus, there had only been one church in the city, and once Silvanus had been consecrated bishop no one challenged him.[3] What was happening 300 miles away in Carthage was little concern of the ordinary townsfolk. The same appears to have occurred elsewhere: in Limata, where Purpurius remained undisturbed, or in Advocata or Sicilibba, whose bishops are mentioned in the repression of 317.[4] Later, there seems to have been some resistance. In Mauretania, on a site where the modern settlement of Renault stands, an inscription dated to 329 suggests that the rival factions came to blows, and deaths resulted.[5] In Constantine, as we have seen, the Catholics tried to organize a community, but were frustrated.[6]

We find too that the Donatists were exercising the same economic pressure on their opponents as they had been subjected to previously. It will be remembered that one of the causes of the appeal to Constantine had been the exemption of the Caecilianist clergy from municipal obligations. By 330 the Donatists in Numidia were making a regular practice of forcing their opponents to accept these burdens,[7] a proof of their supremacy in the province. Constantine addressed a decree to the *Consularis* of Numidia, Valentius, ordering that this be stopped, but there is no evidence that it was effective.

---

[1] *CIL*. viii. 9708.

[2] At Satafi (Mauretania Sitifensis) a *memoria martyrum* is dated to 322 (*CIL*. viii. 20305) and at Sillègue in the same province Christian inscriptions begin at A.D. 324 (*CIL*. viii. 10930 and 20478).

[3] 'Semper civitas nostra unam Ecclesiam habet; et si habuit dissensionem, nescimus omnino', *Gesta apud Zenophilum* (Ziwsa, p. 185).

[4] *Passio Donati*, 7 and 12 (*PL*. viii, cols. 755–57).

[5] *CIL*. viii. 21517; Monceaux, *Histoire littéraire*, iv. 473.

[6] Optatus, Appendix x (Constantine's letter to the Catholics in Constantine).

[7] Ibid. (Ziwsa, p. 215). See L. Duchesne, *Le Dossier du Donatisme*, p. 613.

The Donatists were even beginning to establish themselves outside Africa. Their venture in Spain,[1] possibly on Lucilla's estates, led to nothing, and the remainder of the West remained true to Caecilian. In Rome itself, however, the Donatists had more success. There had always been a considerable African community in Rome, and this had played an influential part in the Church there. As Cyprian's letters show, the relations between Carthage and the capital were extremely close. Interchanges of visits by clergy were frequent. For this reason, apart from any theological ground, an African religious movement would tend to spread to Rome, and the Donatists were favoured by the suspected lapse of successive Catholic bishops during the Persecution. As has been shown, there were grounds for thinking that not only Bishop Marcellinus but also Miltiades and Silvester had either been *traditores* themselves or had communicated with *traditor* clergy, and the Donatists adopted exactly the same attitude towards them as they had towards Caecilian. In the first place, they sent *interventores* to Rome to investigate on the spot, and to take over the administration of the see until a Council could be called.[2] In this case a Council never met, but the incident shows that the Donatists had no intention of confining themselves to Africa. They only came to do so when the remainder of the West continued to recognize Caecilian. At Rome the *interventores* had no success, and so Donatus dispatched one of the original consecrators of Silvanus of Cirta, Victor of Garba, to establish himself as true bishop of Rome.[3] The apostolic succession had now been restored, though during the century of his existence the Donatist Bishop of Rome was to rank below the primates of Carthage and Numidia.[4]

Failure overseas, except at Rome, was balanced by almost complete success in Africa. 'Donatus wished to gain all Africa',[5] wrote Augustine sixty years later, and it seems that he very nearly succeeded.[6] It is unfortunate that we have no friendly critic to describe his rule between the years 330 and 347. One

[1] Augustine, *Contra Litteras Petiliani*, ii. 97. 247 (*PL.* xliii, col. 346).

[2] Idem, *De Unico Baptismo*, 16. 28 (*PL.* xliii, col. 610).

[3] Optatus, ii. 4. Date of Victor's arrival is uncertain.

[4] At the Conference of Carthage the Donatist bishop of Rome signs the nominal roll after the Bishop of Carthage and the Primate of Numidia (*Gesta Coll. Carth.* i. 149).

[5] Augustine, *Psalmus contra Partem Donati*, line 94, 'Nam Donatus cum volebat Africam totam obtinere' (*PL.* xliii, col. 27).

[6] Cf. Jerome, *De Viris Illustribus*, 93, 'paene totam Africam decepit'.

is left to speculate what was the effect of his ascendancy in Carthage on the general policy of the Emperors towards the factions in the Christian Church at this period. The position he achieved in his own country has, however, been described by Optatus,[1] and his words are impressive. 'He claimed for himself sovereign authority (*Principatum*) at Carthage, he exalted his heart and seemed to himself to be superior to other mortals, and wished that all, even his own allies, should be beneath him.' His bishops hardly dared take Communion in his presence, while Donatus himself is described as 'performing some ceremony in private', and afterwards conversing with them perfunctorily. He was looked upon as someone not less than God, and among the people he was rarely called 'bishop', but was known as 'Donatus of Carthage'. Augustine in one of his sermons even stated that Donatists reacted more sharply to an insult against the name of Donatus than to a blasphemy against Christ.[2]

Allowing for exaggeration designed to feature the 'pride' of Donatus, it is clear that the latter held a position even greater than that enjoyed by Cyprian. As a prophet and religious leader who could claim to converse directly with the Lord,[3] and yet at the same time maintained a stringent control over the faithful, one may recognize in Donatus an African forerunner of Mahomet.

Yet the situation in the last years of Constantine's reign was not free from difficulty. There were three problems which faced Donatus: first, the independence of the Church in regard to the Emperor and his officials must be upheld; secondly, the schism and apparent isolation of Africa from the rest of the Christian world needed to be explained, and thirdly, the difficulties felt by otherwise loyal colleagues on the rebaptism question required settlement.

While the Caecilianists in theory and practice leant heavily on the secular arm,[4] Donatus after A.D. 316 maintained the African Christian tradition of hostility to the world represented by the Roman authorities. The latter could be abused at will if they interfered in the affairs of the Church. In 336 the *Praefectus*

---

[1] Optatus, iii. 3 (Ziwsa, p. 76).

[2] *Sermo* 197. 4. Cf. *Contra Epistolam Parmeniani*, ii. 2. 5, 'Si verba dant Christo, cor autem Donato.'

[3] See Augustine, *In Ioannis Evang. Tract.* xiii. 17 (*PL.* xxxv, col. 1501), 'Et Pontius fecit miraculum et Donatus oravit et respondit ei Deus de caelo.'

[4] Indicated by Optatus, iii. 3 and 4. See below, pp. 177 ff.

praetorio of Italy, Gregorius, seems to have attempted to repress the Donatists. Donatus defied him. The opening line of his letter of protest read: 'Gregory, pollution of the senate and disgrace of the prefecture'.[1] The rest is lost; but whatever the contents, the prefect climbed down and Donatus was left undisturbed. Perhaps Constantine feared the result of provoking powerful clerics at Carthage as well as at Alexandria.

In Africa, meanwhile, nothing was left undone to propagate Christianity and the name of Donatus. Travellers arriving from up country are said to have been asked by the bishop 'how his community was faring in their neighbourhoods'.[2] Instructions and letters were sent to the clergy in the remotest parts. At the same time, a literary war was carried on against the Caecilianists. The latter, at some date after 330, retaliated by compiling a dossier of the main documents on the origins of the dispute, including some drawn from official sources, such as the vindication of Felix of Aptungi and the trial of Bishop Silvanus. This has survived to a large extent under the title of *Gesta Purgationis Caeciliani et Felicis*, and remains one of our chief sources on the early years of the schism.[3] On some of these issues the Donatists also may have produced their legal *Acta*, the existence of which can be traced from allusions in Augustine's works,[4] but Donatus himself seems to have concentrated on a reasoned defence for the separation from Caecilian. This work, like everything else he wrote, is lost, but the trend may be partly reconstructed from a chapter in Augustine's *Contra Epistolam Parmeniani*.[5] The fragment shows that Donatus was following a traditional line of African theology. The Christian Church was a small body of the saved surrounded by the unregenerate. Its progress had been described in the Parable of the Tares. The field was the world, the tares the false Chris-

---

[1] Optatus, iii. 3 (Ziwsa, p. 73); L. Duchesne, *Early History of the Church*, ii. 188.

[2] Optatus, iii. 3 (Ziwsa, pp. 77–78). Optatus also asserts in the same passage that at this time the Donatists actually styled themselves 'Donatistae'.

[3] On the date of compilation, Duchesne, *Mélanges*, x, 1890, pp. 625 ff. In Egypt Athanasius was using similar dossiers of material drawn from official archives to confound his opponents.

[4] These must have included the *Acta* of the Martyrs of Abitina, an account of the apostasy of Pope Marcellinus, and the condemnation of Felix of Aptungi by a 'proconsul Vincentius'. See Augustine, *De Unico Baptismo*, 16. 27, and *Contra Cresconium*, iii. 69. 80.

[5] ii. 2. 5; P. Monceaux, *Histoire littéraire*, v. 124.

tians, and the wheat the elect. The tares had increased, and it was necessary for the true Christians to separate themselves from them. The result of the acceptance of Caecilian by clergy in other provinces of the Empire was merely that for the time being the field of God was to be found in Africa alone.[1] It might seem paradoxical that at the moment of the conversion of the Emperor a Christian leader should solemnly have asserted that the number of Christians had in fact diminished,[2] but the alliance of Church and Roman Empire was not one that appealed to the mass of African Christians. Indeed, such an idea must have seemed blasphemous to the numbers who regarded Christianity in terms of a military service by a chosen few in everlasting combat against the hosts of paganism and idolatry. Donatus' hard and narrow logic carried conviction.

At this time Donatus' authority was acknowledged by nearly 300 bishops—over three times the number which had assembled for councils in the age of Cyprian. We have evidence for one council attended by 270 bishops which he summoned probably towards the end of Constantine's reign.[3] The question, as in the previous period, was the validity of baptism[4] given by a priest not in communion with the 'Catholic' (in this case Donatist) Church. The problem seems not to have been whether a *traditor*'s sacrament was valid—everyone was agreed that it was not—but the case of Christians who had been baptized before the separation from Caecilian, or by clergy who for one reason or another had remained in communion with him. When they acknowledged Donatus, were they to be rebaptized? The situation was most complicated in Mauretania (as it had been in Cyprian's time), probably because the Persecution had been less severe there, and feelings for or against Caecilian were consequently less bitter. Donatus himself believed that there could be no baptism outside his communion, and therefore

---

[1] *Contra Epistolam Parmeniani*, ii. 2. 5, 'Donatus autem dicit, agrum Dei in sola Africa remansisse.'

[2] Ibid., 'Donatus autem dicit, zizania quidem crevisse, frumenta vero esse diminuta.'

[3] Augustine, *Ep.* 93. 43. Nothing is known about this great meeting except what can be gathered by the chance references in this letter to the Rogatist bishop, Vincentius of Cartenna.

[4] The constant preoccupation with the magical element of baptism was not confined to the Donatists. It will be recalled that Constantine himself had postponed baptism until his deathbed in order to avoid the peril of post-baptismal sin.

favoured rebaptism of former Caecilianists,[1] but Mauretanian prelates such as Deuterius of Macri pointed out difficulties.[2] Many congregations were ready to reject Caecilian if they could do so without undergoing what they considered a second baptism. This demand was obstructing the work of reuniting the African Church under Donatus' leadership. For seventy-five days the debates went on, the decisions of previous councils were reviewed, and finally Donatus allowed himself to be persuaded into accepting the Mauretanian case. Rebaptism was not obligatory in every instance. This says a great deal for his wisdom and sound sense, as well as for the authority he exercised. The debate might well have led to a schism, but clearly Donatus' object was the unity of the Church in Africa, and he was prepared to meet reasonable requirements of colleagues if that would further this aim.

This great council, clearly one of the greatest in African Church history, ended harmoniously. Whatever may have been Donatus' attitude towards individual prelates, he did not attempt to exercise 'tyrannical terror' over bishops assembled under the inspiration of the Spirit in a Council. Here again we see the follower of the traditions of Cyprian, a tradition which tended to be abandoned by Caecilian and his apologist Optatus of Milevis.[3]

The death of Constantine saw Donatus in the ascendant. Caecilian disappears into obscurity after Nicaea, and for the next quarter of a century we hear almost nothing of the Catholic Bishop of Carthage and, indeed, of the Caecilianists as a whole.[4] During these years Donatist Christianity was the religion of African town and village alike. The Church presided over by Donatus seemed to be founded upon a rock.

[1] Augustine, *Retractationes*, i. 21.

[2] Id., *Ep.* 93. 43.

[3] Cyprian's views on the validity of a Sacrament given outside the Church are not mentioned at all in Optatus, and Cyprian himself is passed over with two perfunctory references.

[4] It is interesting that Silvester, who was Bishop of Rome for twenty-one years (314–35), and must have known of Caecilian's vindication, never seems to have stirred himself in his favour. It is particularly strange in view of the fact that he had been represented at the Council of Arles.

XII

THE CONSOLIDATION
OF DONATISM

A.D. 337–63

THE half-century which followed the death of Constantine was one of steady development for the Donatist Church, disturbed but not halted by periods of intermittent repression. For the facts we are once more mainly in the hands of Optatus of Milevis, the two editions of whose *De Schismate Donatistarum* were written in all probability in 365–7 and 385 respectively.[1] Some of his statements may now be checked through recent archaeological research, and by the non-African writers Zosimus and Ammianus Marcellinus. Of the Donatists themselves, Tyconius is the only writer of note whose work has survived in this period, but Tyconius sheds little light on the history of the movement, except what may be gathered by inference. Something of the spirit which animated it may, however, be gained from the writings of the martyrologists during the persecution under Macarius in 346–7, and in particular by the *Passio Marculi*,[2] written probably about A.D. 348.

Incomplete though the evidence is, enough exists to trace the main lines of the history of Donatism during this period. At the death of Constantine in May 337, Donatus was still at the height of his power. Caecilian probably had died, and his successor Gratus is shown from the little we know of him to have been a pleasant but colourless personality. Donatus' authority by now extended to every corner of Roman Africa, but was most solidly entrenched in Numidia and in Carthage itself. So firm were the traditions on which he had built, that despite the affair of Paul and Macarius and the succeeding period of Caecilianist ascendancy between 347 and 361, Donatism remained for another fifty years the predominant religion of North Africa. Throughout this period the Donatists also maintained

---

[1] I have accepted the dating arrived at by P. Monceaux, *Histoire littéraire*, iv. 450–3.

[2] P. Monceaux, ibid. vi. 69–81, considers this was written within a few months of Marculus' death in Nov. 347. It probably had a liturgical use.

themselves in Rome, the Popes being regarded as successors to the *traditor* Marcellinus.

In the early part of Constans' reign Donatus took steps to improve his relations with the Church outside Africa. He even hoped that he would be recognized by the Emperor as Bishop of Carthage. A connexion was established with the semi-Arians, and Donatus himself may have signed the Synodal Letter of the Council of Serdica-Philippopolis in the autumn of 342.[1] At the time, it was by no means impossible that the creed of Eusebius of Nicomedia would be recognized by the Emperors. It is interesting that the Donatists were the only representatives of Western Christianity to join the semi-Arians at Philippopolis, while the African Catholics under Donatus' rival, Gratus, remained with the Westerners and Hosius at Serdica.[2] The doctrinal similarities between Donatus' *De Spiritu Sancto*[3] and the semi-Arian position may not have been merely opportunist.

At this stage the Donatists were recruiting from all classes of the population. Despite the scandals which had accompanied the breach with Caecilian, many literate Africans regarded the Donatist Church as the true Catholic Church in Africa, and the successor of the Church of Cyprian's time. It appeared also to be a purer and nobler communion than its rival.[4] Philosophers such as Tyconius, as well as lesser figures like Vitellius Afer and Macrobius, Bishop of Rome, were Donatists despite persecution or quarrels with their own Church. Clergy, who like Rogatus of Cartenna formed a schism, seem to have had no more thought of joining the Catholics than schismatic Moslems in French North Africa would have of becoming Christians.

The Donatist Church was also beginning to acquire property.[5] There was thus a danger of losing her former enthusiasm and relapsing into the placidity of an established institution. The

---

[1] Dating, Lietzmann, *Geschichte der alten Kirche*, Bd. iii. 195.

[2] Thirty-six Catholic bishops, including Gratus of Carthage, were at Serdica. It is interesting to note that the two parties carried their differences to the length of supporting rival doctrinal theses at this Council. The possible participation of the Donatists in the Arian Synod is recorded by Augustine, *Ep.* 44. 3. 6, and *Contra Cresconium*, iii. 34. 38, iv. 44. 52, and discussed by J. Zeiller, *CRAI.*, 1933, pp. 65–72. For Gratus at the orthodox synod, Athanasius, *Apol. contra Arianos*, 50, *PG.* xxv, col. 317.

[3] Jerome, *De Viris Illustribus*, 93 (*PL.* xxiii, col. 694), 'de Spiritu sancto, Ariano dogmati congruens'.

[4] Augustine, *Ep.* 208. 6, on the 'quasi laudabilis conversatio' of the Donatists.

[5] Augustine, *In Ioannis Evang. Tract.* vi. 25 (*PL.* xxxv, 1436), mentions properties acquired in the reign of Julian which the Catholics confiscated after the Conference of Carthage.

outlook and interests of the educated leaders were not always the same as those of the peasantry who formed the backbone of the Church, and whose inarticulate yearnings influenced its distinctive doctrine. Considering, however, that apart from divergence of interests, there was often a language barrier between the Donatist bishop and his flock, it is remarkable that there was not more schism and disruption, especially during the periods of persecution.

The relations with the Imperial authorities also denote a more orderly process at work during the second half of the fourth century. The Donatists, indeed, supported the cause of Firmus during his revolt in 372. Donatus could demand haughtily, 'What had the Emperor to do with the Church?', but it would be mistaken to see in the Donatism of the mid-fourth century a consciously anti-Imperial movement with political aims. The Donatists had no hesitations about appealing to Julian for the restoration of their Church. Imperial officials were numbered among their sympathizers, and one of them at least, Flavian, the *Vicarius Africae* in 377, was a communicant. Hostility was directed not against the Empire, but against the 'world' generally, the domain ruled over by Satan, and represented by corrupt officials, oppressive landowners, 'sons of *traditores*'. In the light of history we know that the official and land-owning class and the Catholic Church represented the Roman Empire in North Africa in the fourth century, and that 'barbarism' was as much the village cultures of the inland areas of the Mediterranean basin as the pressure of the German tribes on the frontiers. But such political reasoning cannot be attributed to the Donatists of the period. Their outlook was fixed on what might happen in the next world. The Roman Empire was to them the symbol of the imperfection of the present transitory phase. There is no evidence that they envisaged its overthrow even in Africa.

Signs were not lacking that the latent tensions between the literate puritan element and the country populations in the Donatist Church would soon come to a head. In the year 340 one first hears of the strange revolutionary fringe of Donatism,[1]

---

[1] P. Monceaux, *Histoire littéraire*, iv. 179, dates the beginnings of the Circumcellion movement to A.D. 316–17, but I find no firm evidence for this. The 'barbarians' against which Ursatius fought were probably Aures mountaineers. Had they been Donatists, more would probably have been heard about the affair.

the Circumcellion movement. There is little doubt that today one would regard these Circumcellions as 'terrorists', having much the same relation to the Donatist Church as, for instance, Irgun Zvai Leumi had to Zionism in 1946–1948. They were alternately stirred up and discouraged by the Donatist leaders. When it was convenient they were disowned and the fact was loudly proclaimed;[1] when there was some tough work to be done, like sacking a Catholic church or a Roman villa, or bringing troublesome dissenters to heel, the Circumcellions would be called in. From now on, they form the permanent background to the controversy; their presence rendered alike Augustinian rhetoric, Imperial decree, and religious debate academic and futile.

All authorities are agreed as to the main features of the Circumcellions.[2] They were peasants from Upper Numidia and Mauretania,[3] and they were Donatists. Their field of action was the countryside, and native settlements such as the *castella* of Fussala and Sinitum in northern Numidia were among their headquarters.[4] Augustine describes them as *agrestes*, peasants who had thrown up their holdings and were living by terrorizing the great estates.[5] Their activities in this regard have already been noted, and Augustine has left more than one graphic description of the ruthless treatment meted out to unpopular landowners. Optatus of Milevis gives exactly the same account for the period 340 and the following years. They were fighting against clearly defined economic grievances. 'No one could feel secure in his estates', he writes; 'the debtor's bond (*chirographia*) lost its force. In those days no creditor had the

---

[1] Augustine, *Contra Epistolam Parmeniani*, i. 11. 17; *Contra Litteras Petiliani*, i. 24. 26; *Contra Cresconium*, iii. 49. 54.

[2] See Augustine's classic description, *Contra Gaudentium*, i. 28. 32, 'Quis enim nescit hoc genus hominum in horrendis facinoribus inquietum, ab utilibus operibus otiosum, crudelissimum in mortibus alienis, vilissimum in suis, maxime in agris territans, ab agris vacans, et victus sui causa cellas circumiens rusticanas unde et nomen Circumcellionum accepit.'

[3] Praedestinatus, *De Haeresibus*, 69, 'in partibus Numidiae superioris et Mauretaniae'. See H. von Schubert, 'Der sogennante Praedestinatus', *TU*. xxiv. 4, Leipzig, 1903, 63. On their native nomenclature, 'Miggin', 'Sanae', &c., see J. H. Baxter, 'The Martyrs of Madaura', *JTS*. (Oct. 1924), pp. 21 ff.

[4] Augustine, *Ep.* 209 and 105.

[5] Id., *Contra Gaudentium*, i. 28. 32 (*PL*. xliii, col. 725); Possidius, *Vita Augustini*, 10 (*PL*. xxxii. 41). Cf. Tyconius, apud Beatus, 26. 3, cited from Hahn, *Tyconius-Studien*, 68–69, 'Hi, graeco vocabulo Cotopices dicuntur, quos nos latine circumcelliones dicimus, eo quod agrestes sunt. Circumeunt provincias . . . .'

liberty of exacting payment of a debt.'[1] More than that, creditors were warned to release debtors from their obligations.
If not, the Circumcellions exerted due pressure. In the same
spirit, slaves and masters found their positions reversed. Rich
men driving comfortable vehicles would be pitched out and
made to run behind their carriages, now occupied by their
slaves.

The Circumcellions, however, were, above all, religious fanatics.[2] They derived their name from the fact that they lived
'around the shrines'[3] (circum cellas) whence they got their food.[4]
This latter fact has caused a good deal of difficulty, because
until recent discoveries in Algeria it was not thought possible
that large numbers could be fed at churches or chapels. The
cellae were therefore believed to be farm-houses or barns.[5] Excavations at Mechta Azrou and Bir Djedid on the High Plains,
however, provide examples of martyrs' shrines which also
included ample space for storing grain, and contained silos dug
in the sacristy or adjoining building.[6] In other churches, such
as Henchir Behir and Hr. el Beguer, troughs containing offerings of food lined the central nave, and fragments of storage-
jars were found in other parts of the church.[7] We may therefore
imagine the Circumcellions, as Tyconius describes them, 'visiting the tombs of the saints, as they believed, for the safety of
their souls',[8] and being fed there. Perpetual pilgrimage, or
membership of a 'maraboutic family', dwelling round a spot
hallowed by the tomb of a saint is the hall-mark of religious
life as understood by the Berbers today. Pilgrimage and burial

---

[1] Optatus, iii. 4, 'nulli licuit securum esse in possessionibus suis; debitorum
chirographia amiserant vires, nullus creditor illo tempore exigendi habuit potestatem'. See v. Nathusius, Zur Charakteristik der afrikanischen Circumcellionen, Greifswald,
1900, on this aspect of the movement.

[2] Cf. R. A. Knox, Enthusiasm, pp. 61–64.

[3] For cella as a martyr's shrine, CIL. viii. 9585 (Cherchell); cf. Augustine, Contra
Cresconium, iv. 66. 83 (PL. xliii, col. 592–3). Salvius of Membressa's 'cellulas et
agellos' were probably 'little churches and plots of ground'.

[4] Augustine, Contra Gaudentium, i. 28. 32 (PL. xliii. 725), 'victus sui causa'.

[5] See C. Saumagne, 'Ouvriers agricoles ou rôdeurs de celliers: les Circon-
cellions d'Afrique', Annales d'histoire économique et sociale, vi, 1934. Cf. P. Monceaux,
Histoire littéraire, iv. 180.

[6] A. Berthier, Les Vestiges du Christianisme, p. 129.

[7] Le Commandant Guenin, 'Inventaire archéologique du Cercle de Tébessa',
Nouvelles Archives des Missions, tome xvii, Algiers, 1909, pp. 81–85.

[8] Tyconius, apud Beatus, p. 26; cited from Hahn, Tyconius-Studien, pp. 68–69:
'Sed ut discimus, diversas terras circuire et sanctorum sepulchra pervidere quasi
pro salute animae suae.'

by a martyr's tomb are known to have been among the usual Donatist practices.[1]

The lives of the Circumcellions were in fact devoted to martyrdom.[2] What Tertullian had preached they put into practice. They were renowned as much for over-observance of ritual as for violence.[3] Psalms and shouts of 'Praise to God' ('Deo laudes') were their battle-cries.[4] Inscriptions and texts show them to be *agonistici*,[5] or *milites Christi*[6]—soldiers of Christ. Naturally, bishops and clergy would be their leaders on raids against Catholics and pagans. Martyrdom was prepared by ascetic and communal practices. Possidius regarded them as spurious 'ascetics'.[7] They adopted a monastic-looking habit,[8] and besides their clubs, 'Israels', they carried martyrs' relics which they sold.[9] The women also, who accompanied them, were *sanctimoniales* (in vows of chastity),[10] whose incidental conduct might possibly be compared with that of the Berber holy women or *merabtas*. The Circumcellion was a strict adherent to the letter if not to the spirit of the Commandments. His drunkenness may also be regarded as in the nature of a ritual act designed to attract the *baraka* latent in a martyr's tomb. We know from both archaeological and literary sources that drinking and dances were characteristic of the celebrations in honour of

---

[1] Cf. P. Monceaux, *Bull. Arch. du Comité*, 1908, 86–104 (*accubatorium* at Dougga, a Donatist see, *Gesta Coll. Carth.* i. 180), and A. Bigeard, *Recueil de Constantine*, 1907, 11–19 (description of the cemetery basilica at Cedias, also· a Donatist see, *Gesta Coll. Carth.* i. 180).

[2] Thus their name 'Biothanatoi', Philastrius, *Diversarum Haereseon Liber*, lvii. 85 (*CSEL*. xxxviii. 46; *PL*. xii. 1197–8). Cf. Tyconius, op. cit., p. 68, 'Et isti [Circumlions] non vivunt aequaliter ut ceteri fratres, sed quasi amore martyrum semetipsos perimunt, ut violenter de hac vita discedentes et martyres nominentur.'

[3] Id., cited from Hahn, op. cit., pp. 68–69; P. Monceaux, *Histoire littéraire*, v. 206.

[4] Augustine, *Ep.* 108. 5. 14.

[5] Optatus, iii. 4; Augustine, *Enarratio in Ps. 132*, 6 (*PL*. xxxvii, col. 1732). *Agon* was a technical term for a martyr's struggle. Cf. Cyprian, *Ep.* 10. 4, on Mappalicus.

[6] P. Monceaux, *Revue de Philologie*, 1909, pp. 116 and 132 (inscription from Henchir Bou Said, 'Donatus Miles Christi').

[7] *Vita Augustini*, 10 (*PL*. xxxii. 41), 'velut sub professione continentium ambulantes'; W. Thümmel, *Donatismus*, pp. 86–88.

[8] Isidore, *De Officiis ecclesiasticis*, ii. 15, 'De Monachis' (*PL*. lxxxiii, cols. 796–7), 'Quintum genus [monachorum] est Circumcellionum, qui habitu monachorum usquequaque vagantur. . . .'

[9] Isidore, loc. cit., 'alii membra martyrum, si tamen martyrum venditant'. The club was carried as Scripture forbade them to carry a sword. The name 'Israel' may be a corruption of 'Azael' = 'strength of God'.

[10] Augustine, *Ep.* 35. 2 (*CSEL*. xxxiv. 2. 28). Cf. *Contra Epistolam Parmeniani*, ii. 3. 6 (*PL*. xliii. 53); *Contra Gaudentium*, i. 36. 46 (*PL*. xliii. 735).

martyrs.[1] As Cyprian pointed out, holy drunkenness such as that of Noah was not mere self-indulgence.[2]

All this, however, was in preparation for martyrdom, by every means including suicide. Again we see how very clearly Tertullian expressed the latent religious ideas of the African natives. The Circumcellion merely represented Donatist doctrine in its extreme form. Warned by a dream or revelation that his time was at hand, a Circumcellion would go forth and stop a traveller, or better still, more reminiscent of the heroic age of Christianity, a magistrate.[3] The unfortunate would be given the choice of killing or being killed. Others would rush in on a pagan festival and offer themselves for human sacrifice.[4] These became martyrs automatically, and similarly those who perished in attacks on villas or Catholic churches. As Augustine put it, they lived as robbers, died as Circumcellions, and were honoured as martyrs.[5] The alternative was mass suicide. Crowds would fling themselves over precipices or drown in the Chotts, or even burn themselves alive.[6] Between 1937 and 1940 exploration of the mountainous country around Nif en-Nisr, near Ain Mlila on the High Plains, brought to light a collection of roughly hewn inscriptions.[7]

---

[1] Augustine, *Sermo* 311. 5 (*PL.* xxxviii–xxxix, col. 1415), 'ubi jacet tam sancti martyris [Cyprian] corpus, invaserat pestilentia et petulentia saltatorum. Per totam noctem cantabantur nefaria'. *Ep.* 29. 11 (Leontius) (*CSEL.* xxxiv. 1. 121). On Circumcellion drunkenness, *Contra Cresconium*, iv. 63. 77, 'Negas eas quas dixi tyrannicas vestrorum in fundis alienis dominationes et bacchationes ebrietatum', *Contra Litteras Petiliani*, i. 24. 26. For a parallel with pagan ceremonies, Augustine, *Ep.* 199. 11. 37, 'perstrepunt lascivi cantus, organa, tibiae, lyrae, citharae, tesserae, multa et varia genera sonorum atque ludorum' (*CSEL.* lvi. 276). For archaeological evidence, see M. Barry's report on Morsott, *Recueil de Constantine*, 1899, pp. 391–430.

[2] *Ep.* 63. 11 (*CSEL.* iii. 710). Cf. H. Lewy, 'Sobria Ebrietas', *Zeitschrift für N.T. Wissenschaft*, 1929, pp. 140 ff.

[3] Theodoret, *Haereticarum Fabularum Compendium*, v. 6 (*PG.* lxxxiii. 423); Augustine, *Ep.* 185. 3. 12 (*CSEL.* lvii. 11), and also *De Haeresibus*, 69 (*PL.* xlii, col. 43).

[4] *Contra Epistolam Parmeniani*, i. 10. 16 (*PL.* xliii, col. 45); *Contra Gaudentium*, i. 28. 32 (*PL.* xliii, col. 725); *Ep.* 185. 3. 12. For Circumcellion assaults on pagans, probably mid-fourth century, see J. H. Baxter, 'The Martyrs of Madaura', *JTS.* (Oct. 1924), pp. 21 ff.

[5] Augustine, *Ep.* 88. 8 (*CSEL.* xxxiv. 2. 414), 'vivunt ut latrones, moriuntur ut Circumcelliones, honorantur ut martyres'. For a parallel to the asceticism practised by the Circumcellions, cf., in Asia Minor, the Messalians and Patriciani (suicides and rites typified by ecstatic dances), L. Duchesne, *Histoire ancienne*, ii. 583; Philastrius, *De Haeresibus*, 85. To the Moslem Berber there would have been nothing incongruous in a holy man being a robber as well as a contemplative.

[6] *Contra Gaudentium*, i. 22. 25; i. 27. 30; and i. 28. 32.

[7] A. Berthier, op. cit., p. 215; L. Leschi, *Revue Africaine*, lxxxii, 1940, pp. 35–40.

Some of these were simply boulders lying at the foot of a precipice. Each was marked with a name, the calendar month, and the word *reditum* or *red(itum)*. It is thought that this may mean 'ransom' or 'rendering' of the soul to God, and that we have at this site evidence of Circumcellion ritual suicides.

The Circumcellions indicate the union of social and religious discontent in the Donatist movement. Why the outbreak should have started in A.D. 340 is not known, though, as has been pointed out, the situation of the African peasants tended to become yearly more miserable. We gather from Optatus that social war devastated the province. The 'leaders of the saints' Fasir and Axido terrorized southern Numidia.[1]

The Donatist leaders took fright. They appealed to the military commander Count Taurinus to intervene. The Circumcellions, they complained, would not accept ecclesiastical discipline.[2] Taurinus complied, and sent his troops to the markets, *nundinae*, where the trouble-makers would assemble and agitate. These markets were great open fairs often established by landed proprietors, such as that by the important spring at M'chira.[3] Similar institutions exist in North Africa today. Villagers congregate not merely to exchange goods but to hear news from other parts, and these places were ideal for the spread of rumours and revolutionary ideas.

At one of these markets, Octava in Numidia, which had long been a Christian centre, the crowd resisted.[4] The soldiers used force and a number of people were killed. They were at once regarded as martyrs by the Donatist lower clergy, and one, Clarus, priest at the village of Subbula (Locus Subbulensis), defied his bishop and buried them within the walls of his church. First, he had their names inscribed on whitened stone tables (*mensae*).[5] This act had a particular religious significance, and was an honour reserved for martyrs and clergy. The Donatist bishops forbade the practice, but in vain. To judge from

[1] Optatus, iii. 4, 'Fasir et Axido duces sanctorum'.

[2] Ibid., 'dicuntur huiusmodi homines in ecclesia corrigi non posse.'

[3] *CIL.* viii. 8280. The *nundinae* may also have had a religious significance. In central Numidia, at Henchir Oued Kherouf an inscription records that a fair (*nundina*) and village (*vicus*) were associated with a temple of Caelestis (M. Piquet, *Recueil de Constantine*, xlvi, 1912, p. 284). In Cappodocia fairs were held round a martyr's tomb. Cited from W. L. Clarke, *The Ascetic Works of St. Basil*, Cambridge, 1925, p. 211.

[4] Optatus, iii. 4. Octava was represented by a bishop at Cyprian's Council in 256.   [5] Ibid.

discoveries made in the chapels of southern Numidia, the burial
of bodies within the precincts of the church and the dedication
of *mensae* to Circumcellions and other 'unofficial' martyrs were
almost universal. The outlook of the extremists was to prevail
in other ways besides, for later in the century Taurinus was
numbered among the persecutors of Donatism.[1]

THE MACARIAN PERSECUTION

While this was happening in Numidia, Donatus made a
decision which had an important bearing on the future history
of the Donatist Church. About the year 346 he approached the
Emperor Constans for recognition as sole Bishop of Carthage.
In the light of events in the next two years this must seem an
extraordinary move, but Optatus' precise description admits
of no other interpretation, and, as Seeck points out, Donatus
had a sound reason for his act.[2] In the first place, he could
claim to be in communion with at least some of the more
important bishops in other provinces, and further, he was now
senior Bishop of Carthage. If Caecilian had some right as
Mensurius' archdeacon to claim the primacy of Africa against
Donatus, the same could not be said for Gratus his successor.
It could also be argued that Miltiades' Council had laid down
that where there were two rival bishops the junior must give
way—regardless of whether he was a Donatist or a Caecilianist.

The Emperor did not reject Donatus' approach out of
hand. As his father had done before him, he decided to send
a commission to Africa to investigate and report. Two Imperial notaries, Paul and Macarius, were chosen for the
duty, and probably reached Africa in the spring of 347. The
choice could not have been worse, and one is led to suppose that in the meantime the African Catholic bishops, who
according to Hosius[3] swarmed at Constans' court, had primed
the commission before it started. The ostensible object of
the visit was to bring funds for the decoration of the African
churches and relief of the poor, and the money was to be
distributed to both parties without distinction.[4] The question

---

[1] Augustine, *Contra Litteras Petiliani*, ii. 92. 202; Optatus, iii. 1.

[2] Optatus, iii. 1, 'Donato Carthaginis, qui provocavit, ut unitas proximo tempore fieri temptaretur'. Also, iii. 3. O. Seeck, *Untergang*, iii. 337 and 521. Seeck's
notes on this incident are particularly useful.

[3] Canon 8 of Council of Serdica. See below, p. 183.

[4] Optatus, iii. 3, p. 73.

of Unity was to be discussed later. From the outset, however, Paul and Macarius showed their sympathy for Donatus' opponents. They attended Gratus' services, and apparently intervened openly to sway public opinion in his favour.[1] This was too much for Donatus. When at last they did contact him, he told them plainly that the 'Emperor had nothing to do with the Church', and dispatched instructions to all his clergy to ignore the Commission and refuse any alms they might offer.[2] In addition, he appears to have sent a letter of protest to Constans.

Meanwhile, Carthage was seething with rumours. It was being spread that the Emperor's bust had been placed on the altar of Gratus' church and incense offered to it; further, that the Commissioners were attempting to usurp the functions of bishops.[3] Hatred of idolatry and association of Imperial officials with persecution were thoughts that came readily to the mind of the populace. Excited spirits were prepared to believe the worst. The chance of provoking persecutions in the name of the Church was readily seized upon.

Tales of what was happening in Carthage quickly reached Numidia, and the news of the approach of Paul and Macarius roused the populace to expectant fury. As they made their way along the high road between Theveste and Thamugadi at the foot of the Aures mountains their reception became increasingly hostile, and they were forced to call in the aid of the *Comes* Silvester with the troops under his command.[4]

The Donatists, however, were determined on resistance. Donatus the Bishop of Bagai called in the Circumcellions from all round[5] and withdrew to what appears to have been a fortified storehouse-basilica, of which numerous examples exist in Numidia.[6] From here he defied the Imperial authorities. When Macarius ordered the *metatores* (billeting officials), who were particularly hated, to go forward and investigate, trouble came to a head. There was fighting, and finally the soldiers rushed the basilica and massacred its defenders. Bishop Donatus was

---

[1] Optatus, vii. 6.　　　　　　　　[2] Id., iii. 3, p. 73.
[3] Id., iii. 12; vii. 6.　　　　　　　[4] Id., iii. 4.
[5] Ibid. He summoned them out of the fairs by town-criers, *praecones*.
[6] These buildings, more examples of which have been found in Tripolitania, consist of a central courtyard, one side of which is occupied by a basilica, the others by store-rooms. In some cases there appear to have been a parapet and towers set at each corner. They could be closed by means of a heavy circular stone which was rolled across the narrow entrance.

among the killed, and his body is stated by the Donatists to have been thrown down a well.[1]

According to Donatist sources, Macarius now proscribed Donatism in Numidia. The writer of the *Passio Marculi* states that he published *judicia* (decrees) of 'barbarous severity', in which the leading Numidian Donatists were singled out for abuse. Faced with the real prospect of suppression, the Donatist bishops held a council. They decided to play for time and to protest to Macarius, who meanwhile had set up a headquarters at Vegesela (Ksar el Kelb), the centre of a great landed estate near Bagai.[2] The meeting took place on 29 June 347. The Donatist delegates led by a Bishop Marculus upbraided the Commissioner. Stung to fury, Macarius had them bound to pillars and flogged like criminals. One of the delegates, Felicianus, may have succumbed to the ordeal.[3] The others were put under arrest, and Marculus was conveyed round the countryside with the object of exciting ridicule. Shortly afterwards he was imprisoned at Nova Petra[4] and finally, on 29 November 347, executed.[5] He became one of the great heroes in the Donatist saga.

Meantime, events had been moving rapidly in Carthage. On 15 August 347 the Proconsul published an Imperial decree proclaiming Unity between the two Churches under Bishop Gratus.[6] There were scenes of riot and tumult. Optatus speaks of the arrival of 'bowmen', which suggests the employment of regular troops of a type which were later to serve Constantius and Julian so well.[7]

---

[1] Optatus, iii. 4; Augustine, *In Ioannis Evang., Tract.* xi. 15.

[2] *Passio Marculi* (*PL.* viii, col. 761); P. Cayrel, *Mélanges,* li, 1934, pp. 136–40.

[3] Felicianus is referred to on an inscription on a reliquary found at Ain-Dalaa near Bagai. I am inclined to accept Monceaux's view that the reliquary was dedicated in honour of the bishop, now that a basilica dedicated to Marculus himself has been found (Monceaux, *Histoire littéraire,* iv. 475).

[4] Probably in south-west Numidia. See S. Gsell, *Atlas archéologique de l'Algérie,* f. 27, no. 62.

[5] Dating, O. Seeck, *Regesten,* p. 195. The Donatists alleged that Marculus was thrown over a cliff (*Passio Marculi* (*PL.* viii, col. 764) and Augustine, *Contra Cresconium,* iii. 49. 54). The Catholics claimed that he threw himself over. Optatus, however, agrees (iii. 6) that both he and Donatus of Bagai were 'occisi'. His death in this manner by whosesoever agency would explain the particular method chosen by the Circumcellions to commit suicide. Marculus himself managed to find his way into the Catholic martyrology (Bede, vi. Kal. Decembris).

[6] *Passio Maximiani et Isaaci,* i (*PL.* viii, col. 768). The text of the decree has not survived.

[7] Optatus, iii. 1, 'Venerunt tunc cum pharetris armigeri, repleta est unaquaeque civitas vociferantium; nuntiata unitate fugistis omnes', &c.

But once order had been re-established, the task of restoring the Catholics to power proved surprisingly easy. Donatus saw his life's work collapsing around him. His bid for supreme power had ended suddenly and in utter disaster. He himself and other leaders were caught and exiled. Many of his clergy remembered the injunction concerning flight in persecution and acted on it. The rout of the Donatists was complete.

The sudden collapse of Donatism in Carthage and Proconsular Africa is attested by Catholic and Donatist writers alike.[1] Granting the latter's tendency to emphasize the vigour and ruthlessness of the Macarian persecution as a proof of their own righteousness, there is little reason to doubt its severity and momentary effect. In this respect the events of 347–8 resemble the persecution of 303–5. Both took their victims by surprise, in both there were apostasies and mass flights, and in both the cowardice of the majority was redeemed in the eyes of later generations by a few resolute individuals. In either case a long period of security preceding the persecution had induced over-confidence and slackness. So much is admitted by the writer of the *Passio Maximiani et Isaaci.*

There were probably additional reasons for the débâcle. By 347 Caecilian and nearly all the main actors in the original dispute had died. A new generation had grown up, and with it a movement towards reuniting the divided factions in the African Church. Donatus, as we have seen, apparently took the first step in this direction himself, and it is unlikely that the proclamation of the fact of unity could have caused any deep resentment. Moreover, the Donatists had been faced by the defiance of their own extremists in Numidia, and had appealed to the Imperial authorities for help. They had manœuvred themselves into a contradictory position. Donatus' bluff was called and the penalty of exile was inevitable.

Resistance in Carthage developed slowly. Later,[2] possibly the following year, pressure against the Donatists was renewed. This time the decree proclaiming unity was torn down with the same defiance as the Christians had torn Diocletian's edict from the walls of the cathedral of Nicomedia. The culprit, Maximian,

---

[1] Optatus, iii. 1; *Passio Maximiani et Isaaci* (*PL.* viii, col. 768).

[2] The writer of the *Passio Maximiani et Isaaci* (*PL.* viii, col. 768) records this incident separately from the Edict of Union ('Diabolus iterum fremens', &c.). On the other hand, Seeck, *Untergang*, iii. 338, prefers August 347 for both publication of the decree and Maximian's demonstration.

was arrested, but by now the crowd was on his side. Insults were flung at officials and the *traditor* clergy, and a man named Isaac, who had been particularly abusive, accompanied Maximian to prison. Both are said to have been executed. Their martyrdom was recorded in *Acta* written with the same intensity of feeling that characterized the Acts of the Abitinian martyrs. The details of their sufferings, and the account of the multitudes that were alleged to have kept vigil round the prison show that little had changed in popular outlook over the previous fifty years. For the Donatist leaders abroad, the heroism of these 'resisters' provided an alibi for their own errors and weakness.

Donatus himself never set foot again in Africa. His death in exile enabled his followers to claim him as a martyr as well as a religious reformer.[1] He remained a powerful figure to the end, and far from his Church dissolving in faction at his death, probably in A.D. 355, there seems to have been no difficulty in accepting a non-African priest named Parmenian as his successor.[2] Parmenian was to prove an ideal choice.

An estimate of Donatus' work can only be given on the broadest lines. Augustine placed him as a matter of course alongside Cyprian as a 'precious jewel' in the Church.[3] The association is not inapt. The main lines of Cyprian's teaching on the nature of the Church and on the Sacraments were preserved by Donatus, but probably were carried by him to conclusions with which Cyprian would not have agreed. Both men were gifted with spiritual and administrative talents of a high order, and both shared the same exalted view of the bishop's office. The curious incident of the dispatch of a Numidian bishop to Rome suggests that Donatus, too, considered that the unity of the Church entailed contact in some form with the see of Peter. When Victor of Garba died, he took care to send a successor.

But whatever Donatus' intentions, the effect of his separation from Caecilian was to bring the most flourishing of the Churches in the West permanently out of line with the other Latin Christian communities. Augustine could fairly point out that

---

[1] Augustine, *Ad Donatistas post Collationem*, 16. 20.

[2] Optatus, ii. 7. I have accepted Monceaux's view that he was not a native of Africa (*Hist. litt.* v, chap. v).

[3] Augustine, *Sermo* 37. 3 (*PL.* xxxviii, col. 223), 'Lapis pretiosus erat Cyprianus; sed mansit in hujus ornamento. Lapis pretiosus erat Donatus.'

Cyprian's controversy with Stephen had not involved a schism.[1]
In claiming that true Christianity had by circumstances become
restricted virtually to a single province, Donatus was anticipating the road taken by Schnoudi of Atirpe and the Coptic
Church after Chalcedon in 451. The immediate result, however,
was that during the fourth century the African Church ceased
to exert the influence on Latin Christian thought that it had in
the time of Tertullian and Cyprian. Even Augustine could not
turn back the trends to which Donatus had given so powerful
an impulse. For their part, the Bishops of Rome no longer found
themselves face to face with a rival ecclesiastical power in
Africa. In the third century Spanish and Gallic Christians had
appealed to Cyprian at Carthage to settle ecclesiastical disputes.
Now, Rome was able to develop unhindered its jurisdictional
claims over the Christian Churches in the West. North Africa,
on the other hand, took a long step towards eventual cleavage
from its neighbours on the northern shores of the Mediterranean. With Donatus of Carthage begins the cycle of events
which led to the division of the Mediterranean between the
rival creeds represented by Pope and Prophet.

THE CATHOLIC ASCENDANCY, A.D. 348 TO 361

The Catholic triumph, however, was complete to all appearances. Unity was proclaimed in synods held throughout the
African provinces. In 348 or 349, Bishop Gratus summoned a
Council at Carthage which was to crown his work of pacification. It was attended by fifty bishops, including possibly a
number of former Donatists. Gratus in his opening address
thanked 'the servants of God', Paul and Macarius, for their
holy work,[2] and welcomed the return of Unity as proclaimed
by the Emperor. The Council then proceeded to enact canons
forbidding rebaptism and the honouring of 'unworthy persons'
as martyrs. But as a gesture of reconciliation, Gratus also included *traditores* in his condemnation. It was well meant, and
had the conflict been merely over the behaviour of individuals
a generation previously it might have succeeded.[3] For the time

---

[1] Augustine, *De Baptismo contra Donatistas*, v. 25. 36 (*PL*. xliii, col. 194).
[2] 'ministros sancti operis famulos Dei, Paulum et Macarium'. Cited from *PL*.
viii, col. 774.
[3] Duchesne, *Early History of the Church*, ii. 194.

being, however, Africa had returned at least nominally to the unity of the Catholic Church in the western provinces.[1]

The next thirteen years are among the most difficult to reconstruct in the story of Donatism. It seems clear, however, that the Catholics were unable to exploit their victory to the full. Gratus himself was a man of only moderate ability and was indifferently supported. He does not, for instance, lead the discussion at his Council as Aurelius and Augustine were wont fifty years later. He is simply one of a dozen or so orators who address the meeting. His name is associated with no revival of religion, and the Catholics failed almost completely to impress the African Christians with claims to superior sanctity and doctrine. From an independent and friendly source, Hosius of Cordoba, we learn that the Africans more than any other Catholic bishops spent their time at Constans' court, lobbying for sinecures for their friends, and indulging in extravagance and nepotism. Gratus was unable to control them.[2] The decrees of Gratus' Council at Carthage show that discipline was lax in other respects. Clergy were in the habit of wandering from see to see offering their services where prospects of gain were best. Bishops for similar motives attempted to usurp each other's congregations.[3] Others were acting as moneylenders,[4] a fact which gains significance when placed against the background of the prevailing economic misery in the countryside.

In matters of doctrine also, the African Catholics seem to have been somewhat ill advised. At this moment there was no philosophic or theological dispute with the Donatists. Both inclined towards the semi-Arians. Four African bishops were among the signatories to the semi-Arian formula of Sirmium in 358,[5] while Gratus' successor at Carthage, Restitutus, presided at the Council of Ariminum (Rimini) in October 359, and played his part in its support of Constantius' creed.[6]

Here and there the African Catholics made gains. At Curubis

---

[1] Mansi, *Concilia*, iii. 144; Monceaux, *Histoire littéraire*, iii. 221.

[2] Canon 8 of Council of Serdica (Mansi, *Concilia*, iii. 67).

[3] Canon 10. 'Multi [episcopi] enim transcendunt sua et usurpant aliena ipsis invitis.' The motive was 'avaritiae cupiditatem'.

[4] Canon 13.

[5] Sozomen, *Historia Ecclesiastica*, iv. 15; Monceaux, *Histoire littéraire*, iii. 217.

[6] He thereby raised the prestige of the see of Carthage. There were 400 western bishops present. It was the first and last time that a bishop of Carthage presided over a representative synod of the western provinces.

(Kurba), on the Tunisian coast, hallowed by association with Cyprian, the Donatists dated the first emergence of a Catholic community to this period of repression.[1] At Thagaste the same may have been true.[2] There the results were to be more serious for their cause. If Monnica had been a Donatist like some other members of her family, Augustine's life-history would have been considerably different. On the whole, however, there is little trace of a permanent change of allegiance, and the opportunity of vindicating Caecilian passed away for a generation.

Concerning the Donatists during these years two things stand out: first, that as in the previous period of repression between 317 and 321 effective measures were not taken against them outside Carthage, and second, the importance which the Donatist Bishop of Rome now assumed in the leadership of his Church.

In Numidia it seems that the Donatists did not take long to recover from the shock of Macarius' decrees. As early as 348/9 the Catholic Bishop of Madauros (Mdaorouch) complained at Gratus' Council at Carthage that under cover of 'reconciliation' the junior bishop (presumably the ex-Donatist) had deprived him of his entire flock. He was their 'father' while the lawful bishop had become known as their 'father-in-law'.[3] Farther south, the name of Marculus had become a watchword. At Vegesela, the site of the ill-starred conference with Macarius, a great basilica was built in his honour. Over the chancel arch were inscribed the defiant words, 'Deo laudes omnes hic dicamus'.[4] At Nova Petra pilgrims visited the spot where the bishop was supposed to have been executed.[5] Sixty years later, in June 411, the Donatist bishop, Dativus, could tell the Imperial Commissioner that he had 'no Catholic opponent in his diocese, for Marculus is there, whose blood God will

---

[1] *Gesta Coll. Carth.* I. 187 (*PL.* xi, col. 1328).

[2] Augustine, *Ep.* 93. 5. 17, mentions that Thagaste was once 'wholly Donatist', but was won over by fear of Imperial edicts. The most probable time for this to have taken place would be between 348 and 361, having regard to Augustine's own upbringing in a Catholic household.

[3] Canon 12 of Gratus' Council.

[4] The discovery and excavation of this church is described by P. Cayrel, 'Une Basilique donatiste de Numidie', *Mélanges*, li, 1934, pp. 132 ff., and P. Courcelle, 'Une seconde campagne de fouilles à Ksar el Kelb', ibid. liii, 1936, pp. 161-83.

[5] *Passio Marculi* (*PL.* viii, col. 765). Marculus himself was regarded as a prophet (Augustine, *Contra Litteras Petiliani*, ii. 14. 32).

avenge at the Last Day'.[1] Elsewhere, in south-western Numidia fanatical Donatist bishops, such as Felix of Zabi (Zabi) and Januarius of Flumen Piscensis, bided their time in possession of their sees, and hoped that their revenge would not be too long postponed.

The 'days of Macarius', the *tempora Macariana*, left as deep a mark on the mind of the Donatist Numidians as did the Great Persecution. Reading the words of the sect's apologists in the time of Augustine one can see the extent to which this single event added to the ill feeling between the two parties. The misdeeds wrought by Paul and Macarius are the theme alike of Parmenian, Petilian, Cresconius, and the host of lesser writers against whom Augustine inveighed. The Catholic Church became known as the 'pars Macarii', and the Catholics as 'Macariani'.[2] It was like 'Cromwell in Ireland'. A spirit of brooding hatred was engendered which no gesture of conciliation could erase.

Apart from the maintenance of popular favour, the Donatists were able to produce at least one writer of note, Vitellius Afer.[3] The work for which Gennadius considers him worthy of mention, the *De eo quod odio sint mundo servi Dei*, has perished, but that he could write at all in this period is of interest as showing the comparative ineffectiveness of the repression. It is also remarkable that Gennadius describes Vitellius' doctrinal orthodoxy as beyond reproach, a judgement which could hardly have been passed on some of his African Catholic contemporaries.

But in this period the Donatist Church owes less to Africa than to Rome. With the death of Donatus the leadership passed to two men, Bishop Pontius, Donatus' companion in exile, and Macrobius, Bishop of Rome. Parmenian, who was consecrated Donatus' successor by the exiled bishops, was a stranger to Africa, possibly even a Spaniard or Gaul by birth, and played little part at this stage.[4]

The leadership of Pontius and Macrobius, despite conditions

---

[1] *Gesta Coll. Carth.* i. 187.

[2] Augustine, *Contra Litteras Petiliani*, ii. 39. 92, and ii. 92. 208; *Ep.* 87. 10.

[3] Gennadius, *De Scriptoribus Ecclesiasticis*, 4 (*PL.* lix, col. 1059), 'Vitellius Afer, Donatianorum schisma defendens, scripsit "De eo quod odio sint mundo servi Dei". In quo, si tacuisset de nostro velut persecutorum nomine egregiam doctrinam ediderat.'

[4] Optatus, ii. 7, 'Hispanum aut Gallum', another indication that Donatus had no intention of confining his Church to Africa, if he could secure acceptance of his views in other provinces.

imposed by exile, appears to have been vigorous. Both men represented distinct types of Donatist bishop. Pontius was a seer, a worker of miracles, and a prophet. He seems to have kept together the small group of senior bishops which accompanied Donatus overseas, and in 361/2 he took the lead in addressing an appeal to the Emperor Julian. Otherwise, little is known about him, though he may have still been living at the time of the Council of Bagai in 394. To judge from the anti-Donatist works of Augustine, his prestige in fifth-century Africa was second only to that of Donatus himself, with whom he became closely associated in the popular mind.[1]

Macrobius was an entirely different personality. At one time he was a presbyter in the Catholic Church and had begun to establish a reputation as a moralist and an authority on Church discipline.[2] At this stage, however, he evidently fell under the influence of the stern moral teaching of Donatus, and became a Donatist. The Macarian persecution caught him at Carthage, and like many of his colleagues he fled overseas.[3] But in his case this did not mean an interruption in his activity. The small Donatist community in Rome needed a bishop and Macrobius was chosen. He appears to have found his flock in a sad state, with dwindling numbers and lax discipline. The church appears to have been a catacomb excavated in a hill outside Rome, a circumstance which earned the Donatists in Rome the name 'Mountaineers' (*Montenses*) or 'Rock-dwellers' (*Rupitae*).[4] In view of the tendency of his previous works, one would be inclined to agree with Harnack and ascribe the pseudo-Cyprianic *De Singularitate Clericorum* to his pen.[5] It was a tract admirably suited to a small austere group such as Macrobius led.

---

[1] Augustine, *Ad Catholicos Epistola*, 19. 49, 'Mirabilia fecit vel Donatus vel Pontius', also 11. 28 and *In Ioannis Evang. Tract.* xiii. 17.

[2] Gennadius, *De Scriptoribus Ecclesiasticis* (*PL.* lix, col. 1060), 'librum scripserat ad Confessores et Virgines, moralis quidem, sed valde necessariae doctrinae et praecipue ad custodiendam castitatem aptissimis valde sententiis communitum ac postea ab Ecclesia catholica desciscens Donatistarum in urbe Roma occultus episcopus fuit'.

[3] In his *Passio Maximiani et Isaaci* (*PL.* viii, cols. 767–74), Macrobius refers to 'secessio nostra' (at col. 774).

[4] Optatus, ii. 4; Augustine, *Ad Catholicos Epistola*, iii. 6. The use of the term *spelunca* to describe the Donatist meeting-place in Rome may simply be a term of abuse. The Donatists were to tax the Maximianists with meeting in a *spelunca* during the crisis of 393, though there can be little question of the latter actually using a cavern for their services.

[5] A. Harnack, 'Der Pseudo-Cyprianische Traktat de Singularitate Clericorum',

By 356, however, the situation had improved, and Jerome records Donatist activity in Rome in his *Chronicle* for this year.[1] Macrobius had begun to restore contact with the Donatist communities in Africa. He sent letters of encouragement, and about this time probably wrote the *Passio Maximiani et Isaaci* with the object of strengthening the Carthaginians against accepting the edict of Unity.[2] Thus, to some extent the continuity of organized existence was maintained during these years, and Macrobius himself was to have the satisfaction of seeing Donatism fully restored in Africa.[3] Meantime, the close links between Rome and Carthage were once more in evidence, and for the first and last time in its history, the Donatist Church was governed from Rome.

THE REIGN OF JULIAN, 361–3

The long period of persecution and eclipse ended in the autumn of 361. On 3 November Constantius died at Mopsucrene in Cicilia, and civil war between him and his nephew Julian was thereby averted. The latter was left the undisputed master of the Roman world. Almost overnight the fortunes of the pagans and dissident Christians throughout the Empire changed. Partly, no doubt, animated by feelings of tolerance, but more by a cynical desire of bringing Christianity into disrepute and self-destruction by rekindling the internecine hatreds of the various Christian sects, Julian recalled those who had been banished by Constantius.[4] Athanasius returned to Alexandria on 21 February 362 after the murder of his rival Georgius, and the exiled Anomaean leader Aetius was sent back to Antioch after a private interview with the Emperor at Constantinople. Other exiles such as Lucifer of Calgiari or Eusebius of Vercelli were sped on their way homeward. Therefore, late in 361 or early the following year, the Donatist leaders, headed by Bishops Pontius, Rogatian, and Cassian,

TU. xxiv. 3, Leipzig, 1903. It must, however, be admitted that the style employed by the writer of this work differs considerably from the violence of the *Passio Maximiani et Isaaci.* Cf. H. Koch, *Cyprianische Untersuchungen* (Bonn, 1926), pp. 426 f.

[1] Jerome, *Chronicon* ad ann. 356 (*PL.* xxvii, col. 501).

[2] *Passio Maximiani et Isaaci* (*PL.* viii, col. 768 (top)).

[3] Macrobius was still living in 365, when Optatus published the first edition of the *De Schismate Donatistarum*, Optatus, ii. 4.

[4] Lietzmann, *Geschichte der alten Kirche*, iii. 268 ff. On Julian's motives, Ammianus Marcellinus, xxii. 5. 4.

appealed to Julian, asking that they too should be allowed to return to Africa. Their request was granted. Not only might they return, but the basilicas and other property seized by the Catholics in 347 were to be restored to them.[1]

The letter which Pontius addressed to Julian was in flattering terms. 'Justice alone' swayed his thoughts, he claimed.[2] For once the Donatists found themselves on the same side as their enemies, the pagan Numidian town-dwellers who were celebrating the Apostate's accession with triumphal arches and congratulatory addresses.[3] But in this instance, as in others less creditable, they did themselves no harm in the eyes of their followers. After all, had not Athanasius himself accepted the Apostate's favour? An appeal to the Emperor, whether Constantine or Julian, as the source of justice was considered a reasonable procedure. Neither Optatus of Milevis nor Augustine was able to make much progress with arguments to the contrary. With regard to Donatists and Catholics the Emperor's estimate of Christian charity was sound enough.

The return of the Donatist leaders from exile was like the return of triumphant revolutionary leaders. Their homecoming is described in dramatic sentences by Optatus of Milevis. They came, he says, 'frenzied in anger, tearing asunder the limbs of the Church, subtle in deceit, horrible in slaughterings'.[4] Their arrival put North Africa in the grip of an outbreak of terror and communal fury unparalleled in the relations of the two Churches. The same author, writing only a few years after the events, has left vivid descriptions which remind the historian of the communal outbreaks in parts of India after the end of the Second World War. He tells of congregations who for fourteen years had lived peaceably and apparently as Catholics, suddenly

---

[1] Optatus, ii. 16. Augustine, *Contra Litteras Petiliani*, ii. 97. 224, quotes part of the text of Julian's reply. 'Hoc quoque supplicantibus Rogatiano, Pontio, Cassiano et caeteris episcopis, sed et clericis, accedit ad cumulum, ut abolitis quae adversus eos sine rescripto perperam gesta sunt, in antiquum statum cuncta revocentur.' Also, *Ep.* 105. 2. 9.

[2] Augustine, op. cit., 'apud eum sola justitia locum haberet'.

[3] Inscriptions in honour of Julian have been found in the Numidian towns of Timgad, *CIL*. viii. 2387, and 18684 (a *municipium* on the site of Mr'heb Thala).

[4] Optatus, ii. 17, 'Venistis rabidi, venistis irati, membra laniantes ecclesiae, subtiles in seductionibus, in caedibus immanes.' Optatus has left a vivid account of events of which he at Milevis (modern Mila) may well have had first-hand knowledge. The most revealing passages are ii. 18–21 and vi. 1–8. The phenomenon of sudden mass conversions is noted, 'ex ovibus subito facti sunt vulpes, ex fidelibus perfidi, ex patientibus rabidi . . .', vi. 8.

seized with religious frenzy. Donatism swept Numidia and Mauretania like a forest fire. Bishops, priests, and women in vows (*sanctimoniales*) were rudely deposed. Where they were not killed outright, they were ordered 'to become Christians', they were stripped of their mitres and veils, their heads shaven, covered with ashes (i.e. subjected to ritual penance), and either invested anew by the victorious Donatists or cast out among the crowd of laymen and penitents. The altars at which they had worshipped only a short time before were broken up and burnt, the Communion wine thrown to the dogs or heated into a powerful stimulant and drunk. The Catholic liturgical vessels were thrown out of windows to be smashed, and their fragments sold off at the fairs for what they would fetch. Those who hesitated to participate were taunted with adhering to the 'Macarians' and accused of 'idolatry'. The Donatist leaders saw in such events a just retribution and a necessary purge. As Parmenian pointed out in 363/4, 'Those things which had been touched by the defiled were themselves defiled', and should thus be destroyed.[1] Rebaptism once more became the rule.[2]

At least two major acts of vengeance were perpetrated. In 362[3] one armed band of Donatists led by the bishops of Zabi and Flumen Piscensis on the Mauretanian High Plains moved north-east across the plateau of Metarfa and stormed the walled settlement of Lemellefense (Kherbet Zembia).[4] The Catholic church was sacked and two deacons were slain. Another horde also led by bishops advanced westwards from the area round Constantine, and then through the Kabylie to attack the coast town of Tipasa. This city was at that time, as in 373 and throughout the fifth century, a Catholic stronghold. In this instance, the Donatists appear to have had the full support of the Imperial officials. The *Praeses* of Mauretania Caesariensis,

[1] Optatus, vi. 3.

[2] Augustine is quite explicit on this point. In 408 he wrote, 'usque ad persecutionem per Macarium factam traditoribus sine baptismo communicasse' (*Ep.* 93. 43). The reversion to the original practice is a further indication of the effect of the Macarian persecution on the relations between the two communities.

[3] The Catholic clergy who were the victims of the attack are recorded in the Roman Martyrology on 9 Feb.; the attack on Lemellefense may have taken place in Feb. 363.

[4] The location of Zabi and Lemellefense is known. The latter was the first posting station on the road between Zarai and Aumale and occupied an important stragetic position (Gsell, *Atlas archéologique*, feuilles 25 and 26). Le Commandant L. Jacquot has traced out a possible route taken by the Donatists from observations on the ground (*Recueil de Constantine*, 1915, pp. 129 ff.).

Athenius, with his troops and some of his subordinates are related by Optatus to have taken part in the scenes that followed the entry of the Donatists into the town.[1] Nothing is more indicative of the complete reversal of the situation of the two religions which Julian's accession brought about. The Catholics were ejected with every insult. Their virgins under vows were violated, the Eucharist desecrated, and a Donatist community established. The next year the episcopal leaders of the insurgents returned to view their handiwork. They then went back to Numidia and crowned their success by solemnly deposing the Catholic bishop of Tiddis near Constantine.[2]

Where violence was not used, the law was invoked. Justices were kept busy restoring to the Donatists churches and property seized by the Catholics during the previous fourteen years.[3] Buildings which thereby changed owners were rigorously purified with salt and water, and the walls and altars washed over with a thick coating of adhesive whitewash. The Donatist leaders gained immense popularity. The Numidian population swore by them and called them blessed. Catholic clergy hastened to make their peace, and their congregations followed them. Recalcitrants were summoned before the Council which met at Theveste (Tebessa) in 362. The great cathedral may well have been the scene of the Donatist triumph.[4]

As in more recent outbreaks of communal fanaticism one is tempted to look beneath the surface of religious divergences to the social tensions which divided the two groups. The years of Catholic ascendancy had not been years of prosperity for the mass of the inhabitants of Roman Africa. The laws of the *Codex Theodosianus* over this period tell their own story of grinding misery and of the oppression of the poor by the rich. On two occasions, in 353 and in the summer of 361, there seems to have been an attempt at actual revolt.[5] The citizens

---

[1] Optatus, ii. 18, 'nonnullorum officialium et favore et furore iuvante et Athenio praeside praesente cum signis catholica frequentia exturbata . . .'.

[2] Ibid. 19. Tiddis is about thirteen miles west-south-west of Constantine.

[3] Id. iii. 3.

[4] Id. ii. 18. There is, however, no evidence to show that the Council was held in the basilica itself, though this would be a fair assumption. On the deposition of Catholic bishops, ibid. 25.

[5] *Cod. Theod.* x. 8. 4, to Iuvenalis, *Rationalis Numidiae*; Seeck, *Regesten*, pp. 41 and 199, dates this rescript to June 353, identifying the *hostis publicus* referred to as Magnentius; *Cod. Theod.* i. 36. 14, to Flavian, *Proconsul Africae*, 3 Aug. 361, 'Gravis ista commotio', &c.

were ordered to repair their town walls.[1] In February 359 Constantius instructed that the villagers dwelling on Imperial estates, that is, over a large part of Numidia and Mauretania Sitifensis, should be freed from all 'extraordinary burdens' to which they were being subjected.[2] But as against this, the Imperial officials such as the notary Gaudentius were building up for themselves reputations for villainy and extortion at the expense of the inhabitants, and their example was being followed eagerly by their subordinates. Among Julian's first measures of pacification in Africa was to order the execution of Gaudentius and his brother the *Vicarius Africae*.[3] This was accompanied by the grant of a general remittance of taxation in kind to the provincials, a concession of direct benefit to the village population.[4] In Asia Minor, Gregory of Nazianze notes that the countryfolk looked to Julian for justice. The same may have been true in Africa.[5]

The effect of the restoration of the Donatist leaders was to increase the religious and social feuds between members of the two communities. A barrier of fear, hatred, and superstition separated Donatist and Catholic. No greetings were exchanged (a much more significant gesture in the Middle East than in western Europe), no Catholic might be buried in a cemetery held by the Donatists, there was no intermarriage, except where the Catholic was prepared to abandon his faith.[6] At Hippo Regius, where the Donatists gained a complete ascendancy, the Donatist *inquilini* (tenants) refused to bake bread for their Catholic masters.[7] The stigma of being the 'Macariani'

---

[1] *CIL.* viii. 9282 (Thanaramusa); *Cod. Theod.* vi. 15. 3.

[2] *Cod. Theod.* xi. 16. 9, to Taurus, *Praefectus Praetorio.* An inscription from Timgad, dated to Julian's reign, records steps taken to remedy abuses connected with the forwarding of petitions (*CIL.* viii. 17896).

[3] Ammianus Marcellinus (ed. Loeb), xxii. 11. 1. On unscrupulous officials in Africa in this period, *Cod. Theod.* vi. 29. 1 and xi. 7. 8.

[4] Ibid. 28. 1, 'Excepto auro et argento cuncta reliqua indulgemus.'

[5] *Oratio*, 5. 21 (*PG.* xxxv, col. 689). One particular abuse affecting Africa, which Julian gained the admiration of the provincials by restricting, concerned the use of the public post by the wealthy. The villagers would be obliged to supply fodder and sometimes the animals themselves for the benefit of wealthy Africans, including Catholic bishops, who were abusing a privilege reserved for officials (*Cod. Theod.* vii. 5. 7 and 10; cf. Gregory of Nazianze, *Oratio*, 4. 75 (*PG.* xxxv, col. 599)).

[6] Optatus, iv. 5 and vi. 7. Cf. Augustine, *Enarrratio in Psalmum 54.* 20, and *Sermo* 46. 7. 15.

[7] Id., *Contra Litteras Petiliani*, ii. 83. 184. While all this may have been merely 'unlovely manifestation of Evangelical zeal' (Knox, *Enthusiasm*, p. 67),

o

was one which was to cling to African Catholicism as long as
the religious strife lasted.

there was probably in addition a ritual motive for avoiding contact with the
Catholics, that is, fear of contagion. We notice that the Catholics had the same
fear of contact with Manichees (Augustine, *Confessions*, iii. 11. 19). The idea has
survived in Roman Catholic as well as Protestant concepts and is shown by the
wording of decrees, 'Vitandus', issued against individuals (e.g. against the Abbé
Loisy in 1907).

XIII

THE AGE OF PARMENIAN

A.D. 363-91

THE position which Parmenian, the new Donatist bishop of Carthage, was called upon to fill was no easy one. So long as Julian was Emperor the Numidian extremists were in control, and Donatism was a recognized religion of the African provinces, but with the Emperor's death on 26 June 363 the situation changed once more, and the brief spell of power and Imperial favour ended.

Parmenian, however, was to show himself equal to the situation. The year and a half of undisputed authority had evidently done much to remove the initial disadvantages under which he had arrived in Africa. His opponent, Optatus of Milevis, makes the most of the fact that he was a foreigner and therefore unfamiliar with the early history of the controversy and with African conditions in general. Yet by 364 he was the acknowledged spokesman of the Donatist Church, and throughout his long period of office, which lasted until 391/2, his authority was never seriously challenged.[1] He was to bring Donatism successfully through the crisis of Firmus' revolt, the excommunication of Tyconius, and the Rogatist schism. By the end of his rule, his Church had attained the height of its power and prosperity.

From all accounts, he was a firm and honourable man, a stranger to intrigue and violence, and contemptuous of the value of brutality.[2] He was a great orator, like nearly all the Donatist leaders,[3] and though more moderate in his views than most, he gave nothing away when it came to denouncing the African Catholics. Like his predecessors, he took care that the essential tenets of Donatism penetrated the mass of his followers. The 'new psalms' which he wrote, probably in rhyming couplets, for that purpose were very popular and were being

---

[1] For Augustine's view, *Sermo* 46. 8. 17 (*PL.* xxxviii, col. 279), 'Extulit se superbia Donati, fecit sibi partem, subsequens eum Parmenianus illius confirmavit errorem.'
[2] Monceaux has summarized available literary evidence on Parmenian. See article 'Parmenianus', in *Journal des Savants*, Jan. and Apr. 1909, pp. 19 ff. and 157 ff.; also, in *Histoire littéraire*, v. 220 ff.
[3] *Contra Cresconium*, i. 2. 3.

sung in Augustine's time and much later.[1] In the mid-fifth century 'Praedestinatus,' the Pelagian writer of the *De haeresibus*, refers to the Donatists outside Carthage as 'Parmeniani'.

Parmenian deserved the reputation he had achieved by the next century. With Tyconius he shares the honour of maintaining the intellectual predominance which the Donatists enjoyed in Africa down to the time of Augustine. He was responsible for a clear advance in Donatist theology which raises the community above the level of an unprogressive sect. It seems that very soon after his arrival in Africa he found himself obliged to defend his Church's claims to be the true representative of Christianity in Africa. It must be imagined that Restitutus and his colleagues had recovered from the shock of the Donatists' sudden return to power in 361. Parmenian defined his position in five books, probably entitled *Adversus Ecclesiam Traditorum*.[2] As is usual with Donatist writings, these have not survived, but fragments are quoted by Optatus of Milevis in his reply. The books themselves probably dealt with Baptism, the Unity of the Church, the crime of *traditio*, the villainy of the recent persecution by Paul and Macarius, and the meaning of the text 'Let not my head be anointed with the oil of a sinner' (Psalm cxl. 5—LXX). But out of these rather commonplace headings there emerged an original theory of the attributes of the Church and a further definition of its relationship with the world surrounding it.

Parmenian based his ideas on the familiar symbolism of the Church as the Bride of Christ, but he introduced a new element into his argument. Like a human bride, the Church possessed certain endowments (*dotes*),[3] and the claim of a Christian community to represent the true Church depended on whether or not it possessed these endowments. They were five in number.

---

[1] Augustine, *Ep.* 55. 18. 34 (*CSEL.* xxxiv. 2. 209); and Praedestinatus, *De Haeresibus*, 43, 'Parmenianos a Parmeniano qui per totam Africam libros contra nos conficiens et novos Psalmos faciens circumibat'. Praedestinatus was probably writing about 435 (H. von Schubert, 'Der sogenannte Praedestinatus', *TU.* Bd. xxiv. 4, 1903, p. 63). Augustine's own 'Psalmus contra Partem Donati', written for his congregation at Hippo in 393, was in rhyming couplets.

[2] See A. Pincherle, 'L'Ecclesiologia nella Controversia Donatista', *Ricerche Religiose*, i, 1925, pp. 35–55, and E. Buonaiuti's criticism of this article in *Il Cristianesimo nell' Africa Romana*, 332.

[3] I have no direct evidence that Parmenian used this comparison, but in view of his gift of employing homely illustrations to point out doctrinal truths, it seems a possible explanation.

First, there was the *cathedra*, representing the authority and unity of the episcopacy. It may seem astonishing that Parmenian should have opened with this claim, when he must have known that, only three or four years before, his opponent Restitutus had presided at Ariminum over the assembled bishops from the western provinces—but he had apparently no hesitation in relying on the arguments used by Cyprian in the *De Unitate*.[1] Moreover, he could in fact point to the presence of a Donatist episcopal succession at Rome as proof that unity with the see of Peter was being maintained.[2] After the *cathedra* came the *angelus*, presumably the Angel who hovers over the waters of baptism and in the Apocalypse stands at the side of the elders.[3] Then followed the *fons* or baptismal font, the *sigillum* or seal, without which the baptismal font could not be opened, and finally the altar.[4] While, so far as is known, the Donatists had previously rested their claims to be the true Church on their opposition to the *traditores*, they had now come to define their own concept of the Church, and to work out a logical defence of their position. The Catholics had nothing to say against Parmenian's theology, and were obliged to argue their case from historical facts, where for the moment they were on the defensive.[5]

Which of the rival Churches in Africa possessed these 'endowments'? Parmenian maintained that the African Catholics had proved themselves to be false Christians. First, they had renounced salvation by having betrayed the Word of God to pagan magistrates, and, secondly, they had called in the armed forces of the secular power against the Church. Parmenian again seems to have cited the *De Unitate*.[6] He who bore arms against the Church automatically put himself outside it. Return to the Church could only be gained by penance followed by a new initiation by baptism. Thus the insistence on the rebaptism of Catholics fitted logically into Parmenian's general theory of

[1] A. Pincherle, op. cit., pp. 37 ff.

[2] Optatus, ii. 4.

[3] As referred to in Tertullian, *De Baptismo*, 4 and 6; Revelation v.

[4] Which Parmenian equated to the Bride's navel in Song of Solomon vii. 2 (Optatus, ii. 8).

[5] See Optatus, i. 4 and 5.

[6] A. Pincherle, op. cit., pp. 40–43, draws attention to Parmenian's indictment of the Catholics as 'unfruitful branches', and the similar language used by Cyprian in *De Unitate*, 5. The denunciation of those who bore arms against the Church is evidently modelled on *De Unitate*, 17.

the nature of the Church in which penance and baptism were inseparably linked. We shall find the same view developed by Tyconius a few years later.

From Parmenian's ideas on the nature of the Church followed automatically his views on its relation with the State. In this he had nothing to add to what had already been proclaimed by Tertullian and Donatus. But in demanding complete separation of the Christian Church from the State, Parmenian did not mean a purely negative attitude of resignation. As we know from an anonymous sermon once attributed to Optatus of Milevis, Parmenian's colleagues were preaching that the true Christian *must* expect a life of continuous persecution. His fate was that of all just men from Abel onwards.[1] That entailed continuous struggle with false brethren and the secular powers. One such period of open conflict had, in Parmenian's view, been the return of the Donatist leaders from exile. Acts of violence if committed by clergy in the name of the Church against 'persecutors' were legitimate, and in a different category from the action of soldiers.[2] The paradox of 'aggressive suffering' has a strangely modern ring,[3] and in the ideas of Parmenian one finds an early trace of the conception of 'holy war', the *jehad* in the name of Islam.

Optatus' reply to Parmenian's five books reads today like a logical and convincing argument. It is doubtful if it did so to his contemporaries. With the Catholics discredited as 'Macariani', his proof that the Donatists were really the schismatics might have sounded odd to a Numidian audience. The use of troops by Macarius and Donatus' death in exile were well-known facts; Optatus was driven to justify these measures by requiring the almost complete dependence of the Church on the civil power.[4] The Numidians were not ready for such a change. The conversion of the State itself to Christianity necessitated a restatement of relationships, and opposite views were preached in Africa by Parmenian and Optatus. It is, however, doubtful whether the latter's arguments disturbed the Donatists.

[1] A. Pincherle, 'Un sermone donatista attributo a S. Ottato di Milevi', *Bilychnis*, xxii, 1923, pp. 134-48.

[2] Optatus, ii. 18, 'aliud sunt milites missi, aliud episcopi ordinati'.

[3] When support of a 'Peace Committee' is perfectly consistent with an attitude of ferocious aggression against 'imperialists' and 'enemies of peace and democracy'.

[4] Optatus, iii. 3, p. 74.

Parmenian did not bother to reply, and contemporary chroniclers pass over the author of the *De Schismate Donatistarum* in a short and undistinguished note.[1]

Meantime, the accession of Valentinian and Valens in October 364 had brought changes among the high officials in Africa. Whatever leanings the Emperors may have felt towards the Arians in the west, they had no sympathy for the Donatists. In the new *Comes Africae*, Romanus, the latter found an enemy who was prepared once more to restore Catholicism with the aid of the troops under his command.[2] Tyconius regarded the persecution that followed as a revelation of Antichrist.[3] For the poor, extortion and corrupt administration were added to the hardships caused by the renewed period of repression and insecurity. Few Imperial representatives in Africa left so evil a name as Count Romanus.[4]

The persecution caused a renewal of Circumcellion activity. As in the previous generation, their excesses frightened and alienated the more conservative Donatists. There were protests, and in Mauretania Caesariensis, Rogatus the Bishop of Cartenna took the law into his own hands and declared that the drunken orgies of the Circumcellions disgraced the Church. He and nine colleagues decided to break away from the main body and establish their own community, where traditional purity based on non-violence would be maintained.[5] Cartenna was a long way from Carthage, and doubtless Parmenian would have found it difficult to reassert his authority against these 'Rogatists', as they came to be known. In 372, however, retribution overtook them from an unexpected quarter.

In that year, as we have already noted,[6] the crushing weight of continuous heavy taxation coupled with the exactions of the Imperial officials drove the population of Mauretania Caesariensis to revolt. Their leader Firmus,[7] son of Nubel, was chief of

---

[1] See Jerome, *De Viris Illustribus*, 110.

[2] For the persecution by Romanus see *Gesta Coll. Carth.* iii. 258; *Contra Litteras Petiliani*, iii. 25. 29.

[3] Tyconius, quoted from Bede (*PL.* xciii, col. 132–3), 'Si in Africa factum est, ita fieri oportet in toto mundo, revelari Antichristum sicut nobis ex parte revelatum est.'

[4] Ammianus Marcellinus (ed. Loeb), xxix. 5. See above, p. 72.

[5] Augustine, *Ep.* 93. 11 and 49.   [6] See *supra*, p. 72.

[7] On Firmus see P.–W. *Realenzyklopädie*, vi, col. 2383; Ammianus Marcellinus (ed. Loeb), xxix. 5. 44; S. Gsell, 'Observations géographiques sur la révolte de Firmus', *Recueil de Constantine*, xxxvii, 1902, pp. 21–46.

the Jubaleni, a clan which probably dwelt in the region of the Mitidja, south-east of Icosium (Algiers), and whose name suggests some kinship with the last independent king of Mauretania, Juba. For the next twenty-five years the sons of Nubel through Firmus and Gildo were to play a predominant part in North African history. The remains of turreted castles belonging to Nubel and to Firmus' unfortunate brother Sammac have survived. Inscriptions from them show the family to have been semi-independent feudatories, boasting a veneer of Latin culture, ready to defend Rome against barbarians less civilized than themselves, but equally prepared to champion the African natives against the Imperial authorities.[1] Firmus and his younger brother Gildo may perhaps be regarded as the forerunners of the Kabyle chieftains who in the last years of the fifth century were styling themselves *Rex Romanorum et Maurorum* and appointing *praefecti* and other 'Imperial' officials. In Africa as in other provinces in the western half of the Empire, care of Roman administrative tradition was passing from the decaying Roman cities to the native feudatories.[2]

Firmus was in fact proclaimed 'king' by the rebels.[3] He took Icosium on the coast, and extended his hold from the Kabylie, as far eastwards as Calama, and westwards into the valley of the Chelif to Tigava (Kherba). On the coast, his brother Mazuca captured Caesarea, and for a brief moment the capital of Juba's kingdom was once more in Moorish hands.[4] For three years the rebel leader held out against the Roman armies which were sent against him. It was not until 375 that he was betrayed by one of his feudatories into the hands of the *Comes* Theodosius, who had been dispatched to Africa with fresh forces after Firmus appeared likely to establish his position.[5]

The Donatists lent their support to the rebel, as legitimate Emperor, and in return for the help which he had received

---

[1] *CIL*. viii. 9255, found in the valley of the Ouad Sahel at M'lakou. S. Gsell, *Atlas archéologique*, feuille 6 (Fort National), No. 148, and *Monuments archéologiques*, i, 102 (castle at Kouah). The possibility of Nubel's descent from Juba is suggested by Claudian (ed. Loeb), *De Bello Gildonico*, 331–2, 'Iterum post me coniurat in arma | progenies vesana Iubae.'

[2] *CIL*. viii. 9835. Cf. J. Carcopino, *Le Maroc antique* (Paris, librairie Gallimard, 1943), pp. 298–9.

[3] Orosius, *Historia adversus Paganos*, vii. 33, 'Maurorum gentibus regem constituens'. Also *CIL*. viii. 5338 (Calama), which suggests that he was proclaimed 'Augustus'.

[4] Ammianus Marcellinus, xxix. 5. 18 and 42.　　　[5] Ibid. 44; S. Gsell, art. cit.

Firmus repressed the Rogatists around Cartenna.[1] Their schism was not stamped out, but it never emerged from the status of an obscure 'Quietist' movement to trouble the main Church.[2]

The Catholics, as perhaps was to be expected, welcomed Theodosius as a deliverer. In their view, Firmus' rule in Mauretania had been a tyranny, a 'labes tyrannidis', the Moorish king was a 'degenerate barbarian', and his followers 'a crowd of brigands', mutineers against law and order.[3] The indignation and fear which Firmus inspired among them are summed up in two texts, the *Passio Sanctae Salsae* written to celebrate the rebel leader's check at Tipasa, and that on a mosaic in the Catholic basilica in Tigava in the Chelif valley. Here his final defeat became the theme of a verse forming part of the pattern of the mosaic.[4] Firmus' reverse at Tipasa, where it was alleged that the martyr Salsa rejected his prayers and saved the town from capture, was long remembered.

The collapse of Firmus' revolt brought another short period of repression of Donatism. Already in February 373 the Emperors had forbidden the practice of rebaptism;[5] now on 22 April 376 a law was addressed to Hesperius, Proconsul of Africa, forbidding the Donatists to hold services either in the towns or in the open countryside.[6] As a result, some of the Donatist leaders went into exile, among them a Bishop Claudian, who a few months later was elected Bishop of Rome. The alarm, however, did not last long. By one of those swift changes of fortune which show how obscure were the relations between the Donatists and the Imperial representatives, Theodosius was overthrown. Orosius hints that the Donatists had a hand in this,[7] but there is no convincing evidence, and his execution at Carthage in 376 may have been for treason.[8]

---

[1] Augustine, *Contra Epistolam Parmeniani*, i. 10. 16, and *Contra Litteras Petiliani*, ii. 83. 184.

[2] In Augustine's time, Rogatus' successor Vincentius still maintained himself with a few colleagues (Augustine, *Ep.* 93. 21, written c. A.D. 408).

[3] *Passio Sanctae Salsae* (cited from Gsell, *Mélanges*, xiv, 1894, pp. 311–12). Firmus was a 'degener gentilis', and his followers, 'catervae praedonum', in revolt against 'fas et ius'.

[4] *CIL.* viii. 21497; Monceaux, *Histoire littéraire*, iv. 450.

[5] *Codex Theodosianus*, xvi. 6. 1, to Julianus, Proconsul of Africa. See also Augustine, *Ep.* 105. 9.   [6] *Cod. Theod.* xvi. 5. 4. For dating, see Seeck, *Regesten*, p. 116.

[7] Orosius, *Historia adversus Paganos*, vii. 33; Pauly–Wissowa, *Realenzyklopädie*, 'Theodosius'.

[8] The evidence is discussed by E. A. Thompson in his *The Historical Work of Ammianus Marcellinus*, C.U.P., 1947, pp. 87–95.

His death meant the loss of a valuable ally for the Catholics, for the senior Imperial official in Africa was now the *Vicarius* Flavian, who was an ardent Donatist.[1] A law dated 17 October 377 was addressed to him which re-enacted all previous legislation against the Donatists and aimed particularly at stamping out the movement on the great landed estates.[2] Naturally, this remained a dead letter, and when Flavian considered the time had come to quell some of the more turbulent of his co-religionists, the Donatists retaliated by suspending him from Communion. With such officials holding power in Africa, the question of punishing the sectaries for their support of an unsuccessful rebellion soon ceased to be practical politics.

For the remainder of Parmenian's tenure of office the Donatist Church enjoyed peace from outside interference. In Africa the Catholics continued to lose ground;[3] overseas, they were discredited. Restitutus' championship of the Creed of Ariminum involved them in controversy with both Rome and Alexandria. Restitutus himself was probably the target for Athanasius' *Ad Afros*, and in 378 he was summoned by Pope Damasus to Rome to explain his doctrinal waywardness. Whether he recanted or died, we do not know.[4] Be this as it may, the African Catholics were in no mood to try conclusions with the Donatist majority. As Restitutus' successor they chose a quiet, colourless individual named Genethlius, who desired nothing more than to avoid friction between the two communities. He was even stated to have used his influence to prevent the renewal of legislation against Donatism.[5] Some of his leading colleagues were men of the same stamp, such as Augustine's predecessor at Hippo, Valerius.[6] They were reconciled to ministering to the needs of a faithful minority without attempting to interfere with their rivals.

As a result, for a short while the relations between Donatists and Catholics improved. Augustine relates how, in his early years as a presbyter at Hippo, Donatists as well as Catholics

[1] Augustine, *Ep.* 87. 8, 'Flaviano quondam vicario, partis vestrae homini, quia legibus serviens nocentes, quos invenerat, occidebat, non communicastis.'

[2] *Cod. Theod.* xvi. 6. 2.

[3] Optatus, vii. 1, on the situation of African Catholicism, *c.* 385.

[4] L. Duchesne, *The Early History of the Church*, ii. 374–5.

[5] Augustine, *Ep.* 44. 5. 12, 'nescio quam constitutionem datam contra illos [Donatists] compresserit et effectum non habere siverit'.

[6] He was old and decrepit, a Greek who could hardly speak Latin and knew no Berber or Punic (Possidius, *Vita Augustini*, 5 and 8).

would bring their disputes to him for settlement,[1] and members of the two faiths would live together in the same household and would discuss their differences amicably in each other's homes.[2] Rarer still, in this age of bitter religious strife, there was even a certain amount of good-humoured, if rather contemptuous, toleration. 'You would be a good fellow, if you weren't a *traditor*. Think things over, man, and become a Christian'—so the Donatist would greet a member of the rival communion.[3] The clergy of each had come to regard the Orders of the other as sacred; Donatists would even attend a Catholic service.[4] On at least one issue, hatred of the Manichees, the two communities found themselves on the same side.[5] In the big cities, young members of the two communions studied and played together.[6] Even the origins of the dispute were being forgotten. The generation which had suffered under Macarius was dying out, and its place was being taken by men who could bring themselves to a wider view, less prejudiced and less fanatical. The leader of these moderates was the philosopher Tyconius.

In Tyconius the Donatist Church produced one of the great theological minds of the fourth century.[7] He is the only member of his community whose ideas influenced Christian thought outside North Africa. Little is known about his life. He was probably a native of Proconsular Africa and he was a layman—an interesting fact in view of the tendency of Donatist clergy to form themselves into a caste apart, and in view of Tyconius' awe of the Church as an institution. He died about the year

[1] Augustine, *Ep.* 33. 5.

[2] Id., *Ep.* 35. 2 and 33. 5.

[3] Id., *De Baptismo*, ii. 7. 10.

[4] *Ep.* 33. 5, 'per coronam nostram nos adjurant vestri, per coronam vestram vos adjurant nostri'. The 'corona' was the distinctive headgear worn by the clergy. To swear by it would be a mark of deep respect. For Donatists at Augustine's services, Possidius, *Vita*, 7.

[5] Ibid. 6 (*PL.* xxxii, col. 38).

[6] As Augustine and his friend Vincentius, the Rogatist Bishop of Cartenna; *Ep.* 93. 1, 'cum me adulescentem vivo adhuc Rogato, cui successisti, apud Carthaginem noveras'.

[7] Much has been written on Tyconius. I think the following the most useful: F. C. Burkitt, 'The Book of Rules of Tyconius', *Cambridge Texts and Studies*, iii. 1, 1894; T. Hahn, 'Tyconius-Studien', *Studien zur Geschichte der Theologie und der Kirche*, Bonwetsch und Seeburg, Leipzig, 1900; P. Monceaux, *Histoire littéraire*, v. 165–219; E. Buonaiuti, *Il Cristianesimo nell' Africa Romana*, pp. 335–40; W. Bousset, *Die Offenbarung Ioannis*, Göttingen, 1906, pp. 56 ff.; A. Pincherle, 'Da Ticonio a Sant' Agostino', *Ricerche Religiose*, i, 1925, pp. 443–66; A. Batiffol, *Le Catholicisme de Saint Augustin*, i. 110 ff.

390, and his main writings would date between 370 and 380. The most lucid account of his work is contained in Gennadius' notes.[1] The four major books that he wrote are mentioned, and a tribute is paid to his character and learning, but apart from this summary, and details derived from Augustine on his quarrel with Parmenian, nothing has so far come to light.

The two books most interesting for the study of Donatism are lost. From Gennadius' reference to his quotations from 'former Councils' to defend his point of view, it seems clear that the *Expositiones Diversarum Causarum* as well as the *De Bello Intestino* were concerned with the Donatist versus Catholic controversy. Gennadius adds that from these works 'it was recognizable to all that he belonged to the Donatist party'. The *Liber Regularum*,[2] which is the forerunner of medieval allegorical interpretation of Scripture, has survived, and also a considerable part of the Commentary on the Apocalypse (*Commentarius in Apocalypsin Joannis*).[3] It is from the last mentioned that Tyconius' ideas can most easily be assessed.

Augustine and many who have followed him appear to have misunderstood Tyconius, and attributed to him ideas which it is most unlikely that he held. He certainly did not write *invictissime* against the Donatists,[4] whatever his differences with Parmenian may have been on the precise manner of the separation of the just from the false brethren within the Christian Church. Like Parmenian in his controversy with Optatus, Tyconius was concerned exclusively with the nature of the Church. The doctrinal issues debated in the rest of the Empire regarding the nature of the Trinity appear to have been foreign

---

[1] Gennadius, *De Scriptoribus Ecclesiasticis*, 18 (*PL*. lviii, col. 1071). 'Tichonius natione Afer, in divinis litteris eruditus, juxta historiam sufficienter, et in saeculari-bus non ignarus fuit; in ecclesiasticis quoque negotiis studiosus. Scripsit *de bello intestino* libros tres et *expositiones diversarum causarum*, in quibus ob suorum de-fensionem antiquarum meminit Synodorum. E quibus omnibus agnoscitur dona-tianae partis fuisse. Composuit et Regulas ad investigandam et inveniendam intelligentiam Scripturarum, septem, quas in uno volumine conclusit. Exposuit et Apocalypsin Joannis ex integro, nihil in ea carnale, sed totum intelligens spiri-tuale. . . . Mille quoque annorum regni in terra justorum post resurrectionem futuri suspicionem tulit.'

[2] Text, see Burkitt, op. cit., and Migne, *PL*. xviii, cols. 15–65.

[3] The two main sources are the MS. Spicilegium Casinense, iii. 1, 'Tyconii Afri Fragmenta Commentarii in Apocalypsin', and the work of Beatus of Libana 'In Apocalypsin' (American Academy of Rome, 1930). I have made use of Hahn's citations from the earlier edition by H. Florez, Madrid, 1770.

[4] Augustine, *De Doct. Christ.* iii. 30. Also, *Contra Epistolam Parmeniani*, i. 1. 1. On Tyconius as a Donatist, see Hahn, *Tyconius-Studien*, 99.

to him: the whole of his *Liber Regularum* is concerned to show
that every sentence in Scripture, every allusion however seemingly remote, refers to the Church—and through the Church
to the individual's salvation. He was in agreement with Parmenian and his fellow bishops on the attributes of the true
Church. These were composed of suffering and penance, and
the persecutions suffered by the Donatists under Count Romanus
and the Proconsul Hesperius[1] merely presaged greater trials
which would precede the coming of Antichrist. The inscription
found in a chapel at Timgad referring to the *sancti et penitentes*
defending 'their Mother' (?= the Church) seems to indicate that
the ideas represented by Tyconius were also to be found in the
African Church generally.[2]

The difficulties with Parmenian were not caused by a dispute
on the qualities of the true Church, and whether the Donatists
possessed those qualities. The Church in Africa had been proven
in persecution, and would be manifest throughout the world:
'ex Africa manifestabitur omnis ecclesia'.[3] The Gospel preached
in Africa would later be preached everywhere. In the Millen-
nium, when the Just would reign on earth, the Donatists would
play a leading part. But the problem that presented itself to
Tyconius was the apparent paradox of the Church represented
in Scripture as 'an unspotted bride', and at the same time as
'a field containing both wheat and tares'. In practice, what was
to be the relationship between the Christians and the *traditores*?
Was separation possible, or not? Tyconius pointed out that
Scripture showed the Church to be 'bipartite', composed of good
and evil members. The Bride of Christ in the Song of Solomon
(i. 5) was both 'black and comely',[4] the seed of Abraham was

---

[1] The allusion in Bede's *Epistola ad Eusebium* (*PL.* xciii, col. 133) to the confiscation of Donatist property and the exile of Donatist leaders in the reign of Valentinian, and Tyconius' protest in his *Commentarius in Apocalypsin*, suggests that this
was written *c.* 380. His quarrel with Parmenian may have been some years later.

[2] The inscription is dated to fourth/fifth century, and was cut on the foot of
what had once been an ornamental stone table. The text, as amended by Mon-
ceaux, *CRAI.*, 1924, p. 80, reads, 'B(onis) B(ene). | et gaudet Pe | trus et Laza | rus. |
rogo te | Domine | su(b) veni | Criste tu | solus me | dicus sanctis et peniten | tibus
ma(t) re(m) manib(us) | et pedibus de (fendentibus).' Also P. Monceaux, *CRAI.*,
1920, pp. 75–83, and S. Gsell, *Revue Africaine*, lxix, 1928, pp. 20–22. The salutation
Bonis bene suggests Donatist usage. The invocation of Christ as *solus medicus* is
interesting in view of the Lambiridi inscription from near by. In the third century
A.D. Hermes Trismegistos was evidently regarded as *solus medicus*. Cf. *supra*, p. 97.

[3] Cited from A. Pincherle, *Ricerche Religiose*, i, 1925, p. 53.

[4] Cited from Burkitt, op. cit., p. xiv.

both 'royal and servile', the Church existed not only 'in the south where the Lord made his flock to lie down', but also, figuratively, 'in the north', in the shadow. This bipartite nature of the Church was represented by the 'saints', or elect, and the false Christians. These two elements would be in eternal conflict until the Day of Judgement.

So far there was nothing in Tyconius' view that would arouse the opposition of his fellow Donatists. But Tyconius was not content to confine his definition of the two aspects of the Church to 'African Christians' and 'sons of *traditores*'. The Donatism of Tyconius extended beyond satisfaction at being hated 'by the world' to an analysis of the meaning of the Kingdom of Satan.[1] The real division was not so much between two Churches as between two societies,[2] each made up of individuals but governed by contrary wills, the one destined to salvation, the other to destruction. 'Satan dwells everywhere: the throne of Satan is evil men.'[3] The distinction between the righteous and unrighteous was not predestined in individual cases:[4] each could be a member of the *Civitas Dei* or the *Civitas Diaboli*. Penitence, contemplation, and consideration of Eternity were possible for all, and were the means by which Grace was acquired and the means too of preparation for the first resurrection experienced in the sacrament of baptism. In the last resort it was penance, or the continuous striving to do God's will, which divided the true from the false Christians.[5]

Thus the division between Christians was a moral one. The true Christian, fortified by the Spirit and regenerate by baptism, had no need to separate himself physically from the unjust. The righteous 'did not hear the wicked'; they would suffer persecution but, tried like gold in the furnace, they would prevail. The saints should stay in the world, not flee from it like monks.[6] It was even necessary that there should be heretics and hypocrites in the Church, as a means of proving the just. These were not there to be tolerated, but fought. The separation,

---

[1] A. Pincherle, 'Da Ticonio a Sant' Agostino' , p. 463.

[2] Beatus, p. 506, cited from Hahn, p. 23, 'Ecce duas civitates, unam Dei, et unam Diaboli.'

[3] Beatus, p. 116, l. 7, 'Ubique Satanas habitat. Thronus autem Satanae homines mali sunt.'

[4] Hahn, op. cit., p. 24.

[5] Cf. Beatus, p. 179, cited from Hahn, pp. 47–49, 'Una pars est quae paenitentiam agit et altera est saecularium' and 'semper ecclesia in paenitentia est'.

[6] Beatus, p. 186, cited from Hahn, pp. 53–54.

however, would take place at the Last Day, and then the Church in Africa would come into her own.

These are the ideas of a thinker and a deeply religious man. With their emphasis on the moral value of the *individual* rather than the institution they belong to the Donatist tradition, but they pass beyond it. In pointing to the universal character of the Church, and the need for postponing separation from the unjust until the Last Day, Tyconius appeared to be calling in question Donatus' separation from Caecilian. Parmenian was disturbed, and took the matter up with him, quoting the usual Donatist proof-texts to show the necessity for 'parting from evil brethren'. Tyconius, however, was not convinced, and continued to publish his writings. Finally, about the year 385, Parmenian summoned a Council and he was excommunicated.[1] We know the facts only; of the background, nothing has survived.

The verdict had no immediate effect on the fortunes of the Donatist Church. Tyconius formed no sect of his own, and did not join the Catholics.[2] His spiritual home was probably with the Maximianists, but he seems to have died before 393 when Maximian's movement started. His repudiation meant, however, that the progress in African theological thought, which up to now had been predominantly Donatist, passed over to the Catholics. Augustine, as he readily admits, built his concepts of Grace and of the Two Cities on foundations laid by Tyconius.[3] He read the *Liber Regularum* with enthusiasm.[4] It seems clear that much of his thought in his formative years between 386 and 396, as illustrated by the comments on the Pauline Epistles which date from that period, was influenced by Tyconius' teaching. Time and again, in unexpected places such as in the midst of a speculation on the significance of the numbers 40 and 50 in the Bible (*De Diversis Quaestionibus*, lxiii), Augustine lets drop some aside which hints at the source of his exegesis. With Ambrose, Tyconius may perhaps have shared the honour of finally winning Augustine from Mani to Christ.[5]

The Donatists, on the other hand, failed to benefit from their great theologian. From now on they tend to become narrower

[1] Augustine, *Contra Epistolam Parmeniani*, i. 1. 1; *Ep.* 93. 44.
[2] Id., *De Doct. Christ.* iii. 30.
[3] Ibid., 46.
[4] Id., *Ep.* 41. 2 (to Aurelius).
[5] See in particular A. Pincherle, *Ricerche Religiose*, viii, 1932, pp. 139–42, and 'Da Ticonio a Sant' Agostino', ibid., 463–5, by the same author.

in their outlook. The greatness of the Church was seen not in the fulfilments of God's promises to Abraham, but in the impressive size of the cathedrals of Timgad and Bagai.[1] The bishops assumed pretensions to infallibility, at the same time as their mental horizon became more bounded. 'What we wish is holy', they thundered, and the faithful echoed in reply, 'Great is the Church in Numidia: we are Christians and we alone.'[2]

The mass of the Africans and the Circumcellions desired no compromise with the world or the 'sons of *traditores*', but the leaders and the educated laity were to find themselves in increasing difficulty in defending their position with logical arguments. The thesis which Augustine propounded on every occasion, that the African Catholics were in fact in communion with the Church throughout the whole Roman world, and that the final separation of the good from the evil members of that Church must wait until the Last Day, was to be a telling one, especially when reinforced by Imperial sanction. But this stage was not reached for another twenty-five years, and meanwhile power was in the hands of the Numidians.

One further incident disturbed the final years of Parmenian. In 376/7 Claudian had been elected Donatist Bishop of Rome. He arrived at an opportune moment, for Pope and anti-Pope were engaged in bitter legal battles, and Claudian was able to take advantage of the situation to conduct active propaganda among the poorer classes. Damasus and his predecessors he denounced as pagans, and many submitted to rebaptism. The Catholics were forced to admit their rival was having a certain amount of success, which they ascribed to judicious bribery.[3]

It was not long, however, before Damasus got the upper hand of Claudian. At a Council held in the autumn of 378 the Pope formally invoked the assistance of the Emperor. Gratian dispatched a rescript to the *Vicarius Urbis*, Aquilinus, in which he ordered the removal and punishment of all who were hostile to the Pope, including the unfortunate Catholic Bishop of Carthage, Restitutus.[4] Claudian's sentence was relatively mild.

---

[1] Augustine, *Enarratio in Ps. 21*, 26 (*PL.* xxxvii, cols. 177–8).

[2] Id., *Contra Epistolam Parmeniani*, i. 2. 3; cf. *Sermo* 46. 16. 40.

[3] Letter drawn up by the Italian bishops present at Damasus' Council at Rome between 9 Aug. 378 and 19 Jan. 379 (Mansi, *Concilia*, iii. 626), 'sed contemptis iudicibus et quidem saepe constrictus residet tamen sollicitans pretio frequenter pauperiores, et redemptos rebaptizare non veretur'.

[4] *Relatio Gratiani*, quoted ibid. 627–8.

He was simply ordered to return to Africa without penalty.[1] Other trouble-makers were dealt with severely, the undisciplined Bishop of Parma being exiled 'beyond the bounds' of the Empire and the anti-Pope Ursinus' principal ally, the fiery Jewish high priest Isaac, being sent to a 'corner of Spain'.[2]

It even appears that Claudian was able to last the course a few more years; Optatus of Milevis, re-editing his work about A.D. 385, would hardly have failed to point the downfall of the Donatist bishopric of Rome, especially as Parmenian had laid stress on the fact that the Donatists were in communion with the Apostle's see. But soon after, Claudian returned to Africa. The official Papacy was too strong. On 8 January 386 Damasus' successor Siricius sent a long letter to a Catholic Council which was meeting in Carthage, informing them of numerous conversions among the Donatist congregation in Rome.[3] Unfortunately Claudian was evidently too much of an individualist to work under Parmenian's rigid, and perhaps somewhat unimaginative, discipline. He broke with the Bishop of Carthage, formed a schism, and established his own community, the 'Claudianists'. His followers continued to be a source of annoyance to the official Donatists for some years.[4]

The quarrels with Tyconius and Claudian were incidental to the general quiet which characterized the history of Donatism between 377 and 391. But even so, events were taking place in southern Numidia which were to usher in the decisive conflict between the rival Churches. The result was to settle the future not only of Donatism but of Christianity itself in North Africa.

[1] Ibid. 628, 'repetere tantummodo patriam hactenus, remota severitate, praecipimus'.

[2] 'Parmensem episcopum protinus ultra fines debuisset extrudere. . . . Isaacem remotus Hispaniae angulus titulo damnationis inclusit', ibid. 628. On Isaac see L. Duchesne, op. cit., 370–2.

[3] Siricius, *Ep. V ad Episcopos Africae*, para. 8 (ed. Migne, *PL.* xiii, col. 1159).

[4] The Claudianists were schismatics in 392. One of the charges brought against Primian, Parmenian's successor, by his Maximianist accusers was that he had readmitted the Claudianists to communion without consulting his colleagues (Augustine, *Sermo ii in Ps. 36*, 20 (*PL.* xxxvi, col. 379)).

XIV

THE RULE OF OPTATUS AND GILDO
A.D. 386–98

Two appointments in no way connected with each other opened the decisive period of strife between the Catholics and the Donatists. In 386 the Emperor Theodosius nominated Firmus' younger brother Gildo[1] as *Comes Africae*, and two years later a priest named Optatus was elected Bishop of Thamugadi (Timgad), the most important Donatist bishopric in southern Numidia.[2]

There was nothing in the nature of these appointments to suggest that Gildo and Optatus would come together. However, by A.D. 396 they were allies in an attempt to impose the extreme doctrines of Numidian Donatism on all North Africa. In 398 they were joint leaders of a revolt against Honorius which if successful might have led to the transfer of the allegiance of the African provinces from Ravenna to Constantinople. But at the moment when the army in Africa was placed under his command Gildo had a sound record of service to the Emperor. He had taken an active part on the side of the elder Theodosius against his brother Firmus.[3] During the war against Magnus Maximus in 387–8 he had at first kept on good terms with the latter,[4] but his lapse was speedily forgiven and in 392 one of his daughters, Salvina, married into the Imperial family.[5] The hazard of confiding the command of the Roman army in North Africa to the care of the most powerful native chieftain in the provinces promised to be justified.

The new Bishop of Thamugadi, on the other hand, did not take long to show his true colours. Though Augustine must be considered a prejudiced witness, there would seem to be little doubt that Optatus represented from the first the arrogant

---

[1] On Gildo, see Otto Seeck, 'Gildo', Pauly–Wissowa, *Realenzyklopädie*, vii, cols. 1360–3; Pallu de Lessert, *Fastes des Provinces africaines*, ii. 256–64.

[2] See P. Monceaux, *Timgad chrétien*, 65–70.

[3] Ammianus Marcellinus, xxix. 5. 6, 21, and 24.

[4] Pacatus, *Panegyricus* (ed. Baehrens), 38. 2; Seeck, 'Gildo', in Pauly–Wissowa.

[5] Jerome, *Ep.* 79. 2 (*PL.* xxii, col. 724). She was a Catholic and one of Jerome's correspondents.

fanaticism of Numidian Donatism, and was himself bent on accomplishing social as well as religious revolution by violent means. His views were thus akin to those of the Bogomil and Albigensian leaders who in the Middle Ages combined religious dissent with social reform, and whose ideas have inspired some of the national peasant movements in eastern Europe today. For ten years he was the undisputed master of southern Numidia.[1] On each anniversary of his consecration as bishop he held an audience in regal state in Thamugadi at which he received the congratulations of his colleagues and the enthusiasm of the crowds.[2] To give such occasions an appropriate setting, it seems likely that he built on a rise overlooking the town from the south-west one of the largest cathedrals ever erected in Christian Africa. It stood 200 feet long by 50 feet across; in front of the great nave was a spacious atrium, and to one side was built a richly decorated baptistery; the whole was surrounded by a wall and a suite of buildings, possibly for housing pilgrims or storing food.[3] The Donatists saw the glory of the Divine Kingdom represented by this church; it served as a symbol of their power in Africa.

Apart from this outward display, Optatus was capable of harnessing and directing the latent religious enthusiasm of the Numidian country-dwellers. In his cathedral a mosaic records 'How great is the praise of his name'.[4] An orator, like most other prominent Donatist bishops, he knew well how to sway the passions of the multitude.[5] Under his inspiration the Circumcellions became something of a military force. Their clubs and staves were supplemented by swords, spears, and other weapons,[6] their services were at the disposal of the clergy and bishops to crush incipient schisms or to overawe the Catholics and possessing

[1] Augustine, *Contra Epistolam Parmeniani*, ii. 2. 4, 'Optatum Gildonianum decennalem totius Africae gemitum'.

[2] Id., *Contra Litteras Petiliani*, ii. 23. 53, 'cujus [Optati] natalitia tanta celebratione frequentabatis'; also *Contra Epist. Parmeniani*, iii. 6. 29.

[3] The mosaic indicating that the basilica was built by Optatus is published by E. Albertini, *CRAI.*, 1939, p. 100. Previously the buildings around the church itself were believed to have belonged to a monastery. See P. Monceaux, *Timgad chrétien*, 29 ff.

[4] Albertini, op. cit., 102, 'quanta [laus] nomini [illius].'

[5] Augustine, *Ep.* 51. 3; *Contra Epistolam Parmeniani*, iii. 6. 29, col. 106.

[6] Ibid. i. 11. 17, 'quam multa quotidie agunt per furiosos ebrosiorum juvenum greges, quibus principes constituunt, qui primum tantummodo fustibus, nunc etiam ferro se armare coeperunt, qui Circumcellionum notissimo nomine per totam Africam vagantur', &c.

classes. In this period their depredations became endemic. Optatus seems to have intended to create a new social order with Circumcellion aid.[1] In Augustine's bare words, he redistributed lands, settled marriage disputes, evicted unpopular heirs, and punished oppressive landowners by forcing them to abandon their estates.[2] The fact, however, that he was able to do these things in a complex and primitive native society, where disinheritance could lead to a blood feud, suggests a quite extraordinary power, which Augustine himself could never claim to possess. The Catholics naturally saw him as an embittered tyrant, 'scorching all Africa with tongues of flame'.[3] His rule may perhaps be likened to that of another Numidian, the Kharedjite leader Abou Aziz, who dominated tenth-century Algeria. The blow which Optatus and his Circumcellions dealt to the power of the romanized landowners in southern Numidia must have been a severe one. In this period we hear of villas being destroyed and Circumcellions controlling the countryside.[4] In alliance with Gildo the formation of a predominantly 'native', non-Roman power in Africa became possible: Donatism would have been the religion and motive force in such a kingdom.

Even so, it was in these ten years between 388 and 398 that Donatism came nearest to achieving complete mastery in Africa. There are the formal statements of Possidius, Augustine's biographer, that in 390 the majority of Africans were Donatists,[5] and the admission made by Optatus of Milevis[6] in his final book against the schismatics, that the Catholics were 'few' in North Africa. More interesting, perhaps, are the asides let slip by Augustine in the heat of argument, that at this time the Donatists had the upper hand even in the Roman cities such as Constantine,[7] Hippo, Rusiccade, and Calama.[8] The Donatists

---

[1] Optatus as leader of bands of Circumcellions, *Contra Litteras Petiliani*, i. 24. 26.

[2] Ibid. ii. 23. 53, 'pupillos evertit, aliena patrimonia prodidit, aliena matrimonia separavit'; also, 35. 82.

[3] Ibid. 33. 78, 'linguis igneis miserabilem Africam incendit'.

[4] Possidius, *Vita Augustini*, 10.

[5] Ibid. 7 (*PL*. xxxii, col. 39), 'convalescentibus haereticis, praecipueque rebaptizante Donati parte majorem multitudinem Afrorum.'

[6] Optatus, vii. 1, 'sufficiebat [ecclesia] et in Africa, licet in paucis'.

[7] Augustine, *Sermo ad Caesareensis Ecclesiae Plebem*, 8, 'Pars Donati quando praevalebat Constantinae . . .'. Also, *Ep*. 34. 5.

[8] Id., *Contra Litteras Petiliani*, ii. 83. 184, 'apud Hipponem quoniam Catholicorum ibi paucitas erat'; ibid. iii. 57. 69, 'etiam Rusiccadiensem vel Calamensem vel cujuslibet alterius civitatis aliquem de parte vestra'.

themselves were fully alive to the strength of their position. When in February 395 Primian the Metropolitan of Carthage brought a case at the Proconsul's court against a dissident bishop, his advocate could plead that 'nearly the whole world acknowledged the name and worship of the Catholic Church, cleansed from error by Donatus of venerable memory'.[1] He won his case. With 420 or so bishops the Donatists had acquired a quasi-official standing in North Africa.[2]

During this period too, there is evidence that many literate Africans continued to prefer Donatism to Catholicism. Augustine's early letters contain many instances of conversions including those of Catholic clergy to Donatism, but few, if any, of Donatists becoming Catholics;[3] Augustine himself was unable to prevent some of his own subordinate clergy from leaving the Catholic fold. In about the year 395 the Donatists achieved what was to be their greatest individual success. At Constantine they kidnapped a rising young Catholic advocate named Petilian and submitted him to rebaptism. His co-religionists were powerless to intervene, and Petilian, apparently convinced that the hand of God was in the event, placed his talents at the service of his new faith.[4] He soon became one of its leaders, and, during the period of repression which succeeded the downfall of Gildo, the only defender who could make an impression on Augustine. It is interesting to note that in this long-drawn-out conflict both champions were converts to their faith.

It seems that, in the countryside also, the last decade or so of the fourth century saw Donatism reach the climax of its influence. Unfortunately, the historian has not been well served by the archaeologist in Algeria. While the field-work, involving the actual discovery of Christian buildings in the Numidian villages, has been excellent, the stratigraphy enabling

---

[1] *Contra Cresconium*, iii. 56. 62, col. 529, Titianus dixit: 'Peregrinus presbyter et seniores Ecclesiae Mustitanae regionis tale desiderium prosequuntur: Cum Ecclesiae Catholicae sanctitatem vir memoriae venerabilis ab errore perfidiae Donatus assereret, in ejus nomen et cultum mundi pene totius observantia nutrita coaluit.'

[2] The numbers were made up of 310 bishops who were present at the Council of Bagai, together with about 100 dissident Maximianist bishops, and ten or so Rogatists, Claudianists, and others.

[3] Augustine, *Ep.* 23. 2 (rebaptism of a deacon); *Ep.* 35. 2 and 4 (conversion of a sub-deacon and *sanctimoniales*). At Milevis the Donatists held a Council in 396, indicating considerable strength in the area (*Ep.* 34. 5).

[4] *Sermo ad Caesareensis Ecclesiae Plebem*, 8.

churches to be dated accurately on excavation has not progressed
so well. The canons of dating at the outbreak of the Second
World War were still very much where Gsell had left them half
a century previously.[1] Even so, it is possible to date a large
number of village churches to 'end of fourth century–early fifth
century', mainly through the type of chrism used in the decoration of the chapel. A form similar to that employed in Optatus'
basilica at Thamugadi, and therefore probably nearly contemporary, has been found in many other Numidian churches, at
Henchir Gourai,[2] Ksar Sbehi,[3] Hr. el Ateuch,[4] Foum el Amba,[5]
Hr. el Guis,[6] Ksar Tibinet,[7] Bekkouche,[8] and elsewhere;
the church of Bishop Argentius at Lamiggiga (Pasteur) dates
also to this period.[9] All of these churches contained reliquaries
and bones of martyrs, and in some the community is put
beyond doubt by the presence of Donatist inscriptions. Even
though so many of their writings have been lost, the enthusiasm
which the Donatist leaders inspired in these remote villages can
still be gauged from these humble and silent ruins. And yet
this period of Donatist ascendancy was not one of continuous
persecution for the Catholics. Whatever may have been the
situation in Optatus' own diocese, farther north the Catholics
were generally left in peace. There is a contrast between what
Augustine wrote about the period after the downfall of Gildo
and what he wrote at the time. The examples of comparative

---

[1] The French have been faced with two major difficulties: first, that of super-
vising the unskilled native labour by which the actual excavations must be carried
out; secondly, the lack of co-operation by the army and local civil authorities,
who too often have used Roman sites as quarries. Nevertheless, there has been a
tendency to rely solely on inscriptions to date sites, to neglect the study of pottery
types and the evidence of coins, and to concentrate too much on obtaining the
plan of a building without digging to the lower layers to establish its history. Much
evidence has been lost by such methods. As long ago as 1894, Gsell established a
rough canon for dating Christian buildings. The Constantinian monogram flanked
by α ω was regarded by him as denoting a late-fourth-century date, in contrast to
the Greek monogram used in Vandal and Byzantine times. But the margin of
error remains regrettably wide.   [2] S. Gsell, *Monuments antiques*, ii. 200.

[3] Ibid. 217.

[4] M. Simon, 'Fouilles dans une basilique chrétienne de Numidie', *Mélanges*, li,
1934, p. 171.

[5] A. Berthier, *Les Vestiges du Christianisme*, 76–77. A *Deo laudes* inscription was
found in the church.

[6] S. Gsell, *Le Musée de Tébessa* (Paris, 1902), p. 10.

[7] P. Monceaux, *Bull. Arch. du Comité*, 1909, p. 246.

[8] H. Jaubert, 'Évêchés de Numidie', *Recueil de Constantine*, xlvi, 1912, p. 152.

[9] P. Monceaux, *CRAI.*, 1908, pp. 308–9. Argentius was Donatist bishop without
Catholic challenger in 411 (*Gesta Coll. Carth.* i. 188).

harmony between the two communities which have been quoted as characteristic of the last decade of Parmenian's rule are derived mainly from Augustine's correspondence of the period 392–7.[1] His letters show that the Donatists did not oppress their Catholic neighbours in northern Numidia, that religious questions could be discussed in relative calm, and that Catholic councils were able to meet even in towns such as Hippo where there was a Donatist majority.[2] There was personal friction, as is usual where two antagonistic religious groups occupy the same area,[3] and the Catholics, always ready to claim toleration for themselves, were not prepared to grant the same privilege to the Donatists a decade later. But taking the evidence as a whole, it does not seem that Optatus of Thamugadi really extended his direct influence to the rest of Numidia until he had decided to be finished with the Maximianists, and Gildo had thrown off his last ties of allegiance to the court of Ravenna; these events took place in 397.

The position of the African Catholics was to be made less hopeless by the divisions and crises which now assailed their opponents. Parmenian of Carthage died in 391 or 392. His successor Primian was a man of extreme views and ruthless violence, less able than his predecessor, but secure in the favour of the Carthaginian crowd and the Numidian bishops.[4] Soon after his election a party of opposition began to form round one of his deacons, named Maximian.[5] The latter was a descendant of Donatus the Great,[6] and evidently had the support of many

---

[1] Particularly *Ep.* 33–35, 43–44; Possidius, *Vita*, 5 and 6. See *supra*, p. 201.

[2] Catholic Councils were held at Hippo in 393 and Carthage in 397.

[3] For instance, *Ep.* 34, which quotes a particularly horrible case.

[4] The character-sketch given by Monceaux, *Histoire littéraire*, vi. 57 ff., seems overdrawn. Primian was not a nonentity. In a period of severe crisis he held his Church together, and prevented mass defections to Catholicism before the Conference of 411. He retained the loyalty of his bishops, and the rank and file of the Donatist community became known as 'Primianists' during his rule. He was also a sufficiently able speaker to make Augustine lose his temper—a fairly rare feat. See Augustine, *Sermo iii in Ps. 36*, 19 (*PL.* xxxvi, col. 394). He was nevertheless a violent individual and clearly from the first the nominee of an extremist group.

[5] What would appear to be a fairly detailed account of the origins of the dispute is contained in Augustine, *Sermo ii in Ps. 36*, 19–21 (*PL.* xxxvi, cols. 377 ff.). Of modern writers, Monceaux, *Histoire littéraire*, iv. 58 ff., 299 ff., and vi, pp. 111 ff., gives a full, if rather unimaginative, account of Maximianism.

[6] Primian at the time of the outbreak was 'recens ordinatus' (Augustine, *Sermo ii in Ps. 36*, 20). Maximian was 'Donati propinquus' (*Ep.* 43. 9. 26). A rivalry between the 'orthodox' Donatists, led by descendants of the 'prophet', and the Numidians should not be ruled out of account in assessing the causes of the schism.

of the wealthier members of the Donatist community in Carthage, including, as Augustine delighted to point out, a rich and influential woman who played the part of a second Lucilla.[1]

At first the conflict was kept within the bounds of the Donatist church at Carthage. Primian attempted to coerce his presbyters into framing a charge against Maximian and three other deacons. They refused, whereupon Primian declared Maximian excommunicate at a time when he was ill and had no chance to defend himself.[2] The new Donatist Primate then embarked on a course of conduct little calculated to win the respect of the more solid members of his community. The Claudianist schismatics were readmitted to communion,[3] as were people who were known to have committed incest.[4] The *seniores* of the Church of Carthage protested. They did so in vain; Primian had them beaten and continued in a wild career of violence. He forced one of his presbyters to disinherit his son in his favour, and another was thrown down a Carthaginian sewer for having administered sacraments to the sick[5] (probably without the Primate's permission).

The indignation of the congregation increased. The *seniores* met in council and decided to take a stand in favour of Maximian. The latter seems to have been in every way a more fitting character than Primian, though he had little popular support on his side.[6] The decision was to send a circular letter to the Donatist episcopate outlining the Primate's misdeeds and demanding that a Council be summoned. Forty-three bishops, presumably from towns near Carthage, arrived in the capital in answer to the *seniores'* invitation. The Council met probably towards the end of 392. Primian refused to recognize its authority and defied a thrice-repeated summons to appear. He was luckier than Caecilian, for he had the populace and, more

---

[1] Augustine, *Ep.* 43. 9. 26; *Sermo in Ps. 36*, 19 (*PL.* xxxvi, col. 377).

[2] Ibid. 20, 'in Maximianem diaconum, virum sicut omnibus notum est innocentem, sine causa, sine teste, absentem ac lecto cubantem'.

[3] Ibid., 'quos Claudianistas appellaverunt, cum eos a Primiano in communionem receptos'. Cf. *Contra Cresconium*, iv. 9. 11.

[4] Ibid., 'Ad nos non pertinet si illos, nescio quos, incestos ad communionem admisisti.'

[5] Ibid., 'quod Fortunatum in cloacum fecerit mitti, cum aegrotantibus baptismo succurrisset'.

[6] Augustine, probably for the sake of propaganda, compares Maximian to Arius and Donatus as a 'great preacher of heresy' (*Enarratio in Ps. 35*, 9 and 124. 5— *PL.* xxxvi–xxxvii, cols. 347 and 1662). The Council of Cebarsussa did, however, declare him innocent of the charges brought by Primian against him.

curiously, the local officials on his side, including the legate of the Proconsul. The police and mob searched the houses of Maximian's supporters and stormed the church where the *seniores* and dissentient bishops were meeting.[1] After a rather undignified flight these reassembled in a house somewhere in the suburbs of Carthage, and there passed a preliminary condemnation on Primian (a *praeiudicium*). This was communicated to their colleagues throughout Africa.[2]

The Council of forty-three had left it open to Primian to clear himself before a more formal gathering.[3] This met on 24 June 393 at Cebarsussa in Byzacena under the presidency of the Primate of Byzacena, Victorinus of Munatiana.[4] Meantime, about 100 Donatist bishops had signified their adherence to Maximian. Nearly all of them had their sees in Proconsular Africa, Byzacenia, and Tripolitania. They included the bishops of such large communities on the coast as Hadrumetum (Sousse), Tacape, Oea, Leptis Magna, and Sabratha, and also representatives from the Roman cities of the upper Mejerda valley, such as Assuras and Membressa. The province of Byzacena was particularly pro-Maximian. On the other hand, his cause made little headway in Numidia and Mauretania, Perseverantius of Theveste being apparently the only Numidian bishop of standing who joined him.[5] The dispute began to take on a regional character, the more conservative and tolerant Donatists of the Romano-Punic cities of the coast and the Tunisian coastal plain protesting against the violence and brutality of the Numidian nominee in Carthage. The provincial composition of the Maximianist party was sufficiently striking even for contemporaries to note.[6]

[1] Augustine, quoting the Sentence of Cebarsussa, in *Sermo ii in Ps. 36*, 20, 'Qui [Primian] usquequaque rebelli animo, calcitrans in malo permansit, ut, conducta multitudine perditorum, atque impetratis officialibus, basilicarum januas obsedissent qui ingrediendi nobis atque agendi solemnia interdicerent facultatem'. Also *Contra Cresconium*, iv. 47. 57.

[2] Ibid. 7. 8, 'et sic nondum audentes ultimum praecipitare judicium, sed quodam praejudicio consulentes'.   [3] Ibid. 6. 7.

[4] *Sermo ii in Ps. 36*, 20. Victor signs the decree of Cebarsussa first, as *senex*.

[5] This list of signatories at Cebarsussa includes only Pancratius of Badias (Numidia) and Pomponius of Macri (Mauretania Sitifensis) apart from the Byzacenans and clergy from the Proconsular Province.

[6] Augustine, *Ep.* 93. 8. 24, 'omnes vos Maximianistae superabunt, quorum schisma in Byzantio [sic] et in Tripoli exarsit.' Also *Ad Catholicos Epistola*, iii. 6, 'Si in paucis Tripolitanis et Byzacenis et Provincialibus; Maximianistae ad eam [Ecclesiam] pervenerunt'. Augustine is arguing the universal character of the Catholic Church as against the provincialism of the sects.

The fifty or more bishops[1] who assembled at Cebarsussa were in fact almost exclusively drawn from the two provinces of Byzacena and Tripolitania. The sentence passed by the Council on Primian has been preserved for us in full,[2] by the accident of Augustine's using it in reply to an attack made against him by the Donatist Primate during the stormy debates which took place in Carthage in the autumn of 403. It is a reasonable document drawn up by civilized beings who had a sense of responsibility. The language employed is studiously moderate. The Council points out that it had to investigate the complaints made by the *seniores* of the church of Carthage against Primian, and that it would have far preferred to find that Primian was the innocent party in the dispute. Unfortunately, the Primate's scandalous conduct and peculiar wickedness left them no choice but to proceed against him. Primian's crimes were then recalled factually and without rhetorical flourish. The Primate was condemned, and clergy were given till the following December and laity till the following Easter in which to withdraw from communion with him; those who remained obstinate after those dates would be readmitted to the Church only after penance. The document concludes with the signatures of the fifty-three participants. Soon afterwards Maximian was solemnly consecrated in Primian's stead.

Some of his supporters were to regret their zeal for honest conduct. The Numidians and Mauretanians would have none of it. Gamalius the Primate of Numidia backed by Optatus of Thamugadi, Crispinus of Calama, and possibly the veteran seer Pontius[3] began to rally support for Primian. The unfortunate experiences of a few wealthy clerics in Carthage were no justification for a schism, which involved the rejection of a leader who scarcely more than a year previously had been solemnly enthroned as Primate of Africa. A 'universal Council' of the Donatist church was summoned to concert action against the

---

[1] Fifty-five bishops sign the Council's decree. On the other hand, Augustine states in *Contra Cresconium*, iv. 6. 7, that 'centum vel amplius' were present. There may have been confusion in Augustine's mind between the 'Council of forty-three' and that of Cebarsussa. The Council of Cebarsussa may simply have been the adjourned meeting which the Primianists broke up at Carthage. The location of Cebarsussa is not known.

[2] Text reconstructed in Migne, *PL.* xi, cols. 1183–89.

[3] Pontius signs the decree of Bagai immediately after the Primates of Numidia and Carthage. He must therefore have been a senior bishop. Optatus' own signature comes fourteenth. Pontius was not a common name in North Africa.

Maximianist rebels. On 24 April 394, 310 bishops mainly from Numidia and Mauretania assembled in the great cathedral of Bagai in southern Numidia.[1] The Primate of Numidia presided, but with him in a place of honour was Primian himself, not only vindicated but also a participant in the judgement which was to be pronounced against his enemies.[2]

Like the decree of the Council of Cebarsussa a large part of the conciliar decision of Bagai has survived. Various fragments were quoted by Augustine against the Donatists over the next fifteen years, so that nearly the whole document can be reconstructed. It is interesting to compare the two Sentences, for the contrasts they contain are the measure of the difference in outlook which separated the Numidians from the more cultivated Maximianists in the Proconsular Province. The judgement passed by the latter was a fair statement of a case designed to prove that Primian was completely unfit to remain in office. His continued presence would lay the Church open to contagion and defilement such as were suffered in the days of Caecilian.[3] In both cases the remedy was the same, separation 'from the brother who walked idly'. The decree of Bagai was very different. That Maximinian and his supporters were 'schismatics' was taken for granted, and this in itself was sufficient to warrant their condemnation. No attempt was made to meet their case, nor even to vindicate Primian. Instead, the Maximianists were subjected to concentrated invective, abuse driven home by an apt reference to a Biblical text. As schismatics, their fate would be similar to that of the Egyptians who perished in their thousands at the crossing of the Red Sea, or of the rebels against Moses—Dathan, Korah, and Abiram (Numbers xvi. 32).[4] Their 'mouths were filled with bitterness and cursing',

---

[1] *Contra Cresconium*, iv. 58. 69, 'Numidae et Mauri quam plurimi paucis Byzacenis et Provincialibus'. The text of the Sentence of Bagai has been pieced together from various references in Augustine's works, in Migne, *PL*. xi, cols. 1189–91.

[2] Augustine, *Contra Cresconium*, iv. 6. 7, 'tamquam judex innocentissimus considebat.'

[3] 'Praeter alia illicita ejus admissa, quae pro honestate styli nostri siluimus a sacerdotali choro perpetuo esse damnatum; ne eo palpato, Dei Ecclesia aut contagione, aut aliquo crimine maculetur': Sentence of Cebarsussa (Migne, *PL*. xi, col. 1188). The liturgical reason for Primian's expulsion should not be overlooked. It may provide a clue why the Maximianists as a body never sided with the Catholics against the Donatist majority; their reasoning was purely Donatist.

[4] Augustine, *Contra Cresconium*, iv. 16, and *De Gestis cum Emerito*, 10, col. 705, 'Maximianum fidei aemulum, veritatis adulterum, Ecclesiae matris inimicum, Dathan, Chore et Abiron ministrum, de pacis gremio sententiae fulmen excussit.'

they were 'adulterers of truth', they were 'sacrilegious', they must be regarded as 'vipers', the 'poison of asps was under their lips',[1] they were 'a pestiferous wound' in the body of the Church.[2] The ferocity of these statements combines well with what we know of the Circumcellions and of those Donatist clergy who were their leaders. It was the work of men who brooded on violence and delighted in fanatical strife.[3] It was also the technique of the Donatist sermon in Numidia, as described by Optatus of Milevis: a Biblical text, in this case Rom. iii. 13–15, followed by invective against the enemies of the faith.[4] And yet the judgement of Bagai was drawn up not by an untutored Berber but by one of the most fastidious of Latin stylists, Bishop Emeritus of Caesarea.[5]

As a result of the Council, the condemnation of Primian was reversed. Instead, Maximian and twelve of his coadjutors who had consecrated him bishop, together with the dissenting Carthaginian clergy, were declared excommunicate in the most solemn terms, 'by the will of God who presides [over the deliberations] and by the authoritative voice of the universal council'.[6] Then, imitating perhaps the Maximianists in making a show of magnanimity, the Council granted a period of grace until Christmas 394 to all those who would dissociate themselves from the arch-schismatic. If they made their peace within that time all would be well.[7] The judgement was received with

[1] 'Venenum aspidum sub labiis eorum, quorum os maledictione et amaritudine plenum est, veloces pedes eorum ad effundendum sanguinem'—De Gestis cum Emerito, 11, col. 705 (PL. xi, col. 1190).

[2] Ibid., 'tabescentis vulneris putredo pestifera'.

[3] The spirit is not unlike that of Communist polemic directed at 'deviationists'. The position of 'deviationists' and 'schismatics' has much in common.

[4] Optatus, iv. 5, 'Nullus vestrum est, qui non convicia nostra suis tractibus misceat, qui non aut aliud initiet, aut aliud explicet. Lectiones dominicas incipitis, et tractatus vestros ad nostras injurias explicatis; profertis Evangelium, et facitis absenti fratri convicium; auditorum animis infunditis odia, inimicitias docendo suadetis.'

[5] Augustine, De Gestis cum Emerito, 10, col. 704, 'ab isto Emerito est dictata sententia ubi illi [Maximianistae] damnati sunt'. On Emeritus as a Latinist see P. Monceaux, Histoire littéraire, vi. 117.

[6] De Gestis cum Emerito, 11, 'Dei praesidentis arbitrio, universalis concilii ore veridico, damnatos esse cognoscite.'

[7] Ibid., 'Eos autem quos sacrilegi surculi non polluere plantaria, hoc est, qui a Maximiani capite, proprias manus verecundo fidei pudore retraxerunt, ad matrem Ecclesiam redire permisimus.' This was an important stipulation which I think referred to all Maximianists, including the twelve condemned by name. The Donatists themselves thought so (Contra Cresconium, iv. 28. 35). This view provided them with a partial answer to Augustine's charge that there was no logic in their

great enthusiasm and was passed by a shout of acclamation, contrary to the usual practice whereby each bishop gave his own vote. Some, it was stated, were impressed as much by the diction and turn of phrase employed by the drafter as by the condemnation itself.[1]

Armed with this formidable pronouncement, Primian and the Numidians made short work of the Maximianists. In Carthage Primian had the city magistrates turn his rival out of his house, while the mob destroyed his church.[2] A special hostility was directed against those bishops who had taken part in the consecration of Maximian. Before the year was out, Primian had appointed a new bishop of Membressa in the valley of the Upper Mejerda, in place of Salvius, one of the chief adherents of Maximianism in the area.[3] The law was invoked. Primian was able to bring a case against Salvius before the Proconsul Herodes. His advocate, Nummasius, argued that all church property in Membressa should be put at his candidate's disposal, on the grounds that the Maximianists had been declared schismatics by an ecclesiastical council.[4] The Proconsul decided in favour of Primian's contention,[5] a fact which shows that at this time the Donatists had achieved something in the nature of recognition that they were the 'Catholic Church' in Africa. The Catholics looked on, apparently unable to assert their own claims. The precedent, however, was to stand them in good stead in a few years' time. Primian then turned to two other of Maximian's friends who were bishops of towns in the same area. On 2 March 395 Herodes heard the case against Praetextatus of Assuras and Felicianus of Musti, which was instituted by his clergy in Musti.[6] Again the decision went to the Primianists: Praetextatus and Felicianus were to be expelled from their churches, which were then to be handed over to the substitutes consecrated by Primian. But, as the Catholics were to find later

refusal to reunite with the Catholics while they had no qualms about receiving back the Maximianists.

[1] *Contra Cresconium*, iv. 2. 2 and 4. 4.

[2] Ibid. iii. 59. 65, iv. 47. 57.   [3] Ibid. iv. 4. 5.

[4] Ibid. iii. 59. 65, 'Instructi sunt advocati, adita judicia et tamquam in haereticos excitata'. This was at precisely the time when the Imperial Government were confirming the privileges of the African Catholics; see *Codex Theodosianus*, xvi. 2. 9, of 23 March 395 to Hierius, *Vicarius Africae*. (The Proconsuls concerned were pagans: Augustine, *Contra Litteras Petiliani*, ii. 58. 132 (*PL.* xliii, col. 303).)

[5] *Contra Cresconium*, iv. 4. 4 (*PL.* xliii, col. 549).

[6] Ibid. iii. 56. 62, cols. 529–30. See also *PL.* xi, col. 1191.

on, it was one thing to win a lawsuit, quite another to have the judgement executed in face of a hostile population. Salvius and his two colleagues remained firm. Primian's lawyers had to plead twice more, before the Proconsul Theodorus in December 396,[1] and seemingly in the following year before his successor Seranus.[2] Even then it was might rather than right that decided the issue.

In 397, however, Gildo was virtual ruler of Africa. The new Proconsul Seranus declared in explicit terms that the judgement pronounced at Bagai against the Maximianists was valid and that, unless contrary decisions existed, it should be obeyed.[3] This time, the execution of the order was entrusted to the local enemies of the citizens of Membressa, the people of the neighbouring town of Abitina. The medicine was effective. Salvius was forcibly removed from his church. Dead dogs were hung round his neck, and he was paraded through the streets of Membressa in mock triumph. A Primianist was installed in his place. Salvius, however, had not forfeited public sympathy. He was venerable and respected. A new church was soon built for him, and he was able to maintain himself a short while longer.[4]

By this time the quarrel between the rival groups of Donatists had become merged in the wider political scene. The exact reasons which caused Gildo to tread the same road of rebellion as his brother a quarter of a century previously are obscure. In 391 he was still the loyal servant of Theodosius. His services were rewarded by his special appointment as *magister utriusque militiae* in Africa,[5] but during 392 his views began to change. In that year Eugenius revolted against Theodosius and estab-

---

[1] *Contra Cresconium*, iii. 56. 62, col. 530. The hearing took place on 22 Dec. 396 (Seeck, *Regesten*, p. 290).

[2] *Enarratio in Ps. 21. 31* (*PL.* xxxvi, col. 181); *Contra Cresconium*, iv. 3. 3. Augustine claims that the *legatus* of Carthage and four 'if not more' Proconsuls listened to the Donatists' claims. He gives Seranus the titles of both 'Vicarius' and 'Proconsul', and it seems that he did in fact hold both offices at different times during the period 393–7 (Pallu de Lessert, *Fastes*, ii. 218–19).

[3] *Contra Cresconium*, iv. 48. 58, col. 579, 'Seranus proconsul dixit: "Lis episcoporum secundum legem ab episcopis audienda est : episcopi judicaverunt. Quare non aut sub satisfactione ad chorum reverteris vetustatis, aut ut habes scriptum terga persecutoribus prodis?" ', i.e. rejoin his colleagues or resign.

[4] Ibid. 49. 59, cols. 579–80; *Contra Epistolam Parmeniani*, iii. 6. 29, cols. 106–7.

[5] He has this title in a rescript addressed to him on 20 December 393 (*Codex Theodosianus*, ix. 7. 9; Seeck, *Untergang*, v. 282).

lished himself in Italy. Gildo remained neutral as he had in the conflict with Magnus Maximus. He continued to receive his master's edicts, but he kept Rome and Italy well supplied with grain.[1] His attitude enabled him to keep a foot in each camp, and the defeat of the usurper did not involve his own fall. On 19 January 395, however, Theodosius died at Milan, and Gildo gradually broke off his connexion with the Imperial house.

The objects he had in mind are uncertain. Jornandes indicates that he hoped to obtain the control of the African provinces for himself.[2] From Claudian and others one gathers that he contemplated transferring Africa from the suzerainty of Honorius to that of Arcadius in the East.[3] In so doing, he would have been following the precedent set by the rebel Alexander in 308 who seems to have declared Africa part of the dominions of Galerius. The objectives were not incompatible, for had he succeeded, the arm of Constantinople was unlikely to have reached farther than it did during the Vandal period. Like Gaiseric after him, he could have withdrawn Africa from all but the most formal ties with the Empire. There is nothing, however, to show that Gildo was ever in revolt against the Empire as such, or had conscious aims beyond gratification of the personal ambition of acquiring an enormous landed estate.[4]

Until the end of 396 he appears to have acted cautiously. Italy was gradually put on rations.[5] The Imperial writ continued to run, and the officials in Africa received their appointments and rescripts from Ravenna. Yet during this time, if not before, an alliance had come into being between the Primianists and Count Gildo. The moving spirit in this arrangement was Optatus of Thamugadi.

[1] Symmachus (ed. Seeck, *MGH.* iv), *Ep.* vi. 1; and Claudian, *De Bello Gildonico* (ed. Loeb), 245–50.

[2] Iornandes, *De Regnorum et Temporum Successione Romana*, 320 (ed. *MGH.* v. 1. 41), 'ac si juvenile regnum utriusque despiciens, sibi velle coepit Africam optinere.' Also Orosius, vii. 36, and Zosimus, v. 13.

[3] Claudian, *De Bello Gildonico*, 4–6; *In Eutropium*, i. 399–400; *De Consulatu Stilichonis*, i. 271–3.

[4] This was so vast that after his execution its administration was put into the hands of a special office, the *comitativa Gildoniaci patrimonii* (*Notitia Dignitatum* (ed. Seeck), occ. xii. 5). Cf. *Cod. Theod.* vii. 8. 7 and ix. 42. 16.

[5] Claudian, *De Bello Gildonico*, 70, 102, and 127; also *De Consulatu Stilichonis*, i. 278 and 309.

By 397, however, as in the reign of Julian, the Donatists had
the machinery of Imperial administration and the army on their
side. The Proconsul Seranus and Gildo were more than favourable to them; the Numidians merged their interests completely
with those of Gildo, as they had twenty-five years before with
those of Firmus. The relationship between Optatus and Gildo
was summed up in a sentence by a Donatist bishop—'Optatus
Comitem Deum habet'.[1] First the Catholics and the landowners
who supported them, and afterwards the Maximianists were to
feel the effects of this alliance. The Circumcellions blazed into
activity.[2] Gangs of youths, often led by Donatist clergy, attacked
the dwellings of the rich. Villas were burnt to the ground and
estates plundered. From Claudian one gathers that Gildo was
as unmerciful as Optatus towards the richer landowners.[3] An
effort seems to have been made to root out the Catholic minority
in Numidia. Augustine tells of the sack of local churches, and a
wholesale attack on Catholic property.[4] In vain the Catholics
appealed to the Imperial authorities. On 15 June 392 an
edict had laid down that heretical clergy were liable to a
fine of 10 lb. of gold.[5] The Catholics attempted to invoke
this law against Optatus. They put their case to Seranus, but
the Donatist bishop defied them and refused to answer any
charge.[6]

He had other intentions. Though Primian had been able to
install his own nominees in some of the towns held by the
Maximianists, the bishops of Musti and Assuras still defied him.
Optatus was determined to end this situation. At the head of
a motley army of Circumcellions and soldiers, the Numidian
bishop crossed into Byzacena and advanced northwards to
Assuras. Panic seized the population. They besought their
unwilling bishops to yield;[7] riots broke out in the threatened

[1] Augustine, *Contra Litteras Petiliani*, ii. 23. 53, col. 277, and ii. 83. 184.

[2] For Circumcellion activity in the years 397–8, see *Contra Epistolam Parmeniani*
(written A.D. 399), iii. 3. 18, col. 96, also i. 11. 17 and ii. 9. 18; *Contra Litteras
Petiliani*, i. 24. 26.

[3] *De Bello Gildonico*, 163–71.

[4] *Contra Litteras Petiliani*, ii. 83. 184 (*PL*. xliii, col. 316), 'Ipsa Ecclesia catholica soli-
data principibus catholicis imperantibus terra marique, armatis turbis ab Optato
atrociter et hostiliter oppugnata est.' *Ep*. 29. 12 (destruction of a Catholic church
at Hasna).

[5] *Codex Theodosianus*, xvi. 5. 21. Cf. ibid. 2. 29 and 5. 28.

[6] *Contra Litteras Petiliani*, ii. 83. 184.

[7] *Contra Cresconium*, iii. 60. 66 (*PL*. xliii, col. 532).

towns. Optatus backed the Primianists with dire threats of what might take place should he allow his forces to attack. Then the unexpected happened. The Maximianist prelates yielded, and were promptly restored to their sees as Primianist bishops after taking an oath of allegiance to the Carthaginian Primate.[1] Primian's own nominees quietly stood down and elected to serve under their former rivals.[2]

Flushed with this victory, which is further evidence for the immense power which he wielded, Optatus returned to Thamugadi in triumph. On his way he was accompanied by Felicianus of Musti and Praetextatus of Assuras. Other Maximianist bishops seem to have followed their example and made their peace with Primian. The Donatist Primate himself was at Thamugadi to meet Optatus and together they celebrated the tenth anniversary of Optatus' consecration by a great Council.[3] The event struck the imagination of contemporaries. Optatus sat enthroned in state in the raised apse of the vast cathedral which he had probably built, surrounded by his clergy, settling disputes, and, amid the enthusiastic cries of the multitude, letting his will be known to his colleagues by what Augustine describes as 'nutu regali'.[4] This moment may well be regarded as the culminating point in the history of the Donatist Church.

How was it that Optatus was able to treat the Maximianist bishops so leniently despite the sentence passed against them at Bagai in 394? Personal prestige played a decisive part. 'Optatus wished it',[5] was the explanation given by the ordinary Donatist when challenged with the facts by Augustine. The dominating personality of Optatus is clear from everything that has survived concerning him. The mosaicist at Timgad records that he 'received orders from the priest of God, Optatus'.[6] So, too, did the Maximianists. In the Donatist view, they were simply schismatics, a perfect example of Tyconius' definition of

---

[1] Ibid. and iv. 25. 32.

[2] *De Gestis cum Emerito*, 9. Rogatus of Assuras later joined the Catholics.

[3] Augustine, *Ep.* 108. 5 (*CSEL.* xxxiv. 2. 616), 'Quos duos [Praetextatus and Felicianus] non unus Primianus sed multi coepiscopi vestri, cum frequentissima numerositate Tamugadensis Optati natalicia celebrarent'.

[4] *Contra Epistolam Parmeniani*, ii. 3. 7, col. 54.

[5] *Contra Cresconium*, iv. 25. 32, 'Optatus hoc voluit, Optatus hoc fecit.'

[6] 'Haec iubente sacerdote Dei Optato peregi', E. Albertini, *CRAI.*, 1939, p. 101. The Donatist uses the same term 'sacerdos' for 'bishop' as was usual in Cyprian's time.

a schism. Theirs was a local affair ('in aliquibus provinciis aut in una civitate'), a division of minds within the same communion brought about by the schismatics' believing themselves to be of a superior sanctity.[1] The Maximianists had broken from Primian because they considered him personally unworthy, and therefore liable to administer sacraments which were spiritually valueless. Their position was wholly different from that of the Catholics, who were in Donatist eyes betrayers of the Christian faith and regarded as defilers of the holy places (*loca sancta*) in every province.[2] It was evidently permitted to grant a certain amount of discretion in reconciling clergy who had gone over to Maximian, even after the time-limit set by the Council of Bagai had expired. The Donatists regarded Maximianism as a purely internal affair, and the Maximianists themselves, despite persecution by the Primianist majority, showed little tendency to make common cause with the Catholics. By 411 many of the more prominent members of the schism had rejoined Primian.[3] Augustine's propaganda, 'Maximianistarum baptismus acceptatur, orbis terrarum baptismus exsufflatur',[4] may have sounded less logical to his African contemporaries than it would to modern critics.

But the Donatist ascendancy rested on the narrow basis of Gildo's success. Optatus and his friends overestimated the chieftain's power. In the autumn of 397 Gildo resolved on a trial of strength with the representatives of the Empire in Italy. The corn-fleet was held back, and Rome was thereby threatened with famine. This time Stilicho acted. He could not surrender Africa to Arcadius. Gildo was declared a public enemy by the

---

[1] Cited from T. Hahn, *Tyconius-Studien*, 68–69, n. 1. 'Scisma a scisura animorum vocatur, eadem enim religione eodem cultu, eodem ritu credit ut ceteri sancti, sed solo congregationis delectatur discidio, id est cum ceteris sanctis, qui in ecclesia sunt, unum non habet consilium, quia plus se sanctum putat quam ceteros in ecclesia.'

[2] Ibid., 'Diaboli schisma est et falsi fratres; et si schisma in aliquibus provinciis aut in una civitate, aut non multo plus. Non de his dicimus, qui per universas provincias loca sancta occupaverint et polluerint, quae aperte patitur ecclesia'. Cf. Cresconius (*Contra Cresconium*, ii. 4. 6 (*PL*. xliii. 470)) on the same issue, 'schisma vero eadem sequentium separatio'. Hence the Donatist contention concerning Maximianism, 'nec causam causae, nec personam praejudicare personae', quoted by Augustine in *Breviculus Collationis*, iii. 16. 28.

[3] Among reconciled Maximianist bishops who took part in the Conference of Carthage in 411 as Donatists were: Gaianus of Tiguala (*PL*. xi. 1286), Donatus of Ad Palmam, Pomponius of Macri, and Pancratius of Badias (*PL*. xi. 1325).

[4] *Contra Epistolam Parmeniani*, iii. 6. 29, col. 108.

Senate, and an expedition was prepared against him.[1] But
there was no need for the *magister militum* to conduct the campaign in person, or even to use the army which he had collected.
Gildo, like Firmus before him, had quarrelled with one of his
brothers and, with a violence which appears to have characterized the blood-feuds of the Numidians, had murdered two
of his children.[2] The offended man Mascazel sought refuge in
Italy. He came under the influence of the governing group
of Catholics[3] and was entrusted with part of the expedition
against Gildo, setting out with a small force of Gallic troops in
the winter of 397–8.

There was evidently no serious fighting for some months.
Gildo established his headquarters in Theveste, where he
gathered an army in the expectation that he would have to
meet Stilicho. Perhaps he even contemplated taking the offen-
sive and attacking Spain.[4] Meantime, violence against the
African Catholics increased, and on 25 April 398 Honorius
ordered the death penalty against those who engaged in sacking churches.[5] The decisive moment was now at hand. The
late spring found Gildo still at Theveste, and either he under-
estimated his brother's abilities, or he let himself be taken by
surprise. Mascazel reached the Ardalio River (Oued Soumma)
between Theveste and Ammaedara (Haidra) unopposed. There,
probably in the gorges of Gourai, the armies met, and Gildo
suffered total defeat (April/May 398.)[6] Panic seized his levies,
and they fled without striking a blow. Their leader became a
helpless fugitive. On 31 July 398 he was caught at Thabraca
(Tabarka) on the Tunisian coast, whence he was attempting
to escape overseas, and was either strangled or committed
suicide.[7] His henchman Optatus shared his fate. He was

[1] Claudian, *De Bello Gildonico*, 16 and 66; Symmachus, *Ep.* vi. 58; Seeck, *Untergang*, v, pp. 286–90.   [2] Orosius, vii. 36. 4 (*CSEL*. vii. 533–4).
[3] Ibid., and Paulinus, *Vita Ambrosii*, 51 (*PL.* xiv, col. 47). Monks accompanied
his expedition.
[4] A move hinted at by Claudian in *De Consulatu Stilichonis*, i. 19, 'Vicinum quod
nescit Hiberia Maurum'.
[5] *Codex Theodosianus*, xvi. 2. 31. The wording of the rescript indicates that attacks
on Catholic churches by armed mobs were on such a scale that the police (*stationarii*) could not be expected to control them, and that regular forces under the
Comes Africae would have to intervene.
[6] Orosius, vii. 36; Gsell, *Atlas archéologique de l'Algérie*, feuille 29, no. 110. Dating,
Seeck, *Untergang*, v. 289.
[7] *Chronica Minora* (ed. Mommsen), i. 298. By an irony of fate Gildo was eventually
buried in the Catholic church at Lamzelli (*Gesta Coll. Carth.* i. 206 (*PL.* xi. 1343–4)).

disowned by his colleagues and executed as a rebel.[1] The common people, however, regarded him as a martyr.[2]

Thus ended the Donatist bid for supremacy in Africa. Whether Donatism would have developed into a national Church like that of the Copts in the Nile valley, had Gildo triumphed, must be left to speculation. Creative genius, religious enthusiasm, popular support, and vigorous leadership were not lacking in that period among the Donatists. But they had no practical solution to the problem of the relationship between Church and State. Rebels in fact against the Roman Empire, they could evolve no alternative system of government in which Donatism would have had the same place as Catholicism secured in the Roman world. Lacking a conscious *political* aim themselves, they had to await the 'hand of God' in the form of an outside invader to remove their oppressors, and neither the Goths nor the Vandals nor the Arabs suited their ends. Fanaticism and fatalism were not the foundation on which a new system of society could be built. Meantime, the Catholics were able to take full advantage of the favour of the Imperial Government. The possible inconvenience of relying on another native potentate was quickly removed by Mascazel's murder.[3] Henceforth, command of the armies in Africa was in the hands of pro-Catholic officers. In their Primate, Aurelius, and in Augustine of Hippo the Catholics at last possessed men who could meet the Donatists in debate, and who had the political sense to make the most of the armoury of anti-heretical legislation that lay to hand. The schismatics were given no mercy. The next thirteen years were to see them driven on to the defensive and relentlessly harried. The great edifice which Donatus and Parmenian had so laboriously built up was undermined by the superior tactics and personal ability of the Catholics. The Conference held at Carthage in June 411 into which they were manœuvred merely sealed their fate. We pause to study the outlook of the architect of their defeat, St. Augustine of Hippo.

---

[1] *Contra Litteras Petiliani*, ii. 23. 53, col. 278, 'te autem, etiamsi tibi displiceat quidquid fecit Optatus, furem tamen tenemus, non per calumniam nostram, sed per sententiam tuam'. On his execution, ibid. ii. 92. 209.

[2] Augustine, *Ep.* 76. 4, 'quem cum modo martyrem dicitis'. Inscriptions in his honour in the cathedral of Timgad were not defaced.

[3] Orosius, vii. 36. He is discreet about the reasons behind Mascazel's fall from grace. Stilicho is said to have had him pushed into a fast-flowing river after a conference. Cf. Zosimus, v. 11. 5.

XV

ST. AUGUSTINE AND THE DONATISTS

THE years 391 to 392 may be regarded as decisive in the history of the two Churches. Up to this moment, the Donatists had not only succeeded in drawing the mass of fanatical Christianity in the bazaars and villages to them, but on the whole they had produced the abler and more learned leadership. They could claim with some justice to be the true successors of the primitive Church and of Cyprian, and Donatists such as Tyconius and Vitellius Afer had maintained something of the theological and moral pre-eminence of the African Church of the third century. Their laity, too, as St. Augustine was to find at Hippo[1] and at Thubursicum Bure,[2] were well instructed, and ready to enter into theological debate. The Catholic Church, on the other hand, had shown little power of attraction. So far as is known, neither Tyconius nor the Maximianists in 394 showed any inclination to cross over to it, even when they had been condemned as schismatics by the majority of their own community.

But in 391/2 both Parmenian[3] and his rival Genethlius[4] died, and in the ensuing elections it was the Catholics who made the wiser choice. Aurelius, the new Catholic Bishop of Carthage, does not seem to have been outstanding either as a scholar or a theologian, but he had the qualities of an organizer, and he was blessed with longevity which enabled him to guide the Catholic Church in Africa on a continuous course until the Vandal invasion.[5] But above all, he had the friendship and loyal

---

[1] *Retractationes*, ii. 28 (*PL*. xxxii, col. 642)—the circle led by Centurius.

[2] *Ep*. 43 and 44. One of Augustine's major opponents, Cresconius, was a grammarian.

[3] Dating, Monceaux, *Histoire littéraire*, iv. 53.

[4] Possibly on 7 May 391 (Seeck, *Regesten*, 278).

[5] Aurelius' reputation as a centralizer and organizer long outlived him. Ferrandus of Carthage, writing his *Vita Fulgentii* in the mid-sixth century, records that Aurelius claimed among his other rights that of personal responsibility for drafting and signing the encyclical letters from the Councils of Carthage over which he presided (*Vita Fulgentii*, 41 = *PL*. lxv, col. 138). His own view of his office is summed up in his statement: 'Ego cunctarum Ecclesiarum, dignatione Dei, sollicitudinem sustineo.' Canon 55 (*Codex Canonum*). See also Tillemont, *Mémoires*, 13. 155.

support of one of the outstanding men in human history, Augustine, Bishop of Hippo. The association between these two started on Augustine's return to Africa after Cassiciacum in A.D. 388.[1] Aurelius was then deacon. It lasted throughout their lives. The development of the Donatist controversy from that date is intimately bound up with the work of the Bishops of Carthage and Hippo. On the Catholic side, the Proconsular Province and Numidia co-operated in a manner rare in African church history.

But Augustine's long conflict with the Donatists presents the historian with a problem. The energy with which he pursued them is remarkable. From his first discussions with the local Donatist clergy during his presbyterate until his final exchanges with Gaudentius of Thamugadi, not a year passes without some anti-Donatist tract or sermon. When in 401 the arrival of Stilicho's brother-in-law Bathanarius as *Comes Africae* enabled the Catholics to begin to reap the fruit of Gildo's failure, Augustine set on one side the treatises on Genesis and against the Manichees which he had been writing, and concentrated on the Donatists alone.[2] For ten years he spent all his energies as a writer and a diplomat in combating them, his object being first to defeat their leaders in argument and then, as a result of a general conference, to persuade the mass of the Donatist Church to reunite with the Catholics. If they refused, the secular arm would stand ready to deal with them. There was hardly a Donatist leader whom he did not personally try to convert. One can see the hand of Augustine and his close companions in the tactics agreed upon in the annual Catholic Councils, in the missions to the Imperial Court, and in the propaganda used to convince the populace. Augustine's fervour abated only when he believed that the Donatist Church was ceasing to exist. Then he began to turn to other topics, to the Pelagians and the Arians. After 420 the Donatists are mentioned but seldom in his writings. It might seem that Augustine believed that his life's work hitherto, the overthrow of the schismatics, had ended in victory.

This, however, is hardly a true picture. The Donatist Church

[1] *De Civitate Dei*, xxii. 8. 3. See Gustave Bardy, *Saint Augustin, l'homme et l'œuvre*, Paris, 1946, p. 141.

[2] See ibid. 325 ff. Monceaux, *Histoire littéraire*, vii, is an indispensable work for a detailed study of Augustine's relations with the Donatists; also G. G. Willis, *Saint Augustine and the Donatist Controversy* (S.P.C.K., 1950).

had at least a century and a half of existence after Augustine died, and interestingly enough the early and mid-fifth century appears to be the classic period of church building in the home of Donatism on the High Plains. One has the impression that the triumph of the Catholics in 411 was a personal triumph of Augustine and his friends, and that this triumph did not outlast the death of their leader.

We gather from Augustine's friend and biographer Possidius of Calama, as well as from a hint dropped by Victor Vitensis, that Augustine's last days were clouded by a feeling of disappointment and fear for the future of the Church.[1] The heresies were dormant, not dead, and Arianism and paganism were aiding the Donatists to destroy his work. At his death in 430 African Catholicism was experiencing terrible destruction at the hands of the African barbarians and the Vandals. Heraclius, whom he had seen so solemnly enthroned as his coadjutor on 26 September 426,[2] leaves no mark upon history. Fifty years later, at the time of Huneric's Council in 484, Hippo was not included in the list of African sees then in existence. Though the name of Augustine remained connected with Hippo until the time of el Bekri (eleventh century), it does not appear to have had much practical effect on the fortunes of Catholicism.[3] The work of Donatus and Parmenian was preserved in popular imagination after their deaths, a great church was erected to the honour of Bishop Marculus, the Donatist leaders were long believed able to perform miracles, and legends concerning them maintained the spirit of their followers during the persecutions which followed the Conference of Carthage.[4] But this does not appear to have been the case after Augustine's death. Victor Vitensis does not mention him in connexion with Catholic resistance to the Vandals. No saga grew up round his

---

[1] Victor Vitensis, *Historia Persecutionis*, i. 3 (*CSEL.* vii. 6), 'qua tempestate Hipporegiorum obsessa est civitas, quam omni laude dignus beatus Augustinus, librorum multorum confector, pontifex gubernabat. Tunc illud eloquentiae, quod ubertim per omnes campos ecclesiae decurrebat, ipso metu siccatum est flumen, atque dulcedo suavitatis dulcius propinata in amaritudinem absinthii versa est'. Cf. Possidius, *Vita Augustini*, 28.

[2] Dating, Seeck, *Regesten*, 352.

[3] El Bekri, *Description de l'Afrique septentrionale*, tr. de Slane, Algiers, 1913, p. 116.

[4] *In Ioan. Evang. Tract. XIII*, in which Augustine alludes to miracles performed by Donatus and Pontius, was written after the Conference of Carthage, about A.D. 417.

name or those of his closest associates, Alypius or Possidius of Calama. As yet, no *memoria* erected in his honour to serve as a place of pilgrimage has been found. Tipasa, hallowed by the shrine of Salsa farther along the coast, remained a centre of Catholic pilgrimage for the whole Mediterranean area until the mid-sixth century:[1] Hippo is no more difficult of access. In Byzantine times, Augustine's fight against the Donatists is not mentioned in African church literature. So far as African Catholicism is concerned, he appears as a majestic but rather solitary figure, the leader of a movement which was already in decline.

The ultimate failure of Augustine's efforts in Africa calls for an explanation. Was it merely the untimely incursion of the Vandals that wrecked his work, or do the causes lie deeper, in Augustine himself, in his background, and in his appreciation of the Donatist movement?

Augustine was first and foremost an African, and was influenced throughout his life by the Berber background of his upbringing. The researches of French archaeologists have shown that Thagaste, his birthplace, was one of the centres of Libyan or proto-Berber culture. In no other area of North Africa are Libyan cemeteries, identified by Libyan and bilingual Romano-Libyan inscriptions, so numerous. Six Libyan inscriptions have been found in Thagaste itself.[2] Augustine's Berber descent shows itself in numerous small ways, in the name of his mother Monnica, a Berber name, perhaps derived from the Libyan deity Mon worshipped in the neighbouring town of Thibilis,[3] and in Augustine's tendency to follow Berber tradition and to attribute a nearer relationship to a brother than to a son.[4] The rather odd name which he gave his own son, 'Adeodatus', is intelligible only with reference to the Berber usage of naming children with a name connected with the worship of Baal—Adeodatus=Iatanbaal.[5]

---

[1] To judge from the funerary inscriptions found in the great cemetery around the church of St. Salsa, pilgrims came from as far afield as Syria. Many came from Gaul during the fifth and sixth centuries.

[2] P. Rodary, 'Recherche des inscriptions libyques dans la région de Souk Ahras', *Premier Congrès*, 173–81 and 415–23. Published in detail in J. B. Chabot, *Recueil des inscriptions libyques*, Paris, Imprimerie Nationale, 1940, p. 116, nos. 524–9.

[3] *CIL.* viii. 14911 and 17798. Cf. J. Toutain, *Les Cultes païens*, iii. 41.

[4] *Sermo* 46. 12. 29 (*PL.* xxxviii. 286), 'etsi non frater diaboli, certe adiutor et filius'.

[5] Toutain, *Les Cultes païens*, i. 252.

More than that, this native background colours much of Augustine's political and religious thought. One remembers the passionate interest he showed in the story of Dido when he was a boy.[1] He goes on to rebuke the grammarian Maximus of Madauros for his lack of sympathy and understanding for his native country;[2] Augustine's answer to Maximus in 389 is one of the most interesting and revealing of his letters. Later, as a mature thinker he appears to reject the Roman Empire as a political ideal. While grieving over the sack of Rome by Alaric as a tragic and significant event, he finds himself on the side of previous generations of African Christian apologists in maintaining that the city's rise was due to injustice—to unjust wars, aggressions and robberies.[3] His ideal was a series of small kingdoms, each living securely within its own boundaries, but all members of the Roman Catholic community. It may have been something of this idea, only from the Donatist standpoint, that moved Gildo and Optatus of Thamugadi during their rebellion of 397–8. In the fifth and sixth centuries, however, these ideas were translated into fact. In the far west, in what had once been Mauretania Caesariensis, a series of native Christian kingdoms grew up, centred on the old Roman foundations of Volubilis and Tiaret.[4] Though he probably never knew it, Augustine's thought as set out in the fourth book of the *De Civitate Dei* was fully in line with the developments which were even then taking place on the fringes of Roman Africa.

Augustine's attitude towards the cult of the martyrs provides an interesting example of the development of his outlook, and suggests what appears to be a steady reversion to original Berber type as he grew older. When he came back to Thagaste in 388 he was returning from three years in Italy, and before that, since 374, he had lived most of his life among cultivated latinized companions in Carthage. Whatever the effect of the translation of the bones of Gervasius and Protasius while he was at Milan may have been on his development towards Catholicism,

---

[1] *Confessions*, i. 13. 20.

[2] *Ep.* 17. 2. To his opponent in later years, Julian of Eclanum, Augustine is 'Philosophaster Poenorum'. *Contra Julianum*, Opus Imperfectum, v. 11.

[3] *De Civitate Dei*, iv. 3 (*CSEL*. xl. 165–6). Cf. J. N. Figgis, *The Political Ideas of St. Augustine*, Longmans, 1921, p. 53, and N. H. Baynes, 'The Political Ideas of the *De Civitate Dei*', Historical Association Pamphlet, No. 104, London, 1936.

[4] I have accepted Carcopino's views on the later history of Mauretania Caesariensis.

he showed at first that he had little time either for African martyrs or for miracles connected with them. In A.D. 390/1 he declares in the *De Vera Religione* that wonders were not seen any more as in Apostolic times, otherwise men would cease to be impressed by them.[1] He was then thirty-six. Shortly afterwards, when he had become a presbyter, he took firm action to prevent his congregation at Hippo celebrating the feast of the martyr Leontius in the traditional manner,[2] and he wrote in 392 to Aurelius at Carthage suggesting that the banquets held in the churches in honour of the martyrs (*parentalia*) should cease.[3] As regards miracles, he was equally rationalistic. In A.D. 400 he told his hearers that the physically blind were not healed by Divine miracle at the present time,[4] and in a letter written about the same period to a Donatist relative he poured scorn on Donatist credulity. 'If anyone brings them a lump of earth from the East, they will worship it.'[5]

Twenty years later Augustine appears to have changed his views entirely. In *De Civitate Dei*, xxii. 8, he fills his readers with stories of the dead being raised, the blind receiving back their sight, and other wonders performed by the bones of St. Stephen and the sacred earth which Paulus Orosius had fetched from Palestine at his behest.[6] The new churches which he was building in Hippo were all dedicated to martyrs, the Eight Martyrs,[7] the Twenty Martyrs,[8] Sts. Protasius and Gervasius,[9] and St. Theognis.[10] It is only from Augustine that one hears of the 'Twenty Martyrs'. Following his Donatist opponents, he elevated clergy such as the deacon Nabor who were killed in the religious strife to the rank of martyrs.[11] Indeed, except that Augustine admitted foreign saints into his canon and seems

---

[1] *De Vera Religione*, 25. 47 (*PL.* xxxiv. 142) possibly a Manichee belief.
[2] *Ep.* 29.   [3] *Ep.* 22.
[4] *Sermo* 88. 3 (*PL.* xxxviii. 540), 'Modo caro caeca non aperit oculos miraculo Domini.' The reference to blindness is all the more interesting when one recalls that Augustine was probably aware that cures were claimed to have taken place during the translation of the bones of Sts. Protasius and Gervasius.
[5] *Ep.* 52. 2, 'unde [from the East] terra si eis adferatur, adorant'.
[6] He relates some twenty-five stories of resurrections and cures from various ailments. See also the later Sermons, 318. 6, 323. 3, and 324. J. Zellinger, *Augustin und Volksfrommigkeit*, Muenchen, 1933, p. 52, has some interesting views on the development of this aspect of Augustine's outlook.
[7] *Sermo* 356. 10 (*PL.* xxxix. 1578).   [8] *De Civitate Dei*, xxii. 8. 9.
[9] Ibid. 8.   [10] *Sermo* 273. 7 (*PL.* xxxviii. 1251).
[11] On Nabor see P. Monceaux, 'Enquête sur l'épigraphie chrétienne', *Revue Africaine*, 1909, p. 423; and De Rossi, *Inscriptiones Christianae*, ii. 461.

always to have rejected those such as Miggin and Sanae who were exclusively revered by the Donatists, there is little to distinguish his beliefs in this respect from those of his rivals.

But if Augustine shared a common background and some of the underlying beliefs of his opponents, there was much also that stood in the way of his securing a true appreciation of their ideas. By the mid-fourth century the Roman town in the Algerian Tell, where Augustine was born, was ceasing to be the centre of local trade and community life. The latinized minority had become isolated by speech and economic interest from the Libyan peasant population that surrounded it. Augustine himself belonged to this minority. For all his intellectual distaste for Rome he became increasingly a Roman official in outlook as he grew older. His father Patricius was a *municeps*, a member of the *ordo* of his town, and he had a certain amount of property;[1] his neighbour Julian was a Senator;[2] the friends of his family were rich men, such as Alypius, Romanianus,[3] and Nebridius; at Carthage and in Italy he moved in those circles, and his letters and sermons throughout his life are addressed to an educated audience and to members of senatorial families such as Melania, Albina, Proba, Italica, or Juliana. On the other hand, he was out of touch with the agricultural workers whence the Donatists drew their following. He could not preach to them, since he knew little Punic and no Libyan,[4] and his methods of bringing them into the Catholic fold gradually became confined to strong-arm tactics through the agency of the great landowners.[5]

As one reads the long series of anti-Donatist treatises, letters, and sermons, one gets the impression that Augustine regarded Donatism as a 'heresy', to be fought by the same methods as might be used against the Manichees or Pelagians. If only he

---

[1] *Confessions*, ii. 3. 5, Patricius' property is described as 'tenuis'. He was a *curialis* (Possidius, *Vita*, 1, 'de numero curialium'—*PL.* xxxii. 35).

[2] *Ep.* 99. 1, 'de domo clarissimi et egregii iuvenis Iuliani quae nostris adhaeret parietibus'.

[3] Romanianus is thus described; 'essentque inter nos praedivites, Romanianus maxime communiceps noster' (*Confessions*, vi. 14). Augustine himself appears to have been able to use a private postal service for his correspondence with Nebridius (*Ep.* 10. 1).

[4] He quotes a Punic proverb in *Sermo* 167, 3. 4 (*PL.* xxxviii. 910), and was aware of the importance of appointing priests who spoke the African language, but there is no trace of his own knowledge of Berber.

[5] *Epp.* 58. 1, 88. 10, and 112.

could bring the leaders to debate, hold a Council with them, and have their opinions formally condemned then all would be well. Unity would be restored, the Donatists would hand over their churches, the acquiescent would retain their dignity as bishops, the rest would be heavily fined and rendered harmless. The matter would be ended by the due process of Roman law. But Augustine may have misread the psychology of the movement. It seems clear if one follows him on his various journeys that he never went to Lower Numidia until he visited Count Boniface at his headquarters about A.D. 422. Nothing suggests the division between the Tell and the High Plains more clearly than this. Augustine's area of activity lay almost exclusively among the romanized cities of the coast and river valleys where Catholicism was already strong. He would travel to Carthage through the coast towns of Thabraca, Hippo Diarrhytos, and Uzalis,[1] or westwards by sea to Caesarea. Alternatively, he would follow the Seybouse valley to Calama (Guelma) or the valley of the Rummel to Constantine. Once, he got as far as the upper reaches of the Mejerda, to Musti (Henchir Retbou) and Assuras (Zanfour),[2] but the great Donatist centres of Timgad and Theveste (Tebessa) lay beyond his reach and ken. He makes odd mistakes about Numidia, asking where the shady mountains are (if he had seen the Aures or even the Djebel Fedjoudj he would have known) or, even more extraordinary, asserting that olives did not grow in Numidia, when in fact Numidia was the chief olive-exporting centre of the Mediterranean.[3]

Limited by his environment and class, Augustine failed to appreciate the religious ideas and background of his Donatist opponents. He thought he was dealing with mental aberrations hardened into custom, from which people could be jolted by mild persecution.[4] He was in fact faced with a 'communal' issue of the bitterness which characterizes religious faith in the Near East. He tried to treat suicidal fanatics such as the priest Donatus

[1] *Sermo* 359 was preached on behalf of Bishop Florentius of Hippo Diarrhytos. Thabraca and Uzalis are mentioned in *Sermo* 62 and *Sermo in Ps.* 36.

[2] *Contra Cresconium*, iii. 60. 66 (*PL.* xliii. 532), 'Mustitani et Assuritani, sicut ab eis praesens audivi'.

[3] *Sermo* 46. 39 (*PL.* xxxviii. 293), 'non olivetis fertiles, non caeteris nemoribus amoenos. Unde ergo mons umbrosus in Numidiae partibus?'

[4] This is shown particularly in *Ep.* 93. 2 and 5. Note also the attitude adopted towards Cresconius. 'Expergiscimini aliquando' ('Wake up a bit'), *Contra Cresconium*, ii. 20. 25.

of Mutugenna with the same cheerful *bonhomie* as could be applied to the intellectual quirks of an episcopal colleague.[1]

A further point should be noticed. It often happens even in French North Africa today that a landowner living among his tenants gets much nearer to their outlook than revolutionary idealists from Metropolitan France who would emancipate them. Men of senatorial rank such as Celer had themselves become Donatists along with their farmers until the persecution suggested the wisdom of conversion.[2] But Augustine was not typical of this landowning-citizen class either. He had none of the civic pride that characterized Nectarius of Calama,[3] or of the devotion to the Roman past of his teacher Maximus of Madaura.[4] Neither he nor his intimate friends show in their letters that they gave a thought to their duties towards Thagaste as *curiales*. Alypius joined the *militia* of the Imperial service in Italy as an assessor, an act which a whole series of laws forbade *curiales* to do.[5] The ideal of Augustine and his friends was not the safeguarding of the city state or even the active farming of a villa, but *otium liberale*[6]—the mere enjoyment of the fruits of a great rural domain. This entailed the maintenance for their own benefit of a system which Optatus of Thamugadi and other Donatist clergy were attempting to overthrow.

Thus Augustine's circle had tended during the formative years of its members to cut itself off from the outlook both of many of the romanized citizens and of the countryfolk. They became Manichees, at a time when Manichaeism was regarded by the authorities with that horror and dread which they reserved for parricides and practisers of the black arts.[7] Yet for some years Augustine was an active and proselytizing member of the sect.[8] It is interesting, in assessing that atmosphere which

---

[1] *Ep.* 173. Rebecca West's *Saint Augustine* (Nelson's Short Biographies, 1938), pp. 132–45, contains a suggestive study of Augustine's mental approach to the Donatists.   [2] *Epp.* 56 and 57.

[3] *Ep.* 90. 1, Nectarius to Augustine, 'Sed quoniam crescit in dies singulos dilectus et gratia civitatis', &c.   [4] *Ep.* 16.

[5] *Confessions*, vi. 10. The *Codex Theodosianus* contains numerous laws designed to prevent African *curiales* from migrating into the Imperial service. Cf. xii. 1. 26, 27, 31, 41, 73, 95, 178.

[6] *Confessions*, vi. 14. Augustine's choice of Cassiciacum for his retirement in 387 is also indicative of this attitude.

[7] *Codex Theodosianus*, xvi. 5. 7 and 18. Cf. *Contra Litteras Petiliani*, iii. 25. 29 (prosecutions before the Proconsul Messianus).

[8] *Confessions*, bk. iii; P. Aflaric, *L'Évolution intellectuelle de S. Augustin*, Nourry, Paris, 1918, pp. 77–78.

Augustine represented, that, while Donatists and Manichees seem to have kept clear of one another, there is evidence for a considerable amount of interconversion between Catholics and Manichees. Apart from Augustine himself and Alypius,[1] successive bishops of Constantine, Profuturus and Fortunatus, were ex-Manichees.[2] This fact did not escape the notice of the Donatists.[3] Towards the end of Augustine's life, one of his deacons was converted to the sect.[4] When one considers that at the beginning of the eighth century Pope Gregory II[5] refused to receive African Catholic clergy on the grounds that they might have been Manichees, one begins to wonder whether perhaps there was not some intellectual link which bound African Catholicism to Manichaeism, just as Tertullian alined Gnostics and Catholics in opposition to his Church of the martyrs.

Augustine's Manichee preoccupations perhaps prevented him from understanding the background of the Donatist movement when he was at a receptive age. It is curious, for instance, that we do not know when he first began to learn about his opponents. We gather that at one period there was a considerable Donatist majority in and around Thagaste.[6] The Donatists maintained a bishopric there in the early fifth century, and some of Augustine's relatives, such as his cousin Severinus, were Donatists.[7] So, too, was Vincentius, one of his student friends at Carthage.[8] Yet the Donatists are not mentioned once in the *Confessions*, i.e. he seems to have had no significant contact with them in his youth. As soon as he was elected to the priesthood, Augustine studied and digested the Catholic *Acta* concerning the origins of the schism, but his knowledge of the sources of Donatist doctrinal tradition for some time remained rudimentary. When he wrote *De Baptismo contra Donatistas*, in 400, it is clear that, while his own ideas may have been influenced by Cyprian, he had not understood fully how those of his opponents could be

---

[1] *Confessions*, vi. 7. 12.

[2] *De Unico Baptismo*, 16. 29 (*PL*. 611), 'Proinde, si Profuturus ante paucissimos annos defunctus et Fortunatus qui in corpore adhuc est atque illi successit episcopo, quomodo Manichaei fuerunt . . .'.

[3] *Contra Litteras Petiliani*, iii. 16. 19. For Donatist views on Mani, ibid. ii. 18. 40, and *infra*, p. 256.

[4] *Ep*. 236. Also *Contra Litteras Petiliani*, iii. 17. 20, referring evidently to the conversion of a Catholic *sanctimonialis* to Manichaeism, and *Contra Fulgentium*, 13 (*PL*. xliii. 768).

[5] Gregory, *Ep*. 4 (Mansi, xii. 239).

[6] *Ep*. 93. 5. 17.

[7] *Ep*. 52.

[8] *Ep*. 93. 1.

inspired from the same source. He believed at that time that Donatus had invented the practice of rebaptism and falsified the text of Ecclesiasticus xxxiv. 30.[1] In fact, the Donatists were using the Cyprianic Bible. As late as 408, Augustine apparently believed that Cyprian had recanted his views, but that someone had suppressed this recantation.[2]

We have given this background of St. Augustine in order to try to answer one question—Did his arguments carry conviction? We know that he grasped the fact that the Donatist masses must be converted if any permanent results were to be obtained. His essays in 'political warfare', such as the *Psalmus contra Partem Donati,* and the use of the walls of confiscated Donatist churches for displaying copies of Imperial edicts or his own anti-Donatist works, show that he meant to reach the widest possible public. He went, too, to immense efforts to secure accurate information about those subjects on which he believed he could carry most conviction. For instance, he visited the main centres of Maximianism in the Mejerda valley to obtain first-hand accounts of events, in order to argue more effectively Donatist inconsistencies in their treatment of Maximianists and Catholics.[3] On his own assessment, a considerable number of conversions were gained through this particular line of attack.[4] Again, among the ordinary people the constant appeal for 'peace' and 'unity' may have found a responsive chord. We have seen how the 'Unity of the Church' was the aim of Donatus and the constant preoccupation of Parmenian. It may not be an accident that Augustine's most popular tract (written possibly by clergy on his staff) was the *Ad Catholicos Epistola, De Unitate Ecclesiae.*[5] The watchword 'peace' served Donatists as well as Catholics, as is shown by the inscription describing Bishop

---

[1] Augustine admits that in 397 he was not a real specialist ('nondum expertus') in the Donatist theory of Baptism (*Retractationes*, i. 21). Three years later, when he compiled the *De Baptismo*, he was still unaware of earlier decisions in favour of the Donatist practice. (See *De Baptismo*, iii. 1. 2, 'quod et consuetudo Ecclesiae pristina non habebat'.) On the other hand, he had read and digested the works of Tyconius, which he quotes frequently in his writings of this period. For the influence of Cyprian on Augustine's early works, cf. H. Koch, *Ricerche Religiose*, viii, 1932, pp. 317–37. The first sure reference to Donatism is contained in *Ep.* 20 (A.D. 390).

[2] *Ep.* 93. 10. 38 (*CSEL.* xxxiv. 482–3). Also *Contra Cresconium,* ii. 31. 39 (*PL.* xliii, col. 490), on Cyprian's *Ep.* 69–75.

[3] *Contra Cresconium,* iii. 60. 66.   [4] *Ep.* 185. 4. 17 and 18.

[5] On the authorship of this work, see Karl Adam, *Theologische Quartalschrift,* xci, 1909, pp. 86–115. I consider it to have been written either by Augustine himself or by one of his clergy.

Marculus' basilica as an 'aula pacis'.[1] It became, however, the refrain of Augustine's *Psalmus contra Partem Donati*. The fury with which Petilian of Constantine reacted to Augustine's effort to appropriate these ideas into a purely Catholic vocabulary suggests that this approach was not in vain.[2]

Less successful probably were Augustine's tracts on the Sacraments. The distinction between 'regular' and 'valid' sacraments, of membership of the Church 'visible' and 'invisible', so clear to a modern, or to a fourth-century student of Plotinus, was probably beyond the grasp of the native Berber; the simple metaphor used by Cyprian of the Church as the Ark—within the saved, outside the drowning multitudes—conveyed the situation to them.[3] A sculptured pillar from a Donatist church at Oued R'zel in central Numidia shows the peasant's interpretation of the Ark and the Dove, as symbols of the Church of the saints watched over by the Holy Spirit.[4] The Donatists had their own answer to Augustine, founded on valid African tradition, and they had orators and pamphleteers who could fix it firmly in the minds of the people.

Partial success only could be gained by arguments with Donatist opponents. Augustine was at his most effective when he was speaking of the wider world he knew from first-hand experience. He had been to Milan. He knew of the persecution which St. Ambrose had suffered at the hands of the Arians. 'Was not this "for righteousness' sake"?' he asks. He could speak too to his opponents of the Council of Arles and correct their mistakes about the orthodoxy of the decisions made at Serdica. He must have been impressive to individuals who heard him.[5] But even so, he somehow just misses the mark. He repeats his close-knit arguments year after year with increasing disdain for his opponents, and back come the same answers. There are conversions balanced by lapses. In the end, success of one party over the other depended on two factors, the ability to maintain clergy permanently with a congregation, and the ability to apply

---

[1] P. Cayrel, *Mélanges*, li. 128–9.

[2] *Contra Litteras Petiliani*, ii. 17. 38, 'Sic, sic improbe persecutor, quocumque te velamine bonitatis obtexeris, quocumque nomine pacis bellum osculis geras, quolibet unitatis vocabulo hominum genus illicias: qui hactenus fallis ac decipis, vere diaboli filius es, dum moribus indicas patrem.'

[3] Cyprian, *Ep.* 74. 11.

[4] A. Berthier, *Le Christianisme antique*, plates xxiv and xxv.

[5] See *Epp.* 43 and 44, his description of his debates with the Donatists at Thubursicum Bure.

force. As in other aspects of his thought Augustine gradually reverts to type. The 'liberal' phase of his outlook did not last long: he ended, as he began, by accepting the ultimate logic of his beliefs.

His own explanation of how he came to accept forced conversions and persecutions by the State is given in his long letter to Vincentius, the Rogatist Bishop of Cartenna[1] (c. A.D. 408).

> For originally my opinion was, that no one should be coerced into the unity of Christ, that we must act only by words, fight only by arguments, and prevail by force of reason, lest we should have those whom we knew to be avowed heretics feigning themselves to be Catholics. But this opinion of mine was overcome not by the words of those who controverted it, but by the conclusive instance to which they could point. For in the first place, there was set over against my opinion my own town, which although it was once wholly on the side of Donatus was brought over to the Catholic unity by the fear of the Imperial edicts. . . . There were so many others which were mentioned to me by name, that from the facts themselves, I was made to own that to this matter the word of Scripture might be understood as applying, 'Give opportunity to a wise man and he will become wiser.'

The 'opportunity' was coercion, and this was not so mild as Augustine would lead his readers to think.[2]

Like many personal confessions the explanation is probably true, but not the whole truth. Possidius records that even at the outset of his career Augustine was occupied day and night with plans for converting the Donatists.[3] In 392 there was little hope of Imperial assistance for Catholicism in Africa. Gildo was in command. Augustine therefore seems to have continued the same approach used by Optatus only a few years before, in the second edition of his *De Schismate*. The points in common between the two communities were stressed. Like Optatus, Augustine appealed to the Donatists as 'brethren', fellow believers in Christ, listening to the same Gospel, singing

---

[1] *Ep.* 93. 5. 17 (tr. Dods, *Letters of St. Augustine*, i. 409–10).

[2] Thus Nectarius of Calama, a pagan philosopher, describes to Augustine the effects of coercive measures by the Imperial authorities, after the religious riots of A.D. 408. *Ep.* 103. 4, 'Reflect on the appearance presented by a town from which men doomed to torture are dragged forth; think of the lamentations of mothers and wives, of sons and fathers; think of the shame felt by those who may return, set at liberty indeed, but having undergone the torture' (tr. Dods, op. cit. ii. 63).

[3] Possidius, *Vita*, 9.

R

the same Psalms, intoning the same Alleluia, responding with the same 'Amen'. Only the quarrels of the dim past prevented unity.[1] This, however, was for the public. To his friend Alypius, to whom he wrote at this same period, he was already describing the Donatists as 'heretics'[2]—and therefore liable to the legal consequences of the existing anti-heretical legislation.

In the next few years, the years of Gildo's ascendancy, Augustine continued outwardly to champion reason and discussion as the best means of converting Donatists. In his *Retractationes*[3] he claims that he did not wish the schismatics to be brought back to Catholicism by the violent intervention of the secular power. Nevertheless, he provoked the quarrel.[4] The period 393–8 was spent in attempting to bring prominent Donatists to debate, and Augustine's success at Thubursicum Bure may have convinced him of the value of a general conference as a means of restoring unity.[5] But even at this stage he was ready to appeal to the authorities if he thought it would be of any use. In about the year 396 the conversion of a member of his congregation to Donatism, though in admittedly disgraceful circumstances, caused him to appeal to the governor of Numidia and the magistrates of Hippo to 'take note of this sacrilegious act'.[6] Augustine, however, seems to have been no more successful than his colleagues at Carthage who were attempting to prosecute the Donatist primate as a heretic before the *Vicarius* Seranus.[7]

We do not know the contents of his writings against 'the heretic Donatus' in these years.[8] Perhaps they showed some evolution towards advocating force as a means of conversion. However, by 399 the transition had been completed, and one is

---

[1] *Enarratio in Ps. 54*, 16; dating, Bardy, *Saint Augustin*, 183. Cf. also *Ep.* 22, to the Donatist bishop Maximian of Sinitum, with its disapproval of the methods of Paul and Macarius. On this question, Willis, op. cit. 122–35.

[2] *Ep.* 29. 11, 'basilica haereticorum'.

[3] *Retractationes*, ii. 5, 'non mihi placere ullius saecularis potestatis impetu schismaticos ad communionem violenter arctari'.

[4] The Donatists of Hippo, as Possidius points out in *Vita*, 9, only wanted to be left in peace.

[5] *Ep.* 43 and 44. For the germ of his later ideas, see *Ep.* 34. 5—debate between the representatives on each side.

[6] *Ep.* 34 and 35 addressed to Eusebius.

[7] *Contra Litteras Petiliani*, ii. 83. 184 (*PL.* xliii. 316). On Seranus, see above, p. 220. But the attempt to have Primian made liable to the fine of 10 lb. of gold as a heretic must have taken place before 397 when Seranus was Proconsul.

[8] *Retract.* i. 21, 'Contra Epistolam Donati Haeretici'.

left with the possibility that with the failure of Gildo's revolt Augustine found himself free to advocate courses which in his heart he may have approved previously. The text from St. Luke's Gospel, 'Compel them to come in', which has served orthodoxy so well, stood ready to hand.[1] In the *Contra Epistolam Parmeniani* the Donatists are openly identified with heretics, and told that if the kings of this world could legislate against pagans and poisoners they could legislate against them.[2] This was six years before the Emperor and his ministers decided to assimilate the Donatists formally with other heretical sects. The African Catholics were, however, 'plus royalistes que le Roi' at this moment, and it was good to remind the Donatists of the disadvantages of resisting the lawful powers.

From then on, persecution by the Imperial authorities was defended and encouraged. Examples of its successful application no doubt fortified Augustine's conscience, but one is inclined to doubt whether the arguments of his Catholic colleagues ever influenced his view decisively. Between 393 and 398 he was clearly moving towards the acceptance of coercion as a legitimate weapon. His mind may have been made up by other considerations—not least by his home experiences[3] and the harsh ritualism he had experienced as a Manichee. Persecution became connected with his theological views, with his concept of the freedom of the human will; severity, he urged, was necessary to ensure that man used his freedom aright. 'Whoever', he went on in one of his most pungent phrases, 'is not found within the Church, is not to be asked why, but either he is to be corrected and converted or, if brought to book, let him not complain.'[4] Donatist 'heresy' had become a disciplinary matter, to be punished as 'inveterate schism'.[5]

The truth possibly is that, while the complete destruction of Donatism remained Augustine's first aim from the moment he

---

[1] Quoted by Augustine, *Ep.* 93. 2. 5, to justify 'positive methods' against the mentally lazy Donatists. So also the terrible argument that persecution saved the heretic from eternal punishment (*Ep.* 173. 1).

[2] *Contra Epistolam Parmeniani*, i. 10. 16.

[3] His mother, for instance, refused to have meals with him when she heard that he was a Manichee, *Confessions*, iii. 11. 19 (tr. E. B. Pusey, 47).

[4] 'Quisquis igitur in Ecclesia non invenitur, jam non interrogetur, sed aut correctus convertatur, aut correptus non conqueratur', *Contra Litteras Petiliani*, ii. 85. 189 (*PL.* xliii. 318).

[5] *Contra Cresconium*, ii. 7. 9 (*PL.* xliii, col. 471), 'haeresis autem schisma inveteratum' (i.e. not intellectual difference).

took up his office at Hippo, events forced him to elaborate a
theory of persecution to support his acts. He had to meet the
Donatist argument that the very fact of being persecuted made
their Church the chosen of the Lord. Thus he tells his readers
in A.D. 402 that 'not every persecution was wrong', and he
constantly draws attention to the need of being 'righteous' as
well as being persecuted—and only a member of the Catholic
Church could be 'righteous'.[1] The emphasis is on the Church.
Augustine informed a Manichee opponent in A.D. 400 that he
would not even believe in the Gospel unless he were instructed
to do so by the authority of the Catholic Church;[2] twenty
years later he told Emeritus, Donatist Bishop of Caesarea, that
he persecuted openly, 'because he was a member of the Church'.[3]
The Church had full powers of *correptio* against its erring
children.[4] In an age when the Last Judgement had a very real
place in human imagination, Augustine believed that he would
be personally answerable if he failed to bring the Donatists
back to Catholicism.[5] The appeal to the secular power thus
takes its place as one further method in bringing about this
end. Popular propaganda, debate, personal appeal, general
Council, political pressure were all employed as the moment
demanded.

The unity which Augustine restored was deceptive and short-
lived. One is left with the impression that the Donatists were
opposed by the monastery of Hippo, while the rest of the Catholic clergy went on their normal way. Augustine and his friends
occupied the key bishoprics, took the lead in the conciliar
debates, represented the Church at the Imperial Court, and
maintained the struggle against sundry intellectual disturbers of
the peace, such as the Arians and the Pelagians. The rest of the
episcopate murmured 'Placet, placet', while the same routine

---

[1] *Ad Catholicos Epistola*, 20, 53 (*PL.* xliii. 432), 'Non omnem persecutionem esse
culpabilem'. For the need for 'righteousness', *Contra Epistolam Parmeniani*, i. 9. 15
(*PL.* xliii. 44).

[2] *Contra Epistolam Fundamenti*, 5. 6 (*PL.* xlii, col. 176), 'Ego vero Evangelio non
crederem, nisi me catholicae Ecclesiae commoveret auctoritas.'

[3] *Sermo ad Plebem Ecclesiae Caesareensis*, 8 (*PL.* xliii. 696), 'Persequar plane quia
filius Ecclesiae'. Augustine also used the famous phrase attributed to him, 'No salvation outside the Church', on this same occasion—'Extra Ecclesiam catholicam
totum potest praeter salutem', ibid. 6, col. 695.

[4] *Ep.* 185. 2 and 6, Willis, op. cit. 134.

[5] *Ep.* 43. 2, 'erit igitur mihi ad defensionem testis haec epistula in iudicio Dei',
i.e. would be produced on the Day of Judgement as evidence in his favour.

went on and ecclesiastical abuses continued to flourish. At the same time the independence of the African Church over against the Roman see was vanishing. When the African Catholics on Augustine's inspiration explicitly threw Cyprianic teaching and tradition overboard, unconditional acceptance of the full Roman sovereignty became inevitable.[1] In their last days the African Catholics were dependent on outside support for both material aid and spiritual direction.

[1] This was hardly Augustine's aim. It will be noticed that he reproves the Donatists for being out of communion less with Rome than with the Apostolic sees generally (cf. *Ep.* 52. 3, 53. 2 and *Contra Litteras Petiliani*, ii. 1. 3). The particular virtue of Rome was that 'semper apostolicae cathedrae viguit principatus' (*Ep.* 43. 3. 7). This did not imply the right to interfere in the internal affairs of the African Church, and against these Roman interventions from A.D. 417 onwards Augustine protested, but in vain. It is interesting that the Roman legates threatened to call in the secular power against the hesitant African bishops led by Augustine.

XVI

THE ECLIPSE OF DONATISM

A.D. 399–410

ELEVEN years saw the defeat of the Donatist movement in North Africa. It is one of the few periods in the history of the ancient world in which the historian is able from contemporary sources to follow step by step the events which he is recounting, to catch a glimpse of the personalities of the chief actors and the motives that guided them. The tactics pursued by the two Churches can be reconstructed in their detail. The great personal duel between Augustine and Petilian of Constantine becomes alive amidst the arid dialectic of the Augustinian anti-Donatist tracts. At the same time, the canons of the annual Catholic Councils provide the background of the internal condition of the victorious Catholic Church. The laws of the *Codex Theodosianus* shed light on the policy of the Imperial Court, and provide a clue towards understanding the mission of the Imperial mandatory Marcellinus to Africa in 411. Finally, the student has the incomparable *Acta* of the Council of Carthage over which Marcellinus himself presided in June 411. This is a verbatim account of the proceedings, revealing both the conflicting ideas of the two Churches and the outlook and personal beliefs of the advocates who defended them. It is a priceless document, dated as it is to the very eve of the collapse of classical culture in North Africa.

In the first place, the political situation in Italy and in the western provinces generally was unfavourable to the continued tolerance of Donatism. A grateful Senate celebrated Stilicho's 'liberation' of Africa from Gildo's bondage,[1] and so long as he remained in power Honorius' minister saw to it that the 'liberation' should be enjoyed permanently. The experiment of placing the armed forces under the command of a native prince was discontinued: by July 401 Stilicho had appointed his own brother-in-law Bathanarius as *Comes Africae*.[2] Gildo's supporters were proscribed, and for the decade succeeding the rebellion Donatists

---

[1] *CIL.* vi. 1730; Pallu de Lesert, *Fastes*, ii. 260–2.
[2] Seeck, *Regesten*, 304.

were liable to be denounced to the authorities as 'satellites' of Gildo.[1] Moreover, the massive invasion of the western provinces of the Empire by the Germanic tribes and the wars with Alaric and Radagaisus rendered the government at Ravenna increasingly dependent on Africa both as a source of supply and a possible refuge. The victory of Catholicism in Carthage became a political as well as a religious necessity. Legislation in the form of the edict of 15 June 392[2] stood ready at hand to crush the Donatists under ruinous fines and deny them the right of holding services—but first they must be proved to be heretics. The Catholics needed time to put their own house in order before they dared take this step.

A beginning had been made in the years of Gildo's supremacy. The canons of Genethlius' Council, held on 16 June 390, show how much was required.[3] The defects of the Catholic Church in Africa were as gross as they had been fifty years previously. The same spirit of indiscipline and strife lamented by Bishop Gratus in 348 still prevailed in the ranks of the clergy. Preferment in the Church was tending to become secularized and regarded as an 'honour', the equivalent of the municipal 'honours' held by *curiales*.[4] Bishops were using the Church's money as their own,[5] there was a perpetual scramble to secure possession of the richer sees,[6] and in some favoured cities rival factions of clergy quarrelled over the spoils of office. There were difficulties in the way of bringing clergy to justice. An accused priest could defy bishop and council alike and take his case to the Imperial Court, where it would not be difficult to find some official to give him patronage.[7] Augustine commenting on the

[1] *Cod. Theod.* ix. 40. 19 (11 Nov. 408); cf. Augustine, *Contra Cresconium,* iii. 13. 16.

[2] *Cod. Theod.* xvi. 5. 21.

[3] I have used here the text published by G. Bruns, *Canones Apostolorum Conciliorum Selecti,* Berlin, 1839, p. 121 (= Bruns, *Canones*).

[4] *CIL.* viii, 20905 (Tipasa)—Bishop Alexander, 'aetatibus honoribusque in Æclesia Catholica functus'. Cf. inscription drawn up in exactly the same terms from the church of the Catholic bishop Cresconius at Cuicul (Djemila) (E. Albertini, *Bull. Arch. du Comité,* 1922, pp. xiv–xv).

[5] Bruns, *Canones,* canon 31, 'Ut episcopus rebus ecclesiae tanquam commendatis non tanquam propriis utatur'.

[6] Canon 27 in Breviary of the Council of Hippo (Bruns, p. 144), 'Ut episcopus de loco ignobili ad nobilem per ambitionem non transeat'.

[7] Canon 7 of the Council of 390, 'ausi fuerint ad comitatum pergere' (ibid., p. 119; cf. Augustine, *Ep.* 64. 4. Other bishops, such as Cresconius of Villa Regia and Equitius of Hippo Diarrhytos, defied successive councils which sought to depose them (Bruns, pp. 171 and 175). Equitius was still in possession of his see in 404 (*PL.* xi. 1204).

condition of the Catholic element in Hippo during 392 could
write: 'As to strife and deceit, what right have I to speak,
seeing that these vices prevail more seriously among our own
order than among our congregation?'[1] The Conciliar decrees
of the next five years show that he was speaking the bare truth.

Aurelius set about cleansing this Augean stable. In 393 he
held a Council at Hippo, where Augustine, though at this time
only a presbyter, preached to the assembled bishops.[2] An effort
was made to tackle some of the more grotesque abuses, connected with paganism, simony, and various forms of immorality.
It was resolved too that a Council should be held every year,[3]
a step which enabled Aurelius to maintain both a continuity of
policy and contact with his colleagues throughout his rule.

More important, however, in the process of consolidating
African Catholicism were the new episcopal appointments
during the next five years. On becoming presbyter in the spring
of 391, Augustine had established a seminary at Hippo at which
he and his friends lived a community life and trained in every
aspect of their duties as priests.[4] It was from this seminary that
the bishops of the leading Catholic sees in Numidia were now
chosen. In 394 Alypius, Augustine's lifelong friend and companion on his journey to Italy, became Bishop of Thagaste.[5] In
January 396,[6] after a momentary hesitation on the part of Megalius, the Catholic Primate of Numidia, Augustine himself became
coadjutor to the aged Valerius at Hippo, and next year its sole
bishop.[7] By 397 his friend and pupil Severus[8] had been elevated to
the see of Milevis. Another of his pupils, Profuturus,[9] was elected
Bishop of Constantine, and on his death about the year 400

---

[1] *Ep.* 22. 2. 7 (*CSEL.* xxxiv. 1. 59), 'De contentione et dolo quid me attinet
dicere, quando ista vitia non in plebe sed in nostro numero graviora sunt'. Also
Ep. 23. 5, in which he refers to the Catholic Church as 'quae per totam Africam
tabefacta miserabiliter jacent'.

[2] *Sermo* 'De Fide et Symbolo'. In itself it is a tribute to Augustine's extraordinary
gifts, and possibly a turning-point in his attitude towards the Donatists. His *Psalmus
contra Partem Donati* was written later, in the autumn of the same year.

[3] Council of Hippo, canon 5 (Bruns, *Canones*, p. 137). Councils were held in
Carthage in 397, 398, 400, 401 (twice), 402 (at Milevis), 403 (twice), 404, 405,
407, 408 (at Milevis), 410, and 411.   [4] Possidius, *Vita*, 3.

[5] Augustine, *Ep.* 24. Alypius was responsible for Augustine's contact with Paulinus of Nola and Jerome.

[6] Augustine, *Ep.* 32. 7. Cf. G. Morin, *Revue bénédictine*, xl, 1928, p. 366; G. Bardy,
Saint Augustin, 188–9.

[7] *Contra Litteras Petiliani*, iii. 16. 19 (*PL.* xiii, col. 357); Possidius, *Vita*, 8.

[8] *Ep.* 31. 9.   [9] *Ep.* 32. 1.

Augustine kept control of the see through his admirer Fortunatus.[1] Also about the year 400 his biographer Possidius became Bishop of Calama.[2] Thus, by the end of Gildo's revolt, all the chief Donatist strongholds in Proconsular Numidia had been occupied by an able Catholic opponent awaiting the opportunity to strike at Donatism.

The effect of these appointments on the fortunes of the Catholics in the next twelve years was far-reaching. In North Africa it is doubtful whether the native was much impressed by technical transgressions of the clergy against discipline of the type complained of in ecclesiastical councils. He was impressed, however, by the presence of a bishop. As the controversy grew in intensity, we shall notice how each side attempted to create new sees and to increase the numbers of their bishops. In certain cases, as at Tucca and at Fussala in northern Numidia, the presence of a bishop was in itself sufficient to rally former convinced Donatist villagers to the Catholic cause. Fussala is a particularly interesting case, because Augustine's choice, Antonius, was a worthless character against whose excesses the inhabitants appealed in vain, but they did not return to Donatism.[3] In this struggle, however, the Catholics started at a disadvantage. A conciliar decree of 401 admitted that 'in some parishes there were no clergy at all, not even an illiterate deacon'.[4] Too few of the Catholic clergy understood the Libyan language.[5] With rare exceptions they were drawn from the limited Latin-speaking minority.[6] Nevertheless, despite all handicaps the Catholics in 398 were at once able to derive a certain advantage from the embarrassments in which their opponents found themselves after the defeat of Gildo.

Donatism, however, was by no means ripe for collapse. The Donatist leaders during this period, Petilian of Constantine,

---

[1] *De Unico Baptismo*, 16. 29.

[2] Dating, P. Monceaux, op. cit. vii. 59. Augustine's affection for Possidius, *Ep.* 101.

[3] Augustine, *Ep.* 209 (*CSEL.* lvii. 347).

[4] Letter to Anastasius and Venerius dispatched on behalf of the Council. The ordination of former Donatists was required, 'maxime quia tanta indigentia Clericorum est, multaeque Ecclesiae ita desertae sunt, ut ne unum quidem diaconum vel illiteratum habere reperiantur' (*PL.* xi, col. 1196).

[5] Augustine had great difficulty in finding clergy for outlying areas for this reason (*Ep.* 84. 2).

[6] Samsucius of Turres, mentioned by Augustine in *Ep.* 34, is the only Catholic bishop who is stated definitely to have been unversed in Latin literature.

Emeritus of Caesarea, Primian of Carthage, were able and resolute individuals, men who appear to have remained unshaken
in their faith throughout years of setback and persecution.
From Augustine himself they earned grudging recognition as
'tam malae causae pertinacissimi defensores'.[1]

These leaders were supported by an educated and devoted
laity, active propagandists in their cause. Probably many regarded the persecution as in the natural order of things, the
events which would precede the coming of Antichrist and the
ushering in of the last days.[2] For three generations Donatists
had been impressed by their leaders that their lot on earth was
persecution by their enemies; even Tyconius had written, 'In proportion as the just are persecuted, the unjust feast and rejoice.'[3]
Now, this precise situation was coming to pass. Individuals
might break down, and Augustine made much of these cases.
The survival of the Donatist Church as such must be attributed
largely to this factor—that the events of 400–20 had been long
foretold and were to some extent expected. For the rest, Donatism, if narrow in outlook, had not lost its spiritual vigour. In
the towns, especially in Carthage, minor sects and conventicles
flourished: Maximianists, Claudianists, Rogatists, Tertullianists,
Urbanists, Abelonians, and even Trigarists[4]—evidence for the
abounding religious enthusiasm and ecclesiastical anarchism
which characterized both Christian and, later, Moslem Africa.
Behind this literate and articulate minority was the vast multitude of Berber peasants who knew no leader but the Donatist
priests. Embittered by incessant extortion and unrelieved mis-
government, these vented their wrath on the Catholics in proportion as the repression of their faith was intensified. The
violences of the Circumcellions grew every year; the activities
of 'terrorist bands' covered 'nearly all Africa', according to Possidius.[5] The destruction of the Roman landed civilization must
be laid at their door, and in this they were a far more terrible
enemy than the Bagaudae in Gaul and Spain.

[1] Augustine, *Ad Catholicos Epistola*, 1 (*PL.* xliii, col. 391).

[2] Possidius, *Vita Augustini*, 9.

[3] Cited from *In Apocalypsin*, i. 10, by A. Pincherle, 'Da Ticonio a Sant' Agostino', 445.

[4] Augustine, *Ad Catholicos Epistola*, 3. 6; *De Haeresibus*, 86; *Contra Cresconium*, iv.
60. 73; and *Tractatus in Ioannem*, x. 6. The Trigarists are recorded on an inscription
from Setif, *CIL.* viii. 8650; P. Monceaux, *Histoire littéraire*, iv. 477.

[5] Possidius, *Vita*, 10, 'erant in ingenti numero et turbis per omnes pene Africanas
regiones constituti.'

In 399 Augustine himself had already been actively campaigning against the Donatists for six years. As early as 393 he had composed his *Psalmus contra Partem Donati* in rhyming verse for his congregation at Hippo.[1] It was a work aimed at the ordinary citizen and set out the Catholic arguments furnished by Optatus of Milevis in a popular and vivid style. A year or two later he had written the *Contra Epistolam Donati*, which has not survived.[2] In this same period he had attempted to hold conferences with Donatist clergy in the immediate neighbourhood, with Maximin of Sinitum[3] and his colleague at Hippo, Proculeianus.[4] His sermons became well known and were reported back to the local Donatist clergy. In 397 he went farther afield and debated with leading Donatist laymen in Thubursicum Numidarum on the frontier of Proconsular Africa.[5] At the same time, he was opening his correspondence with highly placed Donatist clergy, such as the Bishops Honoratus[6] and Fortunius.[7] His reputation was already considerable and open debate with him was avoided. As his biographer claims, even in these years, thanks to Augustine, the Catholic Church in Africa began to raise her head once more.[8]

After Gildo's defeat the position of the African Catholics improved rapidly. The first step taken by the Emperors was to identify the Donatists with other dissenters proscribed by law: on 25 June 399 a rescript was addressed to the *Vicarius* Sapidianus to this effect. The privileges of the Catholics were confirmed, and penalties threatened against their opponents.[9] About the same time the Catholics won the first of a series of lawsuits which opened the way for the eventual confiscation of Donatist property for their benefit. A Catholic landowner claimed the reversion of his sister's property, which the latter had left to a Donatist bishop named Augustinus.[10] Circumcellions had prevented the Catholic from taking possession. The case found its way to the Imperial Court, where judgement was entered in favour of the Catholic on the grounds that no heretic could benefit from a legacy. Though Donatism had not yet

---

[1] See Migne, *PL.* xliii, cols. 25–52. It is written in the same type of verse as that used by Africans composing epitaphs in this period; see G. G. Willis, op. cit., 36–40.
[2] Referred to in *Retractationes*, i. 21, as is another lost work entitled *Adversus Partem Donati*, written in this period.   [3] *Ep.* 23.   [4] *Ep.* 34.   [5] *Ep.* 43 and 44.
[6] *Ep.* 49.   [7] *Ep.* 44.   [8] Possidius, *Vita*, 7 (*PL.* xxxii, col. 39).
[9] *Contra Epistolam Parmeniani*, i. 12. 19 (*PL.* xliii, col. 48); *Cod. Theod.* xvi. 2. 34.
[10] The story is quoted by Augustine in *Contra Epistolam Parmeniani*, i. 12. 19.

officially been described as a heresy, the general laws against heresy were in fact being applied against Donatists. When towards the end of 399 Augustine preached before a Catholic Council at Carthage, he drew the attention of his hearers to the incongruous alliance of Donatists, Jews, and pagans, all equally the sufferers from the renewed Catholic activity.[1]

Augustine's correspondence in the years 399 and 400 throws some light on his methods against the Donatists during this period. The approach is still persuasive, the emphasis less on the 'heresy' of Donatism than on the points in common uniting the two Churches. He continues to invite debates with prominent Donatists. He writes in turn to Proculeianus, the Donatist Bishop of Hippo,[2] to Crispinus of Calama,[3] and to his own cousin Severinus.[4] He takes it for granted that Donatists have only to hear about the scandalous origins of the schism, or the inconsistency of their Church in its dealings with Maximian, to join the Catholics. He evidently expected that any landowner, whether Donatist or Catholic, would enforce Catholicism on his tenants.[5] The strategy remained: discredit the Donatist leadership and tradition and in particular Donatus himself,[6] win over the Latin-speaking minority, and force conversion on the masses.

By 401 these methods were beginning to show results. Petilian, in a circular letter addressed to his clergy at Constantine, indicates that a number of the wealthier members of the congregation were conforming to Catholicism in order to save their possessions from confiscation.[7] His rival at Constantine, Fortunatus, seems to have been active, well informed, and not too scrupulous. A former Manichee like his predecessor,[8] he served Augustine faithfully as an agent.[9] He was well aware

[1] *Sermo* 62 (*PL.* xxxviii, cols. 422–3). The temple of Caelestis at Carthage was turned into a church in 399.

[2] *Ep.* 34.   [3] *Ep.* 51.

[4] *Ep.* 52.

[5] The underlying supposition in his letter to Celer, *Ep.* 57, who at this time was at least under Donatist influence if not actually a Donatist.

[6] Attacks on Donatus personally at this time are numerous. Apart from two full-scale works, Donatus' memory is attacked in *Sermones* 37. 3, 197. 4, and in *Enarrationes in Pss.* 65, 5, 75, 7, and 85, 14.

[7] Petilian, quoted in *Contra Litteras Petiliani*, ii. 98. 225 (*PL.* xliii, col. 335), 'Vos, vos, miseri appello, qui persecutionum metu perterriti, dum vestras divitias non animas quaeritis, non tam fidem perfidam traditorum diligitis, quam contra ipsorum malitiam, quorum vobis patrocinia comparastis', &c.

[8] Augustine, *De Unico Baptismo*, 16. 29 (*PL.* xliii, col. 611).

[9] It was through Fortunatus that Augustine got the facts about Splendonius

of the existence of anti-heretical legislation, and in his new capacity as Catholic bishop he kept the Donatists in a state of nerves by bringing charges of heresy against them before the city magistrates.[1] The year saw the conversion of at least one prominent Donatist bishop, Maximian of Bagai, to Catholicism.[2] There were also numerous defections among both serious believers and the large floating population of semi-Christians who made up the majority of the inhabitants of the cities of Roman Africa.[3]

These accessions of strength confronted the Catholics with a serious problem. As early as 393 the Council of Hippo had considered whether converted Donatist clergy could be admitted to the Catholic priesthood. The provisional decision had been one of expediency; if the individual concerned had not rebaptized converts to Donatism, or if he brought his congregation over with him, he should retain his office.[4] Evidently Aurelius did not feel entirely sure of himself, for at the Council of Carthage in 397 an embassy was sent to Rome and Milan to secure the advice, if not the consent, of their bishops to admit former Donatists to Catholic Orders. It was pleaded that the lack of clergy made this necessary.[5] Both Venerius of Milan and Anastasius of Rome had, however, frowned on this request and the matter had been allowed to rest. In July 401 the situation had deteriorated. Despite the changes in their fortunes, the ranks of the Catholic clergy were not filling up, and Aurelius' Council decided at least to attempt to obtain permission for those who had merely been baptized as Donatists in infancy to become Catholic priests.[6] It appears, however, that the reply

a renegade priest from Gaul whom Petilian had ordained presbyter. The incident is an interesting example of the connexion between the African Catholics and the Church in Gaul at this time. (Augustine, *Contra Litteras Petiliani*, iii. 38. 44 (*PL*. xliii, col. 371), also ii. 92. 228.)

[1] *Gesta Coll. Carth.* i. 139 (*PL*. xi. 1316). He earned the reputation of being a 'persecutor'.

[2] Augustine, *Ep*. 69. Maximian was allowed to remain as Catholic bishop of the town.

[3] For people passing from one Church to the other, Augustine, *Sermo* 252. 4–5; conversions among the more serious-minded, *Ep*. 93. 1. 3. *Ad Catholicos Epistola*, 25. 74 (*PL*. xliii, col. 444), indicates a return of a considerable number to Catholicism.

[4] 'Decretum Hipponensis Concilii' quoted from *PL*. xi, col. 1185.

[5] Canon 48, *PL*. xi, col. 1192. The same reason was put forward by the Council of Hippo.

[6] Text printed in full, ibid., cols. 1195–7.

of an Italian Council which considered Aurelius' representations was negative, and so, on 13 September 401, a full Council of
the African Catholics was called to consider further action.[1]
The decision was practical. Elaborate deference was paid to the
wishes of the oversea Churches, ex-Donatist clergy were in principle to be reduced to the ranks of the laity, but each Catholic
bishop was empowered to make exceptions where the situation
demanded.[2] The exceptions did in fact become the general
rule.[3]

The Council of 401 is also important in other respects. It was
the first time that the Catholics carried the struggle into the
opposing camp. It was agreed that missionaries should be sent
throughout Africa to spread the Catholic teaching, and, in order
that these missionaries should not be without local material, an
appeal was made to the provincial authorities to open inquiries
in the African cities on the exact relationship between the
Donatists and the Maximianists in their area.[4] Augustine himself
set a vigorous example by going down to Assuras and Musti
in the Upper Mejerda valley to investigate details of the cases
of the ex-Maximianist clergy on the spot.[5]

Activity, however, in this year was not confined to the Catholics. Indeed, the interest of the period lies partly in the fact that
it is not the story of a relentless and one-sided persecution of
an already beaten adversary, but that both Churches were of
approximately equal strength and both were in a position to
give and take heavy punishment. The Donatists would not
admit that they were other than the Catholic Church in Africa.
They would not accept the anti-heretical laws as applying to
themselves. Their leaders set out to assert this in as telling a
manner as possible. Crispinus, the Donatist Bishop of Calama
(Guelma), found himself in a position to acquire the lease of
part of an Imperial estate, in his diocese but near the boundary

---

[1] Text in *PL.* xi, cols. 1197–9.

[2] Canon 2, 'id est, ut ordinati in parte Donati, si ad catholicam correcti transire
voluerint, non suscipiantur in honoribus suis secundum transmarinum concilium,
sed exceptis his per quos catholicae unitati consulitur', ibid., col. 1198. Augustine's
personal view of the problem at this time is given in *Ep.* 61 and 245. 2 (to Possidius
of Calama).

[3] Even nefarious characters such as Bishop Quodvultdeus were apparently
accepted during this period (*Contra Litteras Petiliani*, iii. 32. 37).

[4] *PL.* xi, col. 1198.

[5] Augustine, *Contra Cresconium*, iii. 60. 66, 'Mustitani et Assuritani, sicut ab eis
quoque praesens audivi' (*PL.* xliii, col. 532).

of the sees of Calama and Hippo. As if in an anticipation of the Reformation principle of *cujus regio ejus religio*, he proceeded to rebaptize eighty families of *coloni* who worked on the estate. Augustine raged at this stroke of audacity, attributing Crispinus' success to bribery.[1] The Catholics were not yet strong enough to intervene and invoke anti-heretical legislation against him, but the event had taken place too near Augustine's own diocese for Crispinus ever to be forgiven.[2]

Meantime, the theoretical defence of Donatism was being undertaken by Petilian of Constantine. It might appear that there was much in common between Petilian and Augustine. Both men were converts to their cause;[3] both believed that they had been called to their work by the special grace of God;[4] neither felt any doubt that his was the true Church, and that no quarter could be given to the heretics who persecuted it. In their private lives each practised what he preached. Both lived solely for their Churches, and both left the stage of history with their life's work seemingly in ruins. Petilian's *Epistola ad Presbyteros*, written about 400/1, was the first step in his ten years' duel with Augustine. Only once, at the Council of Carthage in 411, did the two men meet face to face, and curiously enough Augustine, otherwise so ready to debate with the Donatist chiefs, never accepted Petilian's challenge to him made in 402.[5]

The entire text of the *Epistola ad Presbyteros* has survived, and has been skilfully reconstructed by Monceaux (*Histoire littéraire*, v. 311–28) out of the relevant passages of Augustine's reply contained in the second book of the *Contra Litteras Petiliani*. Petilian's object was to put his clergy on their guard against the Catholics and to prove that Donatus' community was the true Catholic Church. Without preliminary salutations

---

[1] Augustine, *Ep.* 66. 1, 'Crispine, carum fuit pretium tuum ad emendum timorem Mappaliensium'; *Contra Litteras Petiliani*, ii. 83. 184 and 99. 228. The incident therefore took place about A.D. 401.

[2] Augustine places the event 'juxta Hipponem nostram', ibid. 99. 228 (*PL.* xliii, col. 337'). In his letter to Crispinus (*Ep.* 66), Augustine refers to the penalty of 10 lb. of gold which Crispinus 'could have been compelled to pay'. Three years later the penalty was to be enforced.

[3] P. Monceaux, *Histoire littéraire*, vi. 6 ff.

[4] *Contra Litteras Petiliani*, ii. 92. 202 (*PL.* xliii, col. 324), 'nam gratia Dei in nobis non est pauper'. Petilian abandoned his fortune to the poor on entering the Donatist ministry.

[5] Petilian attacked Augustine 'quod numquam mecum comminus disputaverit'.

and introductory phrases, Petilian comes straight to the point. The validity of baptism depends on the worthiness of the minister.

What we look for is the conscience of the giver, giving in holiness, to cleanse that of the recipient. For he who knowingly receives faith from the faithless receives not faith but guilt. For everything consists of an origin and root, and if it have not something for a head, it is nothing, nor does anything well receive second birth, unless it is born again of good seed.[1]

The line of thought is very similar to that represented by both Tertullian and the African bishops who spoke at Cyprian's Council in September 256—the impossibility of the Holy Spirit who was present at baptism dwelling in an unclean environment.[2] The true Church, Petilian went on, was that which maintained the purity of the Sacraments. The word 'Catholic' referred to what was whole, regardless of geographical extent.[3] The Catholics had as their origin Caecilian and their root in the *traditores*. The taint of apostasy lasted for ever. Their clergy were not clergy at all, and ordination at the hands of a *traditor* minister merely transmitted infection. The Catholics were, indeed, worse than Judas, for Judas had only betrayed Christ in His mortal body, and then had repented and hanged himself: the *traditores* had betrayed Him in spirit, by committing His Gospel to the flames[4]—an indication of the meaning placed by contemporaries on the act of surrendering the Scriptures to the pagan magistrates. It was betrayal of the Testament of God.

The Catholics, however, unwittingly performed one service: they had allied themselves with the secular powers. These were no different in spirit from the pagans of the previous age.[5] Through the persecution that resulted from this alliance, the true Church was purified.[6] In one of the most biting sentences of the whole epistle, Petilian sought to unmask the real motives that lay behind Augustine's appeal for unity and peace.[7] Then, taking each of the beatitudes, Petilian denounced his opponents

---

[1] *Contra Litteras Petiliani*, ii. 2–5; for the addition of 'sancte' and 'sciens' in Petilians's definition of true baptism, ibid. iii. 20. 23. The translation used is from Marcus Dods, *The Works of Aurelius Augustine*, iii. 256–7.

[2] See p. 138, *supra*.

[3] *Contra Litteras Petiliani*, ii. 38. 90.

[4] Ibid. 8. 17.   [5] Ibid. 92. 202.

[6] Ibid. 71. 159.

[7] Ibid. 17. 38.

as the real breakers of the peace and the executioners of the innocent.[1] It was they who called in Ursatius, Macarius, and the other military commanders, and these had perished, punished by God.[2] But their victims were the responsibility of the Catholics—'Nor indeed does the hand of the butcher (*carnifex*) glow save at the instigation of your tongue'.[3] By all tests, the Catholics were the schismatics and traitors to the Church.

This was a violent document, the mixture of dialectic, jargon, and invective strangely reminiscent of the Communist approach to backward and semi-literate communities. And like its modern counterparts, Petilian's tract had its effect on the populace. The impression was not confined to Constantine. Its fame spread to neighbouring dioceses, including Augustine's. Donatist laymen hailed it as 'a new gospel'. Members of Augustine's own congregation learnt passages by heart, and repeated them to the bishop.[4] None of Augustine's own works seems to have struck such a chord—a further clue, perhaps, towards understanding the eventual failure of his work in Africa. The language spoken by Petilian was the language the Africans understood, that of Augustine was not.

Immediately after the second book against Petilian comes the long address to the Catholics on the unity of the Church. As Parmenian and Optatus, so Augustine and Petilian turn over once more the issue, 'Where is the Church?'[5] The Catholics give the same answer as they did sixty years before—the Church is that community which is spread throughout the world; the sects are confined to single provinces. The arch-crime was schism, and the Donatists as schismatics were destined for correction in this world or punishment in the next.

Petilian answered both works with a sermon attacking Augustine personally, the *Ad Augustinum*; this is one of the most interesting pieces in the whole controversy between these two men. The investigations made by Augustine and his agents about the situation in Petilian's diocese are well known and have been commented upon.[6] The extent of Petilian's own researches and the significance of his reply have only now been

---

[1] Ibid. 63–71 (*PL.* xliii, cols. 306–10).
[2] Ibid. 92. 202.   [3] Ibid.
[4] *Ad Catholicos Epistola*, i. 1. 1; cf. *Contra Cresconium*, i, chaps. 1 and 2.
[5] *Ad Catholicos Epistola*, ii. 2, 'Inter nos autem et Donatistas quaestio est, ubi sit hoc corpus, id est, ubi sit Ecclesia.'
[6] P. Monceaux, *Histoire littéraire*, vi, pp. 8–9.

S

brought to light through the work of Professor P. Courcelle.[1] It seems that Petilian not only was acquainted with the *Confessions*, and possibly the *Contra Academicos*, but also was in possession of copies of some of Augustine's letters.[2] It would be interesting to know how he obtained these. From this material he built up a picture of Augustine as a man who had not only once been a Manichee priest but who still remained one at heart, and whose only baptism had been at the hands of a Manichee Elect.[3] He had been forced to flee the country to avoid prosecution on the charge of infamous heresy.[4] Under the smooth disguise of the Christian bishop lurked the Manichee rhetorician.

To make his point perfectly clear to his audience, Petilian linked his charges with the question of baptism. Augustine had misquoted him by omitting the words 'sancte and 'sciens' from the passage already cited: 'What we look for is the conscience of the giver, giving *in holiness*, to cleanse that of the recipient. For he who *knowingly* receives faith from the faithless receives not faith but guilt.'[5] Petilian told his hearers that this misquotation was deliberate: Augustine had a bad conscience about his own baptism, as well he might if he had received it from a Manichee.[6]

The effect of these revelations may well be imagined. To a Donatist, it was bad enough for a Christian bishop to include texts from pagan authors in his sermons and writings. This in itself would make Augustine's conversion suspect, but the possibility that he might also be a Manichee in secret would discredit anything he said. On his own admission he had been 'falsus et fallens'[7] in the past. What was his position now? Moreover, Petilian's charges did not sound fantastic to his audience. Many people in Constantine would know that two successive Catholic bishops of their city had been Manichees, and both had been Augustine's friends.[8] They knew too that in 395 the

---

[1] P. Courcelle, *Recherches sur les Confessions de Saint Augustin*, Paris, 1950, pp. 238–45.

[2] Possibly *Ep.* 31, to Paulinus of Nola and his wife; P. Courcelle, op. cit. 239, n. 3.

[3] *Contra Litteras Petiliani*, iii. 24. 28; P. Courcelle, op. cit. 241.

[4] *Contra Litteras Petiliani*, iii. 25. 30. The Manichee Secundinus made the same accusation against Augustine in 405: *Epistula ad Augustinum*, 2 (*CSEL*. xxv. 2. 895).

[5] *Contra Litteras Petiliani*, iii. 23. 27.   [6] P. Courcelle, op. cit. 241.

[7] *Contra Litteras Petiliani*, iii. 17. 20. Cf. *Confessions*, iv. 1.

[8] *De Unico Baptismo*, 16. 29.

Catholic primate, Megalius of Calama (Guelma), had taken Bishop Valerius to task on hearing of his intention to appoint Augustine as coadjutor.[1] It was not by any means unknown for Catholic clergy and laymen to be secretly Manichees.[2] Conversion from Catholicism to Manichaeism and vice versa, as we have seen, was not rare at this time. Petilian gave his Church a lead which was followed. The attack on Augustine's past became general in Donatist polemic, just as the scandals of Primian were in that of their opponents.[3] Augustine's third book against the letters of Petilian fell on stony ground. The Donatist bishop remained supreme in the capital city of Numidia, and his words rallied the Donatists far beyond the borders of the province.[4]

The next two years saw the struggle mount in violence. The Catholics at their Council held in Carthage on 13 September 401 had decided to send missionaries into the Donatist areas to preach on the history of the Maximianist schism:[5] they were met by Circumcellions. Against this illegal violence they could appeal to the secular arm in the person of Stilicho's brother-in-law, Count Bathanarius. Hardly a week passed without some new outrage and reprisal. At Thubursicum Bure (Teboursouk) the Catholic bishop, Servus, who had been trying to take back property seized by the Donatists, was chased out of his diocese and did not find a safe retreat until he reached the Imperial Court.[6] Donatist clerics who conformed to Catholicism were liable to be seized, and subjected to refinements of ritual torture.[7] One presbyter was kidnapped, beaten, and left on view in a cage for twelve days until

---

[1] The Donatists had a copy of the letter in their own archives (*Contra Cresconium*, iii. 80. 92). Cf. *Contra Epistolam Parmeniani*, ii. 4. 9, for Manichee influence in Augustine's polemic.

[2] Augustine reveals an instance among his own clergy (*Ep.* 236). Cf. Pope Leo I, *Sermo* 42. 5 (*PL*. liv, col. 279).

[3] The attack was taken up by Cresconius (*Contra Cresconium*, iii. 78) and Primian of Carthage (*Sermo iii in Ps. 36*, 19 (*PL*. xxxvi, cols. 393–4)).

[4] On Petilian's popularity in Constantine, Augustine, *Contra Litteras Petiliani*, iii. 11. 12, and 59. 71. Cresconius, who wrote in support of Petilian in A.D. 401–2, was a native of Proconsular Africa, 'Afer in Africa' (*Contra Cresconium*, iv. 71. 83).

[5] Text quoted from Migne, *PL*. xliii, col. 810.

[6] *Contra Cresconium*, iii. 43. 47 (*PL*. xliii. 521–3); the incident probably took place in A.D. 403. For Circumcellion savagery in these years see *Ad Catholicos Epistola*, 19. 50 and 20. 54.

[7] e.g. cutting out their tongues so that they could no longer preach, or blinding them with lime and vinegar, a mixture very likely used to seal up reliquaries. *Contra Cresconium*, iii. 42. 46.

released by a Donatist bishop.[1] Even in the far west, in Mauretania Caesariensis, an inscription from Tiaret recalls the names
of those who were killed in 401 during the riots between
the two Churches.[2] A Donatist Council attempted in vain to
check these deeds of fanaticism.[3] In self-defence the Catholics
began taking hostages in the towns and estates where they held
a majority.[4] Roman Africa was fast falling a prey to social and
religious war.

In the summer of 403 the Catholics attempted to break the
deadlock. On 24 August Aurelius presided at a further general
Council held in the Basilica Restituta at Carthage. A document
was drawn up, to judge by its phrasing probably by Augustine,
summoning the Donatists to a conference. The language of the
invitation, however, was not such as to secure a ready acceptance. The Catholics could hardly assume that their opponents
had much right on their side. They were therefore ordered to
appear 'by authority of the Catholic Council'.[5] They were
to be corrected and converted, their slothful error was to be
finished with.[6] They were to choose delegates to defend their
assertions, but, pointed out the Council, 'the light of truth should
shine forth of its own accord'.[7] If the Donatists refused this offer,
they showed that they mistrusted their own cause. They were
not, however, given much time to decide whether they 'mistrusted their cause' or not. On 13 September, at the instance
of the same Council, a deputation was sent to the Proconsul
Septiminus.

This time the Catholics repudiated recourse to anti-heretical
legislation. They requested the Proconsul merely that 'the
heretics of the community ("pars") of Donatus should be

---

[1] *Contra Cresconium*, iii. 48. 53; *Ep.* 88. 6.

[2] Published by S. Gsell, *Bull. Arch. du Comité*, 1908, ccii. Cited by P. Monceaux, *Histoire littéraire*, iv. 474.

[3] *Contra Cresconium*, iii. 45. 49; the attempt to curb the extremists was evidently
as useless as that undertaken at the time of the Macarian persecution.

[4] *Contra Litteras Petiliani*, ii. 83, 184; *Ad Catholicos Epistola*, 20. 55.

[5] Text in Migne, *PL.* xi, cols. 1200–1, 'Convenimus vos ex concilii nostri catholici
auctoritate missi, de vestra correctione gaudere cupientes'. The choice and placing
of some of the scriptural quotations, e.g. Isaiah lxvi (lxx) ('Ye are our brethren')
and Matthew v, suggest that Augustine may personally have influenced the drafting of the document.

[6] Ibid., 'finem veternosus error accipiat'.

[7] Ibid., 'Si enim hoc fraterne acceperitis, veritas facile dilucescat. Si autem hoc
facere nolueritis diffidentia vestra facile innotescat.' For an able discussion of this
decree, P. Monceaux, *Histoire littéraire*, vi. 128–31.

admonished "in a kindly manner", so that they could meditate upon their error, and not neglect to recognize it'.[1] They were then to be summoned by the magistrates to appear 'honourably' before the municipal courts, so that they might discuss their point of view with the Catholics in public.[2]

Septiminus granted the Council's request, ending on a rather ominous note that by the friendly activity of the law superstition would be destroyed.[3] Secular authority had now been called in, and the Donatists once more faced the same situation which had confronted them in 317 and 347.

To be summoned before the magistrates, who were in many towns pagans, was an order reminiscent of earlier persecutions: it was met with defiance. For once, the Donatist Bishop of Carthage gave a lead. In the autumn of 403 he issued a circular letter to his clergy outlining his reasons for refusing to confer with his Catholic opponent.[4] The Catholics, he claimed, had put forward the sacred letters of numerous Emperors, the Donatists offered only the Gospels. 'Your ancestors', he told them, 'had exiled our fathers', and now they were sharpening their swords for a renewal of persecution and were seizing on Donatist property. The true Church is that which endures persecution, not that which persecutes. Therefore 'It would be an indignity for the sons of martyrs to meet with the descendants of *traditores*.'[5]

At the same time Primian found himself at grips with Augustine himself. The latter had participated at the Council and was preaching in the Catholic churches in Carthage. He attacked Primian in a lengthy *Primiano Commonitorium*,[6] a document which provides our most detailed information about the Maximianist schism and in particular its origins.[7] Primian, however, replied in kind. Taking his cue from Petilian, Augustine's own doubtful past, the excesses of his youth at Carthage,[8]

---

[1] *PL.* xi, col. 1201, 'leniter eos volumus admonere ut errorem suam cogitando et agnoscendo non negligant.'

[2] Ibid., 'per magistratus . . . honeste conveniri'.

[3] Ibid., col. 1202, 'ut rebus in medio prolatis amica legis moderatio servetur, superstitione supplosa'.

[4] P. Monceaux, *Histoire littéraire*, vi. 131; *Ad Donatistas post Collationem*, i. 31.

[5] I have used Monceaux's reconstruction (*Histoire littéraire*, vi. 131). Also Duchesne, op. cit., iii. 91.

[6] Possidius, *Indices Operum Sancti Augustini*, 3 (*PL.* xlvi, col. 8).

[7] *Sermo ii in Ps. 36*, 19–20 (*PL.* xxxvi, cols. 375–81).

[8] *Sermo iii in Ps. 36* (*PL.* xxxvi, cols. 394–5).

his Manichaean days and excursions into pagan philosophy were set before the Carthaginian populace with a violence of tone and invective that made their victim wince. It was nearly seven years before Augustine preached in Carthage again.

Returned to their dioceses in the winter of 403/4, neither Augustine nor Possidius of Calama gave the Donatists time to assemble a Council and consider the Catholic demands. Both Proculeianus and Crispinus were at once summoned before the magistrates. This manœuvre to force a discussion failed, for the two bishops first insisted on consulting a Council of their Church, and then on receipt of both Primian's and their Council's orders refused to consider the matter.[1] Their example was followed by the Donatists all over Africa.

The Numidian Catholics then sought other means of securing their ends. Probably during the spring of 404, Possidius of Calama, Augustine's biographer, opened a vigorous campaign in his diocese.[2] Augustine, as has been noted, had already attempted to have pressure brought to bear on the Donatist peasantry through friendly landowners there, but this had proved vain.[3] So too did Possidius' efforts. It was not long before he was ambushed by Circumcellions, led by a Donatist presbyter, and barely escaped with his life.[4]

The incident presented the Catholics with a chance of involving their opponents in a test case. It gave Augustine, too, a golden opportunity for squaring accounts with Crispinus personally. Granted that the Donatist bishop was responsible for the action of his presbyter, could he be made liable to the fine of 10 lb. of gold as a heretic? He was brought before the municipal magistrates, but from them the case was transferred to Carthage.[5] Here the Catholics made a false step, for they allowed their case to be managed by the *defensor Ecclesiae*.[6] Crispinus denied the charge of heresy. The question between the Donatists and their opponents was one of schism, he claimed. The *defensor* could not refute him, and he carried the day.[7] It was the last legal triumph which the Donatists were to enjoy.

---

[1] *Contra Cresconium*, iii. 46. 50 (*PL*. xliii. 523); *Ep*. 88. 7 (*CSEL*. xxxiv. 413).
[2] *Ep*. 102. 2. 4 (*CSEL*. xxxiv. 598).
[3] *Ep*. 57 and 58 to Celer and Pammachius respectively.
[4] The incident is told in full in *Contra Cresconium*, iii. 46. 50 (*PL*. xliii. cols. 523-4).
[5] Ibid. iii. 48. 52.   [6] The *defensores Ecclesiae* were laymen.
[7] Possidius, *Vita Augustini*, 12 (*PL*. xxxii. 43), 'apud Proconsulem se negaret haereticum'.

Augustine had worked up a tremendous interest in the case;
'all Africa was waiting on the outcome',[1] and failure would have
had incalculable results. An appeal was therefore made once
more to the Proconsul. Matters this time went better for the
Catholics: Crispinus was pronounced a heretic, and duly
ordered to pay 10 lb. of gold in accordance with the law of 392.[2]
Augustine and Possidius were content, however, that the precedent should be established, and they intervened to save their
adversary from the actual payment of the fine. They returned to
their respective bishoprics, Possidius to turn his mercy to account
by a further campaign of preaching throughout his diocese.[3]
Crispinus for his part had also seen the importance of the
occasion. He at once set sail for Ravenna to appeal against the
sentence before the Emperor himself. The reception he received,
however, could have left him few illusions as to what was in
store for his colleagues. Not only was the fine reimposed, but
a second levied against the Proconsul and his *officium* for neglect
of duty.[4] Once again, however, the Catholics intervened to
prevent the sentence taking effect. On no account must the
Donatist leaders be allowed to represent themselves as martyrs.[5]

THE EDICT OF UNITY, A.D. 405

The incident involving Possidius was not isolated. The year
404 saw yet further deterioration of both religious peace and
public order throughout Numidia. The Circumcellions made
the whole diocese of Hippo unsafe. Villas were besieged and destroyed,[6] Catholic priests ambushed and beaten, their churches
attacked, and converts treated with that mixture of malignant
torture and ridicule which seems to have characterized the
Romano-Berber of the day.[7]

---

[1] Ibid., 'et per totam Africam expectante'.
[2] *Contra Cresconium*, iii. 47. 51 (*PL*. xliii. 524).
[3] P. Monceaux, *Histoire littéraire*, iv. 500.
[4] *Contra Cresconium*, iii. 47. 51; *Ep*. 88. 7; Possidius, *Vita*, 12 (*PL* xxxii. 44).
Crispinus eventually remained bishop, to die just before the conference at Carthage
in 411.
[5] *Contra Cresconium*, iii. 47. 51 (*PL*. xliii. 525), 'tandem intelligat quod Christi
martyrem non facit poena sed causa'.
[6] Augustine, *Ep*. 88. 6 (*CSEL*. xxxiv. 412); *Contra Cresconium*, iii. 46. 50; and
Ep. 111. 1.
[7] Augustine, *Ep*. 105. 2. 3; *Contra Cresconium*, iii. 48. 53 (*PL*. xliii, col. 525)
(the presbyter Restitutus); and *De Gestis cum Emerito* (*PL*. xliii, col. 704) (Bishop
Rogatus). Cf. *Ep*. 105. 2. 4, regarding Maximin of Sinitum in 405. The Donatists

In this atmosphere of growing exasperation, the annual Catholic Council met at Carthage on 16 June 404.[1] A policy of open persecution was decided. Many were in favour of a repetition of Macarian tactics, but Augustine and his friends knew better. At all costs recourse to the death-penalty was to be avoided.[2] Therefore the instructions which the Catholic delegates to the Imperial Court, Evodius and Theasius,[3] received aimed once more at economic measures designed to withdraw the support of the educated classes from Donatism. Military protection 'without any dissimulation' for all Catholic property and churches was demanded.[4] The penalty of 10 lb. of gold was to be applied to Donatist clergy in whose dioceses Circumcellion outrage took place, but not otherwise.[5] All landowners who allowed the dissidents to hold services on their estates were to be similarly fined.[6] Donatists were to be deprived of all testamentary rights; but their children, if they converted themselves, should enter on their inheritances.[7] The Proconsul and Vicar were to be warned of what was expected from them.[8]

The Emperor's Court had already made up its mind when the Catholic envoys arrived.[9] An incident had occurred which convinced them more powerfully of Donatist fury than any words the delegates might have used.

Maximian of Bagai had soon found himself in difficulties when he joined the Catholic camp. In 402 he formally resigned his see at the Council of Milevis,[10] and Augustine wrote to his

---

sent the town-crier round with the message, 'Quisquis Maximino communicaverit, incendetur domus eius.'

[1] *Codex Canonum Ecclesiae Africanae*, 93; Bruns, *Concilia*, 181–3.

[2] Cf. *Ep.* 185. 7. 25 (*CSEL*. lvii. 24) and *Ep.* 100. 2.

[3] Evodius was a close friend of Augustine.

[4] *Codex Canonum*, 93, quoted from Migne (*PL*. xi, col. 1203), 'Sed nos illud poscimus, ut catholicis Ecclesiarum ordinibus per civitates singulas, et vicinorum quorumque possessorum per diversa loca sine ulla dissimulatione tuitio praebeatur'.

[5] Augustine, *Ep.* 88. 7.

[6] *Codex Canonum*, 93; Bruns, 182, 'seu etiam in possessores, ubi eorum congregatio deprehenditur'.

[7] 'absque interdicto huius legis capiendae hereditatis aditus pateat, si adhuc in errore haeretico constitutis aliquid donationis vel haereditatis obvenit, his sane exceptis qui lite pulsati putaverint ad catholicam transeundum'. Bruns, 182.

[8] *Codex Canonum*, 93 (*PL*. xi. 1204).

[9] Augustine, *Ep.* 88. 7, 'sed cum legati Romam venerunt, iam cicatrices episcopi catholici Bagaitani horrendae ac recentissimae imperatorem commoverant, ut leges tales mitterentur, quales et missae sunt'.

[10] *Codex Canonum*, 88; Bruns, *Concilia*, 178 (*PL*. xi. 1199–1200).

brother Castorius suggesting that he should take it up.[1] The plan evidently fell through, for in 403 Maximian was again in possession. This time he provoked his former friends beyond endurance. Attempting to take possession of a chapel on the Fundus Calviensis near the city, he found himself surrounded by Circumcellions. In vain he hid beneath the altar of the church: it was broken over him, and he was hauled out and severely manhandled.[2] At the same time the Catholics had provoked trouble in the city, which was a prey to riots.[3] In the end Maximian recovered from his injuries and escaped to Ravenna, where in company with Servus of Thubursicum he presented compelling testimony to the bitterness of the African religious feud.

Between 12 February and 5 March 405 Honorius dispatched an edict and three *decreta* to Africa. Unity was once more proclaimed; the Donatists were pronounced heretical. All Donatist property must be handed over to the Great Church, all Donatist meetings and services were prohibited, houses in which they were found to be held were confiscate, the clergy were made liable to exile. The death penalty was not to be enforced, but lessees and bailiffs on estates where Donatist services were conducted were to be flogged with leaden whips.[4]

A Donatist was forbidden to bequeath his property or receive anything under the terms of a will, nor was he allowed to avoid the intention of the law by accepting goods as 'presents'. In the same way they were deprived of the right of making contracts.[5] Catholic children of Donatist parents could, however, succeed to their fathers' confiscated estates. As if in allusion to the baptism of the Mappalian *coloni* by Crispinus of Calama four years previously, it was decreed that slaves fleeing to a Catholic

---

[1] *Ep.* 69 (*CSEL.* xxxiv. 243).

[2] *Contra Cresconium*, iii. 43. 47 (*PL.* xliii. 521); *Ep.* 185. 7. 26 and 27 (*CSEL.* lvii. 25).

[3] *Gesta Coll. Carth.* iii. 258 (*PL.* xi. 1413), 'Postremo, in uno tantum oppido Bagaiensi eorum causa multorum Christianorum sanguis effusus est'.

[4] *Cod. Theod.* xvi. 5. 37 and 38, xvi. 6. 4 and 5, xvi. 11. 2, 'coerciti plumbo'. See F. Martroye, *La Répression du Donatisme*, 104 ff. The decrees were applicable to Manichees as well as Donatists. They served as a precedent for Zeno's *Henoticon* seventy years later.

[5] *Cod. Theod.* xvi. 6. 4, 'non solum testandi sibi, verum adipiscendi aliquid sub specie donationis vel agitandorum contractuum in perpetuum copiam denegatam, nisi pravae mentis errorem revertendo ad veram fidem consilii emendatione correxerint'.

church from such a ceremony should be rewarded with their
freedom.[1] The hand of Augustine can be seen in the most important of the clauses. Quoting and replying to the Donatist
assertion that they were at all events only schismatics, Honorius
answered that by rebaptizing they insulted Catholic mysteries
and hence became heretics.[2] They were thus liable to all the
previous anti-heretical legislation and placed on the same level
as the Manichees.[3] Dire punishment threatened attempts at
popular resistance,[4] and judges who refused to carry out the
terms of the decree were to be fined up to 20 lb. of gold. To
justify these measures in the eyes of the people, the Government
at Ravenna made use of another favourite Augustinian argument—the appeal of the exiled Donatist leaders to Julian. It was
ordered that copies of the rescript assuring them toleration,
which they received at his hands, should be prominently displayed in Carthage.[5]

The decrees were severe, putting all those who did not accept
the official Catholic viewpoint outside the protection of the
law. Wherever possible they were rigorously enforced. The
Donatist chronicler of the *Liber Genealogus* records 26 June 405
as the day on which they were promulgated in Carthage.[6] The
Donatist primate Primian, Petilian of Constantine, and others
followed in the wake of the founder of their community sixty
years before, and went into exile.[7] On 23 August Aurelius, now
left in sole possession of the city of Carthage, instructed, in the
name of the Catholic Council which he had assembled, that a
delegation should be sent to Ravenna to convey the thanks of
the Catholics to the Emperor.[8] At the same time letters were to be

---

[1] *Cod. Theod.* xvi. 6. 4, 'servis, si qui forsitan ad rebaptizandum cogentur,
refugiendi ad ecclesiam catholicam sit facultas'. Cf. Augustine, *Ep.* 66; *Contra
Litteras Petiliani*, ii. 83. 184.

[2] *Cod. Theod.* xvi. 6. 4. Cf. Augustine, *Contra Cresconium*, ii. 4. 5 and 6 (*PL.*
xliii. 469–70), and *Ep.* 105. 3. 12.

[3] *Cod. Theod.* xvi. 5. 38, 'Nemo Manichaeum, nemo Donatistam, qui praecipue
(ut comperimus) furere non desistunt in memoriam revocet'.

[4] Ibid., 'et si turbae forte convenerint, seditionis concitatos . . .'.

[5] Ibid. 5. 37. Dating, F. Martroye, *La Répression du Donatisme*, 113. Augustine, *Contra Epistolam Parmeniani*, i. 12. 19 (*PL.* xliii, cols. 47–48); *Contra Litteras
Petiliani*, ii. 97. 224 (*PL.* xliii, cols. 334–5).

[6] *Liber Genealogus*, 627 (ed. Mommsen, *MGH., Chronica Minora*, p. 196).

[7] Augustine, *Ep.* 88. 10.

[8] *Codex Canonum Ecclesiae Africanae*, 94. Text in Migne, *PL.* xi, cols. 1211–12. The
mission was sent despite the fact that at the same Council letters from Pope Innocent I were read, protesting against the frequent journeyings of the African episcopate to Italy.

dispatched to the local authorities in Africa urging on them the task of speeding the reunion of the two Churches.[1]

The persecution was to last with slight intermissions up to and beyond the Conference of 411. From Augustine's works and from the statements made at the Conference it is possible to form a general impression of its effectiveness during the next five or six years.[2] On the whole the Catholic gains were local and partial, depending very much on the personal qualities of the individual Catholic bishop, and to a surprising extent they were balanced by losses to Donatism. The division of North Africa into fixed, watertight areas, the Catholics predominating in the settled urban country and the Donatists on the Numidian High Plains, became more pronounced. Each side evidently concentrated on eliminating the minorities of the other in his own territory.

At Hippo, Augustine applied the Edicts of Unity with a characteristic vigour.[3] Bishop Proculeianus found himself deprived of his basilica, whose walls were then used for the display of Augustinian tracts.[4] In the surrounding countryside, Augustine secured the conversion of the hill village of Thiava[5] and the Donatist bishopric of Sinitum.[6] In addition he gained adherents among the minority of Donatist landowners.[7] Farther south in Thagaste, Alypius enforced unity, and around Milevis and near Constantine the Catholics also gained ground, establishing six 'shadow' bishoprics.[8] Some other towns in the same

[1] Ibid., 'Ut quia apud Carthaginem tantum unitas facta est, dentur etiam litterae ad judices, ut et in aliis provinciis et civitatibus operam impendi jubeant unitati'.

[2] Particularly *Contra Cresconium*, ii. 10. 12 (*PL.* xliii, col. 473); *Ep.* 93. 5. 16; and *Gesta Coll. Carth.* i. 116, 130, and 135. A canon of the Council held in June 407 provides for converted Donatist communities (Migne, *PL.* xi, cols. 1212–15).

[3] See *Sermo ii in Ps. 101*, 9 (*PL.* xxxvii, col. 1310). The Donatists were told that 'it was their deeds, their pride and their vanity', which had brought persecution on them. 'You have wandered', Augustine said, 'that is why you are trampled under the foot of men.' In *Enarratio in Ps. 145*, 16, he tells them that it was no use their priding themselves on being persecuted, because they were merely victims of their own wickedness in 'repulsing Christ'.

[4] *Retractationes*, ii. 27 (*PL.* xxxii, col. 643), 'eumque libellum sic edidi, ut in parietibus basilicae quae Donatistarum fuerat prius propositus legeretur'. It did not remain for long unanswered; see *Retract.* ii. 28. [5] *Ep.* 83.

[6] *Ep.* 105. 4. This was only temporary. In 411 the Donatists were once more in control.

[7] e.g. Celer, who was a Donatist when Augustine wrote *Ep.* 56 to him but was evidently a Catholic by the time Augustine compiled *Ep.* 139.

[8] *Gesta Coll. Carth.* i. 65, 130, and 165 (*PL.* xi), and similar occurrences are

area we know from the proceedings of the Conference of Carthage were reconciled to Catholicism.[1] These local gains were fairly impressive in their sum total, and there is no reason to accuse Augustine of exaggeration when he wrote to his friend Vincentius, the Rogatist Bishop of Cartenna, that there were many cities once Donatist, now Catholic, vehemently detesting the diabolical schism and ardently loving the unity of the Church.[2] In Augustine's view, the persecution was justified by its results. To some, it had proved a happy deliverance from the bondage of custom.[3] It had made people rethink their position and in this part of Numidia had unfrozen the frontiers between the two communities.

In areas where there were traditional Catholic majorities, such as in Proconsular Africa and in parts of the province of Byzacena, there were also considerable Catholic gains. Some bishops were able to use violent methods to coerce the Donatist minority. One Donatist bishop found himself handed over to the executioner by his Catholic rival, and was only spared by the intervention of the local civil authorities;[4] in another town the Catholic bishop declared that if anyone mentioned the name of Donatus in his diocese he was stoned.[5] In important centres such as Bulla Regia[6] and Gratianopolis[7] Donatist congregations were reduced to almost nothing or compelled to submission. But more often, the Catholics appear to have waited until the death of the local Donatist cleric before attempting to take over the congregation:[8] they would appeal

reported at i. 116 (Liberta). Petilian's view of these tactics is expressed in *Gesta Coll. Carth.* i. 165, 'aut in dioecesibus passim multas imagines erigunt, ut numerosi esse videntur'.

[1] e.g. the towns of Boseta (*Gesta Coll. Carth.* i. 120) and Vozari (ibid. 129).

[2] *Ep.* 93. 5. 16 (*CSEL.* xxxiv. 461). Cf. *Codex Canonum*, 117, A.D. 407.

[3] *Ep.* 93. 1. 2, 'ut tamquam de somno lethargico emergent' (*CSEL.* xxxiv. 447). Also Mansi, *Concilia*, iii. 795.

[4] *Gesta Coll. Carth.* i. 142 (*PL.* xi, col. 1318), 'Scriptum sit si ipse Florentius bene agnoscit, qui me persecutus innocentem, quem apprehendit et in custodiam officii dedit necandum ubi, triennium temporis feci.' The victim, Bishop Victor, was one of the Donatist archivists of the Conference of 411.

[5] *Gesta Coll. Carth.* i. 133, 'Nomen si illic auditum fuerit Donatistarum lapidatur' (*PL.* xi, col. 1302). For other scenes of violence, *Gesta Coll. Carth.* i. 133 and 135.

[6] Ibid. 135.

[7] Ibid. 135, 'e diverso Deuterius est, solus sine plebe'.

[8] e.g. at Vina in Proconsular Africa, (ibid. 129) and Quiza in Mauretania Caesariensis (i. 143). Other gains were Sufasar (i. 135) and Turres in southern Byzacena (i. 121). It was at this period that the Tertullianists in Carthage gave up their church to Aurelius.

to Imperial legislation to prevent a new election, and then present the inhabitants with a monopoly of religious life. It was in fact this particular tactic, coupled with the planting of Catholic 'cells' in Donatist areas, that caused Petilian most concern.

In the circumstances an increase of Catholic strength could be expected, but it is also interesting that despite the Imperial laws the Donatists continued to make a certain amount of headway. In northern Numidia they secured control of the town of Thibilis, where the former Catholic bishop brought his whole congregation over to them.[1] On the Numidian High Plains, the Conference of Carthage reveals two instances where Catholic clergy had become Donatist bishops.[2] In other centres, the Donatists succeeded in ridding themselves of opposition by more or less forcible means.[3] At Liberalia in south-western Numidia they seized the Catholic basilica.[4] In Byzacena two important towns became Donatist, and progress was made even in the Proconsular province.[5] In Mauretania the persecution does not appear to have altered the balance of forces either way to any extent.

It seems likely that local officials were not interested in enforcing the legislation if it meant antagonizing the population.[6] The nine days of commotion at Calama against Bishop Possidius, 1 to 8 June 408, showed how little was needed to cause a bitter religious riot to break out. In any case, the persecution did not extend to literary works. The controversy between Augustine and Petilian was carried on through Petilian's *De Unico Baptismo*, in which the writer justified the Donatist practice of rebaptizing their converts, and Augustine's answer in 410–11.[7] Previously, in about A.D. 406 Augustine had written four books in reply to the tract of a Donatist layman Cresconius, who had written under the inspiration of Petilian's works.[8] It is in this

---

[1] Ibid. 198 (*PL.* xi, col. 1337).

[2] At Voseta and Zarai (*Gesta Coll. Carth.* i. 202 and 203).

[3] e.g. at Rusticana and Rotaria (ibid. 187 and 198).

[4] Ibid. 133 (*PL.* xi, col. 1309).

[5] At Silemsila, *Gesta Coll. Carth.* i. 201, the Catholic see had been reduced to a presbyterate. The towns in Byzacena were Mesarfilta and Maxliana.

[6] For instance, prominent Donatists in Mauretania and southern Numidia were left unmolested. In 406 Augustine wrote to Januarius, the Donatist Primate of Numidia, inviting him to summon his colleagues to a conference with the Catholics (*Ep.* 88).

[7] i.e. after Petilian had returned from exile. Dating, Migne, *PL.* xliii, cols. 593–4.

[8] On Cresconius, P. Monceaux, *Histoire littéraire*, vi, ch. ii.

work that he claimed that heresy was not merely doctrinal error but 'inveterate schism'—the view of a bureaucrat. In his own diocese too Augustine had to face Donatist pamphleteers, but most remarkable of all during these years is the Donatist chronicle, the *Liber Genealogus*. The writer shows a real Carthaginian patriotism. He notes the foundation of Carthage along with events of Biblical history.[1] There is a strong anti-Catholic bias, as when he comments on the schism between Rehoboam and Jeroboam that 'there was strife between them all the days of their life, as now between the true Christians and the false Catholics'.[2] He shows that the tradition of the apostasy of Pope Marcellinus in A.D. 304 was still very much alive among the Donatists, and he indicates whom they considered to be the real martyrs during the various pagan persecutions. Catholic persecutions appeared to the writer as merely a continuation of the latter. The *Liber Genealogus* is an interesting example of the intense literary warfare which each side was conducting at this time.

The last entry in the first edition of the *Liber Genealogus* concerns the arrival of renewed persecution in Africa in 405. In their exile, however, Primian, Petilian, and their colleagues were trying hard to have the Imperial decisions reversed. In January 406 they reached Ravenna and, like Crispinus of Calama two years previously, stated their case to the Emperor's advisers. At Court they found an African Catholic bishop, Valentinus, and they suggested that they might be allowed to debate the issue of the schism with him before the *Praefectus Praetorio* as judge.[3] On 30 January, however, this was refused, but the incident shows that Donatist opinion had developed during the previous three years and by this time both rival Churches in Africa were prepared to accept the award of a non-ecclesiastical authority, i.e. the Emperor or his representative, as to which was the true 'Catholic Church'. The only matter in dispute was the fairness of the judge appointed.

The Donatists appear to have secured partial success in Ravenna, for they were evidently allowed to return home to Africa. For the next two years the pressure was relaxed and

---

[1] See Monceaux, op. cit., vi. 247–58.

[2] *Liber Genealogus*, 546 (*MGH.* ix. 192).

[3] *Gesta Coll. Carth.* iii. 141 (*PL.* xi, col. 1388) and 170; Seeck, *Untergang*, v. 364. This action by the Donatists enabled the Catholics to claim at the Conference in 411 that *both* communities had appealed to the Emperor.

significant incidents are few. The persecution was formally extended to the Donatists in Rome by a rescript to the *Praefectus Praetorio* Curtius on 15 November 407,[1] but in Africa the Catholics, while continuing to urge the Donatists to confer with them,[2] concentrated their energies on reorganization and Church discipline. It is clear that, at this time, many of the bishops were finding that too much of their lives was spent travelling to Carthage to attend Councils.[3] Augustine himself lamented the 'feebleness' of his congregation, which he dared not leave, no doubt for fear of apostasies.[4]

It should be recalled too that the Donatists were not the only sufferers from persecution. The Catholics were also waging a truceless war on Manichees, Jews, and pagans, whose property and places of worship were equally liable to confiscation. It seems that a blind eye was often turned on the methods used to enforce the decrees which favoured the Catholics. From the *Codex Theodosianus* it is clear that the executive power lay in the hands of soldiers, and their depredations at the expense of the rest of the provincials provided a contrast to the Catholic arguments concerning the 'blessings of unity', secured through the 'work of charity'.[5]

By the middle of 408, the areas where the various persecutions had been enforced were simmering with discontent. On 1 June savage riots, ostensibly pagan-inspired, broke out in Calama, Possidius' see.[6] They lasted nine days, and lives were lost. On 16 June Aurelius assembled another Council at Carthage and sent Fortunatianus, Bishop of Sicca, near the Numidian border of Proconsular Africa, to the Emperor to plead for more drastic measures against heretics and pagans.[7]

Before he could return, however, the Catholics had suffered a further blow through the arrest and execution of Stilicho on 23 August 408.[8] While expediency rather than belief had

---

[1] *Cod. Theod.* xvi. 5. 43.

[2] Augustine, *Contra Cresconium*, iv. 66. 82 (*PL.* xliii, col. 593), 'sed ad collationem vocamus'.

[3] *Codex Canonum*, 95; Bruns, 184.

[4] *Ep.* 95. 1 and 97. 4. See G. Metzger, *Die afrikanische Kirche*, Tübingen, 1934, p. 67.

[5] Robberies by soldiers and *agentes in rebus* in Africa at this time, *Const. Sirmond.*, 12 (*Codex Theodosianus*, p. 917, ll. 5 ff.).

[6] Augustine, *Ep.* 90 and 91.

[7] *Codex Canonum*, 107; Bruns, 188. Dating, Monceaux, op. cit. iv. 381.

[8] Zosimus, v. 34. 7.

inspired the religious policy of the all-powerful minister, the African provincials had adopted the convenient fiction that the Emperor himself was well disposed to their Church, but that he had been misled by bad advisers.[1] This was not to be the last time in history that revolutionaries have employed this inverted theory of ministerial responsibility.

The natural corollary to this view was that Stilicho's fall entailed the complete reversal of the policy that had been attributed to him.[2] The anti-heretical laws were consequently no longer valid. This seemed evident with the recall of the *Comes* Bathanarius. In the next two months all those who had suffered any form of repression from the Catholics broke forth in jubilation and revenge. In northern Numidia and Proconsular Africa there was a general outburst against the Catholic clergy. Two bishops, Macarius and Severus, were killed, and apparently in the same incidents the Catholic delegates to the Imperial Court in 404, Evodius and Theasius, were severely beaten.[3] Other clergy had to flee for their lives and were forced to seek refuge at Ravenna.[4] Converts from Donatism were subjected to murderous assaults.[5] Gildo's former sympathizers began to stir again and Gildo's memory was once more celebrated.[6] At Hippo, where Augustine had restored 'unity' in 405, the tables were turned. The successor of Bishop Proculeianus, Macrobius, entered the city in triumph escorted by a bodyguard of Circumcellions.[7] The beggars had come to town, the new and non-Roman forces in Africa were making their presence increasingly felt.

Augustine, however, once more showed himself equal to the situation. His contacts and friendships had for long extended far beyond the borders of Africa. He was well acquainted with members of the rival groupings at Ravenna and knew whom to

[1] Augustine, *Ep.* 97. 3 to Olympius, 'noverint, sicut dixi, homines vani, quorum et adversantium salutem requirimus, leges quae pro Christi ecclesia missae sunt, magis Theodosii filium quam Stilichonem curasse mittendas'.

[2] Id., *Ep.* 100. 2, 'noverint haeretici Donatistae, manere leges contra errorem suum latas, quas iam nihil valere arbitrantur et iactant'.

[3] Mansi, *Concilia*, iii. 810. Theasius and Evodius were particularly unpopular among the Donatists; Petilian denounced them as being the 'permanent emissaries' who demanded blood and proscriptions from the Emperor (*Gesta Coll. Carth.* iii. 141 (*PL.* xi, col. 1388)).

[4] *Ep.* 97. 2.

[5] Such as Bishop Marcianus of Urgi (*Ep.* 105. 2. 3). Other incidents are recorded in *Ep.* 108 and 111.

[6] *Cod. Theod.* ix. 40. 19.   [7] *Ep.* 108. 5. 14.

approach with the maximum of effect.[1] Possidius of Calama had
already been dispatched to Ravenna to protest against the riots
in his episcopal town. In the spring or early summer of 408
when Stilicho's power was tottering we find Augustine in lively
correspondence with his supplanter and murderer, the *Magister
Officiorum*, Olympius.[2] The latter is recorded by Zosimus,
albeit an unfriendly critic, as a man of insinuating craft who
was able to mask his intrinsic villainy by an ostentatious devotion to the Catholic Church.[3] Stilicho's executioner Heraclian
was rewarded for his services by his appointment as *Comes
Africae*.

Augustine's diplomatic approaches found ready acceptance.
Olympius promised his aid to the African Catholics. On 13
October 408 Aurelius was able to dispatch a strong delegation
to Ravenna with every hope that the situation would be speedily
restored.[4] He was not disappointed. On 11 November imprisonment and execution were once more ordered for the supporters
of Gildo.[5] On 24 November two decrees reminded Jews and
Donatists that previous legislation was still valid, and that they
were liable to a 'just penalty', a phrase which at that time would
bear the interpretation of death.[6] On 15 January 409 a further
law warned the Imperial officials in Africa of punishment in
store, should they fail to carry out the previous orders.[7]

The Emperor had at last appointed an official on whose zeal
for the Catholic cause he need have no cause for doubt. The
Proconsul Donatus was himself an African and owned landed
estates near Hippo in Augustine's diocese.[8] The child of mixed
Catholic and Donatist parents, he evidently possessed something
of the psychology of the convert, including a desire to repress
in general the religion which he himself had rejected, and yet
from whose influence he could never free himself. Donatus

---

[1] Augustine's friends included Paulinus of Nola and the Consul for the year 408,
Fl. Anicius Bassus.

[2] *Ep.* 96. Indicated by the words 'litteras nostras te accepturum esse praesumus',
and (*Ep.* 97. 1) 'Quamvis mox, ut audivimus te merito sublimatum'.

[3] Zosimus, v. 32.

[4] Mansi, *Concilia*, iii. 810. Augustine meanwhile was in personal touch with
Olympius through one of his presbyters, *Ep.* 97. 3.

[5] This would also include the Donatists (*Cod. Theod.* ix. 40. 19).

[6] *Cod. Theod.* xvi. 5. 41 and 44. The law demanded the infliction of *supplicium
justae animadversionis* which, as Augustine in *Ep.* 100. 2 shows, was interpreted by
the Proconsul to mean the death penalty.

[7] *Cod. Theod.* xvi. 5. 46; *Const. Sirmond.* 14.

[8] Augustine, *Ep.* 112. 3 (*CSEL.* xxxiv. 2. 659). See also *Ep.* 100.

intended that the new sanctions against the Donatists should include death. The Catholics, however, had asked for 'proper and Christian measures' only, and Augustine at once protested. He was careful to point out on this occasion that he was acting from expediency. He feared the Donatist power of revenge, and he feared too that additions would be made to the Donatist roll of martyrs. 'You will help us greatly in our work and in our dangers,' he told Donatus, 'and you would prevent them from being sterile, if you were to repress this vain and proud sect in a manner which does not let it feel that it is suffering for truth and justice.'[1]

The Proconsul did his best, but despite his vigour the laws do not seem to have been applied any more effectively than those issued before. In northern Numidia the Donatists continued to regain lost ground. At Hippo Augustine found Macrobius a vigorous opponent, and suffered the humiliation of seeing some of his own clergy go over to Donatism.[2] On the great estates surrounding the town social unrest prevailed. The sermons of the Donatist clergy had begun to instil in the colonate a deep sense of injustice. In these years we read more of the fanatical outrages of the Circumcellions, burning, pillaging, and rebaptizing. Forty-eight Catholics were rebaptized in one village on a single day.[3] Augustine himself felt uncertain of his hold over some of his congregation.[4]

Early in 410 external events again caused the legal pressure on the Donatists to ease. Olympius had fallen in 409, and for a brief while pagan influence dominated at Ravenna. Meanwhile Alaric had threatened Rome twice, and on 3 November 409 the *Praefectus Urbi* Priscus Attalus renounced his allegiance to Honorius. On Alaric's demand he was elected Emperor by the Senate.[5] Like other usurpers who held Rome before him, his

---

[1] *Ep.* 100. 2 (*CSEL.* xxxiv. 538), 'Plurimum autem labores et pericula nostra quo fructuosa sint adjuvabis, si eorum vanissimam et impiae superbiae plenissimam sectam non ita cures imperialibus legibus comprimi, ut sibi vel suis videantur qualescumque molestias pro veritate atque justitia sustinere. . . .'

[2] *Ep.* 106, 'Audivi, quod quendam subdiaconum nostrum rebaptizare disponis'.

[3] *Ep.* 111. 1, 'multos etiam rebaptizari compellunt. pridie, quam ista ad te dictavi, ex uno loco per huiusmodi terrores quadraginta et octo animae mihi rebaptizatae nuntiatae sunt'. Cf. *De Unico Baptismo*, 12. 20, for similar happenings about this time.

[4] *Ep.* 124. 2, 'populus Hipponenis . . . ex magna ac paene ex omni parte ita infirmus'.

[5] Zosimus, vi. 7. 1. Attalus was a pagan, who allowed himself to be baptized as an Arian. Seeck, *Untergang*, v. 401; *Regesten*, 318.

position depended largely on the supplies he could draw from Africa. In the winter of 409/10 these were denied him by Heraclian. Attalus, however, feared the results of allowing Alaric to take his army to conquer Africa by force as the latter had proposed. Instead, he dispatched Constans, a member of the Roman aristocracy, to Africa to displace Heraclian as *Comes Africae*. The latter was well able to fend for himself, and by mid-April 410 Constans had been captured, tried, and executed. For the time being Africa had been denied to the anti-Imperial coalition of Alaric and the Senate dominated by Attalus and his friends.

Honorius expressed his appreciation of the provinces' loyalty by a decree dated 25 June 410 which forgave the Africans all arrears of taxation.[1] He may also previously have granted to both Donatists and pagans a certain measure of religious freedom. This now proved highly objectionable to the Catholics, and on 14 June 410 Aurelius dispatched a delegation which included two of the fiercest anti-Donatists, Possidius of Calama and Florentius of Hippo Diarrhytos, with a protest to the Emperor.[2] They demanded first the withdrawal of any legislation in favour of toleration, and secondly that the Donatists be brought to a final conference.[3] Suppression by force had failed, and the Catholics returned to the policy they had attempted seven years before by their appeal to the Proconsul Septiminus. It was the policy which had the entire approval of Augustine.

Despite his difficulties in Gaul and Italy, Honorius listened to the delegation. On 25 August, the day after Alaric entered Rome, he sent a short but exceedingly sharp rescript to Heraclian. Heresy was to be put down in 'blood and proscription'.[4] This was followed by the dispatch of Count Marcellinus, a high official of the Imperial Chancery, who was also a friend of Augustine's, to supervise the arrangements for a joint

---

[1] *Cod. Theod.* ix. 28. 6.

[2] Mansi, *Concilia*, iii. 810, 'legationem susceperunt contra Donatistas Florentius, Possidius, Praesidius et Benenatus episcopi, eo tempore quo lex data est, ut libera voluntate quisquis cultum christianitatis exciperet.' The text of the 'Edict of Toleration' has not been preserved.

[3] Ibid. It is interesting that at the Conference the Catholics refused to disclose the full terms of the instructions given to their delegates on this mission. Augustine (*Gesta Coll. Carth.* iii. 160) indicated that it might be wrong for the Donatists to know the details.

[4] *Cod. Theod.* xvi. 5. 51. Dating, Seeck, *Regesten*, 320.

conference. On 14 October a further short edict showed what was expected of him. 'On the removal of the seditious superstition', all previous decrees enacted for the benefit of the 'Catholic law' were to be enforced in their entirety.[1] With these instructions the Emperor's 'mediator' sailed for Africa.

[1] *Cod. Theod.* xvi. 11. 3, 'novella superstitione submota integra et inviolata custodiri praecipimus.'

XVII

THE CONFERENCE OF CARTHAGE

A.D. 411

THE choice of the Count Marcellinus as president of the conference which was to decide the future of Donatism was eminently satisfactory to the Catholics. One is even tempted to see further evidence of the resiliency and political skill of Augustine in the appointment. Like many other high officials among Augustine's friends, Marcellinus was at heart a theologian, and had for some time at least been an admirer of the Augustinian system. He seems to have been a sincere and upright man devoted to the Catholic cause. In 410, evidently before he replied to Petilian's *De Baptismo*, Augustine had dedicated to Marcellinus his treatise on sin and free-will entitled 'De Peccatorum Meritis'.[1] The following year, at about the time the Conference was opening, he was to address to this same admirer the greatest of all his works, *De Civitate Dei*.[2] After the Conference was over, Marcellinus consulted his friend on every step in the tactics to be pursued to destroy Donatism throughout North Africa.[3] It is hardly to be wondered that from the outset the Catholic bishops regarded the Count as a faithful member of their flock, a son devoted to the interests of their Church.[4] With such a man as president, the Conference could only have one result.

Events now moved swiftly and surely towards their climax on the night of 8/9 June 411. Alone among the crowd of wealthy refugees who were pouring into Africa from Rome, Marcellinus

---

[1] *Retractationes*, ii. 33 (*PL*. xxxii. 644). The *De Baptismo* is recorded in *Retractationes*, ii. 34. The dating A.D. 410 is that preferred by Migne, but must be considered approximate.

[2] *De Civitate Dei*, Prologue; Pauly–Wissowa, *Realencyclopaedie*, xiv. 2, col. 1445. For Marcellinus' interest in the doctrine of Free Will, see *Ep*. 143.

[3] Augustine, *Epp*. 133 and 139.

[4] *Ep*. 128. The Catholic bishops addressed Marcellinus as 'Honorabili et dilectissimo filio'. After his execution in 413 Augustine wrote of him, 'The report that he would approve himself an eminent Christian both in heart and practice when commissioned to serve the Church came before him to Africa, and this good report followed him still when he had come' (*Ep*. 151. 8 (ed. Dods, p. 258)).

had a definite task to perform. On 19 January 411 he issued a pronouncement calling the conference for 1 June of the same year.[1] To make the Donatists amenable, he promised that in the meantime all basilicas that had been confiscated should be restored to them.[2] In many places the Catholics refused this concession.[3] 'Why return to heresy what would soon be shared in unity?' they argued.

Primian had been able to return to Carthage, and he saw that the only course open to the Donatists was to obey and hope that an appeal to the rights of their case would prevail.

Probably in the same month as the issue of the Commissioner's Edict, he sent out instructions to his colleagues. It was a short, urgent message. They were to leave everything else and hasten to Carthage, for therein lay their best chance of success.[4] Two hundred and eighty-four bishops responded to the appeal.[5] Some of them, like the Bishops of Oea and Cellae, had had to make long journeys, others, as Quodvultdeus of Cessita[6] and Maximian of Bennefa, arrived dying men, to expire at Carthage[7] or on the return journey to their sees. By 18 May, the last day before the four-month time-limit prescribed by Marcellinus expired, all had arrived. On that day they made a magnificent entry into the capital, the last triumph the Donatist Church was to enjoy.[8] But all there knew how grave the situation was. Feeling on both sides was rising, but among the Donatists, if one may believe Augustine, it was one of resignation

---

[1] *Gesta Coll. Carth.* i. 5. Dating, ibid. 27.

[2] Ibid. 5. The Donatists were granted the right to bring complaints against depredations on the part of the Catholics.

[3] Ibid. iii. 18 (*PL.* xi, col. 1355), *Ep.* 128. 4.

[4] *Ad Donatistas post Collationem*, 24. 41 (*PL.* xliii. 678), 'quo praetermissis omnibus properarent convenire Carthaginem ut scirent se decepisse quod haberent optimum in causa quicumque venire noluissent'.

[5] The tally is a little confusing. In fact, 316 Donatist bishops are mentioned during the course of the proceedings. Two hundred and seventy-nine signed the *mandatum*, but five of the seven Donatist mandatories Emeritus, Petilian, Protasius, Montanus, Gaudentius, and Adeodatus do not appear to have done so with the rest, and thus were not counted in the total of those present. Some sees, such as Ala Milaria in Mauretania, which are known through archaeological evidence to have been Donatist at this time are not represented (S. Gsell, 'Les Fouilles à Benian', p. 50); *Gesta Coll. Carth.* i. 213 (*PL.* xi. 1349); *Breviculus Collationis*, i. 14 (*PL.* xliii. 620). In 412 the Donatists still claimed 400 bishoprics.

[6] *Gesta Coll. Carth.* i. 208; *Breviculus Collationis*, i. 14 (*PL.* xliii. 619–20).

[7] *Gesta Coll. Carth.* i. 133 (*PL.* xi. 1304–5).

[8] *Ad Donatistas post Collationem*, 25. 43 (*PL.* xliii. 679), 'cum tanta speciosi agminis pompa'.

and despair. 'Woe unto us, unity is come!'[1] was the atmosphere when in the last week of May Augustine preached to his supporters on the subject of charity and peace.[2] The Catholics had arrived some days later than their adversaries, late enough in fact to give pretext for the charge that they had forfeited their right to debate through contumacy.[3] They left nothing undone to prevent accidents. Between 18 May and 30 May, the date of their second preliminary Council, they had sent two letters to the Arbitrator.[4] These were sent by way of accepting the Commissioner's regulations for the holding of the Conference, and commented on an alleged Donatist refusal to do the same. They contained, however, a full statement of the Catholic case, and even went so far as to ask that the work of unifying the Churches in Africa should begin before the Conference met.[5]

Meantime, on 25 May, the Donatists had met in the basilica assigned to them, the Theoprepia, and had drawn up their reply to Marcellinus.[6] They chose their representatives, but for some reason only included their primate at the last minute, Victor of Tabora standing down in his favour.[7] On the 30th the Catholics met for the same purpose. Two days later the Conference opened in the 'Thermae Gargilianae'.[8]

Both sides had put forward almost their full numerical strength. The Catholics mustered 286 bishops against their opponents' 284. Champions who had previously fought out their literary battles at long range now faced each other as

---

[1] *Sermo* 357. 3 (*PL.* xxxviii–xxxix. 1583).   [2] *Sermones* 357 and 358.

[3] *Gesta Coll. Carth.* i. 29 (*PL.* xi. 1268–9); *Breviculus Collationis*, i. 8 (*PL.* xliii. 616).

[4] *Ep.* 128 and 129 (*CSEL* xliv). Cf. *Breviculus Collationis*, i. 7 (*PL.* xliii. 616), 'In eisdem litteris etiam tota ipsa causa comprehensa est.'

[5] *Ep.* 128 (*CSEL* xliv), 'etiam ante Collationem, si fieri potest, corda hominum vel infirma vel dura, pia charitas aut sanet, aut edomet'. Their offer to resign their sees if beaten should not perhaps be taken very seriously in the circumstances.

[6] The Donatist Mandate contained no anti-Catholic arguments. It was simply a delegation of powers (*Gesta Coll. Carth.* i. 150).

[7] Ibid. i. 201 (*PL.* xi. 1340).

[8] One can get some idea of what the *thermae* looked like from an example complete with barrel-vaulted roof which was excavated by Ward Perkins at Sabratha in 1948. The windows are small, and the atmosphere in the room where over 500 people were gathered must have become stifling. The Thermae Garglianae may have been larger. Literature on the Conference:

P. Monceaux, *Histoire littéraire*, iv, ch. iv; L. Duchesne (tr. Jenkins), *Early History of the Christian Church*, iii. 95–99; J. Sparrow Simpson, *St. Augustine and African Church Divisions* (Longmans, 1910); P. Batiffol, *Le Catholicisme de Saint Augustin*, i, pp. 306 f.

delegates across the floor of the great bath-building. It was, it seems, the first and only occasion that Augustine and Petilian met, but in the crowded, murmuring ranks of the bishops which were soon to line each side of the building these two men stood out as leaders. Both in their particular ways accepted the responsibility for the future of their communities. There were many others, however, who recognized hated rivals, people who for years had dogged each other's footsteps as leaders of hostile communities in small, semi-isolated townships. At times the tension mounted to breaking-point as old memories revived and thoughts of vengeance forced their way to the surface. The future not only of those who were present but of Christianity itself in North Africa was to hang on the outcome.

But of the contending parties, all the advantages lay with the Catholics. They came to the Conference sure at least of a legal triumph. For the Donatists to have won would have meant a decisive change in the religious policy of the Emperors, a change which would not have been confined to Africa. For six years the opposition had been officially proscribed. This was the occasion to give that proscription its judicial form. Augustine and his colleagues had planned and worked for this day. Four years before, Augustine had explained his attitude to Januarius, Donatist Primate of Numidia. 'Yet in wishing for this conference with you, we seek not to have a second final decision, but to have it made known as already settled, to those who meanwhile are not aware that it is so.'[1] The 'final decision' had been given long ago in Constantine's reign. The Conference was merely an opportunity for the Donatists to submit on relatively favourable conditions. The Catholic tactics were therefore directed throughout towards having the questions at issue settled by a small meeting of delegates with as much speed and as little show as possible. Doctrinal matters would be settled from Scripture, historical questions by an appeal to documents. The only thing that they feared was that the conference should be bogged down in legal arguments, and possibly in the end broken up by mob violence.[2] When the second session had

---

[1] *Ep.* 88. 10 (ed. Dods, p. 373).

[2] Augustine, *Breviculus Collationis*, i. vii (*PL.* xliii, col. 616), 'Cum tamen illic ex Catholicis episcopis illi soli adessent, quos edicto suo Cognitor definierat; ut si aliquis tumultus existeret, quod Catholici valde metuebant, non illis imputaretur qui paucissimi adessent, sed eis potius qui multitudinem praesentem esse voluissent.' Also *Gesta Coll. Carth.* i. 81 (*PL.* xi. 1278).

produced no decision, this was a possibility that began to emerge.[1]

The Donatists, on the other hand, had only accepted the conference as the alternative to the continuance of proscription and repression. If they had refused the Imperial summons they would have stood self-condemned. However much they may, as a Church, have prided themselves on suffering, they show that as individuals they welcomed a respite. In contrast to the Catholics, who leave the impression of abiding by a well-thought-out scheme of attack, the Donatists prepared their case indifferently. They even included documents which could help their opponents,[2] and, as already mentioned, they seem even to have been unable to decide until the last moment whether to include their Primate among the delegates chosen for the actual debate. Perhaps they felt that Primian was too vulnerable on the Maximianist issue—perhaps there were other grounds.[3] They appear too to have been uncertain whether to treat the conference as a Council, in which the voice of every bishop should be heard, and in which their numbers would be of some avail, or as a lawsuit, whence they could appeal once more to the Emperor in the event of condemnation. In the earlier stages, the more constructive alternative seems to have prevailed. In the second and third sessions, after they had failed to secure the acceptance of their idea of a Council, their main object appears to have been to prolong proceedings in the hope of wearing down their opponents. In this they were to be disappointed, and Petilian and Emeritus found their match as advocates in the superb debating skill of Augustine, seconded by Alypius of Thagaste.

Any hopes the Donatists may have had of winning their case and establishing that theirs was the true Church, at least in Africa, were dashed as soon as the proceedings opened. Marcellinus read a long Imperial rescript which set out the reasons why the conference had been called.[4] The object of the meeting

---

[1] *Gesta Coll. Carth.* ii. 72 (*PL.* xi, col. 1363).

[2] For instance, they tried to prove that Caecilian had himself been condemned by Constantine, quoting Optatus, i. 26. The Catholics, however, forced them to read on a bit farther, where Caecilian was declared innocent. See Augustine, *Breviculus Collationis*, iii.20. 38 (*PL.* xliii, col. 647). The debate, however, showed that the Donatist central organization was still intact. Primian's deacons were very well informed about even remote communities.

[3] Such as old age. On the incident, Monceaux, *Histoire littéraire*, vi. 150.

[4] *Gesta Coll. Carth.* i. 4 (*PL.* xi, cols. 1260–1).

was to 'confirm the Catholic faith'. The Donatists were named as those who 'had discoloured Africa with vain error and super-fluous dissension'.[1] Their beliefs were a *superstitio*; in vain they had previously been adjured to correct their depraved menta-lities. The conference gave them a final chance of recognizing the truth. Meantime, all former laws against heresy were to remain in force.[2] The Donatists were in fact told bluntly that they could either accept a conference on those conditions or be judged contumacious.[3]

The rules which Marcellinus had drawn up for the debate were designed to produce an orderly discussion, after which he would be able to give a clear-cut decision on the lines of the Imperial edict. Each side was to choose seven speakers to whom were to be allocated seven deputies who would act as specialist advisers, but who did not have the right of speaking. In addi-tion, four invigilators were entitled to supervise the drafting of the records. Each side therefore would be represented by eighteen persons. The remainder of the bishops were to be kept away until called to attend a final plenary session at which the verdict would be announced. To make the proceedings still more definitive, no speech, remark, interruption, or any single word was to be uttered without the speaker certifying to its accuracy on the record. This record was to be kept by clerks from the city offices at Carthage, and it appears that they did their work well.

The Donatists, however, had considerable mental reservations about accepting these rules. It seems clear that they had in mind a Council of Bishops, somewhat on the lines of Cyprian's Council of 256, or Secundus' of 312—a meeting at which every bishop would give his views in turn individually. If this proce-dure had been adopted it could have been made quite obvious that they had sufficient weight of opinion and justice on their

---

[1] *Gesta Coll. Carth.* i. 4 (*PL.* xi, cols. 1260–1). 'Neque enim aliud aut belli laboribus agimus, aut pacis consiliis ordinamus, nisi ut verum Dei cultum orbis nostri plebs devota custodiat, ut etiam Donatistas vel terrore vel monitu olim implere convenerat, qui Africam, hoc est, regni nostri maximam partem, et saecularibus officiis fideliter servientem, vano errore et dissensione superflua decolorant.'

[2] *Gesta Coll. Carth.* i. 4 (*PL.* xi, cols. 1260–1), 'id ante omnia servaturus ut ea quae circa Catholicam legem vel olim ordinavit antiquitas . . . novella subreptione submota integra et inviolata custodias'.

[3] *Gesta Coll. Carth.* 1. 4 (*PL.* xi, cols. 1260–1). 'Quod si intra praestitutum tempus studiose Donatistarum episcopi declinaverint convenire trini edicti vocatione contumacium tempora concludantur.'

side for the Emperor to revert at least to the position adopted by Constantine in 321. The subsequent debate between delegates would have developed into a stalemate.

When, therefore, the proceedings opened, the Donatists were present in force; the Catholics, however, had their eighteen delegates only. Marcellinus invited the Donatists to state whether they had chosen their representatives to negotiate with the Catholics under the terms of the rescript. Emeritus of Caesarea, a long-winded, pedantic, and exasperating speaker, replied that the case should not be decided on the model of a lawsuit but according to the precepts of the Scriptures.[1] He wanted a full Council to be held in the presence of all the bishops. The Catholics opposed this vigorously, and their motive, as stated by Augustine in his short account of the conference written later in the year, was that they feared that the mass of Donatist bishops and the mob might disturb proceedings.[2] They were not, however, able to have their way entirely, and the Donatists managed this part of the proceedings with skill. After both sides had read the Mandates with which they had provided their representatives for the debate, Petilian stated that his colleagues wanted to see the Catholic signatories. They were not satisfied that every individual who claimed to be a bishop was in fact such.[3] He quoted examples from his own experience of how the Catholics had set up 'shadow' or titular sees with the sole object of increasing their apparent numbers. He wanted these interlopers to be confronted by Donatist bishops in the same area and exposed. At the same time, he claimed, the Catholics had been misinforming the Emperor about the numerical strength of their adversaries. Marcellinus could now satisfy himself that the Donatists were not merely a trivial sect.[4]

On this occasion the Catholics objected, and Alypius made a determined effort to start the debate proper, but Marcellinus intended to give the Donatists the utmost latitude within the framework of the Imperial rescript.[5] He assented to Petilian's request, and the rival clergy, having been collected from all over Carthage, began to file in from opposite ends of the building. As a secretary read out each name, the bishop who had been

[1] *Gesta Coll. Carth.* i. 31 (*PL.* xi, col. 1269). He changed his ground later on.
[2] *Breviculus Collationis,* i. vii, (*PL.* xliii, col. 616).
[3] *Gesta Coll. Carth.* i. 59, 61 (*PL.* xi, cols. 1273–4).
[4] *Gesta Coll. Carth.* i. 65 (*PL.* xi, cols. 1274–5) and i. 165 (*PL.* xi, col. 1323).
[5] *Gesta Coll. Carth.* i. 89 and 93 (*PL.* xi, cols. 1278–9).

called stepped forward. If he had an opponent in his diocese, the latter faced him and said, 'I recognize him', with or without some opprobrious comment. The whole of the rest of the day's proceedings were occupied by this vast identification parade. From the little incidents which arose as two bitter rivals confronted each other, one gathers much about the life of the Churches in the remoter parts of the North African provinces.

The Catholics were called first. On the whole, matters were fairly orderly. The bishops behaved like well-disciplined functionaries. They came forward, identified themselves, and stood down. Some curious little asides are recorded. At the outset there was confusion over the identity of one cleric's see. Which Summa did Bishop Felix claim as his?[1] This was quickly straightened out, and from then on Marcellinus had matters under control. The Catholics in the Proconsular province and from Byzacena began to reveal their strength. Catholic bishops came forward with the confident assertions that 'in my see, I have no rival bishop, nor have ever had one',[2] or that 'the whole city has been Catholic from time immemorial'.[3] In some cases the Donatist minorities had been reduced to insignificance, in others the Donatists had not been able to replace clergy who had died. Like their opponents, the Catholics had seldom hesitated to use force to achieve results when the local situation had favoured them. In some places they were alleged to have been increasing their numbers by accepting Donatist clergy who had been expelled from communion for adultery and other crimes.[4]

As might be expected, the Numidian sees provided most material for recrimination. At one town near Milevis the newly appointed Catholic bishop was accused of 'terrorizing' the inhabitants;[5] in another town, it was alleged that Donatist dwellings had been destroyed; there was a bitter exchange between Petilian and his Catholic rival at Constantine, Fortunatus. The

---

[1] *Gesta Coll. Carth.* i. 113–16 (*PL.* xi, col. 1281).

[2] *Gesta Coll. Carth.* i. 120, 'Aptus episcopus plebis Tigiensis. Idem dixit "Praesto sum. Nec habui nec habemus episcopum Donatistam"' (*PL.* xi, col. 1282).

[3] *Gesta Coll. Carth.* i. 121, 'Urbicosus episcopus Eguilguilitanae. "Praesto sum sed Catholica est omnis ex vetustate"' (*PL.* xi, col. 1284).

[4] *Gesta Coll. Carth.* i. 129–30. 'Niventius episcopus plebis Tunugabensis. "Praesto sum. Non habeo contra me episcopum." Primianus episcopus dixit. "Damnatus est in causa adulterii, tamen illic fuit usque ad annum praesentem"' (*PL.* xi, col. 1298).

[5] Ibid. i. 134, '"Per violentiam unde exclusit omnes clericos et presbyteros. . . . Etiam mei terrore succubuerunt omnes, qui in eodem loco constituti erant." Severianus episcopus Ecclesiae catholicae. "Mentitur"' (*PL.* xi, col. 1311).

latter accused the Donatist leader of breaking up the altars in the Catholic churches.[1] In a number of instances the Donatist greeted the Catholic bishop with the words, 'I recognize my persecutor.'

When the secretary had finished there were two hundred and sixty-six Catholic bishops on the roll. It was now the Donatists' turn. The concourse was becoming visibly more weary, as up to then the proceedings had been conducted standing. Marcellinus attempted to persuade both parties to be seated. On behalf of the Donatists Petilian refused the offer, though with more grace than usual. Christ had stood before His judge, he urged; the Donatist clergy, aged and ailing though many of them were, would stand before theirs. He asked that the names of the Donatist bishops should be read without further delay.[2]

The same procedure was repeated though, as the day wore on, tempers became more frayed and incidents multiplied. If anything, the Donatists were less disciplined and more arrogant than their opponents. They were at pains wherever possible to show that they had no rivals in their sees. Often enough they answered the roll, 'I have no *traditor* against me.' There was early trouble when Felix, Donatist Bishop of Rome, came forward to sign.[3] He was immediately challenged by Aurelius of Carthage. This time, Petilian did not insist. The position of bishops in provinces overseas should not be prejudiced, and the Catholics contented themselves with affirming that they were in communion with Innocentius. A few minutes later Marcellinus and the Catholics made a final vain effort to bring these proceedings to a close. The Donatists, however, were adamant. There had been much debate about comparative numbers. They intended to show that in Numidia at any rate the Catholics had no hold.[4] Marcellinus had to give way and the roll-call continued. Soon afterwards the second exchange took place between Petilian and Alypius, to which attention has already been drawn.[5] Alypius objected to the presence of Donatists from village bishoprics, and Petilian replied; the Catholics had tried to establish themselves in the country districts but had failed

[1] *Gesta Coll. Carth.* i. 139 (*PL.* xi, col. 1316).
[2] *Gesta Coll. Carth.* i. 145 (*PL.* xi, cols. 1319–20).
[3] Felix signed the register third after the Numidian Primate and the Donatist Bishop of Carthage. He had escaped to Africa with other refugees after the sack of Rome by Alaric in the previous year.
[4] Petilian, *Gesta Coll. Carth.* i. 165 (*PL.* xi, col. 1323).   [5] See *supra*, p. 49.

through lack of support. At this stage, Alypius was rivalling
the Donatists in producing legalistic and time-wasting arguments. A moment later he was on his feet again, objecting to
the signature of a Donatist presbyter in place of the bishop of
the diocese who was blind, and there was further commotion
when one of the Catholic leaders in Numidia accused a Donatist of murdering a rival.[1] There were many more charges
and counter-charges before the list drew to its close. Then, one
final incident in which the Donatists were alleged, with a certain
amount of justification, to have introduced the name of a corpse.[2]
They prevaricated, and this made matters worse. The Catholics
for the first time became really conscious of the need to present
the Commissioner with evidence that they had a majority, and
Alypius started an intensive search for stragglers in the Catholic
camp. In a mood of growing exasperation the count began.
The first figures were 266 Catholics to 279 Donatists—the
Donatists were in a majority of thirteen.[3] Then the Catholics
sprang a surprise. They claimed that some bishops were absent
through illness or other cause but nevertheless had signed the
Mandate. Alypius had those who could walk brought in, and
one way or another a further 20 signatures were added; so it
was 286 to 279.[4] The names of five Donatist delegates brought
their total to 284. Both parties now made a final effort to include more names of absent clerics, but this time Marcellinus
cut matters short. It was late, and the meeting broke up for an
adjournment until 3 June.

The Conference reassembled for its second session. This time
the Donatists had their way, and the proceedings never
really began. At the outset they showed that they were determined to obstruct, and again turned an invitation from the
President to seat themselves into a wrangle over ritual purity.[5]
They quoted the words of the Psalmist that the righteous should
not sit down with sinners, and Marcellinus let them stand.

---

[1] *Gesta Coll. Carth.* i. 187 (*PL.* xi, col. 1330).

[2] *Gesta Coll. Carth.* i. 207–8 (*PL.* xi, cols. 1344–6). The Donatist Bishop of Cessita
died *en route*, having deputed a colleague to sign the Mandate on his behalf. It
took a considerable amount of wrangling to elicit this explanation.

[3] *Gesta Coll. Carth.* i. 213–14 (*PL.* xi, col. 1350).

[4] *Gesta Coll. Carth.* i. 215–16 (*PL.* xi, col. 1350).

[5] *Gesta Coll. Carth.* ii. 3 (*PL.* xi, cols. 1353–4). The Donatists had some justification. To be seated could be interpreted that they were at peace with their opponents. At the Council of Cirta this gesture ended the dispute between Secundus of
Tigisis and his colleagues; Optatus, i. 14.

They then complained that the minutes of the first day's proceedings were not ready, and demanded an adjournment. The Catholics were not able to refuse, though delay was no advantage to them. Outside the populace was becoming restive, as the Donatists had put about the rumour that their opponents had been late in drawing up their original acceptance of the Conference and had therefore become defaulters.[1] Marcellinus, however, scrupulously fair on matters of procedure and detail, declared an adjournment for six days. When the final meeting opened the Donatists could hardly claim that they had been refused the necessary time in which to prepare their case.

At first light on 8 June both sides faced each other for the decisive encounter. The debate went on without apparent intermission until nightfall.

The *Acta* which were drawn up at the time make difficult reading, and naturally Augustine's *Breviculus Collationis*, which was written as a sort of guide to the general reader, does less than full justice to the Donatists. Petilian's plan of action seems to have been the following. The Conference was from thenceforward to be regarded as the preliminary hearing of a lawsuit, which in any case should be referred back to the Imperial Court.[2] Meantime, proceedings were to be made as complicated and intricate as possible. The immediate objective was to secure that the Catholics should be put into the position of the accusing party, on the grounds that they had first demanded the conference and eight years before had submitted their request to the Proconsul Septiminus. Once that point was made, the Donatists would challenge the personal worth of their accusers and thus, on Donatist standards, their fitness as clergy.[3] Petilian had prepared a good deal of evidence against two members at least of the Catholic delegation, Augustine and Fortunatus of Constantine. Both were former Manichees, and in the case of Augustine he could make the point that the Catholic Primate of Numidia, Megalius, had once refused to consecrate him bishop.[4] If the debate developed on the general nature of the Church,

---

[1] *Gesta Coll. Carth.* ii. 72 (*PL.* xi, col. 1363).

[2] The Donatist line of argument is elaborated by Montanus, bishop of Zama, in *Gesta Coll. Carth.* iii. 62 (*PL.* xi, col. 1373).

[3] Emeritus episcopus dixit, 'Ecce jam professus es partem. Dic quando petisti, dic per quos petisti', *Gesta Coll. Carth.* iii. 60 (*PL.* xi, col. 1373), also iii. 85. Augustine, *Ad Donatistas post Collationem*, i. 44 (*PL.* xliii, col. 679).

[4] Augustine's answer, *Gesta Coll. Carth.* iii. 247 (*PL.* xi, col. 1406).

the Donatists would assert their view that the true Church was that which kept its Sacraments pure,[1] and that the fact that their opponents had induced various congregations in other provinces to enter into communion with them was not relevant. They had used the six days' adjournment to prepare a comprehensive brief.[2] Marcellinus was called upon to arbitrate in an affair between Africans as to which community *in Africa* was to be regarded as the rightful claimant to the Catholic name.[3] Once that was established, communion with the outside world would follow automatically.

For what must have been several hours Petilian and Emeritus of Caesarea attempted to gain their argument. Augustine, however, who up to now had taken little part in the debate, began to come into his own. Together with the Imperial Commissioner he systematically frustrated this manœuvre. Taking his stand on the Emperor's order which he had recited on the first day of the Conference, Marcellinus informed the Donatists that for the time being, though without prejudice, he must regard their opponents as the 'Catholic Church', and that they themselves should bring forward their objections to that claim.[4] Augustine then spoke. While agreeing that the Catholics had demanded a conference in A.D. 403 and again in the previous year, he insisted that the Donatists while at Ravenna in 406 had also requested one themselves. Marcellinus accordingly ruled that as both sides had asked for the conference to take place, neither could be regarded as the accuser in the legal sense.[5] Augustine then urged that the documents dealing with the origins of the dispute be investigated. Despite Petilian's protest, he carried his argument that these documents would show clearly that the Donatists had originally made accusations which they had failed to prove, and further, by failing to abide by Constantine's decision, had broken the unity of the Church.[6]

---

[1] *Gesta Coll. Carth.* iii. 102. Speech by Gaudentius of Thamugadi (*PL.* xi, cols. 1381–2).

[2] *Gesta Coll. Carth.* iii. 258. This is one of the most lucid statements of Donatist doctrine that we possess. See below, p. 321.

[3] Ibid. iii. 99. Speech by Emeritus of Caesarea (*PL.* xi, cols. 1380–1).

[4] *Gesta Coll. Carth.* iii. 92 (*PL.* xi, col. 1379) and iii. 103, where he appears to accept the Catholic claim that 'Catholic' meant 'universal in extent' and not 'whole' in respect of doctrine.

[5] Ibid. iii. 117 (*PL.* xi, col. 1384).

[6] Ibid. iii. 176–9 (*PL.* xi, cols. 1393–4); Augustine, *Ad Donatistas post Collationem,*

Once this procedure had been adopted, the Catholics were never in much danger. On the purely historical issue, the Donatists could claim only that Caecilian had been condemned by an African Council, that the Emperor Constantine had not been over-impressed by Caecilian personally, and that he had eventually granted them a grudging toleration. The Catholics, however, could point to the favourable judgements at Rome and at Arles, followed by the Emperor's own rescript to the *Vicarius Africae* Eumalius in November 316. The Donatists were forced to prevaricate their way out of one situation by asserting that there were two clerics called Donatus, and that it was the 'other Donatus', and not Donatus the Great, whom Miltiades' Council had condemned in 313. This, however, lost them the only point they had been able to score.[1] Petilian had previously produced documents which indicated that Miltiades had himself been a *traditor* and had employed *traditores* among his clergy, and hence that his judgement in favour of Caecilian had been prejudiced, if not invalid. The Catholics were taken momentarily off their guard, but immediately rallied by arguing that if there were two different individuals called Donatus, it was quite likely that there were two deacons in Rome called Strato, and that Miltiades' deacon of that name had not been a *traditor* at all.[2] In addition, when the argument shifted to points of doctrine, the Catholics naturally found Marcellinus favourable to their interpretations. The Commissioner was prepared to accept their view that the true Church was that which was extended throughout the world, and that the field referred to in the Parable of the Tares was to be identified with the Church and not with the world.[3] That is to say, the Church on earth was a mixed body containing good and evil, and not, as the Donatists claimed, a society of the elect 'without spot or wrinkle'. When pressed by the Donatists, Marcellinus fell back on the argument that he would deliver a general judgement and not a verdict on each individual

---

25. 44 (*PL.* xliii, col. 680). He describes the Donatists' fear of approaching the main issue in the picturesque phrase, 'similar to that experienced by demons on the approach of an exorcist'.

[1] *Gesta Coll. Carth.* (chapter headings), iii. 539–40 (*PL.* xi, col. 1256); Augustine, *Breviculus Collationis*, iii. 20. 38.

[2] *Gesta Coll. Carth.* (chapter headings), iii. 492–522 (*PL.* xi, cols. 1255–6); Augustine, *Ad Donatistas post Collationem*, 13. 17.

[3] *Gesta Coll. Carth.* iii. 275–7 (*PL.* xi, col. 1417).

question, as they would have preferred.[1] Further, he allowed the
Catholics to use evidence of Donatist inconsistency taken from
their handling of Maximianism, despite the fact that the Donatists claimed that this was a purely internal schism, and bore
no analogy to their differences with the Catholics.[2] He was not
prepared to accept the view that the sin of being a *traditor*
descended on all African Catholics, just as the sin of Adam had
compromised all mankind.[3]

The conference turned more and more on the events of a
hundred years previously, and here the Catholics gradually
gained a decisive advantage. Finally, Marcellinus asked whether
the Donatists had any documents to produce against the Catholic *Acta* showing that both Felix of Aptungi and Caecilian had
been declared innocent of *traditio*, and they were unable to say
more than that some of the evidence had been destroyed.[4] They
then demanded that a decision be given on each individual point
which had been made during the debate. But by this time the
Catholics were in full cry. The Donatist objections were brushed
aside. 'If there is nothing more to be read let the two parties
retire', Marcellinus ordered.[5] Then, that same night, by the light
of lamps and candles, without summoning another session, he
had the delegates recalled and pronounced sentence in favour
of the Catholics.[6] The great Conference was over.

On 26 June, Marcellinus announced his decision to the
authorities throughout the African provinces.[7] The *ordines* of the
cities, private proprietors, bailiffs and lessees of Imperial states,
the headmen (*seniores*) of villages, all were enjoined to enforce
the ban on Donatist assemblies and to confiscate Donatist property. The Donatists for their part carried out their plan of
appealing direct to the Emperor.[8] But if they had hoped that
Honorius' difficulties would stand them in good stead, they were
disappointed. At Ravenna the Emperor received Marcellinus'

---

[1] *Gesta Coll. Carth.* iii. 278 (*PL.* xi, col. 1417), 312–14, and 579 (headings) (*PL.* xi, cols. 1249 and 1258).

[2] *Breviculus Collationis*, iii. 8. 11 (*PL.* xliii, cols. 629–30).

[3] *Gesta Coll. Carth.* iii. 313 (*PL.* xi, col. 1249).

[4] *Gesta Coll. Carth.* (chapter headings), iii. 584 (*PL.* xi, col. 1258).

[5] *Gesta Coll. Carth.* iii. 585 (*PL.* xi, col. 1258).

[6] Ibid. iii. 587; Augustine, *Ad Donatistas post Collationem*, 12. 16 and 35. 58 (*PL.* xliii, col. 689), 'nocte dicta sententia est'. The Donatists complained bitterly of this, and alleged that they were held as prisoners during the final act.

[7] Printed in *PL.* xi, col. 1418.

[8] Possidius, *Vita*, 13; Augustine, *Ad Donatistas post Collationem*, 12. 16.

report and acted upon it. On 30 January 412 he dispatched an edict to Seleucus the *Praefectus Praetorio* proscribing Donatism. The Donatist clergy were to be exiled and, separated one from another, dispatched to remote corners of the Empire. Donatism was henceforth a criminal offence, punishable by a scale of fines ranging from 50 lb. of gold for a member of the senatorial class to 5 lb. for a plebeian. Circumcellions were to be mulcted 10 lb. of silver. *Coloni* and slaves could be beaten with rods. All Donatist property was to be handed over to the Catholics, but, as in previous edicts, the death penalty was not prescribed.[1]

The victory of Augustine was therefore complete. The Donatists had been brought to a conference, out-argued, and proscribed by the due process of the law. The real test, however, was to be the use to which he could put his success. Previous experience had shown that it was one thing to defeat the Donatists in debate, another to convert the North African provinces to Catholicism.

[1] *Codex Theodosianus*, xvi. 5. 52.

XVIII

THE AFTERMATH OF THE
CONFERENCE

A.D. 412–29

IN the seventeen years which remained of Roman rule in Africa the Catholics left nothing undone to make their success lasting. In contrast to the situation in previous periods of 'Unity' they had the full support of the chief military and executive officials in Roman Africa. Marcellinus, his brother the Proconsul Apringius, Count Macedonius, the Tribune Dulcitius, Counts Darius and Boniface were all to be numbered among Augustine's friends, and were zealous in putting down Donatism. As a first step the results of the great Conference were given as much publicity as possible. Complete copies of the official report were posted up on the walls of the Theoprepia, the principal Donatist church in Carthage, and sent to the provincial capitals.[1] Augustine himself, realizing that people would not be bothered to read the enormous volume of the report, at once compiled a précis in three books in which the salient facts were brought out for the benefit of the educated layman.[2] He also addressed a lengthy tract to the Donatists themselves, emphasizing the fairness of the proceedings and urging them to pay no heed to the rumours which were being put about by their leaders.[3] In northern Numidia, Augustine's friends at Constantine, Milevis, and Thagaste were displaying equal activity, taking over both the congregations and property of their rivals. On 14 June 412 a Council of Catholic Numidian bishops met at Constantine and addressed a further warning to the Donatists not to delay reconciliation with the Great Church.[4]

But defeated though they were, the Donatists did not rally *en masse* to the Catholic side. As after the publication of the Edict of Unity in 405, the greater part of the defections were from among the town communities. Augustine enjoyed a great personal triumph when he preached in Constantine to former

---

[1] Augustine, *Ep.* 139. 185. 2. 6.   [2] Id. *Retractationes*, ii. 65.
[3] Id. *Ad Donatistas post Collationem*, 1. 1 (*PL.* xliii, col. 651).
[4] Augustine, *Ep.* 141.

members of Petilian's congregation, and at Hippo he again drove the Donatist bishop from the city.[1] In Cuicul (Djemila) the Catholic bishop, Cresconius, erected a large and ornate basilica for former Donatists, and an inscription in verse preserved in a mosaic proclaimed that unity had been secured.[2] At Hippo Diarrhytos, Bishop Florentius also constructed a new church for converts, and this he named 'Florentia' in memory of his achievement.[3] Even in the towns, however, the Donatists were often able to maintain cohesion. The first reaction to Marcellinus' sentence was that 'the Imperial Commissioner had been bribed' and that, in any event, he was merely carrying out an Imperial order.[4] Rumours and propaganda were sedulously put about and, to judge from Augustine's recriminations, not without effect. He rails at those who delayed conversion out of 'superstitious regard for family tradition', obstinacy, pride, and such like.[5] The Donatist episcopate, too, seems to have been able to avoid the worst punishments ordered by the Emperor. Petilian, if out of Constantine, nevertheless remained in Numidia, and was able to keep contact with his fellow bishops by irregular councils.[6] In Mauretania he was supported by Emeritus, with whom Augustine now found himself obliged to enter into controversy.[7] New Donatist ordinations did in fact take place. Donatist pamphleteers were as persistent as ever, and Donatist bishops remained in control of such centres as Caesarea and Thamugadi as well as the more obscure settlements like Ala Milaria (Benian) in Mauretania.

The real resistance, however, to Catholicism took place, as might be expected, in the Numidian countryside. In some instances the Donatist episcopate which had previously been moderate rallied to the cause of the extremists. Macrobius of Hippo, who had stood out and rebuked the Circumcellions, himself became the leader of a Circumcellion band, and despite the

---

[1] Augustine, *Epp.* 139. 2 and 144. Cf. *Ep.* 142.

[2] E. Albertini, *Bull. Arch. du Comité*, 1922, pp. xxvi–xxxii. The mosaic indicates the feeling of triumph felt by the urban Catholics at this moment:

'Undique [se] visendi studio cristiana decurrit
Aetas in unum congeriem, Deo dicere laudes.'

[3] Augustine, *Sermo* 359. 9, 'basilica Florentia' (*PL.* xxxix, col. 1597).

[4] Augustine, *Ad Donatistas post Collationem*, 1. 1, *Ep.* 141. 1.

[5] Id. *Contra Gaudentium*, i. 33. 43.

[6] Ibid. 37. 48.

[7] He wrote *Ad Emeritum post Collationem*, c. 414. The text has not survived, but the gist is contained in *Retractationes*, ii. 72.

Imperial decree kept the Donatist churches open on the estates.[1] Terrible acts of vengeance were perpetrated in the outlying areas of Augustine's diocese against those who rallied to Catholicism. Augustine himself speaks of his colleagues as sharing 'the toils and dangers' of the church in Numidia, and he relates specific instances of Donatist fanaticism immediately following the Conference.[2] Generally averse to using physical compulsion against his opponents, he was driven to urge that force and constraint be used against 'the uncharitable wretches'.[3] But the fury of the Circumcellions was not to be quenched by the forces that still remained to the Roman power.

In 413 the Catholics suffered a political setback. From the moment he gave his decision against the Donatists, Count Marcellinus had been taking an active part in destroying their influence. Naturally, he had accepted Augustine as his adviser, and had put into practice Augustine's theories as to how the obstinate should be treated. Hard labour replaced mutilation or death among the scale of penalties.[4] In the spring of 412 he appears to have been in Numidia trying cases of Donatists accused of violent crime, and throughout the year he kept in constant touch with Augustine.[5] The friendship between the two men is strikingly revealed in Augustine's letters of this period. But next year North Africa was swept into the maelstrom of intrigue and civil war which racked the declining years of the Empire, and Marcellinus was among the principal victims.

Since he had frustrated Attalus' attempt to set foot in Africa Count Heraclian had become one of the most feared men in the western provinces. He was all-powerful in Africa but his rule was harsh, and he was hated not only by the provincials but by the immigrants who had fled from Rome. He retained Honorius' trust, however, and in January 413 was declared Consul.[6] Nevertheless, rumours of his misrule had begun to reach Ravenna, and Heraclian feared recall. Like others before him he found the easiest method of bringing pressure

---

[1] Augustine, *Ep.* 139. 2.   [2] Ibid. 4, also 133 and 134.
[3] *Contra Gaudentium*, i. 33. 43; *Sermo* 138. 3; *Ep.* 185. 6. 23.
[4] Ibid. 133. 1. Augustine also wrote to Marcellinus' brother Apringius, the Proconsul, in the same sense.
[5] Ibid. 136, 139. The cases of the Circumcellions may, however, have been referred to Marcellinus for trial in Carthage, rather than during his visit to Numidia.
[6] Seeck, *Regesten*, p. 324.

to bear on the Emperor was to ration the corn fleet. At first
this proved successful, and as late as 12 June Honorius was
still dispatching rescripts to him in Africa.[1] But just at this time
the greater part of the mobile forces in Italy were engaged in
Gaul against the usurpers Jovinus and Sebastianus and against
the Franks. Heraclian considered that the moment had come
to bid for Imperial power himself. He sailed from Carthage
with an enormous fleet, landed near Rome, and advanced on
Ravenna. The only troops available to Honorius were under
the command of the *Comes Domesticorum*, Count Marinus, but
these were deployed skilfully, covering the main pass through
the Apennines by which Heraclian must gain the Flaminian
Way in his march to Ravenna. The decisive encounter took
place at Ocriculum (Otricoli), and once again Honorius' luck
held. Heraclian was repulsed, his army scattered, and he fled to
his ships. Marinus gave him no respite. On 5 July Honorius
condemned him to death. Marinus followed him to Carthage,
arrested him, and he was executed.[2]

Then follows a curious and tragic incident reminiscent of the
fate of Count Theodosius after his defeat of Firmus in 376. The
story is told in Augustine's letter 151 to the *Praefectus Praetorio*
Caecilian. Marinus had evidently been ordered to make a
thorough purge of Heraclian's supporters in North Africa. For
reasons which may have been personal, and are at any rate not
at all clear, his suspicions were directed to Marcellinus and his
brother Apringius, the Proconsul of the previous year. Both were
suddenly arrested at the conclusion of a private interview with
Marinus. The African Catholics intervened. Augustine hastened
to Carthage; a bishop was sent to intercede at the Imperial
Court. Caecilian was himself in Carthage and Augustine used
all his influence on behalf of his friends. It was in vain. Marcellinus and Apringius were brought from prison, given a summary trial, and, on 13 September, beheaded.[3]

This was a great personal blow to Augustine, who immediately
left for Hippo and put his thoughts on record in a letter to
Caecilian. It was the severest diplomatic setback he was to
suffer in his lifetime. But were the Donatists to blame? Augustine
suspected that they were behind the denunciation which led
to their enemy's arrest.[4] Orosius and Jerome are still more

[1] Seeck, *Regesten*, p. 326.   [2] Id. *Untergang*, vi. 52–53.
[3] Augustine, *Ep.* 151. 6.   [4] Ibid. 3–9.

blunt.[1] Certainly in two cases, those of Count Theodosius and Marcellinus, they had the satisfaction of seeing their persecutor executed at the Emperor's own orders. Coincidence is not, however, evidence and the mystery of the real reasons behind Marcellinus' death must remain unsolved.

This time, however, no change of policy towards the Donatists resulted. Rescripts dispatched to Julianus the Proconsul of Africa on 17 June[2] and 30 August 414[3] reminded the provincials that the death of Marcellinus did not mean the vindication of Donatism, and the anti-heretical legislation of the previous twenty years was repeated. The African Catholics, supported by the new military commander, *Comes* Macedonius, kept up the pressure. From Augustine's sermons and correspondence of this period and the canons of the Catholic Councils we learn of the frequent seizure of Donatist estates. Augustine justified these measures by appeal to Scripture; the wealth of the sinner had been laid up for the righteous (Proverbs xiii. 22). He told the Donatists that the bequests of pious benefactors had been made 'to the Church', not 'to the party of Donatus'.[4] In 418 the Council of Carthage urged the Catholic bishops not to delay the spoliation of their rivals. Those who neglected their duty in this respect would come under ecclesiastical censure.[5]

The late summer of the same year witnessed a supreme effort by Augustine to win over his opponent, Emeritus of Caesarea. The story of his visit to the capital of Mauretania and what happened there is graphically recounted by Augustine himself.[6] Evidently there had been some major ecclesiastical conflict among the Catholics at Caesarea, and Augustine, accompanied by Alypius and other friends among the Numidian episcopate, went as Papal Legate to investigate—an astonishing piece of evidence for the growth of Papal authority in the African provinces in the last decades of Roman rule. Emeritus, who was in hiding in the province, heard of Augustine's arrival and met him.[7]

[1] Orosius, *Historiae*, vii. 42; Jerome, *Contra Pelagianos*, 3. 6. 19 (*PL*. xxiii, col. 616).
[2] *Cod. Theod.* xvi. 5. 54 to Julianus, Proconsul.   [3] Ibid. 55.
[4] Augustine, *In Ioannis Evang. Tract.* vi. 25; *Ep.* 185. 9. 36 and 37.
[5] *Codex Canonum*, Canons 121, 123, and 124. 'Ita placuit, ut quicumque negligunt loca ad suam cathedram pertinentia in catholicam unitatem lucrari . . . '.
[6] *Sermo ad Caesareensis ecclesiae plebem* and *De Gestis cum Emerito* (*PL*. xliii, cols. 690–706). See also P. Monceaux, *Histoire littéraire*, vi. 174 ff.—an excellent description.
[7] Quite possibly, as Augustine says, out of a desire to see him (*Contra Gaudentium*, i. 14. 15).

After exchanging greetings, the Donatist bishop made the enigmatic remark, 'I cannot refuse what you wish, but I can wish what I wish.'[1] The two went into a basilica, where Augustine preached to the congregation, many of whom had known the Donatist as their bishop. Emeritus was present. Augustine implored him to make up his mind. The congregation was moved. 'Here or nowhere!' they shouted, but Emeritus kept silent.[2] He did, however, consent to come to the church of Deuterius, the Catholic bishop, two days later, ostensibly for a discussion. The day came, 20 September 418, a huge congregation assembled, including some who were Donatists at heart. Augustine was supported by Alypius,. Possidius, and three Mauretanian bishops.[3] Had he succeeded, it would have been his greatest hour. Donatism would have suffered a crushing blow. In the eyes of posterity Catholicism would have triumphed in the most convincing of ways, in the moral and intellectual victory over the champion of a rival view. But this was not to be. Emeritus also rose to the occasion. Whatever may have been his hesitations the previous day, he showed no signs of weakness now. Augustine evidently expected a short discussion, ending with Emeritus and Deuterius walking out as joint bishops in the unity of the Catholic Church. He was disappointed, and one can read the rising note of disappointment throughout his sermon. He made every point he could: Emeritus' drafting of the savage decree of Bagai, his inconsistency in freely accepting the Maximianists back into the Donatist fold, then his part at the recent Conference at Carthage, and finally even an appeal to his feelings as an African. It was in vain.[4]

Emeritus left Augustine to speak and remained impressive in his silence. Augustine raged at his 'cruel obstinacy'[5] but could do nothing. The Donatist had faced persecution and prevailed.. The man who in the last quarter of a century had been identified with the triumphs and defeats of his Church, whose character shows so much the mixture of barbarism and culture

[1] Augustine, *Sermo*, 'Non possum nolle quod vultis, sed possum velle quod volo' (*PL*. xliii, cols. 689–90).

[2] Augustine, *Sermo*, 'Aut hic, aut nusquam.'

[3] *De Gestis cum Emerito*, i.

[4] Ibid., particularly chaps. x and xi, cols. 704 to 706. Emeritus reminds one of Cranmer in 1556. Both were old men at the moment of ordeal, both were tempted to deny their life's work for the sake of personal security; both hesitated before the choice, and both finally triumphed over themselves.

[5] Ibid. 12, 'Constantem se putat fortitudo crudelis.'

that underlies Donatism, possessed in the hour of trial the courage of his convictions. The Catholics consoled themselves by spreading rumours of his conversion. These Augustine had to deny.[1]

The occasion for this came two years later. An attempt was being made by the tribune and notary Dulcitius to force the Donatist bishop, Gaudentius, to surrender the cathedral of Thamugadi. It is the last incident in the annals of Donatism of which there exists a full record. Gaudentius was successor to the famous Bishop Optatus.[2] He had taken a part, but not too prominent a one, in the directing counsels of the Church, and had been one of the Donatist mandatories at the Conference of Carthage. Here his remarks had been shrewd and to the point. After the sentence he had evidently returned to Thamugadi and remained in undisturbed possession of his see. This situation lasted until A.D. 420. Then the Imperial officials felt themselves strong enough to penetrate into an area that had seen the discomfiture of Paul and Macarius three-quarters of a century before. Dulcitius arrived at Thamugadi and demanded the surrender of the Donatist cathedral. He was met with a blunt refusal. Supported by his congregation, Gaudentius retired to the safety of the walls of his citadel whence, from its position on a vantage-point overlooking the whole town, he could defy the authorities.[3] In the event of force being used, he declared his intention of burning the building with himself and everyone else inside.[4] Dulcitius in perplexity appealed to Augustine, and a lively controversy ensued between Gaudentius from his fortress and Augustine in his study at Hippo. Many months must have elapsed while the two works *Contra Gaudentium* were being written, and at the end of them the reader is none the wiser as to the outcome. Archaeological evidence, however, suggests that the cathedral of Thamugadi was not burnt down,[5] and Augustine for his part makes no reference to any surrender by Gaudentius.

[1] Augustine, *Contra Gaudentium*, i. 14. 15 (*PL.* xliii, col. 712).

[2] *Contra Gaudentium*, i. 38. 51 (*PL*, col. 758), 'tuus decessor Optatus'. See essay by Monceaux, *Histoire littéraire*, vi. 190 ff.

[3] At this time the cathedral and outbuildings covered about five acres. There was plenty of room for storing oil and grain.

[4] *Contra Gaudentium*, i. 1 (*PL.*, col. 707).

[5] Some traces of burning were found over the cathedral area, but these may well belong to the sixth century and not to the period of Gaudentius.

The story of Donatism in Roman Africa closes as it began on a note of defiance. From a hint dropped by Augustine, in his long epistle to Count Boniface dated about A.D. 417, we learn that some of the Donatists were taking the first steps towards political separation from the Roman Empire. These were coming to regard the Goths as possible liberators, and were considering the points in common between Donatism and Arianism.[1] As in Gildo's day, a more distant master was preferred to the representatives of Ravenna. When the Vandals arrived they may not have been wholly unwelcome to the Donatist population.

It is no easy matter to assess the extent to which the Catholics were able to enforce Unity during this final decade of Roman rule. Augustine himself sometimes appears to regard Donatism along with Manichaeism as 'finished and done with'. In his letter to Count Boniface already mentioned, he writes as though, except for a few pockets of resistance, church unity had been completely restored.[2] But in 420 he admits to Gaudentius that many of the conversions were feigned.[3] His own mind certainly was turning away from the Donatist problem to doctrinal matters—to the dispute with Pope Zosimus and to the final great controversy with Julian of Eclanum. Some of the evidence regarding the African towns which has been quoted seems to justify Augustine's view. Canons enacted at the Catholic Council at Carthage in May 418 show not simply that Catholic bishops were taking vigorous measures to bring about Unity, but that a number of former Donatist sees were being organized on terms approved by the Catholics.[4] These terms were not dissimilar to those which Bishop Gratus had attempted to enforce during the first period of Unity, 348–61. Reconciled Donatist bishops were allowed to keep their flocks, and where there were two bishops in a see the younger should give way.

Unfortunately, events in the cities were of little moment for the future history of North African Christianity. Time was against the Catholics. The steady pressure of political and

[1] *Ep.* 185. 1. 1.

[2] Ibid. 7. 30. These 'pockets' have become 'regiones' by the time Augustine writes to Gaudentius (*Contra Gaudentium*, i. 23. 26).

[3] Ibid. Some such converts persevered, however, even when they had the chance of returning to Donatism. This latter point indicates that the persecution may have been sporadic in these years rather than continuous.

[4] Cf. Augustine, *De Gestis cum Emerito*, 4, on the situation at Carthage, Hippo, Thagaste, and Constantine.

economic factors began to assert itself. The towns, as we have already seen, were ceasing to exist, and the Catholic bishopric was based on the Roman *civitas*.

There are indications too during these years that even where the Catholics had made gains their position was not secure. The letter which Bishop Honoratus wrote to Augustine about the year 428 is very instructive.[1] Both Honoratus and another cleric named Quodvultdeus had asked what was to be done in the event of barbarian invasion. 'If the Lord has commanded us to flee, in those persecutions in which we may reap the fruit of martyrdom, how much more ought we to escape by flight, if we can, from barren sufferings inflicted by the hostile incursions of barbarians.'[2] A little before they had argued: 'I do not see what good we can do to ourselves or to the people by continuing to remain in the churches, except to see before our eyes men slain, women outraged, churches burned, ourselves expiring amid torments in order to extort from us what we do not possess.'[3] A few years previously Augustine in a letter to Count Boniface had referred to 'hordes of African barbarians plundering and destroying without resistance'.[4] The Donatists were not mentioned, but even before Gaiseric had landed, Roman Africa was being threatened by these new and implacable forces.

The villages, however, where Donatism was strongest remained comparatively prosperous and unscathed. It would be unwise therefore to underestimate the importance of evidence provided by Augustine of the violence of Donatist resistance in the countryside. The story of the priest Donatus of Mutugenna throwing himself down a well rather than see Augustine was perhaps typical of many such acts of fanaticism.[5] One even hears of conversions to Donatism in this period.[6] The vehemence with which Augustine describes the outrages of the Circumcellions and the Donatist *sanctimoniales* who accompanied them suggests comparative helplessness. As he admits in his controversy with Gaudentius, if the Donatists were fewer they were

[1] *Ep.* 228 (ed. Dods, op. cit., p. 427), and Possidius, *Vita*, 30.

[2] Ibid. 4. Quodvultdeus may be Aurelius' archdeacon at Carthage who became bishop in 437. P. Courcelle, *Les Grandes Invasions germaniques*, p. 102.

[3] Ibid. 5.   [4] *Ep.* 220. 7.

[5] *Ep.* 173. Also *Ep.* 185. 7. 30.

[6] Id. *Tractatus in Ioannis Evangelium*, x. 5 (*PL.* xxxv, col. 1469), 'cum audis, "Mitte illum foras de Ecclesia", dicis, "Duco me ad partem Donati"'. Also, ibid. xiii. 13–14 (*PL.* xxxv, cols. 1499–1500).

none the less more tenacious.[1] The Donatist leaders stood firm, and one learns that their conduct influenced the masses.[2] In the countryside, archaeologists have yet to find clear evidence for the transformation of a Donatist church into a Catholic one. Unlike some of the basilicas in the towns, the village churches tend to show continuous occupation from their date of erection until the seventh century. In these circumstances, to assume that Unity was enforced would probably be mistaken; Donatism may have remained the religion of a large proportion of the African villagers in the fifth century as well as in the fourth. Perhaps, after all, the Circumcellions had the last word.

[1] *Contra Gaudentium*, i. 12. 25.   [2] *Ep.* 185. 7. 30.

XIX

THE LAST PHASE

DONATISM IN VANDAL AND BYZANTINE AFRICA

WITH the exchange of letters between Augustine and Gaudentius the continuous thread in the story of Donatism is interrupted. For the next century and a half the Donatists might have ceased to exist, so silent are the records. In 428 they are named among other dissenters in the great catalogue of heretics to whom Theodosius II forbade places of worship or the ministration of clergy.[1] With the arrival of the Vandals in 429 there is a long period of obscurity, lit only by fleeting references in Victor of Vita,[2] in a letter of Pope Leo I of August 446 to the bishops of Mauretania,[3] in Fulgentius of Ruspe,[4] and in the Arian writer Fastidiosus in the first decades of the sixth century.[5] The Donatists appear to play no part in the great issues which divided the African Church in the sixth century—in the Three Chapters controversy and in the dispute over the Byzacenan primacy. Then, quite suddenly, after an interval of more than 150 years one comes upon a series of letters from Pope Gregory to the bishops and Byzantine officials in Africa which tell an entirely different story. The Pope is gravely concerned at the situation in Africa: Donatism and also Manichaeism[6] have again taken root, and the Catholics in Numidia are in urgent need of help. But with Gregory's death there is no sequel, and this time darkness descends for good.

The historian is thus confronted with a problem. What happened to the Donatists during the Vandal and early Byzantine period? Was there a sudden revival of the movement at the

---

[1] *Codex Theodosianus*, xvi. 5. 65.

[2] Victor Vitensis, *Historia Persecutionis Africanae provinciae*, iii. 71 (*CSEL*. vii. 107). Nicasius, a Donatist convert to Arianism in A.D. 484.

[3] Leo, *Ep*. 12. 6 (*PL*. liv, col. 653). See also *PL*. xi, cols. 1434–38, for other references.

[4] Fulgentius, *Contra Sermonem Fastidiosi Ariani ad Victorem*, 10 (*PL*. lxv, col. 518).

[5] Fastidiosus, *Sermo* (*PL*. lxv, col. 375).

[6] The reference to Manichaeism comes from one of Gregory's letters, *Ep*. ii. 37, in which he forbade the bishop of Squillace to ordain Africans lest they turned out to be members of that sect.

end of the sixth century, or had Donatism merely lain dormant to burst into activity as the results of Gregory's attempts to direct the internal administration of the African Church? Is there in fact a continuity in the religious history of Numidia from the fourth to the seventh century, or was Augustine's victory more enduring than one has been led to suppose?

At present there can be no clear-cut answer. The probability is that in Proconsular Africa and in Byzacena Donatist and Catholic found themselves alike the victims of Arian persecution, and that to some extent the old lines of controversy were blurred in common suffering. The Catholics may have been able quietly to absorb their former rivals or at least reduce them to an insignificant minority. In Mauretania, too, the spread of Christianity to the native kingdoms which were coming into being appears to have been mainly Catholic as opposed to Donatist. A large number of Mauretanian bishops, for instance, attended the Catholic Council summoned at the behest of King Huneric at Carthage in 484.[1] There is at present no direct evidence for a Donatist movement in the fifth century of equal strength, though this may be accidental. In Numidia, on the other hand, existing evidence indicates that Donatism, or at least the Donatist religion whatever were its outward allegiances, survived and prospered until the native farmers were driven from their villages by the advance of nomadic tribes of the Zenata in the seventh century A.D.

In the Vandal period, the main theme in African church history is the comparatively rapid decline of the Catholic Church from the pre-eminence gained in the last generation of Roman rule. Augustine, as we have shown, had some foreboding that his work would hardly outlast him. His biographer Possidius, writing about A.D. 435, saw the beginnings of the collapse. The arrival of the Vandals seems to have caused an immediate and spontaneous outbreak of feeling against Catholicism in which the clergy were the chief sufferers. In view of Augustine's letter to Count Boniface it is hard to credit the Vandals alone with the destruction of Catholic churches that was taking place.[2]

---

[1] While thirty-five Catholic bishops from Mauretania Caesariensis attended the Conference of Carthage in 411, their number had increased to 124 at the Council of 484, but thereafter contact between Mauretania and the east declined. At the Council of Carthage in 525 Mauretania was represented by one bishop only, that of Mina (Relizane).

[2] Augustine, *Ep*. 220. The bishops, such as Simeon of Furni Major, Pampinian

Possidius describes the situation as he saw it while Augustine was still alive. Very many churches, he says, were burnt to the ground,[1] and he goes on, that 'Of the innumerable churches, he [Augustine] saw only three survive, namely those of Carthage, Hippo, and Cirta, which by God's grace were not demolished. These cities, too, still stand, protected by human and divine aid, although after Augustine's death the city of Hippo, abandoned by its inhabitants, was burnt by the enemy' (i.e. the Vandals).[2] There has been much discussion about this passage, especially its reference to Hippo. Possidius, however, was an eyewitness of what he wrote, and it may be assumed that in the Numidian Tell, where the Catholic effort had been greatest during the previous twenty years, there was a considerable revulsion of feeling. While Possidius does not mention the Donatists in this connexion, we gather from Augustine that a barbarian invasion overthrowing the Catholic hegemony would not have been unwelcome to them.[3]

Fifty years later, about the year 487, Victor, Bishop of Vita in Proconsular Africa, gives a similar account of the sudden destruction of Catholicism in the early years of the Vandal conquest. We have the impression that Gaiseric saw the Catholics as his enemy from the outset. He raged, we are told, 'in particular against the churches and basilicas of the saints, and the cemeteries and monasteries'.[4] Bishops were slain, nobles and priests were destroyed for the sake of their wealth[5]—an interesting association of the two classes at this period—churches were closed down or taken over for Arian worship, and the Imperial laws against heresy were enforced by Gaiseric's successor Huneric against the Catholics themselves. The Catholic clergy was diminished by progressive persecutions, and by 460 the

of Vita, and Mansuetus of Uruci, who were murdered at this time, were all in towns which were off the Vandals' immediate line of march. The church of Uppenna in Central Tunisia seems to have been among those destroyed in the Vandal period.

[1] *Vita Augustini*, 28, 'aedificia ecclesiarum quamplurimis locis ignibus concremata'.

[2] Ibid. This passage is discussed at length in an article by H. V. M. Dennis in *JRS*. xv, 1925, pp. 261 ff. See also Bishop Quodvultdeus of Carthage's *Sermo de Tempore Barbarico* (*PL*. xl, col. 200) on the situation in Carthage at this time. (Identification, G. Morin, *Revue Bénédictine*, xxx, 1914–19, pp. 156–62).

[3] Augustine, *Ep*. 185. i. i.

[4] Victor Vitensis, i. 1, 'praesertim in ecclesiis basilicisque sanctorum, coemeteriis monasteriisque sceleratius saeviebat.' Also I. 12.

[5] Ibid. i. 2 and 4.

number of bishoprics occupied in Vandal Africa is said to have
declined from 164 to three.[1] Victor doubtless exaggerated certain
incidents so as to emphasize the oppressive features of the Vandal
rule. He does not, however, leave the impression of the same
strenuous resistance on the part of the Catholics to Arian 'Unity'
as that maintained by the Donatists against the Catholics in the
previous century. There were evidently a certain number of conversions from Catholicism to Arianism among the wealthier
romanized classes.[2] Even in those areas which had been most
favourable to its growth, African Catholicism does not seem to
have had the inner strength to maintain the impetus provided
by Aurelius and Augustine. It was very quickly driven on to the
defensive.

The Donatists, however, appear to have been unable to take
advantage of the discomfiture of their opponents. For a generation or so an active Donatist community continued to exist, as
indicated by the controversy between Donatist and Catholic
which has been preserved in the *Contra Fulgentium*, and by the
successive editions of the *Liber Genealogus* between 427 and 463.[3]
But by the time Victor of Vita wrote (*c.* 487), references to
Donatists in Carthage have become rare. A century and a half
later Gregory, writing to Dominicus of Carthage, leaves the
impression that Donatism was not a live problem for the latter's
diocese, but only in other provinces.[4] In Proconsular Africa and
in Byzacena the Donatists never seem to have recovered from
the generation of persecution instituted by Augustine, and in the
Vandal period pass out of the history of these two provinces.[5]

[1] Ibid. i. 9. In 484 the figure was 54 in Proconsular Africa, compared with
220 in 419.
[2] Victor mentions a number of officials with Roman names, such as 'Antonius'
and 'Proculus', who were carrying out Gaiseric's anti-Catholic policy. Victor
Vitensis, i. 39 and 44.
[3] On the dating of the *Contra Fulgentium*, C. Lambot, *Revue Bénédictine*, lviii, 1948,
p. 186. For the *Liber Genealogus* see P. Monceaux, *Histoire littéraire*, iv. 102.
[4] Gregory, *Ep.* v. 3 (ed. Ewald and Hartmann, Berlin, *MGH.* 1891).
[5] One should perhaps qualify this statement by reference to the curious inscriptions probably of Vandal date from a basilica at Ammaedara (Haidra) in western
Tunisia. These record a number of martyrs who are specifically claimed to have
been executed in the Diocletianic persecution. There are, however, no known 'Am-
maedarenses', and the list appears on neither the Kalendar of Carthage nor the
Martyrology of Jerome. There is also the formula 'De donis Dei et sanctorum eius',
and a certain prominence given to ordinary members of the congregation rather
than to priests, suggesting Donatist inspiration. L. Poinssot in *Bull. Arch. du Comité*,
Séance of 20 Feb. 1934, while suspecting Donatist influence, draws attention to the
late date of this inscription.

In Mauretania also, the situation does not seem to have favoured Donatism. As Carcopino has shown, the end of the third century probably saw the evacuation of Roman military rule from western Mauretania (the area now covered by the Spanish zone and the northern part of the French zone of Morocco).[1] From this time on this area, which included such towns as Volubilis and Lixus, was ruled by native chiefs, though it retained an astonishing degree of romanization. In 456 the remaining parts of Mauretania fell to the Vandals, and thereafter became gradually separated from Roman administration and ecclesiastical influence. But, in contrast to the territories farther east, the fifth and sixth centuries are the great age of Christianity in Mauretania.[2] It seems, even, that the withdrawal of Roman administration gave a new lease of life to Roman civilization. A development took place which may have been paralleled by developments in other territories such as Wales, Brittany, and Abyssinia on the extreme edge of the Roman orbit. Native chieftains styled themselves *rex Romanorum*, or *princeps*, and appointed local *praefecti*[3] and even officials such as 'dispunctors' under them. Inscriptions on their tombs were in Latin, and Latin remained the written language of the towns. These chieftains and many of their subjects appear to have been Christians. Apart from the large increase in the numbers of bishops, there is a wealth of dated inscriptions of this period in Mauretania. The pyramidal tombs of members of some native royal house near Tiaret were ornamented with Christian symbols.[4] At Volubilis and elsewhere Christian inscriptions continue into the seventh century.[5]

Mauretania has left no saga of local Christian saints such as

[1] J. Carcopino, *Le Maroc antique*, pp. 233 ff.
[2] Ibid. p. 291; Diehl, *ILCV*. iii. 270–2, quotes some fifty Christian inscriptions from western Mauretania dated between A.D. 450–650.
[2] *CIL*. viii. 9836 (from Altava). In fifth to sixth century Wales, chieftains continued to use Latin names, and distinguished themselves by Roman titles such as *magistratus*.
[3] For instance, the *praefectus* Iugmena who with the Zabenses built the church at Berrouaghia in 474. He still used the Roman provincial method of dating. Cf. E. Albertini, *CRAI.*, 1925, p. 261; also, *CIL*. viii. 8828, 'Flavius Capito, princeps'.
[4] S. Gsell, 'Le Christianisme en Oranie', *Bulletin du Cinquantenaire de la Société de Géographie et d'Archéologie d'Oran*, April 1928, pp. 17–32. See also *Monuments antiques de l'Algérie*, ii, pp. 418–25, by the same author.
[5] Carcopino, op. cit., p. 294. See also M. Vincent's article on Aquae Sirensis, datable Christian inscriptions from which extend to A.D. 577 (*Cinquième Congrès international d'archéologie*, Algiers, 1936).

those who evangelized Wales and Brittany in this period. We know little of the form of Christianity practised. The evidence at present, however, suggests a Catholic rather than a Donatist allegiance.[1] There, big Catholic centres continued to flourish. Tipasa, as stated, developed into a great centre of pilgrimage around the tomb of the martyr Salsa. Many of the 15,000 graves in the cemetery which grew up around the shrine date from the sixth century, and include those of pilgrims from Gaul and Syria.[2] Then there is the phenomenal increase in the number of Catholic bishoprics in fifth-century Mauretania, which contrasts with their decline elsewhere. We know, too, of Donatists joining the Catholic ranks, such as Bishop Maximinus, of whom Pope Leo demanded a confession of faith.[3]

Donatism indeed had not died out in the fifth century. The excavations at Benian (Ala Milaria) revealed the presence both of a fifth-century Donatist church and a Donatist bishopric unrecorded at the Conference of Carthage. The church was built between 434 and 439 on a prominent point in the city in memory of a Donatist martyr, the *sanctimonialis* Robba, who died in 434, and contained the bodies of a number of Donatist clergy. The last was that of the presbyter Donatus, 11 March 446.[4] A dozen years later, in 458, the bishops of southern Gaul were troubled by the possibility of Donatists being among the refugees from Mauretania, fleeing from Gaiseric.[5] But that is the last direct mention we have for Mauretania. The legacy of Donatism may, however, be preserved in the puritanical work of Victor of Cartenna on the subject of penance. The *De Paenitentia*[6] cannot be claimed for certain as Donatist, but,

---

[1] We know, for instance, something of individual Catholic bishops in these remote areas. The Bishop of Tanaramusa is described as 'multis exiliis probatus' and was killed in battle against the Moors on 9 May 495 (*CIL.* viii. 9286). The tomb of Bishop Reparatus of Castellum Tingitanum (Orleansville), who died in A.D. 460 has also been unearthed. On the other hand, contact with Rome seems to have ceased about A.D. 480. The parallel with the Celtic Church in Wales is again indicated.

[2] L. Leschi, *Algérie Catholique*, Dec. 1936, pp. 74–84. See *supra*, p. 230.

[3] Leo, *Ep.* 12. 6 (A.D. 446), quoted from *PL* xi, col. 1434.

[4] *CIL.* viii. 21570–4; S. Gsell, *Les Fouilles de Benian*, Algiers, 1901, pp. 46 ff. Pilgrims, however, seem to have visited the shrine for some years later (*CIL.* viii. 21571–2 (graffiti)).

[5] Leo, *Ep.* 168. 18 (*PL.* liv, col. 1209).

[6] See B. Poschmann, 'Abendländische Kirchenbüsse', in *Münchener Studien zur historischen Theologie*, 1912, p. 166. To Victor penance was the means of rising towards the status of confessor, 'negotium confessionis'. Victor does not speak of

written from Cartenna, the centre of Rogatist exclusiveness, it betrays the harsh and uncompromising attitude towards the sinner which one associates with the Donatists.

In Numidia, as one might expect, there is more evidence for the continuance of an active Donatist community throughout Vandal and Byzantine times. We have already noted the strength of Donatist resistance to Augustine and the Imperial officials in the last two decades of Roman rule. It is reasonable to assume that, with the victory of the Vandals in 435 and their occupation of Numidia, pressure against the Donatists would be relaxed, though we know from a passage in Victor Vitensis that the Circumcellions were unpopular.[1] The new rulers of Numidia were not numerous. Outside Constantine itself no traces of the Vandals have been found in the province.[2] They made little or no effort to disturb native institutions that had taken root in the Roman period. For instance, the inscribed potsherds found at Ouled-Sidi-Thil, south of Tebessa, dated about the year A.D. 500 show that the Mancian colonate was still the established unit of native land-tenure at this time.[3] The Roman municipalities, such as Timgad, indeed declined further, and the sites may even have become deserted, but the Romano-Berber villages continued to prosper. The change of overlords appears to have brought no real modification in the life of the Numidian peasant.

The religious life of the villages seems also to have gone on without disturbance. Excavations undertaken on a large number of sites in southern and central Numidia suggest that the Christian churches decayed gradually, better buildings being replaced by poorer, until the villages themselves were deserted. There is no evidence for a wholesale destruction, but some for increasing poverty and neglect. The churches follow the same pattern as the Berber irrigation and field systems. The

reconciliation of the penitent sinner through the Church, but only through God Himself. The acts of penance which he describes are severe. 'Saccum indue, cinerem asperge, in jejunio semper ora, in oratione jejuna', &c. It may also be not without significance for the survival of the Donatist spirit in western Mauretania, that in the eighth century these parts were strongly Kharedjite. It was on the Sebou river that the sectaries gained their great victory in 741.

[1] Victor Vitensis, iii. 10.

[2] Some Vandal brooches and jewellery which were found in a cemetery outside Constantine have been preserved in the Musée Gustave Mercier.

[3] Published by E. Albertini, *Journal des Savants*, Jan. 1930, 'particelles agrorum ex culturis mancianis'.

religion and society alike gradually decayed in face of the growing pressure of the nomads. But the Vandal and early Byzantine period must have been a time of considerable prosperity for the churches. To quote but one example, the magnificent silver reliquary found in the church dedicated to the Apostles at Ain Zirara suggests a comparatively wealthy community.[1] The Vandal period is represented by big new churches at Ain Ghorab,[2] Ain Ateuch,[3] Henchir Tarlist,[4] and Kherbet oum el Ahdam,[5] and the Byzantine by new building at Henchir el Akhrib,[6] Er-Rouis,[7] and Sila,[8] to mention but three basilicas on which full reports have been written. The workmanship in these buildings is still good. The decline of Numidian Christianity would not appear to have set in until the end of the sixth or the beginning of the seventh century.

The community to which individual churches belonged in this period is difficult to assess, except where there are inscriptions recording the watchwords of one or the other. There are, however, a number of Biblical texts which one can ascribe to the Donatists with some certainty. At Ain Zirara, for instance, the dedication to the Apostles Sts. Peter and Paul is followed by the words '(Semper De)o laus et g(loria)'.[9] It may be argued that, however conciliatory the Catholics were in the Vandal period, they would not have allowed the inclusion of their opponents' notorious watchword *Deo laus* to appear on the inscription dedicating these most sacred relics. There is some evidence that

[1] This is one of the finest single Christian objects ever discovered in North Africa. The reliquary was a small silver box. The figure of Christ was represented on the lid and various Christian symbols on the sides. Described by P. Monceaux in his *Enquête*, no. 274. Also, H. Jaubert, *Recueil de Constantine*, xlvi, 1912, pp. 212–14.

[2] Monceaux, op. cit., no. 267; Jaubert, op. cit., pp. 165–7.

[3] M. Simon, *Mélanges de l'École de Rome*, li, 1934, pp. 143–77.

[4] M. Labrousse, 'Basilique et reliquaire d'Henchir Tarlist', *Mélanges*, li, 1934, pp. 250 ff.

[5] Monceaux, *Enquête*, 317. At Kherbet Bahrarous, the writer came upon sarcophagi in the church marked with a Latin cross probably of Vandal date.

[6] S. Gsell, *Mélanges*, xxiii, 1903, pp. 1–25; Jaubert, op. cit., pp. 141–4.

[7] Jaubert, op. cit., pp. 196–7. The dedication of relics in the Church to 'Maxima, Secunda and Donatilla', who are prominent in Donatist martyrology, suggests the possibility of this Numidian church being Donatist.

[8] F. Logeart and A. Berthier, 'Deux basiliques chrétiennes à Sila', *Recueil de Constantine*, lxiii, 1935–6, p. 259. This by no means exhausts the list of Vandal and Byzantine churches on the High Plains. Christian inscriptions of the later period in this area seem to be almost as numerous as those which can be attributed to the fourth and early fifth centuries.

[9] *CIL.* viii. 17746; Jaubert, op. cit., p. 213.

the cult of Sts. Peter and Paul in Numidia was Donatist.[1] The same argument may be applied to an inscription from Ain Ghorab. The church of the Apostles was also dedicated to the Holy Spirit, with whom was associated a figure well known in Donatist martyrology, the lector of the Abitinian Christians, Emeritus.[2] At Ain Fakroun a Byzantine inscription testifies to the believer's faith in God in face of persecution,[3] and at Henchir el Ogla a fifth-century inscription records that a church was the 'abode of the saints' ('sanctorum sedes'), and that 'he who seeks in purity shall receive'.[4] The Donatists were always the 'saints', and the emphasis on the need for 'purity' by the recipient of baptism corresponds with their attitude. A similar fifth–sixth-century inscription was found in a church at Ain Seguer near Tebessa,[5] and it seems probable that the church at Sila which records a 'Saint Donatus' and the deposition of relics of 'uncanonical' martyrs in May 585 was also Donatist.[6] Other churches that have been excavated show little evidence for change of ritual through the Vandal and Byzantine periods. Rather, the cult of martyrs becomes even more intense. Apostles, eastern saints such as Menas, Laurentius, and Julianus are honoured alongside native martyrs such as Miggin and Baric. Whatever the outward allegiance of these Byzantine Numidians —and the presence of eastern saints suggests Imperial and orthodox leanings in some parts—the 'atmosphere' of Numidian Christianity remained Donatist.

Such then is the background to the final events in the history of Donatism of which record has survived. The Byzantine reconquest meant the return of the Catholics to a position of unchallenged supremacy. Arianism seems to have disappeared overnight. At least, we hear very little of Arians, and like the Vandals themselves they left no mark on North Africa. By

---

[1] See article by the writer, *JRS*. xxx, 1940, pp. 32–49, 'The *Memoriae Apostolorum* in Roman North Africa', and *infra*, p. 320.

[2] On Ain Ghorab see L. Leschi, 'Basilique et cimetière donatistes de Numidie', *Revue Africaine*, lxviii, 1936, p. 35.

[3] *CIL*. viii. 18742 (Ain Fakroun is on the High Plains; Gsell, *Atlas archéologique*, Constantine, no. 491).

[4] P. Monceaux, *Bull. de la Soc. nat. des Antiquaires de France*, 1909, p. 222.

[5] *CIL.* viii. 10701 = 17617.

[6] The 'uncanonical' martyrs recorded at Sila are Regulianus, Baric, and Celsus. In addition, numerous burials had taken place within the walls of the church. This practice had been condemned in the fourth century by Catholics and Donatists alike, but was carried on by Donatist extremists (Logeart and Berthier, *Sila*, pp. 36–37).

Imperial edict in 535 the privileges of the Catholic Church and of the see of Carthage were restored to what they had been before the Vandal conquest. Donatists, Arians, and Jews were proscribed.[1] The real beneficiary, however, was the see of Rome, which seems not only to have acquired considerable landed wealth in the reconquered African provinces[2] but to have begun to exercise a direct control over the internal affairs of the African Church both in Proconsular Africa and in Numidia.[3] It is due to this fact that the most recent events in the history of Donatism have been preserved.

It seems that for some years before Gregory's accession the Papacy had been worried at the survival of Donatism in Numidia. An effort had been made by Pope Pelagius II to strengthen the organization of the Catholic hierarchy by modifying the practice which both Churches shared, whereby the Primate of the province was the senior bishop and not necessarily the bishop of the most important town.[4] From the administrative viewpoint it was obviously inconvenient to have as Primate a bishop of some out-of-the-way settlement or someone so old as to be ineffective. The Numidian Catholics were, however, unwilling to accept a change, and possibly as a result of their opposition the Pope had resorted instead to the appointment of legates who were to report direct to him. The most important of these was Columbus, who may now with some probability be placed as Bishop of Nicivibus (N'gaous) in an area which two centuries previously had been the 'deep South' of Donatism.[5]

---

[1] Justinian, *Novel*, xxxvii. 5 and 8, 1 Aug. 535.

[2] The extent of these estates is not fully known, though Gregory himself refers to them as 'non parva' (*Ep.* 1. 73 to Gennadius). The largest single unit appears to have been around Hippo, and they were evidently important enough to warrant the appointment of a special agent, Hilarius, for the Papal patrimony in Africa. The *Liber Pontificalis* (ed. Duchesne), i. 375, lists seven *massae* to the value of 4485 gold *solidi* as belonging to the Papal estates.

[3] For instance, through encouraging appeals by bishops and lower clergy direct to Rome, and ordering the calling of provincial councils. The subject is admirably dealt with by Homes Dudden in *Gregory the Great*, Longmans, 1905, pp. 298 and 414–28. I have used Dr. Homes Dudden's analysis of Gregory's policy towards the Donatists, and consider that this work has not been superseded on the subject of Pope Gregory and the African Church. See also the chapter 'La Fin de l'Afrique chrétienne' in vol. v of A. Fliche and V. Martin's *Histoire de l'Église*, 1947.

[4] Gregory, *Ep.* i. 75 (*PL.* xi, col. 1435).

[5] Columbus' see is not mentioned in Gregory's Letters. In 1902, however, an important inscription was found in a church at Henchir Akhrib recording the dedication of relics of Sts. Julian and Laurence, 'per manus Columbi episcopi sanctae ecclesiae Nicivensis', in the year 581 or 582. Columbus is not a common

In the first year of his office as pope we find Gregory writing to the Patrician Gennadius, Exarch of Africa, requesting him to take firm action against the heretics.[1] Gennadius, however, seems to have considered that he had sufficient on hand in defending the African provinces against Berber tribes. He had no wish to stir up trouble among the natives within the provincial boundaries, and Gregory's appeal went unheeded. In the next year, 591, Gregory was confronted with an abundance of evidence for the renewed strength of Donatism in Numidia. Disgruntled deacons of the church of Pudentiana near Macomades complained that their bishop had accepted a bribe from the Donatists, and had allowed a Donatist bishopric to be established in his town.[2] In another south Numidian town, Lamigigga, the Catholic bishop was alleged to have handed over churches to the care of Donatists.[3] Gregory ordered Columbus and Hilarius his agent to call together a Council, and if the bishops were proved guilty they were to be deprived and excommunicated. In addressing Columbus, the pope admitted that 'Donatism was spreading daily', and that Catholics were submitting to rebaptism.[4] Over the two centuries which separate Augustine from Gregory the characteristic features of the struggle between the rival Churches remained the same.

In 593 Gregory made his greatest effort to crush the movement. Failing to find support from Gennadius, he wrote to his subordinate, the *Praefectus Praetorio* Pantaleo:[5]

African name, and it is a reasonable supposition that the Columbus of Niciva and Gregory's legate ten years later are one and the same man. This view is perhaps strengthened by the fact that the places mentioned in connexion with Donatism at this time are all in southern Numidia, where Columbus could be expected to give information to the Pope at first hand. See H. Jaubert, *Recueil de Constantine*, op. cit., pp. 66–67 and 141–4.

[1] Gregory, *Ep.* i. 72. Gennadius was one of a line of distinguished generals who maintained the Byzantine reconquest for over a century. In 579 he co-operated with the *Praefectus* Thomas in defeating the Moorish king Garmul. A dated inscription from a church at Sila of 8 May 585 refers to him as *magister militum*, thus placing the introduction of the exarchate in Africa between 585 and 590. In 591 he was exarch, and he held this office as late as 596. He clearly saw that the task of maintaining Byzantine authority in Africa would become impossible if, added to the threat of Moorish attacks, he roused the opposition of the Donatist peasantry in the frontier districts.

[2] Ibid. ii. 46.   [3] Ibid. i. 82.

[4] Ibid. ii. 33, 'Porro autem praesentium latorum insinuatione didicimus Donatistarum haeresim pro peccatis nostris quotidie dilatari, et valde plures, data per venalitatem licentia, post catholicum baptisma a Donatistis denuo baptizari' (*PL.* xi, col. 1436).

[5] Gregory, *Ep.* iii. 32. Translation quoted from Homes Dudden, op. cit., p. 417.

With what rigour the law punishes the execrable wickedness of the Donatists Your Excellency is well aware. It is no light sin, then, if those whom the purity of the faith and the severity of human laws alike condemn, find under your rule the means of creeping up again into importance. We have learnt that the audacity of these people has so increased in your province, that not only do they expel with pestilential force the bishops of the Catholic Faith from their churches, but they even venture to rebaptize those whom by a true confession the water of regeneration has already cleansed.

He then exhorts him to enforce the anti-heretical laws against the Donatists. In Numidia the situation was returning to what it had been under Constantine.

At the same time the Pope tried to goad the Catholics into action. In August 593 a synod was held under the presidency of the Numidian Primate, Adeodatus, but with Columbus as its most influential member. The record shows that the orthodox had themselves failed to put their house in order. As in the past, simony, corruption, and vice prevailed.[1] Columbus had been instructed to concert action against the Donatists, and at the same time rid the Numidian Church of abuses such as the election of boys and immoral persons to vacant prelacies. Evidently the Numidian Church thought differently about these matters, for in September Gregory informed the Exarch Gennadius that 'many things are being done in the Council of Numidia contrary to the usage of the Fathers and the ordinances of the canons'.[2]

Gregory, however, did not give up. In 594 he wrote to Columbus and the new Primate of Numidia, Victor, urging them to hold another Council against Donatism.[3] He sent the same orders to Dominicus, Bishop of Carthage, and here it was at least decreed that bishops who were negligent in searching out and punishing heretics should be deprived.[4] The Donatists, however, had means to hand to deal with clergy who too readily accepted Gregory's orders. One such, Bishop Paulus, soon found himself in difficulties. In 594 he appealed to the exarch for assistance against the Donatists, but the Imperial authorities preferred to side with the latter. Paulus was prevented from leaving his diocese to submit his appeal to Rome.

---

[1] Gregory, *Ep*. iii. 47 and 48; also *Ep*. xii. 8 and 9 (bishops accused of simony).
[2] Ibid. iv. 7, quoted from Homes Dudden, op. cit., pp. 421–2.
[3] Gregory, *Ep*. iv. 35.   [4] Ibid. v. 3.

Charges were framed against him, and he found himself excommunicated by a Catholic Council.[1] Religious zeal and lack of tact were more unpopular with the local officials than heresy and schism.

By 596 the situation had become even less favourable. A further letter from the pope to Columbus repeats the story of the spread of Donatism,[2] but in August Gregory wrote to the Emperor Mauricius himself.[3] The Imperial commands against the Donatists were being disregarded 'by carelessness or connivance'. The bribes of the Donatists 'so prevail in the province that the Catholic Faith is publicly put up for sale'.[4] The exarch, far from taking action himself, was complaining of bishops who brought these things to his notice. The emperor's personal assistance was requested, 'to issue strict orders for the punishment of the Donatists and to arrest with saving hand the fall of the perishing'. Whether this appeal was successful or not we do not know. Except for Bishop Paulus' repeated effort to have his case heard in Rome, there is no further literary record of Donatism. We are left with the impression of the movement resurgent and triumphant in southern Numidia, and then there is silence.

The days of Christianity itself were by now drawing to their close.[5] The farming villages were no longer secure against the incursions of Moorish nomads. The contrast between the great cathedrals which the fourth and fifth centuries produced and the primitive chapels which housed the African Christians two hundred years later is striking. Orthodoxy in the seventh century is represented by the church of the Patrician Gregorius at Timgad; on the High Plains the last age of Christianity produced the miserable structures which French archaeologists discovered at Meharza and Henchir Guesses.[6] Two final records of Christian Numidia deserve mention. On a farm at the foot

---

[1] The incident is recounted in detail in Homes Dudden, op. cit., pp. 424–5.

[2] Gregory, *Ep.* vi. 34.   [3] Ibid. 61.

[4] Ibid., 'hoc etiam subjungentes quod in praefata provincia Donatistarum praemiis praevalentibus fides catholica publice venundetur'. It would be interesting to know where the Donatists got their money from.

[5] Eloquent of this phase is a Byzantine inscription from Ain Nechma, just outside Guelma (Calama). It reads, 'Hic memoria pristini altaris'. Published in *Recueil de Constantine*, 1882, p. 46. The stone itself is in Guelma Museum.

[6] The dating is not certain, but the opinion of M. Berthier, Curator of the Musée Gustave Mercier at Constantine, who excavated both, was that they belonged to the latest age of North African Christianity.

of the Djebel Teioualt, five miles south of Telergma airfield, a chance discovery brought to light one of the most interesting Christian inscriptions ever found in Algeria. It consists of a flat piece of lead 20·5 cm. long and 5·3 cm. wide, covered on both sides with a text closely written, but in painful and inaccurate Latin. It is dated 8 February 637, the twenty-sixth year of the reign of Heraclius, and records the deposition of relics of numerous martyrs accompanied by considerable ceremony. The mention of several bishops who were present shows that an episcopal organization still existed, and that the religion in the last age of Numidian Christianity was still that of martyrs and holy men.[1] The second text is as obscure and tantalizing as anything in this final phase of Christianity in North Africa. It is dated to A.D. 722,[2] a generation after the final defeat of the Berber resistance to the Arab invaders, and ten years after the overthrow of the Christian Visigothic kingdom in Spain. Apparently, numerous African clergy were making their way to Italy, and their presence was causing the pope, Gregory II, some concern. He writes, 'Aliqui rebaptizati saepius sunt probati'. The reference is to rebaptism, and clergy who had undergone this were suspect to His Holiness. This could, however, hardly refer to anyone else but the Donatists. The necessity of rebaptizing their converts was one of the main distinctions between them and the Catholics both in the fourth and sixth centuries. If this interpretation is true, then there is formal evidence for the survival of Donatism up to the very end of African Christianity.

Our summing up of this long period must be inconclusive. We do not know the real extent of Donatist survival in Vandal and Byzantine times. Certain it is that Donatus' work did not lead to the foundation of a permanent national Church on the lines of the Coptic Church in Egypt. Possibly Rome and Ravenna were too close for the development of a national dissident Church to have taken place. The direct power of the Papacy in the internal affairs of the African Church, already appreciable in the last decade of Augustine's life, continued to grow. The efficiency

---

[1] First published by J. Bosco and Mme Alquier in *Recueil de Constantine*, lviii, 1927, pp. 209–19. Complete text reproduced by Berthier in *Les Vestiges du Christianisme en Numidie*, pp. 121–2.

[2] Gregory II, *Ep.* iv (*PL.* lxxxix, col. 502), 'Afros passim ad ecclesiasticos ordines praetendentes nulla ratione suscipiat, quia aliqui eorum Manichaei, aliqui rebaptizati saepius sunt probati.'

of the Catholics had the paradoxical result of being a factor in the permanent loss of north Africa to Christendom. We have seen how Pope Gregory's arm stretched into the farthest corners of Byzantine Numidia. His able lieutenants kept him thoroughly posted on the strength of anti-orthodox influences. His correspondence taken by itself merely confirms what one had been led to expect, i.e. that in southern Numidia Donatism survived. If the movement was to survive anywhere it would have been in the area immediately north of the Aures mountains where it had held unchallenged mastery in the fourth century. On the other hand, the actual advance of the movement in this period is extraordinary. The historian, too, would have liked to know the fate of Donatism in the other provinces, particularly in the remote areas of Mauretania Caesariensis and in Tripolitania. In the latter province Christianity survived until the eleventh century.[1] In these places the answer will only become known, if ever, by the slow method of excavation and archaeological research. The literary records are silent.

[1] On the En-Gila inscriptions and other evidence of the survival of Christianity after the Arab invasions, see W. Seston, 'Sur les derniers temps du Christianisme en Afrique', *Mélanges*, liii, 1936, pp. 101–21, and M. Paribeni, *Africa Italiana*, vi, 1935, p. 79.

XX

TWO CITIES . . . TWO CHURCHES

THUS Donatist and Catholic remained divided from each other until both were swept away by Islam. The questions that separated them were those of will and outlook, not doctrine and philosophy. It was the nature of the Church as a society and its relationship to the world rather than its distinctive beliefs that formed the heart of the controversy. In the eastern provinces of the Empire the fact that Donatus had written a work 'On the Trinity'[1] which appeared to agree with the Arian view would immediately have led to ferocious controversy. To judge from the deliberate subordination of Christ to the Creator on some of the Numidian and Tripolitanian inscriptions,[2] the Catholics had a case against their opponents. The Donatists, however, might have replied by pointing to the part played by their opponents at the Council of Ariminum. But doctrine was not the issue. Both Optatus and, in his earlier years, Augustine lay stress on the unity of belief. The Catholics conceded that their opponents possessed the 'endowments' (*dotes*) of the Church.[3] Parmenian was a 'brother' as well as a schismatic bishop.

Yet, to contemporaries, the two Churches seemed to stand in relation to each other as two rival societies inspired by contrary wills: an illustration of the everlasting clash between the 'Church of Judas' and the 'Church of Peter'.

From the pages of the *De Civitate Dei* the student is familiar with Augustine's concept of the two cities, and of the definition of a given society by its aim and its collective will.[4] He should

---

[1] Jerome, *De Viris Illustribus*, 93, 'de Spiritu sancto Ariano dogmati congruens'. Augustine, *Ep.* 185. 1, 'And if some even of them have said that the Son was inferior to the Father, yet they have not denied that He is of the same substance.'

[2] Indicated by the use of the disjunctive 'atque' in 'Dei *atque* Christi' on inscriptions from Msuffin in Tripolitania and Hr. Bou Sboa in Numidia. Others, as that at Oued R'zel, differentiate between 'Dei Omnipotentis et Christi Salvatoris'. See above, p. 103, note 9.

[3] Optatus, i. 4, ii. 6, iii. 9, and iv. 2. See Cresconius in *Contra Cresconium*, ii. 3. 4 for the Donatist view. Cf. Augustine, *Enarratio in Ps. 54*, 10.

[4] *De Civitate Dei*, iv. 3–10, v. 22, and xix. 12–22. N. H. Baynes, 'The Political Ideas of St. Augustine's *De Civitate Dei*', Historical Assoc. Pamphlet, 104, London, 1936.

bear in mind, however, that these ideas are partly Donatist by origin. They were evolved from the need of justifying the separation of the Church as a company of the Elect from a Church worldly if universal in extent, allied with worldly powers and polluted with the stain of *traditio*.

At Cyprian's Seventh Council of Carthage in September 256 one finds in the statements of some of the bishops present traces of the idea of a Church of Judas standing in opposition to the Church of Peter. Therapius of Bulla Regia argued, for instance, that to concede that heretics possessed baptism was to make Judas the Bride of Christ.[1] Firmilian of Cappadocia held the same view in his correspondence with Cyprian.[2] The first generation of Donatists took the argument a step farther. They saw an exact parallel in the rejection of Judas and the fall of Caecilian.[3] Maiorinus and Donatus dispossessed Caecilian just as Matthias took over the bishopric of the fallen apostle. They saw, too, how a rival (Catholic) Church could exist parallel to their own, its doctrine orthodox, and yet in the service of the Devil.[4] Donatus' community was merely the continuation of the African Church as it existed before the Great Persecution. The Caecilianist party had put themselves outside, as Judas had done.

Gradually, in the hands of the great thinker Tyconius, these ideas crystallized into a conception of two Churches, representing two societies, world-wide in extent, but ever opposed to each other. Not everyone who called himself a priest, said Tyconius, was one. Since the foundation of the Church there had been Judas and Peter. Two altars, yet Christ divided. These rival Churches, sprung from different origins, had 'different heads', which could be interpreted as Donatus and Caecilian.[5] The taint of *traditio* descended, like Original Sin, from

---

[1] *Sententiae Episcoporum*, 61 (*CSEL*. iii. 1, 455): 'Qui haereticis ecclesiae Baptismum concedit et prodit, quid aliud quam sponsae Christi Iudas extitit?'

[2] *Ep*. 75. 2 (*CSEL*. iii. i, 811).

[3] Petilian in Augustine, *Contra Litteras Petiliani*, ii. 8. 17 and 18. 40. The Donatists added the phrase 'quando ordinatio facta est Matthiae' to Cyprian, *Ep*. 67. 4.

[4] Tyconius, *Commentario in Apocalypsin* (Hahn, *Tyconius-Studien*, p. 65). This, I would suggest, is the interpretation of the 'three parts' of the 'Ecclesia generalis' which Tyconius' predecessors ('maiores nostri') asserted in 'una est Dei, duae vero diaboli, diaboli schisma et falsi fratres; et ecclesia est, quae pars Dei, hae duae partes intro videntur esse, sed foras sunt'.

[5] Tyconius (apud Beatus), 184, 'non ... omnes sacerdotes sacerdotes sunt, non

one generation to the next.[1] Tyconius, indeed, regarded the
Churches less from a local point of view than as an aspect of a
wider struggle between the wills towards good and evil. 'One
aimed at serving Christ, the other at serving the world. The
one desires to dominate in this world, the other flees from this
world. One kills, the other is killed. Each labours in common,
the one to have whence it may be condemned, the other
whence it may be saved.'[2]

These views, as we have seen, ranged beyond the restricted
confines of the Donatist Church. Tyconius believed that all
men possessed the power to be righteous, not merely the Donatists. The question was where their will belonged, 'whether of
sin unto death or obedience unto righteousness'.[3] There could
be 'secretly wicked' in the Donatist Church itself, and possibly
true Christians outside its communion, especially overseas,
where the name of Caecilian was unknown. Christ's inheritance could not be confined to Africa. Christ and Satan were
everywhere; their thrones were in the minds of men.

Tyconius' theories did not gain general acceptance within
the Donatist Church, but he did express in a few sentences the
differences of religious will and approach to society which
characterized the two Churches. Under the terms *traditio* and
'persecution' there are summed up those deep divergences in

omnes diaconi diaconi sunt. Attendis Petrum, sed et Iudam considera. Stephanum
suspicis, sed et Nicolaum respice. . . . Sic in specie ostendit genus, et genus revocat
ad speciem. Habet Petrus imitatores discipulos, habet et Iudas, habet Stephanus
imitatores diaconos habet et Nicolaus. Petrus praedicat Evangelium Christi, praedicat et Iudas. Baptizat Petrus in nomine Trinitatis, baptizat et Iudas. Habet
Petrus in ecclesia postestatem solvendi et ligandi peccata, habet et Iudas sedu-
cendo servos Domini fornicari et manducare idolis immolata. Ecce in una domo,
duo altaria. Ecce communis lectus et divisus Christus.' See also *Contra Fulgentium,* 23
(*PL.* xliii, col. 772), and *Gesta Coll. Carth.* iii. 258 (*PL.* xi, col. 1412).

[1] *Gesta Coll. Carth.* iii. 313 (chapter headings).

[2] Tyconius (apud Beatus, 507. 15–33), Hahn, 29, 'perspicue patet duas civitates
esse et duo regna, et duo reges Christum et diabolum; et ambo super utrasque
civitates regnant. . . . Hae duae civitates, una mundo, et una desiderat servire
Christo, una in hoc mundo regnum cupit tendere, et una ab hoc mundo fugere: una
flagellat, altera flagellatur; una occidit, altera occiditur; una ut justificetur adhuc,
altera ut impie agat adhuc. Hae utraeque ita laborant in unum, una ut habeat
unde damnetur, altera ut habeat unde salvetur.' Cf. Tyconius (apud Beatus 533),
Hahn, 28, 'quia semper et ecclesia fuit et bestia'.

[3] Tyconius, *Regulae,* 7 (Burkitt), 82. 'Omnia enim quae fecit Deus bona sunt,
horum diabolus usum non naturam mutavit'. Beatus, 'Babylonem civitatem diaboli dicit; civitas diaboli populus ejus, et omnis corruptela et opera nequitiae,
quam in persecutionem sui et humani generis exquirit.' A. Pincherle, *Da Ticonio
a Sant' Agostino,* 458–59.

religious and social outlook which prevented reunion, despite
a similarity in formal belief.

The Donatists claimed to be 'the Church of Peter' in Tyconius' sense of the term, and they never regarded themselves as
other than the Catholic Church in Africa, sanctified by the
martyrs and purged of its errors by Donatus.[1] They were consciously the continuators of the African Church presided over
by Cyprian.[2] Their characteristic doctrines may be traced back
in their detail to this period. The Church was conceived as a
mystical union of the righteous inspired by the Holy Spirit and
instructed by the Bible. It was governed by bishops and clergy
whose function was to lead their flock to the goal of Christian
life, which in the last resort was martyrdom. The religion of
praise and exultation which the Donatists professed is well
illustrated by an inscription from a church at Thamallula
(Tocqueville), a *castellum* in Mauretania Sitifensis, 'Praise ye the
Lord and exult, ye righteous, and let us glory in the Lord with
a true heart',[3] or again, in the words of the Donatist *Acta
Saturnini*, 'In our Church, the virtues of the people are
multiplied by the presence of the Spirit. The joy of the
Spirit is to conquer in the martyrs and triumph in the confessors.'[4] The question of territorial extent was secondary to
that of maintaining the purity of the Sacraments. That it was
not lost to sight, however, is shown by Cresconius' pleasure in
the gradual conversion of the world to Christianity and the
defeat of the heresies, such as Arianism, Marcionism, &c.[5]

In matters of organization, Cyprian, the example of one who
was both bishop and martyr, was the model which the Dona-

---

[1] *Acta Saturnini*, 20 (*PL*. viii. 703), 'beatissimorum martyrum successio gloriosa,
quae est Ecclesia sancta, una et vera catholica, ex qua martyres profecti sunt.'
Cf. Petilian in *Gesta Coll. Carth*. iii. 92 ff. and *Contra Cresconium*, iii. 56. 62. Near
the site of Marculus' basilica at Vegesela an inscription was found mentioning
an *ecclesia chatolicorum*, in this instance probably the Donatists' (*CIL*. viii. 2311),
P. Courcelle, *Mélanges*, liii, 1936, p. 190. On the distribution map of bishoprics in
Numidia I have shown other inscriptions where the words 'catholicus' or 'pax'
occur as Catholic. Further research, however, may necessitate modification.

[2] *Contra Cresconium*, ii. 31. 39, and iii. 2.

[3] S. Gsell, *Bull. Arch. du Comité*, 1908, p. ccxvi; J. Gauthier, *Bull. Arch. du Comité*,
1909, pp. 54–58; comment by Monceaux, *Histoire littéraire*, iv. 455.

[4] *Acta Saturnini*, 20 (*PL*. viii, col. 703). Cf. Optatus, iii. 6, on the sacred character
of oaths sworn by the Donatists in the name of the martyrs.

[5] *Contra Cresconium*, iv. 61. 74. Cf. Rogatus of Cartenna's view, quoted by Augustine, *Ep*. 93, 22. *Contra Cresconium*, iii. 34. 38, also shows that the Donatists condemned the Arians as such.

tists followed. As Tyconius pointed out, the bishops were the
'guardians of the law', without whose aid none could enter the
New Jerusalem.[1] Thus their word was unchallenged, and what
they decreed in Council under the guidance of the Spirit was
ipso facto 'holy'. They spoke, like Crispinus of Calama, 'patriar-
chale sermone'.[2] On the other hand, they were expected to
participate actively in 'holy war' against the forces of evil,
whether in the shape of Catholic clergy or oppressive landowners. Donatist bishops and priests were always in the fore-
front of the Circumcellion bands. They led the great forays of
362 and 363 in reprisal against the persecution of Paul and
Macarius, and when challenged, Parmenian replied that their
acts could not be placed on the same level as those of the
Imperial officials.[3] The Donatist idea of a true bishop is characterized by the writer of the *Passio Marculi*. He was a man 'predestined to Salvation', 'who had the Gospel ever on his lips and
martyrdom in his heart'.[4] An ascetic, he led a dedicated and
sacramental life.

Martyrdom and devotion to the Word of God as contained in
the Bible were the heart of Donatism. These, as much as 'the
authority of the Church', were the means of uniting clergy and
people. We have already noted in passing the tendency of the
Novatianists to regard themselves as 'evangelicals'.[5] The tendency was developed among the Donatists.[6] Knox has quite
rightly drawn attention to the form used by the Donatist bishops
in their letters to their clergy, as 'fellow presbyters who have
been appointed with us ministers in the gospel', and to the laity
as 'the people that shares our warfare in the truth of the
gospel'.[7] The ability to combine the concept of an *Ecclesia*
governed by a hierarchy, with the non-hierarchical community
devoted to the Spirit is probably one of the clues to the Donatists' power of survival.

[1] Tyconius, apud Hahn, *Tyconius-Studien*, p. 63. Augustine, *Sermo* 46. 10. 21, on
Donatist reliance on their bishops.

[2] Crispinus, quoted by Augustine, *Contra Cresconium*, iii. 46. 50. Cf. *Contra Litteras Petiliani*, ii. 241.   [3] Optatus, ii. 18; Ziwsa, p. 52. See *supra*, p. 196, n. 2.

[4] *Passio Marculi* (*PL*. viii. 762), 'Erat illi assidua et jugis oratio, erat continua de
devotione meditatio. Habebat in sermone Evangelium, in cogitatione martyrium.'

[5] See *supra*, p. 129.

[6] For Donatists as 'evangelicals' see *Contra Cresconium*, ii. 1. 2; *Contra Litteras
Petiliani*, ii. 1. 2 (*CIL*. viii, 21572 (Benian)).

[7] R. A. Knox, *Enthusiasm*, pp. 67–68. Knox, however, perhaps underestimates the
tendency that was equally strong in popular Donatism towards organization as a
Church. The word 'ecclesia' is common enough on southern Numidian inscriptions.

In their church services the Donatist clergy used the same Bible, the Old Latin text, as that in use in Cyprian's time. The Latin Vulgate was read only by the Catholics in Africa.[1] As in the earliest days of African Christianity, the sermon and reading from Scripture played a considerable part in what is known of the Donatist services. Probably the Acts of Donatist martyrs would also be recited. The idea was not simply instruction, in the modern sense of the term, but the lector or priest was believed to be transmitting the Spirit in his utterances. It is interesting that on the Henchir Taghfaght inscription (near Khenchela in central Algeria) and at Ain Ghorab, Emeritus, the lector among the Abitinian martyrs, is styled *gloriosus consultus* ('glorious pleader') and associated with the Apostles Sts. Peter and Paul.[2] In Cyprian's time we hear of boys and illiterates being employed as 'readers' on the same grounds, that they 'talked by the Spirit'.[3]

In other ways the Donatists held fast to traditional ceremonies. The old penitential discipline of the *exomologesis* was retained,[4] and so also the *agape*, especially in connexion with ceremonies at the tombs of the martyrs.[5] On the other hand, feast-days introduced by the Catholics during the fourth century, such as the Epiphany, were ignored,[6] and the institution of monasticism opposed.[7]

In his daily life the Donatist Christian was continually reminded in sermons that nothing essential had changed now that the Roman Empire had accepted Christianity. The text of a sermon that has survived, dated probably to *c.* A.D. 350 and preached on the anniversary of the Holy Innocents, informs the congregation that they were members of a brotherhood (*fraternitas*). They were always in 'battle' against the Devil, they would always suffer persecution, as the righteous had suffered

[1] For instance, as Burkitt points out, at Carthage in 411 the Donatists quoted from the Old Latin text and the Catholics from the Vulgate (Burkitt, *Texts and Studies*, 1894, pp. lx f.). Cf. P. Monceaux, *Histoire littéraire*, vi. 224.

[2] *CIL.* viii, 17714 and 2220. Cf. article by the writer, *JRS.* xxx, 1940, p. 43.

[3] Cyprian, *Ep.* 27. 1, concerning the lector Aurelius. Cf. *Eps.* 16. 4 and 33; *CIL.* viii. 453 (Ammaedara). Visionaries among Donatist lower clergy, Augustine, *Ep.* 53. 1.

[4] *Passio Donati et Advocati* 2 (*PL.* viii. col. 753).

[5] H. Leclercq, 'Agapes', *Dictionnaire d'Archéologie*, i. 1, col. 830. Cf. C. Vars, 'Morsott', *Recueil de Constantine*, 1899, p. 401. For a find of chalices at Bou Takrematem, see A. Berthier and M. Martin, 'Nouvelles recherches archéologiques à Bou Takrematem', *Recueil de Constantine*, 1935-6, p. 224.

[6] Augustine, *Sermo* 202. 2. See A. Pincherle, *Bilychnis*, xxii, 1922, p. 143.

[7] Augustine, *Enarratio in Ps. 132*, 6.

from the time of Abel to that of Herod. In their lives they were to be wedded to poverty and penance and were to hope only for a rebirth through martyrdom.[1] Similar views were expressed by the writer of the sermon on the martyrdom of Donatus and Advocatus (A.D. 320)—the only difference between the pre- and post-Constantinian epoch was that in the one the Devil used force, now he had allies in the Christian camp itself and could rely on fraud; but for the true Christian the result was the same.[2]

The most lucid summary of the Donatist outlook was compiled under the threat of immediate proscription by the authorities. It is contained in the letter to Count Marcellinus which one of the Donatist assessors, Bishop Habetdeus, read at the third session of the Conference of Carthage.[3] It was drawn up during the adjournment between the second and the final session as an answer to the Catholic statement which had been read at the beginning of the proceedings. It is a complete *professio fidei*. It opens, 'Januarius and the other bishops of the catholic truth that suffers persecution but does not persecute.' In Tertullian's, as in the Donatist, view, persecution was the Divine means of separating just from unjust on earth.[4] Then follow the arguments that the Church even on earth was a body of the righteous, of the necessity of separation from the corrupt, of the contagion of sin, and the worthlessness of the sacraments dispensed by a sinner, and, above all, the uselessness of baptism administered outside the Church. Finally, after a brief reference to the Maximianists, there is the catalogue of persecutions which the Donatist Church suffered at the hands of the Roman governors. It is noticeable that in another place Petilian draws no distinction between the persecutions in pagan and Christian times.[5] The fact of having suffered in both periods justified the Donatist claim of having safeguarded the pure tradition of the African Church, and thus to the title of the Catholic Church, the true repository of the endowments of the Apostles.[6]

---

[1] Quoted from A. Pincherle's article 'Un Sermone donatista attribuito a S. Ottato di Milevi', *Bilychnis*, xxii, 1923, pp. 134–48.

[2] *Passio Donati* (*PL*. viii, col. 753), '[Diabolus] eos quos aperta persecutione superare non potuit callida fraude circumvenire molitus est.'

[3] *Gesta Coll. Carth.* iii. 258 (*PL*. xi, cols. 1408–14); also quoted in *PL*. xliii, cols. 834–839, together with Augustine's reply.

[4] Tertullian, *De Fuga*, i. Cf. *Contra Gaudentium*, i. 20. 22 and *CIL*. viii. 18472 (Ain Fakroun).

[5] *Contra Litteras Petiliani*, ii. 92. 202 (*PL*. xliii, cols. 323–4).

[6] So Gaudentius at the Conference of 411, *Gesta Coll. Carth.* iii. 102.

The African Catholics represented a contrary outlook.[1] Many of the individual beliefs of the primitive African Church were retained, but their character and the underlying will expressed were drastically modified. Once the premiss of the Church as a body of the Elect had been dropped, then most of the puritanical beliefs with which this concept was associated automatically became obsolete. The way was open for integration within the Roman Empire and alliance with the social and political institutions of the State. An attitude which under Tertullian and Cyprian had been more in the nature of a reaction to rigorist ascendancy became the 'official' view of the African Church.

A single instance of this process may be quoted, the Catholic attitude towards the cult of martyrs. Augustine, as we have seen, showed special reverence for local saints at Hippo, and clergy who had been killed by the Donatists were regarded as martyrs.[2] But there must have been many who would have agreed with the words of Caesarius of Arles, that actual death was not always necessary for the gaining of the martyr's crown. 'Non martyrium sola effusio sanguinis consummat.'[3] At Tipasa, for instance, even at the shrine of Salsa, this view was taught. On the mosaic covering the tomb of Bishop Alexander almsgiving was claimed as the equivalent of martyrdom. At the same time writers of Catholic *Acta Martyrum*, like the *Passio Fabii Vexilliferi*, implied that though the martyr's death served as an example to pious minds, it was not to be expected. Veneration for the martyr sufficed to make the believer a partner in his rewards.

But such veneration was rigorously controlled and purged of all enthusiasm.[4] The riotous celebration of martyrs' anniversaries was prevented,[5] the visions and revelations granted to the martyrs pushed to one side,[6] while emphasis was laid on their wealth and noble birth[7] instead of their threats against the

---

[1] See G. G. Willis, *Saint Augustine and the Donatist Controversy*, chap. iv, an excellent summary.   [2] See above, p. 232.

[3] Caesarius of Arles, *De Martyrio*, 1; Augustine, *Sermo* 224. 1 (*PL*. xxxix. 2159).

[4] For mistrust of popular martyrs by Catholics, *Optatus*, i. 16; also *Codex Canonum Eccl. Af.* 60 and 83, *Sermo* 318 (against excavation of martyrs' bones).

[5] Augustine, *Ep*. 29; *Sermo* 273. 5, 311. 5.

[6] For instance, in the Short Latin *Acta* of the *Passio Perpetuae*; Augustine, *Sermo* 280. 1 (*PL*. xxxviii. 1281), mentions without comment the 'divinis revelationibus' which were granted to the saints.

[7] As Crispina, 'feminam divitem et delicatam', *Enarratio in Ps. 120*, 13. She was

Roman magistracy. At the same time, inroads were made on the purely African element in the cult. Foreign saints, as Protasius and Gervasius of Milan,[1] were introduced. It might seem as though the concession to popular ideas was used to teach the belief in the universality of the martyrs' virtues, and therefore of the Christian Church.

To the opponents of Donatism the Catholic Church meant the One visible Church universal.[2] In the Old Testament the Lord had promised that his inheritance would be world-wide: 'In thy name shall all nations be blessed'; 'I will give thee the heathen for thine inheritance'; while Christ had told His disciples that they would be His witnesses unto the ends of the earth. The Church must therefore be 'diffusa'.[3] True, that entailed the presence of evil members within the Church, but that also was in accordance with Christ's will. The Church could be likened to a lily among thorns, a net within the sea of the world containing every kind, a threshing-floor including chaff as well as grain, a field in which wheat and tares grew.[4] Separation of the good from the bad would be by the Lord, and then not till the Last Day, not by Donatus at the present time.[5] Meanwhile it was necessary to maintain Christian unity through unity of the Sacraments, in the bond of peace, though the true believer should dissociate himself from the ways of evil brethren.[6] The sin of one man did not infect his fellows, and therefore schism, a breach of unity, even on the grounds of creating a purer congregation was inexcusable. It was the outstanding example of lack of charity.[7]

Turning to the breach with Caecilian, the Catholics pointed

'clarissima . . . nobilis genere'. The Donatist *Acta* make no mention of her alleged wealth. Also Fabius the Standard-Bearer (*Passio*, 2), described as 'generosae stirpis beatiore lare progenitus'.

[1] *De Civitate Dei*, xxii. 8 (*CSEL.* xl. 597–603).

[2] See F. W. Sparrow Simpson, *Saint Augustine and African Church Divisions* (Longmans, 1910), 70–90; G. G. Willis, *St. Augustine and the Donatist Controversy*, chap. iv.

[3] *Contra Epistolam Parmeniani*, i. 1. 1; *Ad Catholicos Epistola*, 8. 22 and 25. 75; *Ep.* 43–44. 87. 10; Optatus, ii. 9.

[4] These comparisons are made by Augustine in his letter to Vincentius, *Ep.* 93, 28 ff.; *Contra Cresconium*, ii. 34. 43; *Gesta Coll. Carth.* iii. 275–81, in answer to the Donatist statement of belief.

[5] *Contra Litteras Petiliani*, iii. 2. 3 (*PL.* 349), 'Ager enim est mundus non Africa, messis finis saeculi, non tempus Donati.'

[6] *De Baptismo*, iv *passim*; *Contra Litteras Petiliani*, ii. 15. 35; *Contra Cresconium*, ii. 36. 45.

[7] Ibid. ii. 6. 9; iii. 19. 25; iv. 4. 5; 13. 19: *Contra Litteras Petiliani*, ii. 23. 54; ii. 46. 108.

out that the rest of the world, especially the Apostolic sees, had maintained communion with him, and therefore had shown that they regarded him as the true representative of the Church.[1] However, even if the charges against him were proven, that did not invalidate the sacraments which he gave, or justify schism. The sacraments were of Christ, dispensed indeed through His ministers, but pure in all circumstances, just as their source, Christ Himself, was pure. They were valid in themselves, even if in extreme cases they had been given as a joke, or by Judas Iscariot.[2] They might have been *irregularly* administered, but that did not compromise their divine source and character.

Today it can be realized that Augustine and his colleagues were laying the foundations for a subtler and perhaps finer view of the Church than that taught by Cyprian and the Donatists. It contained a measure of hope for those not in Catholic communion. It established the holiness of the attributes of the Church irrespective of the human agents who ministered them. But it led automatically away from African tradition, and under the prevailing conditions in the last decade of Roman rule the African Catholics were not able to maintain the independence that had characterized the Church in Africa when there had previously been unity. They became progressively more dependent on the Roman see in ecclesiastical questions and on the Roman authorities for material support. Papal legates attended African Councils, and demanded that African clergy should have the right of appeal to Rome. They intervened in the internal affairs of African dioceses and invoked the aid of local secular authorities to enforce their decisions. African bishops, on the other hand, continued to frequent the Imperial Court. At the death of Augustine the alliance between Church and Empire had become complete.

This was the real heart of the controversy. In the last resort the differences between Donatist and Catholic turned on the relations between Church and society, between Christianity and the Roman Empire. The two communities provided contrary answers. First, the attitude of the Catholic Church to the

---

[1] *Ep.* 44. 2. 3. Cf. *Contra Cresconium*, ii. 37. 46.

[2] *Tract. v in Ioann. Evang.* 18 (*PL.* xxxv. 1423), 'Et [baptisma] quod dabatur a Paulo, et quod dabatur a Petro, Christi est; et si datum est a Juda Christi est.' *Ad Catholicos Epistola*, 21. 58; *De Baptismo*, vii. 53. 101–2; Willis, op. cit., pp. 154–60.

Roman Empire was modified after 312, while the Donatists retained the antithesis preached by Tertullian and Cyprian. Secondly, partly as a result of this, the outlooks of the two Churches on social questions became progressively more opposed as the fourth century wore on.

On both these issues the Catholics were influenced by the origins of the schism. It will be recalled[1] how, at the outset, Constantine freed members of the Caecilianist party from the financial obligations to which members of city councils were subject. In a period of increasing economic strain for the remainder of the provincials the privileges of the Catholic Church were augmented. In 349 clerics and their children were exempted from all fiscal obligations in respect of their city.[2] The Church was granted a share in the *annona* paid by the provincials.[3] Its clergy were allowed to use the public transport system in the same way as Imperial officials, a privilege which contemporaries considered greatly abused.[4] Other exemptions included that of providing supplies in kind to soldiers and officials (the *parangaria*),[5] and freedom from all *sordida munera*.[6] Clerics had the right to engage in trade.[7] In 359 a demand by the Council of Ariminum for exemption from all forms of taxation was refused,[8] though the Church was exempted from all 'new taxes'.[9]

From these facts one can understand that the Catholics tended to abandon the assimilation of the Empire to the outside 'world' hostile to Christianity. Where previous generations of African Christians had seen the Emperor and his officials as personifications of the Devil, Augustine told the Donatists, 'There is no braver soldier of Christ than the Emperor.'[10] Persecution was not the divine means of separating just from unjust, but the execution of the Emperor's edicts.[11] The latter was 'God's avenger'. He had become 'most merciful and most

---

[1] See above, p. 146.
[2] *Cod. Theod.* xvi. 2. 9.
[3] Sozomen, *Hist. Ecc.* v. 5 (*PG.* lxvii, col. 1227).
[4] Ammianus Marcellinus, xxii. 5. 4; Julian, *Ep.* 31. 4.
[5] *Cod. Theod.* xvi. 2. 10.   [6] Ibid. 15.
[7] Ibid. 8.   [8] Ibid. 15.
[9] Ibid. 2. 8.
[10] *Enarratio in Ps.* 21, 4 (*PL.* xxxvi, col. 172), 'non est fortior miles [Christi] quam imperator'.
[11] *Contra Epistolam Parmeniani*, i. 10. 16; 12. 19 (*PL.* xliii, cols. 45 and 48). See N. H. Baynes, *Political Ideas of St. Augustine's De Civitate Dei*, pp. 12–13.

religious'.[1] He had the duty of suppressing heresy, and those who suffered thereby died as criminals, not martyrs.[2] Persecution was only meritorious if suffered for 'righteousness' sake'—and the Donatists were a 'sect' and therefore not 'righteous'.[3]

The theory of alliance between Catholic Church and Roman Empire, however, was stated in its most uncompromising form not by St. Augustine but by Optatus of Milevis. In answering Donatus' denial of the State's right of interference in the affairs of the Church, Optatus asserts, 'For the State (*respublica*) is not in the Church, but the Church is in the State, that is, the Roman Empire which Christ in the Song of Songs calls Lebanon.' The Roman Empire was the protector of the virtues of the priesthood.[4] The Donatists replied through Tyconius. The Catholics were 'evil priests working with the kings of this world. Relying on royal favour they have renounced Christ, and as it were, condemned by the law, they confess and speak through their works, "We have no other king but Caesar".'[5]

In practice we find evidence for the close association of the Catholics with the official classes. Of Augustine's friends, Bishop Evodius was a former security official (*agens in rebus*)[6] and Hilarius was a senior administrator (*vir Tribunitius*).[7] Inscriptions relate of Catholic Churches being built by the 'nobility'. Where they were not pagan, the city magistrates were likely to be Catholics, even in Numidia.[8] If chances of Donatist victory faded with the downfall of Gildo, the African Catholics depended for their own survival on the survival of the Roman authority.

The Donatists maintained African tradition on the subject of relations with the State. The separation of the Church from the outside world was a necessity. It was not merely that 'the Emperor had nothing to do with the Church', but his right to legislate for the Church could be denied. In 420 Gaudentius pointed out that God had given the duty of teaching Israel to

---

[1] *Ep.* 97. 3.

[2] *Ep.* 87. 7 (*CSEL.* xxxiv. 403); *Ep.* 185. 5. 19.

[3] *In Ioannis Evangelium Tract.*, vi. 25; *Enarratio in Ps. 145*, 16.

[4] Optatus, iii. 3; Ziwsa, p. 74; see E. L. Woodward, *Christianity and Nationalism*, p. 36.

[5] Tyconius, apud Hahn, op. cit., p. 71.

[6] Augustine, *Confessions*, ix. 8.17.

[7] Id. *Retractationes*, ii. 11.

[8] Y. Allais, *Djemila*, 29–30. Cf. A. Audollent, *Carthage romaine*, 599, *CIL.* viii. 11650, and Augustine, *Ep.* 99, 139 and *Vita*, 24 ('Honorati' of Hippo Regius).

prophets and not to kings.[1] The outlook which this betrays could never lead to a relationship such as that which prevailed between medieval Papacy and Empire, but might eventually uphold a theocracy or Caliphate. The Donatists were instructed that Christians had nothing in common with rulers, nor bishops with the Court.[2] As Tertullian had declared 150 years before: 'Nothing could be more foreign to the Christian than the State.'[3] To become a Donatist, as to become a Christian, in those days entailed the complete renunciation of pagan literature, knowledge, and way of life. One finds plenty of quotations from the classics in Augustine, but none in the works of Petilian and Emeritus, and almost none in Cyprian. As the writer of the *Passio Marculi* expressed the matter, the Christian had no need for books other than the Bible.[4] No wonder Donatists urged their Catholic compatriots to 'become Christians'.[5] Nothing illustrates better the clash of ideas between the two Churches than their respective attitudes towards the Imperial Government and classical civilization.

Equally self-interest and accumulation of wealth allied the Catholics to the great landowners, and hence to the maintenance of the social *status quo* in Africa. Inevitably the geographical distribution of the two Churches influenced their social composition. If the Berber-speaking peasants from Numidia predominated in Donatism, their Latin-speaking masters dominated the Catholic party.[6] This is evident from Augustine's sermons. He preached to his congregation in a faultless Latin without trace of barbarism.[7] He speaks to leisured and propertied folk, people with their villas equipped with marble and tapestries who could understand allegories drawn from the life of an owner of some wealthy estate.[8] On one occasion he reproved his congregation at Hippo for 'failing to clothe the

---

[1] *Contra Gaudentium*, i. 34. 44, 'Deus Prophetis praeconium dedit, non regibus imperavit.'

[2] Parmenian, quoted by Optatus, i. 22, 'Quid Christianis cum regibus, quid episcopis cum Palatio?'

[3] Tertullian, *Apol.* 38.

[4] *Passio Marculi*, 1.   [5] Optatus, iii. 11.

[6] An example of this may be found in the situation in Hippo in 362, when Donatist tenants refused to bake bread for their Catholic deacon (*Contra Litteras Petiliani*, ii. 83. 184). For Donatist *coloni* on Catholic Church estates, Augustine, *Ep.* 35. 4.

[7] Cf. H-I. Marrou, *Saint Augustin et la Fin de la Culture antique*, p. 78.

[8] Augustine, *in Ps. 33*, 14 (*PL.* xxxvi, col. 316), 'lectis eburneis'; *Sermo* 51. 4. 5 and *in Ps. 48*, 8.

poor'.[1] He could maintain, however, that riches were in themselves no bar to entry into the Kingdom of Heaven.[2] Those
who argued the necessity of poverty were denounced as heretics.[3] Augustine, indeed, was never tired of emphasizing the
wealth of his heroes such as Joseph of Arimathea and the
martyr Crispina.[4] The besetting sin of his congregation appears
to have been avarice.

This outlook of complacency was shared by other members
of the Catholic community. In contrast to the monastic movement in other Roman provinces, the Catholic monasteries in
Africa were established of set purpose in fertile and populated
areas, as near Hippo.[5] The monks were to have their lives
made easy under the patronage of a wealthy landowner. Far
from the desert being the homeland of the monk, monasteries
were to be built 'where orchards promised a good return'.[6] The
contrast between this type of monasticism and that in Egypt
and Syria is significant of the difference of outlook between the
Church of Augustine and that of Athanasius and Cyril.

Evidence suggests, moreover, that the wealth of the Catholic
Church was considerable in the fourth century. A law of Constantine, dated A.D. 321, legalized bequests to the Church,[7] and
it seems that it was the custom in many dioceses for wealthy
families to leave part of their property to it.[8] On ordination,
priests would without fail hand over their estates to the keeping
of the church in which they served.[9] The scandalous scenes at
Hippo when the congregation attempted to force ordination
on the rich nobleman Pinian indicate the benefit expected from
the recruitment of a wealthy presbyter.[10] From the Councils of
the African Catholics we learn that the wealth of some of the
sees was a motive behind episcopal translations.[11] Clergy moved
from place to place with the object of arriving at the one best paid.
At Hippo, though the Catholics were in a minority, Augustine

---

[1] Ep. 122. 2.   [2] Sermo 48. 6 (PL. xxxviii, col. 319–20).
[3] Ep. 157. 31 (CSEL. xliv. 478).
[4] Sermo 46. 17. 41 (PL. xxxviii, col. 295); Enarratio in Ps. 120, 13.
[5] Ep. 211. 6. Social inequalities were maintained in these monasteries.
[6] Ferrandus, Vita Fulgentii, 28 (PL. lxv, col. 131).
[7] Cod. Theod. xvi. 2. 4.
[8] Augustine, in Ps. 103, 16; Sermo 359. 9; Ep. 262.
[9] Canon 49 of Council of 397, Mansi, Concilia, iii. 892.
[10] Augustine, Epp. 124, 125, 126. The Church at Thagaste had a great windfall
when Melania took the veil.
[11] Gratus' Council, Canon 10; Mansi, Concilia, iii. 147. Cf. Augustine, Ep. 208. 2.

administered five churches and property estimated at twenty times that of his father who was a *curialis*.[1]

A landowner on a large scale itself, the Catholic Church was at one with the romanized landowning interest as a whole. Some bishops acted as bailiffs on senatorial estates,[2] others put their lands under the patronage of a landowner in order to secure his protection from the tax-collector.[3] But more important than all this was the fact that without the aid of the senatorial landowners it would have been impossible to put down Donatism in the countryside. It was to men such as Pammachius, Festus, Donatus, and Celer, owners of great estates in the diocese of Hippo, that Augustine turned in his efforts to have tne Edict of Unity of 405 enforced.[4]

Thus practical issues prevented the Catholics from making any serious move to alleviate the prevalent social misery and oppression. It is interesting that the petitions for remission of taxation made on behalf of the provincials in the reign of Honorius originate with the pagan Council and not the bishops, who spent so much of their time at court.[5] With the arrival of the Vandals 'priests' and 'nobles' had become intimately associated in the public mind.[6] Possidius relates, probably from first-hand knowledge, that the Church was 'hated because of its lands'.[7]

From Augustine's correspondence and sermons it is evident that the Catholic clergy were fully alive to the intolerable conditions of life endured by the mass of the provincials. The bishop paints a vivid picture of the greed of the rich, their ostentatious luxury, and their exploitation of the poor.[8] He saw how farmers were pillaged by bailiffs, forced to pay double rents, refused justice, and finally evicted.[9] He warned his listeners of the trouble they were storing up for themselves, and

---

[1] *Ep.* 126. 7.

[2] Council of Carthage 397, Canon 15 and Council of Carthage 419, Canon 16.

[3] *Ep.* 96. 2.   [4] *Epp.* 58, 89, 112 and 139.

[5] In 401 the legate on behalf of the curials was Mecilianus (*Cod. Theod.* xii. 1. 166); in 414 the 'viri inlustri' Flavian and Caecilian (*Cod. Theod.* vii. 4. 33); in 445 the delegation of Numidians and Moors was led by Palladius, a count and tribune, and Maximinus, a pagan priest, 'vir sacerdotalis', *Novel* 13.

[6] Victor Vitensis, I. 2 and 14.

[7] Possidius, *Vita Augustini*, 23 (*PL.* xxxii, col. 53), 'Dum forte (ut assolet) de possessionibus ipsis invidia clericis fieret'.

[8] Augustine's sermons, *in Ps. 39*, 7 (*PL.* xxxvi, col. 438); *in Ps. 48*, 8 (*PL.* xxxvi, col. 561–2); and *in Ps. 38*, 2 (*PL.* xxxvi, col. 413).

[9] *Ep.* 247 and *Ep.* 251; *Sermo* 302. 16.

he attempted to intervene to prevent gross cases of injustice.[1]
But the system itself was inviolate. A slave's relation to his
master was divinely ordered, as that of wife to husband, and of
subject to ruler.[2] He might be beaten, chained to a mill, and
cast into prison[3] at the pleasure of his master, but to seek to
better his condition was against 'apostolic discipline'.[4] The
hardship suffered by the poorer classes was no excuse for their
revolt. They were told that they lived 'at the expense of the
rich',[5] that poverty was necessary in a Christian life, that they
had no right to murmur against those who fed and clothed them
so bounteously.[6] The knowledge that Donatist teaching inspired
their efforts towards a freer life did not increase the bishop's
sympathy. Peasant revolt, to Augustine, was an 'audacia rusticana'.[7] His friend and pupil Paulus Orosius describes the Gallic
Bagaudae as a 'rustic band' stirring up a 'most pernicious
tumult'.[8] The same attitude prevailed among many of the
Gallic and African clergy of the time. In face of the sufferings
of the provincials provoked by the senators and Imperial officials 'the majority of the clergy either say nothing, or if they
do speak, their words are no more effective than silence',[9] commented Salvian. The duties imposed by wealth were acknowledged in theory[10] but neglected in practice. It is, perhaps,
interesting to note that elsewhere even the noblest examples
among the Catholic episcopacy, men such as Synesius, would
seldom interfere to prevent administrative oppression unless the
offending official had committed heresy or blasphemy as well.[11]

---

[1] See G. Metzger, *Die afrikanische Kirche*, Tübingen, 1934, p. 70.

[2] *Contra Gaudentium*, i. 19. 20.

[3] *Sermo* 161. 9 (*PL*. xxxviii–xxxix, col. 883), 'Timet servus offendere dominum suum, ne jubeat eum verberare, jubeat in compedes mitti, jubeat in carcere includi, jubeat eum in pistrino conteri.'

[4] *Ep.* 108. 18 (*CSEL*. xxxiv. 632).

[5] *Ep.* 157. 38 (*CSEL*. xliv. 484), 'Puto enim, quod quidam eorum, qui haec impudenter . . . garriunt, a divitibus Christianis et piis in suis necessitatibus sus-tentantur.' Cf. *in Ps. 103*, 16—the rich compared to Lebanon, in whose branches the poor sheltered.

[6] *Ep.* 157. 38 (*CSEL*. 485), 'Sicut autem ipsi qui divitum religiosis obsequiis aluntur atque vestiuntur—neque enim ad suas necessitates nihil accipiunt nisi et eis qui res suas vendunt.'   [7] *Ep.* 108. 18 (*CSEL*. xxxiv. 632).

[8] *Historia adversus paganos*, vii. 25 (*CSEL*. v. 488).

[9] *De Gubernatione Dei*, v. 5. 20 (*CSEL*. viii. 108), 'nam aut tacent plurimi [sacer-dotes] eorum aut similes sunt tacentibus'.

[10] Augustine, *in Ps. 124*, 7.

[11] Synesius, *Epp.* 57 and 72 (*PG*. lxvi. 1383 and 1433); O. Seeck, *Untergang*, ii. 175 ff. and notes. Also A. Piganiol, *L'Empire chrétien*, p. 408.

The Donatists, as we have seen, adopted a different stand-point. It would be misleading to think of the Donatist Church as poorly endowed with this world's goods. They drew their members from Imperial officials as well as peasants, and on the whole their laity in the towns were as well educated in classical literature as their opponents. The Church possessed its lands, accepted legacies, and fought to retain its wealth.[1] For long periods the Circumcellions were unpopular, and the Donatist leaders were no less institutionalized and law-abiding than had been the bishops of the Christian Church in the pagan period a century before.

Yet, as Martroye has long ago pointed out, one of the causes of Donatism was probably the suspicion that the Caecilianists had surrendered not only sacred objects but equally the sense of social justice which had inspired the primitive Christian community.[2] The Donatists retained that sense. Their sermons emphasized the necessity of personal poverty. From Petilian we learn that evangelical poverty was enjoined on clergy and people alike.[3] The deeds of Optatus of Thamugadi were not a cause for scandal until Gildo and he had suffered defeat.

There is a curious duality in the Donatist leaders. Outwardly they were cultivated men, Latinists like Emeritus of Caesarea, moral preachers such as Macrobius of Rome, former lawyers such as Petilian of Constantine. Yet at heart they were revolutionary leaders, and their powers of ferocious oratory raised them in the esteem of congregations whose mother tongue in many cases they could not speak.[4] Their sermons consisted of Scriptural text coupled with invective against their enemies.[5] The same men who could write dull disciplinary tracts could instil boundless hatred of the Catholics in a *Passion* of Donatist martyrs. Like the Kharedjite leaders of the eighth and ninth centuries, they represented the will of an oppressed and

---

[1] For Donatist landed property, see Augustine, *In Ioann. Evang. Tract.* vi. 25; *Contra Epistolam Parmeniani*, i. 12. 19; *Ep.* 185. 9. 36.

[2] P. Martroye, 'Une tentative de révolution sociale en Afrique', *Revue des questions historiques*, lxxvi, 1904, p. 399.

[3] *Contra Litteras Petiliani*, ii. 99. 207. Cf. ii. 98. 227.

[4] As instanced by Macrobius of Hippo. He rebuked the Circumcellions through an interpreter in 408. Four years later he became their leader (Augustine, *Ep.* 108). Nothing suggests that Donatist leaders such as Petilian and Emeritus spoke Berber, but of their ability to use Latin as an effective means of expression there is no doubt.

[5] Optatus, ii. 25 and iv. 5. Cf. Petilian in *Contra Litteras Petiliani*, ii. 63. 141 and ii. 68. 153.

embittered people whose religious fantasy and lust for revenge they understood and knew how to direct.

Donatism and Catholicism represented opposite tendencies in early Christian thought. The Churches were in fact two societies, differing fundamentally in outlook on both religious and social questions. Did 'Catholic' refer to the purity of sacraments, or to the extent of the Church over the inhabited world? Was the Church 'within the Roman Empire', sustaining and sustained by the Christian Emperors, or was the Empire the representative of the outer 'world', whence the Christian must separate himself in order to progress in the faith? Were social evils and injustices to be fought in the name of Christ, or were they to be tolerated for the sake of Christian unity? To all these questions Donatists and Catholics gave different answers. The issues were not those of 'truth' versus 'heresy', but of two opposed attitudes to society, attitudes which have persisted throughout the history of the Christian Church down to the present day.

EPILOGUE

THE question has often been asked by historians, from Gibbon onwards, how far the Christian Church was responsible for the eclipse of the classical world and the transition to the Early Middle Ages. In our view the problem has been misconceived. Christianity did not prevail until the Greco-Roman cities which had for so long been the centres of classical influence were themselves falling into irretrievable decay, and their predominance was passing to revived native, prehistoric units of society. In Africa we have seen that Christianity was an episode in the religious history of the Berbers which lasted some 400 years. Its victory was associated with the rise in the latter part of the third century A.D. of settled farming communities which occupied the inland plains. At the same time the once powerful romanized middle classes were falling between the senatorial landed aristocracy on the one hand and a large artisan population on the other. Its disappearance coincides with the desertion of both cities and villages in face of ever-increasing attacks by the Berber, and later by the Arab, nomads from the Sahara. Christianity was a symptom of a period of great historical change, not its cause.

But within this framework two contradictory interpretations of the Christian message took root. The germs of Catholicism and Dissent, the authority of an institution as against the authority of the Bible or of personal inspiration, existed from the earliest moments of the Christian Church. In Africa it has been possible to carry the argument a stage farther, and to show that the difference of interpretation was interwoven with other differences, such as geography, culture, and economic circumstance.

Catholicism was centred in the cities and villas of Africa. Far from being a destructive force, the Catholics time and again rallied to the defence of authority against the native rebels. They defended established institutions and preserved the use of the Latin language. Roman society found its last interpreters in the Catholic bishops, and in St. Augustine Christianity and classical culture were blended in a harmony never subsequently attained. The survival of the Catholic Church, however, depended in Africa as in other parts of the Mediterranean on the survival of the material institutions of the Empire. When these failed, as they did in the fifth and sixth centuries, Catholicism had no appeal for the masses of the native population. It had no message of effective social reform. The Catholic Church in Africa ultimately suffered the fate of its counterpart, the Melkite Church in Egypt.

Beyond the city walls on the fringes of Greco-Roman society a different type of Christianity became the religion of the inhabitants. We have seen how Donatism was concentrated among the crowded villages of Numidia, the heir of the old national religion of Saturn and Caelestis. But in other parts of the Empire similar developments took place. Despite the great distances which separated the adherents, despite differences of language and culture, the dissenting non-Catholic form of religion that emerged in the various provinces had many features in common. Donatism in Africa, Montanism and Novatianism in Asia Minor, and certain aspects of Coptic Monophysitism, all seem to belong to a common stream of Christian thought both in respect of economic background and belief. Certainly the analogies between the asceticism practised by the Donatists and the Novatianists in Asia Minor were sufficiently pronounced to attract the notice of contemporaries.[1]

The Christianity of the sects was the real enemy of the Empire. This was not a political enmity, for a different form of human society could not be imagined at the time. But the Emperors were regarded by men like Petilian as the 'kings of this world',[2] and the Christian must renounce the society of this world in its entirety. The dissenters thus created a set of values different from those of classical society and also from Catholicism, which sought to harmonize classical and Christian concepts. Christian poverty and martyrdom, for instance, represented not merely virtuous conduct or personal heroism, but were ritual acts, perhaps one might say magical acts, designed to secure for the Elect the vision of Paradise and immediate admittance to the 'Vine of the Lord'. Renunciation of pagan philosophy was one part only of renunciation of the world. As

---

[1] Epiphanius, *Panarion*, 59. 13 (ed. Holl, Leipzig, 1922, pp. 378–9); R. A. Knox, *Enthusiasm*, p. 52, may be mistaken in thinking that 'the Donatists never held the cardinal doctrine of Novatian, that apostasy from the faith was an unforgivable sin'. *Traditio* was apostasy. See *Acta Saturnini*, 18.

[2] *Contra Litteras Petiliani*, ii. 27. 53.

Tertullian showed, 'idolatry' could include nearly all forms of contemporary society.

In addition to this, the dissenters were drawn in the main from the oppressed and primitive groups in the population. In Egypt one finds in the Life of Schenute of Atirpe[1] that same denunciation of alien landowners and military oppressors as in the sermons of the Donatist leaders. Circumcellions and Coptic monks often found themselves fighting similar enemies. Orthodoxy was hated, among other reasons, because of its association with oppressive government and extortions against the peasants. In Egypt and in Africa there is also the reversion to the native language and art in preference to the language and art of the rulers. There seems to be little doubt that if Latin was the language of the inscriptions, Berber was used in the Donatist services in the country districts, just as Coptic was used in the Monophysite liturgy.

In some parts of the Mediterranean Christian dissent may have prepared the way for Islam. If the Moslems were able to absorb the populations which they conquered into a mould so different from the classical, it was because by the seventh century A.D. the masses had already renounced Greco-Roman culture, or had remained untouched by it. With primitive people who considered government in terms of theocracy, the Koran merely replaced the Bible, the Kadi and Emir the dissenting clergy, and martyrdom could equally be attained in holy war against the infidel Franks as against infidel pagans and Catholics. In Africa the marabout and his koubba succeeded the *cellae* or shrines dedicated to the martyrs, and the maraboutic 'family' succeeded the Circumcellion band. Perhaps, too, the taste for Arab love-songs and poetry was easily acquired by those for whom the 'Song of Songs' seems to have had so powerful a fascination. The basic concepts which had governed the native's life for generations could survive better under Islam than under Greco-Roman society or Catholic Christianity.

In these circumstances one can see in Donatism one of the movements which led to the extinction of classical culture over a large part of the Mediterranean. The crude fanaticism of the Donatists represented the outlook of the majority of the North Africans of their day. The Catholic victory in the great Conference of 411 produced a 'revolutionary situation' which, if

---

[1] J. Leipoldt, 'Schenute von Atirpe', *TU.* xxv, 1904, pp. 167 ff.

anything, hastened the decline of Catholicism on the arrival of the Vandals. In the end neither Donatist nor Catholic prevailed, and Islam entered into the African heritage with no opposition of strength equivalent to that of the Monophysite Church in Egypt. If the Islamic conquest was the final act in the division of Rome and Carthage, and of the southern and northern halves of the Mediterranean, then the Donatists and the dissenting sects contributed powerfully to that result. Donatism was not merely a schism, it was part of a revolution.

APPENDIX
EXTANT DONATIST TEXTS

A. Acta Martyrum

Name	Where edited	Relevant literature
Acta Crispinae	Franchi di Cavalieri, Studi e Testi, ix, 1902, pp. 23–35.	P. Monceaux, Histoire littéraire, iii. 159; Mélanges Boissier, p. 383.
Passio Maximae Secundae et Donatillae	Analecta Bollandiana, ix, 1890, pp. 110–16.	P. Monceaux, Histoire littéraire, iii. 148–50.
Acta Saturnini	Migne, PL. viii, cols. 690–703.	E. Buonaiuti, Il Cristianesimo, pp. 295–7; P. Monceaux, Histoire littéraire, iii. 140–2.
Sermo de Passione Advocati et Donati	Migne, PL. viii, col. 752.	O. Seeck, Untergang, iii. 514.
Passio Maximiani et Isaaci	Migne, PL. viii, col. 766.	L. Duchesne, Early History of the Church, ii. 192–3.
Passio Marculi	Migne, PL. viii, col. 760.	P. Monceaux, Histoire littéraire, v. 69 f.; H. Delehaye, 'Domnus Marculus', Analecta Bollandiana, liii. 81.

The Donatist *Passio Cypriani* is analysed by R. Reitzenstein in 'Die Nachrichten über den Tod Cyprians', *Sitzungsberichte der Heidelberger Akademie*, phil.-hist. Klasse, 1913, No. 14, pp. 46–69.

B. Other Texts

Author	Title	Literature
1. Macrobius (Bishop of Rome)	De Singularitate Clericorum.	A. Harnack, TU., 1903, xxiv. 3. (Discussed by H. Koch, Cyprianische Untersuchungen, ch.12.)
2. Unknown Bishop (flor. circa 350)	Sermo in natale Infantium (text published by A. Wilmart, Revue des sciences religieuses, 1922, pp. 271–302).	A. Pincherle, Bilychnis, xxii, 1923, pp. 134–48.
3. Unknown Bishop	Sentence of Council of Cebarsussa 24 June 383 (text Migne, PL. xi, cols. 1189–91).	

Author	Title	Literature
4. Tyconius	*Liber Regularum* (text, Migne, *PL.* xviii, cols. 18–65).	F. C. Burkitt, *Cambridge Texts and Studies*, iii, 1894.
	Commentario in Apocalypsin. Text partially restored in Florez's edition of Beatus of Libana's *In Apocalypsin*, Madrid, 1772, and Souter, in *JTS.*, 1913, pp. 338–58. Sanders's edition of Beatus, American Academy at Rome, 1930, does not help in the reconstruction of Tyconius.	T. Hahn, *Tyconius-Studien*, Leipzig, 1900; A. Pincherle, 'Da Ticonio a Sant' Agostino', *Ricerche Religiose*, i, 1925, pp. 443–66. (Other literature quoted on p. 201, n. 7).
5. Emeritus of Caesarea	Sentence of Council of Bagai, 24 April 394 (text Migne, *PL.* xi, cols. 1189–91).	
6. Petilian of Constantine	*Epistola ad Presbyteros et Diaconos.*	Text reconstructed by P. Monceaux, *Histoire littéraire*, v. 311–28.
7. Gaudentius of Thamugadi	*Epistolae ad Dulcitium.*	P. Monceaux, *Histoire littéraire*, v. 329–33 (text reconstructed).
8. Fulgentius	*De Baptismo.*	P. Monceaux, *Histoire littéraire*, v. 335–9 (text reconstructed); C. Lambot, *Revue Bénédictine*, lviii, 1948, pp. 177–222.
9. Unknown	*Liber Genealogus.*	Mommsen, *MGH.* ix, *Chronica Minora*, Berlin, 1892.

Texts on the origins of the Donatist controversy are collated by H. von Soden, *Urkunden der Entstehungsgeschichte des Donatismus* (Kleine Texte, cxxii, Bonn, 1913).

A Donatist Corpus of Cyprianic writings is commented upon by R. Reitzenstein, *Nachrichten v. der königlichen Gesellschaft zu Göttingen*, phil.-hist. Klasse, Heft iv, 1914, pp. 85–92.

The Donatist letter to Count Marcellinus at the Conference of Carthage, June 411, is to be found in Migne, *PL.* xi, cols. 1408–14, and xliii, cols. 834–8. *Ep.* iii of Pseudo-Cyprian, 'ad Plebem Carthaginensem' (*CSEL.* iii. 3, p. 273), may also be an early Donatist work.

BIBLIOGRAPHY

I. ORIGINAL SOURCES

(Donatist texts have already been quoted in the Appendix and are
not repeated here.)

Acta Martyrum: ed. R. K. Knopf and G. Krüger, *Ausgewählte Märtyrerakten*,
1929, Tübingen.

AMMIANUS MARCELLINUS: *Rerum Gestarum qui supersunt*, Loeb Classical
Library, tr. J. C. Rolfe, 1935–9.

AURELIUS AUGUSTINUS: Anti-Donatist works, A.D. 393–412.
Ad Catholicos Epistola de Unitate Ecclesiae.
Ad Donatistas post Collationem.
Contra Cresconium.
Contra Epistolam Parmeniani.
Contra Gaudentium.
Contra Litteras Petiliani.
De Baptismo contra Donatistas.
De Unico Baptismo.
Gesta cum Emerito.
Psalmus contra Partem Donati.
Sermo ad Caesareensis Ecclesiae Plebem.

These works are to be found in Migne, *Patrologia Latina*, vol. xliii,
and also in *CSEL*. li, lii, liii. The text of the *Patrologia* has been used
throughout.

Enarrationes in Psalmos: *PL*. xxxvi–xxxvii.
Epistolae: *CSEL*. xxxiv, xliv, lvii, lviii.
In Ioannis Evangelium Tractatus: *PL*. xxxv.
Retractationes: *PL*. xxxii.
Sermones, *PL*. xxxviii–xxxix.
De Haeresibus ad Quodvultdeum: *PL*. xlii.

Of the Anti-Donatist works, *De Baptismo contra Donatistas*, *Contra
Litteras Petiliani*, and *Ep*. 185 (to Count Boniface) have been translated
by the Rev. Marcus Dods, Edinburgh, 1872, *The Anti-Donatist Works of
St. Augustine.*

A number of letters concerned with the Donatist controversy are to
be found in the Rev. J. G. Cunningham's *Letters of Saint Augustine*,
Edinburgh, 1872, vols. i and ii.

There is an index to Augustine's Anti-Donatist letters and sermons
in Migne, *PL*. xliii, cols. 757–60.

PSEUDO-AUGUSTINUS: *Contra Fulgentium*: *PL*. xliii.

CHURCH COUNCILS IN AFRICA: G. Bruns, *Canones Apostolorum Conciliorum
Selecti*, Berlin, 1839.

J. D. Mansi, *Sacrorum Conciliorum Collectio nova et amplissima*, Florence,
1759.

Extracts of Conciliar decisions referring to Donatism are to be found
in Migne, *PL*. xi, cols. 1185 ff., and xliii, cols. 802 ff.

CLAUDIUS CLAUDIANUS: *Poems*, Loeb Classical Library, tr. M. Platnauer, 1932. Two volumes.

Codex Theodosianus: Ed. Mommsen and Meyer, Berlin, 1905.

CYPRIANUS: *Opera Omnia*, ed. Hartel, *CSEL*. iii. English translation, *The Writings of Cyprian*, Ante-Nicene Christian Library, Edinburgh, 1868–9.

EUSEBIUS: *Historia Ecclesiastica*, ed. Schwartz, 1908, tr. Lawlor and Oulton, Loeb Classical Library, 1927.

Gesta Collationis Carthaginensis: ed. Migne, *PL*. xi, cols. 1223 ff.

POPE GREGORY: *Epistolae*, ed. Ewald and Hartmann, *MGH*., 1891–3.

HERODIAN: *Ab Excessu divi Marci*, ed. K. Stavenhagen, 1922.

Liber Pontificalis: ed. Duchesne, 1886–92.

OPTATUS: *De Schismate Donatistarum*, Lib. VII, *CSEL*. xxvi, tr. O. Vassall-Philipps, Longmans, 1917.

PAULUS OROSIUS: *Historiarum Libri adversus Paganos*, *CSEL*. v, or ed. Zangemeister, Teubner, 1889.

POSSIDIUS: *Vita Augustini*, *PL*. xxxii, or ed. Weisskotten, Princeton, 1919.

SALLUSTIUS: *Jugurtha*, ed. Ahlberg, Teubner, 1766.

SALVIANUS: *De Dei Gubernatione*, *CSEL*. viii, or ed. E. M. Sanford (English translation), New York, 1930.

Scriptores Historiae Augustae: Loeb, Classical Library, tr. D. Magie, 1922–32, three volumes. Also ed. E. Hohl, Teubner, 1927, two volumes.

SOCRATES: *Historia Ecclesiastica*, *PG*. lxvii, or ed. Hussey, Oxford, 1853.

SOZOMENUS: *Historia Ecclesiastica*, *PG*. lxvii, or ed. Hussey, Oxford, 1860.

TERTULLIAN: *Quae supersunt omnia*, *PL*. i and ii, ed. 1845 and 1879; *CSEL*. xx (1890).

TERTULLIAN and MINUCIUS FELIX: *Apologeticus, De Spectaculis*, and *Octavius*, tr. G. H. Rendall, Loeb, 1931.

TYCONIUS: see Appendix.

VICTOR VITENSIS: *Historia Persecutionis Africanae Provinciae*, *MGH*. iii. 1; *CSEL*. vii.

ZOSIMUS: *Historia Nova*, ed. Mendelssohn, 1887.

Editions of Latin Inscriptions used: see under 'Abbreviations' on page x.

II. GENERAL WORKS OF REFERENCE, PERIODICALS, AND CRITICISM OF SOURCES

Abbreviation	*Text*
AJP.	*American Journal of Philology*, Baltimore, 1880.
Altaner, *Patrologie*	B. ALTANER, *Patrologie, Herders theologische Grundrisse*, Freiburg-i.-Br., 1938, second edition 1950.
Analecta	*Analecta Bollandiana*, Brussels, 1880.
Atlas archéologique	S. GSELL, *Atlas archéologique de l'Algérie*, Algiers, Jourdan, 1911.
Bull. Arch. du Comité	*Bulletin archéologique du Comité des Travaux historiques et scientifiques*. Paris, 1881.

Abbreviation	*Text*

Bruns, *Canones* — G. BRUNS, *Canones Apostolorum et Conciliorum Veterum Selecti*, Berlin, 1839.

CAH. — *Cambridge Ancient History*, vol. xii, Cambridge, 1939.

Congrès (Premier, Deuxième, etc.) — *Actes du Congrès de la Fédération des Sociétés savantes de l'Afrique du Nord.* (First four congresses 1934–8. Reports published in Algiers 1935–9.)

CRAI. — *Comptes rendus de l'Académie des Inscriptions et Belles-Lettres*, Paris, 1858.

Dictionnaire — *Dictionnaire d'Archéologie chrétienne et de Liturgie*, ed. F. Cabrol and H. Leclercq, Paris, Letouzey, 1909. (Particularly valuable for articles under African place-names, e.g. 'Orléansville', 'Morsott', &c.)

Dossier — L. DUCHESNE, 'Le Dossier du Donatisme', *Mélanges*, x, 1890, pp. 590 ff.

Enquête — P. MONCEAUX, 'Enquête sur l'épigraphie chrétienne d'Afrique', in *Mémoires présentés par divers savants à l'Académie des Inscriptions et Belles-Lettres*, tome xii, 1907.

Fastes — PALLU DE LESSERT, *Fastes des Provinces africaines sous la domination romaine*, two volumes, Paris, 1896, 1901.

JRS. — *Journal of Roman Studies*, London, 1911.

JTS. — *Journal of Theological Studies*, Macmillan, 1899.

Mansi, *Concilia* — J. D. MANSI, *Sacrorum Conciliorum Collectio nova et amplissima*, Florence, 1759.

Mélanges — *Mélanges d'archéologie et d'Histoire de l'École française de Rome*, 1881.

Nouvelles Archives — *Nouvelles Archives des Missions et des Explorations scientifiques*, Paris, 1890.

Pauly–Wissowa, *Realencyclopädie* — *Realencyclopädie der klassischen Altertumswissenschaft*, Stuttgart, 1894. (Articles on individuals such as Anulinus, Firmus, Gildo, and Marcellinus.)

Rapport — *Rapport sur les Travaux de Fouilles et Consolidations effectuées par le Service des Monuments historiques de l'Algérie.* Edited by M. Christophle, Algiers, 1932, 1938.

Recueil de Constantine — *Recueil des Notices et Mémoires de la Société archéologique du département de Constantine*, 1858.

Revue Africaine — *Revue Africaine*, Algiers, 1856.

Seeck, *Regesten* — O. SEECK, *Regesten der Kaiser und Päpste*, München, 1919.

III. SECONDARY SOURCES

The field covered by this study is a wide one, and in consequence an enormous bibliography of secondary sources could be built up. There are, however, a number of key works, knowledge of which is essential to the study of Donatism in its African setting.

Most important of all remains the late Professor PAUL MONCEAUX's *Histoire littéraire de l'Afrique chrétienne depuis les origines jusqu'à l'invasion arabe* (Paris, Leroux, 1901–23). This, and the separate articles on North Africa written by this author, are worth very serious attention even though nearly half a century has passed since they appeared.

For the Geography of Donatism and its association with Numidia, the researches of A. BERTHIER and his associates MM. MARTIN and LOGEART are valuable. Their joint *Les Vestiges du Christianisme antique dans la Numidie centrale* (Algiers, 1942) is useful not only for the description of the various chapels explored but for photographs and its introductory chapter. An older work by J. MESNAGE, *L'Afrique chrétienne* (Paris, Leroux, 1912), is useful for its collation of material on the distribution of Catholicism and Donatism.

Apart from MONCEAUX, the works of the late S. GSELL are essential for the study of the African background of Donatism. The *Atlas archéologique de l'Algérie* (Algiers, 1911) is still a basic study of the archaeology of ancient Numidia. Volumes i, ii, v, and vi of Gsell's *Histoire ancienne de l'Afrique du Nord* (Paris, 1913–24) and E. F. GAUTIER's *Passé de l'Afrique du Nord* (Payot, 1937) should also be consulted. The Roman archaeology of Algeria and of Donatism was treated in the years before the Second World War in a series of articles by students of the École française de Rome. Those by P. CAYREL and P. COURCELLE in vols. li and liii of *Mélanges* describe the important Donatist site of Vegesela (Ksar el Kelb).

On the cult of Saturn which preceded Donatism in Numidia, the basic work remains J. TOUTAIN's *Les Cultes païens dans l'Empire romain*, première partie, 'Les Provinces latines', tome iii (Paris, Leroux, 1920). This work has now, however, been supplemented by J. CARCOPINO's article on the N'gaous inscriptions entitled 'Survivances par substitution des sacrifices d'enfants', *Revue de l'Histoire des Religions*, tome cvi, 1932, pp. 592–9.

The account of the origins of the Donatist movement and the place of Donatism in the development of Constantine's religious policy has been described often. N. H. BAYNES's lecture, 'Constantine the Great and the Christian Church' (*Proceedings of the British Academy*, xv, 1929), is very important, especially regarding the chronology of the period A.D. 313–16. Apart from Duchesne's article in *Mélanges*, 1890, noted on p. 341, Otto SEECK's chapter on the origins and development of Donatism in vol. iii of *Geschichte des Unterganges der antiken Welt* (Berlin, 1909) is valuable. In English, the best summary of the history of Donatism is still to be found in the relevant chapters of the translation of L. DUCHESNE, *Histoire ancienne de l'Église*, vols. ii and iii.

The story of Saint Augustine's struggle with the Donatists has been told anew by the Rev. G. G. WILLIS, *Saint Augustine and the Donatist Controversy*

(S.P.C.K., 1950). This is excellent on the ecclesiastical aspects of the controversy but less useful on the Donatists themselves. The older work by W. J. SPARROW SIMPSON, *Saint Augustine and African Church Divisions* (Longmans, 1910), has not been entirely replaced. Of the general works, GUSTAVE BARDY, *Saint Augustin, l'homme et l'œuvre* (Desclée de Brouwer, Paris, 1948), is recommended.

The most valuable studies of the theology of Donatism are to be found in the works of E. BUONAIUTI and his pupil A. PINCHERLE. In particular, Pincherle's 'L'Ecclesiologia nella Controversia Donatista', *Ricerche Religiose*, i, 1925, and 'Da Ticonio a Sant' Agostino' in the same number of the same periodical, are important contributions.

Finally, for the analogies between Donatism and other dissenting Churches, in Later Roman times, R. A. KNOX, *Enthusiasm* (O.U.P., 1950), chapters iii and iv, is stimulating, if not completely accurate, and W. SCHEPERLEN, *Der Montanismus und die phrygischen Kulte* (Tübingen, 1929), is a useful study for the parallel development of popular religion in Asia Minor.

A select Bibliography is quoted below.

A. THE NORTH AFRICAN BACKGROUND

E. ALBERTINI, *L'Afrique romaine*, Algiers, 1937.
—— 'Actes de vente du Ve siècle trouvés dans la région de Tébessa', *Journal des Savants*, Jan. 1930.
——'Un Témoignage de Saint Augustin sur la prospérité relative de l'Afrique au IVe siècle', *Mélanges P. Thomas*, Bruges, 1930.
Y. ALLAIS, *Djemila*, Les Belles Lettres, Paris, 1938.
J. and P. ALQUIER, *Le Chettaba*, Constantine, 1928.
A. AUDOLLENT, 'Voyage épigraphique en Algérie', *Mélanges*, x, 1890, pp. 397 ff.
—— *Carthage romaine*, Paris, 1901.
A. BALLU, *Les Ruines de Timgad. Sept années de découvertes*, Paris, 1911.
J. BARADEZ, *Fossatum Africae*, Gouvernement Général de l'Algérie, Paris, 1949.
W. BARTHEL, *Zur Geschichte der römischen Städte in Afrika*, Greifswald, 1904.
H. BASSET, 'Les Influences puniques chez les Berbères', *Revue Africaine*, lxv, 1921, pp. 340–75.
A. BEL, 'La Religion musulmane en Berbérie', *Esquisse d'histoire et de sociologie religieuses*, tome i, Geuthner, Paris, 1938.
J. BÉRARD, 'Mosaïques inédites de Cherchell', *Mélanges*, lii, 1935, pp. 111–12.
D. VAN BERCHEM, 'L'Annona militaire dans l'Empire au IIIe siècle', *Mémoires de la Société Nationale des Antiquaires de France*, lxxx, 1937, pp. 117 ff.
A. BERNARD, *Atlas de l'Algérie et de Tunisie*, Algiers, 1924.
G. BOISSIER, *La Fin du paganisme*, Paris, 1903.
MME A. BOUGAREL-MUSSO, 'Recherches économiques sur l'Afrique romaine', *Revue Africaine*, lxxvi, 1934 (3e et 4e trimestres).
E. S. BOURCHIER, *Life and Letters in Roman Africa*, Oxford, 1913.
A. H. BRODRICK, *Parts of Barbary*, Hutchinson, 1944.

T. R. S. Broughton, *The Romanisation of Proconsular Africa*, Johns Hopkins, Baltimore, 1929.

J. Cantineau, 'Les Parlers arabes du département de Constantine', *Quatrième Congrès*, Algiers, 1939, pp. 849–65.

J. Carcopino, 'L'Inscription d'Ain el-Djemala', *Mélanges*, xxvi, 1906, pp. 365–406.

—— 'Les Castella de la Plaine de Sétif', *Revue Africaine*, lxii, 1918, pp. 1–22.

—— 'Le Limes de Numidie et sa Garde syrienne', *Syria*, vi, 1925, pp. 30–57 and 118–49.

—— 'Survivances par substitution des sacrifices d'enfants', *Revue de l'histoire des religions*, cvi, 1932, pp. 592–9.

—— 'La Fin du Maroc antique', *Mélanges*, lvii, 1940, pp. 349 ff.

—— *Aspects mystiques de la Rome païenne*, Paris, Artisan du Livre, 1941.

—— *Le Maroc antique*, Librairie Gallimard, 1943.

L. Carton, 'Le Sanctuaire de Baal-Saturne à Dougga', *Nouvelles Archives des Missions*, vii, 1899.

—— 'Travaux d'irrigation et de culture dans la région du Dj. Onk', *Recueil de Constantine*, xliii, 1909, p. 193.

J. Chabot, *Recueil des inscriptions libyques*, Paris, Imprimerie Nationale, 1940.

M. Christophle, *Essai de restitution d'un moulin à huile de l'époque romaine à Madaure (Constantine)*, Algiers, 1930.

S. Dill, *Roman Society in the Last Century of the Western Empire*, Macmillan, 1919. (Particularly book iii, pp. 227–81.)

E. Doutté, 'Notes sur l'Islam maghrébien', *Revue de l'histoire des religions*, xl, 1899, pp. 343–69, and xli, pp. 22–66.

—— *Magie et religion dans l'Afrique du Nord*, Algiers, Jourdan, 1909.

W. H. C. Frend, 'The Revival of Berber Art', *Antiquity*, December 1942, pp. 342–52.

E. F. Gautier, *Genséric, roi des Vandales*, Paris, Payot, 1930 (second ed. 1950).

—— *Le Passé de l'Afrique du Nord. Les siècles obscurs*, Paris, Payot, 1937.

R. Gavault, *Étude sur les ruines romaines de Tigzirt* (Ministère de l'Instruction Publique, fasc. ii, Paris, 1897).

R. G. Goodchild and J. B. Ward Perkins, 'The *Limes Tripolitanus* in the light of Recent Discoveries', *JRS.* xxxix, 1949, pp. 81–93, and xl, pp. 30–39.

H. Graillot and S. Gsell, 'Exploration archéologique dans le département de Constantine', *Mélanges*, xiii, 1893, pp. 461–541, and xiv, pp. 17–86.

S. Gsell, 'Enquête administrative sur les travaux hydrauliques de l'Algérie', *Nouvelles Archives des Missions*, x, 1902.

—— *Monuments antiques de l'Algérie*, Paris, Fontemoing, 1901–2. Two volumes.

—— *Hérodote*, Jourdan, Algiers, 1915.

—— *Histoire ancienne de l'Afrique du Nord*, vols. i–viii, Paris, 1913–28.

Commandant Guenin, 'Inventaire archéologique du Cercle de Tébessa', *Nouvelles Archives des Missions*, xvii, 1909, pp. 75–234.

J. Guey, 'Ksiba et à propos de Ksiba', *Mélanges*, liv, 1937, pp. 67–107.

—— 'Note sur le Limes romain de Numidie et le Sahara au ive siècle', *Mélanges*, lvi, 1939, pp. 178 ff.

F. M. HAYWOOD, *Economic Survey of Ancient Rome, North Africa*, Johns Hopkins, Baltimore, 1938.

C. A. JULIEN, *Histoire de l'Afrique du Nord*, Algiers, 1931.

L. LESCHI, 'Épigraphie du pays des Nemenchas', *Revue Africaine*, lxii, 1921, pp. 262–94.

CHRISTIAN LUCAS, 'Notes on the *Curatores Reipublicae* in Roman North Africa', *JRS*. xxx, pp. 56–74.

WM. MARCAIS, 'Comment l'Afrique du Nord a été arabisée', *Annales de l'Institut d'Études orientales, Faculté des Lettres de l'Université d'Alger*, iv, pp. 1–22.

H.-I. MARROU, 'La Collection Vulpillières à el-Kantara', *Mélanges*, l, 1933, pp. 42 f.

E. MERCIER, 'La Population indigène de l'Afrique sous la domination romaine, vandale et byzantine', *Recueil de Constantine*, xxx, 1895–6, pp. 127–212.

A. MERLIN and L. POINSSOT, 'Deux mosaïques de Tunisie', *Monuments Piot*, xxxiv, 1934, pp. 129–76.

—— 'La Mosaïque du Seigneur Julius à Carthage', *Bull. Arch. du Comité*, 1921, pp. 95–114.

J. MESNAGE, *La Romanisation de l'Afrique: Tunisie, Algérie, Maroc*, Paris, 1913.

P. MONCEAUX, *Les Africains, les païens*, Paris, 1894.

M. F. G. DE PACHTÈRE, 'Le Règlement d'irrigation de Lamasba', *Mélanges*, xxviii, 1908, pp. 373–405.

L. POINSSOT, 'Mosaïques d'el Haouria', *Actes du premier Congrès*, 1935, pp. 183–206.

M. REYGASSE, *Monuments funéraires préislamiques de l'Afrique du Nord*, Paris, 1950.

P. RODARY, 'Recherche des inscriptions libyques dans la région de Souk-Ahras', *Actes du premier Congrès*, 1935.

M. ROSTOVTZEV, *Studien zur Geschichte des römischen Kolonates* (Archiv für Papyrusforschung, 1910, Erste Beiheft), Leipzig, 1910.

—— *Social and Economic History of the Roman Empire*, O.U.P., 1926. (Particularly illustrations of mosaics relating to life on Roman villas in Africa in 3rd–4th century.)

CH. SAUMAGNE, 'Sur la législation relative aux terres incultes de l'Afrique romaine', *Revue Tunisienne*, 1922, pp. 57–116.

—— 'La Paix vandale', *Revue Tunisienne*, nouvelle série, i, 1930, pp. 183 ff.

—— 'Observations sur deux lois byzantines relatives au Colonat dans l'Afrique du Nord', *Actes du deuxième Congrès*, 1936.

—— 'Les Inscriptions de Jenan ez Zaytouna', *CRAI.*, 1937, pp. 292–301.

A. N. SHERWIN WHITE, 'Geographical Factors in Roman Algeria', *JRS*. xxxiv, 1944, pp. 1–10.

C. E. VAN SICKLE, 'Revival of Public Works in Africa in the Reign of Diocletian', *Classical Philology*, 1930, pp. 173–9.

TENNEY FRANK, 'The Inscriptions of the Imperial Domains in Africa' and 'A Commentary on the Inscription of Henchir Mettich', *AJP*. xlvii, 1926.

H. TERRASSE, *Kasbas berbères de l'Atlas et des oasis*, Paris, 1938.

J. Toutain, *Les Cités romaines de la Tunisie*, Paris, 1896.

—— 'Le Sanctuaire de Saturnus Balcarensis', *Melanges*, xii, 1892, pp. 3–124.

—— 'Le Progrès de la vie urbaine sous la domination romaine', *Mélanges Cagnat*, pp. 319–47, Paris, Leroux, 1912.

—— *Les Cultes païens dans l'Empire romain*, première partie, 'Les Provinces latines', vol. iii, Paris, Leroux, 1920.

A. Truillot, 'Bibliographie de la région de Tébessa', *Recueil des Notices et des Mémoires de la Soc. de Préhistoire et d'Archéologie de Tébessa*, i, 1936–7, pp. 321–53, Algiers, 1938. (A valuable local study.)

A. Vel, 'Monuments et inscriptions libyques relevées dans les ruines de Tir Kabbine (Ain Mlila)', *Recueil de Constantine*, xxxix, 1905, pp. 193–229.

P. Westermarck, *Ritual and Belief in Morocco*, Longmans, 1926.

J. Zellinger, *Augustin und Volksfrömmigkeit*, München, 1933.

B. Donatism and the History of Christianity in North Africa

K. Adam, *Der Kirchenbegriff Tertullians*, Paderborn, 1907. (Forschungen zur christlichen Literatur.)

A. Alföldi, *The Conversion of Constantine and Pagan Rome* (tr. H. Mattingly), O.U.P. 1948.

G. Bardy, *Saint Augustin, l'homme et l'œuvre*, Desclée de Brouwer, Paris, 1948.

—— *La Conversion au Christianisme durant les trois premiers siècles*, Aubier, Paris, 1949.

P. Batiffol, *La Paix constantinienne et le Catholicisme*, Paris, 1914.

—— *Le Catholicisme de Saint Augustin*, Paris, 1920.

J. H. Baxter, 'The Martyrs of Madaura', *JTS*. xxvi (Oct. 1924), pp. 21 ff.

N. H. Baynes, 'Optatus', *JTS*. xxvi 1924.

—— *Constantine the Great and the Christian Church* (Proceedings of the British Academy, xv, 1929).

—— *The Political Ideas of St. Augustine's 'De Civitate Dei'*, Historical Association Pamphlet, No. 104, 1936.

—— 'The Great Persecution', essay in *CAH*. xii, pp. 646–77.

Archbishop E. W. Benson, *Cyprian, His Life, His Times, His Work*, Macmillan, 1897.

A. Berthier, 'Fouilles dans une chapelle chrétienne à Oued R'zel', *Actes du deuxième Congrès*, Algiers, 1936, pp. 375–85.

—— and M. Martin, 'Édifices chrétiens de Bou Takrematem', *Actes du premier Congrès*, Algiers, 1935, pp. 137–51.

—— and F. Logeart, 'Deux basiliques chrétiennes de Sila', *Recueil de Constantine*, lxiii, pp. 235–84. (Useful for Christianity in Byzantine Africa.)

—— M. Martin, and F. Logeart, *Les Vestiges du Christianisme antique dans la Numidie centrale*, Algiers, Gouvernement Général de l'Algérie, Direction des Antiquités, 1942. (Reviewed by W. H. C. Frend in *JRS*. xxxiv, 1944, pp. 152–3, and S. G. F. Brandon in *JTS*. xlvi, 1945, pp. 125–8. Contains useful bibliography, and photographs of Numidian chapels.)

M. Besnier, 'L'Empire romain de l'avenir des Sévères au Concile de Nicée', vol. iv, part i, of Glotz's *Histoire générale, Histoire ancienne*, troisième partie, Les Presses Universitaires de France, 1937.

J. Berton, *Tertullien le schismatique*, Paris, 1928.

M. Bévenot, 'Saint Cyprian's *De Unitate*, Chapter IV, in the Light of the Manuscripts', *Analecta Gregoriana*, Rome, 1938.

W. Bousset, *Die Offenbarung Ioannis*, Göttingen, 1906.

J. P. Brisson, *Gloire et misère de l'Afrique chrétienne*, Lafont, Paris, 1949.

E. Buonaiuti, *Il Cristianesimo nell' Africa Romana*, Bari, 1928.

F. C. Burkitt, 'The "Book of Rules" of Tyconius', *Cambridge Texts and Studies*, iii. i, 1894.

H. v. Campenhausen, *Die Idee des Martyriums in der alten Kirche*, 1936.

P. Cayrel, 'Une Basilique donatiste de Numidie', *Mélanges*, li, 1934, pp. 114–42.

Carlo Cecchelli, 'Africa Christiana', article in *Africa Romana*, Istituto di Studi Romani, Hoepli, Milan, 1935. (Excellent photography.)

Dom J. Chapman, 'Donatus the Great and Donatus of Casae Nigrae', *Revue Bénédictine*, 1909, pp. 9–23.

C. N. Cochrane, *Christianity and Classical Culture. A Study in Thought and Action from Augustus to Augustine*, O.U.P. 1940.

P. Courcelle, 'Une Seconde Campagne de fouilles à Ksar el Kelb', *Mélanges*, liii, 1936, pp. 166–97.

—— *Histoire littéraire des grandes invasions germaniques*, Hachette, 1948. (Includes criticism of Salvian and other sources for the early fifth century in North Africa.)

M. C. D'Arcy and others, *A Monument to Saint Augustine*, London, 1934.

H. Delehaye, *Les Origines du culte des martyrs*, Brussels, Soc. des Bollandistes, 1912.

—— *Les Passions des martyrs et les genres littéraires*, Brussels, 1921.

—— 'Domnus Marculus', *Analecta Bollandiana*, liii, 1936, p. 81.

R. Devréesse, 'L'Église d'Afrique durant l'occupation byzantine', *Mélanges*, lvii, 1940, pp. 143–66.

L. Duchesne, 'Le Dossier du Donatisme', *Mélanges*, x, 1890, pp. 590–643.

—— *Histoire ancienne de l'Église* (Paris, 1910–11) (English translation, London, John Murray, 1931).

A. Ehrhard, *Die Kirche der Märtyrer*, München, 1932.

W. H. C. Frend, 'The *Memoriae Apostolorum* in Roman North Africa', *JRS* xxx, 1940, pp. 32–49.

—— 'Note on the Berber Background in the Life of Augustine', *JTS*. xliii, Nos. 171–2 (July–Oct. 1942), pp. 179–81.

—— 'Religion and Social Change in the Late Roman Empire', *Cambridge Journal*, ii, May 1949, pp. 487–97.

G. Gagé, 'Nouveaux aspects de l'Afrique chrétienne', *Études d'archéologie romaine*, Annales de l'École des Hautes Études de Gand, 1937, pp. 181–230.

J. Geffcken, *Der Ausgang des griechisch-römischen Heidentums*, Heidelberg, 1929.

M. M. Getty, *The Life of the North Africans as revealed in the Sermons of Saint Augustine*, Washington, 1931.

T. R. Glover, *Conflict of Religions in the Early Roman Empire*, Methuen, 1909.

H. Grégoire, 'Sainte Salsa', *Byzantion*, xii, 1937, pp. 213–24.

S. Gsell, 'Tipasa', *Mélanges*, xiv, 1894, pp. 290 ff.

—— *Les Fouilles à Benian*, Algiers, 1901. (Donatism in fifth-century Morocco.)

—— 'Chapelle chrétienne d'Henchir Akhrib', *Mélanges*, xxiii, 1903, pp. 3–25.

—— 'Observations géographiques sur la révolte de Firmus', *Recueil de Constantine*, xxxvi, 1902, pp. 21–46.

—— 'Le Christianisme en Oranie', *Bull. du Cinquantenaire de la Soc. de Géographie et d'Archéologie d'Oranie*, 1928, pp. 17–32.

—— *Édifices chrétiens de Thélepte et d'Ammaedara*, Tunis, 1933.

—— 'Les Martyrs d'Ammaedara', *Bull. Arch. du Comité*, 1934, pp. 69–82.

Commandant Guenin, 'Notice sur l'Henchir el Begueur', *Bull. Arch. du Comité*, 1907, pp. 336–53.

—— 'Notice sur une petite basilique à Rouis', *Bull. Arch. du Comité*, 1907, pp. 153–8.

Ch. Guignebert, *Tertullien*, Paris, Leroux, 1901.

T. Hahn, *Tyconius-Studien* (Studien zur Geschichte der Theologie und Kirche, ed. Bonwetsch und Seeburg, Leipzig, 1900).

W. R. Halliday, *The Pagan Background of Early Christianity*, Liverpool, 1925.

A. Harnack, *Mission und Ausbreitung des Christentums in der ersten drei Jahrhunderten*, Leipzig, 1929.

—— *Lehrbuch der Dogmengeschichte*, 5th edition, Tübingen, 1932.

—— 'Das Leben Cyprians von Pontius', *TU*. xxxix, Leipzig, 1913.

C. J. Hefele, *Conciliengeschichte* (transl. W. R. Clarke, Edinburgh, 1872).

K. Holl, 'Die Vorstellung vom Märtyrer und Märtyrerakten in ihrer geschichtlichen Entwicklung', *Gesammelte Aufsätze zur Kirchengeschichte*, Tübingen, 1928. Other articles in this collection are also valuable.

F. Homes Dudden, *Gregory the Great*, Longmans, 1905.

T. G. Jalland, *The Church and the Papacy*, S.P.C.K., 1944.

H. Jaubert, 'Anciens évêchés et ruines chrétiennes de la Numidie et de la Sitifienne', *Recueil de Constantine*, xlvi, 1912, pp. 1–216.

A. H. M. Jones, *Constantine and the Conversion of Europe*, English Universities Press, 1948.

M. E. Keenan, *The Life and Times of Saint Augustine*, Washington, 1935.

H. Koch, 'Cyprian und der römische Primat', *TU*. xxxv, 1910.

—— *Cyprianische Untersuchungen*, Bonn, 1926.

—— 'La Sopravvivenza di Cipriano, Cipriano in Agostino', *Ricerche Religiose*, viii, 1932, pp. 317–37.

P. de Labriolle, *Histoire de la littérature latine chrétienne*, Paris, 1924.

H. Labrousse, 'Basilique et reliquaire d'Henchir Tarlist', *Mélanges*, li, 1934, pp. 224–58.

G. G. Lapeyre, *Saint Fulgence de Ruspe, un évêque catholique sous la domination vandale*, Paris, 1929.

—— and A. Pellegrin, *Carthage latine et chrétienne*, Paris, Payot, 1950.

J. Lebreton and J. Zeiller, 'De la fin du deuxième siècle à la paix constantinienne', vol. ii of *L'Histoire de l'Église depuis les origines jusqu'à nos jours*, published under the direction of A. Fliche and V. Martin, Bloud & Gay, Paris, 1948.

H. Leclercq, *L'Afrique chrétienne*, Paris, 1904. Two volumes.

L. Leschi, 'Reliquaires chrétiens du VIᵉ siècle en Numidie', *CRAI.*, 1934, pp. 236–45.

—— 'Basilique et cimetière donatistes de Numidie (Ain Ghorab)', *Revue Africaine*, lxxviii, 1936, pp. 27–46.

—— 'A propos des épitaphes chrétiennes du Djebel Nif-en-Nisr', *Revue Africaine*, lxxxiv, 1940, pp. 30–35.

—— 'Tipasa', *Bull. Arch. du Comité*, 1940, pp. xi–xxii.

H. Lietzmann, *Geschichte der alten Kirche*, vols. i–iv, Berlin, 1937–44. (Vols. i–iii translated by B. E. Woolf, Lutterworth Press, 1947–50.)

F. Logeart, 'Les Épitaphes funéraires chrétiennes du Dj. Nif en Nisr', *Revue Africaine*, lxxxiv, 1940, pp. 5–29.

H.-I. Marrou, *Saint Augustin et la fin de la culture antique*, Paris, 1938.

F. Martroye, 'Une Tentative de révolution sociale en Afrique', *Revue des questions historiques*, lxxvi, 1904, pp. 353–416 and lxxvii, 1905, pp. 1–53.

—— 'La Répression du Donatisme, et la politique religieuse de Constantin et ses successeurs en Afrique', *Mémoires de la Soc. Nationale des Antiquaires de France*, lxiii, 1913.

J. Mesnage, *L'Afrique chrétienne, Évêchés et ruines antiques*, Paris, Leroux, 1912.

G. Metzger, *Die afrikanische Kirche*, Tübingen, Mohr, 1934.

E. Michaud, 'La Théologie d'Optat de Milève', *Revue internationale de théologie*, xvi, 1908.

P. Monceaux, *Histoire littéraire de l'Afrique chrétienne depuis les origines jusqu'à l'invasion arabe*, seven volumes, Paris, Leroux, 1901, 1902, 1905, 1912, 1920, 1922, 1923.

—— 'Inscriptions chrétiennes du Cercle de Tébessa', *Recueil de Constantine*, xlii, 1908, pp. 193–237.

—— *Timgad chrétien*, Paris, Imprimerie Nationale, 1911.

—— 'L'Épigraphie donatiste', *Revue de philologie*, xxxiii (avril–juillet), 1909, pp. 112–61.

K. von Nathusius, *Zur Charakteristik der Circumcellionen*, Greifswald, 1900.

E. M. Pickman, *The Mind of Latin Christendom*, Oxford, 1937.

A. Piganiol, *L'Empire chrétien, 325–395 (Histoire romaine*, tome iv, deuxième partie). Same series as Besnier's work already quoted. Presses Universitaires de France, 1947.

A. Pincherle, 'Un Sermone donatista attribuito a S. Ottato di Milevi', *Bilychnis*, xxii, 1923, pp. 134–48.

—— 'L'Ecclesiologia nella Controversia Donatista', *Ricerche Religiose*, i, 1925, pp. 35–55.

—— 'Da Ticonio a Sant' Agostino', *Ricerche Religiose*, i, 1925, pp. 443–66.

—— 'Il Decennio di Preparazione di Sant' Agostino', *Ricerche Religiose*, vi, vii, viii, and ix, 1930–3, especially articles in viii, pp. 118–43, and ix, pp. 399–423.

B. Poschmann, 'Abendländische Kirchenbusse', *Münchener Studien zur historichen Theologie*, 1912.

R. Reitzenstein, 'Die Nachrichten über den Tod Cyprians', *Sitzungsberichte der Heidelberger Akademie der Wissenschaften*, phil.-hist. Klasse, B. 1913.

—— 'Ein donatistisches Corpus Cyprianischer Schriften', *Nachrichten von der kgl. Ges. zu Göttingen*, phil.-hist. Klasse, 1914, Heft 4, pp. 85–92.

CH. SAUMAGNE, 'Ouvriers agricoles ou rôdeurs de celliers? Les Circon-cellions d'Afrique', *Annales d'histoire économique et sociale*, vi, 1934, pp. 351 ff.

E. SCHWARTZ, *Kaiser Constantin und die christliche Kirche*, Leipzig, 1936.

E. SECKEL, 'Die Karthagische Inschrift, *CIL*. viii, 25045, Ein kirchen-rechtliches Denkmal des Montanismus', *Sitzungsberichte der Preuss. Akad. der Wiss.*, 1921, 989–1021.

O. SEECK, 'Quellen und Urkunden über die Anfänge des Donatismus', *Zeitschrift für Kirchengeschichte*, x, 1889, pp. 526 ff.

—— *Die Geschichte des Unterganges der antiken Welt*, Berlin, 1907–20. Parti-cularly vol. iii, *Religion und Sittlichkeit* (Berlin, 1909), chapter xi on Donatism, and notes.

W. SESTON, 'Le Monastère d'Ain Tamda et les origines d'architecture monastique en Afrique du Nord', *Mélanges*, li, 1934, pp. 74–113.

—— 'Sur les derniers temps du christianisme en Afrique', *Mélanges*, liii, 1936, pp. 101–24.

—— *Dioclétien et la Tétrarchie*, Paris, Boccard, 1946.

M. SIMON, 'Fouilles dans la basilique de Henchir el Ateuch', *Mélanges*, li, 1934, pp. 143–77.

H. VON SODEN, *Das lateinische Neue Testament in Afrika zur Zeit Cyprians*, Bonn, 1909.

A. SOUTER, 'Tyconius' Text of the Apocalypse; a partial reconstruction', *JTS* xiv, 1913.

F. W. SPARROW SIMPSON, *Saint Augustine and African Church Divisions*, Long-mans, 1910.

H. B. SWETE (editor), *Essays on the Early History of the Church and the Ministry*, Macmillans, 1926.

—— *The Holy Spirit in the Ancient Church*, Macmillan, 1925.

E. A. THOMPSON, *The Historical Work of Ammianus Marcellinus*, C.U.P. 1947. (Useful on the revolt of Firmus.)

W. THÜMMEL, *Zur Beurteilung des Donatismus*, Inaugural-Dissertation, Halle, 1893. (Reviewed by S. Gsell in *Mélanges*, xv, 1895, p. 325.)

LE NAIN DE TILLEMONT, *Mémoires pour servir à l'histoire ecclésiastique des six premiers siècles*, Paris, 1701–12.

C. H. TURNER, 'Adversaria Critica, Notes on the anti-Donatist Dossier and Optatus', *JTS*. xxvii, 1925.

D. VOELTER, *Der Ursprung des Donatismus*, Freiburg and Tübingen, 1883.

REBECCA WEST, *Saint Augustine*, Nelson's Short Biographies, 1938.

G. G. WILLIS, *Saint Augustine and the Donatist Controversy*, S.P.C.K., 1950.

M. ZEPF, 'Zur Chronologie der anti-donatistischen Schriften Augustins', *Zeitschrift für die neutestamentliche Wissenschaft*, xxviii, 1929, pp. 46–61.

C. ZIWSA, *Praefatio in Optatum*, CSEL. xxvi, Vienna, 1893. (Useful preface to *CSEL*. edition of Optatus' works.)

C. Donatism and Other Ascetic and Dissenting Movements in the
Roman Empire

E. Amélineau, 'Le Christianisme chez les anciens Coptes', *Revue de l'histoire des religions*, xiv, 1886.

J. G. C. Anderson, *Paganism and Christianity in the Upper Tembris Valley*. (Studies in the History and Art of the Eastern Provinces of the Roman Empire, Aberdeen, 1906.)

W. M. Calder, 'Philadelphia and Montanism', *Bulletin of the John Rylands Library*, vii, 1923, p. 309.

—— 'The Epigraphy of the Anatolian Heresies', *Anatolian Studies*, Manchester, 1923, p. 59.

H. Grégoire, 'Du nouveau sur la hiérarchie de la secte montaniste d'après une inscription grecque trouvée près de Philadelphia en Lydie', *Byzantion*, ii, 1925, p. 329.

K. Holl, edition of Epiphanius' *Panarion*, Leipzig, 1922.

A. Harnack, article 'Novatian' in Herzog-Hauck, *Realencylopädie für protestantische Theologie und Kirche*, Leipzig, 1896–1913.

K. Heussi, *Der Ursprung des Mönchtums*, Tübingen, Mohr, 1934.

R. A. Knox, *Enthusiasm*, O.U.P., 1950, chapters iii and iv.

P. de Labriolle, *La Crise montaniste*, Paris, 1913.

J. Leipoldt, 'Schenute von Atirpe', *TU*. xxv, 1904.

W. Schepelern, *Der Montanismus und die phrygischen Kulte*, Tübingen, Mohr, 1929.

E. L. Woodward, *Christianity and Nationalism in the Later Roman Empire*, Longmans, 1916.

J. Zeiller, 'Donatisme et Arianisme. La Falsification donatiste du Concile arien de Sardique', *CRAI.*, 1933, pp. 65–73.

IV. BIBLIOGRAPHY TO THE SECOND IMPRESSION

J.-P. Brisson, *Autonomisme et Christianisme dans l'Afrique romaine de Septime Sévère à l'invasion vandale*, Paris, 1958.

P. R. L. Brown, *Augustine of Hippo*, a biography, London, 1967.

—— 'Religious Dissent in the Later Roman Empire. The case of North Africa', *History*, 46, 1961, pp. 83–101.

Y. M. J. Congar (ed.), *Œuvres de saint Augustin*, 28, Traités anti-donatistes i, (Bibliothèque augustinienne), Paris, 1963.

Ch. Courtois, 'Saint Augustin et le problème de la survivance de punique', *Revue Africaine*, 94, 1950, pp. 259–82.

H. J. Diesner, *Kirche und Staat im spätrömischen Reich*, Berlin, 1963.

—— *Der Untergang der römischen Herrschaft in Nordafrika*, Weimar, 1964.

W. H. C. Frend, 'The Roman Empire in the eyes of the Western Schismatics', *Miscellanea historiae ecclesiasticae* i, Louvain 1961, pp. 5–22.

A. H. M. JONES, 'Were ancient heresies national or social movements in disguise?' *JTS*. n.s. x. 2, pp. 280–98.

A. MANDOUZE, 'Encore le Donatisme!' (discussion of J.-P. Brisson's work), *L'Antiquité classique*, 29, 1960, pp. 61–107.

R. A. MARKUS, *Saeculum: History and Society in the Theology of St. Augustine*, Cambridge, 1970.

E. TENGSTRÖM, 'Die Protokollierung der collatio Carthaginensis', *Studia Graeca et Latine Gothoburgensia*, xiv, Göteborg, 1962.

—— 'Donatisten und Katholiken, soziale, wirtschaftliche und politische Aspekte einer nordafrikanischen Kirchenspaltung', *Studia Graeca et Latina Gothoburgensia*, xviii, Göteborg, 1964.

A. C. DE VEER, 'L'exploitation du schisme maximianiste par S. Augustin dans sa lutte contre le Donatisme', *Recherches augustiniennes*, 1965, pp. 219–37.

B. H. WARMINGTON, *The North African Provinces from Diocletian to the Vandal Conquest*, Cambridge, 1954.

INDEX